Indian Myths & Legends
from the
North Pacific Coast of America

"Passing on the Legends." A composite photograph produced by B.W. Leeson consisting of images taken among Native people of the west coast of B.C.

Vancouver Public Library, Vancouver, B.C. No. 14062.

On the cover: Nanaimo Indian Village, 1858.

Watercolour by J.M. Alden. British Columbia Archives, Victoria, B.C. PDP 2144.

Indian Myths & Legends from the North Pacific Coast of America

A translation of Franz Boas' 1895 edition of
Indianische Sagen von der Nord-Pacifischen Küste Amerikas

Edited and Annotated by
RANDY BOUCHARD and DOROTHY KENNEDY

Translated by
Dietrich Bertz

With a Foreword by
Professor Claude Lévi-Strauss

TALONBOOKS
2002

Translation copyright © 2002 B.C. Indian Language Project and Dietrich Bertz
Editing and annotation copyright © 2002 B.C. Indian Language Project and
                                    Randy Bouchard and Dorothy Kennedy

Talonbooks
P.O. Box 2076, Vancouver, British Columbia, Canada V6B 3S3
www.talonbooks.com

Typeset in Times
Printed and bound in Canada on 30% post-consumer recycled paper

Third revised printing: September 2013

Talonbooks gratefully acknowledges the financial support of the Canada Council for the Arts, the
Government of Canada through the Canada Book Fund, and the Province of British Columbia
through the British Columbia Arts Council and the Book Publishing Tax Credit.

This book has been published with the help of a grant from the Humanities and Social Sciences
Federation of Canada, using funds provided by the Social Sciences and Humanities Research
Council of Canada.

Library and Archives Canada Cataloguing in Publication

Boas, Franz, 1858–1942.
    Indian myths & legends from the North Pacific Coast of America

    Includes bibliographical references.
    ISBN-10: 0-88922-553-2
    ISBN-13: 978-0-88922-553-4

1. Indians of North America—British Columbia—Folklore. 2. Legends—British Columbia.
3. Indian mythology—British Columbia. I. Bouchard, Randy. II. Kennedy, Dorothy I. D.
III. Bertz, Dietrich. IV. Title.

E78.N78B62513 2002   398.2'089'970711   C2001-911127-4

To Lilo
and
To Ralph

Contents

ILLUSTRATIONS

Maps

Foreword

The foreword which Mr. Randy Bouchard and Dr. Dorothy Kennedy have honoured me by requesting for this volume gives me an opportunity, first of all, to pay tribute to the monumental task being accomplished under their direction by the British Columbia Indian Language Project. I do not claim to be familiar with all its wealth of information, but whether it be a question of the myths already collected or of the fascinating studies dedicated to the traditional sources of our knowledge concerning the marine resources and their uses, in every instance the directors of the Project and their collaborators are bringing a new impetus to the study of the peoples of British Columbia and their languages. It is even more admirable that this progress should be made with the consent and the cooperation of those most concerned—the members of the Indian Nations—for this prefigures a time when anthropology, instead of being a study conducted by outsiders, will become a deepening under-standing by a people itself of its own age-old cultural heritage. If anthropology, born in the Western world and developed by it, were one day to disappear as a scientific discipline, it could blissfully go to its last rest secure in the knowledge that, thanks to an undertaking like the British Columbia Indian Language Project, other George Hunts will take up the torch among the Kwakiutl and other Henry Tates and William Beynons among the Tsimshian, and that these great examples will have their own followings elsewhere, on the coast or in the interior.

Of the various tasks undertaken by the Indian Language Project, one of the most remarkable is, without a doubt, the translation into English of Franz Boas' *Sagen* by Mr. Dietrich Bertz. Of all the works on American Indians, this is the one for which the lack of a translation has been the most keenly felt, not only because not all specialists in American studies have a good reading knowledge of German, but also because the difficulty is even greater with myths where every word counts, since you can never predict what is going to happen from one line to the next, and also because this book, which is more than a century old and has never been republished, is not to be found in every library and is awkward to use due to the poor quality of its print. Now, this is one of the richest collections of mythological texts available for the whole of the American continent, and it is doubly valuable because of the time at which it was compiled. A true epitome of the mythology of the Pacific Coast and part of the interior, Boas' *Sagen* allow us to categorize and compare an enormous number of more recent versions of myths from tribes as far apart as the Fraser Valley Salish in the south and the Tlingit in the north.

These versions are often substantially different from those collected by other investigators, and by Boas himself, at later dates. For having failed to pay enough attention to one of them, I had to revise my original analysis of the Tsimshian myth of Asdiwal fifteen years later.[1] Quite recently, a text from the *Sagen* enabled me to clarify and enlarge on an interpretation I advanced a few years ago on the role of shellfish in myths relating to the giant ogress of the Kwakiutl and the Bella Bella.[2] By making the *Sagen* accessible to a greater number of readers, those in charge of the Indian Language Project are unquestionably ensuring a new interest in studies devoted to the mythologies of the Pacific Coast by encouraging researchers to examine these texts which have been neglected for too long. A careful examination of them cannot fail to suggest new similarities, comparisons and hypotheses.

This translation of Franz Boas' first major work is also a brilliant homage to the memory of a great ethnologist without whom our knowledge of the cultures of the Pacific Coast would still be only rudimentary. Like any scholar, he sometimes made mistakes in his work, but whenever he had the opportunity, he was always the first to correct his previous judgements. These instances when he was feeling his way are hardly worth mentioning in comparison with the prodigious mass of data he collected and published over a period of more than half a century on societies which, through the magnificence of their art, the originality of their economic system and the richness of their social organization and religious practices, earned themselves a prominent position in the great scheme of humanity.

Did Boas himself see them this way? I remember one occasion when I was invited to dinner at his Grantwood home. I was as in a dream in front of the magnificent carved, painted chest in his dining room and I said imprudently that, in his life as an ethnologist, his sojourns with people capable of creating such a masterpiece must have been an extraordinary experience. With his legendary puritanism, he answered drily, "They were Indians, like any others," and I did not dare continue. He was probably reluctant to allow any kind of hierarchy to be introduced among cultures which his oft-proclaimed relativism bound him to respect equally. It seems to me, however, that by devoting his most important books year after year to the Pacific Coast, he betrayed an unspoken predilection for cultures which reminded him of his youth, and about which he wrote so much, that although

---

1. Pp. 223–231, *Anthropologie Structurale Deux*. Paris: Plon (1973).
2. Structuralisme et empirisme. *L'Homme, Revue Française d'Anthropologie*. Vol. XVI, No. 2–3 (1976).

a number of texts came out posthumously, even today there is still unpublished material waiting to be released.

The incident I have just related took place a few weeks before he died. Since I witnessed this directly, perhaps the time has come for me to describe its circumstances which will remain engraved on my memory forever. Boas was a host at a luncheon at the Columbia University Faculty Club in honour of Paul Rivet, then a refugee in Columbia, who was passing through New York on a mission for General de Gaulle. I was invited along with a few other people, including Mrs. Yampolski, Boas' daughter, Ruth Benedict, Gladys Reichard and Ralph Linton. It was December 21, 1942. The city was in the grip of a bitter cold spell and Boas arrived from Grantwood wearing an astonishing faded fur hat that must have dated back to his travels among the Inuit. The meal began gaily; you could tell that Boas was happy to see an old friend again and to be surrounded by former students, some of whom had followed in his footsteps. The conversation was going along at a good pace when suddenly, in mid-sentence, Boas jerked violently backwards, as under the effect of an electric shock, and fell over, taking his chair with him. I was sitting next to him and hurried to help him up, but he remained motionless. Rivet, who had been an army medical officer, tried in vain to revive him; he was only able to pronounce him dead. Boas' son Ernst, a professor at Columbia, arrived a little later. Leaving Mrs. Yampolski and him to their sorrow, we withdrew in silence, grief-stricken at the loss of the greatest ethnologist of all time.

I relived these memories as I leafed through the translation of the *Sagen*, a work which Boas published at the age of thirty-seven. (He was eighty-three when I first visited him in the office which, as a professor emeritus, he had kept at Columbia.) And, when I thought of the fantastic number of books and articles which followed and the diversity of their subject matter, which ranged from physical anthropology to folklore, from archaeology to linguistics, from geography to ethnology, from the most minute description of objects and customs to far-reaching theoretical ideas, I said to myself that, on this December 21, 1942, a handful of people of whom I was one had been given the dramatic privilege of witnessing the passing of a man who was not only the honoured master of their discipline, but the last of those intellectual giants produced by the nineteenth century, the likes of whom will probably never be seen again.

Claude Lévi-Strauss
of the Académie française,
Professor at the Collège de France.
September 2001

L'avant-propos

L'avant-propos que M. Randy Bouchard et le Dr. Dorothy Kennedy m'ont fait l'honneur de me demander pour ce volume m'offre d'abord l'occasion de rendre hommage à l'oeuvre monumentale que, sous leur direction, le British Columbia Indian Language Project est en train d'accomplir. Je ne prétends pas en connaître toutes les richesses, mais, qu'il s'agisse des mythes actuellement recueillis ou des passionnantes études consacrées aux savoirs traditionnels sur les ressources marines et leur emploi, dans tous ces cas, les responsables du Projet et leurs collaborateurs impriment à l'étude des peuples de la Colombie Britannique et de leurs langues un nouvel élan. Il est encore plus admirable que ces progrès se fassent avec l'assentiment et le concours actif des principaux intéressés, c'est-à-dire les membres des nations indiennes; car on voit ainsi apparaître le moment où l'anthropologie, d'étude menée par le dehors, se changera en un approfondissement de leur propre culture par ceux-là-même dont elle constitue l'héritage millénaire. Si l'anthropologie devait un jour disparaître en tant que discipline scientifique, née dans le monde occidental et développée par lui, elle pourrait s'endormir avec sérénité de son dernier sommeil, certaine que, grâce à une enterprise comme le British Columbia Indian Language Project, d'autres George Hunt reprendront le flambeau chez les Kwakiutl, d'autres Henry Tate et William Beynon chez les Tsimshian, et que ces grands exemples feront aussi école ailleurs, que ce soit sur la côte ou dans l'intérieur du pays …

Parmi les entreprises de l'Indian Language Progect, l'une des plus remarquables est, sans conteste, la traduction en anglais des *Sagen* de Franz Boas, menée à bien par M. Dietrich Bertz. De tous les ouvrages concernant les Indiens d'Amérique, c'est, en effet, celui pour lequel l'absence de traduction se faisait le plus durement sentir. Non seulement parce que tous les américanistes ne lisent pas l'allemand de façon courante, et que la difficulté s'accroît encore pour de mythes où chaque mot compte, car, d'une ligne à la suivante, on ne peut prévoir ce qui va se passer; mais aussi parce que ce livre, vieux de plus d'un siècle et jamais réédité, ne se trouve pas dans toutes les bibliothèques, et que sa médiocre qualité typographique en rend l'usage incommode. Or, il s'agit là d'une de plus riches collections de textes mythiques dont on dispose pour l'ensemble de l'Amérique, rendue doublement précieuse par l'époque à laquelle son auteur l'a rédigée. Véritable somme de la mythologie de la côte du Pacifique, et pour partie de l'intérieur, les *Sagen* permettent d'inventorier et de comparer un nombre énorme de versions, toutes contemporaines, de mythes répandus depuis les Salish de la vallée du Fraser au sud jusqu'aux Tlingit vers le nord.

Ces versions présentent souvent des différences substantielles avec celles que d'autres enquêteurs, et Boas lui-même, obtinrent à des dates plus récentes. Pour avoir prêté une attention insuffisante à l'une d'elle, j'ai dû, après quinze ans, remanier mon analyse du mythe tsimshian d'Asdiwal.[3] Tout récemment, c'est un texte des *Sagen* qui allait me permettre de préciser et d'élargir l'interprétation avancée par moi quelques années auparavant, sur le rôle des coquillages dans les mythes relatifs à l'ogresse géante des Kwakiutl et des Bella Bella.[4] Nul doute qu'en rendant les *Sagen* accessibles à un plus grand nombre de lecteurs, les responsables de l'Indian Language Project n'assurent le renouveau des études consacrées aux mythologies de la côte du Pacifique, en incitant les chercheurs à se pencher sur ces textes trop longtemps négligés, et dont l'examen attentif ne manquera pas de leur suggérer des rapprochements, des comparaisons, des hypothèses.

Et puis, cette traduction du premier ouvrage important de Franz Boas consitue en elle-même un éclatant hommage à la mémoire du grand ethnologue sans lequel notre connaissance des cultures de la côte du Pacifique serait restée rudimentaire. Comme il arrive à tout savant, il s'est parfois trompé sur leur compte, mais, chaque fois qu'il en eut l'occasion, il fut le premier à rectifier ses jugements antérieurs. Ces tâtonnements ne comptent guère au regard de la masse prodigieuse d'informations qu'il a rassemblées et publiées pendant plus d'un demi-siècle, sur des sociétés qui, par la splendeur de leur art, l'originalité de leur vie économique, la richesse de leur organisation sociale et de leurs pratiques religieuses, tiennent une place de premier plan sur la grande scène de l'humanité.

Les considérait-il lui-même comme telles? Il me souvient qu'invité à dîner dans sa maison de Grantwood, je me pris à rêver devant le magnifique coffre sculpté et peint qui ornait sa salle à manger, et je lui dis imprudemment que, dans sa vie d'ethnologue, ses séjours chez des gens capables de créer un tel chef d'oeuvre avait dû représenter une expérience exceptionnelle. Avec son puritanisme légendaire, il me répondit sèchement: "Ce sont des Indiens comme les autres," et je n'osai répliquer. Sans doute ne voulait-il pas permettre qu'une hiérarchie quelconque fût introduite entre des cultures que son relativisme souvent proclamé l'obligeait à respecter au même titre. Il me semble pourtant qu'en consacrant années après années ses livres les plus importants à la côte du Pacifique, il trahissait une dilection inavouée pour des cultures qui lui rappelaient sa jeunesse, et sur lesquelles il a tant écrit que même

---

3. Pp. 223–231, *Anthropologie Structurale Deux*. Paris: Plon (1973).

4. Structuralisme et empirisme. *L'Homme, Revue Française d'Anthropologie.* Vol. XVI, No. 2–3 (1976).

après plusieurs ouvrages posthumes, encore aujourd'hui des inédits attendent leur publication.

Les propos que je viens d'évoquer furent échangés quelques semaines avant sa mort. Témoin direct de celle-ci, le moment est peut-être venu pour moi d'en décrire les circonstances, restées à jamais gravées dans ma mémoire. Boas offrait au Faculty Club de Columbia University un déjeuner en l'honneur de Paul Rivet alors réfugié en Colombie, et qui passait par New York pour remplir une mission dont le Général de Gaulle l'avait chargé. J'y fus convié avec quelques autres personnes parmi lesquelles figuraient Mme. Yampolski, fille de Boas, ainsi que Ruth Benedict, Gladys Reichard et Ralph Linton. C'était le 21 décembre 1942. Un froid intense régnait sur la ville, et Boas arriva de Grantwood coiffé d'un étonnant bonnet de fourrure toute décolorée qui devait bien dater de son voyage chez les Inuit. Le repas commença gaiement; on sentait Boas heureux de retrouver un vieux camarade, et d'avoir autour de lui d'anciens élèves, certains devenus ses successeurs. Les conversations allaient bon train quand, au milieu d'une phrase et comme mu par une secousse électrique, Boas se rejeta violemment en arrière et tomba à la renverse, entraînant sa chaise dans sa chute. Placé à côté de lui, je me précipitai pour le relever, mais son corps restait inerte. Rivet, qui avait été médecin militaire, essaya en vain de le ranimer; il ne put que constater son décès. Son fils Ernst Boas, professeur à Columbia, arriva peu après. Les laissant Mme. Yampolski et lui à leur douleur, nous nous retirâmes en silence, accablés par la perte du plus grand ethnologue de tous les temps.

Je revis ces souvenirs en feuilletant la traduction des *Sagen*, ouvrage que Boas publia à l'âge de trente-sept ans (il en avait quatre-vingt-trois quand je lui fis ma première visite, dans le bureau que, comme professeur emeritus, il avait conservé à Columbia). Et, considérant la masse fantastique de livres et d'articles que suivirent, la diversité de leurs thèmes qui vont de l'anthropologie physique au folklore, de l'archéologie à la linguistique, de la géographie à l'ethnologie, de la description la plus minutieuse d'objets et de coutumes à d'amples vues théoriques, je me dis que, ce 21 décembre 1942, quelques-uns, dont je fus, eurent le privilège dramatique de voir s'éteindre sous leurs yeux non seulement le maître vénéré de leur discipline, mais le dernier parmi ces géants de l'esprit que le XIXe siècle sut produire, et comme on n'en verra probablement jamais plus.

Claude Lévi-Strauss
de l'Académie française,
Professeur au Collège de France.
Septembre 2001

ACKNOWLEDGEMENTS

One anonymous reviewer of the *Sagen* translation manuscript remarked that "the publication of *Indian Myths and Legends* is almost equivalent to the discovery of a group of hundred-and-fifty-year-olds from these Native groups, all in full possession of their faculties and anxious to share their knowledge with anthropologists." It is unfortunate that the paucity of Boas' *Sagen* fieldnotes means that not many of these mythtellers can now be identified. In a few cases, we know their identity and this is provided at the beginning of each translated section. Apart from the mythtellers, however, we owe considerable gratitude to numerous members of B.C. First Nations who assisted us both directly and indirectly in the preparation of this volume.

Indian Myths and Legends has been completed with the support of many individuals, acting in many capacities, whose names are listed below in alphabetical order. We have also benefited greatly from the comments of numerous anonymous assessors who participated in reviews of various drafts of the manuscript over the years. As we have spent more than two decades working on this volume, we also take this opportunity to thank and offer apologies to any individual whose contributions we have inadvertently overlooked.

We gratefully acknowledge the assistance of the following (those of our Native consultants and colleagues who are now deceased are identified by the abbreviation "dec'd" following their name): Arthur Adolph; Helen Akrigg; Dr. Philip Akrigg (dec'd); John and Merle Alexcee; Dr. Aimee August (dec'd); Bill Arnouse (dec'd); Dietrich Bertz; Franziska Boas (dec'd); Robert Bringhurst; James Bryant; Peryl Cain; Diane Carr; Mary Charles (dec'd); Mary Clifton (dec'd); Professor Douglas Cole (dec'd); John Dewhirst; Chief Adam Dick; Jeannie Dominick (dec'd); Amelia Douglas (dec'd); Chief Charley Draney (dec'd); Dr. Richard Dauenhauer; Nora Dauenhauer; Agnes Edgar (dec'd); Carl Edgar, Sr. (dec'd); Francis and Annie Edwards (dec'd); Bill Edwards (dec'd); David W. Ellis; Dr. Brent Galloway; Marina and Howard Gerwing; Eric and Freda Green; Arnold Guerin (dec'd); Professor Emeritus Erna Gunther (dec'd); Roy Hanuse, Sr. (dec'd); Elizabeth Harry (dec'd); Jim Henderson (dec'd); Mamie Henry; Lucy Hovell (dec'd); Maggie Hunt (dec'd); Willie Hunt; Slim Jackson (dec'd); Sophie Jacobs (dec'd); Dr. Wolfgang Jilek;

Dr. Louise Jilek-Aall; Lucy Johnson; John Johnson, Sr.; Norman Johnson, Sr. (dec'd); Juanita Judson; Chief Harvey Jules (dec'd); Grant Keddie; Della Kew (dec'd); Dr. Michael Kew; Helen Knox (dec'd); Wilfred Knott; Dr. Robert Levine; Professor Claude Lévi-Strauss; Dr. George Louie (dec'd); Barbara McDonell; Charlie Mack (dec'd); Professor Emeritus Ralph Maud; Dr. Marie Mauzé; Professor Pierre Maranda; Charlie Matilpi (dec'd); Dr. Louis Miranda (dec'd); Rose Mitchell (dec'd) and Chief Bill Mitchell (dec'd); Sam Mitchell (dec'd); Christopher Paul (dec'd); Tommy Paul (dec'd); Susan Peters (dec'd); Susan Pielle; Louis Phillips (dec'd); Diana and Bud Recalma; Kim Recalma-Clutesi; Victoria Reece; Baptiste Ritchie (dec'd); Hans Roemer; David Rozen; Denis St. Claire; Stanley Sam; Dan Savard; Klaus Schmidt; Dr. Daisy Sewid-Smith; Chief Adam Shewish (dec'd); Dr. Margaret Siwallace (dec'd); Hilda Smith; David Stevenson; Dr. Arnoud Stryd; Professor Emeritus Wayne Suttles; Chester Thomas (dec'd); Professor Nancy J. Turner; Cecil Wadhams; Felicity Walkus (dec'd); Isaac and Adeline Willard (dec'd); Ambrose Wilson (dec'd); Peter Webster (dec'd); Joe Williams (dec'd); Evelyn Windsor.

We offer our sincerest thanks to Professor Claude Lévi-Strauss for writing the Foreword to this volume and for his sustaining interest in our research over the years. Lévi-Strauss' eloquent testimonial and description of the death of Franz Boas is a major contribution to this volume. For assistance in translating the initial draft of Professor Lévi-Strauss' Foreword, the Translation Bureau of the Government of Canada is acknowledged, as are several scholars of French for their additional review of that translation: Professor John Greene; Mirella Gazzoni; Professor Ralph Baldner (dec'd); and Professor Jennifer Waelti-Walters. We are additionally grateful to Professor Lévi-Strauss for his own revisions and confirmation of both the French and English versions of his Foreword in September 2001.

We also wish to acknowledge with thanks the following foundation, corporate and government sources who provided modest grants that permitted some of the work on the *Sagen* translation manuscript to proceed between 1980 and 1982: W. Garfield Weston Foundation; Canada Council (Explorations Programme); Samuel and Saidye Bronfman Foundation; Jackman Foundation; Alcan Canada Limited; Chevron Canada Limited; Esso Resources Canada Limited; Amax of Canada; H.R. MacMillan Estate Trust; F.K. Morrow Foundation; Petro Canada Limited; Westwind Charitable Foundation; Leon and Thea Koerner Foundation; Laidlaw Foundation; McLean Foundation; Winspear Foundation; Nova, an Alberta Corporation; Westcoast Transmission Company Ltd.; Trans Mountain Pipe Line Co.; Teleglobe Canada.

Thanks are also due to the Community Heritage Development Program of the British Columbia Heritage Trust for their Publication Assistance Supplement granted in June 2001.

Our annotations in this volume draw upon the considerable manuscript materials we have obtained from archival institutions throughout North America over the past three decades. The helpful assistance provided by the staff of the following institutions is especially acknowledged: American Philosophical Society Library, Philadelphia; British Columbia Archives, Victoria, B.C.; National Anthropological Archives, Smithsonian Institution, Washington, DC; National Archives of Canada, Ottawa; Royal British Columbia Museum, Victoria, B.C.; Special Collections Division of the University of British Columbia Library, Vancouver, B.C.

Photographs appearing in this volume have also been obtained from institutions throughout North America. We acknowledge the professional assistance provided by the staff of these institutions and we thank them for permission to publish the photographs that appear here: Alberni Valley Museum, Port Alberni, B.C.; American Museum of Natural History, New York; American Philosophical Society Library, Philadelphia, Pennsylvania; British Columbia Archives, Victoria, B.C.; Canadian Museum of Civilization, Ottawa; City of Vancouver Archives, Vancouver, B.C.; Milwaukee Public Museum, Milwaukee, Wisconsin; Museum of Northern British Columbia, Prince Rupert, B.C.; National Anthropological Archives, Smithsonian Institution, Washington, DC.; National Archives of Canada, Ottawa; Powell River Museum, Powell River, B.C.; Royal British Columbia Museum, Victoria, B.C.; University of Washington Library, Seattle, Washington; Vancouver Public Library, Vancouver, B.C.

Randy Bouchard and Dorothy Kennedy
B.C. Indian Language Project
Victoria, British Columbia, Canada
May 2002

Franz Boas, 1887.

EDITORS' INTRODUCTION

In *Indianische Sagen von der Nord-Pacifischen Küste Amerikas* Franz Boas collected together the numerous stories he had been publishing in German periodicals hospitable to his research. The *Sagen* volume constitutes, in effect, the myths and legends Boas obtained in his first four trips to British Columbia: 1886, 1888, 1889, and 1890.[1]

SUMMARY OF BOAS' FIELD TRIPS

Though *Indianische Sagen* itself has very few signposts as to where, when, and how the stories were collected, beyond the grouping under tribal name, Ronald P. Rohner's (1966; 1969) work enables us to place most of them within the right field trip and thereby learn something of the circumstances of the gathering.[2] The fact is that, in the four field trips involved, the itineraries of which are conveniently tabulated in Rohner (1966:153–158), Boas never spent more than approximately three weeks at any one place outside of his base in Victoria, and often only a day or two. He worked under severe restrictions and against many obstacles. In 1886, the twenty-eight-year-old Boas was, of course, relatively inexperienced. He had been a year with Eskimos (Inuit) in Baffinland (1883–1884) where his observations went far beyond his discipline, which at that time was geography, as *The Central Eskimo* (Boas 1888a) attests. But the only aboriginal Northwest Coast people he had seen were the Bella Coola (Nuxalk) "exhibited" at the Berlin Royal Ethnographic Museum, where he was a docent in geography in 1885–1886. Boas did "field" research with them in that museum setting and published on their language and culture.[3]

---

1. See Douglas Cole (1999) for a biography of Boas which places his scholarly work in the context of his life, influences, and motivations.

2. This part of the Introduction has drawn from the summary of Boas' itinerary while working on the *Sagen* that was prepared by Ralph Maud for his book *A Guide to B. C. Indian Myth and Legend* (Maud 1982:50–53).

3. For a list of Boas' publications by year, see H. A. Andrews *et al.* (1943). One other item not in Andrews' bibliography that came out of Boas' Berlin encounter with the Bella Coola (Nuxalk) was an article by Stumpf (1886) for which Boas provided a number of Bella Coola songs.

As it happened, these Bella Coola contacts stood him in good stead. On 18 September 1886 Boas disembarked from the steamer *North Pacific* and, after settling into his hotel, made his way through the streets of Victoria to find that shop windows were displaying photographs of these same aboriginal dancers. A further search fortuitously led him to a couple of these Nuxalk men, themselves visitors to Victoria. It soon became apparent to Boas that Victoria was a magnet to "endless Indians of various tribes" (Rohner 1969:20), both resident and visitors. After only two days in the city, Boas declared in a letter to his parents: "I am now convinced that this trip will have the results I desire" (Rohner 1969:21). The task Boas set for himself involved making a general ethnological map and collecting museum specimens. Yet once on the ground in this uncharted cultural landscape, his parameters quickly expanded and "he began to ask about the language," which he confided in his letter-diary home, "in the beginning is always hard work" (Rohner 1969:21). By the second day, Boas had recorded a text.

Speed was essential, since Boas had very little money (from personal sources only). He had budgeted for a three months' general reconnaissance of the coast tribes. That's why Victoria was so useful; he could get most of what he wanted right there. With little time allotted, Boas' pace was frantic. He called upon the assistance of all whom he met for introductions to the aboriginal camps, sometimes extracting from his guides promises for future texts and translations to be sent on to him. On his second day in Victoria, before even knowing the lay of the city, he "mapped out a whole campaign in order to interest as many people as possible in my work." "Tomorrow," he wrote, "I shall visit Dr. Tolmie ... the Indian Agent Dr. Powell, and the catholic priest. I must further try to enlist photographers and perhaps the school teacher ... " (Rohner 1969:22). So shamelessly did he seek out cooperation from local residents that Boas later wrote of himself: "I am as well known here in Victoria as a mongrel dog. I look up all kinds of people without modesty or hesitation" (Rohner 1969:88).

In the early weeks Boas' selection of Native consultants was guided mostly by the advice of his White contacts. They steered him toward those aboriginal people who were, foremost, willing to talk with Boas, in possession of adequate cultural and linguistic knowledge, and importantly, had an ability to speak slowly, using both English (or Chinook) and the indigenous language. Sometimes, desperate to find an informant, Boas combed the Indian camps in search of mythtellers. Following a particularly disappointing day in September 1886, Boas confessed in his letter-diary that he had "crawled into a Bella Coola tent and obtained a few nice facts" and then added, "I have the least trouble with this tribe because I know their language a little" (Rohner 1969:26). In spite of this bravado, these letters home express a feeling of unease at taking advantage of the congregated Tsimshian,

Kwakwaka'wakw (Southern Kwakiutl), Nuxalk, Haida, and Tlingit, as well as the local Lukungun (Songhees and Esquimalt) people, while knowing full well that the quality of life in the back streets of Victoria was detrimental to obtaining clean texts.

There were many frustrations. On 25 September 1886 Boas described what he called "the worst day since I have been here," having spent the "entire day running about in search of new people" (Rohner 1969:25). Reflecting on these lost hours, Boas lamented: "I am unhappy for every moment lost, but one cannot butt one's head against a stone wall; I must bear these fruitless hours patiently" (Rohner 1969:26). It is positively refreshing to read that after sixteen days of hustling about, Boas has finally left Victoria and sailed north on the *Boskowitz*. Though he thought it "the most horrible ship I have ever experienced" (Rohner 1969:47), his work continued aboard with at least one Nuxalk mythteller who was heading home to Bella Coola, from whom he transcribed "the long-drawn-out tale" of the supernatural carpenters (Rohner 1969:31).

Stopping first with the Nahwitti on Hope Island at the northern end of Vancouver Island, Boas spent 6–17 October 1886 living in a chief's cedarplank house while gathering texts. A small boat then took him to Alert Bay on Cormorant Island from 18–23 October, after which he returned to Victoria from 26 October to 2 November, again looking for his Nuxalk friends who continued "explaining the grammar of the texts" he had been collecting (Rohner 1969:50). During the period 4–10 November Boas was among the Cowichan, followed by a stay at Comox from 12 November to 2 December 1886. He returned south, stopping at Nanaimo from 4–9 December, and then carrying on to Victoria, where he attended the funeral of his friend Dr. W. F. Tolmie, before sailing to Vancouver. It was, in the end, a great success. He had enough data to complete an ethnological map of the B. C. coast.[4] He had packed off sufficient museum specimens to pay for the trip, and his facility in acquiring field data had increased to the point that he was having trouble keeping up with his transcriptions. In the final days of this first trip to the Northwest Coast, Boas was to announce: "My manuscript has reached page 326. Now I must go to bed; I am murderously tired" (Rohner 1969:73).

The other trips which are reflected in *Indianische Sagen* are similar to the first, and can be briefly summarized. They were all conducted under the auspices of the British Association for the Advancement of Science and the initially strict supervision of Horatio Hale.[5] Boas was not to attempt a thorough study of any one tribe, but to compile a general synopsis, i.e. continue the kind of rushing around that he

---

4. This important map, in different formats, was published twice in 1887 (see Boas 1887e; 1887f). Both versions of the 1887 map are reproduced here, along with the map that appeared originally in the 1895 *Sagen* publication. (See pages 55–58.)

5. See Gruber (1967) for a serious article on this amusing situation.

had proved himself good at. The pace remained hectic. Arriving in Vancouver on 31 May 1888, he wasted no time in organizing the local missionary to introduce him to the Squamish chief. On June 3 he was off to Victoria and by 9 June had made a trip to Cowichan and environs. He left Victoria on 15 June for Port Essington, on the northern British Columbia coast, returning south on 29 June. After another brief visit to Cowichan, Boas was off again to Vancouver on July 12, only to leave for Lytton in the B.C. interior that same night. He occupied himself in Lytton 13–15 July, then travelled to Golden and Windermere in the Kootenays before heading east by train. During this field trip, in addition to collecting artifacts and texts, Boas had been also asked to measure heads and collect skeletal remains, two disagreeable tasks which sapped his energies. He was happy to head home.

By 18 July 1889 Boas had begun his third field trip and his letters from Victoria reveal business as usual. Complications meant that he didn't leave the city until 30 July, but the itinerary never let up after that: Port Alberni (2–12 August), Alert Bay (25 August–3 September), and Kamloops (8–14 September).

For the 1890 trip some funding came from the United States Bureau of Ethnology in Washington D.C., so Boas was in Oregon and Washington most of June and July; thereafter in New Westminster (31 July–10 August), Ladner (11–21 August), and back in the U.S. till mid-September.

Boas' Methodology

With this sense of the frenzy of the work, we can look at the actual process Boas employed in recording the *Sagen* texts. The immediate obstacle facing him was his lack of familiarity with both the indigenous languages and Chinook Jargon, the trade language that had developed on the Northwest Coast beginning in the late eighteenth century to facilitate communication among the races, and was being used extensively among the aboriginal peoples themselves.[6] Boas appreciated that "the visitor who leaves the much-travelled tourist roads in British Columbia has to depend completely on this means of intercourse" (Rohner 1969:6), and after only eleven days' study of Chinook Jargon in the province, he was able to write: "I am gradually learning to understand this language quite well" (Rohner 1969:28). Still, the Jargon's somewhat limited capacity for eliciting Native texts was clearly evident. "Unfortunately this language is incomplete," Boas commented. "It is characteristic of Chinook that one must guess the meaning of a sentence; one never knows what is subject and what is object. Even verbs and nouns can often not be distinguished, and one has to be very alert in listening to their mythical tales" (Rohner 1969:28). When planning his trip north to Alert Bay, Boas promised him-

---

6.   See Silverstein (1996:127–130) for a brief description of Chinook Jargon.

self that he would "try as quickly as possible to pick up something of the language … A mixture of Chinook and the native language is quite useful for purposes of communication" (Rohner 1969:28). He was obviously a quick learner. After only two weeks at Comox, for example, Boas was able to announce on 27 November 1886: "I am beginning to understand something of what the people say and try to say something myself once in a while" (Rohner 1969:67).

Boas (1895b:v) states explicitly in his Preface to the *Sagen* that Chinook Jargon was the medium by which he recorded many of the stories. We know from his let-ter-diary that he transcribed quickly in the field, then immediately recopied the materials once in the solitude of his lodgings—and that he constantly berated him-self for falling behind. Looking upon the mass of information he obtained from Nahwitti and Alert Bay potlatch guests, Boas wrote: "I shall have to work hard in Victoria, reread everything, and, if possible, copy it. Otherwise I shall lose control of my material" (Rohner 1969:45). When he later arrives in Victoria, he says of this task: "Tonight I shall copy some of the material I have brought from Newetti. All that stuff is beginning to make me feel very stupid. The Eskimo tales are innocent compared with these. I have recorded one hundred and nineteen, among them a whole bookfull that have not been copied. At any rate the results of my trip will make a presentable book" (Rohner 1969:50).

Boas provides little guidance on which stories he recorded from the Chinook Jargon and which he transcribed directly from the indigenous language. Though he writes in his own Preface that "many legends of the Kwakiutl tribes and the Tsimschian were translated into German directly from the original languages," we have not found evidence to confirm his statement with regard to the numerous Kwakwaka'wakw (Southern Kwakiutl) texts that appear in the *Sagen*. Two Tsimshian-German texts, however, are now in the collections of the American Philosophical Society Library (Freeman Item Pn5a.6).[7] Pentlatch manuscripts from the American Philosophical Society (Freeman Items B63c, S2j.3), as Dale Kinkade (1992:164) has commented, also illustrate that Boas sometimes transcribed both texts and word lists in the indigenous language and provided on-the-spot German glosses. There are texts in both Pentlatch-German and Pentlatch-English, with word lists presented also in English-Pentlatch.[8] Stories in the Pentlatch manuscript mate-rials transcribed in the indigenous language appear with the briefest of interlinear

---

7. See John F. Freeman's (1966) *Guide to Manuscripts of the American Indian in the Library in the Library of the American Philosophical Society.*

8. Kinkade (1992:167–172) provides an English version of one of the APS' Pentlatch texts based on the Native original, then compares it with a translation of the German version. To Kinkade's com-parison could be added Boas' own English translation, as given in his Pentlatch manuscript mate-rial held by the National Anthropological Archives (Ms. No. 740) of the Smithsonian Institution, Washington, DC.

translation and appear terse in comparison with the German translations offered by Boas in the *Sagen*, which we assume must be the same stories elicited through Chinook Jargon, though no trace of this transmission process remains among his Pentlatch manuscripts.

Manuscript materials remaining from Boas' 1890 fieldwork in the Fraser Valley that are held by the American Philosophical Society (Freeman Item Pn 4.b 5) reveal that Boas often took notes using a type of shorthand, with indigenous terms transcribed phonetically, flora and fauna identified in Latin or English, and English retained for additional notes and common local place names. The one brief story in this APS manuscript that is transcribed in Halkomelem, with interlinear English translation, does not appear in the *Sagen*; the available evidence suggests that Chinook Jargon was also the language of transmission for the Lower Fraser River materials in the *Sagen*, and likely for most of the other texts as well.

Boas' skills in getting down texts were phenomenal, but there were some lost opportunities. His letter-diary demonstrates that he had witnessed smokehouse oratory at its best, in conditions conducive to proper performance: oral accounts from high-ranking Nahwitti chiefs telling of their descent group's breadth and greatness; and two-hour speeches by Cowichan household heads praising their own generosity. Still, Boas did not always recognize their value. "If I had understood their language," he wrote after a particularly-animated evening at Cowichan, "it would have been an excellent occasion for me to learn to make 'after dinner' speeches" (Rohner 1969:56). Our own patience is tried by Boas' impatience with the Cowichan men reciting their people's ancestor legends: "I was up there again yesterday and almost became impatient because of the long-drawn-out manner in which they told the stories. It really was a test of patience" (Rohner 1969:55). Boas should have been more grateful for what he was hearing—stories now back in their proper setting in the aboriginal villages, being told by authorized tradition-bearers.

The authenticity of the stories gathered in the field is indicated, for one thing, by the fact that there was considerable debate regarding the propriety of who, if anyone, should be speaking with the foreigner. At Nanaimo Boas recorded in his diary in November 1886 that he entered a house to find the Natives "all assembled in front of the fire discussing the case of 'Boas.'" Much rumination later, a leader who had previously forbidden these people to tell Boas their stories, announced in Chinook Jargon that he would now help him. And apparently he "really kept his word" (Rohner 1969:56). Boas commonly discovered that once his intentions had been understood and agreed to by the villagers, not only was assistance graciously forthcoming, but also considerable effort was extended on his behalf. Working conditions were obviously good at Nahwitti on Hope Island, for Boas was to write soon after his arrival that "everyone is most anxious to tell me something" (Rohner

1969:39). One household head told Boas that since he was a "chief" from a distant land, a dance would be held to celebrate his visit, an event that furnished Boas with data sufficient to write a description of the dramatic performance.[9] It was in such surroundings that Boas began to recognize the association of certain types of stories and objects of material culture with distinct groups of people, particularly the affiliation of ancestor legends, masks, and house decorations with specific, identified numayms (descent groups) of Kwakwala-speaking tribes. Such knowledge was localized. In these communities, leaders of such groups continuously displayed and confirmed their status relative to others, and in such situations, Boas quickly found that he had much to learn about Native protocol, including just whom to consult. While Boas was at Nahwitti he heard that one particular leader was "most unhappy" with him because he had not paid this chief a visit. Apprised of the situation, and with "all manner of trinkets along," he approached this chief and "told him that I knew he was a great chief and that he should tell me the story of his family as the other chiefs had done" (Rohner 1969:37).

It is of interest whether Boas offered remuneration for the time he spent with aboriginal mythtellers collecting texts for the *Sagen*. His letters indicate that money was always favourably received, and Boas sometimes took along tobacco and cotton as well. One of the existing notebooks of Boas' (1890b) Fraser Valley work among the Halkomelem contains a detailed list of expenditures that includes the repeated item "Indian," likely referring to Native honoraria. At Nahwitti, Boas held what he described as his own "potlatch," at which he distributed tobacco after feeding the assembled men a feast of boiled rice and receiving their speeches with appropriate decorum (Rohner 1969:30, 37). However, Boas did not appreciate that ornamented house fronts and poles were also property belonging to an individual or group, and that compensation for the privilege of photographing or sketching them was expected. His misunderstanding occasionally led to verbal altercations (Rohner 1969:53), and most often he resorted to subterfuge in order to obtain his much desired photographs.[10]

Sometimes the remuneration issue could be taken care of by a bit of *quid pro quo*. Chief Joseph of the Squamish Mission Indian Reserve in North Vancouver, for example, told his stories only after Boas assured him that at some time he might go to England to deliver a message from the Chief to Queen Victoria. Having established this point, Chief Joseph then dictated a communication for the Queen and instructed Boas to deliver it to the sovereign the next time he happened to be in

---

9. See Boas (1888j) "On Certain Songs and Dances of the Kwakiutl of British Columbia."

10. The whereabouts of photographs Boas took at Cowichan is not known. Boas attended a potlatch at Fort Rupert in 1894, accompanied by the Victoria photographer, O.C. Hastings; photographs appearing in Section XVII in this volume were taken at that time.

her country. Boas wrote out Chief Joseph's complaint about his people's loss of ancestral lands, only satisfying the chief once he had read it back verbatim, and adding the words "Chief Joseph says so and so ... " (Rohner 1969:86–87).

MANUSCRIPT MATERIALS

No pre-publication manuscript of the entire *Sagen* has been found. Nevertheless, some fieldnotes obviously used for compiling the *Sagen* survive from Boas' first four trips to the Northwest Coast. In addition to the Pentlatch and Lower Fraser River fieldnotes mentioned above, several other manuscripts dated to this period are currently held either by the National Anthropological Archives (NAA) of the Smithsonian Institution, or by the American Philosophical Society Library (APS), Philadelphia. These manuscripts are incomplete and reflect different stages in Boas' recording process. Some are similar to the shorthand fieldnotes remaining from his Lower Fraser River research and are thus difficult to interpret, other than for terms that appear in English, Latin or the indigenous language. Boas' Bella Coola notes (Freeman Item Pn 4.b 5), for example, contain shorthand notes, vocabulary, and a few sample Nuxalk language texts with brief interlinear English translation, but only a few of the *Sagen* myths are included. This same notebook contains a few pages of Masset Haida vocabulary, although the Skidegate Haida language materials obtained while recording the *Sagen* texts can be found in an NAA manuscript (No. 4117-b).

The Çatlōltq (Island Comox) materials Boas collected at Comox are a step removed from notes taken in the field. Boas organized a list of vocabulary alphabetically and rewrote the texts in a neater script with English interlinear translation (NAA Ms. No. 719). Vocabulary slips compiled at this time also reflect revisions undertaken after leaving the field (NAA Ms. No. 711-b). Boas prepared similar vocabulary slips for Pentlatch (NAA Ms. No. 711-a) and Nanaimo (Ms. No. 712-a). Two texts appearing in the *Sagen* were recorded in the Nanaimo dialect of Halkomelem, with English translation, and are included with grammatical notes in another NAA manuscript (No. 738). Only a few of the Tlingit notes have been located, although an NAA manuscript (No. 4118-b) remaining from this time contains several pages of materials Boas recorded with Mrs. Vine, a Stikine Tlingit woman. These manuscript texts, however, transcribed only in English, appear more like abbreviated notes than variants of the *Sagen* texts, and were likely explanatory notes Boas recorded to provide cultural context to the stories themselves. Judging by the clarity of the handwriting and the use of English glosses for the alphabetical vocabulary, the Tlingit notes suggest that this was work Boas completed after the initial recording process. A manuscript version of two of the *Sagen*'s Tsimshian stories, recorded in the original language with interlinear German translation, is held by the APS (Freeman Item Pn 5.a 6). This document was subsequently published in 1894 by A.C. Graf von der Schulenburg under the title *Die Sprache der Zimshīan-Indianer in Nordwest-America.*

There is some overlap between the Comox language texts in the National Anthropological Archives (Ms. No. 719) and the Comox stories appearing in the *Sagen*. If Boas derived the *Sagen* texts from these original Comox-English language versions, then it is evident that he took considerable liberties in fleshing out the stories for his audience. Yet considering that the tales are mostly of the "Mink Marries" series (story 4 in this collection)—myths that continue to be known commonly amongst Comox-speaking people—it is probable that the *Sagen* texts came from versions other than the original language texts, likely through Chinook Jargon and possibly from the same mythtellers. The Comox language versions contain a few items of special note. One in particular is found in the Mink and the Whale story (No. 4, part 15 in Section VIII of the present volume). Here in the fieldnote, Boas uses shorthand instead of English to translate what is presumably the word "genitals," which appears in the *Sagen*, yet is subsequently translated incorrectly by Boas (1888h:369) as 'belly.' Even Boas' use of the term "genitals" shied away from what he really knew the word to be, and it was another three decades before Boas revealed that Mink used his grandmother's vulva for bait (Boas 1916:1020).

Mention of manuscript versions of the specific *Sagen* myths known to exist appears in each relevant Section Introduction in this volume. Moreover, these versions are referred to in our annotations when they assist in clarifying specific terms Boas used in the *Sagen* publication.

EARLIER PUBLICATION OF INDIVIDUAL SECTIONS OF THE *SAGEN*

Overwhelmed with the amount of work required to complete the task he had set for himself of compiling what would eventually become the *Sagen*, Boas wrote to his parents from the field, confiding: "I have a real horror of writing this book." He goes on in this letter of 23 November 1886 to explain: "It entails an enormous amount of work, and it is going to take a long time to work it out completely. I am afraid that the journals will have to serve first" (Rohner 1969:64–65). This is what happened. Boas presented the myths and legends collected during his 1886, 1888, 1889 and 1890 field trips in a series of German periodicals prior to his publication of the entire collection in 1895 under the title *Indianische Sagen von der Nord-Pacifischen Küste Amerikas*. The following chart provides citations for the initial publication of these materials:

Group	Where Previously Published	Pages of Original Publication	Pages of 1895 *Sagen*
Shuswap	*Verhandlungen der Berliner Gesellschaft für Anthropologie, Ethnologie und Urgeschichte 1891*	Vol. 23:532–546	1–15
Ntlakyapamuq	*Verhandlungen 1891*	Vol. 23:546–549	15–18
Lower Fraser River	*Verhandlungen 1891*	Vol. 23:549–576	18–45
Cowitchin	*Verhandlungen 1891*	Vol. 23:628–636	45–54
SnanaimuQ	*Verhandlungen 1891*	Vol. 23:636–638	54–56
Sk·qōmic	*Verhandlungen 1891*	Vol. 23:639·643	56–61
Lku′ñgEn	*Verhandlungen 1891*	Vol. 23:643–645	61–63
Çatlōltq	*Verhandlungen 1892*	Vol. 24:32–60	63–90
Tlahū′s	*Verhandlungen 1892*	Vol. 24:60–62	90–92
Tlaā′men	*Verhandlungen 1892*	Vol. 24:62–63	92–94
Ē′ek·sen	*Verhandlungen 1892*	Vol. 24:63–65	94–95
PEntlatc	*Verhandlungen 1892*	Vol. 24:65–66	95–97
Nutka	*Verhandlungen 1892*	Vol. 24:314–344	98–128
Lē′kwiltok·	*Verhandlungen 1892*	Vol. 24:383–388	129–134
Nimkisch	*Verhandlungen 1892*	Vol. 24:388–407	134–153
Kwē′qsōt'ēnoq	*Verhandlungen 1892*	Vol. 24:407–410	153–156
Kwakiutl	*Verhandlungen 1893*	Vol. 25:228–240	157–169
Tlatlasik·oala	*Verhandlungen 1893*	Vol. 25:241–265	170–194
Nak·o′mgyilisala	*Verhandlungen 1893*	Vol. 25:430–444	194–208
Awi′ky'ēnoq	*Verhandlungen 1893*	Vol. 25:444–468	208–232
Hē′iltsuk·	*Verhandlungen 1893*	Vol. 25:468–477	232–241
Bilqula	*Verhandlungen 1894*	Vol. 26:281–306	241–266
Bilquala	*Verhandlungen 1895*	Vol. 27:189–195	266–272
Tsimschian	*Verhandlungen 1895*	Vol. 27:195–216	272–293
	Zeitschrift für Ethnologie 1888	Vol. 20:232–247	294–305
Haida	*Verhandlungen 1895*	Vol. 27:217–222	306–311
Tlingit	*Verhandlungen 1895*	Vol. 27:222–234	311–328
Die Entwickelung der Mythologien der Indianer	*Verhandlungen 1895*	Vol. 27:487–523	329–363

Boas also published excerpts and variants of these texts elsewhere, notably in the German periodicals *Globus* and the *Zeitschrift der Gesellschaft für Erdkunde zu Berlin*. In a seven–part series published in *Globus* in 1888, Boas presented "Die Mythologie der nordwest–amerikanischen Küstenvölker" ('The Mythology of the Northwest-American Coastal Peoples') (Boas 1888c), a comparative discussion of Northwest Coast mythology that included examples of myths from several coastal tribes, some of which appeared also in the *Verhandlungen der Berliner Gesellschaft für Anthropologie, Ethnologie und Urgeschichte*, and subsequently in the *Sagen*, and others of which appeared uniquely in this 1888 collection. Variants of the *Sagen* Tlingit texts appeared also in 1888, in an article entitled "Einige Mythen der

Tlingit" ('Some Myths of the Tlingit') (Boas 1888e), published by the *Zeitschrift der Gesellschaft für Erdkunde zu Berlin*.

Boas provided his own English translations for only a few of the *Sagen* stories. The Çatlōltq texts, gathered at Comox, were published in English in an 1888 volume of the *American Antiquarian* (Boas 1888h). The journal's editor, however, excised several words from the text: the reference to the "toothed-vagina" in the second version of what appears in the *Sagen* as story 3, Tlā́ik·, has been replaced by several asterisks.

Despite sections of the *Sagen* being published piecemeal between 1888 and 1895, it had long been Boas' intention to present the texts as a collection that would include chapters providing their ethnographic context. In a 12 June 1887 letter and lengthy enclosure to Major J.W. Powell, Director of the Bureau of Ethnology in Washington, DC, Boas summarized his research approach and set out his long-term publication objective (Boas 1887c). This important document, which includes a list of texts Boas had recorded to date in English and in the aboriginal languages, is reproduced below in its entirety, exactly as Boas wrote it;[11] illegible terms are indicated with a [?]:

Dear Sir,

I beg to submit to you the enclosed plan of publication and hope it will enable you to form an opinion of the character of my work.

I want to add a few remarks what do not belong to the plan. About six years ago, after I had finished my studies I laid out a plan for my future work. The leading question for this plan was: is it possible to apply the method of natural science, more particularly of physics to psychology. This led me to researches on psychophysics and induced me to follow a certain method of ethnological researches. I believe the fundamental question is: How far does our influence of the surroundings exist. In studying this question I found it necessary to limit my inquiry to a study of the influence of geographical surroundings upon migrations and certain stages of ideas. Even this I found to be extremely complex and began to inquire into their psychological elements. Studying the literature from this standpoint I found that I could not understand the questions and facts without practical experiences, I considered it necessary to study on the spot a people living in a [?] area of [?] forms character. I considered the Eskimos the best race for these studies and consequently went there. After my return I carried on my researches from the same point of view. The longer I studied the more

---

11. Boas' transcriptions of Native terms appearing in the enclosure to this June 1887 letter occasionally are inconsistent within the document, itself, and are sometimes different than they appear in the *Sagen*. While we do not comment on these inconsistencies here in the Introduction, we do discuss them throughout the *Sagen* collection itself.

I became convinced that the phenomena such as customs, traditions, and migrations are far too complex in their origin as to enable us to study their psychological causes without a thorough knowledge of their history. I considered it necessary to see a people, among which historical facts are of greater influence than the surroundings and selected for this program Northwest America.

I write this in order to explain to you the special line of study what I pursue, and to show you that my explorations were not made at random. This will also explain to you the foundation of my criticism of Prof. Mason's method, what will be set forth more fully in the next issue of 'Science.' In connection with these remarks it may be of interest to you to see some of my psychophysical papers, what I send along with this letter.

Yours very truly,

Dr. Franz Boas

Enclosure:

The native tribes of the North West coast of America between Juan de Fuca Strait and Alaska

Part I Ethnology

I   The tribes of the North West coast of America between Juan de Fuca Strait and Alaska
Mode of life; distribution; historical account.

I intend to give only a brief sketch of their mode of life, as much has been written on this subject and reliable accounts exist. A few new observations on the plan of houses, boats etc. will be embodied in the sketch what is necessary as a foundation of the following parts. The chapter on distribution will contain my observations on this subject: tribal names, gender, synonymology, extinct tribes, migrations. The historical account will contain the history of exploration, intertribal wars, census etc.

II   Traditions and customs

A. Material

1.   Tlingit

The raven legend: The raven obtains the daylight. The raven obtains the water. The deer obtains the fire. How the raven became black. The raven cheats the whale. The raven and the butterfly. The raven and the shadows. The raven and the fishermen. The raven and the cormorant. The raven gives a feast.

The Kuštā′qa (sea otter) legend: The boy who was stolen by the Kuštā′qa. The medicine man's visit to the Kuštā′qa.

The land of the souls.

2. Tsimpshian

The raven legend: The raven obtains the daylight. The raven and the man made of cedarbark. The raven steals a girl.

The origin of the whale gens.

The origin of the bear gens.
The origin of the cannibal ceremonies.
Lā̌′ek (the story of the deserted boy).
Tsaχatilā̌′o, a long story referring to the exploits of a woman and her son.

3. Bilχula

The raven legend: The raven obtains the daylight. The raven and the beautiful girl. The raven and his four sisters. The raven and the fisherman. The raven and the cormorant. The raven and the deer. The raven and the panther. The raven and the bird aiχaoχōnē. How the raven became black. The raven gives the finishing touch to the salmon. The raven marries the salmon. The raven invents the nets.

The Masmasalaniχ legend: The origin of the mountains and trees. Masmasalaniχ teaches man how to build boats, how to carve, etc. Masmasalaniχ does not succeed in opening the river of Nut′el.

The sun and mink legend:
Snē̄nē̄′iq. (= Tsōnō′qoa of the Kwakiutl). Two legends.

Vávalis.
The dog's children.
The man in the moon.
Origin of the stars.
The deserted woman.
Qaeā′ns.
The boy who visited the salmon.
The woman who followed her husband into the grave.
Saχsakyaiā′laiχ; or the origin of the cannibalism.

4. Wik'ē′no

The raven legend: The origin of the daylight. The raven obtains the water. The deer obtains the fire.
The Masmasalaniχ legend.
The sun and mink legend.
Origin of the mosquitoes and the origin of the cannibalism.
Qē̄q'tsunuχ′skyā′na.

Lā′lχ′emitḻ.
The moon.
Mēmaōṯlemē′.
Haughaug, a spirit of the Elaχō′tla (cannibals).
The Thunderbird.
Mitḻa and the moon.

5. Ṯlatḻasiqoala and Naqomgilis

The raven legend: The birth of the raven; he obtains the daylight; the water; he makes the tides; makes the salmon; the raven and his sisters. He deserts his sister Hā′taqa; the raven and the trustful girl. His son Qē′χemtḻ. He kills the gum. He kills the Thunderbird; he takes the squirrel for his mother. The raven and mink kill the grizzly bear; the raven and the fishermen. The raven gives a feast; he goes fishing; the raven and his sister Hā′taqa; Kuē′χakila. The raven and Hoialikyā′nē. Ṯlē′nēmitenutḻ, the raven's son. Hā′taqa's dance. The raven creates the earth. The raven and Qawatiliqala. The raven and Nūmas.

The Q'ā′niqilaq legend: The birth of Q'ā′niqilaq. Q'ā′niqilaq meets the Sisiutḻ, Hē′likilikyala, Lōṯlematḻ; he transforms Ṯlē′χekyotḻ into a deer, mā′yus into a coon; he kills Ts'ē′giš; transforms Yä′q'enḏemakš, transforms four girls into ducks; meets Ēyañ′ika, Omeatḻ, Nōmasinoslis, Koana′lalis. He revives his brother Nomō′gois. He meets Tleχyō′likila. He transforms a fisherman into a crane. He becomes a star at Çatḻōltχ. He teaches men the use of oars. The origin of salmon at Tsawitte.

The Thunderbird.
Twins.
Hē′likilikala.
Nā′laqanaq and the wolves.
Tsẹntsẹngatḻaχs kills Hataqa.
Kya′lqamistal, the first Hā′mats'a.
Kyā′loyagamē, the moon.
Qoaχī′la and Qomō′qoa.
Taχstatḻ and the frogs.
Baā′kumi.
Nutḻẹmkχ.
Taχstatḻ and the wolves.
Q'ōmq'ōmkilskya and the thunderbird.

The mink legend. The mink and the sun. The mink's matrimonial experiences. The mink and the ghosts.
Nīmasenχilis.
Tikyá.

Kumsnŏ́utl meets Çŏ́çēneus. He meets the codfish; the squid. He paints the raven.

The beaver and the frogs.
The great flood.
Xoāēχoē. The ancestor of the Çatlŏltχ.
The deer and the wolves.
The deer obtains the fire.
Qōmŏ́qoa.

The raven legend. The raven and the bird Anan. The raven and the Blue Jay. The raven and the seal. The raven and the deer. The raven as medicine man. The raven and the gull.

Ā́leχs.

Tlā́ŏqoqt the ancestor of the Tlā́amen.

The Thunderbird, the ancestor of the Pentlatc. Xoā́tqum. The Mink kills the thunderbird.

The hunters (Pentlatc).
Baχbakuanusiuae.
Tāl.
Tlŏ́menatso and the Aihōs.
Qatēnats.
Haliotis and Copper.
Qatḗmot (Eeqsen).

12. Qauistsin

Siā́lasta. The ancestors of the Qauistsin.

Swuχ'as. The Thunderbird. Siḗtlqē.

Xäls. meets the deer; he meets Spāl; he meets Q'ḗsēq.

The two boys and the whale.
The deserted boy.
Sχoḗtē.
Siḗtlqē.
Tiŏ́χtset.
The woman and the salmon.
The origin of the fire.

B. Customs as observed and derived from traditions.

Social organization—Chiefs, the people, clans. Gentes. Property. Birth, marriage, death. Transformation of customs and traditions by marriage.

The Potlatc.

Dances. More particularly among the Bilχula, Wik'ḗnō, Tlatlasiqoala, Kwakiutl. The meaning of the dancing implements.

C. Examination and comparison of traditions and customs.

I cannot give the contents of this part, as it will contain the final results of my work. The problem I had in view in visiting the Northwest coast was to study the reasons why tribes of different linguistic stocks participated in a common culture. My method is to inquire into the peculiarities of the single tribes which are obtained by a thorough comparison of language, customs and folklore. The latter I consider of great importance, as it recalls customs which easily escape notice, or are extinct; and is the best means of tracing the history of the tribes. I am analysing the numerous traditions enumerated above and comparing their elements. As yet I cannot say what the results of the comparison will be. Only a few points have become clear: the raven legend belongs to the northern part of the coast. Sun worship was the original form in the south. The cannibal occurrences belong to the Tsimpshian and Kwākiūtl. A third element what I cannot yet account for is the Masmasalanuχ legend of the Bilχula, an unrelated tribe of Selish lineage. It is not impossible that Tinne influence extends here. The Hēiltsuk and Wik'ēnō who are of Kwakiutl lineage are influenced by the Bilχula. The Çatloltχ are influenced by the Kwakiutl.

I have systematically collected from the point of view explained above. I may mention here that my collection is not complete, as it does not embrace the Puget Sound tribes, the Chinook, the Selish of the interior, the northern Tinne and the Kutena, what must be studied in the same way, in order to know the culture of the coast tribes as far back as it is possible by my method.

I include the Tsihelish, Nokwallis and the tribes in the southern part of British Columbia as far north as Seymour Narrows in the Coast Selish; their numerous dialects are closely related to each other, but differ considerably from the languages of the interior and other parts of the coast. I believe the Chinook will be found to be also of Selish lineage.

It would be difficult to obtain new material in those places where I have been. Generally I did not leave until I had collected sufficient material for my purpose.

III The art of the Northwest tribes

I make it a point of my researches to study the meaning, use and style of the carvings and paintings of the natives. The traditions and notes on the dances will be accompanied by numerous illustrations of masks, paintings, heralds, posts etc. with full explanations. I had photographs from Berlin, sketches from London and New York with me and obtained considerable amount of material in this line. I intend to discuss in this chapter the conventional style of implements and to trace their distribution. The results will corroborate and complete the inquiry contained in the foregoing chapter.

Part II Linguistics

My principal study in this line was the Selish languages.

I have comparative vocabularies of the following dialects:

1. Bilχula
2. Kwākiutl
3. Çatlōltχ
4. Peͺntlatc
5. Sī′ciatl
6. Snanaī′muχ
7. Sqχō′mic
8. Lquñgeͺn

containing from 700 to 1100 words. Words contained in texts are not included in this number. For all dialects I have grammatical notes and collections of sentences (the Sī′ciatl, Sqχō′mic and Lquñgen excepted).

Texts

Bilχula

Sṇēṇē′iq. about 180 words.
The raven and the salmon. 140 words.
The raven and the deer. 100 words.
The raven obtains the daylight. 100 words.
The boy and the salmon. 480 words.
Vavalis. 800 words.

All texts with full grammatical explanations and explanatory sentences.

Kwākiutl

25 songs and sentences. Dr. George M. Dawson had informed me that he and Rev. Hall of Alert Bay were going to publish a grammar of the language. Therefore I did not collect grammatical elements. Unfortunately I found out after my return from Kwakiutl territory that Mr. Hall himself does not know much about the language. Therefore I do not know whether I can give a satisfactory account of the language.

Çatlōltχ

Kumsnō′otl. 160 words.
The Mink and the clams. 40 words
The mink and the bear. 200 words
The mink and the wolf. 230 words
The mink and the whale. 160 words.
The jealous man. 380 words.

Qomoqoa. 180 words.
The mink and the fog. 55 words.
The mink and the eagle. 60 words.

Pe̜ntḻatc
The sun and the gum. 50 words.
The beaver and the frogs. 90 words.
The great flood. 120 words.
Tlaiq. 410 words.
The Thunderbird. 130 words.
The raven and his sisters. 75 words.

Snanaī′muχ
The whale steals the woman. 250 words.
The mink and the ghost. 100 words.

Tsimpshian
The raven steals the girl. 320 words
The cannibal. 250 words

A short vocabulary of the Tsimpshian.

Besides this I have a few scattered notes, what might be added as notes.

PUBLICATION OF THE *SAGEN*

While the *Verhandlungen* and *Zeitschrift für Ethnologie* journals published the individual sections of the *Sagen* texts between the years 1891–1895, Boas' correspondence indicates that he had been searching several years for a publisher who would print the entire collection in one volume.[12] Colleagues also offered Boas their views on suitable literary outlets. For example, a German colleague, Professor G. Gerland, recommended in a letter of 19 May 1887 the names of several publishers and anthologies, including: Asher & Co.; F.A. Brockhaus; Trübner's (for an English version); *Brinton's Library of Aboriginal American Literature*; and the French series, *Littérature populaire de toutes les nations*. Gerland urged Boas to publish soon, and though Boas was hesitant, especially considering the salacious nature of some of the stories, Gerland reassured him that German publishers would not be influenced by considerations of prudery in regard to a work of such scholarly dimensions (Gerland 1887). Still, Boas' concern was justified. The following year, the editor of the noted journal *American Antiquarian* excised terms regarded as "not suitable for publication" from Boas' article "Myths and Legends of the Çatloltq of Vancouver Island" (Boas 1888h:206).

---

12. We acknowledge with thanks the assistance that Dietrich Bertz provided in 1974–1977 in compiling this information on Boas' efforts to publish the *Sagen*.

Some potential publishers rejected Boas' *Sagen* manuscript on the ground that sales would not justify the expense. Hermann Costenoble of the *Verlagsbuchhandlung* in Jena replied on 21 November 1887 to Boas' inquiry that he generally refused "travel material" because it didn't sell, pointing to Aurel Krause's *Die Tlinkit-Indianer* (1885), the publication of which resulted in considerable losses. Others were nevertheless interested. Dr. G.M. Dawson of the Canadian Geological and Natural History Survey wrote to Boas on 30 March 1887: "Referring to the publication of your matter on B.C. Indians. It would be territorially appropriate to have it published in Canada & if you think the Royal Society Proceedings would be a suitable medium I should be gratified to introduce your paper, & give the requisite notice of it to the Council" (Dawson 1887b). Two years later Dawson still promoted publication of the *Sagen*, but realized that he, personally, had little to offer. On 10 January 1889 Dawson wrote: "I should be glad if possible to present your views in respect to the publication of B.C. myths etc. but you will understand that it is impossible for me to speak ... as to the action of the R.S. Can. in the matter as I am not even a member of the particular section under which they would come ... Have you ascertained from Mr. Hale or from Sir Daniel[13] whether it may not be possible to publish the matter in connection with British Association work?" (Dawson 1889). Boas did publish material with the Royal Society (Boas 1888g) and the British Association for the Advancement of Science (Boas 1890a; 1891d; 1894b), but these works contained only brief abstracts or a few examples of the numerous myths he had obtained for the *Sagen*.

Alternate publication plans for the *Sagen* collection were set in motion by Boas when he was in Europe in 1889. He succeeded in placing the work with a Leiden firm, and sent them the final manuscript at the end of 1890. After receiving no response, he discovered that this Dutch publisher had issued a circular requesting 100 American subscriptions before commencing printing. Boas demanded the return of his manuscript. Soon after, he made arrangements with the editor of the Verhandlungen der Berliner Gesellschaft für Anthropologie, Ethnologie und Urgeschichte (the journal of the Berlin Anthropological Society) to publish installments over several years, then provide 150 offprints which Boas could sell as bound separates (Cole 1999:141, 310).

Finally, Verlag von A. Asher & Co. of Berlin accepted the entire collection for publication, drawing together the sections of mythology that had been published

---

13.   Horatio Hale, the philologist and ethnologist from Clinton, Ontario, and Sir Daniel Wilson of the University of Toronto, along with G.M. Dawson of the Geological Survey of Canada, sat on a committee of the British Association for the Advancement of Science regarding the northwest tribes of Canada. The chairman of this Committee was Oxford University's Edward Burnett Tylor, the leading anthropologist in the United Kingdom (Cole 1999:110).

separately between 1891–1895 and printing the complete work under the title *Indianische Sagen von der Nord-Pacifischen Küste Amerikas* (Boas 1895b).

An Evaluation of the *Sagen*

The *Sagen* in its entirety is an extremely rich collection, although it is uneven. There is little in some of these myths and legends to distinguish them as particularly good examples that might reflect the original narrative form or personal style of the storytellers. The patterned repetition found commonly in the mythology of the region (such as incidents occurring four times) that is occasionally evident in the indigenous language texts, is sometimes absent in the *Sagen*, or present in an abbreviated form, along with an explanatory note. Boas sometimes took shortcuts. For example, where he regarded a story to be identical to that found in another area, Boas at times would state simply: "See legends of the Nootka. The name of the man killing his wife is QuakQū́kolatc here."[14] His focus, clearly, was on the plot summary and not the structure of the narrative event, and we can be thankful that he retained as many variants in the *Sagen* as he did.

Still, sections of the *Sagen* are superb. Texts from the Nahwitti and other Kwakwaka'wakw (Southern Kwakiutl) tribes—particularly the Nimpkish—present some fine examples of numaym ancestor legends, resplendent with genealogies and the identity of carved figures on the remaining village poles. Boas struggled with the task of recording the details of these people's histories, sometimes uncertain of the stories' completeness, yet the results are rewarding. In those areas where he spent enough time, Boas provides us with impressive collections of mythology. Legends of Raven and Mink told by the Tlatlasikwala and Nuu-chah-nulth (Nootka) are humourous examples of this genre. Stories from the Lower Fraser River, Shuswap, Comox and Pentlatch certainly indicate that Boas had found some exceptional mythtellers in those areas, and that he took the time to check his transcriptions and his understanding of the texts.

All in all, having worked with Boas' *Sagen* for more than two decades, we still marvel at what this brilliant young man accomplished under arduous conditions. And we, like Professor Lévi-Strauss, believe these texts have been neglected far too long.

Boas' Orthography

The general reader may be intimidated by the frequent use of indigenous terms in the *Sagen*. A myriad of information about mythical characters, places, species of flora and fauna, songs, crests and totems is recorded in 15 different languages. Over

---

14. See Section XIII of the present volume.

the years we have vacillated whether to update Boas' transcriptions with either an anglicized or phonetic orthography in the texts, or to retain his original transcriptions of all indigenous language terms. We have decided on the latter, mainly to retain this important aspect of his work. The astute reader may note inconsistencies in Boas' transcriptions of a single term between, for example, two Kwakwala-speaking tribes. Still, Boas' contributions in this area are especially impressive considering that the science of linguistics was in its infancy at the time of his field work. In 1886, very few studies of Northwest Coast languages were available for Boas to consult, and seldom did he find the research of missionaries, Indian Agents and settlers sufficient to do more than acquaint him with the complex phonologies of the numerous Native languages. A standardized orthography for these languages had not yet been developed. Much later Boas wrote of this early work: "During the early years of my own work on the coast of British Columbia I had not mastered sufficiently the art of clear phonetic perception and rendering, and for this reason the material is not as good as it might be" (Boas and Haeberlin 1927:4:117).

The several extant versions of Boas' Pentlatch texts indicate that in his earliest work he employed an orthography of his own creation that he then altered for the recopied versions going into the *Sagen*, so that the following symbols were modified from fieldnotes to publication: Ȼ →ç; X→q; X̣→x̣; Q→K̲; š→c; tl→l';ẹ→ě. The latter are the symbols used in the *Sagen*, although he returned to q for the uvular stop. In a letter to his elder sister, Toni, written from the field, Boas recommended further modifications to the orthography that included altering ẋ to h and X̱ to q̲, changes that are reflected in transcriptions left from his 1890 Fraser Valley work and in the vocabulary slips he was compiling (Rohner 1969:105). Obviously Boas recognized the importance of these numerous terms to the texts.

In our own *Sagen* annotations, where indigenous language terms have been recognized by the contemporary speakers of these languages with whom we have consulted, we provide an updated transcription written in the Northwest Coast version of the International Phonetic Alphabet, as well as the recognized translation of the term. The phonemic inventory adopted for each language is, for the most part, that presented in the Northwest Coast and Plateau volumes of the Smithsonian Institution's *Handbook of North American Indians*. The footnoted transcription appears, in most cases, for only the first occurrence of each Native term in each section of the *Sagen*. Where we have consulted Native speakers regarding a certain term but found that it was not recognized, this has been indicated. There are, however, some instances where we did not have an opportunity to confirm Boas' transcription with a Native speaker, and could not confirm its accuracy with contemporary linguistic or ethnographic studies. In these cases, Boas' original transcriptions appear without comment.

HISTORY OF THIS TRANSLATION

The history of the present volume began in 1973 when the British Columbia Indian Language Project commissioned Dietrich Bertz of Victoria to prepare an English translation of Franz Boas' *Indianische Sagen* which had been published in German in 1895. Mr. Bertz finished the initial draft of this translation in 1974, and completed a revised translation in 1977, in close collaboration with us, incorporating the Foreword presented here that was initially written in 1976, at our request, by Professor Claude Lévi-Strauss of the Collège de France. Around 1980, as part of the editing process, we again cross-checked with Mr. Bertz every line of the 1977 draft against the original German.

We began developing publication plans for the *Sagen* translation in the late 1970s, at the same time seeking clarification of copyright issues by initiating legal inquiries in Canada, the United States, and Germany. Subsequently, the sole surviving executrix of Franz Boas' estate, his daughter Franziska Boas (now deceased), transferred to the British Columbia Indian Language Project, by contract dated 25 June 1979, the Boas estate's world rights, title and interest to the underlying German work of the *Sagen*. We also obtained permission to publish a translation of the *Sagen* from the relevant publishers in Germany: A. Asher & Co.; Springer Verlag; and the Berliner Gesellschaft für Anthropologie, Ethnologie, und Urgeschichte.[15]

Throughout the years we have provided numerous photocopies of the 1974 and 1977 drafts of the *Indian Myths and Legends* translation to the First Nations communities from which these stories originated, to scholars in the field, and to public institutions throughout Canada and the United States. We began the task of annotating this translation in the mid-1970s. We took specific sections of the translation into the field to review with our Native consultants—at that time we were undertaking research with about half of the British Columbia First Nations whose stories are represented in the *Sagen*. For those First Nations with whom we were not directly involved, we were assisted by colleagues. This kind of consultation enabled us to feel more confident about our own transcriptions, and to confirm the translations that Boas gives for the many hundreds of Native terms in 15 indigenous languages. The identity of the numerous aboriginal individuals with whom we have consulted is mentioned both in the Acknowledgements and in the first footnote to each section. The indigenous language terms appearing in our annotations, as mentioned previously, have been transcribed by us in the International Phonetic

---

15. Prior to the present volume's publication, only two portions of the *Sagen* translation were previously published: a representative collection of the translated texts appeared in a literary quarterly (see Boas 1981); and a revised version of Professor Claude Lévi-Strauss' *Sagen* Foreword was published in an anthropological journal (see Lévi-Strauss 1984).

Alphabet, using the phonemic inventories set out in the relevant chapters of the Smithsonian Institution's Northwest Coast and Plateau volumes of the *Handbook of North American Indians*.

Our annotations for the texts have focussed on providing assistance to the reader by clarifying various terms, including: indigenous terms, especially those designating place names and aboriginal social groups; explanation of Native personal names; translation of phrases and songs that appear in the texts; identification of flora and fauna, especially those that are subjects of the stories; and comments on Boas' use of specific German terms that were not easily translated or require some manner of explanation. We have purposely not drawn the reader's attention to variants appearing in other myth collections[16] (including our own publications), except where this type of direction offers distinct clarification. Instead, our objective has been to assist the reader through a dense but rich volume that for far too long has remained inaccessible.

The task of editing and annotating this translation has been extraordinarily time-consuming—much more so than we originally envisioned when we approached a potential publisher around 1980. At that time, a major university press solicited peer review comments on several draft annotated sections of the translation. These same materials were sent out for peer review by funding sources we approached for publication subvention, including the Social Science Federation of Canada (as it was then known), the National Endowment for the Humanities in the United States, and the British Columbia Heritage Trust. The reviews recognized the contribution that the translation made to the existing knowledge of Northwest Coast and Plateau Native peoples; the assessors spoke highly of the translation, itself, and of our annotations, and all of them recommended publication of this work. Consequently the annotated *Sagen* translation was accepted for publication, and all three subvention sources committed financial support.

Yet it is only now, two decades after the initial publication acceptance and subvention commitment, that the final publication is being realized. This demands explanation. The timely completion of the manuscript in the early 1980s was hampered by a lack of sufficient funds being made available to enable us to complete our additional fieldwork, annotation, and editing. This resulted in the entire Boas project being put aside for a number of years, and the publication subsidies expiring. Modest grants from foundation, corporate, and government sources permitted some of this work to proceed between 1980–1982, but the voluminous manuscript languished on our resumes as a labour-of-love to which we

---

16. Occasionally in the *Sagen*, Boas himself refers to analogs; a listing of variant texts can be found in Section XXVI of this volume and in Boas' 1916 publication, *Tsimshian Mythology*.

returned on those occasions when we had the spare time and funds to devote to this academic undertaking.

Work resumed on the *Sagen* translation manuscript between 1991–1994 with funds provided to the B.C. Indian Language Project by Employment and Immigration Canada's "Challenge" program to subsidize student summer employment. This funding contribution assisted us in hiring research assistant Peryl Cain to word-process the entire manuscript, which was then proof-read by Juanita Judson.

Sporadically throughout the rest of the 1980s–1990s, as time and funds permitted, we continued with our work that had begun in the mid-1970s of confirming Native terms with aboriginal elders throughout the Northwest Coast and Plateau. As well, we made some progress with our annotation and editing, taking into consideration the discerning comments that had been provided to us both by colleagues and by anonymous assessors as part of the peer review process.

It was during 2000–2001, however, that our work on this translation had a new impetus. We benefited greatly during this time from the expert editorial assistance of our colleague Dr. Ralph Maud, Professor Emeritus in the English Department of Simon Fraser University and author of several books and articles on B.C. First Nations mythology. Ralph worked closely with us to undertake a definitive review of the entire manuscript and to prepare the Section Introductions. Also during 2000–2001, Klaus Schmidt of Victoria graciously volunteered his time to make a final line-by-line check of the entire translation against the original *Sagen*. This resulted in further refinements to the translation, including standardization of certain translated terms. As well, Klaus translated a number of other German articles containing variants of some of the *Sagen* tales that were published in several periodicals between 1886–1894. The completed manuscript was proof-read by BCILP research assistant Diane Carr, who also took charge of selecting and ordering the archival photographs for the publication (many of them the work of early B.C. photographers, and a few of them never before published). Diane also helped us to compile the References Cited section (in lieu of an Index, we have included an Appendix which provides a full listing of the stories appearing in each section).

It was also during 2000–2001 that Karl Siegler of Talonbooks, who had maintained a strong interest in the *Indian Myths and Legends* translation over the past two decades, offered to publish this collection, and the B.C. Heritage Trust, whose 1980 subvention for this translation had expired in 1982, again committed publication funding, as did the Aid to Scholarly Publications Programme of the Social Sciences Federation of Canada, whose 1981 subvention had expired in 1985.

Textual Notes

Since it has been our aim to be faithful to the text of the *Sagen* volume as published in 1895, the translation has been quite literal. Occasional idiosyncrasies have been pointed out in footnotes, but to avoid tedious repetition we have made certain translation decisions that operate throughout and should be listed as prefatory information. These are mainly concerned with the fact that Boas had the problem of using a European language sometimes to denote things that did not exist in Europe but were the familiar stuff of life on the Pacific coast and often entered the story-telling. Some examples are as follows:

(1) *Delphin* 'dolphin': but the species found in Pacific waters in our area of concern is the porpoise (Harbour porpoise or Dall porpoise); thus "porpoise" is the preferred translation.

(2) *Dohle* 'jackdaw': Boas consistently used this word instead of *Krähe* 'Crow' throughout, though his storytellers undoubtedly meant to indicate Crow—there are no jackdaws in the Pacific Northwest area. It has been thought best to translate *Dohle* as 'Crow' without always reiterating this circumstance in a footnote.

(3) *Elch* 'elk; moose': since there were formerly no moose in our area of concern, except for the far north of the province, 'elk' is the usual translation. Moose occurs only once in the *Sagen*, in a Tsimshian story where Boas uses the term *Elenthiere*, meaning literally 'elk or moose-like animal.'

(4) *Fett* 'fat': liquid oil is sometimes being talked about, so we have translated it as 'oil' where necessary to the context.

(5) *Finwal* 'finwhale': this is a neologism created by Boas (comprised of English "fin" and German *Wal* 'any whale') to indicate an orca or killer whale (*Delphinus orca*), and we have translated accordingly. Boas reserves the German *Finnwal* for other species of whale, including the common finback whale (*Balaenoptera physalus*).

(6) *Geschlecht* 'social group': this general word of many uses receives some peculiar to the aboriginal societies involved in the legends, so that 'tribe,' 'lineage,' 'family,' 'village,' 'descent,' 'race,' 'origin,' or "numaym" are sometimes appropriate. This also applies to the equally multi-use synonym, *Stamm* 'family; tribe; race; stock; clan; household group; etc.'

(7) *Hirsch* 'deer; red deer': this is generally translated as "deer," although on those occasions where the animal's identification is more plausibly an elk, this term has been translated as such and footnoted.

(8) *Kranich* 'crane': Boas' mythtellers were generally referring to the Great Blue Heron, common in the area, and a frequent character in Northwest Coast

mythology: we have felt it best to translate it most often as "heron," especially when guided by the indigenous language term. Sometimes Sandhill Crane is meant, and we have translated accordingly, with an explanatory note.

(9) *Kupferplatte* 'sheet of copper': this is Boas' way of rendering the unique Northwest Coast "copper," a shaped sheet of beaten copper of great value in potlatching; thus "copper" would be the appropriate translation.

(10) *Mantel* 'cape; coat; cloak; outer covering': in accordance with the reality of aboriginal life, this general word has been translated most often as 'cape' but sometimes as 'blanket.' Wherever it has implications of exchange value, the proper word would be 'blanket.' Occasionally, Boas does use the German *Decke* 'blanket,' and in one story he makes a distinction between *Kragen* 'collar'—in that instance referring to a cape of cedar bark—from *Fellmantel*, meaning 'fur cape.'

(11) *Muschel* 'shellfish; mussel; shell': most often edible shellfish is being referred to, but often a shell is meant, and occasionally the reference is specifically to mussels, so we have translated accordingly.

(12) *Panther* 'panther': there are no panthers in this area of North America, so we translate this as "cougar," the animal that the mythteller would have had in mind; on several occasions where the indigenous term for 'wolverine' is also given, we use the translation 'wolverine' rather than 'cougar.'

(13) *Präriewolf* 'prairie wolf': this is the German equivalent for 'coyote,' the popular trickster of the stories, so 'coyote' has been consistently used. In one story, Boas used the English term "coyote," and in another he refers to "der Coyote."

(14) *Reibe-Feuerzeug* 'friction lighter': the proper English equivalent for this created word would be 'fire-drill.'

(15) *Schellfisch* 'haddock': there are no haddock in these waters, so the informants would be referring to the commonly-fished red snapper (sometimes called "red cod"); hence the translation "red snapper."

(16) *Taucher* 'diver; grebe; loon': often the Western or other species of Grebe, and sometimes the Common Loon, would be the species concerned, so we have translated accordingly, guided by the advice given to us by the aboriginal residents of each area; where adequate information has not been available, we have simply left it as 'diver.'

(17) *Unterirdisches Haus* 'underground house': This is a direct translation of the German term used to describe a 'semi-subterranean pithouse.' In the stories we have retained the less formal language "underground house."

(18) *Wappen* 'coat of arms; armorial bearings': the heraldic equivalent on the northwest coast would be "crest."

Since the German of the *Sagen* capitalizes all nouns, it leaves open the problem of what should be capitalized in an English translation. We have determined the following:

(1) persons or places receive capital letters as customary, e.g. G'anō;

(2) personal names, including animals and myth figures, receive a capital letter, whereas animals in groups or identified as a member of a group do not: e.g. Beaver or Porcupine; a beautiful duck (mē'ek·); Raven Clan; a big raven;

(3) when a name is given in an indigenous language and the parenthesis that follows it is presented as a translation (with or without the equal sign [=]), the parenthetical words are capitalized, except where the brackets contain an explanatory note:

e.g. KsEmtsiâlk (= female kingfisher) (*Sagen*:273)

NEmōmhā't (= Gut Devourer) (*Sagen*:273)

Hōk·qsāug·am Negno'q (the one not believing in Negno'q) (*Sagen*:280)

Laqaquwā'se (the double-headed fish) (*Sagen*:276)

Wulbatlketl k·ā'aq (= der *enthauptete Rabe*) (*Sagen*:278) (= the beheaded raven)

ADDITIONAL NOTES

The final section of the *Sagen*, "The Development of the Mythologies of the North Pacific Coast Indians," appears here in translation without comment. This section represents Boas' initial recognition of mythic motifs as isolatable episodes that recur over wide areas, continuously borrowed and shared among diverse groups of people. Some of his conclusions in this chapter have since been shown to be erroneous, and Boas, himself, subsequently revised and greatly expanded this analysis in Tsimshian Mythology (Boas 1916), a volume readily available to students of folklore. This chapter of the *Sagen* is important in the history of science, nevertheless, for demonstrating Boas' departure from earlier theories on mythology that were rooted in evolutionary dogmas and psychological assumptions. We have therefore left it intact as an artifact of a genre of anthropology based on the comprehensive collection and comparison of similar data from broad geographical areas.[17]

---

17. Boas' own summary of this final section of the *Sagen* was given as an address to the American Folk-Lore Society in December 1895, published the following year as "The Growth of Indian Mythologies" (Boas 1896), and subsequently reprinted in *Race, Language and Culture* (Boas 1940:425–436).

A comment on the title is also necessary. One reviewer of the translation observed that the term *Sagen* translates quite well as 'myths,' whereas we have chosen to say 'myths and legends'—a translation that Boas, himself, used.[18] We say 'myths and legends' to emphasize the distinction between different types of stories that is commonly made in the languages of the indigenous peoples from whom Boas recorded these texts. Some aboriginal people regard the connotation of the term "myth" to be "fairytale," thus inferring an intrinsically false or childish character to the stories. In some cases, the tales presented here might well be classified as children's stories, but we hope that our use of "legend" indicates that many of the texts recorded by Boas possess more epic dimensions, particularly the accounts of First Ancestors and their encounters with wondrous beings.

Our use of the term "Indian" in the title (translated from the German "Indianische") also requires comment. During the past two decades, aboriginal people in Canada have increasingly sought recognition of themselves as members of "First Nations." This contemporary terminology, which is not used in the United States, conveys Canadian aboriginal peoples' sense of having indigenous governments parallel with the structure of the dominant nation-state. Today in Canada the term "First Nation" has largely replaced the term "Indian," which is seen by some indigenous people and some non-Natives as pejorative, but which remains current in ordinary daily conversation by both "Indians" and "Whites" alike. In the present edition, we tend to use the synonyms "indigenous," "aboriginal," and "Native," but occasionally make reference to "First Nations," "tribes," and "Indians," as well, following the context of the people's own usage of these terms. For the most part, we have used the names of specific groups, as used by the members themselves. In the title, however, we have employed the more literal translation "Indian," the term used by Boas, and also the term used in the title of the well-distributed 1974 and 1977 drafts of the translation. This, after all, is an historic volume that must be presented as an artifact of its own time.

Randy Bouchard and Dorothy Kennedy
Victoria, British Columbia, Canada
May 2002

---

18. See Boas 1888h, "Myths and Legends of the Catloltq of Vancouver Island," comprising Boas' own English version of some of the stories appearing here in Section VIII of the *Sagen*.

Translator's Note

I was asked to provide a close and exact translation and this I endeavoured to do, even though invariably this goes at the expense of style. There are only a few instances where currently accepted terms have been used instead of the literal meaning. Thus I give 'pitch' and 'double-headed serpent' rather then 'gum' or 'resin' and 'double-headed snake,' used by Boas in other texts of the late 1800's. He refers to *Hirsch* and *Tintenfisch* throughout, literally 'elk or wapiti' and 'squid', which I usually give as 'deer' and 'octopus', basing this (and the capital letters for supernatural items and beings) on his own later style, notably with the Hunt texts (Boas and Hunt 1902–1905). He uses the term 'canoe' only once, giving it in English spelling, otherwise using *Boot* or *Kahn*, which I render as 'boat.'[1] Similarly he employs the term 'doctor' only once, otherwise using *Schamane* most of the time, or else *Krankenbeschwörer* and *Heilkünstler*, which I give as 'shaman' and 'medicine man.' Ambiguities are inherent in such terms as *Muschel*, which could be several (but not all) varieties of 'shellfish,' or simply 'any seashell' (i.e. the outer shell without the living organism) and *Reinigung*, which could denote ritual purification as well as simple cleaning. Finally, the motif index at the very end, compiled by Boas, lost its alphabetical order in translation and was not rearranged because of the many references to its entry numbers throughout the final discussion.

My sincerest appreciation goes to Ronald Knott and Colleen Casey Stewart for reading the first draft of the translated texts in their entirety, and to Lilo Berliner for sustaining interest. I also wish to express my gratitude to my family for their understanding and forbearance all along, and heartfelt thanks especially to my wife Shirley-Ann for sharing the tedious task of final proof-reading my 1977 translation.

Dietrich Bertz
Victoria, British Columbia, March 1977

---

1. In subsequent editing of the translation, we have chosen to use the gloss most culturally appropriate, thereby substituting 'canoe' for 'boat' (see the Editors' Introduction).—eds.

Boas' Preface to the Original 1895 Edition

The legends contained in the following collection were noted down by me from the lips of Indians during repeated trips to the Pacific coast of America. A large number were told through the medium of the Chinook Jargon, while many legends of the Kwakiutl tribes and the Tsimschian were translated into German directly from the original languages. The Shuswap legends I noted down with the help of an old French Indian half-blood. Communications from the lips of whites have been used only in a few instances and then with reference to sources.

The collection appeared first in *Zeitschrift für Ethnologie* and *Verhandlungen der Berliner Gesellschaft für Anthropologie, Ethnologie und Urgeschichte*, as follows:

Zeitschrift für Ethnologie 1888	pp.	231–247
Verhandlungen der Berl. Ges. Für Anthrop., Ethnol. und Urg. . . 1891	¨	532–576
¨ . . . 1891	¨	628–645
¨ . . . 1892	¨	32–66
¨ . . . 1892	¨	314–344
¨ . . . 1892	¨	383–410
¨ . . . 1893	¨	228–265
¨ . . . 1893	¨	430–477
¨ . . . 1894	¨	281–306
¨ . . . 1895	¨	189–234

The following alphabet has been used to render Indian words and names: Vowels are used as in German; E stands for Lepsius ę. The following consonants require an explanation:

g·	velar g;
k·	velar k;
q	as ch in German *Bach*;
H	as ch in German *ich*;
Q	between q and H, lips in position for u;
c	the German *sch*;
ç	the English th in thin;
tl	plosive, dorso-apical l;
'	lips in position for u;
,	pause.

The author has published additional communications about the physical anthropology, ethnology and languages of the North Pacific coast of America as follows:

Zur Ethnologie von Britisch Columbien. *Petermann's Mittheilungen* 1887. Nr. V.

Die Sprache der Bella Colla Indianer. *Verhandl. der Berl. anthropol. Ges.* 1886. Pp. 202–206.

Mittheilungen über die Bilqula-(Vilχula-) Indianer. *Original Mittheilungen des Museums für Völkerkunde*. Berlin.

Chinook Songs. *Journal of American Folk Lore* 1888. Pp. 220–226.

The Houses of the Kwakiutl Indians, British Columbia. *Proceedings of the U.S. National Museum* 1888. Pp. 197–213.

Notes on the Snanaimuq. *American Anthropologist* 1889. Pp. 321–328.

Fourth Report of the Committee of the British Association for the Advancement of Science on the North Western Tribes of Canada 1889. Pp. 1–10.

Fifth Report of the same Committee 1890. Pp. 1–96.

Sixth Report of the same Committee 1891. Pp. 1–163.

Seventh Report of the same Committee 1892. Pp. 1–40.

Ninth Report of the same Committee 1894. Pp. 1–12.

Tenth Report of the same Committee 1895. Pp. 1–71.

Petroglyph von Vancouver Island. Sagen der Kootenay. *Verhandl. der Berl. anthropol. Ges.* 1891. Pp. 158–172.

Notes on the Chemakum Language. *American Anthropologist* 1892. Pp. 37–44.

Vocabularies from the North Pacific Coast. *Trans. Am. Philos. Soc.* Philadelphia 1891. Pp. 173–208.

Vocabulary of the Kwakiutl Language. *Trans. Am. Philos. Soc.* Philadelphia 1892. Pp. 34–82.

Chinook Jargon. *Science* Vol. XIX. New York. 1892. P. 129.

Notes on the Chinook Language. *American Anthropologist* 1893. Pp. 55–63.

Classification of the Languages of the North Pacific Coast. *International Congress of Anthropology*. Chicago 1893. Pp. 339–346.

Chinook Texts. *Bulletin of the Bureau of Ethnology*. Washington 1894. Pp. 1–278.

Bella Coola Texts. *Trans. Am. Philos. Soc.* Philadelphia 1895. Pp. 31–48.

Zur Mythologie der Indianer von Washington und Oregon. *Globus* 1893. Vol. 63. Nr. 10–12.

Above: *Britisch Columbien*. Boas' map reproduced from the 1895 *Indianische Sagen*.

Over: *Die Indianerstämme von Vancouver Id. und an der Küste von Britisch-Columbia. Nach eigenen Forschungen gezeichnet von Dr. Franz Boas* ('Indian Tribes from Vancouver Island and on the Coast of British Columbia. Drawings based on Dr. Franz Boas' Research'). *Petermanns Geographische Mitteilungen,* 1887.

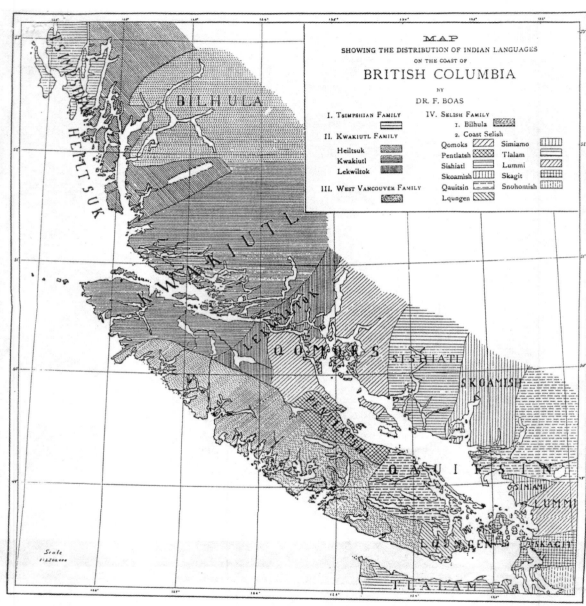

Map showing the distribution of Indian languages on the coast of British Columbia, by D. F. Boas. *Science*, March 25, 1887.

I. Legends of the Shuswap

"The Shuswap legends I noted down with the help of an old French Indian half-blood"; beyond this comment in the Preface to *Indianische Sagen* (Boas 1895b:v), there is no mention of this Métis interpreter, neither in the body of the text nor in Boas' report on the Shuswap for the British Association for the Advancement of Science (Boas 1891d:632–647, 683–692). We know that in Kamloops for the week 8–14 September 1889 Boas was unhappy. It was his last stop on the trip; he was eager to get home, but he had to include the Shuswap in his report, to "please old Hale" (Rohner 1969:114). We know that he used the "French Indian half-blood," but we do not know what this man's skills were or what his attitude might be to the Shuswap storytellers, about whom we unfortunately know nothing.

Unidentified Shuswap woman using a stone scraper to soften a hide stretched on a frame fastened between the support posts of a cache, Kamloops, B.C., 1928.
American Museum of Natural History Library, New York. Neg. No. 411796
(Harlan I. Smith photo).

I. Legends of the Shushwap. Collected in Kamloops.[1]

1. Tlē'esa[2]

There was once a young woman who had four sons. The eldest was called Tlē'esa. The young men wanted to wander throughout the world, so their mother threw a magic substance over them in order to make them strong. She hit the three youngest but missed the eldest and he was at once changed into a dog. Then she foretold everything that would happen to them.

Presently the young men set out and wandered from Shushwap Lake down the South Thompson River.[3] Soon they reached the home of "Woodchuck" (*Arctomys monax*),[4] which stood right between two rocks. When someone came, Woodchuck

---

1. Kamloops is situated at the centre of Shuswap traditional territory, at the confluence of the North and South Thompson Rivers. What Boas transcribes as "Shushwap" is most often written as "Shuswap" (Boas, himself, uses the spelling "Shuswap" elsewhere in the *Sagen*) which is an anglicization of the Native term applied both to this Plateau group and to the language they speak. Shuswap traditional territory encompassed the region bordered approximately by Enderby, Pavilion, Soda Creek, the Rocky Mountains, and the Big Bend area of the Upper Columbia. The Shuswap, Thompson and Lillooet languages together comprise the Northwestern group of the Interior Salish Branch of the Salishan Language Family (Teit 1909:449–463; 1914:284; Bouchard and Kennedy 1979:ix; Boelscher Ignace 1998:203–205; Kinkade *et al.* 1998). A contemporary transcription that refers to the Shuswap is "Secwepemc" meaning 'Shuswap people.'

    In annotating this section, we have drawn upon our 1970s–1980s consultation with the following Shuswap people whose assistance we gratefully acknowledge: Aimee August, Charley Draney, Isaac Willard, Adeline Willard, Bill Arnouse, Harvey Jules, and Joe Williams. For comparative Upper Lillooet information cited in this section, we have drawn upon our 1960s–1980s consultation with Sam Mitchell, Slim Jackson, Francis Edwards, Bill Edwards, and Annie Edwards.

2. "Tlē'esa" is Boas' rendering of tɬíʔse, the Shuswap term for one of the Transformers—cultural heroes with special magical powers who set the world in order for the coming people (see Bouchard and Kennedy 1979:3–5).

3. Given in English as South Thompson River (without quotation marks) in the original *Sagen*.

4. Given in English as "Woodchuck" (with double quotation marks) in the original German text; the Latin identification *Arctomys monax* provided here by Boas was used in the late 1800s for the Virginian woodchuck, a species not found in this area. The species referred to here is very likely the yellow-bellied marmot (*Marmota flaviventris*), known commonly as a "groundhog," whose main habitat is broken rocks, stone piles and rocky talus slopes (Cowan and Guiguet 1973:119–120; Banfield 1974:110). In other Shuswap variants of this same legend, the name of this animal is given as 'marmot' (Teit 1909:648) or 'groundhog' (Bouchard and Kennedy 1979:3–5).

retreated into his house and if anyone followed to catch him, the rocks slammed together and killed the intruder. When Tlē'esa saw many Woodchucks playing on the boulders, he said, "I will go and catch them." Tlē'esa's brothers warned him and reminded him that their mother had told them that Woodchuck would kill anyone who attacked him. But he was not to be restrained and ran off to catch them. The Woodchucks retreated into their house between the rocks. So Tlē'esa took his stone-tipped spear and wedged it sideways between the rocks, which thus could not slam together any more. Then he caught the Woodchucks, killing them with the club[5] suspended from his wrist. He then threw them out of the crevice and his brothers picked them up. Tlē'esa said, "Henceforth you shall no longer kill people. You shall be woodchucks and serve as food for people." While he was still fighting the Woodchucks in the crevice, his brothers lit a huge fire, roasted the animals and had eaten the best when Tlē'esa finally emerged from the crevice. Tlē'esa did not say anything but took what was left.

Then they continued downriver. When they arrived at Ducks[6] they saw a woman sitting there on a rock, singing. Tlē'esa said, "I want to catch her." Again his brothers warned him, but he would not be restrained. He climbed up the mountain and collected many pine cones. The woman laughed at him and walked backwards just as quickly as he climbed up the mountain. His brothers followed him. Finally, the woman stopped. When Tlē'esa came close to her, suddenly an enormous number of rattlesnakes crawled from her orifices[7] and advanced upon him, but he killed them all with his pine cones. While he was still fighting the snakes, his brothers ran on and seized the woman for themselves. Tlē'esa said nothing to his brothers. He merely said to the woman, "From now on you will no longer kill anyone. If a man desires you, he will take you and you shall not be able to harm him."

The brothers continued downriver. When they reached a spot just above Kamloops, they saw an underground house[8] with a tall pole beside it. Here lived

---

5. *Hammer* ('hammer') in the original *Sagen*, but better translated as 'club' in this context. Boas (1891d:638) indicates that one of the weapons formerly used by the Shuswap was "a stone club, consisting of a pebble, sewed into a piece of hide, and attached to a thong, which was suspended from the wrist."

6. Given in English as Ducks (without quotation marks) in the original *Sagen* text. "Ducks" was the former name of the settlement now referred to as Monte Creek, located along the south side of the South Thompson River about 16 miles (approximately 26 km) east from Kamloops. This place was named "Ducks" after the pioneer family of Jacob Duck who settled here in 1863 (Akrigg and Akrigg 1997:178).

7. Boas (1916:1017) summarizes this same legend as "woman with toothed vagina."

8. "The Indians live in such houses during winter" [Boas' original footnote]. Given in the original German as *unterirdisches Haus*, literally 'underground house,' although a more formal translation would be 'semi-subterranean pithouse'; a description of this type of dwelling can be found in Teit (1909:492–493).

Grizzly Bear[9] and Coyote.[10] The Bears watched their arrival and the three brothers entered. They tied up Tlĕ′esa outside the entrance and covered him all over with stone knives, even his tail and his teeth. After a while Bear invited them to a contest; they were to climb the pole in front of the house. First, the second brother climbed up, together with Bear. When they had almost reached the top, Bear grabbed him and killed him. His corpse fell from the pole. When Tlĕ′esa saw this, he became furious, howling and baring his teeth. Thereupon Coyote cried, "I'm afraid the dog will devour us; he is getting too wild." Tlĕ′esa merely touched Coyote with his body and the latter at once began to bleed. The stone knives had cut him. Now the third brother climbed the pole with Bear. He did not fare any better than his brother before him and the fourth brother also met with the same fate. Now only the dog, Tlĕ′esa, was left. He cut the rope with which he was tied and climbed up with Bear. When they had almost reached the top, he cut Bear in half so that one part fell down on the right and the other on the left. Four Bears climbed in competition with him, but he killed them all. He then joined the limbs of his brothers back together, jumped over them, and they were brought back to life.

The brothers wandered on and arrived at Cherry Creek.[11] There they saw an underground house in which Rabbit[12] lived. Tlĕ′esa said, "I will go inside; I want to eat Rabbit for supper." Again his brothers warned him, but he was not to be restrained. He took a flat stone and with it covered his belly and chest and then entered. The brothers stayed outside and peeped into the house. Rabbit lay on his back with his legs crossed. He had some meat lying behind him. When he saw Tlĕ′esa enter, he called out, "Hello stranger! Where do you come from? Where are you going?" Tĕ′esa answered, "Oh, I am just travelling around for pleasure." "You must be hungry, there is meat here behind me; take some!" As Tlĕ′esa stepped forward in order to take some of the meat, Rabbit kicked him in the chest. This was how he used to kill all strangers who visited his house. His leg always kicked straight through the chest. But this time he broke his leg on the stone covering Tlĕ′esa's chest. He began to wail. Tlĕ′esa grabbed him by the other leg, smashed it into the wall and called out, "So far you have killed people. Now I will kill you and

---

9. *Ursus arctos horribilis.*

10. Appears here in the original *Sagen* only as Coyote (without quotation marks).

11. Given in English as Cherry Creek (without quotation marks) in the original text. Cherry Creek enters into the south side of Kamloops Lake about 14 miles (approximately 22 km) west from Kamloops.

12. *Kaninchen,* 'rabbit,' in the original *Sagen*, although Boas' (1916:1017) summary of this same legend refers to it as 'kicking hare,' Teit's (1909:649–650) version identifies it as 'cannibal hare,' and the variant recorded in Bouchard and Kennedy (1979:6) uses the term 'rabbit.' The actual species that predominates in this area is the snowshoe or varying hare (*Lepus americanus*) which is commonly referred to as a "rabbit."

then I will eat you!" He flung him outside the house. His brothers picked him up and cooked him and ate him before Tlē'esa came back out.

The brothers continued and arrived at Savaners (?) Ferry.[13] Here a huge elk[14] straddled the river and killed anyone who tried to cross. He pulled the canoes ashore and devoured them.[15] When the brothers arrived here, they did not know how to continue. Tlē'esa said, "I will build a raft and float down." His brothers did not want him to do it, but he paid no attention to them and built a raft. When he was finished, he stepped onto it and let it drift downstream. When he got close, Elk slurped up Tlē'esa and his raft. So his brothers wept because they thought he was dead. But the logs of the raft passed straight through Elk. Tlē'esa lit a fire inside and cooked himself a good meal. Then he reached for Elk's heart and squeezed it. Elk swayed from one bank of the river to the other. When the brothers saw this they said to each other, "What has happened to Elk?" When he swayed again to the side where the brothers were standing, Tlē'esa cut off his heart and Elk fell down dead. The brothers skinned him and cut him open. When they were about to cut open the stomach, Tlē'esa shouted, "Take care and don't cut me!" So they opened the stomach carefully and discovered that Tlē'esa had cooked himself a meal inside. The brothers ate it all up.

They now crossed the river. Soon they saw a "tobacco tree."[16] As soon as anyone tried to get tobacco, one of the tree's branches began swinging around in circles and killed him. Tlē'esa took a small stick and walked up to the tree. When the branch began swinging, he lopped it off with the stick and tossed it into the river. Then, using his stick, he dug up the tree and pushed it over. Now the brothers came up and picked off all the tobacco. Tlē'esa did not get anything.

---

13. The words Savaners (?) Ferry appear in the original *Sagen* in English (with a question mark, and without quotation marks). The community now known as "Savona," situated at the west end of Kamloops Lake, was named after Francis Saveneux who in 1859 established a ferry across the Thompson River where it flows out of Kamloops Lake (Akrigg and Akrigg 1997:236–237).

14. The German term *Elch* refers to both 'moose' (*Alces alces andersoni*) and 'elk' (*Cervus elaphus nelsoni*). It is most likely that Boas' use of the word *Elch* in this legend refers to 'elk' because moose were not found in this region until the 20th century, but elk are native here (Cowan and Guiguet 1973:378; Spalding 1990:6; 1992:10–11). Elsewhere both Boas (1916:611, 1017) and Dawson (1892:32) use the English term 'elk monster' with reference to this same legend.

15. Concerning this same incident, Boas' summary (1916:611) states: "The canoes pass through its body, while the crew is retained and killed."

16. "Before the arrival of the Whiteman the Indians supposedly used the leaves of this tree as tobacco. The genus and species could not be determined" [Boas' original footnote]. This term appears in double quotation marks in the original *Sagen* as "*Tabaksbaum*" which means 'tobacco tree.' The storyteller was likely referring to the species of tobacco identified as *Nicotiana attenuata* (Teit 1909:574; Turner 1997:176–177), although this is a plant and not a tree.

The brothers then walked up along Bonaparte Creek.[17] Here there is a steep rock where Mountain Goat[18] lived. He killed all who tried to catch him. At the foot of the rock there was a dog who bit anyone passing him by. Tlē′esa said, "I want to kill Mountain Goat and mix his fat with my tobacco." The brothers were sure that he would be unable to climb the rock. But Tlē′esa was not to be dissuaded and embarked upon the adventure. When the dog tried to bite him, he pierced him with his stick and threw him to the ground, shouting, "You will no longer kill anyone! Henceforth people shall make use of you." Tlē′esa climbed the rock. When Mountain Goat saw him, he tried to push him off. But he pierced him with his stick and smashed his head with his club. Then he pushed him down the mountain and said, "You shall no longer kill anyone. Henceforth people will kill you and eat you." Mountain Goat landed at the bottom, ripped in pieces. The brothers picked him up and took all the fat, which they mixed with their tobacco. Thus nothing was left for Tlē′esa.

The brothers continued and arrived at "Johnny Wilson's Place."[19] They were going along the top of the mountainside and saw a man walking on the riverbank below. So the brothers said to each other, "Let's play a trick on him! They flung huge boulders at him. When the dust had settled they could see him walk on, as if nothing had happened. They tried to hit him, one after the other. But they couldn't do anything to him even though they finally caused a large rockslide. So Tlē′esa went down to have a look at the stranger. He noticed that he carried on his back a small basket, no larger than a fist. He said, "Who are you? We've tried to play a trick on you but were unable to do so." The stranger replied that his name was Tkumenaā′lst,[20] and invited Tlē′esa and his brothers to share a meal with him. He put roots and berries in his basket and placed stones in the fire. When the meal was ready, one of the brothers said, "I'll take one bite and it will all be gone." But when he had taken one spoonful from the basket, it filled right up again at once. After they had all eaten their fill, they wandered on together.

17. Given in English (without quotation marks) in the original *Sagen*; present-day maps refer to this as the Bonaparte River.

18. *Bergziege* 'mountain goat,' although Boas (1916:612, 1017) himself uses both 'mountain goat' and 'mountain sheep' when discussing this legend, and Teit's (1909:647) Shuswap variant refers to 'mountain sheep.' Formerly both mountain goat (*Oreamnos americanus*) and mountain sheep (*Ovis canadensis*) were found in this area. The location of the steep rock referred to here is not known.

19. Appears in English (with double quotation marks) as "Johnny Wilson's place" in the original *Sagen*; the area referred to is near today's Highway 97, about a mile (1.6 km) south from the Highway 99 intersection.

20. The name of this stranger, tq̓ʷəmnélst is found in other Shuswap variants of these Transformer stories as the name for one of the brothers of "Tlē′esa" (Dawson 1892:31–32; Bouchard and Kennedy 1979:3–5).

Soon they arrived at Hat Creek.[21] Here there is a steep rock wall. Tlē'esa said, "Let's play here for a bit." Tkumenaā'lst asked what they were going to play and Tlē'esa answered that they should try to run their heads into the rock. The three brothers tried it first. They made slight dents in the rock. Then Tlē'esa tried, and his head went into the stone right past his ears. But Tkumenaā'lst's head went in even further, right up to his shoulders.[22]

Then they continued and came to Fountain Trail.[23] Here Eagle had her nest on a steep rock.[24] Tlē'esa said, "I want to get her feathers and trim my cape with them." His brothers warned him, but he was not to be dissuaded. He took his staff, some red and some white paint,[25] and sat down at the foot of the rock face. Then his brothers saw how Eagle swooped down on him. She carried him up and circled with him in order to dash him against the rock. But when she flew up to the rock in order to smash Tlē'esa against it, he braced his staff against the rock and thus escaped unhurt. He had put some red paint in his mouth and spat it onto the rock so that Eagle and the brothers mistook it for his blood. Eagle flew around with him once more in a wide circle in order to dash him against the rock. Again Tlē'esa braced his staff against the rock and this time spat white paint on it. Eagle and the brothers mistook it for his brains. She took him to her nest and flew away again. The young Eagles wanted to devour him. So he showed them his club and said, "Don't dare touch me or I will kill you. When your mother returns, ask her to sit at the edge of the nest, and should she ask why you haven't eaten me, don't tell her that I am still alive!" The young Eagles were afraid and promised to obey. Soon the old one returned and brought them bears and deer. When she saw Tlē'esa still in the nest, she asked her young ones why they hadn't eaten him. Then she flew away again. Tlē'esa shared the bears and deer with the young ones. When the old one returned

---

21. Given in English (without quotation marks) as Hat Creek in the original *Sagen*.

22. This distinctive rock was formerly located along Highway 99, adjacent to Hat Creek, about five miles (approximately 8 km) west of this creek's confluence with the Bonaparte River, but is said to have been destroyed subsequently by highway construction (after the early 1970s). This same rock and the actions of the Transformers associated with it were identified in 1846 (Anderson 1878:50) and 1888 (Dawson 1888; 1892:32) as the source of Hat Creek's early name, "Rivière aux Chapeaux" (literally, 'creek of the hats').

23. Given in English as Fountain Trail (without quotation marks) in the original *Sagen*. Mayne (1859) indicated that this trail connected the area now known as the town of Cache Creek with the Upper Lillooet Interior Salish settlement at Fountain, upriver from the present town of Lillooet.

24. This bird is identified as the Bald Eagle (*Haliaeetus leucocephalus*). It has not been possible to determine the exact location of the steep rock referred to here by Boas. However, a Shuswap variant of this same story provided by Teit (1909:649) and additional information given in Dawson (1892:35) suggest the rock in question is adjacent to Pavilion Lake.

25. *Rothe Farbe*—'red paint,' referring to red ochre paint. The white paint was obtained from a white clay or chalk (Teit 1909:476).

again, the young Eagles asked her to sit on the edge of the nest. Then Tlē'esa killed her with his club and she fell down from the rock face. Tlē'esa's brothers picked up Eagle and plucked out all the feathers, leaving none for Tlē'esa. Meanwhile Tlē'esa sat in the nest and wondered how to get down again. Finally he said to the young Eagles, "Carry me down, but hold me firmly and do not hurt me, otherwise I will kill you!" The Eagles were afraid and obeyed. He tied himself to the Eagles and they flew with him from the nest and descended slowly to the ground. Before he could get around to plucking their feathers, his brothers had come and taken them all.

The brothers wandered on and arrived at the Fraser River.[26] There they saw a young girl dancing on the opposite bank. They sat down in a row on the shore and watched her. There they remained sitting until they were changed to stone.

2. Coyote[27]

1) Once the sun shone too hot and scorched the whole earth. So the animals decided to make another sun. All the birds tried, but none was judged good enough. Finally Coyote cried out, "Now let me try!" He went towards the sunrise and climbed into the sky. But his tail was so long that it had not quite reached the horizon when his body was already high in the sky. When he was high enough to look over the whole earth, he started to gossip and told all he saw. So the animals said, "No, you talk too much. You mustn't be the sun." In the end, Tsqtskna'sp (a climbing bird with red wings, tail and cheeks)[28] became the sun.

2) A long time ago it was extremely cold on earth. On the upper reaches of the river there was a large glacier which gave off icy cold. All the animals went out to kill the man who made the cold, but they all froze to death. Finally only Coyote and his cousin Fox[29] were left. Coyote wanted to go and kill Cold, but Fox warned him against it. Coyote wrapped himself in warm clothing and set off. He passed all the frozen animals and the closer he got to the glacier, the colder it became. Finally he

---

26. Given in English as Fraser River (without quotation marks) in the original *Sagen*. Our Native consultants said that the Transformers reached the Fraser River and were then turned into rocks at the place called Moran which is located about 10 miles (16 km) up the Fraser from Pavilion.

27. Appears in the original in English as Coyote (without quotation marks).

28. Boas (1916:728) identifies this bird as a Red-shafted (Common) Flicker (*Colaptes cafer*). While this identification is consistent with other sources, Boas' transcription "Tsqtskna'sp" is not consistent with the Shuswap name given for this bird given by Teit (1909:664, fn.1) as "Tcoktceqwa'sp," which is very likely the same term given by Kuipers (1982) as cəqʷcq̓ʷésp. This suggests either that the storyteller was referring to a different bird, or that Boas mistranscribed its Shuswap name.

29. *Vulpes fulva*, the red fox.

saw before him the house from which the cold came. He became very cold, even though he wrapped himself tighter in his blankets. He had passed all the frozen animals and had finally reached the house. He could hardly bear the cold, but entered it all the same. Then he froze and fell down dead. Cousin Fox waited for him for four days. Since he didn't return, Fox thought that Coyote had frozen. He wrapped himself in warm clothing and started on his way. He passed all the frozen animals but couldn't find his cousin, Coyote. He ran on, and with each of his steps, fire sparked from under his feet. Dentalia[30] hung from the tip of his tail and rattled as he moved. He went up to the house and heard someone speaking inside but was unable to see anything. He entered and stamped his foot once. Fire sparked from the ground and the glacial ice began to melt. A stream of water ran down and extinguished the fire. So he stamped once more. Again fire sparked from the ground and melted the ice. When he had stamped four times, all the ice had been melted and it became warm again. Coyote came to life again, stood up and said, "I've been asleep for a long time." "Yes," answered Fox, "You were frozen." Fox took him under his arm and ordered him to stay very still. After the fire had burned out and all the water had run off, they returned and brought all the people back to life.

3) Now Coyote always looked at Fox as if he wanted to say something. Fox knew quite well what he wanted but kept quiet. Finally Coyote begged, "Please, cousin, lend me your tail." Fox replied, "No, I won't; you might come to harm." But Coyote promised to be careful, so Fox finally gave him his tail and took Coyote's. But he warned him never to turn around and look at the tail as long as he had it. Coyote promised. When he had the tail he ran around with it and enjoyed the rattling of the dentalia. In the end the temptation became too great for him and he looked at the tail to see whether it suited him. He thought he looked fine and was very happy. But when he ran on, he suddenly felt himself becoming very weak and noticed that his entrails were trailing from his anus. So he called for his cousin. When Fox saw what had happened, he said, "Ah, you have looked at your tail." He put the entrails back into Coyote's belly and took the tail away from him again.

4) Coyote was very poor. Once he visited his cousin, Fox, who owned a beautiful cape trimmed with eagle feathers. Coyote wished to have it. Fox knew at once what Coyote had in mind but pretended not to know. Coyote said, "I've been missing you, cousin! So I have come to see you." Fox said nothing. Coyote repeated his remark four times without getting a reply. Fox ignored him completely. So Coyote grew angry and resolved to play a trick on Fox. Fox had risen and gone away. So Coyote ran after him, snatched the cape from him and put it on himself. Fox paid no attention at all but calmly went on. Coyote looked at himself, thinking, "Now I am

---

30. A tusk-shaped marine mollusc of the genus *Dentalium*, used as an item of wealth on the Northwest Coast and as a highly-valued trade item on the Plateau.

handsome." He returned home, slowly at first, then he began running. As he ran, a wind came up which grew stronger as he ran faster. The feathers of his cape were blown about and finally the wind blew him straight up into the air. When he fell down again, Fox came running and took his cape away from him. Coyote was almost dead. Fox said, "Now you see what happens to you. You always try to play tricks on me, yet you know full well that you can't do anything to me."

5) Buffalo[31] had two wives. He was so old that his horns were almost worn away. Once the wolves stole his wives. He wanted to pursue them but didn't know where they had gone. Coyote met him and teased him about his mishap. This angered Buffalo and he rushed at Coyote, wanting to gore him. He fled, and Buffalo ran after him. Now when Coyote grew tired, he ran into a hollow, defecated and ordered his excrement to become a tree. This happened, and he climbed up. When Buffalo saw him sitting up in the tree, he pushed it until it toppled. In the meantime Coyote had rested and ran on. When he grew tired again, he made a second tree and took refuge in it. In this way, he escaped four times. When the fourth tree fell over, he said to Buffalo, "Enough of this, friend. I will help you to get your wives back. I will make you young and handsome." Buffalo agreed. So Coyote grabbed one of his horns and pulled it. When it was nice and long, he also lengthened the other one. Thus Buffalo got nice sharp horns again. Then Coyote made the hair on his head beautiful. He pulled his legs and his tail, and Buffalo resembled a handsome young bull again. Then Buffalo said to Coyote, "Now I will make you handsome." He pulled on his muzzle and ever since then Coyote has a long snout and small, narrow eyes. In addition, he pulled his legs and his tail longer. Then he said, "I've finished, my friend. Now let us go to the water and see what we look like." When Buffalo saw himself he was very happy. But Coyote did not like his long nose one bit. Then Buffalo said, "Let's look for my wives. If you know where they are, you shall have one of them." Coyote answered, "Do you see that valley? Four wolves live there; they have stolen them. It is very difficult to get them back, but just leave it to me! Follow me!" They went up into the valley. Soon they saw two women digging for roots. Then Coyote made a dense fog so that no one could see them. They went up to the women and when they were there, Buffalo said, "I've come to fetch you," and they took the women along. They climbed one of the mountains bordering the valley and the fog followed them. When they arrived on top, the fog disappeared. It was not long before the Wolves missed the women and started following the tracks. Soon they came close to the fugitives and saw Buffalo, Coyote and the women. They caught up with them and attacked Buffalo. He tossed them into the air and slit their bellies open so their entrails spilled out. Coyote jumped back and forth for joy at this. They

---

31. Buffalo are not known to have occurred in this area; however, legends about buffalo reached the Shuswap through diffusion from the Plains and from other areas of the Plateau.

went on. Soon Buffalo said, "Friend, let's separate here! I've promised one of my wives to you. Take this one; she is the better one." He continued, "I will teach you how to handle her. You may kill her when you are hungry; cut off a piece of meat and roast it. But after you have killed her, you will have to sit on her, light a fire beside yourself and cook the meat. You must not get up until you have finished your meal, then she will get up again at the same time as you." To begin with, Coyote followed Buffalo's directions. But one day, after he had killed his wife, and when his fire was burning low, he thought to himself, "Why shouldn't I collect some wood?" He rose and went away. When he returned, he spied an old woman who had eaten everything but the bones and who was running away as Fox. So he reflected, "Even though I've lost my wife, at least I've still got her bones." He gathered them up and carried them along. When he became hungry, he lit a fire and began to crack the bones with stones in order to eat the marrow. While he was thus occupied an old woman came along and said, "This kind of work is not fit for a big chief like you; let me do it." Coyote agreed and gave her the bones and the stones. He stretched out beside the fire. When he turned around, the old one had put almost all the marrow into her basket. Coyote thought she would let him know when she was finished and turned back towards the fire. Since he didn't hear a sound for a long time, he turned around again and saw the old one running away, eating at the same time. He ran after her, but when he caught up with her she punched his chest so hard that he fell down. He got up again and thought, "This is bad! But at least I'll boil my bones in order to get the fat from them." He took the bones, broke them up and was about to throw them into the water to boil, when Fox came up again in the form of an old woman and said, "Such work is not fit for a big chief like you; let me do it." Coyote agreed and left the cooking to her while he sat down by the fire to wait for her to call him. But when he turned around he saw Fox running away again, drinking the fat. He pursued him, but Fox punched his chest so that he fell down. So Coyote became very sad and went away. But the woman rose up again and returned to Buffalo.

6) Once Coyote came to a house in which "Foolhen"[32] lived with her children, Ruffed Grouse,[33] Prairie Chicken,[34] and Blue Grouse.[35] Their mother had just gone

---

32. Given in English in the original as "Foolhen" (in double quotation marks); this is the Spruce Grouse, also known as the Franklin's Grouse (*Canachites Canadensis*).

33. Appears in the original *Sagen* in English as "Woodpartridge" (with double quotation marks), but this is probably the Ruffed Grouse (*Bonasa umbellus*); no species of partridge is native to British Columbia.

34. Given in the original as *Prairiehuhn* which means 'Prairie Chicken.' However, the bird referred to is the Sharp-tailed Grouse (*Pedioecetes phasianellus*) as it is this species that is widely miscalled the "Prairie Chicken."

35. The German term *Rebhuhn* used here refers to the common partridge but it is likely the Blue Grouse (*Dendragapus obscurus*) that the storyteller is actually referring to—the common partridge is not native to British Columbia.

out when Coyote arrived. He asked the children, "Have you anything to eat?" "No, we have nothing." "Where is your mother?" "She is in the forest, searching for berries." "And you really have nothing to eat?" "No, we have nothing." "I've cut my foot; would you give me some pitch to put on the wound?" The children gave it to him. He took it, glued their eyes shut with it, and left them. So the poor children got lost in the forest. When their mother returned, she found them wandering all over the forest and brought them home again. Then they told her how Coyote had tricked them. The old one and the children followed his tracks and saw that he was follow-ing a path which led past a steep slope. The mother first told Blue Grouse to hide in the grass; she hid Prairie Chicken a bit further along, Ruffed Grouse still further on, and at last she herself hid in the grass. She had instructed her children what to do. It was not long before Coyote came along, and at once Blue Grouse flew up right in front of him. He was so startled that he nearly fell over the cliff. The others did the same. When Ruffed Grouse rose up he just managed to keep his balance. When he walked on, he said, "I nearly fell down." Then the old one flew up and Coyote top-pled to the bottom. The hens thought that he was dead. They flew down and were very astonished to find him still alive. The old one asked, "What are you doing here?" "Oh," he replied, "someone frightened me and I fell down the cliff." The old one said, "I've done it because you glued my children's eyes closed. Now see how you can get away. We won't help you." And with this they flew away. When they had gone, Coyote got up again and ran away.

7) Coyote said, "I need to have some fun. I'll play with my eyes." With this he plucked out his eyes. He threw them up and caught them again. One time when he threw them up very high, Crow caught his eyes and flew away with them. There Coyote stood, without eyes, and didn't know what to do. He groped around and found a bush of rose hips. So he picked a couple of rose hips and put them in for eyes. Now he could see again and walked on. Soon he came to a hollow from which smoke rose. An old woman sat there and asked him where he came from. He answered that he was just travelling around and asked her whether she lived there by herself. "No," she answered, "I have four daughters, but they have gone to watch the games." "What games?" asked Coyote. "Oh, many people are dancing over there," she replied, pointing out the location. "Why are they dancing?" "They are gambling for Coyote's eyes. Crow has stolen them." "I would like to see that," replied Coyote, "will you show me the way?" The old one obliged and he went to the place where all the dancers had gathered. The people all sat around in a circle. After someone had danced with the eyes, he passed them on to his neighbour, who then started to dance. Coyote sat down by the door and waited his turn. Then he sang while he danced, "How beautiful these eyes are. I have never seen any like them before." They danced four times in turn. When it was his fourth time around, he took

the eyes and ran out the door. Then he threw them up high and, on their own, they fell back into their sockets and grew back on at once. The animals pursued him but were unable to catch him. Once safe, he sat down and laughed because he had his eyes back. He sang, "I knew I would be victorious over you. Here are my eyes back. Here I have my property back."

8) Coyote came to a house in which he could hear voices. He entered but didn't see anyone. When he followed the direction of the voice, he found a talking hair in one corner. He took it and threw it to the ground. Then he heard talking again but didn't see anyone. He called to the voice, "Make yourself visible and give me some food," but no one became visible. When he followed the direction of the voice, he came upon a speaking comb stuck to the wall. He took it and flung it to the floor. Finally he found four salmon skins filled with oil. "Just what I've been looking for," he said, taking them and drinking up all the oil. Then he walked on along the river. After a short time he became thirsty, so he stepped down to the river, drank his fill and climbed up again. After a short time he became thirsty again, so he thought, "It is too inconvenient to go down to the river each time, so I will walk along the bank, then I will be able to drink easily." After a while even this seemed too inconvenient to him; he thought, "I would rather walk along in the water, then I will only have to bend down." He did so, but still remained thirsty. So he walked into the water up to his chest. After a short while even this was too much effort for him and he walked far enough into the river that the water ran right into his mouth. He drank so much that he finally burst.

9) Coyote had a small kettle standing in the rocks just where the trail led up the South Thompson River. Once someone came along and threw his kettle into the water. But it returned all by itself. Then some people stole it, but it always returned by itself. But finally someone carried it away and it did not return.

10) Once Owl came down the South Thompson River. Coyote could hear him coming and singing, "Hĭ hĭ, I am the one who kills and eats all the people." Coyote stopped and said to himself, "He is dangerous. He will eat me. I will sing the same song as he does; maybe he will get scared." When the two met, Coyote said, "It seems you are just as powerful as I am. I also eat all the people. Stop here a bit and let's play a game. We will both vomit to see what is in our stomachs." Owl agreed and suggested that Coyote should begin. "Alright," he said, "but we must keep our eyes closed until we are finished. Don't open your eyes until I call out." Owl closed his eyes and Coyote vomited. He had nothing but grass in his stomach. Then Owl vomited and brought up nothing but human flesh. Quickly Coyote changed over the vomit and then called Owl. When Owl looked, he said, "I've vomited grass," and he was afraid of Coyote, in front of whom the regurgitated human flesh lay. Both were changed into rocks which can still be seen today. Their mouths are wide open.

3. Lynx and the Girl

There once was a girl who refused to have anything to do with men, although she had many suitors. She lived in an underground house and her place was just beneath one of the posts. Lynx[36] also lived in the same village, in a small hut. He would have liked to have this girl, but didn't know how to get her, since her parents always guarded her. One night he sneaked onto the house and there urinated so that it ran down the post by which the girl was sleeping. It ran right into her mouth. So she became pregnant and nobody knew how it had come about. She gave birth to a boy. When the boy turned four, the girl's parents decided to find out who the father was. They put a bird at the top of the ladder leading into the house. Then they asked all the men to try and hit the bird with their arrows. They promised their daughter in marriage to whoever hit the bird. Everyone shot but nobody was able to hit it. Finally everyone had tried but Lynx, who was an old man and lay quietly beside his fire. The girl's parents sent for him, but he replied, "Why should I come? The young men were unable to hit the bird; how then should I manage to do it? My eyes are half blind, after all." Yet finally he had to come. He was given a bow and arrow and he let fly without even looking and hit the bird. Everyone cried out, "Lynx will marry the girl." Her parents prepared a seat for him beside the fire. When he was seated there, they addressed the assembly, "We are going to abandon our daughter, her husband and her child." They packed their meagre belongings. Then they kicked Lynx so that his bones broke and his body was all disfigured. They extinguished all the fires and left. But the girl's grandmother, Magpie,[37] pitied her. She placed a glowing coal in a mussel shell,[38] added some food and hid it. The people had taken all their provisions, which had been hidden under the rocks, and believed that the three must starve to death. When the wife sat there all by herself, she started to weep. She searched in the ashes for fire, but couldn't find any. It grew dark and her child started to cry. Then she heard someone calling from the corner of the house. She followed the voice and found the shell which had been calling her. She took the coal and the food and lit a fire. When she cooked the food, it grew so much that she and her child had ample to eat. When they were satisfied, she stepped over Lynx four times and he became well again at once. Only his face was still disfigured. She passed her hand over his head (?)[39] and it also mended. Then he went hunting and caught much game. Then he caused deep snow to fall so that the people who had abandoned them could not catch anything and soon were in great difficulties, where-

---

36. Canada lynx *(Lynx canadensis canadensis)*.

37. Black-billed Magpie *(Pica pica)*.

38. Given in the original as *Muschelschale* 'mussel shell'; in this area, the genera referred to are either *Margaritifera* or *Anodonta*, referred to collectively as freshwater shellfish.

39. The question mark after *Kopf* ('head') is in the original; it is unexplained.

as he had plenty of meat. His wife dried it and hid it in many caches. She put all the best pieces into one cache which was intended for Magpie. For the others she kept only the hides and bones; for Coyote she kept feet, stomachs and entrails. After some time Magpie returned to the deserted village in order to find out how her grand-daughter was getting on. She feared that she had died already and consequently was very much surprised to see the boy playing with a ball as white as snow. She soon noticed that it was made of deer fat. She hid, and she was so hungry that when the ball rolled past her, she pounced upon it and gobbled it up. The boy cried out, "Magpie has stolen my ball." When Lynx heard this he came out of the house and asked her, "Why did you take my son's ball away? If you are hungry, come inside; I'll give you food." They went inside and Magpie was given meat and fat. When Magpie was satisfied, she took the leftovers home to give to her children. She collected lichen from pine trees[40] and roasted it. She gave it to her children with deer fat. When she distributed the food, the children started shouting and quarrelling, "You have given my brother more than me!" Raven,[41] who shared the house, heard this and asked, "What are you talking about?" Magpie answered, "Oh, it's nothing; it is just the children quarrelling." So Raven sat down again by the fire and drowsed. But he peeked over and noticed that the children were eating deer fat. So he sprang up and called out, "Where did you get the fat?" So the old one told how Lynx had more than enough food. Then they all returned to the abandoned ones. Lynx gave everyone the food he had saved for them and then he hunted for them.

4. Rabbit

Rabbit and his grandmother lived in an underground house. Grizzly Bear lived beside them with his two children. Once Rabbit had run out of food and said to his grandmother, "I'll go to Bear's cache and steal what I need." Grandmother warned him, but he wouldn't listen. He looted the cache, leaving nothing in it but one basket full of wasps and one full of ants. When he arrived home, he ordered his grand-mother to cook and roast, and he gave a huge feast. The following morning, Bear went to his cache and found that it had been thoroughly looted. He asked all the neighbours whether they knew who the thief might be, but received no answers. Finally Bear went to Rabbit. "Someone has raided my cache," he said. Rabbit

---

40. Given in the original German text as *Tannen* ('pine-trees' or 'fir-trees') but more likely 'pine trees' in this context. Although the Shuswap gathered black tree lichen (*Alectoria fremontii*) from both fir and pine trees, they were particularly fond of this lichen when it was found growing on ponderosa pine (*Pinus ponderosa*) (Palmer 1975:47).

41. *Rabe* 'raven,' the Common Raven (*Corvus corax*).

retorted, "Someone has raided my cache." Bear continued, "I'm asking you, Rabbit! Don't you know who did it?" Rabbit answered,"I'm asking you, Rabbit! Don't you know who did it?" Now Bear grew angry and shouted, "I think you did it!" "Yes," Rabbit replied then, "I did it. I stole everything and ate it up." So Bear became furious and wanted to fight Rabbit. The latter hid his grandmother under a basket, put on his cape and ripped off one of his legs which he used as a club. Then he put pine wood on the fire so that his house filled with smoke, and then he started to fight. He hopped around Bear. Once Bear caught hold of him and squeezed him. But Rabbit jumped away again and made Bear lose his breath so that finally he became exhausted. Then Rabbit beat him to death with his club and also killed the small Bears.

5. Muskrat[42]

Tsatl[43] had a grandson, Muskrat. In the same village there also lived a chief who had a very beautiful daughter. All the men wanted to marry her, and Muskrat, too, wished to have her. But he was very ugly and all the girls mocked him. The chief's daughter had just reached puberty and still lived in her hut. One day, when Muskrat was loitering about the hut, he heard the girl sing, "Muskrat has small eyes. His tail is flat and his legs are bandy. He has a fat belly!" In short, she derided Rat's[44] ugly figure. So he resolved to take revenge. He went home and fashioned himself snow-shoes as they are used by various tribes. Then he made himself arrows like those of different tribes. When night came he put the snowshoes on, one kind after another, and ran around the hut where the girl was. Then he took his bow and arrows and killed her with all the different arrows. Next morning the girl's mother sent her youngest daughter, Tsk·a'ноya (= A Bit Foolish),[45] to her sister in the hut in order to bring her fire. The little girl went to the hut and called her sister, but received no answer. So she opened the door and saw her sister lying there, pierced by many arrows. She ran back to her mother and told her what she had seen. Everyone came running. They saw the tracks of snowshoes of enemy tribes and recognized their arrows. Consequently they believed these had attacked and killed the girl. They brought the corpse into the house and called the medicine men in order to try and heal her, but all efforts were in vain. Finally they called Muskrat, who lay asleep by his fire. He had foreseen this and had already dug many holes for himself in the

---

42. Muskrat (*Ondatra zibethica*).

43. This term is not now recognized.

44. In this instance, Boas uses the German term *Ratte* 'rat' rather than the term *Moschusratte* 'muskrat' used throughout the rest of this same legend.

45. The term Tsk·a'hoya is not now recognized.

banks of a lake. He entered the house and at once began to dance and sing. He sang: hē ōinē′ ōinē′ hē, and climbed up the house ladder. Then he descended again and said, "The spirits almost spoke to me." Everyone shouted, "Dance once more." Again he sang: hē ōinē′ ōinē′ hē, and climbed up the ladder. When he came down, he said again, "The spirits almost spoke to me." He danced a third and a fourth time. The fourth time, he climbed right to the top of the ladder and here sang: "hē ōinē′ ōinē′ hē. I have killed the girl." Then he ran away. All the animals pursued him— Fox, Hare,[46] Coyote, Wolf[47] and Eagle. When they had almost caught up with him, he jumped into the lake. Coyote sprang in after him and thought that he had caught him, but it turned out to be only a bunch of aquatic plants. Muskrat popped up, first here, then there, and swam first to this hole, then to that hole and continued singing,"I have killed the girl." The animals were not able to catch him.

6. The Mountain Goats

There once was an old man in Kamloops who went to hunt mountain goats. He climbed about in the mountains and finally grew very tired. He lay down to sleep and began to dream that he heard two beautiful women singing while they approached. He woke up and actually saw two women. They came near and said, "We were looking for you; come with us." The old man didn't answer. So they asked him again to come along and after they had invited him four times, he rose and accompanied them. The women were actually Mountain Goats. He left his bow and quiver of arrows hanging in a small spruce tree. Soon they arrived at a steep cliff. The women told him that this was their home and began to climb up. The man was unable to follow. So they turned around and gave him a pair of shoes and now he was able to climb up without any trouble. When they arrived at the top, the women showed him their house on a nearby cliff and he entered with them. He saw many Billy Goats and Nanny Goats[48] at rest there, and he himself was changed into a Billy Goat. At night he tried to sleep with two of the Nanny Goats, but they told him he had to wait until the mating season. When the mating season arrived, he fought and defeated all the Billy Goats. He had all the Nanny Goats to himself. After some time they said to him, "The mating season has finished and you must not come to us any more." Now all the other Billy Goats returned again. After a while the man became homesick. The Goats soon noticed and asked him what made him so sad. But he only lay there and wouldn't answer. So they said, "You are longing for your home.

---

46.   Boas uses the German term *Hase* 'hare' in the original *Sagen*.

47.   Wolf *(Canis lupus)*.

48.   Boas in the original *Sagen* distinguishes *Böcke*, which in this context has been translated as 'Billy Goats,' from *Ziegen*, translated here as 'Nanny Goats.'

We are going to take you back. Now pay attention; in future you must never again shoot young mountain goats. They will recognize you and play with you. But you may hunt us old ones. When you want to climb a steep rock, just spit in your palms and on your feet." They took him to the vicinity of his village. The people there had searched in vain for his body in the mountains and had long given him up for lost. Initially he was unable to return to the village because he fled instinctively as soon as he scented humans. But he was discovered in the end. The people saw him sitting outside the village and said to each other, "Doesn't he resemble the man who got lost in the mountains?" They fetched him and after some time he told his adventures. Now when he went out to hunt, the young mountain goats always ran to meet him.

7. The Salmon Fisherman

There once was an old man who always caught salmon with a spear adorned with red woodpecker feathers. Woodpecker, Tsk·usk·oa′sp,[49] said to the other birds, "Let's steal his spear." They sent out the bird TsutsuspEla′n[50] first. He changed into a salmon and swam towards the old man, who didn't pay any attention to him at all. Then they sent out the bird Tsk·oā′k·En.[51] He, too, changed into a salmon and swam towards the old man, who didn't pay attention. Tsk·usk·oa′sp, himself, had just as little success. Finally they sent Tsuqk·i′n,[52] the Woodpecker who was black with a red head. He also changed into a salmon and swam towards the old man, who speared him and pulled him towards the shore. But Tsuqk·i′n broke off the spear point and swam away with it. The old man became very sad. He went downriver and asked everyone whether they had seen a salmon who had broken off his spear and taken it away. He promised a large reward for its return. Finally he also came to Tsuqk·i′n, who had changed back into his real form. He asked him, "Haven't you seen a salmon who swam away with my spear?" Tsuqk·i′n answered, "What are you going to give me if I get it back for you?" "Whatever you want. I own four capes; you may choose one of them." He showed them to him in turn and Tsuqk·i′n

---

49. While Boas identifies "Tsk·usk·oa′sp" as 'woodpecker,' we are aware of no independent confirmation of the species referred to by this Shuswap term.

50. Presumably "TsutsuspEla′n" is a type of woodpecker, but no other source has provided this term.

51. Teit (1906:664, fn.2) identifies this bird as the Red-breasted Woodpecker; however this bird is not found here and more likely the species referred to, on the evidence of cognates found in other Interior Salish languages, is a subspecies of the Yellow-bellied Sapsucker (*Sphyrapicus varius*).

52. What Boas transcribes as "Tsuqk·i′n" is the Pileated Woodpecker (*Dryocopus pileatus*). Kuipers (1989:170) transcribes this same Shuswap term as cəqʷqín and also identifies this bird as the Pileated Woodpecker. Teit (1909:663, fn.1) refers to this bird as "red-headed woodpecker," while identifying it as *Ceophlaeus pileatus*.

selected the last one, which was covered all over with red feathers. Tsuqk·i′n took it and returned the spear. The cape made him very vain and now he went downriver again with the other birds. On the way, they saw a trout lying half-dead on the shore. Tsuqk·i′n sent Tsk·usk·oa′sp to catch it. The trout lured him deeper and deeper into the river, then grabbed him and carried him upstream, where it disappeared with him into a rock. In reality it was the Water Spirit, OkElmuqō′luq,[53] who had only assumed the shape of a trout. The birds followed them in order to free their comrade. When they reached the rock into which the trout had disappeared with Tsk·usk·oa′sp, Tsuqk·i′n told TsutsuspEla′n to peck with his beak against the rock, calling out at the same time, "Ām Tsuqk·i′n." But the bird called out his own name and therefore flattened his beak on the rock. The same happened to Tsk·oā′k·En, who, instead of calling out what he had been told, shouted, "Ām Tsk·oā′k·En." So Tsuqk·i′n hit the rock, himself, while calling out,"Ām Tsuqk·i′n." At once a crack opened and he could see Tsk·usk·oa′sp lying inside a cave, barely alive. He hit the rock once more and the crack opened far enough to admit him. He entered, fought OkElmuqō′luq, killed him and took Tsk·usk·oa′sp back home.

8. The Gambler

There once was a man who had three sons and two daughters. The youngest son was a gambler and lost everything he and his brothers and sisters owned, finally even his sisters' shoes. Since he had nothing left to lose, he gave up gambling. He was so poor that he had nothing to eat and from sheer hunger he licked and swallowed other people's boiling stones. So he resolved to leave, and one night he set out without anyone noticing. He wandered on without any destination. Finally he reached a house where an old woman lived. She said, "You are a stranger." "Yes, I am a stranger," he answered. "Where are you headed?" "I do not know." She fed him and he spent the night under her roof. The following morning the old one told him, "When you go on, you will meet two women who will be singing. Don't pay any attention to them under any circumstances, but continue calmly on your way until you meet an old man." And she told him what to do there. He wandered on and soon heard the women singing. But he remembered what the old one had told him and continued calmly on his way. Soon he met an old man who lived by himself in a house. So he thought, "This is Tsūisk·a′lemuǫ (Cannibal)[54] about whom the old woman told me." He saw that

---

53. Kuipers (1974:236) transcribes this same Shuswap term as x̣qlməxʷúl'əxʷ and provides the gloss 'beings half human half fish, believed to understand the language of the birds.'

54. "Tsūisk·a′lemuǫ" is Boas' rendering of the term c̓əsqélməxʷ (derived from qəlmúxʷ 'Indian; human being') which our Shuswap consultants translated as 'people-killer' (Bouchard and Kennedy 1979:6, 38–41).

he was drying human flesh in front of his house. The old man called out to him, "Hello, you are a stranger." He replied, "Yes, grandfather, I am a stranger." "Where are you going?" "I do not know." Then the old one began to growl, but the young man begged, "Please don't harm me, grandfather; I'm only a poor man." The old one growled four times, but did not harm him. In his house he had four boxes. The old woman had told him that the old man would offer him something from his boxes and that he should only accept something from the last one. Now the old one pointed to the first box and asked, "Have you come to get this?" The stranger said no. So the old man opened it and the stranger saw that it contained human heads. In the same way he declined to take anything from the second and third boxes, which also contained human heads. When the old man offered him the fourth box, he accepted. Then the Cannibal took out a beautiful head covered all over with red feathers. He cut open the young man and removed from his stomach the stones which he had swallowed. He washed him and put the beautiful head on him. He gave him four fir capes and named him Sk·oō'ts.[55] The young man had been very ugly before. He was so repugnant to the girls that they had cut out the pieces of their capes if he touched them by accident. This had happened to him ten times and he had given all the pieces to his mother to keep for him. Before the old man sent him back he told him, "On your way here you saw two girls who are always singing. Everyone wants to marry them, but no one is able to get them. Now, go to them. You shall have them." The young man rejoiced. He returned and again heard them singing. So he approached them. The girls smiled at him when they saw him, he was so handsome. They became his wives and he took them home with him. They continued singing and said to the young man, "You mustn't tire of us, but we have to sing all the time." He arrived home during the night, climbed down[56] with his wives and nudged his father. When his father saw who it was, he woke his wife. They all got up and lit a fire. They were happy to see how handsome their son had grown and how beautiful his wives were. When the people saw him next morning, they said, "We haven't gambled for such a long time. Let's gamble again." The young man agreed. Coyote was already thinking, "I'll win his wives." They began and Sk·oō'ts lost all his and his wives' belongings. He had only a staff left. Then his wife showed him how to play and he won everything back, and the belongings of the other people as well. His wives told him, "All the girls who did not want to have anything to do with you in the past will want you now. But pay no attention to them and rebuff them if they touch you." The girls went to his mother and said that they would like to marry him. When she told him this, he only answered, "I think they only want to have the pieces

---

55. This term is not now recognized.

56. That is, into the underground house.

of fur back which they have cut from their capes." He had them returned to the girls, then mocked them and chased them away.

9. The Moon

Once the moon was a man. He had two wives, Wā′ela and Tsitā′eka.[57] The first one bore him two children; the latter remained childless. Therefore he loved her more than the other, and in the end he completely neglected Wā′ela. One evening, when he was with Tsitā′eka, Wā′ela asked him, "Where would you like me to go with your children?" She asked three times, but the man didn't answer her at all. Now when she asked for the fourth time he grew very angry and shouted, "Sit on my eyes!" So she jumped on his eyes and we can still see her sitting there today in the moon. We can also plainly see the man, his legs and a bundle which he carried on his back.

10. Loon[58]

Once Loon was a great gambler. He lost everything except one necklace of dentalia. Finally he lost even this to Crane.[59] But he didn't want to part with it and dived into the water. Ever since, Loon has had a white band around his neck.

---

57. These two terms, "Wā′ela" and "Tsitā′eka," are not now recognized.

58. Common Loon (*Gavia immer*).

59. Given in the original as *Kranich*, referring to the Common Crane which was identified at this time (*circa* 1890) as *Grus cinerea*. However, this bird has never been known to occur in this region; very likely the species referred to here is the Sandhill Crane (*Grus canadensis*).

II. Legends of the Ntlakyapamuq (Thompson)

These few stories are the result of a three-day visit to Lytton, 13–15 July 1888, during Boas' second B.C. trip. Boas spent his first morning visiting "all the graveyards, and gathered a few bones, but nothing of great value" (Rohner 1969:99). Since he was unable to find "a suitable Indian" right away, he went to the Church of England pastor, Reverend Smith, who arranged for some Ntlakyapamuq (Thompson) people to come to the church, "where they told me stories. I did not get very much, but a little" (Rohner 1969:100). The church atmosphere might have been somewhat inhibiting. What Boas says about Ntlakyapamuq story 3—"I obtained only an insignificant fragment of this important legend"—could apply practically throughout. For instance, Reverend Smith's parishioners, facing the problem of telling about the knot-hole wife in story 2, censored themselves down to two lines of this Transformer narrative and left out the knot-hole.

Summer lodge consisting of tule (*Scirpus acutus*) mats lain over a framework of poles near Spences Bridge, Thompson River, 1914. At the top can be seen the "ears" of the lodge made by a mat stretched between two poles and shifted around the smoke hole as required for controlling the interior ventilation.

Canadian Museum of Civilization, Ottawa. Image No. 26627 (J.A. Teit photo).

II. Legends of the Ntlakyapamuq. Collected in Lytton.[1]

1. The Sun[2]

A man had two daughters. One of them married, but the other refused all suitors. One day her sister asked her, "Why are you so proud? I suppose you would like to marry Sun." "Yes," her sister replied, "I want to marry Sun." She made many capes[3] and moccasins for herself and then set out with a slave girl in search of Sun. For many days and many moons they walked towards the sunrise. Whenever they arrived at a lake, they swam and rubbed themselves with cedar branches. At last they arrived at an ocean. When they had climbed down to the shore, they didn't know where to turn. After a while they saw Sun rise from the water. So she took a large hide, spread it on the water and walked over it towards Sun. Her slave remained on the shore. The mistress soon observed that Sun came out of his underground house.[4] After he left, the girl entered and slept there all day long. Then she hid. In the evening, at sunset, a man suddenly entered. He left the sun outside and stuck the pole, from which it was suspended, in the ground. He didn't discover the strange girl. After the man left again the following morning, the girl returned to the shore

---

1. Lytton, at the confluence of the Fraser and Thompson rivers, is the centre of traditional "Ntlakyapamuq" territory. "Ntlakyapamuq" is Boas' transcription of the term nłeʔképmx which is applied both to this Plateau group and to the Interior Salish language they speak. These people are frequently referred to in the literature as "Thompson." Traditional nłeʔképmx (Thompson) territory encompassed the area along the Fraser River approximately between Spuzzum and 25-Mile (south from Lillooet), along the Thompson River as far as Ashcroft, and along the Nicola River to Nicola Lake. The Thompson are classified as part of the Northwestern group of the Interior Salish Branch of the Salishan Language Family (Teit 1900:167–175; 1914:284; Bouchard and Kennedy 1988a:114–115; Wyatt 1998:191; Kennedy and Bouchard 1998:174–175; Kinkade *et al.* 1998). The contemporary spelling of nłeʔképmx is "Nlha7kápmx" or "Nlaka′pamux."

    In annotating this section, we have drawn upon our 1970s–1980s consultation with the following Nlaka′pamux people: Mamie Henry and Louis Phillips. We gratefully acknowledge their assistance.

2. See Teit (1898:110, fn. 169) for Boas' own English translation of this legend.

3. A description of Thompson clothing is given in Teit (1900:206–220).

4. A more formal translation would be 'semi-subterranean pithouse' rather than 'underground house'; see Teit (1900:192–195) for a description of this type of structure.

and fetched her slave. They cleaned the house and when the man returned at night, he found both girls. He had never seen women before and at first was angry. But then he became at ease and married the girl. They had a son and after some time she returned to her home.

2. Qoē′qtlk·otl[5]

TEmtli′psEm (a bird)[6] had two wives, Grizzly Bear[7] and Black Bear. He had four children with each of them. One day Grizzly Bear killed her husband and Black Bear. When the latter's children saw this, they fled to Bittanny.[8] In those days there lived a man named Sk·oinē′ek·a,[9] near Lytton. He killed old Grizzly Bear. After some time the four young men left Bittanny and wandered upriver. Qoē′qtlk·otl was fully grown now. He transformed all the bad people he met into rocks. When the brothers arrived at Nk·ā′ya (on the left bank of the Fraser River right below the Thompson River),[10] they met a man named G·ōk·oē′la,[11] who had come down from Lillooet. He also transformed all bad people into stones. When G·ōk·oē′la and Qoē′qtlk·otl met, they tried to find out which one of them was stronger. They tried to transform each other, but found that they had equal strength. They became friends

---

5. "Qoē′qtlk·otl" is Boas' rendering of qʷíqʷƛ'qʷəƛ't, the Nlaka′pamux term for the Transformers. A classic discussion of these Transformer figures is Boas' introduction to Teit (1898: 11–12). Although Teit (1898:107, fn. 116) commented that he was "unable to obtain any meaning for this name," Thompson and Thompson (1996:295, 1339) note that qʷíqʷƛ'qʷəƛ't is derived from the Nlaka′pamux root qʷíƛ' meaning 'smile'—they translate qʷíqʷƛ'qʷəƛ't as 'Smiley.' Hill-Tout (1899) translated this same term as 'benign-faced.' Sometimes the term qʷíqʷƛ'qʷəƛ't is used to refer only to the youngest of the Transformers, as here, and sometimes to the group of them as a whole.

6. Thompson and Thompson (1996:354) identify təmɬápsəm (Boas' "TEmtli′psEm") as the Nlaka′pamux term for the Northern Flicker (*Colaptes auratus*). Native people throughout this region generally associate the Northern Flicker with shamans and guardian spirit power. Teit (1912:218, fn. 3) and Hill-Tout (1899:196) use the folk term "red-headed woodpecker" for this species.

7. Grizzly Bear (*Ursus arctos horribilis*) and Black Bear (*Ursus americanis*).

8. Given in English in the original text (without quotation marks) which is actually an English approximation of the Nlaka′pamux term pténi, referring to the Botanie Mountain area north of Lytton. Like "Bittanny," "Botanie" is also an anglicization of pténi.

9. "Sk·oinē′ek·a" is Boas' transcription of sqʷəníʔqʷa, the Nlaka′pamux name of a mythological figure who ferried people across the river in his canoe, but killed them in the process.

10. The place known as nqéye (Boas' "Nk·ā′ya") is actually on the right or west bank of the Fraser River, just below its confluence with the Thompson River.

11. "G·ōk·oē′la" is Boas' rendering of this man's name, q̓ʷəq̓ʷíle, which, as Boas (1916:1017) indicates elsewhere, is the Nlaka′pamux term for 'hog-fennel' (*Lomatium macrocarpum*) (Turner *et al.* 1990:155).

and then went separate ways, one upstream, the other downstream. Qoē'qtlk·otl arrived at MEtslait[12] on the Thompson River. There he met the giant Qaaqa',[13] who was catching salmon. Qoē'qtlk·otll changed into a salmon and swam towards the spot where Qaaqa' was fishing. When the latter saw him, he threw his fishing spear at him. This was just what Qoē'qtlk·otl had wished for. He broke off the point of the spear and swam back with it to his brothers. Then he changed back into his former shape and with his brothers, climbed the mountain at the foot of which Qaaqa' stood. They threw dirt at him but couldn't disturb him. Next morning they saw him standing there just as he had stood the previous day. The place where this happened can still be recognized today; it is the great landslide at Nekā'mEn.[14] At last Qaaqa' went into his underground house. He was offended at the loss of his spear. After awhile the brothers descended and entered his house. They found him sulking in bed. The youngest brother said, "Let's cook our salmon here." So Qaaqa' thought, "Surely this is the salmon I lost." He got up and walked up to Qoē'qtlk·otl, who showed him the spear point, saying, "Look what I have found." He gave the point back to Qaaqa', who was very glad.

The brothers wandered on and pitched camp at night. Qoē'qtlk·otl lay close to the fire. He always wore a cap of beaver fur. The eldest brother took it away and flung it into the fire. Thereupon the river started to rise. The three older brothers grew very much afraid and climbed a mountain. But Qoē'qtlk·otl stayed calmly by the fire. From their mountaintop, the older brothers saw him lying there, even though the land was covered by the flood. After some time Qoē'qtlk·otl made the river go down again.

One day, when the brothers came to a village, Qoē'qtlk·otl changed into a dog. They entered the village and the three elder brothers married three girls. One day a black bear was seen close to the village. The eldest brother took his bone arrow and his bow and wanted to shoot it. But the bear killed him instead. On the days following, the bear came again and the second and third brothers met the same fate. When the bear returned on the fourth day, the dog went out to kill it. He soon caught up with it and jumped straight over it. Thereupon the bear broke into two pieces. The dog ran back to the village, where he jumped over all the people, who also

---

12. Teit (1898:107 fn.121) states that this place, situated about four miles (6.4 km) below Spences Bridge on the south side of the Thompson River, was called Mudslide. Boas assumes here that "MEtslait," which is actually an Nlaka'pamux pronunciation of the English term mudslide, is the indigenous name for this place—in fact, 'mudslide' is a plausible English *translation* of the Nlaka'pamux name for this place, zəxzə'x, which is better translated as 'always sliding.'

13. "Qaaqa'" is Boas' rendering of the Nlaka'pamux term xaʔxáʔ which means 'supernatural power.'

14. What Boas transcribes as " Nekā'mEn'" is nq̓áwmən (anglicized as "Nicoamen" or "Nicomen"), the Nlaka'pamux name of Nicoamen Creek and Nicomen Indian Reserve No. 1 situated along the east side of the Thompson River about ten miles (16 km) upriver from Lytton.

broke into pieces. Then he jumped over the corpse of his brothers, thus calling them back to life. Then the three brothers were transformed into stone.

Once Qoē'qtlk·otl met a man who lived all by himself. So he transformed a cottonwood tree and a birch tree into women and gave them to him.

Almost every rock in the Fraser River Canyon bears a legend connecting it with Qoē'qtlk·otl. They are all transformed humans, animals or canoes.

3. The War With the Sky

I obtained only an insignificant fragment of this important legend. The birds wanted to make war with the sky and shot their arrows towards the dome of the sky in order to make a chain on which to climb up. But not one of them was able to reach the sky. At last the bird Tcitu'c[15] took his bow and arrows and he hit the dome of the sky. Then he made a chain of arrows reaching to the ground and all the animals climbed up along it. Later, the chain broke when only half the animals had safely returned.

4. The Boy and the Sun

A long time ago many people lived in Lytton. Amongst them there was a boy who always quarrelled with his playmates and who caused much trouble and mischief. At last his parents became weary of him and decided to abandon him. The chief ordered his playmates to go into the forest with the boy and glue his eyes shut with pitch, while playing. The boys obeyed and brought him back to the village after his eyes had been glued shut. Then the chief ordered everybody to pack up and they moved to Bittanny.[16] In addition to the boy, they left behind an old woman who was blind and lame. After a little while the pitch melted and the boy was able to see again. He looked about but couldn't see anyone. So he began to weep, because he realized that his relatives had abandoned him. He looked into all the houses and finally found the old woman. She told him that he had been abandoned because he caused so much trouble. The boy made himself snares and caught magpies, mice and rats, on which he and the old woman survived wretchedly. He fashioned three different capes from skins, one from the magpies, another from the mouse furs and one from the rat furs. He put the capes onto the roof of their house. When Sun Man

---

15. "Tcitu'c" is Boas' imperfect rendering of the Nlaka'pamux term c̓əc̓úw 'winter wren' (*Troglodyte troglodytes*); a better transcription of this term is provided in a variant of this story provided by Teit (1912:246), in which "Tsetso'" is translated as 'wren.'

16. The Botanie Mountain area north from Lytton (see the footnote in story 2 of this section).

saw them, he stepped down from the sky and said to the boy, "I would like to give you my bow; give me your capes in return." The boy consented, and from then on hit all the game he wanted so that he became very rich. But in Bittanny, among his people, there was great need. At one point the chief sent a slave to Lytton in order to find out if the boy had died. He was very much surprised to find him still alive and to see how rich he had become. When he reported to the chief what he had seen, the whole tribe returned to Lytton and the boy distributed many provisions among the people.

5. Coyote[17]

Nkia'p,[18] Coyote, had a son who had two wives. Coyote wanted one of them very badly for himself, so he tried to get his son out of the way. One day he sent him out to catch a bird sitting in a tree. When the young man climbed up the tree, Coyote made it grow until it touched the sky. So the young man leaped from the tree top into the sky-land, and the tree at once shrank to its former size. He found himself on a path and followed it. He saw many bright points to the right and left. At first he took them for edible roots and intended to dig for them. But then he realized they were holes and that the wind whistled through them. They were the stars. He walked on for a long time without seeing a living thing. At last he came to a spot where trees had been felled. There he met two old and blind women, Grouse.[19] One of them said to the other one, "I can smell something bad. I think it is Tl'iksE'mtEm[20] (= the climber)." When Tl'iksE'mtEm heard this he grew angry and threw the women into the air and transformed them into birds. He walked still further and met an old man and an old woman, Spider. They gave him a friendly greeting and said, "Your father is very wicked to have treated you like this." Tl'iksE'mtEm was surprised that they knew how he had reached to the sky. He stayed with them and hunted deer for them. In the meantime Spider made him a rope. After a while he became homesick; he lay down on his bed and the old ones were unable to make him eat. So they said, "We will send you back to earth." They put him, together with an ample supply of dried meat, into a small basket, which they tied to the rope. Before lowering him, they said, "Don't open your eyes as long as you are in the sky and while you are passing by clouds, mountains and trees, but be patient until you reach the ground. Then open

---

17. *Der Coyote*, in the original.

18. "Nkia'p" is Boas' transcription of nk̓iyép, the Nlaka'pamux (Thompson) term for 'Coyote.'

19. Although Boas uses the German term *Rebhühner* here, which means 'partridges,' the actual species referred to is grouse—the partridge is not a native species to British Columbia.

20. "Tl'iksE'mtEm" is Boas' transcription of nx̌'ík̓səmtəm, the Thompson name of one of Coyote's sons.

the basket, untie the rope and give it a tug, so that we can pull it up." The young man obeyed, and when he reached the ground, Spiders pulled up the rope. He had come to earth in Lytton but didn't meet anyone because all the people had moved to Bittanny.

The woman stolen by Coyote had a son. She was constantly in tears over the death of her husband. While he was walking from Lytton to Bittanny, the child saw him coming. He ran to his mother and said, "Father is coming!" The mother didn't believe him, but when he finally did arrive, she was overjoyed. Coyote pretended to be glad about his son's return, but the son pondered how he could take revenge. Once the hunters had a streak of bad luck and the village was short of food, so Tl'iksE'mtEm went out and killed many deer. He didn't bring all the game home with him but asked his father to help him fetch it. He gave him an old rotten rope to tie up the game with. When Coyote was crossing the river, Tl'iksE'mtEm made the water rise, and Coyote drowned. His corpse drifted into a salmon weir belonging to four women. Here he transformed himself into a small board. When the women saw it, one of them said, "This is nice; we'll make a bowl from it." They took it home and placed some salmon on it. But no sooner had they put this down, when it disappeared. The board had eaten it. So the youngest woman flung the board into the fire. Then Coyote assumed the shape of a small child and cried. The women picked him up and kept him as their slave. When he grew up, the women always left him to watch the house while they went picking berries. They owned two baskets in which they kept fog and wasps. One day, when the women had left him by himself, he opened the baskets and let the fog and wasps escape.

III. Legends from the Lower Fraser River

"The Indian I have here is a prize," Boas wrote to his wife on 10 August 1890 from the Hotel Douglas, New Westminster. "He is a chief and has a genealogy going back nine generations" (Rohner 1969:127). This family tree is diagrammed in Boas' report to the BAAS and the one named aboriginal consultant there is given as George "StsEē′lis" (Boas 1894b: 454–460). Boas is on record as having been in the Harrison Lake area itself on 6 September 1889 (Rohner 1966:155), but it was only for that one day. When Boas tells us in the headnote to the present section is that the "majority of the following legends were told to me by George Stseē′lis and his wife," it is safe to assume that most, if not all, came from this retired couple living in New Westminster. "He does not work," Boas explained, "but lives on what the tribe gives him as payment for former potlatches" (Rohner 1969:127). Again, because of the family letters, we can go behind the scenes into the actuality of myth-collecting: " … at least once a day I have to listen to a speech about how great he is … The main topic of his conversation is the fact that his wife once gave Princess Lenore, the wife of the former Governor of Canada, five cows which she did not even acknowledge, thus proving herself to be most unworthy." Boas adds: "At times I feel like giving up the whole trip and letting all the Indians run off" (Rohner 1969:127). None of this exasperation gets into the *Sagen*. In any case, Chief George and his wife could tell very good stories. The only caution would be to understand that this is the Chehalis view of things, as Boas (1916:1018) acknowledged by heading all these myths as "Stseē′lis" in *Tsimshian Mythology*. They are a selection from, rather than a representation of the whole of the repertoire of the Lower Fraser River (Mainland Halkomelem) tribes, one which reflects influence of the Lillooet, the immediate neighbours of the Chehalis.

Indians encamped in summer shelters on the banks of the Fraser River near the burgeoning town of New Westminster, *ca.*1867. Both Coast Salish (right) and westcoast (left) styles of river canoes are visible along the shore.

City of Vancouver Archives, Vancouver, B.C. (Frederick Dally photo).

III. Legends from the Lower Fraser River[1]

Most of the following legends were collected in Agassiz, near the mouth of the Harrison River, around Harrison Lake, and in New Westminster. A number of them, which take place above Fort Douglas, should properly be counted with Lillooet legends.[2] But I have placed them here, since I heard them from the lips of a Stseē'lis.[3] Most of the following legends were told to me by George Stseē'lis and his wife.

---

1. Boas' "Lower Fraser River" designates the region traditionally used and occupied by 15–20 Coast Salish groups extending from the mouth of the Fraser River up to the Yale area. These groups speak dialects of the Halkomelem Coast Salish language that is also spoken by the Cowichan and Nanaimo of Vancouver Island. Halkomelem is a member of the Central Coast Salish Division of the Salishan Language Family. The Mainland Halkomelem dialects are differentiated into Upriver Halkomelem and Downriver Halkomelem—the former, from the vicinity of Yale down to the Sumas area, have "l" in their speech, while the latter, from the approximate area of Matsqui down to the Fraser River mouth, have "n" (Boas 1887e:map; 1887f:132, map; 1894b:454–456; Hill-Tout 1903:355; Duff 1952:11–24; Suttles 1955:8–14; 1990:453–456; Galloway *et al.* 1980:1–2; Galloway 1993:1–2; Thompson and Kinkade 1990:34–37; Bouchard and Kennedy 1991b:101–102). The term "Stalo" (anglicized from stá·ləw 'river'), adopted by Duff (1952:11) to designate the Lower Fraser River people, was described by Suttles (1955:8) as a "convenient designation." More recently the term "Stalo" or "Stó:lō" has been used as a political unit to identify many of the Fraser Valley Coast Salish groups.

    In annotating this section, we have drawn upon our consultation in the 1970s–1980s with several Mainland Halkomelem people, and we gratefully acknowledge their assistance: Amelia Douglas; Susan Peters; Mary Charles; Arnold Guerin; and Sophie Jacobs. For comparative Halkomelem, Lillooet and Squamish information cited here, we have drawn upon our consultation in the 1970s–early 1990s with the following Native people: Cowichan/Nanaimo Halkomelem: Chris Paul; Chester Thomas; Lower Lillooet: Charlie Mack; Baptiste Ritchie; Squamish: Louis Miranda. We also acknowledge the assistance provided to us concerning these annotations by Brent Galloway, Wayne Suttles, Wolfgang Jilek, Louise Jilek-Aall, Michael Kew, and Della Kew.

2. There is no "Fort" Douglas; Boas simply misheard the English place name Port Douglas, located at the upper end of Harrison Lake (Kennedy and Bouchard 1998:175). As discussed in a footnote that follows (see story 1, part 1), some sources identify the Port Douglas area as the boundary between Halkomelem and Lillooet (Lower Lillooet).

3. "Stseē'lis," anglicized as "Chehalis," is Boas' rendering of the Upriver Halkomelem term sċɛʔí·ləs, referring to a settlement at the mouth of the Chehalis River. Suttles (1990:455; 2002:pers. comm.) translates sċɛʔí·ləs as 'set on the beach'; Galloway (1993:562, 649) provides the gloss 'on top of the chest; something the chest is on top of.' Traditional Chehalis territory encompassed the area along the Harrison River from below the mouth of the Chehalis River (including the Chehalis River drainage) up into Harrison Lake (Hill-Tout 1904:311–315; Duff 1952:20, 22; Suttles 1990:454–455) (see also part 7 of the "Tribal Legends" portion of the present section).

1. Qäls[4]

1) Above Sk'tsās,[5] right in the mountains, lived Redheaded Woodpecker. His wives were Black Bear and Grizzly Bear. He had three sons and one daughter with Black Bear. Grizzly Bear had no children. The middle son was called Qoā'k·otlk·otl.[6] The youngest son was always crying, and because he couldn't be calmed down, his mother asked him why he was crying. So he answered, "I would like us to move down to the lake." The deity[7] had inspired this wish in him. Bear told her husband the child's wish and they moved down to Sk'tsās. When they had arrived there, Woodpecker built a house. Then Grizzly Bear began quarrelling with her husband and finally killed him. Qoā'k·otlk·otl made himself a cap from beaver fur and the four children left their mother and together wandered up along the Fraser River towards the sunrise. When they had arrived at the sunrise, they walked into the sky and wandered towards the sunset. From there they turned back and wandered east once more. They had received the name Qäls and transformed everyone they met into stones or other things. K·ā'iq,[8] Mink, accompanied them on their travels.

---

4. "Qäls" is Boas' rendering of the term for the 'Transformer' that Suttles (2002:pers. comm.) writes as χɛl's in Downriver Halkomelem and χɛ·ls in Upriver Halkomelem (see also footnote 6 below.)

5. What Boas transcribes here as "Sk'tsā's" and elsewhere as "Sk· tsā's" (Boas 1894b:456) is the term that Hill-Tout (1905:128, plate xv) writes as "S'kutzā's" and translates as 'butting,' "so called because, if one paddled on here, one would run against the head of the lake." Hill-Tout's (1905:plate xv) sketch map indicates that this place was located slightly northwest of the north end of Harrison Lake; Boas (1894b:456) states only that it was "north of the upper end of Harrison Lake." There is some disagreement as to whether this place was within Lillooet territory. While Boas' statement at the beginning of the present section suggests his recognition of Port Douglas, at the upper end of Harrison Lake, as a boundary between the Mainland Halkomelem and the Lillooet, Teit's (1906:195) map of Lillooet territory indicates this boundary around the middle of Harrison Lake. Moreover, Teit (1898–1910) specifically denied Hill-Tout's (1905:127–128) statement that prior to the mid-1800s, villages along the lower few miles of the Lillooet River were within Halkomelem territory; instead, Teit (1898–1910) assigned to the Lillooet the entire area down to where the Lillooet River empties into the head end of Harrison Lake, in the vicinity of Port Douglas (for further discussion, see Bouchard and Kennedy 1977:6–7, Suttles 1990:454, Galloway 1993:map 2, and Kennedy and Bouchard 1998:174–175).

6. "Qoā'k·otlk·otl" is likely the Halkomelem equivalent term for the Transformers that Boas transcribes as "Qoē'qtlk·otl" in Section II of the *Sagen*. While Galloway (2001:pers. comm.) has not recorded this term in his own Halkomelem work, he notes that it may be something like "χʷáqʷəҡ'qʷəҡ'." Boas indicates in the present story that among the Mainland Halkomelem, "Qoā'k·otlk·otl" refers only to one of the Transformers, who are also known singly, and sometimes collectively, as "Qäls" (χɛ·ls or χɛl's—see also footnote 4 above.)

7. *Gottheit* ('deity') in the original *Sagen*, although traditional Coast Salish society did not have the concept of a monotheistic deity or "Great Spirit."

8. "K·ā'iq" is Boas' rendering of qɛ'yəχ (also given as sqɛ'yəχ), the Halkomelem name for 'mink' in legends (the usual term for 'mink' is čɛčíqəl in Upriver Halkomelem, or čɛčíqən in other Halkomelem dialects.

2) First Qäls arrived at Mā′lē, where the village of the QmE′çkoyim is situated today.[9] There they met chief Pä′pk·EltEl[10] who was roasting mussels.[11] Qäls sat down not far from him. A bit of burning wood flew into the face of Qoā′k·otlk·otl and burned him slightly. He asked, "Where is your creek? I'd like to get a little water." Pä′pk·EltEl showed him his creek, which was so narrow that the trees touched above it. But in it dwelt Pä′pk·EltEl's subjects, the octopuses. When Qoā′k·otlk·otl came down to drink water, they pulled him in. Since he failed to return, the eldest brother, after some time, went to look for him. He met the same fate and the youngest did not fare any better. So the girl said to Pä′pk·EltEl, "Oh, make me happy and give me back my brothers." He granted her wish and pulled the three brothers from the creek. Then they transformed Pä′pk·EltEl into an iris.[12] Ever since then there have been many irises near Mā′lē.

3) In K·'oä′lEts[13] (below Yale) there lived a boy who constantly tormented his mother for more food, and although she gave him plenty, still he was never satisfied. He went to everyone and said that his mother had told him to ask for food. Thereupon the people gave him food. But instead of taking it home, he hid it in the forest and ate it by himself. Since this happened day after day, one man finally asked the father, "Say, do you people actually send your son over to us every day to ask for food?" The father was astonished and very much ashamed. He went to all the

---

9. The village site known as máli was actually located immediately west of the main village of "QmE′çkoyim" which is anglicized as "Musqueam" and is known also as sċəlɛ′xʷ (anglicized as "Stselax").

10. Galloway (2001:pers. comm.) suggests that the name Boas transcribes here as Pä′pk·EltEl may be pɛ′pqəltəl, an Upriver Halkomelem pronunciation of a Downriver Halkomelem term, although Suttles (2002:pers. comm.) does not recall hearing the name.

11. Given as *Muscheln* ('shellfish; mussels; shells') here in the original *Sagen*, although Boas (1890b) wrote "tlā′okam mussels" in his original shorthand notes; "tlā′okam" is Boas' rendering of ɬɛ′ẇqəm, the Halkomelem term for 'mussel,' which confirms that he was referring to mussels and not other shellfish.

12. Given in the original as *Schwertlilie*, a general term referring to the genus *Iris*. The only iris in this area today is an introduced species, the yellow flag (*Iris pseudacorus*), that grows in marshy areas around the mouth of the Fraser River. It is not likely that an introduced species would be present in an origin legend. Boas' (1890b) original shorthand notes and also his later publication (Boas 1894b:454) associated "mę′çkoi" (məʔθkʷəẏ, from which the term xʷməʔθkʷəẏəm, "Musqueam," is derived) with the English term 'flag,' a folk name for the iris flower. From the description that Boas was given by the storyteller, he concluded that is was likely an iris, but he may have confused the identification of this plant with that of cat-tail (*Typha latifolia*), or another iris-like plant. Kinkade (1986:60–62), on the basis of linguistic analysis, suggests that məʔθkʷəẏ may actually refer to blackcaps (*Rubus leucodermis*).

13. The term q̇ʷɛ′ləc (Boas' "K·'oä′lEts") is the Upriver Halkomelem name applied to the vicinity of Hills Bar located on the east side of the Fraser River, north of the mouth of Emory Creek, below Yale. The term q̇ʷɛ′ləc is tentatively translated as 'barbecued on bottom or back' (Galloway 2001:pers. comm.)

people and asked them whether his son had come begging to them. When he found
out that his son begged daily in all the houses he decided to abandon him. He asked
everyone to move away with him and to take along all their food as well as the wall
planks of their houses. Then he took his son into the forest on the pretext that he was
going to teach him the use of magic substances. He took along a second boy as a
companion. While his son was purifying himself, the father and the other boy ran
away. In the meantime, the people had loaded their canoes and extinguished the
fires. They set out as soon as the man and the boy returned from the forest. Only the
abandoned boy's old and blind grandmother took pity on him. She took some
chewed fern-roots, wrapped a glowing ember in them and put them in a shell[14] which
she hid under a board. Then she said to her dog, "You stay here. When my grandson returns, scratch this board so that he'll find the fire." Then she, too went into the
canoe and they all set out.

After some time the boy came back from the forest and realized that he had been
abandoned. He sat down and cried. He was without clothing or food. Soon he
noticed the dog scratching the board, and when he looked, he discovered the fire left
behind for him by his grandmother. So he lit a fire and fashioned a bow and some
arrows for himself. He made the bow string from willow bark.[15] He shot birds for
himself, skinned them and roasted their flesh. From the skins he made himself a
cape with a beautiful pattern. One day, when he had lain down to sleep, Sun saw
him and stepped down from the sky in the shape of a man. Sun told him, "I like your
cape. Let's swap; I will give you my cape of mountain goat wool in return. If you
dip one corner of my cape into the river, it will fill at once with schools of herring.
I am the sun; the moon is my brother and the bright star often seen close to the moon
is his wife." They made the exchange and the boy at once tried the new cape's
power. He dipped it into the river, which immediately began to fill with schools of
herring. He caught many, dried them and then built a house which he was able to fill
with food. Then he remembered his grandmother. He beckoned to Crow[16] and gave
him some herring to swallow. Then he told him to fly to his father's village and,
should he see an old woman weeping there, give the herring to her. Crow flew off
and found the boy's grandmother. So he called out, "Mā'o, mā'o", and spat out a

---

14. Given as *Muschel* ('shellfish; shell; mussel') in the original, and translated here as 'shell,' as Coast
Salish variants of this legend specify that the container was a clam shell (see, for example,
Kennedy and Bouchard 1983:12).

15. Boas' (1890b) notes identify this as "sqoā'la willow"—"sqoā'la" is recognized as the term
x̣ʷɛ'lɛ'ɫp referring to the 'short-leaf or Sitka willow' (*Salix sitchensis*) (Galloway et al. 1980:83;
1982).

16. Given as *Krähe* 'crow' in the original *Sagen*; in this area, the species referred to is the
Northwestern Crow (*Corbus caurinus*).

herring. Grandmother was astonished, and Crow told her that her grandson was still alive and that he had sent her the herring.

About this time, a young man travelled back to the old village to find out what had happened to the boy. How he marvelled when he saw the boy's large house and many provisions! The boy invited him to come ashore and told him, "Tell all the people that I am rich now. They may all come back here, except for my father and mother." The young man went back and delivered the message. When the people heard how well off the abandoned boy was, they set out to return to K·'oä'lEts. Raven[17] had two daughters. He told them to comb their hair well and to paint their faces. He wished that the abandoned boy would marry them. Everyone wanted to have him as their son-in-law. At last the boy also allowed his parents to return. But while he gave rich presents to all the people, he gave them nothing and they became very poor. He himself was made chief.

Once he went to hunt for elk. He led his dog by a rope and went upriver. When he spied an elk, he let loose the dog, who pursued it along the edge of the water. Just then, Qäls passed by and transformed the young man and the dog into rocks. He took the elk and flung it into the sky, whereupon it was transformed into the four brightest stars of the Big Dipper.

4) Qäls went on and met a group of children who were weeping because their parents had left them. He transplanted them into the sky and they became the Pleiades.

5) Qäls arrived at Sk'tsās (above the northern end of Harrison Lake).[18] Here there lived Sнä'i, a very powerful man.[19] When he looked along any path, it became very long. When Qäls came close, Sнä'i put on his clothes, made entirely from bear skins, and his snowshoes. Qäls camped not too far from Sнä'i's house. Here their sister remained, while the three brothers went to fight with Sнä'i. First Qoä'k·otlk·otl said, "Let's see who can urinate the farthest." He tried to reach the summit of the mountain, but was unable to do so. Sнä'i, however, urinated over the top of the mountain and thus formed the river which runs from Silver Lake to Spuzzum.[20]

---

17. Boas here distinguishes *Rabe* 'raven,' the Common Raven (*Corbus corax*) from the term he used in the preceding paragraph, *Krähe* 'crow.'

18. See the initial footnote to part 1 of this same story.

19. Teit (1912:292–293) in his collection of Lillooet legends and stories also refers to the Transformers' encounters with "S'cxei" (Boas' "Sнä'i") and identities "the celebrated Dr. Stone on Harrison Lake" as the site where "S'cxei" was changed into stone.

20. Possibly the storyteller is referring to Spuzzum Creek, although the only Silver Lake known in this area is south of Hope, a long distance from Spuzzum and on the east side of the Fraser River.

So Qäls tried to defeat SHä'i some other way. He went to him and said, "Old man, we would like to go downriver to Stseē'lis, but have no canoe. Will you lend us yours? We will return it soon." SHä'i promised the canoe to them and the following morning the three brothers came to fetch it. They persuaded SHä'i to come down-river with them. When they had gone only a little way and had reached the lake, Qäls called the east wind. A raging storm came up and the canoe filled with ice and finally capsized. Qäls hoped that SHä'i would drown. The brothers went ashore and returned to their sister, who had remained in the camp. But SHä'i had reached shore safely with the aid of his snowshoes, which he had tied to his shoulders. He took some diatomaceous earth with which his clothes had been rubbed, crumbled it between his hands, and blew it into the air. Thereupon it started to snow. Then he looked along the path which Qäls had to follow and immediately it stretched out very far. The snow became deeper and deeper and Qäls was almost frozen when at last he arrived at his sister's fire. But SHä'i had returned home easily and quickly on his snowshoes. When the brothers came to the camp, they dropped with exhaustion. Their sister warmed them up and gave them hot "sockeye" (*Oncorhynchus nerka*) oil[21] to drink. So they recovered again. SHä'i had beaten them again.

Now Qäls wanted to kill SHä'i. He asked his sister, "Could you give me some of your menstrual blood?"[22] She said yes and gave it to him. So he put it in the bottom of his pipe and heaped tobacco on it. The youngest of the brothers warned Qoā'k·otlk·otl and begged him to leave SHä'i alone, since he was so powerful. But Qoā'k·otlk·otl paid no attention to him. He went to SHä'i and said, "Yesterday, when the canoe capsized and when it snowed afterwards, we became extremely cold. But the tobacco has warmed us very nicely. Won't you smoke some, too?" And he offered him the pipe. But SHä'i refused, saying that he could not smoke. But Qoā'k·otlk·otl encouraged him to try, and finally persuaded him. He took a puff, and Qoā'k·otlk·otl told him, "You have to inhale deeply and swallow the smoke." He took three puffs and then fell down dead. Qäls ripped out his tongue and threw it away; it became a rock.[23] He ripped out his stomach, tore off his arms, legs and head, threw them away and transformed them into stones.

---

21. Given in the original *Sagen* as a mixed English/German term written as "'sockeye' (*Oncorhynchus nerka*) Fett"; Boas has given the usual Latin name for sockeye.

22. Menstrual blood is associated with strong power.

23. Likely this is a reference to Doctors Point, located on the west side of Harrison Lake about 6 miles (10 km) south from the lake's head end. Teit's (1912:292–293) Lillooet collection of stories also refers to the Transformers' encounters with "S'cxei" (Boas' "SHä'i") and identities "the celebrated Dr. Stone on Harrison Lake" as the site where "S'cxei" was changed into stone. Hill-Tout (1905:128) also identifies the name of this shaman as Doctor Point in his Lillooet materials. Doctors Point was recognized as státłəx, meaning 'standing up' in the Lillooet lan-guage, in a variant of this legend recorded among the Lillooet (Bouchard and Kennedy 1977:7,

6) Farther upriver there lived a man, Swan,[24] with his wife, Great Blue Heron. One day they were sitting in front of their doorway when a canoe passed by with a man, Swallow,[25] sitting in it. Swan asked him, "Where are you going?" He answered, "My wife has died and I am now going into the forest for a whole summer." But in reality the following had occurred. His wife had gone out to collect inner cedar bark and had used the opportunity for a meeting with her lover. Swallow had found out and then taken revenge. He accompanied his wife to the forest on the pretext that he wanted to help her gather bark. When she had climbed a cedar, he tied her to the top of the tree. Then he de-barked it completely so that the trunk became very slippery, and left her. Swan invited him into his house for a rest. After a while, Swan heard a voice in the forest. It was the voice of Swallow's wife. She sang, "AtsElsQuā′Quakue͗′wul (i.e. the stick penetrates my anus),"[26] and her blood flowed down the trunk. Swan went into the forest with his people to search for the voice and at last found the woman. Only after much trouble, one of his men succeeded in climbing the tree and bringing the woman to the ground. She said, "When I am dead, you shall drink my blood, and if it rains, please talk about me." Then she died and was transformed into blackberries. Swan became very angry with Swallow and when he returned in the fall, he said to him, "When you come back with the east wind, I will avoid you and move downstream." At this moment Qäls passed by and said, "Alright, you shall become birds. You, Swallow, shall fly about in the forest in the summer, searching for your wife. Now paint your face like you do when you assume your supernatural power." So he painted himself black and white and stuck long feathers on his back. Then he changed into a bird and ever since flies about in the forest in the summer, looking for his wife with the cry El, El, El.[27]

13–14). Galloway (1993:656) recorded the Upper Halkomelem name for this place as ɬx̣íləx 'standing.' According to Robert Joe of Chilliwack, people had to be careful what they said when passing this rock, otherwise "heavy winds are going to come" (Wells 1987:121). People would leave offerings of food here to ensure there would be good weather while travelling on this lake (Galloway 2001:pers. comm.)

24. In Boas' (1890b) shorthand notes of this story he provides the term "sqᵘōkel," which is his transcription of sx̌ʷə′wqəl, the Upriver Halkomelem term for 'swan' (*Olor buccinator*).

25. The name of this bird in Boas' (1890b) notes is transcribed as "E'lel"—this is ʔɛ́ləl, the Upriver Halkomelem term for 'magpie' (Galloway *et al.* 1980:66; Galloway 1993:504), not 'swallow' (see also story 3 in the present section which makes this same confusion of bird names).

26. Boas' "AtsElsQuā′Quakue͗′wul" may be ɛ́cəl sqʷáqʷəhíwəl, derived from sqʷəhá 'come out through' (Galloway 2001:pers. comm.)

27. "This legend is told when it has been raining for a long time, and the Indians believe that this makes the rain stop" [Boas' original footnote]. Although this cry is identified with a "swallow" here, the species referred to is actually a magpie. The Upriver Halkomelem term for 'magpie,' ʔɛ́ləl (Boas' "E'lel"), is an onomatopoeic representation of the sound made by the magpie (see also story 3 in the present section which makes this same confusion of bird names).

7) Qäls wandered on upriver and came to a house where there lived an old man who had a very small mouth and a very fat belly. His name was Spēpā'ltsEp.[28] When Qäls saw him, he asked, "How did it happen that your mouth is so small?" But he knew no answer to this. Qäls continued, "This is not good for you; you are not able to eat properly. Wouldn't you prefer to go into the forest to hunt?" He replied, "No, I'd rather stay here. I don't like to move much, and I would like people always to be able to find me here." "Alright," said Qäls, "you shall always stay here," and transformed him into the fish, Spā'ltsEp.[29]

8) Qäls walked on and reached a house where there lived an old man with a red face and with red hair on his hands and feet. His name was PētHEl. When Qäls arrived, he hid, and when Qäls journeyed on, he changed into a small snake (with a red belly and a black back) and followed. When Qäls pitched camp in the evening and the eldest brother sat down, he crawled into his anus. "Ha!" cried Qäls, "Are you playing such tricks? Then remain a snake and always do this." Ever since then, PētHEl has been a small snake which always follows people, even into the water, and crawls into their anuses.[30]

9) And Qäls came to a house where there lived an old man, Rattlesnake.[31] He sat in front of his house, hiding something behind his back. Qäls sat opposite him and asked, "Old man, what have you hidden there?" But he did not answer the question and said only, "I've already defeated Marten with it." Qäls asked once more but received no reply at all. So he told him to get up and saw that he was hiding a rattle behind his back. Qäls stuck it to his back and said, "From now on, always carry the rattle," and transformed him into a rattlesnake. Since he had been a shaman, he can still poison people today.

10) He went on and met an old man with a small head, named K·ē'wuq.[32] He asked him, "Do you always stay near your house?" "Yes," he answered, "I don't care for

---

28. The term "Spēpā'ltsEp" used by Boas means 'little mountain whitefish' (*Prosopium williamsoni*) (Galloway *et al.* 1980:68).

29. "Spā'ltsEp" is Boas' rendering of the Halkomelem term spa·'lcəp that has been identified as 'mountain whitefish' (*Prosopium williamsoni*) (Galloway *et al.* 1980:68).

30. "PētHEl" is Boas' transcription of the Upriver Halkomelem term pítxəl identified as 'salamander (esp. western red-backed salamander)' (Galloway *et al.* 1980:72). However, Boas' description of "PētHEl" as "a small snake (with a red belly and a black back) ... which always follows people, even into the water, and crawls into their anuses" suggests that in fact the species in question is the red salamander (*Ensatina eschscholtzi*), which was sometimes referred to, with some phobia, as the "bum lizard."

31. Rattlesnakes are not found in the Fraser Valley; they are, however, found in the interior of B.C.

32. "K·ē'wuq" is Boas' rendering of qiwx̲, the Halkomelem term for 'steelhead' (*Oncorhynchus mykiss*) which is subsequently referred to as a "river salmon" in this same story (see also story 3, "Woodpecker and Eagle," of this section).

travelling about." So Qäls transformed him into a river salmon, which always stays in fresh water.

11) Qäls wandered on and met Salamander,[33] an old man with white hair and long nails. "Old man, what do you eat? What do you live on?" Qäls asked him. He answered, "Oh, my grandson, I have nothing to eat at all." "And why do you always kill people by putting your excrement in their mouths? That is very bad. In future, people shall use your excrement as poison." So speaking, he transformed him into a salamander.

12) He wandered on and met a woman who had her genitals on her chest. So Qäls said, "This is no good; genitals shouldn't be close to the mouth. Furthermore you won't be able to give birth like this, because the chest is all bones and not flexible enough." He closed her chest up. Then the eldest brother took birch bark in order to form new genitals. But it wasn't flexible enough. So Qoā′k·otlk·otl took sinews from the neck of the deer and from them made the woman's sexual organs. That is why they are very flexible and stretch during birth.

13) They wandered on and found a man and a woman whose sexual organs were on their foreheads. So he pushed them down to their proper places. If he hadn't done this, people would still have their genitals on their chest or their forehead today.

14) He went on and met Coyote,[34] who had no wife. Coyote had found a knothole, cut it out and used it instead of a woman. When Qäls reached him, Qoā′k·otlk·otl asked, "Grandfather, where is your wife?" "Here," he replied, from his bed. So Qäls lifted the blanket and saw the knothole. "Is this your wife, grandfather? Shall I make you happy? Give me some cedar bark and I will make you a wife from it." Coyote said, "Here, grandson, take this cedar bark and make me happy." Qäls transformed it into a woman, whom Coyote then married.

15) The brothers of Qoā′k·otlk·otl wanted to find out whether he was powerful. One day, when they were journeying up the river, they agreed to test him. In the evening they pitched camp and then teased their brother and pulled his hair. But he didn't pay any attention and lay down and put on his cap of beaver fur. Then the river started to rise and his brother and his sister had to flee up the mountain before the waters, while he remained lying calmly by the fire. Even though everything around was covered by the water, the area around his fire remained dry.

---

33. Boas (1890b) writes "salamander sayī′yaq" in his manuscript version of this story; "sayī′yaq" is Boas' rendering of the Halkomelem term that Galloway *et al.* (1980:72) have transcribed as cəyi·′yəx̣ and identified as 'probably the Pacific giant salamander and/or northern alligator lizard.'

34. Given as *Prairiewolf* in the original *Sagen*.

16) In Stseē'lis,[35] Qäls met a man called Pā'laʜil (One Leg). He was catching salmon in the river. Qäls wanted to have his harpoon head, and transformed himself into a salmon. In this shape, he swam towards the spot where Pā'laʜil was standing. The latter hit him and then he swam away with the harpoon head. He swam back to his brothers and assumed his proper shape. Then they all went to Pā'laʜil, who had gone to bed because he was very sad about the loss of his harpoon head. So Qoā'k·otkl·otl gave it back to him and said, "I want to make you happy. Here is your harpoon head. There shall always be many salmon where you are." With this he transformed him into stone. And he gave him power over the wind; that is why, even today, this stone can cause wind.[36]

Qäls saw One Leg catching salmon and asked him for permission to land near his house. But he refused this request. So the brothers and sister went back and camped some distance from One Leg's house. Then Qoā'k·otkl·otl changed into a salmon and stole One Leg's harpoon head. Thereupon the latter's wife said, "Why don't you go down to the lake with Qoā'k·otkl·otl?" They went and, when they had arrived at the lake, One Leg sprang back to his house in two bounds, while his wife caused the ground to stretch towards Qoā'k·otkl·otl, so that he was unable to return. He nearly froze to death, since it was very cold. His sister then begged One Leg's wife to shrink the ground again, so that her brother might return and she granted her wish. Then the two tried to see who could catch the most salmon in the river. Qoā'k·otkl·otl put his pipe in his mouth and pulled his net through the water and it was filled. Then Qoā'k·otkl·otl gave him his pipe and said, "If you smoke it, you will have better catches." After he had taken one puff, he was changed into stone.

17) When Qäls went up the Harrison River, he came to the place where there lived an old woman called Lᴇqyi'les.[37] Her vagina was set with teeth and with them she bit off the penis of any man who wanted to sleep with her. Qäls camped not too far from her house. When it was dark, K·ā'iq (Mink) sneaked down to the old woman's house. He found her in bed. So he groped about with his right hand under her blanket, in order to feel her genitals. He put his hand into her vagina and she bit it off. So he ran back to Qäls. Even today his footprints can still be seen where he leaped out of the house. He was ashamed and made a fire by himself away from the three brothers' camp. He kept his right arm hidden behind his back. The following morning Qäls continued up the river, with K·ā'iq steering, as always. But because his right hand had been bitten off, he used the left one, and consequently steered so

35. Chehalis.

36. "The above version seems to be incomplete. Therefore I am listing a second one here, but this one doesn't appear to be quite clear either" [Boas' original footnote].

37. "Lᴇqyi'les" is Boas' rendering of the Upriver Halkomelem term ləxʷyəʹləʹs 'always has teeth' (Galloway 2001:pers. comm.) (See also the footnote that follows).

badly that the canoe veered from right to left. Not before they camped again at night did Qäls notice what had happened to K·ā′iq's hand. Then he transformed LEqyi′les into a rock. It still stands beside the Harrison River today.[38] If water is sprinkled on it during nice weather, it will start raining immediately.

18) Qäls wandered on. A bit farther up the Harrison River they saw an old man who was harpooning seals.[39] When they got there, a seal had just surfaced and the old man held his harpoon in readiness to strike. Qäls came up on him from behind and the old one, the canoe in which he was sitting, and the seal were changed immediately into stone.

Tribal Legends[40] from the Lower Fraser River

1) The QmE′çkoyim. Their ancestor, Pä′pk·EltEl, lived in Mā′lē on the north arm of the Fraser River, where the tribe's village still is today. The legend has been recounted in connection with the legend of Qäls.[41]

2) The K·oā′antEl.[42] K·alE′tsEmEs,[43] the first chief, had a daughter who didn't want to marry. But one night a man crept into her bed and she allowed him to stay. It was her father's hammer which had assumed human form. In the morning, before it grew light, he left her again and changed back into a hammer. The following night a man crept into her bed again and slept with her. It was her father's dog who had also assumed human shape. After some time she gave birth to a number of puppies. The dog had been more powerful than the hammer, otherwise her offspring would have

---

38. The place known as ləxʷyə′lə′s is a rock face located on the east side of the Harrison River, north from the old Chehalis Indian cemetery (Galloway 2001:pers. comm.)

39. Seals travel from the Fraser River through the Harrison River and all the way up to Harrison Lake and even Lillooet Lake.

40. Given in the original as *Stammessagen* 'tribal legends'—these legends explain the coming of the First Ancestors of specific clusters of villages, most of which are commonly referred to in this area as "tribes," beginning at the mouth of the Fraser and moving upriver (see Boas 1894b:454 for a list of these villages and their First Ancestors). The First Ancestor legends presented here were all told by George Chehalis and his wife.

41. Boas is referring here to page 19 of the original *Sagen*, specifically story 1 part 2 concerning the Transformers' travels throughout the Mainland Halkomelem world. As previously noted, Boas' "Mā′lē" is máli, a village site actually located immediately west of the main village of "QmE′çkoyim" (xʷmə′θkʷəy̓əm) which is anglicized as "Musqueam."

42. This Native term, anglicized as "Kwantlen," is pronounced q̓ʷá·lx̓′əl in Upriver Halkomelem and q̓ʷánx̓′ən in Downriver Halkomelem. Traditional Kwantlen territory extended on the Fraser from the upper end of the delta upstream approximately as far as the Pitt River (Duff 1952:23–24, 27; Suttles 1990:453–456; Galloway 1993:650).

43. Boas translates "K·alE′tsEmEs" as 'badger' at the end of this same paragraph, but "K·alE′tsEmEs" (sqəlácəməs) actually refers to 'lynx.'

been small hammers. When her father saw this, he grew ashamed and he and the whole family group abandoned her. So the woman built herself a small hut and went down to the beach every day to search for shellfish on which she and her children lived. When she was down at the beach she could hear singing and the beat of the accompanying sticks. She tried several times to get back to the house unobserved in order to find out who was singing, but was not successful. One day, she draped her cape over her digging stick and hung from it the basket in which she gathered shell-fish, so that it appeared as if she were looking for shellfish. Then she sneaked to the rear of the house and heard the following song: "Oh! Mother thinks we are dogs and leaves us daily. She doesn't know that we are humans." She observed six boys playing about. One kept watch by the door and looked towards the beach in order to warn his brothers at once, should their mother return. She saw the dog skins in which the children were normally dressed, hanging up inside. She sprang inside, grabbed the skins and flung them on the fire. So the children had to stay human. They became the ancestors of the K·oā′antEl. Qäls passed that way later and transformed K·alE′tsEmEs into a badger.[44]

3) The K·ē′etsē.[45] Their ancestor was sent down from the sky by the deity. When he came down, there was a great noise up above. His name was Tsatā′sEltEn.[46]

4) The Mā′çQui.[47] Their ancestor, Sk·Elē′yitl (derived from sk·Elā′o, beaver),[48] had a son whom he dressed completely in beaver skins, just like himself. When Qäls came, they fought by standing opposite each other and trying to transform one

---

44. Boas (1890b) was correct to question the identification of this animal as "badger?" in the manu-script version of this text. "K·alE′tsEmEs" is Boas' rendering of the Upriver Halkomelem term for 'lynx,' sqəláčəməs. This animal, Galloway (1993:502) notes, is "regarded as a larger bobcat" which itself is known as sqəčáməs (in story 3 of this section, Boas translates another term, "Sts'ēk·," as 'lynx,' but this is sčε′yk, the mythological term for 'lynx' in Upriver Halkomelem).

45. The term "K·ē′etsē" (anglicized as "Katzie"), transcribed by Suttles (1990:455) as q̓íčəy ('moss') and by Galloway (1993:649) as q̓íčiy ('a many-coloured moss'), refers to the village that stood on the north bank of the Fraser River below Port Hammond. In a broader sense, "Katzie" de-lineated the people of Pitt River, Pitt Lake, and a short stretch of the Fraser above Pitt River, as well as Barnston Island and a small part of the south bank opposite (Duff 1952:24, 27; Suttles 1955:8; 1990:455).

46. Suttles (1955:8) stated that he was unable to identify the term that Boas transcribed as "Tsatā′sEltEn." Possibly this ancestral name was cətε′səltən or c̓ətε′səltən (pronounced cətε′səltəl or c̓ətε′səltəl in Upriver Halkomelem).

47. The "Mā′çQui," anglicized as "Matsqui," whose Halkomelem name is transcribed as mε′θxʷi '(big) flat (opening place)' (Galloway 1993:649), occupied the south bank of the Fraser River between Sumas Mountain and Crescent Island, and the inland area between Abbotsford and Aldergrove, and south (Duff 1952:23; Suttles 1990:455).

48. The Upriver Halkomelem term "Sk·Elē′yitl" (probably sqəlε′yəɬ) is, as Boas notes, derived from sk·Elā′o (sqəlε′·w), 'beaver' (*Castor canadensis*). Likely the translation of sqəlε′yəɬ is 'beaver's child' (Galloway 1993:501; 2001:pers. comm.)

another. Finally Qäls defeated him. Sk·Elē′yitl jumped into the water and thrashed about wildly. He and his son were transformed into beavers.

5) The Lᴇk·′ä′mel (Nᴇk·′ä′men).[49] Their ancestor, IālEpk·ē′lEm,[50] lived with his mother. People in those days didn't yet have fire and were living as if in a dream. When Sun saw this, he took pity on them and descended from the sky in the form of a man. He gave fire to IālEpk·ē′lEm. Then he awoke from his dreamlike existence to real life. Sun taught him and his people all the skills. Later Qäls passed by and fought IālEpk·ē′lEm. They stood opposite each other and tried to transform one another. IālEpk·ē′lEm picked up some white wood ashes, and, sprinkling them over himself, boasted to have become powerful and wise through Sun's help. He was jumping high into the air. So Qäls called out, "In future, do the same in the water," and transformed him into a sturgeon.[51]

6) The Tc'ileQuē′uk·.[52] In Ts'uwä′lē,[53] on the lower Chilluwak River,[54] there lived a chief who had a very beautiful daughter. K·ā′iq, Mink, wished to have her for himself. So he assumed the form of a handsome young man and walked upriver on the shore opposite the village. He carried a harpoon in his hand and fish on his back so that it appeared as if he had just caught them. At just this moment an old man had

---

49. Boas' "Nᴇk·′ä′men," anglicized as "Nicomen," is the Downriver Halkomelem term nəq̓ε′mən, pronounced in Upriver Halkomelem as "Lᴇk·′ä′mel" (ləq̓ε′məʼl, 'level part; part one travels to,' according to Galloway 1993:6, 649) and referring originally to Nicomen Island. Nicomen territory encompassed the area along the north side of the Fraser River from Squawkum Lake to Dewdney Slough, including all of Nicomen Island except the southwest corner (Duff 1952:22–23; Suttles 1990:455, 473). Moreover, the name for this language, "Halkomelem" (given in Galloway 1993:6 as hɛlq̓əmε′yləm, 'going/coming/getting to Nicomen Island'), or, in Downriver, "Hunquminum" (hənq̓əminəm̓, literally 'be Nicomen-ing,' according to Suttles 2002:pers. comm.) is derived from "Nicomen."

50. Boas' "IālEpk·ē′lEm" is likely yaləpqíləm, although Galloway (2001:pers. comm.) is not aware of the term outside of this story.

51. Given as *Stör* 'sturgeon' in the original *Sagen*, and as "sturgeon" in English in Boas' fieldnotes (1890b)—the Halkomelem term for this species, *Acipenser transmontanus*, is sk̫áwəč.

52. "Tc'ileQuē′uk·" (anglicized as "Chilliwack") is Boas' transcription of (s)čəlx̫íq̫ which has been translated as 'going back upstream' by Galloway or as 'upstream head (?)' by Suttles, derived from sčə′lə′x̫ which Galloway glosses as 'quieter water; backwater; slough' and Suttles translates as 'go/come upstream.' Before about 1830, the Chilliwack people occupied the Upper Chilliwack River and Cultus Lake, and Chilliwack villages were confined to the Chilliwack River above Vedder Crossing (Boas 1894b:455–456; Hill-Tout 1903:355–356; Duff 1952:21, 43–44; Galloway 1993:7; Wells 1987:17–18, 48–50, 53, 85, 90, 215; Suttles 1990:455–456; 2002:pers. comm.) But over time the Chilliwack moved down towards the Fraser River until their territory included the Chilliwack River drainage (Duff 1952:20–21, 43–44; Wells 1987:54).

53. This is Boas' rendering of the name for the Chilliwack village site called θ'əwε·′lí, translated as 'dissolve; disappear, melted or wasted away,' and anglicized as "Soowahlie," that is situated at Vedder Crossing (Duff 1952:38; Maud, Galloway and Weeden 1987:40, 221; Galloway 1993:562). This is the setting of this story.

54. Chilliwack River.

sent all the young girls to bathe, among them the chief's daughter. The girls saw the young man, who kept calling "Ps! Ps!" and when they noticed the fish that he was carrying, they asked him to throw one over to them. He fulfilled their wish; the fish fell into the water, swam into the chief's daughter and made her ill. Her father searched for a shaman to heal her. So Mink assumed the shape of a shaman. In the evening he went to the village and when he was seen by an old woman, she said, "Surely he will be able to heal the girl." They called him into the house and he promised to heal her. First, he sent all the people out of the house, leaving only an old woman sitting outside the door to accompany his song with the rhythmic beats of the dancing stick. To begin with, he sang, but then he slept with the girl and she gave birth to a child right away. So Mink leaped at once out of the house. The old woman heard the child's crying and called the people back. They became very angry, took the child and threw him out of the house. But Mink was standing outside with his mountain goat cape spread wide; he caught the child in it and went away with him. After a while the girl's father became sad that he lost his grandson. So he sent to K·ā′iq and begged him to send him back. Mink granted his wish and sent the boy back. He was named T′ē′qulä′tca (from the lower reaches of the river).[55] He became the ancestor of the Tc'ileQuē′uk·.[56]

Later Qäls met T′ē′qulä′tca. They fought and tried to transform each other. Qäls first changed him into a root.[57] But this transformation was not entirely successful. Then he tried to transform him successively into a salmon and a mink, but wasn't any more successful. The mink wore eagle feathers on its head. So finally he changed him into a stone.

7) The Stseē′lis.[58] Their ancestor was called Ts′ā′tsEmiltQ.[59] He had been sent down

---

55. Galloway (2001:pers. comm.) has recorded t'ixʷəlɛ′čɛ (Boas' "T′ēqulä′tca") as an ancestral name and comments that 'from the lower reaches of the river' is a plausible translation.

56. "Up to four generations ago the Tc'ileQuē′uk· spoke the Nooksak language, which is almost identical with that of the Lummi. Hence they must be regarded as only recently assimilated with the other Fraser River tribes. The above legend seems to bear this out, their chief alone stemming from the lower course of the river, while the tribe lived on the upper reaches" [Boas' original footnote]. Boas (1894b:455–456) stated that the Chilliwack spoke Nooksack "until the beginning of this century," that is, until *circa* 1800. Confirmation that the original Chilliwack people spoke Nooksack or a language similar to Nooksack has been provided by Smith (1950:341), Duff (1952:43–44), Wells (1987:40, 87–88, 203), and Galloway (1993:6–7). The Nooksack are a Coast Salish group living to the south of the Chilliwack. The Lummi spoke a dialect of Northern Straits which was mutually incomprehensible with the Nooksack language.

57. Given in the original as *Rübe* which literally means 'turnip,' but translated here as 'root.'

58. As previously noted, "Stseē′lis" is Boas' rendering of the Upriver Halkomelem term anglicized as "Chehalis" referring both to a settlement at the mouth of the Chehalis River, which Boas describes as "the right tributary of the Harrison River," and to the group whose traditional territory encompassed the Harrison Lake, Chehalis River, and lower Harrison River region.

59. Galloway (2001:pers. comm.) concludes that the ancestral name Boas transcribes here as

from the sky by the deity. One of his descendants built a weir in the right tributary of the Harrison River. It stretched right across the river, so that no fish could get past it and go upriver. But upriver in K·oā'lEqt[60] there lived a tribe of whose existence Ts'ā'tsEmiltQ was unaware. Their chief was named K·ulk·E'mEHil.[61] Their ancestors had originally been mountain goats and marten and were then transformed into humans. After Ts'ā'tsEmiltQ built this weir, they suffered great need. Ts'ā'tsEmiltQ had four sons who watched nightly by the weir to catch salmon. They had tied a string around their finger which led to a thin stake stuck below the weir. When salmon swam along the weir to search for a passage, they brushed along the stake, which moved and woke the fishermen. These then immediately blew torches, which they had held in readiness, into flame, and by their light they speared the salmon. When the need in the upper village increased, the son of K·ulk·E'mEHil set out to find out why the salmon failed to come. He managed to get to the weir undetected and, while the men were waiting for the fish, tried to pull out some of the stakes so that the fish could get through. But the sons of Ts'ā'tsEmiltQ noticed that someone was busy at the weir. They blew their torches into flame and caught a glimpse of a young man who was attempting to flee. But they were good runners and caught up with him. So he said, "Oh, brothers! Our village is very poor because no salmon come at all. So my father sent me out to see why the salmon have suddenly failed to come." The sons of Ts'ā'tsEmiltQ answered,"Why don't you all come down and look at our father's land." The young man went back up and the whole tribe accepted the invitation. They went down in a large troop. The sons of Ts'ā'tsEmiltQ married the daughters of K·ulk·E'mEHil and the former gave them a piece of land where they built their houses. Since that time, the two tribes have lived together in Stseē'lis.

8) The Sk·au'ēlitsk·.[62] Their ancestor was called K·ultē'mEltQ.[63] His daughter found

"Ts'ā'tsEmiltQ" is likely ċáċəməltxʷ. The "Ts'ā'tsEmiltQ" story is also presented in Boas (1894b:455) and discussed in Hill-Tout (1904:312–313).

60. While the exact location of "K·oā'lEqt" is not known to us, it was likely on the upper Chehalis River. Hill-Tout (1904:312–315) presents similar accounts which describe fish weirs on the lower Chehalis River and the problems these weirs caused with those living on the "upper reaches" of this river.

61. What Boas transcribes here as "K·ulk·E'mEHil" is the same term that Hill-Tout (1904:311–314) writes as "CwElkúmiHyil" and identifies as the First Ancestor of one of three "septs" (descent groups) from the upper Chehalis River who, together with other septs, comprised the Chehalis. Hill-Tout, however, does not associate "CwElkúmiHyil" with a specific named site (see the preceding footnote). The term transcribed by Boas and Hill-Tout is probably derived from Upper Halkomelem xʷə'mxəl 'fast foot' (Galloway 2001:pers. comm.)

62. "Sk·au'ēlitsk·," anglicized as "Scowlitz," is the term sq̓ə'wləc meaning 'river turn at the bottom' (Galloway 1993:649). Traditional Scowlitz territory encompassed the area around Harrison Bay (where the Harrison River empties into the Fraser) and the lower Harrison River (Hill-Tout 1904:363–366; Duff 1952:20–22; Suttles 1990:455).

63. "K·ultē'mEltQ" is probably qəltíməltxʷ (Galloway 2001:pers. comm.)

the Sqoā′eqoē.[64] He himself was transformed into stone by Qäls.

9) The PELā′tlQ.[65] A woman called Clem (Pelican)[66] lived in Tcā′tcōHil,[67] where there are many rushes. One of them assumed the form of a man and the name Qä′latca (becomes visible).[68] He carried a hammer and an adze[69] and was a skilled canoe-builder. He married the woman and they became the ancestors of the PELā′tlQ. When Qäls came, he transformed Qä′latca into a rock. His hammer and adze can still be seen by his side today.

10) The Pā′pk′um.[70] Their ancestor was called Aiuwä′luQ.[71] When Qäls met him, he transformed him into a mountain goat.[72] This is why there are so many mountain

---

64. "Sqoā′eqoē" is Boas' transcription of the Halkomelem term sx̌ʷáyx̌ʷɛy (anglicized as "sxwaixwe") which refers to a distinctive mask with protruding eyes that is used by the Halkomelem and other Coast Salish groups on certain ceremonial occasions, especially those associated with cleansing.

65. What Boas transcribes as "PELā′tlQ," anglicized as "Pilalt," is the Upriver Halkomelem term pəláɫʷ or pəláɫtxʷ 'buried house' (Galloway 1993:652; Wells 1987:53, 159). Apparently this group took its name from an original village site located at the west end of the little mountain at Agassiz. Prior to about 1840, Pilalt territory encompassed both sides of the Fraser River below Seabird Island, including the broad area around Agassiz and the network of sloughs and islands down the Fraser to the vicinity of the Chilliwack River mouth. But after approximately 1840, the Pilalt scattered themselves along the south side of the Fraser, from Chilliwack to Ohamil (Duff 1952:20–21, 35–37, 42–43).

66. Boas' "clem" is the Upriver Halkomelem term sli·m which refers to the Sandhill Crane (*Grus canadensis*) (Galloway *et al.* 1980:65)—the pelican is not found in this area.

67. Boas' "Tcā′tcōHil," transcribed as "Stcā′tcūHil" by Hill-Tout (1903:400), is likely čéčəwxəl (Galloway 2001:pers. comm.) While Duff (1952:35) commented specifically that he did not obtain this term, Boas' fieldnotes (1890b) suggest this place was near Cheam.

68. Additional information about the term Boas transcribes here as "Qä′latca" and translates as 'becomes visible' is provided in his fieldnotes, where he states that this term is derived from "qē" meaning 'visible' (Boas 1890b). This latter term is likely x̌i, although Galloway (2001:pers. comm.) has not recorded a root with this meaning in Upriver Halkomelem. Notwithstanding, there is indirect support for Boas' translation in the neighbouring Squamish language where we have recorded x̌iʔ meaning 'appear suddenly.' Thus it is possible that Boas' "Qä′latca" is the Halkomelem term x̌iʔlɛ′čɛ.

69. Although the German term *Axt* 'axe' is given here in the *Sagen* (rather than *Dechsel* 'adze'), we have used the translation 'adze' because this is the English term given in Boas' (1890b) manuscript version of this story.

70. "Pā′pk′um," anglicized as "Popkum," is Boas' rendering of pápq̓ʷəm which means 'puffball,' referring probably to the giant puffball (*Calvatia gigantea*) or the gemmed puffball (*Lycoperdon perlatum* or *L. gemmatum*) and possibly other *Calvatia* or *Lycoperdon* species. The area of Popkum Indian Reserve No. 1 was referred to as pápq̓ʷəm because there were a lot of puffballs here (Galloway 1993:562, 653; 2001:pers. comm.) (see also the footnote to the last paragraph of story 3 in this section).

71. "Aiuwä′luQ" is probably the ancestral name ʔɛyəwɛ′ləxʷ (Galloway 2001:pers. comm.)

72. Boas (1890b) fieldnotes confirm the identification of this species as 'mountain goat' by providing

goats on Tlĕ′tlɛk·ē mountain[73] to the southwest of Pā′pk'um.

11) The Siyi′t'a.[74] A bear lived in Sǫuhä′mɛn.[75] He was transformed into a man who took the name Autltē′n.[76] He married and had a daughter. One night he heard a man leave his daughter's bed. He sprang up to see who it was, but the man had disappeared. Then he asked his daughter who it was, but she didn't know, either. So he told her to smear her hands with grease and red paint and to embrace the man with it when he returned. She followed her father's advice and the following morning they all saw that the black dog of Autltē′n was covered in paint. The girl's mother discovered it first and called out, "Look, father's dog has slept with you!" So the girl became ashamed. But Sturgeon also lived in Autltē′n's house. He said, "If he has been with the girl, he can only have been there later on in the morning, because I have always slept with her. If she is pregnant, please believe me that it is my child which she carries." Autltē′n remained completely silent, but the girl was very much ashamed. When she gave birth to a boy, Sturgeon took him and carried him to the water. He threw him into the river and he was at once transformed into a small sturgeon. Old Sturgeon caught him, killed him and cut him up. Then he served him to the people, saying, "Don't throw away any of the bones, but give them all to me." This they did. Then he placed the bones in a bowl and carried them into the water. They came to life immediately and the boy stepped unharmed from the water. He grew up and became the ancestor of the Siyi′t'a.

Autltē′n and his family knew that Qäls would arrive and that he was transforming everything. They said to each other, "He shall not transform us. He is no deity, but

---

the term "pḵ'e′lḵel"—this is p̓q̓ə′lqəl, the Upriver Halkomelem word for 'mountain goat' (Galloway *et al.* 1980:64; Galloway 1993:502).

73. What Boas identifies here as "Tlĕ′tlɛk·ē mountain" is łíłəqɛy 'glacier,' the name by which Mount Cheam was known (Galloway 1993:561, 655).

74. Here in the *Sagen* and elsewhere, Boas (1894b:454) identifies the "Siyi′t'a," i.e. siyə′t'ə (anglicized as "Siyita" or "Tseatah") as a separate group and associates them with Agassiz (see also the footnote that follows, and the preceding story 9). In more recent times, siyə′t'ə, located near the north side of the Agassiz Bridge, has been recognized as a former village site of the Pilalt that is now a reserve of the Cheam Indian Band (Duff 1952:35, 42–43; Galloway 1993:652; 2001:pers. comm.; Wells 1987:97–98).

75. Boas associates "Sǫuhä′mɛn" with Agassiz (see also the preceding footnote). Duff (1952:35), however, noted that probably Boas' "Sǫuhä′mɛn" is the Downriver Halkomelem pronunciation (sxʷʔohɛ′mən) of the Upriver Halkomelem term sxʷʔohɛ′mə′l (anglicized as "Ohamil') 'levelling off of water; more calm; river's widening,' the name of the village to which the Siyita people moved after about 1840. This name, sxʷʔohɛ′mə′l, refers to Indian Reserve No. 1 of the Ohamil Band at Laidlaw (Duff 1952:20–21, 35–37, 42–43; Galloway 1993:653; 2001:pers. comm.; Wells 1987:97–98).

76. What Boas transcribes here as "Autltē′n" is not now recognized. The term may be Ɂawłtín or Ɂawƛ̓'tín (Galloway 2001:pers. comm.)

only the son of a Bear Woman." When Qäls arrived, he pitched camp again, not far from SQuhä'mEn. Qoä'k·otlk·otl went to Autltē'n by himself, having assumed the appearance of an old man. He asked Autltē'n, "What are you doing?" Autltē'n answered, "I am catching salmon in a net between two canoes." Then Qäls asked, "And how do you catch deer?" Autltē'n replied, "I catch them in nets as well." So Qäls asked, "And how do you catch birds?" He said, "In fine nets." Then Qäls asked, "Do you lie on your right or on your left side when you sleep?" "No," said Autltē'n, "I sleep like this, on my back." "And how do you put your legs?" asked Qäls. "I put them up like this." "And how do you hold your hands?" "I put them up to my chin." While he was talking like this, Autltē'n had lain down on his back, legs up high and hands pulled to his chin. Then Qäls transformed him into a rock which can still be seen today in SQuhä'mEn (Agassiz).

12) The QEtlā'tl.[77] Qē'lqElEmas,[78] the first of the QEtlā'tl was very powerful. His people were all river monsters. Once Qäls came to him. The three brothers crossed the river to visit him while their sister stayed on the opposite shore. They managed to cross the river, which is very dangerous at this spot, without mishap. But when they came to Qē'lqElEmas, he called his people and when Qäls saw the dreadful shapes, he fainted. Qē'lqElEmas took a magic substance out of his basket, sprinkled it over Qäls, and revived him.

13) Sk·Elā'o (Beaver), the brother of Qē'lqElEmas, was the first chief of the Spē'yim (Spuzzum, the southernmost village of the Ntlakyapamuq).[79] When he saw that Qäls came to his brother, he dug an underground passage to his house to be able to help him in case of need.

2. Moon and Sun

An old woman named Käiä'm[80] lived all by herself at the mouth of the river flowing from Silver Lake. One day she went down to the river, caught a salmon and took out

---

77. "QEtlā'tl" is Boas' rendering of xǝɫɛ'ɫ, anglicized as "Kuthlalth," which means 'injured people' and refers to the area of Kuthlalth Indian Reserve No. 3 of the Yale Band, located on the east side of the Fraser River adjacent to Lady Franklin Rock, not far upriver from the town of Yale. Galloway's (1993:654) consultants associated this place's name with the Transformers turning people into stone here, or with the occurrence of several battles here in historic times, or with people killed here in a slide.

78. This is the well-known ancestral name xǝ'yxǝlǝma·s (Galloway 2001:pers. comm.)

79. Confirmation of "Spē'yim" as the "southernmost village of the Ntlakyapamuq" (nɫe?képmx) is found in Boas' (1890b) fieldnotes where he identifies the affiliation of this place as "Thompson River." "Spē'yim" is Boas' transcription of spe'yǝm which is likely the Upriver Halkomelem pronunciation of spǝ'zǝm, anglicized as "Spuzzum," the Nlaka'pamux name for this place.

80. "Käiä'm" is Boas' transcription of skayɛ'm, the Upriver Halkomelem term for 'wolverine' (Galloway et al. 1980:65). Boas' (1890b) fieldnote of this text states "Kayilapa (= kayäm),"

the roe. First she took the long piece, squeezed it and said, turning to the sun, "Oh, Sun, I am all alone! Take pity on me and give me companions to live with." Then she took the shorter piece of roe and squeezed it. While she was doing this, she prayed again in the same way to the sun. Then the two halves of the roe were changed into two girls. They grew up and became very pretty. The three women lived all alone. The young girls had never seen a man. But now they were grown up, they wished to have a man very much. Käiā'm died about this time. The girls put her body in a canoe and took it upriver a short distance, as the old woman had told them, and buried her. They put the stone hammer and the wedge of the old one in her grave. Then they returned home and went to bed, each on her own side of the house. But the old woman was not dead at all; after the girls left she rose and took the shape of a young man. She intended to play a trick on the girls. For this purpose she tied together her shrivelled skin, thus making it smooth again. Then she broke her hammer in two and fixed the two pieces as testicles; she added the wedge as a penis. The following morning she climbed into the canoe in which she had been buried and went down to her house. She had tied back her hair, adorned her face with mica and wound marten skins around her head and body. While paddling down the river, she sang, "AuEnā'qoa, auEnā'qoa, aynō'k·sa Kayilā'pa. Hē, hē, yuk· Kayilā'pa."[81] She had assumed the name Kayilā'pa. The girls stepped outside when they heard the song and thought, "A man is coming." Each one of them wanted him for herself. The younger one was the prettier, and when both of them called him, Kayilā'pa followed her. He sat down beside her on the bed; she cooked a fine meal and served it to him. She gave him a beautiful spoon. He held his cape in front of his mouth while he was eating. The girls were puzzled by this and couldn't understand why he was doing it. He did not want to let them see that he was toothless. When they thought that he was finished, they took away the bowl and spoon. When Kayilā'pa got up, they saw that all the food they had given him lay on the ground in front of his place. He had not been able to chew it. This puzzled the girls even more. They went outside and discussed it between the two of them. Both wanted to have him for a husband and finally agreed that he should sleep between them. When they lay in bed, one of them put her arm over his belly, felt for his genitals to make sure that he was a man, and was convinced when she felt the wedge and the halves of the stone hammer. Then she tickled him and he laughed just like Käiā'm used to do. Then she felt that his

---

associates both of these terms as names for wolverine, and suggests the existence of a term kayilɛ'pɛ as the legendary name for 'wolverine.' Galloway (2001:pers. comm.) has not recorded this latter term (see also the footnote that follows).

81. Galloway (2001:pers. comm.) provides a tentative translation of "AuEnā'qoa, auEnā'qoa, ayō'k·sa Kayilā'pa" as 'he isn't starving, he just ran out of everything, Kayilā'pa,' and notes that "Hē, hē, yuk· Kayilā'pa" is comprised of a sung syllable həy həy together with the word yəq meaning 'crawl under.'

skin had only been tied together and thus recognized the old woman who had played this trick on them. The girls were so ashamed that they ran away.

They walked up the creek and after a long journey met an old woman. They saw that she was rocking a baby and soon noticed that she was blind. The two girls stepped up to her and asked, "Whose child are you rocking there?" She replied, "This is my daughter's child." "Where is your daughter?" asked the girls. The old one answered that she had gone away to have a swing. Then the girls asked where the child's father was and learned that he was catching salmon higher up the creek. While they were there, the baby kept on crying and the old woman rocked the branch with the cradle on it continuously in order to calm him. The girls said, "The child is dirty; that is why he keeps crying. We will wash him for you." They took him from the cradle, went to the creek with him and returned after a short while. They told the old one, "The child is clean now and will most likely stay quiet." They pretended to put him back into the cradle, but in reality put in a piece of rotted wood, and stole the child. The old woman kept on rocking the cradle. But since the child didn't stir for a long time, she became uneasy, felt for him and found the piece of rotted wood. Then she called to her son-in-law, "Sk·oā'sk·oāstel![82] Two women have stolen your son." The man could hear that she was calling to him but was unable to make out what she was saying because the creek where he was fishing was too noisy. He shouted, "Huä, huä," took some water in his mouth and sprayed it on the creek, which thereupon became quiet at once so that he was able to hear what the woman was saying. When he heard that her grandson had been stolen, he became angry, hurried home, grabbed the old one by her hair, threw her to the ground and shouted, "In future, when people find you, they shall eat you." She became a root (ts'u'koa),[83] and her hair became the leaves of the plant.

At last the girls arrived at the top of the creek and stayed there. The stolen boy grew up and they made a bow and arrow for him. At first he shot birds, but when he grew stronger, he asked the girls to make him a strong bow. They fulfilled his wish and he then shot deer, bears and mountain goats. When he had grown up, he took both girls as wives.

The stolen boy's mother returned home after she had enough swinging. She became very sad when she found that her son had been stolen. She asked for some of the dirtied inner cedar bark from the cradle, took it to the creek, wept, prayed to

---

82. "Sk·oā'sk·oāstel" is possibly sqʷásqʷastəl (Galloway 2001:pers. comm.), although the term has not been recorded.

83. While linguistically it is more likely that "ts'u'koa" is Boas' rendering of čá·k̓ʷə, the Upriver Halkomelem term for 'skunk cabbage' (*Lysichitum americanum*), rather than θ'ə'k̓ʷɛ, 'spiny wood fern' (*Dryopteris austriaca*) (Galloway *et al.* 1980:77, 82; 1982), ethnobotanical studies suggest that in this region the roots of the latter species were more often used as food than those of the former.

the sun and then squeezed it out so that the filth dripped into the water. It was changed at once into a boy whom she named Sk·u′mtcetl.[84] She was grateful to the sun that it had given her another child. When the boy grew up, she made him a bow and some arrows and he went hunting in the mountains. His mother told him how his brother had been lost and ordered him to be friendly to any stranger he might meet in the forest, because it could turn out to be his brother.

One day Sk·u′mtcetl went far away to hunt for mountain goats. He stayed out overnight and met a stranger who was also hunting mountain goats. They played lehal[85] together. The following day, when he went out to hunt mountain goats again, he met the stranger once more and when he returned home that night he told his mother of the meeting. She said, "If you meet him again, look at him carefully. Your brother has a scar on his forehead which he got when he fell out of the cradle long ago." The following day Sk·u′mtcetl met the stranger again. The latter took him along to his house and they sat down to play. Sk·u′mtcetl saw now that he had a large scar on his forehead, so he said, "You are my brother. Those two women stole you a long time ago. I can recognize you by the scar on your forehead." When his brother thus found out that he had been abducted by the women as a small child, he became so ashamed that he set his house on fire and burned himself to death, his wives and the children he had by them. He became the moon.

He sent Sk·u′mtcetl back home. When Sk·u′mtcetl told his mother what had happened, she became sad. She said, "I will return to the land where the sun sets and where people swing. Henceforth, when the sun wants to send sickness and death among the people, I will pull and shake the land as a sign of what lies in store for you." Sk·u′mtcetl then went into the mountains and became the sun.

When Qäls met Käiä′m later on, he transformed her into stone.

3. Woodpecker and Eagle

TEmE′tlEpsEm, Redheaded Woodpecker,[86] had a wife called LEqyi′les whose vagina was lined with teeth.[87] She was in the habit of biting off the penis of all men who

---

84. What Boas transcribes as "Sk·u′mtcetl" is likely sqʷə′mčəɬ (Galloway 2001:pers. comm.)

85. Given in the original *Sagen* as Lehal; this is a reference to the "bone game" or "stick game" (known commonly by its Chinook Jargon name "lahal"), an Indian gambling game played between two sides in which the players guess in which hand their opponent holds a bone game-piece. This game is widely known throughout the Northwest Coast and Plateau regions.

86. This is the Upriver Halkomelem term for the Pileated Woodpecker, təmə′ɬə′psəm (Galloway *et al.* 1980:68; Galloway 1993:505).

87. As discussed with reference to story 1 part 17 of this section, "LEqyi′les" is Boas' rendering of the Upriver Halkomelem term ləxʷyə′lə′s 'always has teeth' (Galloway 2001:pers. comm.)

slept with her, thus killing them. Ts'ɛ'sk·ɛl, Eagle,[88] was Woodpecker's brother. Woodpecker and Eagle each had a son. The former taught his child to climb trees; the latter taught his to fly up in wide circles. LEky'ɪ̄ā'p, Coyote,[89] lived with them in the village. He was a bad man and was jealous of the skills of Woodpecker's and Eagle's sons. He pondered how he could do them harm. He told his wife to relieve herself and then he transformed her excrement into a beautiful aquatic bird. He made it swim about in front of the two young men in order to tempt them to follow it. Then the bird began to go farther and farther upriver. The young men were unable to get close to it. They managed to shoot at it now and again, but were unable to kill it. Thus it lured them farther and farther upriver until they arrived at last at the sky. Here they met one of the inhabitants of the sky, who took them along to his house.

When Woodpecker and Eagle missed their sons, they became very sad. They called upon all people and all lands to search for them, but they were nowhere to be found. At last they learned from a man that their sons were in the sky. So they wanted to go up to the sky to get back their sons, but they didn't know how to get there. They called a general assembly during which they asked the animals how to get to the sky. First they instructed Pelican[90] to try and fly to the sky. He flew up high but had to turn back without success. Then they instructed Mole (ʔpɛlā'wɛl)[91] to try to get up into the heights by crawling under the water and the ground. But he couldn't accomplish it. Then they made Swallow (ɛ'lɛl)[92] fly up high but he didn't reach the sky, either. Now Eagle himself flew up, but he also had to turn back without success. Then one of the K·stai'muᵩ[93] dwarfs, who live beside the ocean and are extraordinarily strong, made the attempt. But he was not successful. As they were now at a complete loss about how to get up there, T'ā'mia,[94] the grandson of LEqyi'les, stood up and said, "I dreamed last night how we can get up." He pushed his hair back, painted it red, drew a red line from his forehead along his nose to his chin and began

---

88. Boas' "Ts'ɛ'sk·ɛl" is c̓ə'sqəl, the Upriver Halkomelem term for the Golden Eagle (*Aquila chrysaëtos*) (Galloway *et al.* 1980:66; Galloway 1993:504).

89. "LEky'ɪ̄ā'p" is ləkiyɛ'p (often given as sləkiyɛ'p), which Boas translates correctly as 'coyote' in Upriver Halkomelem (Galloway *et al.* 1980:63; Galloway 1993:502).

90. Sandhill Crane—pelicans are not found in this area (see also part 9 of the "Lower Fraser River Tribal Legends" in the present section).

91. Although Boas questions this term, "pɛlā'wɛl" (i.e. spəlɛ'wə'l) is the correct Upriver Halkomelem term for 'mole' (Galloway *et al.* 1980:64; Galloway 1993:502).

92. This is ʔɛ'ləl, the Upriver Halkomelem term for 'magpie,' not 'swallow' (see also story 1, part 6 of the present section).

93. "K·stai'muᵩ" is likely qstáymətxʷ (Galloway 2001:pers. comm.), although this term has not been recorded.

94. This is t'ɛ'miyɛ, the Upriver Halkomelem term for 'wren' (Galloway *et al.* 1980:68; Galloway 1993:505).

singing, while his grandmother beat time: "Wus T'ā'mia tsEnā'! auatsEnsē'sē kulskuli'Ht te suā'yil" (I, T'ā'mia, I'm not afraid to shoot the sky.)[95]

Then he pointed his bow towards the sky's entrance above and shot an arrow. It flew and flew and at last hit the sky just underneath the entrance. He shot a second arrow which hit the notch of the first one; in this fashion he continued until the arrows formed one long chain. His grandmother helped him in this by singing and beating time. When the chain was finished, he wiped the red paint from his face and painted his whole body white with burned bones. Then he transformed the arrows into a broad path leading up to the sky. Now all the people went up to the sky, fought and conquered the inhabitants there and freed Woodpecker's and Eagle's sons. Then they returned home. When they had all arrived safely back down below, they broke up the path on which they had climbed up. They hadn't noticed that Snail had not come with them. Snail arrived at the sky's portal after the chain of arrows had already been destroyed and he had to drop down. Thus Snail broke all the bones in his body and ever since has been very slow.

Eagle and Woodpecker now knew that Coyote had lured their sons into the sky and they decided to take revenge. Coyote lived in an underground house.[96] Woodpecker went there and, without being noticed, hacked through the roof posts as well as the foot of the ladder which had served as the entrance. When Coyote came home, the house collapsed and killed him and his wife.

Grizzly Bear was a friend of Coyote. He thought, "Why have Eagle and Woodpecker killed my friend? I will avenge him." To this end he changed into a dog and went into the hut of the bird, Ts'Elk·ä'k·,[97] who was a beautiful girl. Then he wished that the sons of Eagle and Woodpecker should desire her for their wife. What he wished came to pass, and at first Eagle's eldest son set out to marryTs'Elk·ä'k·. According to custom he sat down beside the door without uttering a word (see *American Anthropologist* 1889, p. 332).[98] Thereupon Grizzly Bear rushed out of the house and devoured him. Since Eagle's son didn't return, the son of Woodpecker thought, "That must be a good country where my friend lives now; I will go there, too." When he arrived at the house and entered, Grizzly Bear rushed upon him and

---

95. The translation of "Wus T'ā'mia tsEnā'! auatsEnsē'sē kulskuli'Ht te suā'yil" is confirmed as: 'I'm already just Wren. I'm not afraid to shoot the sky' (Galloway 2001:pers. comm.)

96. A more formal translation would be 'semi-subterranean pithouse' rather than 'underground house'; see Duff (1952:46–47) for a description of this type of structure among the Mainland Halkomelem.

97. The term that Boas transcribes as "Ts'Elk·ä'k·" is not recognized. Galloway (2001:pers. comm.) points out that it might be ċəlqɛ'q and may be related to sk̫ʷak̫ʷɛ'q, the Upriver Halkomelem name for the American Robin (*Turdus migratorius*).

98. The reference is Boas' "Notes on the Snanaimuq," *American Anthropologist* Vol. 2, 1889, but the page referred to is 322, not 332.

devoured him. Both their younger brothers shared their fate. Since the sons of Eagle and Woodpecker didn't return at all, the old ones knew that they had lost their lives. Each of them still had one very young son. They sent them into the forest to bathe and to rub themselves down with cedar boughs in order to become strong. They obeyed and became very strong. They always thought of their brothers and when they grew up, they set out to look for them.

Once they met an old man, Raccoon (MElE's).[99] He invited them to come into his house and entertained them. He knew that they wanted to look for their brothers and told them, "You must be careful. If you continue in this direction you will get to some houses. On the left side there live bad people; those living on the right side are not quite so bad." The young men went on and soon saw two houses, one on the right, and the other on the left side of the trail. At the right, there lived Quartz Woman and at the left, Grizzly Bear Woman. Both were the wives of Sqāuwä'l (Marten?).[100] They heard Bear Woman call, "Friend, come over to me and delouse me." Quartz Woman came and took Bear Woman's head between her knees, looking for lice. When she had finished, Bear Woman began to delouse her. But she scratched her with her long nails. Quartz Woman grew angry at this and they both started to pull each other's hair and to fight. Since Quartz Woman was nearly losing, she called for help to her brother, who didn't live too far from there. He came and struck his sister's backside so that fire sparked from her. Thus he helped her in her fight against Bear Woman. The latter had the task of guarding the way and of keeping anyone from passing by. Raccoon had caused her to fight with the other woman so that the young men had an opportunity to pass undetected. They went past the houses while the two women were still fighting. When Bear Woman finally discovered them, they had a good head start, but nevertheless she set out in pursuit. Soon the young people arrived at two more houses. To the right of the path there was the house of Sts'ēk·, Lynx,[101] to the left, that of Ts'Elk·ä'k·, where their brothers' bones rested. Lynx wanted to devour them at once. Since they were thus pursued by Bear Woman and Lynx, and couldn't get away in any direction, they clambered up an old pine tree.[102] Bear Woman saw them sitting up there and pretended to be

---

99. This is mə'lə's, the Upriver Halkomelem term for 'raccoon' (Galloway *et al.* 1980:64; Galloway 1993:503).

100. Boas is right to query this as 'marten'—"Sqāuwä'l" is actually sxəwɛ'l, the Upriver Halkomelem term for 'red fox' (*Vulpes fulva*) (Galloway *et al.* 1980:64; Galloway 1993:502).

101. "Sts'ēk·" is Boas' transcription of scɛ'yk, the Upriver Halkomelem name of 'lynx' in mythology (Galloway *et al.* 1980:64) (in part 2 of the "Tribal Legends" portion of this section, Boas provides "K·alE'tsEmEs" as the term for 'lynx'—this is sqəlácəməs, the usual name for the animal 'lynx').

102. In his original fieldnote version of this story, Boas (1890b) provides the English word "pine," along with the term "lä'yitlp" which is lɛ·'yəɬp, the Upriver Halkomelem term for Douglas-fir (*Pseudotsuga menziesii*), not 'pine' (Galloway *et al.* 1980:77; 1982; Galloway 1993:580).

friendly. She called, "Please come down, grandsons." They called back, "If you lie down on your backs and spread your legs, we will come down." Bear Woman and Lynx did what the young men asked because they hoped to be able to catch them afterwards. But they had hardly lain down when the two pelted them with rotted wood. The dust fell into the eyes, mouths, noses and genitals of Bear Woman and Lynx, so that they cried in pain. So the young men quickly climbed down and ran on. When Bear Woman was able to see again, she continued the chase while Lynx turned back. At last the fugitives came to a stream and were unable to cross it. They saw an old man called K·oalē′k·oa, Seagull,[103] on the opposite bank and asked him to ferry them across in his canoe. He came and granted their request at once. Some time afterwards, Bear Woman, who had followed the tracks of the young men, arrived too. When she got to the stream, K·oalē′k·oa was back on the opposite side again. She called to him and asked him to ferry her across. But the old man hammered about on his canoe and didn't react at all. He wanted to help the young men by drowning Bear Woman. To this end he pushed out one of the knots which were in the bottom of his canoe near the bow. When he had done this, he pretended only now to notice Bear Woman's calling, and went across. He sat in the stern of his canoe so that the front of it was lifted up out of the water and thus no water could run in through the hole he made. Then he said to Bear Woman, "Look, my canoe is broken; it has a hole in the front. You'll have to sit on it, otherwise I won't be able to get you across, because my canoe would fill with water." So Bear Woman sat down right on the hole and had to stay there if she didn't want the canoe to sink. Now when she sat there like this, the water ran into her genitals. The man crossed the river at an angle so that they took a long time and the cold water killed Bear Woman before they arrived on the opposite side.

The two young people walked on and soon met two blind women, TēQuamā′is, Partridge,[104] and Lā′k·ɛlak·am, another bird.[105] They were the two wives of K·ā′iq, Mink. He was just out to catch fish when the two arrived, but he returned home

---

103. Likely "K·oalē′k·oa" is Boas' transcription of the Upriver Halkomelem cognate of sqʷəníʔqʷa, the Nlaka′pamux name of the character who also ferried people across the river in his canoe, but killed them in the process (see Section II, story 2). Thus, the Upriver Halkomelem term in question may have been qʷəlíʔqʷa. Together with the fact that the known present-day terms for 'seagull' in Upriver Halkomelem are q̓ʷəlítəq and slílowyɛ (and not qʷəlíʔqʷa), this suggests that "K·oalē′k·oa" (qʷəlíʔqʷa) was used only as a mythological term for 'seagull' in Upriver Halkomelem. "Slē′lawya," the term that appears here in Boas' shorthand notes (1890b), is slílowyɛ, the Chehalis dialect form for 'seagull' (Galloway *et al.* 1980:67; Galloway 1993:505).

104. The German term *Rebhuhn* given here in the *Sagen* refers to the Common Partridge, a species that is not native to British Columbia. "TēQuamā′is" is derived from stíxʷəm Ruffed or Willow Grouse (*Bonasa umbellus*), and may be the term tíxʷəmáyəs meaning 'ruffed grouse eyes' (Galloway 2001:pers. comm.)

105. "Lā′k·ɛlak·am" is Boas' transcription of lɛ′qləqəm, the Upriver Halkomelem term for the Goldeneye Duck (*Bucephala clangula* or *Bucephala islandica*) (Galloway *et al.* 1980:66; Galloway 1993:504).

soon, and said, "Stay with me as my children. I will help you to get back your brothers." That same night he pretended to become seriously ill. He said, "Take me to the shore in my canoe. Give me my harpoon and bury me when I'm dead." The young men obeyed and took K·ā′iq to the shore. When they arrived there, he died and they buried him. Then they returned to the blind women and told them that their husband had died. From then on they had to hunt and gather shellfish for the women. One day, when returning from the hunt, they passed K·ā′iq's grave. They heard him call out, "Have you found a lot of shellfish?" and marvelled that the dead man could speak. A few days later they passed the grave again and this time K·ā′iq asked them, "Have my wives married again?" They replied, "TēQuamā′is has taken another husband, but Lā′k·ɛlak·am is still mourning for you." Then K·ā′iq got up again and ran back home. He took Lā′k·ɛlak·am back again as his wife. Then the youths wandered on and the women gave them magic herbs.

One day, when they were hunting again, they observed smoke rising in the distance and, when they approached, found a house in which Buffalo[106] lived. He said, "I know that you are looking for your brothers. Carry on in this direction and you will get to a cave. The dead live down there, and among them your brothers. We are the guards at the entrance, but we will let you pass." They gave them a magic substance and showed them how they could enter. The youths arrived safely at the cave and entered it. There, among many other people, they saw their four brothers. All the people there were playing together. Then they said to their brothers, "We have been searching for you for a long time. Your bones are resting up there in the house of Ts'ɛlk·ä′k· while you are dwelling down here. Now come back with us." The brothers replied, "We can't come back with you. Although we are strong and powerful down here, we are nothing in the world above." The youths answered, "Each one of us will carry back his two brothers. Then we will go to the place where your bones are resting and we will bring them back to life." So the brothers let themselves be carried back and were brought back to life. Then they returned to the home of their parents, Woodpecker and Eagle.

They had long ago given up their children for lost and had become blind from crying so much. The young people then rejuvenated and healed them. The two youths were outstanding hunters. When they hunted for mountain goats, they were able to kill a whole herd with one shot. They became mighty chiefs.

When Eagle's son grew older, he decided to get married and courted Qut, a small bird.[107] She accepted him, but didn't want to move to his country. She said, "Stay

---

106. Probably the storyteller knew the term "buffalo" through its diffusion from the Plateau. Boas writes "laquaça … buffalo Lillooet lg.[language]" in his fieldnote of this story.

107. The "small bird" whose name is transcribed as "Qut" by Boas is xʷət which is the Halkomelem term for the Swainson's Thrush (*Hylocichla ustulata*) (see also the footnote at the end of this paragraph).

here with us and become a great chief. Send out messengers and invite everyone to a feast." So young Eagle stayed there, built a huge house and invited all the people to a great potlatch. When he was out one day to hunt deer, whose meat was intended for the feast, his uncle, Woodpecker, arrived. He saw Qut and at once desired her for his wife. She became untrue to Eagle's son and accepted Woodpecker's courtship. Now, when young Eagle returned and saw his uncle in possession of the woman, he became very sad and returned to his father. Then Qut told Woodpecker to invite everyone to a feast. He sent out Hare,[108] "Hooknose" Salmon[109] and Suckerfish[110] as messengers. About the time of the winter solstice, all the people arrived and started the feast with the Mē'itla dance[111] in the house of Qut. She was a Siō'wa.[112] She danced and let her guests sing and beat time. Her husband put a large basket in front of her. When she danced she spat into the basket, which became filled at once with berries.[113] Then her husband put another basket in front of her which she filled as well by spitting into it. Thus she made the food with which they gave the feast. Then she gave away many capes.

Among the guests were also "Sockeye" Salmon[114] and his slave, Thunderbird.[115] The latter wanted very badly to have Qut for himself. When the feast had ended,

---

108. Given as *Hase*, 'hare,' in the original.

109. Given in the original *Sagen* as a mixed English/German term written as "Hooknose"-*Lachs* ('coho salmon).' The fieldnote version of this text gives the Native term "ku′qoatç" (Boas 1890b) which is kʷó·xʷəc, identified as the Upriver Halkomelem term for a 'small coho salmon' (Galloway *et al.* 1980:69).

110. Given in the original as *Hecht* 'pike' (not a native species in this region of B.C.), but translated here as 'suckerfish,' because Boas' (1890b) fieldnotes provide the Native term "sqāç" which Galloway *et al.* (1980:70) transcribe as q̓ʷɛ·c, the Upriver Halkomelem name for the 'little sucker with a big salmon-like mouth, prob. largescale sucker' (*Catostomus macrocheilus*).

111. Boas' "Mē'itla" is (s)mɨłə, the Halkomelem term referring both to the 'winter dance' and the 'winter dance season.' For descriptions of winter dancing among the Mainland Halkomelem and other Coast Salish groups see Boas (1894b:463), Kew (1970), Jilek (1974; 1982) and Amoss (1978).

112. "See Sixth Report on the Indians of B.C. in the *Proceedings of the Association for the Advancement of Science*, 1890. Page 28" [Boas' original footnote]. Boas actually refers here to the Lukungun, another Coast Salish group (see Section VII of the *Sagen*). In the referenced report, he states: "There are two classes of conjurers or shaman, the higher order being that of the Sǫunä'am, the lower that of the sī'ōua. The sī'ōua is generally a woman" (Boas 1891d:580 [28]). The former term ("Sǫunä'am") in Upriver Halkomelem is sxʷlɛ·m 'shaman; Indian doctor' and the latter term ("sī'ōua") is syə'wə 'seer; fortune-teller' (Galloway 1993:584).

113. The association of "Qut" (xʷət), the Swainson's Thrush, with berries is well known throughout this region; this bird was believed to ripen the salmonberries.

114. Given in the original *Sagen* as a mixed English/German term written as "'Sockeye'-*Lachs*" ('sockeye salmon').

115. The Mainland Halkomelem term for 'Thunderbird; thunder' is šxʷəxʷá·s (Galloway *et al.* 1980:95), although Boas does not provide the Native word here.

Salmon went to his canoe, lay down in the bow and closed his eyes. Thunderbird stood in the stern. Since they were ready for their departure, Qut came down to the canoe in order to give her guests provisions for the journey, as was the custom. The canoe was so far from the shore that she had to wade into the water up to her knees. Then Thunderbird grabbed her, lifted her into the canoe and took off with his prey.

Since Woodpecker had lost his wife in this fashion, he became very sad and resolved to get her back again. He asked K·á′iq, Mink, who had once been the slave of Sockeye Salmon, for help. Mink said, "I know Salmon's house very well. Close to the landing place of the canoes he has a salmon weir which is guarded by Thunderbird. Salmon sleeps on one side of the fire, Thunderbird on the other side. Let us assume the shape of salmon and swim into the weir. Then they will carry us into their house." Then Woodpecker changed into a coho and Mink into a spring salmon (*O. chouica*).[116] They swam to the weir of Thunderbird and allowed themselves to be caught. Thunderbird flung them into his canoe, together with the other salmon caught in the weir. Then K·á′iq thought, "I wish he would go home now and keep the two of us for himself." He had scarcely thought it when Thunderbird went home and gave the two salmon to his wife, Qut. K·á′iq then thought, "Now I wish that Qut would dry me over the fire and would roast Woodpecker." Thunderbird immediately told her to do this. She sliced both of them open and put K·á′iq on the drying rack, while they roasted and ate Woodpecker. After a short time K·á′iq fell off the rack. Qut put him back up, but he fell off again after a little while. Then K·á′iq thought, "I wish Thunderbird would make his wife throw the bones into the water now." Then he fell off the drying rack again and thought, "I wish that they would think me too dirty now and throw me into the water as well." This is what happened. Thunderbird told his wife to throw both the bones and the salmon, which had fallen down so often, into the water. She obeyed and went into the water up to her knees in order to throw the bones into the ocean properly. Thereupon the two salmon suddenly revived, took Qut by her hands and swam away with her.

When they had arrived back again in her homeland, Qut said, "Let's go up to (Harrison) Lake. I want to get some red paint." She fetched one basket of earth, cleaned it, rolled it into small balls and dried them. Then she made her husband fetch some wood and bark, light a fire and heat stones in it. Then they burned the balls of dried earth on these stones, after having covered them with some soil. Thus she taught her tribe the use and preparation of red paint.[117]

After this they returned to Stseē′lis. On their way they met K·á′iq, whose canoe was deeply laden with deer. Woodpecker asked him, "Where did you shoot these

---

116. The modern terminology is *Oncorhynchus tshawytscha*.

117. Red ochre, used in association with certain rituals among the Mainland Halkomelem and other Coast Salish groups.

many deer?" He answered, "I never shoot deer. When I want to get some, all I have to do is sing: amḗt'aq lɛqlḗ'silats! mḗt'aq lɛqlḗ'silats! (i.e. come down, come down you fat bellies!)[118] and they come down to me and drop down dead."

When they had arrived at Stseē'lis, Qut made them gather many roots. They brought her many baskets full. Then she had a pit dug and red-hot stones, which were covered with grass, thrown in. Then she put roots on the grass, sprinkled them with water and covered them with earth. She took them out the next day and gave them to the people to eat. This is how she taught them to prepare roots. Later she taught the people how to cook in baskets with the aid of red-hot stones.

Now K·ā'iq went home to his grandmother, Sk·ē'i.[119] His younger brother, Qoi'ēqoa,[120] always supplied her with deer. One evening, K·ā'iq said, "There are many fish in the river. Come on, Qoi'ēqoa, let's take the torches and go out and fish." They went out together and when they were in the middle of the water, K·ā'iq said, "Look, what is that down in the water?" Qoi'ēqoa leaned over the side of the canoe in order to be able to see better. K·ā'iq shouted, "Do you see the fish? Jump over the side and catch it." Qoi'ēqoa dived into the water at once. Then K·ā'iq thought, "I wish he would be transformed into a salmon trout,[121] and this came true. Then he killed him and took him home. When he got there, he went up to the house and said to his grandmother, "Go down to the canoe and get the salmon I caught." She obeyed and soon returned with the salmon trout. She said, "I've only found one fish in your canoe." K·ā'iq told her to cut it open. When she picked up her knife, the fish cried, "Don't cut me, Grandmother!" Qoi'ēqoa had not quite turned into a fish. In spite of this, K·ā'iq said, "He is talking nonsense. My younger brother is quite alright." But Sk·ē'i didn't believe him and became very angry that he had killed her grandson. Then they wandered upriver together to get to a country where there was food in abundance. They soon arrived at a house where there lived a beautiful girl

---

118. A tentative literal translation for this is: 'Come home, always-fat-ass! Come home, always-fat-ass!' (Galloway 2001:pers. comm.)

119. This is the Upper Halkomelem term sq̓i?, meaning 'smoked salmon.'

120. The only Upriver Halkomelem term for 'marten' that we are aware of is x̣áqəl (Galloway 1993:502; Galloway *et al.*1980:64); however, in Squamish we have recorded the term x̌ʷíx̌ʷa—the same word that Boas transcribes here as "Qoi'ēqoa"—as the name for 'marten' in legends. Thus it is likely that x̌ʷíx̌ʷa was formerly the Upriver Halkomelem legendary term for Marten, as well.

121. The German word provided here in the *Sagen* text, *Lachsforelle*, is an artificially-constructed term whose literal meaning is 'salmon-trout' which is a folk term used to refer to 'steelhead.' Boas' shorthand notes (1890b) identify the Native name for this 'salmon-trout' as "kē'noq" which is presumably a mis-transcription of the same term that Boas transcribed elsewhere in this section (see part 10 of story 1) as "k·ē'wuq" and referred to as a "river salmon." As previously noted, "k·ē'wuq" is Boas' rendering of qiwx̣, the Halkomelem term for 'steelhead' (*Oncorhynchus mykiss*).

named Pēpahā′m,[122] Frog. Beaver was sitting by the door of the house. He wanted to have Pēpahā′m for a wife. She was busy weaving a beautiful cape. When she had nearly finished it, she said to Beaver, "Why have you been sitting here so long? Go away! I don't want you for my husband. Your feet and hands are too short and your belly is too fat!" Beaver didn't answer, but remained sitting there calmly. The girl continued with her work. After some time, when she turned around and saw Beaver still sitting there, she repeated once more that she didn't want him because of his short hands and feet and his fat belly. So Beaver thought, "I will go home; she is only going to scold me in any case." He went away and sang, "MElmElE′ts qoqōlē′etlp! (i.e. Rise, water, above the trees!)."[123] Thereupon it started to rain. When K·ā′iq saw this, he tied two canoes together and put boards across and paddled away. The water rose higher and higher and the girl climbed up on her loom in order not to drown. Now she called, "K·alā′uya! (Beaver)[124] Come and fetch me!" But he was angry and no longer wanted to have her. He said, "In future your whole body shall be covered with warts." She was transformed into a frog.

K·ā′iq and Sk·ē′i paddled on. When they approached a village, K·ā′iq changed his grandmother into a pretty young girl and piled something onto his canoes which resembled many blankets.[125] He wanted to appear to be a rich chief. He had wound a beautiful fur around his head and coated his face with mica. His grandmother, whom he passed off as his daughter, sat beside him and spun yarn on her knee. When the people saw him they shouted, "A chief is coming!" K·ā′iq and Sk·ē′i went ashore and all the young men wished to have the pretty girl for a wife. During the night, the son of a chief crept to her. He nudged her and said, "Move over a bit; I'd like to lie with you." She let him come over and when he wanted to embrace her, she said, "Give me your copper bracelets, then you may embrace me." He gave them to her, but she wouldn't allow him to embrace her after all. When morning came, the young man left. Then K·ā′iq came to his grandmother and asked, "Did you get the bracelets?" She showed them to him and he put them on. It had all been only a ruse of K·ā′iq's to obtain these bracelets. He went outside, wrapped himself up in a cape and lay down in a way that everyone could see his bracelets. Many women saw him there. At night, the same chief's son crept again to the strange girl. He nudged

---

122. "Pēpahā′m" is pípəha·m, the Upriver Halkomelem term for 'frog' (Galloway 1993:508).

123. Galloway (2001:pers. comm.) provides the tentative literal translation of "MElmElE′ts qoqōlē′etlp!" as: 'Just come fill, high water, fir tree!'

124. "K·alā′uya" is qələ′wiyε which is derived from sqələ′w 'beaver' (Galloway 2001:pers. comm.)

125. Although Boas uses the German term *Mäntel* 'coats; capes' here, rather than *Decken* 'blankets,' we use the translation 'blankets' because in this area, blankets—specifically, mountain goat wool blankets—were items of wealth and symbols of status. We have recorded a similar legend among the Squamish, in which the material piled up in the canoe to imitate mountain goat wool blankets is "old man's beard" lichen (*Alectoria sarmentosa* and *Usnea* spp.)

her, and she moved and let him into her bed. He wanted to turn her over. When he felt her body, he noticed that she was wrinkled all over. So he called, "Surely you are Sk·ē′i!" and he became very ashamed.

And K·ā′iq paddled on with his grandmother. He came to a village where there were many beautiful girls. So he hid in the forest and thought, "I wish they would all come to gather berries." It happened as he wished. Now when the girls went upriver, he changed into a deer and swam along in front of their canoe. He let them catch him and the girls dragged him ashore by the legs. Then he thought, "I wish that the prettiest would skin my hide." This is what happened. When she started to cut open his belly, he winked a bit, jumped up and took her into his arms. The others ran away in fright. His brother, Qoi′ēqoa, who was alive again, observed from the opposite bank that he was sleeping with the woman. Then he saw that she was holding him by his penis and calling to the other girls for help. They came over and ripped out his penis. He was transformed into a rock which can still be seen today above Pā′pk'um on the Fraser River.[126]

4. Brother and Sister

There once was a pretty young girl. Every night a man crept to her and slept with her, yet she didn't know who he was. In order to recognize him, she covered her hands with soot and smeared it on the young man's back without his noticing. The following morning, when all the young men of the village went swimming, she went to the bank in order to discover the one whom she had blackened. But she didn't see any such person. Finally her brother arrived, and when he took off his clothes, she saw that his whole back was black. This made her very ashamed. At night, when the man came to her again, she said, "I know you; you are my brother. I am pregnant. Let's go away from here because we'll be ashamed in front of the people." Her brother agreed. The following day the woman prepared a large bundle of mountain goat wool blankets. Then they went away and she marked their path with pieces of these blankets, which she tied to branches.

They walked inland for ten days. Then they stopped walking and built a house. After some time, she gave birth to a boy. When he grew up he wondered very much why his parents looked so much alike, but was too shy to talk about it. He had become old enough now to go hunting bears. One evening when he returned from a hunt during which he had killed a large bear, he took heart and asked his mother,

---

126. As previously noted (see part 10 of the "Tribal Legends" in the present section), "Pā′pk'um," anglicized as "Popkum," is pápq̓ʷəm, the name applied to an area on the east side of the Fraser River, where the river narrows, about a mile below Seabird Island. Popkum has been identified by Duff (1952:30–34) as the southernmost village of the "Tait" people.

"Mother, is father related to you? He resembles you so much." She told her husband about this and he replied, "It is very bad that he knows that we are related." She answered, "I'm so ashamed that I want to die." "Yes," the brother said, "we will burn ourselves to death." The following day, before he set out to hunt, they told their son that they were brother and sister and how they had escaped. They also told him that they had marked the way to their home with blankets. When the young man had left, they bundled up blankets of mountain goat wool and bear skin together with grease and dried meat. Then they heaped boxes of mountain goat fat around themselves, put cedar boards on them and heaped the blankets on top. Then they set fire to this pyre and burned themselves up.

When the young man returned home at night and found his parents burned up, he thought, "What have I done! If only I had not asked mother about her resemblance to father!" He decided to look for his grandparents. He hoisted the four bundles prepared by his parents on his shoulders and followed the pieces of blanket which marked the way to his grandparents' village.

Having arrived at the village, he hid in the forest and thought, "I wish my cousin would come here." He had scarcely made his wish when his cousin, a young boy, took his bow and arrows and went into the forest. He shot the arrows ahead and then ran after them, picking them up again. One of the arrows landed right next to the young man. So he jumped up, took the arrow and ran towards his cousin. The latter became quite frightened because he didn't know the young man, who was extraordinarily handsome. He told him, "Go to your grandmother and tell her that her son and daughter, who fled long ago, have burned themselves to death. I am their son." The boy rushed to his grandmother, who had become blind from weeping so much for her lost children. He shouted, "Grandmother! I have found my cousin in the woods. He is the son of your lost children." But the old woman beat him because she didn't believe him. The boy ran back to his cousin in the forest and complained that nobody believed him. So the young man gave him a piece of fat and told him to show it to his grandmother. When she saw the fat, she became puzzled and followed her grandson. She saw the young man who told her to lay down blankets all the way from where he stood to her house. She obeyed and he went into the house. He carried in the four bundles which he had brought with him. Then he bathed his grandmother's eyes and she could see again at once and became young once more. He always stayed inside and only went out after midnight because he didn't want to be seen by anyone. He told his grandparents to invite everyone for a feast. He opened the boxes, and, by shaking them, filled the entire house with their contents of mountain goat fat, dried meat, bear skins and mountain goat blankets. When the people had been invited, they said amongst themselves, "What are they going to feast us with? They have no provisions at all." When they entered the house they saw that it was completely filled, but the young man didn't show himself and stayed in his room.

A young girl was very curious and anxious to see him. So she went to the water, relieved herself and transformed her excrement into a beautiful aquatic bird. When the people saw the bird, they tried to catch it, but without success. The young man's uncle also tried to shoot it, but in vain! So the young man got up, took his bow and arrows and aimed at the bird. But even though he usually hit anything he wanted, he missed it. He only hit it on the tenth try. It immediately changed back into excrement. So the young man grew ashamed and decided to go away.

He said to his cousin, "Come, let's go and catch birds." They went out together and when they reached a sandy spot on the river bank, he told his cousin to lie down. Then he slashed his chest with arrowheads and covered him with sand up to his chest. He told him, "I will hide now. Soon eagles will come to you. When they fly towards you from the side, blow at them and you'll be able to chase them away like that. But if one dives straight down on you, close your eyes. He will want to settle down and I'll be able to catch him." His cousin did what he had been told to do. When an eagle came at him from the side, he blew and it flew away. At last one appeared right above his head. Then he held his breath and closed his eyes. The eagle dived down and hooked its claws into his chest. That very moment, the young man rushed from his hiding place, grabbed the eagle and shook it so hard that all its bones and flesh fell to the ground. Then he said to his cousin, "Return home. I am so ashamed that I want to go away. Don't be sad, because I will return one day. You will be able to tell by a red cloud which will appear in the sky." Then he put on the eagle skin and flew up into the sky.

He found a flat country up there and a path, which he followed. Soon he saw smoke rising. He walked towards it and found two blind sisters who were roasting roots for themselves. One of them was just taking roots out of the embers and was about to give her sister a bowl full, when the young man stepped up and took it out of her hand. Since the sister had not received anything, she asked the other one, "Why didn't you give me anything?" She answered, "I gave you a bowl full." "Oh," the other one replied, "surely the son of the couple who burned themselves up is here and took it away." "Yes," he then replied, "I am here." The women said, "We know that you want to go to Sun and marry his daughter, but you must realize that he is very wicked. Many have gone there, but no one has ever returned. We are going to help you." They took dust from a sharpening stone and smeared it on his behind in order to harden it, because the seats in Sun's house were covered with sharp needles which pierced the flesh of anyone attempting to sit down. In addition, they gave him two pieces of meat wound around long bones. They told him to throw them to the two Wolves guarding the entrance. Before he left them, they also told him to return to them for further advice if Moon, who shared Sun's house, should give him tasks. He thanked the women and went on. Soon he came to Sun's house. At the entrance there sat two huge Wolves. He threw the bones to them, which stuck in their throats so that they were unable to bite him. He sprang past them as fast as he could and into the house. He saw six girls inside; three were daughters of Sun, and three were daughters of Moon. Moon's daughters were humpbacked, while Sun's daughters were very beautiful. Moon asked him over to his side, but he went straight to Sun and sat down firmly beside him, squashing all the pointed things on the ground which had killed all former visitors. "Oh," said Sun, "you are more than a man," and gave him his daughter in marriage.

But Moon was angry because he wanted him to marry one of his daughters. He invited the young man to go out with him the following day to split a cedar tree. So the young man went first to his grandmothers and told them what Moon wanted him to do. They gave him two bones and some white paint while telling him what to do with them. He was grateful and treated their eyes with the sap of leaves, which gave them back their sight. Then he returned and the following day accompanied Moon in order to fell the cedar tree. Moon drove his wedges into the trunk and let his hammer drop into the gaping split. Then he told the young man to get it out again. When he had crawled into the split, he knocked out the wedges so that the tree snapped together again. The young man at once braced the two bones against it, so that the tree could do him no harm. But he threw out the white paint, which Moon took to be his brains. He believed him to be dead, and wanted to open the tree up again to pull the body out. But when he had driven his wedge in, he found the young man sitting unharmed inside it.

The following day, Moon told him to go out and catch trout. He first went again to his grandmothers for advice. They gave him a stick into which they stuck many fish bones and told him to take it to Moon. The stick was transformed into a fish. The young man caught yet another trout and took both home with him. Moon ate them and when he started to eat the transformed stick, he choked on one of the fish bones which got stuck in his throat. Sun's daughter told her husband to hit Moon quickly on the back; in this way he made the bones fly out again.

The following day, Moon sent the young man out to catch the red bear, with which he intended to play. Again he went to his grandmothers, who fashioned two bears from a few pieces of wood, and their combs. The latter became their claws. They told the young man, "When you get home, throw the bears onto Moon. They will hurt him badly." He did this and the bears slashed Moon all over. From then on he stopped bothering the young man.

Soon Sun's daughter bore the young man two children. When they grew up, they wished very much to see their grandmother. But their father told them that she had burned herself up. So they asked for their great-grandmother and when they learned that she lived on earth, they wished to go down there. When Sun Man heard of this he gave permission to his daughter and her family to go to earth. He prepared ten heaps of roots and wove a large basket. Then he ordered two old women, Spiders, who lived below Sun, to make a rope. He tied this to the basket and told his daughter and her family to sit inside the basket, into which the daughter put the roots as well. Then he lowered them down and the rope became longer and longer while he was doing so. Finally the basket bumped into the top of a fir tree near Stcuwā'çEl (below Canoe Pass on the south arm of the Fraser River).[127] So they shook the rope a few times as a sign that they had not quite arrived and Sun lowered them a bit more. At last they arrived on earth, safe and sound, and shook the rope for a long time, whereupon Sun hauled it up again. The sky had become completely red while they were coming down. So the young man's cousin said, "My cousin will return now. He told me before he went away that the sky would turn red when he was to return." But nobody believed him, and he was beaten because he spoke of a dead person.

When the basket arrived down there, the young man thought, "I wish my cousin's son would come and play with his arrows." At once he came into the forest, shooting his arrows before him. The young man picked one up, walked towards the boy and asked him, "Do you know that a man disappeared from here once and went into the sky?" "Yes," he answered, "that was my father's cousin." "I am he," the young man said then, "and this is my wife," while he pointed towards her. But the boy was unable to see her because she was shining so brightly. The man then took leaves and washed her face so that it looked like other people's, and they went to the village. The woman passed out four times on their way because she could not bear human scent, even though the houses had been purified carefully according to the wishes of the young man. When they got to the house at last, they cooked the ten heaps of roots which Sun had given them and made so much food that they were able to feast all the households.

The woman always kept in the house and didn't let herself be seen. So the people didn't believe at all that she was Sun's daughter. One man peeped through a crack into her room from sheer curiosity, so she flashed up so brightly that his face was

---

127. "Stcuwā'çEl" is (s)cəẃáθəl ('facing the water'), the Upriver Halkomelem pronunciation of the term whose Downriver Halkomelem form, (s)cəẃáθən, is anglicized as "Tsawwassen." Boas (1890b) provides the Downriver form "Tcuwā'çẹn," i.e. (s)cəẃáθən, in his fieldnote version of this text. Traditional Tsawwassen territory included the Canoe Passage area and much of the South Arm of the Fraser (extending upriver just past Ladner), the delta on the south side of the South Arm, much of Point Roberts, and the present-day Tsawwassen Indian Reserve (Bouchard and Kennedy 1991b:101–102, 109).

all burned. But her husband healed him again. From then on, people believed that she was Sun's daughter.

5. The PōtE′mtEn

In PōtE′mtEn, above Fort Douglas,[128] there lived a woman who had two daughters and several sons. One night two men crept to the girls and already the next day they each gave birth to a child. Nobody knew who the children's fathers were and the girls didn't know who had crept to them either. So they covered their hands in grease and red paint and when the men returned again the following night, they embraced them and reddened their bodies without being noticed. The following morning, when all the young men in the village went to bathe, the young women watched to see whose bodies had been marked in red. The young men threw stones into the water and then dived in to retrieve them. Not one among them had even a trace of red on his body. When the women returned, they passed a spot where a man was building a canoe. There they noticed that the hammer and one of the wood chips were full of red paint and so they knew that these had assumed the form of men and slept with them. So they were ashamed. The following night the men came back. So the women said, "Why do you always leave in the morning? We know who you are." When the men heard this, they stayed with the women and kept their human shape.

The owner of the hammer and the wood chips one day scolded these two men and said they belonged to him. This made the women sad. They made a large basket, sat down inside it with their husbands and children, tied it up and had themselves thrown into the water. The wind and the waves carried the basket along and at last it landed at Puk·pā′k·′ōtl.[129] There they opened the basket and got out. The men prepared planks and built a house. They became ancestors of the PōtE′mtEn.

---

128. As discussed at the beginning of this Lower Fraser River section, Boas notes that a number of these stories "should properly be counted with Lillooet legends." The present story and the one that follows, No. 6, are two such examples, both taking place well inside traditional Lower Lillooet territory. The place identified in the present story by Boas as "PōtE′mtEn" was located northwest from the mouth of the Birkenhead River which empties into the north end of Lillooet Lake. This is certainly "above Fort [Port] Douglas"; in fact, it is about 50 miles (80 km) above Port Douglas.

129. "Puk·pā′k·′ōtl" is Boas' rendering of the Lower Lillooet term pə̓q̓ʷpáq̓ʷuɬ 'food storage caches' which is the name of a former village site located on the west side of the Lillooet River, about 5 miles (8 km) south from the lower end of Lillooet Lake (Kennedy and Bouchard 1998:175).

6. The Dead Woman

In K·'e'luk,[130] below Puk·pā'k·'ōtl, there lived a man who loved his wife very much. She died and was buried. The man became very sad. He cried and fasted. At night, when everyone was asleep, he went to his wife's grave, opened it and lay down beside her. The lynx living on the mountain scented the corpse and hurried over to carry it away. They opened the grave and ran back to their chief, one with the woman's corpse across his back, the other with the man. The chief lived in an underground house,[131] so they dropped the man and the woman down through the entrance. At first the chief wanted to devour the man, but when he got closer to him, he cried out, "He still stinks; he isn't dead yet!" So the man jumped up, drew his knife which he had hidden under his cape, and killed all the lynx. Then he returned home again. He was still very sad because he had lost his wife. He asked his father for five bear skins and made himself one hundred pairs of shoes from them. He took them and set out to get back his wife. He went into the mountains to fast. Then he wandered on further inland. When he had walked for some time, he saw smoke rising in the distance, and when he came closer noticed a house standing in a prairie. Pelican[132] lived there, and asked him, "Where do you want to go?" He replied, "I am searching for my dead wife." "That is a very hard task, my grandson," said Pelican. "Only the dead can find this way easily. The living can get to the land of the dead only at great risk." Pelican gave the man a magic substance in order to help him in his quest and taught him how to use it. The young man wandered on and got to the giant Sā'sk·ats[133] who devoured anyone who tried to pass by. But with the aid of the magic substance, the man managed to slip past. Then he met the double-headed serpent, Atlk·ē,[134] but passed it too, successfully. When he walked on, he met the bird, TlEtscā'wul,[135] who asked him where he was going. When he told him what he intended to do, he said that no living person was able to go to the land of the dead.

---

130. "K·'e'luk" is nq́íl'əqʷ ('head of the river'), the Lower Lillooet name of a former village site located where the southern end of Lillooet Lake drains into the Lillooet River, about 5 miles (8 km) above p̓əq̓ʷp̓áq̓ʷuɬ (see the preceding footnote).

131. See Teit (1906:213) and Bouchard and Kennedy (1977:62–64) for descriptions of "underground houses" (i.e. semi-subterranean pithouses) among the Lower Lillooet.

132. Sandhill Crane.

133. "Sä'sk·ats" is sɛ'sq́əc, the Upriver Halkomelem term for the 'Sasquatch,' a creature said to be large, hairy and human-like in form (Suttles 1987:73–99); the Lillooet term for this same creature is ɬáɬqəč.

134. "Atlk·ē" is Boas' rendering of Ɂə́ɬqiɁ, the Halkomelem term meaning 'any snake.' In his field-notes, Boas (1890b) identified this creature as "stl'alēkam atlkē" (i.e. sx̌'ɛ'ləqəm Ɂə́ɬqiɁ) which would be translated literally as 'supernatural/spiritually-powerful snake.'

135. Boas' "TlEtscā'wul" is possibly ɬəčɛ'wəl or x̌'əčɛ'wəl, although such a bird name has not been recorded in Upriver Halkomelem (Galloway 2001:pers. comm.), or by any known Lillooet source, including our own research.

He advised him to turn back. But the man continued. During the following night he dreamed that if he chewed a certain herb, he would never get hungry. This he did, and found that it stayed his hunger. At last he came to a large lake beyond which the dead were living. He didn't know how to get across and wept. Then he heard a voice which said, "No one is able to bring his body along into the sky. You may come over here once you are dead. But know this: God[136] will make you happy and will give you much clothing and other riches. You may not get your wife back. Sit down, close your eyes, fold your arms across your chest and pray." He did this. Thereupon many clothes, horses and other riches came to him. He took them and returned home. He had become a wise and powerful man.

7. The Dead Woman

A man's wife had died. Because he loved her very much, he set out to go to the sky and search for her. He made many bear skin shoes for himself and went into the mountains. He fasted and every evening swam in ponds and vomited so that he became completely pure. Then he walked on. Soon, when he had worn out almost all his shoes, he met a man who asked him where he was going. He answered, "My wife has died and I am looking for her." Then the other replied, "The way there goes past here. It is very dangerous. Chew this root; it will protect you." He thanked the old man and continued. At last he arrived safely in the land of the dead. He saw them dancing, and caught a glimpse of his wife among them. So he took her back with him. The dead warned him not to sleep with his wife under any circumstances before he reached home. He obeyed and every night they slept on opposite sides of the fire. On the fourth day they found themselves close to their home. He then dreamed that the deity told him to pray. He closed his eyes and prayed. When he opened his eyes again he saw clothes for himself and his wife there on the ground; he saw a horse, a rifle and powder. The following morning they rode home. He had been away for many years. He found that his parents had become blind from all the weeping. But he made them see again.

8. The Origin of Salmon and Fire

In the beginning there was no salmon and no fire. So the animals held a large meeting to discuss how to obtain fire. It was finally resolved to send out Beaver and Woodpecker (ʔTs'ɛ'tɛm)[137] to obtain both. Fire was in the possession of the chief of

---

136. Boas uses here the German term *Gott*, meaning 'God.'

137. Although Boas queries the term that he transcribes here as "Ts'ɛ'tɛm," it is čə'təm, identified as the Upriver Halkomelem term for a 'small woodpecker (probably Downy Woodpecker)' (*Dendrocopos pubescens*) (Galloway *et al.* 1980:68).

the "Sockeye- Salmon," who lived in the extreme west. Beaver and Woodpecker travelled there, the first one swimming, the latter flying. When they got close to the houses, which were standing beside a river, Beaver made Woodpecker fly ahead in order to spy. He returned shortly and reported that there were two houses which were situated on opposite sides of a pond from which the people were in the habit of getting their drinking water. So the two of them made a plan and at once set about to execute it. Beaver dug a tunnel for himself from the pond to the chief's house and then lay down, pretending that he was dead, near the spot where the people used to get their water. Soon the daughter of the chief of the Salmon came out of the house and when she saw the dead beaver, ran back immediately to call the men. They arrived and deliberated among themselves. "Dog Salmon" (*O. keta*)[138] said while turning him over, "Beaver is known to be very clever. I don't believe that he is dead. Surely he wants something from us here." "Coho Salmon"[139] said, "His hands and feet are very clever. With them he closes all the creeks and rivers to us so that we are unable to pass by. When I try to jump across I fall into his traps. Surely he wants something from us." Then Spring Salmon[140] said, "Don't you see that he is dead?" But Coho didn't believe it and said, "Let's tickle him, then we'll find out whether he is alive or dead." So they poked his side so that he almost burst out laughing. Since he didn't move, they carried him into the house and were about to skin him. At this very moment, Woodpecker appeared outside and sat down beside the pond. As soon as the people saw him they wanted to catch him. Then Beaver opened his eyes just a little and when he saw that he was by himself, he sprang up, grabbed Fire and the chief's youngest daughter, who was lying in her cradle, and fled through the tunnel which he had previously dug for himself. At the same time the bird flew away. When they arrived in SEmi⁻ʼmō̄[141] they took some inner cedar bark from the cradle and threw it into the river. That is why there are many salmon here. They threw some inner cedar bark into the water at Pitt River,[142] too, and thus created

---

138. Given in English as "Dogsalmon" (in double quotation marks) in the original *Sagen*. This is the chum salmon, correctly identified by Boas as *Oncorhynchus keta*. In the manuscript version of this same story, Boas (1890b) provides the Native term for this species as "k'oā́'luq" which is k̓ʷá·ləxʷ, the Upriver Halkomelem word for 'dog/chum salmon' (Galloway *et al.* 1980:69).

139. Given in English as "Cohoesalmon" (in double quotation marks) in the original *Sagen*.

140. Although in the *Sagen* Boas provides the artificially-constructed German term *Frühlingslachs* 'spring salmon,' he writes the Native word "soqai" at this place in the story in his fieldnotes (Boas 1890b)—this is sθə́'qi, the Upriver Halkomelem term meaning 'sockeye,' not spring salmon (Galloway *et al.* 1980:69).

141. "SEmiā́'mō̄" is sɛmyámə, anglicized as "Semiahmoo," the name of the Northern Straits Coast Salish group of the Boundary Bay, White Rock and Birch Bay area who were allotted an Indian Reserve in White Rock, near the Canada-United States border.

142. While Boas provides the English term Pitt River here in the original *Sagen*, Boas' fieldnote (1890b) of this story provides the Halkomelem name "ᴋ'ētsē̄" which is his rendering of

many salmon. When they got to Yale, they threw the cradle, together with the child, into the river. That is why large numbers of salmon gather there below the rapids.

Beaver gave Fire to the ghosts. The people didn't know how to obtain it and finally sent out K·áʼiq, Mink, to get it. He borrowed his grandmother's knife, hid it under his cape and went on his way to the ghosts. He went into their house and watched them dance. When the dance was ended, they wanted to bathe and wash. So Mink said, "Stay here; I will get water for you." He took a pail and went down to the shore. When he returned to the house with the full pail and passed one of the two fires burning in the house, he pretended to stumble and poured water over the fire so that it went out. "Oh," he cried, "I've stumbled," and returned to the water in order to fill his pail again. When he got back to the house and passed the other fire, he poured his water out again and it became very dark in the house. So Mink took his knife and cut off the head of the Ghost Chief. He sprinkled dust onto the severed neck so that it wouldn't bleed and ran away with the head. Even before the people had rekindled their fire, the dust was drenched with blood. The chief's mother noticed it and when they had relit the fire, they saw that the chief's head had been cut off. Then the dead chief's mother said, "Follow Mink tomorrow and buy the head back from him." They followed him and came to his house. Mink had constructed ten houses for himself and had his grandmother make him ten different sets of clothes. When the ghosts came, he appeared first on the roof of one house, then on the other, each time in different clothes so that the ghosts thought there were many people there. When they arrived they said to Mink's grandmother, "We would like to exchange our chief's head for capes." But she replied, "My grandson doesn't want any capes." Then they offered him bows and arrows, but the grandmother declined this offer as well. Then the trees wept with the ghosts because they were so sad. The tears of the trees were rain. At last the ghosts offered him a fire drill. This the grandmother accepted and returned the head to them. Since that time, people have had Fire.

9. Mink

Mink wanted to marry the horsetail plant.[143] She said, "No, you can't marry me. What are you going to do when logs come down the river? I bend over, let the log

---

qícəy, anglicized as "Katzie," referring to the people of Pitt River, Pitt Lake, and a short stretch of the Fraser above Pitt River, as well as Barnston Island and a small part of the south bank opposite (Duff 1952:24, 27; Suttles 1955:8; 1990:455).

143. In the *Sagen*, Boas provides the German term *Schachtelhalm* 'horsetail'; in his notes, he describes this as "*Qkʼúla* Equisetum" (Boas 1890b). What Boas transcribes as Qkʼúla is xʷq̓ʷəʼlə, the Upriver Halkomelem name for the plant known as scouring rush, and *Equisetum* is the correct Latin name for this species (*Equisetum hiemale*). But the Upriver Halkomelem term for the horsetail plant (*Equisetum telmateia* and *E. arvense*) is x̣əʼmx̣əm, not xʷq̓ʷəʼlə (Galloway *et al.* 1980:79, 81; 1982).

pass over me and then straighten up again." Mink said, "I can do that, too." "But what are you going to do when a log with many branches comes drifting down the river? It will pierce you and carry you along." "No," said Mink, "I will bend over with you and straighten up again." So Horsetail took him for her husband. Soon a log came floating downriver. Mink clung to Horsetail; they both bent over and let the log pass overhead. But then a log with many branches came. Again Mink clung to his wife. But the log pierced him, drowned him and carried him downstream.

He went to the rotted pine (it consists of nothing but resinous bark) and wanted to marry her. She said, "No, you can't marry me. When I get warm, I perspire and you will become angry." "No," replied Mink, "that doesn't make any difference." So she took him for her husband. In the morning, when it became warm, she started to perspire (i.e. the pitch started to melt) and his chest stuck to hers. He cried out, "Let go of me. Don't hold me so close!" She replied, "I'm not holding you. I'm only perspiring." Then Mink grew angry and beat her. But his hand also got stuck. So he beat her with his other hand, with the same result. He then kicked her with his feet and both feet stuck fast to her. Finally he bumped her with his head and this stuck fast, too. At noon, when the resin became quite soft, he fell down. So he left his wife.

He went to Eagle[144] and wanted to marry her. She had five young ones and lived on top of a cedar tree. He climbed up and when Eagle and her young ones returned from salmon fishing, they found him in the nest. Eagle asked, "What are you doing here?" Mink answered, "I want to marry you." "No," she said, "you can't marry me. I dive down from up here and fly up again. You are not able to do that." "Oh," said Mink, "I can do that, too. I jump down and fly up again." So Eagle took him for her husband. After a short while they wanted to catch salmon. They sat down on a tall tree. Eagle asked Mink, "Do you see the salmon?" "Yes, he replied, "back there, far away." But in reality he didn't see anything. "No," said Eagle, "right here close to us, right below us." "Oh, yes," Mink said then. Eagle said, "I am going to catch it now; come and follow me at once," and swooped down. Mink saw her return immediately with a fish. So he jumped down, too. He smashed his entrails on the tree's branches and lay there dead.

10. Skunk[145]

Skunk had two wives, Snail and Snake. He lived in an underground house. Coyote always passed his house on his way to hunt. Skunk didn't like this and one day

---

144. Boas (1890b) provides the Native term "spā'k'as" in his fieldnotes; this is his rendering of sṗáqəs, the Upriver Halkomelem term for 'mature bald eagle' (Galloway *et al.* 1980:66).

145. Western spotted skunk (*Spilo gale*).

asked him, "Why do you always pass by my house? I don't want you to." The following day he found some red paint in front of his door. Coyote put it there; it was his magic substance. So Skunk cried, "What is the paint doing there? It isn't worth anything." And when Coyote passed by again, he lay in wait for him and urinated into his face. So Coyote ran into the mountains to his friend, East Wind, who told him to paint his face in a certain fashion. Coyote did so, but when he passed the house on the following day, Skunk urinated at him again and nearly blinded him. East Wind's magic substance hadn't been strong enough. Again Coyote called on his guardian spirit, East Wind, for help, but he was powerless against Skunk. So Coyote admitted defeat and promised to pass Skunk's house no more in the future. But he pondered how he could avenge himself. One day, when Skunk was out hunting, Coyote called his friend, East Wind, who brought on a blizzard and Skunk was unable to return home through the deep snow. But an old man, Porcupine, realized that Skunk was close to perishing and took pity on him. He donned his magic regalia and shook out his cape in front of the house. It then began raining and all the snow settled so that Skunk could pass over it easily and go to his house.

11. Mouse

Pelican[146] once gave a huge potlatch. He had Mouse, a young girl with long hair, dance for him on canoes which had been lashed together. He tied fur blankets on poles and tossed them into the water when his guests arrived. So they jumped into the water in order to catch them. When they came into the house, Mouse distributed the food and danced for Pelican. The people beat time and sang while she danced. Then they distributed many blankets again. On the following day the people went back home again. Everyone liked Mouse so much that many wanted to have her. Mink, who was a poor man, put on chief's garb and tied back his hair with mountain goat wool, in order to be taken as a chief from a far country. He wanted to marry her. But she recognized him and rejected him. Then Thunderbird came and courted her. She followed him and he took her back with him to his home. But Thunderbird's first wife was jealous of Mouse and wished to get rid of her. One day, when Thunderbird had gone out with his first wife, Mouse opened the boxes where Thunderbird stored his supply of mountain goat fat, and ate some. When he found this out, he grew angry and flung Mouse down to earth. And that is why Mouse still steals food today.

---

146. Sandhill Crane.

IV. Legends of the Cowichan

Boas was among the Cowichan for a week (4–10 November 1886) during his first season on the coast. He reported that he "could not get the people to talk," and when they did, it was in "a long drawn-out manner" which became "a test of patience" (Rohner 1969:53–55). He finally found a sincere and accomplished story-teller in Somenos, near Duncan. This man "related so well about the first people that I shall try, if at all possible, to stop here on my way back" (Rohner 1969:55–56). The origin story referred to here would be "Siālatsa," story 2. Boas was not able to make another visit, but he had got enough, in spite of obstacles such as when two young men appeared and "laughed when they heard the old man tell stories" (Rohner 1969:55). On another occasion an old woman contradicted the story-teller; where he said a man had lain dead for nine days, and she said ten, "whereupon he became so angry that I could not get another word out of him" (Rohner 1969:55). The woman appears to have won the argument—see the reference to ten days in story 4, which ends abruptly at that point.

View of Coast Salish style canoes, and shed and gabled-roof houses at the Quamichan village, *ca.* 1866.

IV. Legends of the Cowitchin (K·au'ētcin)[1]

1. Qäls[2]

A long, long time ago, a man called Qäls came down from the sky. When he reached the earth he wandered through all the countries and visited all the peoples, rewarding the good and punishing the bad.

1) Once Qäls reached the sea near the mouth of the K·au'ētcin River.[3] There a man called Hā'makos lived on a hill close to Cowitchin Wharf. At the foot of the hill there lived a friend of Hā'makos. When Hā'makos saw Qäls approaching, he called to his friend, "Come to me quickly, before Qäls gets here and transforms you." The friend hurried to run up the hill, but before he reached the top, Qäls had reached him and transformed him into a stone.

2) Qäls went on along the shore, when he saw a woman swimming in the water. A man had hidden behind a boulder and was watching her. He transformed both of them into stones.

3) And he met a man who was sharpening shells in order to use them as tips for his arrows. He asked, "What are you doing?" The man answered, "When Qäls comes, I intend to shoot him with these arrows," because he did not recognize him. Qäls made him hand over the shells, forced them into the man's head and transformed him into a deer,[4] saying, "Now leap away! In future, people shall eat you."

---

1. "K·au'ētcin" is Boas' rendering of qə'wəcən ('warm the back'), anglicized as "Cowichan," referring to the aboriginal people who occupied at least six villages on the lower course of the Cowichan River. The Cowichan speak a dialect of Island Halkomelem Coast Salish which is the language spoken along the eastern side of Vancouver Island between Saanich Inlet in the south and Northwest Bay in the north. Island Halkomelem is also spoken by the Malahat, Chemainus, Nanaimo, and Nanoose (Suttles 1990:455–456).

    While our annotating of this section is based primarily on the available literature, we also draw upon our 1971–1975 consultation with Christopher Paul, whose assistance we gratefully acknowledge.

2. The Transformer; here in the Cowichan area, x̌els (Boas' "Qäls") is a single Transformer character and not several siblings as indicated in the Fraser Valley area (see Section III of the present volume).

3. The Cowichan (Boas' "K·au'ētcin") River flows east into Cowichan Bay near the town of Duncan.

4. In this area, the species of deer is the Columbia blacktail (*Odocoileus hemionus columbianus*).

4) Qäls went on and came to K·umiē′k·en.[5] There he met a man who was called Spâl.[6] He was about to skin a deer, when Qäls said to him, "Skin the deer carefully, for I have killed it, and my arrow is still stuck in it. Don't break it under any circumstances." Spâl rose up abruptly and shouted, "What do you mean? I have killed the deer by myself. It belongs to me; I'll deal with it as I see fit and it's no business of yours." Qäls repeated once more, "Be careful and don't break my arrow!" But Spâl paid no attention to his words, lifted the deer onto his back and went home. Now Qäls took decaying wood and threw one piece at the back and another piece at the antlers of the deer; then he took a stone and conjured it into the deer's stomach. When Spâl arrived home, he put down his load, picked up the deer's stomach and went into the house. He said to his wife, "Go outside and have a look at the big deer I killed." He flung the stomach to his child and it hit the child's body and killed the child because the stomach had suddenly become stone. But the woman found nothing except a heap of decayed wood outside. This had been caused by Qäls.

Qäls now met another man in the forest, who also was about to skin a deer. Qäls went up to him and said, "Skin the deer carefully, for I have killed it and my arrow is still stuck in it. Don't break it under any circumstances." The man promised to pay attention. So Qäls said, "Take the deer on your shoulders and go home. You will see me again later." The man did as he was told. And the deer grew heavier and heavier so that finally he was hardly able to carry it. When he got home he called his wife and asked her to help him unload the deer. They found then that it had become exceedingly fat on his way home and they were able to fill many boxes with the fat.

When Spâl heard of this, he sent his son to his fortunate neighbour with a fish, because he hoped to get some fat as a present in return. But the neighbour did not accept the fish. So Spâl went over personally to offer him the fish, but he was unable to induce the neighbour to accept it. He felt so ashamed about this that he threw the fish away. Spâl went out to hunt again. When he had killed a deer, Qäls walked up to him once more and insisted that his arrow was stuck in the deer. Again Spâl refused to pay attention to the arrow and consequently Qäls transformed this deer into decaying wood as well. The other man[7] obeyed him, however, and he gave him gifts again by making the deer's fat multiply. Then he transformed Spâl into a raven, and the other man into a seagull.

---

5. Boas' "K·umiē′k·en" is q̓ʷəmiyɛ′qən (possibly 'pull out of water at the top'), anglicized as "Comiaken," referring to a Cowichan village located near the junction of the north and south arms of the Cowichan River (Rozen 1985:152).

6. "Spâl" is Boas' rendering of spa·l meaning 'raven' in Island Halkomelem.

7. Boas (1916:717, 1019) identifies the "other man" as Gull, while summarizing this legend as "the arrogant and the modest hunters."

5) And Qäls wandered on. Once he met a man wearing a blue cape, who was known far and wide as an incorrigible thief. Qäls transformed him into a bluejay.[8] He forced two pieces of wood into someone else's head and transformed him into an elk.[9] And he created bears, ducks and many other animals.

6) He went further up the Cowitchin River and arrived at K·ua′mitcan.[10] A powerful chief called K·ē′sek·[11] lived here. When Qäls arrived, K·ē′sek· was standing in front of his house. They stood opposite each other and each tried to overcome the other with his stare. Finally Qäls proved to be the stronger one and K·ē′sek· stepped down into Qā′tsa[12] Lake, where he still lives today. He created the trout in Qā′tsa and from there they swam down the rivers.

7) Everywhere in the Cowitchin River, the works of Qäls can be seen: people and dogs that he transformed into stone; his canoe (now a huge rock in the river) and the peg to which he used to tie his canoe—this, too was transformed into stone.[13]

8) And he wandered on. At last he arrived at the Ts'â′mes[14] people in Lɛk'ū′men[15]

---

8. Boas' reference to "bluejay" is likely a reference to the Stellers Jay (*Cyanocitta stelleri*), known in Island Halkomelem as sk̓ʷíθ'ec.

9. Appears in English as Elk (without quotation marks) in the original *Sagen*. Both elk (*Cervus canadensis roosevelti*) and deer are found in this area (see also story 2 of this section, where Boas twice uses the German term *Elch* 'moose; elk' to refer to elk).

10. Boas' "K·ua′mitcan" is kʷámǝcǝn ('hunchback'), anglicized as "Quamichan," the Island Halkomelem name of a Cowichan village located about five miles (8 km) down the Cowichan River from Duncan, just below the mouth of Quamichan Creek (Rozen 1985:170; Suttles 1990:453). The name is derived from that of the giant cannibal woman who abducted children and carried them away in her basket (Rozen 1985:170).

11. The term Boas transcribes here as "K·ē′sek·" is q̓ísɛq, literally meaning 'tied penis' in Island Halkomelem.

12. "Qā′tsa" is x̣ácǝ, 'any lake,' although this term is also applied specifically to Quamichan Lake; in story 2 that follows, Boas does identify "Qā′tsa" as "Quamitchan" (Quamichan) Lake.

13. The locations of some of these places along the Cowichan River that were created by x̣ɛls (the Transformer) can be found in Rozen (1985).

14. The term Boas renders here as "Ts'â′mes" is likely scámǝs, the name applied by the Cowichan to a local group who formerly lived at Parry Bay, southwest of Victoria, and comprised part of the Lukungun Coast Salish (see Section VII). Elsewhere, Boas (1891d:563) gives this same name ("Ts'â′mes") as "Stsâ′ñges"—this is scánǝs, in the Northern Straits Coast Salish language spoken by the Lukungun (Northern Straits has "ŋ" where Cowichan has "m") (see also the footnote that follows).

15. What Boas transcribes as "Lɛk'ū′men" is lǝk̓ʷǝ′mǝn, the Island Halkomelem term that refers collectively to the aboriginal people living in the general vicinity of Victoria, whose traditional territory extended approximately from Cordova Bay to Parry Bay, and who now reside on Indian Reserves in Esquimalt, adjacent to Victoria. The anglicized term "Lukungun" is derived from lǝk̓ʷǝ′ŋǝn, the name of these people as spoken in their own language, Northern Straits Coast Salish. While Boas gives the Cowichan form "Lɛk'ū′men" (lǝk̓ʷǝ′mǝn) in the present section, he gives the Northern Straits form "Lku′ñgen" (lǝk̓ʷǝ′ŋǝn) in Section VII (see also the preceding footnote).

(near Victoria). They were busy catching flounders. They took the fish ashore and impaled them on sticks which they stuck into the ground. So Qäls asked, "What are you doing there with your fish?" "We want the sun to roast them," they answered. "Don't you know how to make fire?" Qäls asked. When they said no, he taught them how to make a fire-drill and made sure that they understood how to use it.

2. Siā'latsa[16]

In the beginning the earth was uninhabited. But then Siā'latsa came down from the sky to Qā'tsa (Quamitchan Lake)[17] and built a house there. On the following day, Swutlā'k·[18] descended from the sky, then a woman called K·ola'tsiwat. The following day Suk·sā'k·ulak· came down, then Sk·ue͞'lEm,[19] Swik·'em'ā'm, Siai'imk·en, Kto'qcin, Hē'uk·En, Qtlā'set, QaiōtsE'mk·En, and QuitE'qtEn, each one of them on one day. They went to Tsu'k·ola[20] and built houses. But Siā'latsa carried a painted staff with the aid of which he was able to kill monsters and heal the sick. His face was painted with red and black colours. First he met a S'ētlkē (double-headed serpent).[21] He had his men fell and cut up a spruce. Then they dug a deep pit into which they threw the wood. Siā'latsa then went out to lure the S'ētlkē into the pit and there it was burned.

Then he sent Swutlā'k· downriver. He met the Sts'ē'enkoa[22] near T'aētsē'la (the spot where Mr. Lomar's house stands),[23] took a stick of hardwood and with it pierced the monster's tongue. But the Sts'ē'enkoa pursued him all the same. Each time when it had almost caught up with Swutlā'k·, he pierced its tongue. Thus he reached his house, in front of which the deep pit was situated. Sts'ē'enkoa fell into

---

16. What Boas transcribes as "Siā'latsa" is siyálǝcǝ.

17. As previously noted, "Qā'tsa" is x̣ácǝ, 'any lake,' although this term is also applied specifically to Quamichan Lake.

18. "Swutlā'k·" is recognized as swǝ'łaƙʷ (Rozen 1985:194).

19. "Sk·ue͞'lEm" is likely sƙʷǝlx̣íl'ǝm (Rozen 1985:204).

20. What Boas has rendered as "Tsu'k·ola" is the place name cǝ'qʷǝlǝʔ, applied to a grassy area on the southwest side of Mount Prevost (Rozen 1985:190–191).

21. Boas' "S'ētlkē " is sʔǝ'łqiʔ, meaning 'any snake.'

22. "Sts'ē'enkoa" is cínƙʷaʔ 'supernatural lightning monster,' which Boas identifies as 'a mythical bird' near the end of this same siyálǝcǝ story.

23. The place name that Boas renders as "T'aētsē'la" is št'ɛ·'ċɛlǝ 'place to get fish-spreaders,' referring to an area extending north from the north side of the Cowichan River, near the present-day "Silver Bridge" where the Island Highway crosses the river at Duncan (Rozen 1985:181). The storyteller's reference to "Mr. Lomar's" house being at št'ɛ·'ċɛlǝ is actually a reference to W.H. Lomas, the local Indian Agent for the Cowichan area at the time of Boas' visit.

it and was burned as well. Then Swutlā'k· went to the steep rock in Maple Bay and killed another S'ētlkē which lived there.

Once Swutlā'k· went to K·au'ämen[24] near Sâ'menos[25] and there observed many salmon. He told Siā'latsa what he had seen. Then they went to K·au'ämen together and built a house. Siā'latsa had the men fell a tree, and burn and sharpen its lower end. Swutlā'k· then set the tree upright on one side of the river and put up a second one the same way on the other bank. He laid a third trunk across the other two and tied it fast. To this he attached many vertical sticks. Thus he made the first salmon weir and the people had plenty to eat.

Siā'latsa then saw many deer and pondered how he could catch them. He made his people go into the forest and fetch cedar branches. He then ordered them to heat these and fashion ropes from them which he used to make a net. But no one knew what he intended to do with it. When the net was finished, he went into the forest with his men and had it stretched between the trees and fastened to a crossbeam along the upper edge. Then he had the deer driven against the net, and killed them when they got caught in it. But when the men also drove elk[26] into it, these broke through the nets because they were such strong animals. (According to a different version, the cedar ropes broke when they became dry.)

So Siā'latsa pondered how he could catch deer now. He was aware that the monster, Stlā'lak·am,[27] lived on Mount Swuq'ā's.[28] The monster had a needle-sharp horn on its neck. Siā'latsa went up the mountain with all his men. When they caught sight of the monster they ran away in fright. But Siā'latsa said, "Why are you afraid?" and, supporting himself with his staff, went up to the monster. Thereupon

---

24. Boas' "K·au'ämen" is qəwɛ'mən ('warm grease') referring to a former village site situated on the north side of the Cowichan River, adjacent to the present-day Allenby Road bridge near Duncan (Rozen 1985:183, 189).

25. What Boas transcribes as "Sâ'menos" (anglicized as "Somenos") is sʔámənəʔ, the Island Halkomelem name applied to the Cowichan village situated immediately southwest of the present city of Duncan; the same name, sʔámənəʔ, is also applied to Somenos Lake and Somenos Creek (Rozen 1985:183–189).

26. Given as *Elche* 'moose; elk (plural)' here in the *Sagen*, but in this context the distinction is clearly between deer and elk; moreover, moose have never been found on Vancouver Island (see also story 1, part 5, of this section where Boas uses the English term "elk" in the original German text).

27. "Stlā'lak·am signifies something supernatural" [Boas' original footnote]. Boas' "Stlā'lak·am" is sx̣'ɛ'ləqəm, the Halkomelem term commonly translated as 'supernatural'; besides referring to a vague power, sx̣'ɛ'ləqəm can refer, as here, to a particular threatening monster.

28. What Boas transcribes as "Swuq'ā's is swə'q̓əs, derived from wəq̓ás ('stuck on the head'), the name of the supernatural dog that belonged to siyáləcə and had a long horn extending from its forehead. The name swə'q̓əs is applied to Mount Prevost in its entirety; this mountain is situated northwest of Duncan (Rozen 1985:189–194) (see also the footnote that follows).

it fell asleep. He touched it with his staff and named it Wok·'ä's.[29] Then he softly scratched its head and Wok·'ä's twitched its ears contentedly. He had ten men make a rope from cedar branches and put it around the neck of Wok·'ä's. Ten men held the rope and led Wok·'ä's down to Tsu'k·ola.[30] There they found many deer and elk. When Wok·'ä's scented them, it wanted to rush upon them. But the ten men held it back until Siā'latsa ordered them to release the rope. At once Wok·'ä's rushed at the game and killed them by goring their bellies with its horn.

Siā'latsa then had the deer skinned and ordered the men to split the back sinews and pound them with stones until they were soft. Then he had the sinews made into ropes and woven into a new net. But when the men wanted to put the net up, it turned out to be too small. (According to a different version, the people roasted and ate the net during a famine.) Siā'latsa became very angry about this and lay down on his bed. A small boy playing in the village entered the house and saw him lying in bed, full of anger. So he became afraid, ran out and told the people that Siā'latsa was angry and lying in bed. All the people gathered in a house and said to each other, "Siā'latsa is angry with us and will set Wok·'ä's upon us; we had better go away." QaiōtsE'mk·En, Qtlā'set, Hē'uk·En, Kto'qcin, Qoa'qotcin, and Susk·'eme'n went away to SQue'lEn[31] on the Nanaimo River and became the ancestors of the SnanaimuQ. (These names do not agree with those of the Nanaimo families as I investigated them in Nanaimo proper.)[32] Ten others went to Skūts[33] and became the ancestors of the K·o'lk·uisala.[34] Another ten went to S'ē'lak·oatl[35] and became the ancestors of the Tsimē'nes.[36]

Next morning when Siā'latsa got up he found that nobody was there and he had no idea where the people had gone. Even Wok·'ä's, whom he had tied up to the

---

29. "Wok·'ä's" is wəq̓ás, which (as explained in the preceding footnote) is the name of the supernatural dog that belonged to siyáləcə.

30. As previously noted, "Tsu'k·ola" is the place name c̓ə'q̌ʷələʔ, referring to a grassy area on the southwest side of Mount Prevost (Rozen 1985:190–191).

31. The place name transcribed here by Boas as "SQue'lEn" is possibly sx̌ʷíl'ən or sx̌ʷíl'ən; according to Boas, this place was on the Nanaimo River (which is south from the present city of Nanaimo).

32. See Boas (1889b:321) for a listing of the five Nanaimo "clans" (i.e. local groups.)

33. "Skūts" is Boas' transcription of skʷəc ('waterfall'), anglicized as "Skutz," which refers to Skutz Falls, located about 22 miles (35 km) up the Cowichan River from Duncan (Rozen 1985:207–214).

34. Boas' "K·o'lk·uisala" is x̌ʷə'l'q̓ʷsɛ'lə (possibly 'place with snags in river'), anglicized as "Koksilah," where the present-day Island Highway crosses the Koksilah River, south from the town of Duncan (Rozen 1985:221–223).

35. Sílaqʷáʔəɬ (Boas' "S'ē'lak·oatl") is the name for the Chemainus River in its entirety (Rozen 1985:122).

36. "Tsimē'nes" is Boas' rendering of šc̓əmínəs, anglicized as "Chemainus," the Island Halkomelem term referring to the village at Kulleet Bay, northeast from Ladysmith Harbour (Rozen 1985:121; Suttles 1990:455).

house the previous day, was gone. So Siā′latsa went to K·auä′men near S'â′menos and built himself a new house.

In those days there also lived in Sâ′ok[37] a chief who had come down from the sky. He had a daughter. One day he said to her, "Don't eat too much, because I believe that Siā′latsa will come and want you for his wife. I know that there are no women in his country." The girl obeyed, but since Siā′latsa didn't appear, she became impatient. She filled up a basket with berries and seal meat and went off with a slave girl to look for him. After a long walk she arrived at the summit of the mountains on the south side of the Cowichan Valley. From here she could see smoke rising in S'â′menos and K·umiĕ′k·en and thought that Siā′latsa must live there. She climbed down to the river, and when she saw a salmon weir there, she thought that Siā′latsa must have built it. At night she lay down in the forest and slept. The following morning she saw a man pass by who carried a fur cape and a bow and some arrows. So she thought that this had to be Siā′latsa. Without being noticed, she followed him, in order to see where he lived and what he was doing. He entered his house and the girls peeped in through a crack. There they saw that he had carved himself a woman out of wood and that he was giving her food. When Siā′latsa had gone again to hunt, they went into the house to inspect the wooden figure. They found that it held a spindle in its hand and that Siā′latsa had put deer fat in front of it. They ate the fat and hid. When Siā′latsa returned to find that the food, which he had placed in front of the wooden figure, had disappeared, he was very glad because he believed that it would come to life.

The following morning he went out to hunt again, after having put food in front of his wife. The girls came out of their hiding place. The chief's daughter broke up the figure, flung it into the fire, and put its clothing on herself. But the slave girl hid in the forest. When Siā′latsa returned, he was very happy to find his wooden wife alive and he went to bed with her. But soon he noticed a wooden hand in the fire and thus he knew that she was a stranger who had burnt his carving. He became so angry that he grew red in the face and was able to say only, "Ts, ts, ts, ts" (drawing breath in). But after a while he thought that it would actually be better to have a real wife instead of only a wooden one and he became cheerful again. The following morning he called the slave girl from the forest and said, "Don't be afraid; come here to our fire." When Siā′latsa saw the slave girl, he wanted to take her for a wife as well, but the chief's daughter said, "She is a slave and not good enough for you. Give her to one of your men." Siā′latsa agreed. He called his men together and asked, "Who wants to have this girl for a wife?" At once three men rushed up to take her. One of

---

37. What Boas transcribes here as "Sâ′ok" is sɔ′ʔɔkʷ, anglicized as "Sooke," a Northern Straits Coast Salish group living in the vicinity of Sooke Harbour northwest of Victoria (Suttles 1990:454–456; 2001:297–299).

them grabbed her by her right arm, the other by her left and the third around her middle. "Stop," Siā'latsa called out, "only one of you can have her," and he gave her to the one who had grabbed her around her middle.

The wife of Siā'latsa soon bore him a son, then three daughters and then a son again. The eldest daughter was called Tlk·ā'isis. Once the three youngest children tormented her with sharp sticks until she bled; then they licked off the blood. Thereupon the girl became very ill. So Siā'latsa went down to K·umiē'k·en in order to ask K·ulē'miltQ[38] and Ckuâ'wules to paint the girl's face and thus heal her.[39] They replied to his request, "We will fulfil our brother's wish and make his daughter's heart strong." They went up to the house of Siā'latsa and painted his daughter's face. Then they returned to K·umiē'k·en.

But they had painted the girl too much and her heart became too strong. That's how she lost her mind.

One day her youngest brother cried and didn't want to drink any milk. So Tlk·ā'isis thought, "I'll make him eat again." She took a skull, opened it, took out the brain and gave it to the boy, who gobbled it up greedily. And she made a basket with carrying-straps for herself, put snakes, toads and lizards into it and slung it over her back. She hid loathsome vermin ("like a salmon living on bark"??)[40] under her cape and went into those houses where children cried. She asked each weeping child, "Why are you crying? Maybe you are hungry? I'll give you something to eat." Then she took each child and stuffed it into her basket. There the snakes coiled around it.

Siā'latsa was the first to give away blankets and furs. He had two men step out onto a scaffold and distribute the gifts among the invited guests. He made this custom into a strict law and that is why it is still followed today. In addition, he taught the winter dance to his daughter and ordered her to dance it always in the month of SaiE'mtk·Els.[41]

Siā'latsa's son once went up to Mount Qsalā'atsem[42] in order to visit the Thunderbird, SuQoā'as.[43] When he arrived at its house it started raining on earth. He

---

38. Boas' "K·ulē'miltQ" is qʷlímǝltxʷ (Rozen 1985:155).

39. The girl's face is being painted with the red ochre paint used on ritual occasions.

40. This seems to be an image based on the similarity between vermin on old tree bark and spawning salmon in the water.

41. "SaiE'mtk·Els" means literally 'cold moon' in the Cowichan dialect of Halkomelem, referring to an approximate time period encompassing the latter part of December and the early part of January.

42. The Halkomelem term xʷsálǝʔacǝm (Boas' "Qsalā'atsem") applies to the area of Deerholme Mountain, the Koksilah Ridge, and Eagle Heights, situated to the south of the settlement of Deerholme (Rozen 1985:231).

43. What Boas transcribes here as "SuQoā'as" is the Halkomelem term šxʷǝxʷá·s 'Thunderbird; thunder.'

stayed there nine days, but returned on the tenth and recounted what he had seen. Then he carved the Thunderbird upon the post of his house.

The Thunderbird's eyes shine like fire, and when he opens them, lightning flashes. Once SuQoā′as spied a killer whale in the sea and wanted to catch it. A canoe was pursuing the whale at the same time. But the hunters saw how the Thunderbird swooped down and carried the whale away. Once the Thunderbird pursued the Sts'ē′enkoa (a mythical bird, see p. 630).[44] It plunged into a tree and split it from top to bottom in order to crawl in. But the Thunderbird grabbed it and carried it away.

(According to a different version, StE′ts'En,[45] then K·ulē′miltQ,[46] and finally Ckuâ′wules, came down from the sky after Siā′latsa and became the ancestors of the K·uámitcan.[47] The legend of the wooden wife and the chief's daughter from Sâ′ok[48] is also told about StE′ts'En, though the latter was given positively as one of the Qala′ltq[49] ancestors. In K·umiē′ken and S'â′menos I was told the ancestors of the following local groups:[50] the Qala′ltq, presently living in the Tsimē′nes[51] Valley, own a stretch of land between K·ua′mitcan and S'â′menos.[52] Sitqoē′metsten and StE′ts'En

---

44. Boas' page citation refers to the earlier *Verhandlungen* printing of these same Cowichan legends (see Boas 1891c:628–636); page 630 of this 1891 publication is the second paragraph of the present siyálecə story, where the "Sts'ē′enkoa" is also mentioned. As previously noted, what Boas transcribes as "Sts'ē′enkoa" is c̓ínk̓ʷaʔ 'supernatural lightning monster,' but is referred to here by Boas as 'a mythical bird.'

45. Boas' "StE′ts'En" is st'ə́c̓ən.

46. As previously noted, "K·ulē′miltQ" is qʷlíməltxʷ.

47. Quamichan.

48. Sooke.

49. The term transcribed here by Boas as "Qala′ltq," anglicized as "Halalt," is the Island Halkomelem term x̣əlɛ́'l'txʷ 'painted/marked house,' applied to a village formerly situated on the north end of Willy Island, southeast from Chemainus, and to the village these people subsequently moved to at Westholme, just west of Crofton (Rozen 1985:124–127) (see also the footnote below, referring to the village with this same name, x̣əlɛ́'l'txʷ, on the Cowichan River).

50. Boas uses the German term *Stämme* which in this instance we have translated as 'local groups,' meaning a group of individuals sharing a sense of identity and a myth of descent from a First Ancestor (see Suttles 1990:464).

51. As previously noted, "Tsimē′nes" is šc̓amínəs, anglicized as "Chemainus."

52. Boas' statement about the Halalt people of the Chemainus Valley owning "a stretch of land between K·ua′mitcan and S'â′menos" is a reference a Cowichan River village with the same name, x̣əlɛ́'l'txʷ (Boas' "Qala′ltq," anglicized as "Halalt"), located near Duncan where the present-day Island Highway "Silver Bridge" crosses the Cowichan River. Rozen (1985:124–127; 179–180) explains that the reason this name exists in these two difference areas is because the residents of this Cowichan River village initially moved to Willy Island, southeast from Chemainus (perhaps in the early 1800s), and then later to Westholme (Bonsall Creek), just west of Crofton, taking the name x̣əlɛ́'l'txʷ with them.

are supposed to be their ancestors. The K·umiē′ken descend from K·ulē′miltǫ and K·utqä′tse and the Mā′leqatl[53] descend from Soosti′lten.)

3. The Flood

Once it rained for long days and long nights. The sea rose higher and higher and finally covered all the ground. When at last the waters subsided, lakes and rivers remained, and in them the fish.

4. The Thunderbird

Once upon a time there was a man in Tsimē′nes[54] who caught many ducks by setting up a net into which they flew. He carried them home and plucked them in order to feast the people. But a young man called Sqä′lek·en[55] was so impatient that he couldn't wait until he received his portion; instead, he took the entrails, cleaned them and began to eat. When his older brother saw this, he became very angry and beat Sqä′lek·en's face with cedar branches until all the flesh came off the bones and the young man was half dead. Then he covered the wounds with woodchips. When Sqä′lek·en woke up again, he stood up and went first to Cowitchin Bay and there caught ducks in a net. Then he went up Mount Tsō′wan[56] in order to catch mountain goats.[57] But his brother had followed him. He broke Sqä′lek·en's canoe and then whipped him with blueberry bushes.[58] Then he lit ten huge fires in a level place and whipped his younger brother with the branches until his face was all torn to pieces and he left him for dead. Then he returned home.

Sqä′lek·en lay there as if dead for ten days. When he woke up again, he found that the Thunderbird had been with him in the meantime and had given him its eyes.

---

53. What Boas transcribes as "Mā′leqatl" is mɛ′l'əx̣ɛł ('caterpillars'), anglicized as "Malahat," the name of a village situated on the west side of Saanich Inlet just south from Mill Bay; the Malahat village marks the most southerly extent of Island Halkomelem.

54. Chemainus.

55. Boas' "Sqä′lek·en" is sx̣ɛ′ləqən, referred to by Cowichan people as "the man with the flashing eyes" (Rozen 1985:137).

56. What Boas transcribes as "Tsō′wan" is čəwɛ·′n ('land goes right down to the water'), anglicized as Mount "Tuam," referring to the mountain located at the southwest end of Saltspring Island (Rozen 1985:135–137).

57. Mountain goats are not known to occur anywhere on Vancouver Island or in the islands in the Strait of Georgia.

58. The German term used here in the original, *Heidelbeersträucher*, refers to dwarf bilberry bushes, but in the Island Halkomelem area the species referred to is likely either the Alaska blueberry (*Vaccinium alaskense*) or the evergreen huckleberry (*Vaccinium ovatum*).

When he looked around, fire flashed. That same day, when his older brother returned to look at Sqä'lek·en, the latter looked at him and the fire blazing from his eyes killed him. Since that time, everyone who Sqä'lek·en looks at with his flashing eyes has to die.

5. The Boys and the Whale

Once there were two boys, called TEtk·'ē'k·En and TEtk·aiâ'çen. One day they went out in their canoe. They hadn't gone far when they saw a whale surfacing and diving. So they started to shout abuses at it. Thereupon the whale swam up quite close to them, but this did not deter them. It surfaced three times, each time closer to the canoe. The boys did not stop their abuse, so the fourth time that the whale surfaced, it swallowed both the canoe and the boys and swam away. The whale told them, "You may eat my flesh, but be careful not to damage my stomach, otherwise I'll die." But the boys were afraid that the whale would carry them so far out to sea that they wouldn't be able to return. Therefore, they sharpened their stone knife and the older brother said to the younger one, "Lift me up now, so that I'll be able to cut the whale's stomach." The younger one obeyed and his brother killed the whale. It drifted about on the waves. So the brothers thought, "Oh, if only the whale would beach!" And behold, it drifted to the mouth of the Cowitchin River. So the boys inside started to shout, in order that people would notice them. At first no one noticed them. But soon they heard the chopping of an axe close by and it sounded as if someone was building a canoe there. So they shouted again at the top of their voices. The man heard them and went to the village. He said that he had heard two voices but didn't know where they came from. So everyone went with him to the beach and they could hear two voices singing, "Oh, we are sitting inside the whale. Come and free us. It is so hot in here that we are almost scalded." The people went on and soon discovered the whale. The boys' father was among the people. He recognized the voices of his sons and shouted, "Oh, are you there, my sons?" "Yes," they called out, "free us; we are burning up in here." Then the people took their stone knives, opened up the whale and the boys came out. But it had been so hot in the whale's stomach that they had lost all their hair.

6. The Abandoned Boy

There was once a boy who told his father, "I'll go up the mountain and bathe in the pond up there." The father was pleased with this. The boy stayed up there for nine days. But the people saw smoke rising on the mountain and said to the father, "Do you see smoke rising where your son is bathing?" On the tenth day the son returned.

He entered the house and seated himself by the fire. The people could hear rumbling sounds in his body. In a short while the boy went again up the mountain to bathe. Since the people noticed smoke again, his father sneaked after him and so discovered that, instead of bathing, his son had lit a large fire and was roasting and eating fern roots. All the while, snakes were crawling from his anus. The father returned and told the people, "I've seen what my son is up to on the mountain. He doesn't bathe, but instead eats fern roots, and snakes crawl from his anus. Let's move away from here and abandon him." They all agreed, except for the boy's youngest uncle. When the boy returned on the tenth day, the people again heard the noise in his belly and said to each other, "Listen, those are the snakes." When he went back to the mountain again, his uncle sneaked after him and when he also saw that the boy ate fern roots and snakes crawled from his anus, he returned and said, "Let's abandon the boy. Now I can see that he is up to evil things." The canoes were loaded and when everything was ready for departure, the fires were extinguished. Only the grandmother of the boy felt pity for him. She hid a bit of food and some glowing coals in a mussel shell,[59] put this in a corner of the house and said to a dog, "You stay here, and when my grandson returns, tell him that I've hidden the shell in that corner." Then she, too, climbed into the canoe and went away with the rest of the people.

But on the tenth day the young man returned. He sat down and cried because he found the village deserted. The dog crept up to him, nudged him, and ran to a corner of the house. Then it came back and didn't rest until the young man had noticed its behaviour. He followed it and now found the shell in which the glowing coal and the food had been hidden. He lit a fire for himself and pondered who it might be who had taken pity on him. At last he fell asleep and dreamt that he could see a man who called out to him, "Arise and purify yourself!" He awoke and obeyed. While the young man was watching, a man came and stroked the dog's back with his hand. The dog was transformed into a woman with beautiful black hair. After the young man bathed, he became handsome, himself, and had long red hair. He then took the transformed dog for his wife.

While he was asleep, the same man appeared in his dream again and said, "Your fellow countrymen have abandoned you, therefore I have made you handsome and given you a wife. Do you want me to give you food and make you completely happy?" He answered, "My father has abandoned me; please make me happy." The man answered, "Cheer up, even if you own nothing now. I'll give you everything you need, food and good weather. Go to the water where you have bathed, take the inner cedar bark with which you always wash, and beat the water with it. Thereupon

---

59. Given in the original as *Muschelschale* 'mussel shell,' although in some Coast Salish variants of this same legend the container is identified specifically as a clam shell.

many herring will come. Don't be afraid, but throw all of them onto the shore and take them for yourself. I am giving them to you." So it happened, and now the young man didn't suffer want.

When the young man slept again, the stranger appeared in his dream again and said, "Know that your grandmother took pity on you; she gave you fire and food." When the youth awoke he called Raven and ordered him to eat herring. Raven obeyed. When Raven had really filled himself, the young man told him to shake himself so that he would be able to swallow a bit more. Then he said, "Now fly to my relatives. When you see an old woman there who is always weeping, you will know that she is my grandmother. Give her the fish. If your load becomes too heavy, fly up really high; then you'll be able to carry it." Raven did as he was told. When he grew tired, he went high up into the air and here he was able to carry the load without any trouble. He came to the village and soon found the old woman. He called out, "MElā′ō, mElā′ō wa sōkukulē′, mElā′ō!" and dropped the fish. Thereupon the old one stopped crying. She took the fish and hid them until it was dark, because she wanted to keep her son from seeing them. Then she went into the house and stuck the fish onto sticks, as she wanted to roast them. But she didn't put them close to the fire for fear that her son might see them. Raven flew back. Once more, laden with fish, he was sent to the old one by the young man. But this time her son noticed them and asked, "Where did you get the fish?" So she had to admit that Raven had brought them. She added, "I think they come from your son whom we abandoned long ago." The father grew angry and said, "Don't you know how wicked my son was? Surely he is long since dead." But when Raven came for a third time, he told the old one that he was sent by her grandson. The old one said to her son, "See, I was right, your son has sent the fish to me." So the man called all the people together, gave them the herring and said, "My son is rich now; he has sent us this herring. Let us return to our old home."

The people loaded their canoes and the following morning they all set out. When they got close to their home, they saw a handsome man and a woman standing on the shore. The chief said, "This is not my son. This man has red hair." But his youngest brother said, "Oh, don't say that. Who knows who has made him handsome and given him that woman?" They landed and carried their belongings into the houses. Every morning the young man went down to the water and beat it with the bunch of inner cedar bark. Thereupon many herring swam up. He told the people, "Don't be afraid, but help me to get the fish ashore. Then take as many as you need."

One night the stranger appeared again to him in a dream. He asked, "Are you glad that your fellow countrymen, who once abandoned you, have returned again, or would you like to take revenge?" He answered, "I am angry with them, but I am alone and my enemies are many." Thereupon the stranger replied, "Tomorrow, call for a whale; one will come and eat all the herring. Then you will have an opportunity for revenge." And he told the young man in detail what he should do. When he had called the whale and it had eaten all the herring, the people wanted to go out and catch the whale. But the young man said, "Don't bother; I will call and it will come up on land all by itself." This is what happened. Then he called all the people to cut up the whale and placed everyone who had been good to him on one side of the whale and the rest on the other. When they were about to start carving up the whale, he called to it, "Avenge me now!" Thereupon it struck about with its tail and killed everyone who had been bad to the boy.

7. Sqoē′te (Galiano Island)[60]

A long, long time ago, Sqoē′te used to be a tree standing upright whose top reached up to the sky. Down this tree the people descended from the sky, as did deer with white backs and black legs and antlers which bent forward and covered the sides of their faces.[61] When the people had arrived on earth, they pondered how they could bring down the tree. So two men called for the rats (?)[62] and told them to gnaw through the tree. When the rats had gnawed for twenty days, they had almost reached the middle of the tree. The two men then told them to start from the opposite side, and here, too, the rats gnawed a deep hole. While the rats were gnawing, the people sang in order to keep their spirits up. The people were glad that the tree would fall soon and sang, "Oh, let it fall and not break. Many deer will live on the trunk and we will build our houses on it." When the rats had finished their task, they ran out of the tree and it fell over. But the top broke off and formed Ā′wik·sen[63] Island. Many deer then lived on the islands. (The informant, an old man in S'â′menos, maintained that he once had seen one of these deer, but he didn't dare shoot it.)

---

60. Boas gives Galiano Island in English (without quotation marks) in the original *Sagen*. While Boas identifies Galiano Island as "Sqoē′te," no such name has been recorded for Galiano Island (see Rozen 1985:112). Rather, the Native term Boas uses here, sx̌ʷəʔíti? ("Sqoē′te"), has been given as the name by which the Island Halkomelem refer to Lasqueti Island (Rozen 1985:30), which is near Texada Island, and is beyond Island Halkomelem territory. Likely sx̌ʷəʔíti? is the Island Halkomelem pronunciation of Lasqueti Island's name either in Sechelt (where we have recorded it as sx̌ʷəʔítay) or Comox (where we have recorded x̌ʷəʔítay); both the Sechelt and Comox terms mean 'yew tree.'

61. This description does not fit that of the native deer; this characterization, coupled with the storyteller's statement at the end of the legend, indicates that it is likely mythical deer that are being referred to here.

62. Boas queries this word, but in several analogs, rats do gnaw through trees.

63. It is not clear what place Boas is referring to here as "Ā′wik·sen Island." Possibly Boas' "Ā′wik·sen" is ʔɛ·′yqsən ('Douglas-fir point'), the Island Halkomelem term applied to Shingle Point on Valdes Island (Rozen 1985:74–76).

V. LEGENDS OF THE NANAIMO

Boas was in Nanaimo only a few days (4–9 December 1886) but he felt he learned more in one day there "than during the week in Cowichan." By the end of his stay he reports that he has "about 800 words and a few short texts" (Rohner 1969:72–73). This was cause for some pride, since the texts were collected in the Halkomelem language, as can be seen in his manuscript held by the National Anthropological Archives of the Smithsonian Institution (Boas n.d.4). The second and third of the stories are given in Boas' own English translation in his "Notes on the Snanaimuᵠ" publication (see Boas 1889b:326–328).

Unidentified family at entrance to cedar plank house, Nanaimo, 17 August 1866. The carved and painted figures show design elements typical of Salish artists, such as the depiction of mythical or spiritual figures in shallow relief and the use of circles and ovals.
Royal British Columbia Museum, Victoria, B.C. PN5929 (Frederick Dally photo).

V. Legends of the Snanaimuq[1]

1. The Origin of Fire

A long time ago, people had no fire. K·ak·ē'iq, Mink,[2] wanted to fetch it and consequently went with his grandmother to the chief who kept the fire. They landed unnoticed and at night Mink stole up to the house while the chief and his wife were sleeping. But the bird, Tɛ'gya,[3] was rocking the child. Mink opened the door slightly. When Tɛ'gya heard the noise, it called, "Pq! pq!" in order to wake the chief. But Mink whispered, "Sleep, sleep!" Whereupon the bird fell asleep. Then Mink entered the house and stole the chief's child from the cradle. He then went quickly

---

1. What Boas transcribes as "SnanaimuQ" is snənə'ymǝxʷ (anglicized as "Nanaimo"), referring collectively to the aboriginal people whose traditional territory on the east coast of Vancouver Island extended from the Boat Harbour/Dodd Narrows area in the south to the Neck Point/Horswell Bluff area in the north, including Gabriola Island and other adjacent islands and reaching west to the inland mountains (Boas 1887f:map; 1889b:321; Duff 1953–1956; Bouchard 1992:4–5). The Nanaimo speak a dialect of Island Halkomelem Coast Salish which is the language spoken along the eastern side of Vancouver Island between Saanich Inlet in the south and Northwest Bay in the north. Island Halkomelem is also spoken by the Malahat, Cowichan, Chemainus, and Nanoose (Suttles 1990:455–456).

    While our annotating of this section is based primarily on the available literature, we also draw upon our consultation with Christopher Paul in 1971–1975 and with Chester Thomas in 1992–1993, and gratefully acknowledge their assistance.

2. Boas' "K·ak·ē'iq" is qɛ'qɛyx̣ which means, literally, 'little Mink,' although the usual Island Halkomelem name for 'Mink' in Nanaimo mythology is qɛyx̣ (Boas' "K·ä'iq") which is the term that Boas does use in the variant of this legend (No. 1a) that follows here. After the Native term "K·ak·ē'iq" appears in the first line of story 1, Boas provides a half-German/half-English translation, *der Mink* ('the Mink'), rather than the normal German word for 'Mink,' *der Nerz*, that he had been using consistently up until this point in the *Sagen*. All subsequent occurrences of this character's name in Nanaimo story 1, after line 1, are given in English as Mink (without quotation marks) in the *Sagen*. In Nanaimo story 1a of the *Sagen*, Boas uses only "K·ä'iq" which he translates in the first line as *der Mink*.

3. What Boas renders as "Tɛ'gya" appears to be a Nanaimo Halkomelem pronunciation of the Comox Coast Salish word for the Sandhill Crane (*Grus canadensis*)—the Halkomelem term that we have recorded for this same bird is sli·m. Possibly "Tɛ'gya" is a term formerly used in Nanaimo Halkomelem for Sandhill Crane in mythology, although this term does not appear in Boas' (n.d.4; n.d.7; 1889b) Nanaimo materials. The Sandhill Crane's role as "babysitter" here is confirmed elsewhere in Coast Salish mythology, for example, in Squamish.

to his canoe where his grandmother was waiting, and they went home. Each time they passed a village, Grandmother had to pinch the child so that it cried. At last they arrived at Tlāltq[4] (Gabriola Island, opposite Nanaimo).[5] Here Mink had a large house where he and his grandmother lived alone.

In the morning, the chief missed his child and became very sad. He went out in his canoe to look for it, and when he came to a village he asked, "Haven't you seen my child? Someone has stolen it." The people answered, "Last night, Mink came past and a child was crying in his canoe." The chief asked in every village and every-where received this same answer. Thus he finally arrived in Tlāltq. Mink had expected him and, when he saw him coming in the distance, he put on one of his many hats, stepped in front of the house and danced while his grandmother beat time and sang. He then ran back into the house, put on a different hat and came out of another door in a changed shape. Finally he stepped out of the central door as Mink, carrying the chief's child in his arms. The chief didn't dare attack mink because he thought many people were living in the house, and said, "Give my child back to me and I will give you many coppers." The grandmother called out to Mink, "Don't take them." When the chief at last offered him the fire-drill, Mink took it, on the advice of his grandmother. The chief took his child and returned home. But Mink lit a huge fire. Thus people obtained Fire.

1a) In the beginning, the ghosts (of the dead) owned Fire.[6] K·ä'iq, Mink,[7] set out to make war on the ghosts and to rob them of fire. When he got to the houses of the ghosts he heard a child crying in the chief's house. It was in its cradle, suspended from a branch. Mink stole the child and carried it to the house of his grandmother. When the ghosts noticed that their chief's child had been stolen, they pursued the fugitives. They reached K·ä'iq's house and saw him dancing in front of it. He had sprinkled feathers on his head. So the ghosts were afraid and didn't dare attack him. They said, "Let's make a trade; what do you want in exchange for the child?" K·ä'iq's grandmother replied, "My grandson doesn't want to have anything." The ghosts continued, "We don't have any clothing. When we died we were only wrapped in woven blankets.[8] Do you want those? Wouldn't you like to have furs?

---

4.   The term rendered by Boas as "Tlāltq" is recognized as x̣'ɛ·'ltxʷ, the Nanaimo Halkomelem name applied to False Narrows, at the southwest tip of Gabriola Island.

5.   Boas gives the words Gabriola Island and Nanaimo in English (without quotation marks) here in the original *Sagen*.

6.   Elsewhere, Boas (n.d.4) provides a variant of this story in Nanaimo Halkomelem, with a literal English translation.

7.   In Boas' (n.d.7) "Snanaimuq vocabulary," he provides the term "tcitcēk'an" (čəčíqən), which is the normal Island Halkomelem term for 'mink,' and not the name by which 'Mink' is known in mythology, which Boas gives here as "K·ä'iq" (qɛyx).

8.   Elsewhere, Boas (n.d.4) gives the translation, 'blankets of mountain sheep wool,' for the term given here as "swṓk̲oal" (swə́q̓ʷəɫ), meaning 'mountain goat wool blanket.'

They were given to us when we died." "No," K·ä′iq retorted. "We were given only elk[9] hides and tanned deer hides; only the fire-drill was given to us." "Good," K·ä′iq called out then, "that's what I want." They gave him the fire-drill and he returned the child to them.

2. The Origin of Daylight[10]

A long time ago, there was no Daylight because Seagull kept it in a small box, which he guarded jealously. His cousin, Raven, wanted to get Daylight, however. One day, when Raven was walking with Seagull, he thought, "Oh, if only Seagull would get a thorn in his foot." As soon as he had thought this, Seagull cried out in pain because he had stepped on a sharp thorn. Raven said, "Let me see your foot; I will pull out the thorn." Since it was dark, he was unable to find the thorn and there-fore he asked Seagull to open the lid of the box and let out the light. Seagull opened the box a tiny bit so that a faint ray of light came out. Raven pretended that he still couldn't find the thorn and, instead of pulling it out, he pushed it into the foot deeper and deeper, saying, "I need more light." Seagull cried, "My foot, my foot!"[11] and finally opened the box. Thus Daylight was set free, and there has been day and night since then.

3. The Man and the Whale[12]

A harpooner went out to hunt seals every day. He caught many seals and returned home. Then he invited all his friends for a meal. When they had finished their meal, his wife went down to the shore to wash the bowls and to throw away the scraps. She tied on her cape[13] and went into the water a few steps in order to wash a seal-skin. All of a sudden, a killer whale[14] appeared, took her on his back and swam away.

---

9. *Elch* 'moose; elk' in the original, yet clearly 'elk' in this context; moose are not found on Vancouver Island, although both deer and elk are present.

10. Boas (1889b:328) himself provides an English translation of this legend.

11. In the English published version of this story Boas (1889b:328) provides the Island Halkomelem expression, "Sqenä′n, sqenä′n!" (i.e., my foot, my foot!) which is not given here in the *Sagen*.

12. Boas (1889:326–328) provides both an English translation of this legend, and elsewhere, an inter-linear translation of a variant of it (Boas n.d.4).

13. While Boas uses the German term *Mantel* 'cape' here in the original, he uses the English term 'blanket' in his own translation of this story (Boas 1889b:326).

14. The correct Latin identification for this species, *Delphinus orca*, is given by Boas (1889b:326) in his own translation of this legend. In his notes, Boas (n.d.4) gives the Island Halkomelem term "skĕl′ŏ′nĕmähĕn" i.e., q̓əłánəməcən 'killer whale.' Elsewhere, Boas (1916:1019) does use the English term, "killer whale," in summarizing this same story.

Her husband could hear her calling for help, but when he reached the beach and at last launched his canoe, the whale had almost disappeared from sight. He called for his friends and they pursued it, but soon they saw the whale dive, taking the woman down to the bottom of the sea. When they reached the spot where it had dived, the man tied a rope of deer hide[15] around his middle and told his friend, "You stay here and hold the rope. I will go down to the bottom of the sea and bring back my wife. Don't pull the rope up until I am ready to return." Then he jumped into the water. When he reached the sea bottom he found a trail and followed it. After a while he met a number of old women. One of them distributed food which she had cooked in a kettle. The man noticed that they were blind and he took the full bowls from the woman's hand. She thought that all of her companions had received their bowls and asked, "Have all of you got your food?" They answered, "No, we didn't get anything." Then they scented a stranger and called out, "Oh, let yourself be seen, stranger." He asked, "Tell me, grandmothers, hasn't someone carried a woman past here?" "Yes, they went to the house of Killer Whale." He opened their eyes, as a reward. Then they said, "Beware of Heron."[16] "Oh, I'm not afraid of him," he replied, "I have my fish spear."

He went on and met Heron, who was sitting close to the fire, warming his back. The chief kicked him with his foot and Heron fell into the fire, burning his back. He cried out in pain. The man said, "Tell me, Heron, didn't someone carry my wife past here?" "Yes, they went into the house of Killer Whale," answered Heron. So the stranger healed his back and gave him his fish spear in reward. Heron warned him about the slave.

The man went on and arrived at the spot where the slave of Killer Whale was splitting wood for his master. He crawled underneath the log and broke off the tip of the wedge. When the slave saw this he began to cry and called out, "Oh, it's getting dark and I haven't finished my work. My master will surely beat me." Thereupon the man came out and the slave asked, "What is your name, chief? Where do you come from?" "I am searching for my wife." Then the slave said, "I am splitting wood for my master who wants to cook and eat your wife. Oh, please take pity on me and make my wedge whole again, otherwise my master will beat

15. Boas uses the German term *Hirschfell* meaning 'deer hide' in the *Sagen*, and 'deer skins' in his own English version of this story (Boas 1889b:327); in his interlinear translation he provides the gloss 'deer sinews' (Boas n.d.4).

16. The German term *Kranich* that Boas uses here in the original *Sagen* refers to the 'Common Crane,' identified in the late 1800s as *Grus cinerea*. However, this species has never occurred in the Nanaimo area. In his own English translation of this same story, Boas (1889b:327) provides the translation 'Crane,' which he also provides in his interlinear translation (Boas n.d.4). The Native term for 'Crane' that Boas provides in this latter source is "mu'koa," which we have recorded as smə́q̓ʷə, the Island Halkomelem name for the Great Blue Heron (*Ardea herodias*).

me to death." The man fulfilled his request and the slave said, "I want to help you get your wife back. Wait until my master sends me out to fetch water. On my return I will pretend to stumble and will pour water on the fire. Then rush upon the woman and flee!" The man followed the slave's advice. The latter poured water on the fire and then the man fled with his wife. When Whale noticed that they had fled, he ordered Heron to kill them. But Heron missed them on purpose. The man and his wife arrived safely at the top of the rope. He shook it and his friends pulled him up. Then they returned home as quickly as possible. Whale pursued them in vain. They had a long head-start and reached their home safely.

VI. Legends of the Squamish

During his first field trip Boas spent a hurried few days in Vancouver (14–16 December 1886), where at first he "ran about unsuccessfully," until the Methodist minister, Mr. Hall, took him to the "Indian settlement which is next to one of the large saw mills" (probably the old Hastings Mill): "I collected busily during the few hours that were left as well as on Wednesday and Thursday" (Rohner 1969:76). During his next visit, on 1 June 1888, he "hired a boat and travelled over the approximately three-mile-wide inlet in the pouring rain" (Rohner 1969:86). Chief Joseph, of the Mission Reserve there in North Vancouver, gave him the Transformer story and a "young man named Jack," the second story of this section. Still another Squamish consultant, described in a letter of 2 June 1888 as having "lost an arm in a sawmill," provided Boas with vocabulary and grammar (this description suggests that the man in question was Dick Isaacs who was born in 1859 and died in 1947). "By yesterday afternoon," Boas wrote, "I had trained him so well that I really hate to leave. He understood very well what I wanted" (Rohner 1969:87).

"A small wooden church, painted white, stands in the center, and around it stand the small houses, most of them also white. The canoes lie on the shore" (Rohner 1969:86). Squamish Mission Indian Reserve, North Vancouver, 1889.

City of Vancouver Archives, Vancouver, B.C. (W.T. Dalton photo).

VI. Legends of the Sk·qōmic[1]

1. Qā′is

Qā′is, the Sun,[2] created the earth, the sea, humans and fish. He is also called Qā′aqa[3] or Slaā′lɛk·am.[4] In the course of time, the people became evil and didn't obey the commandments of Qā′is any more. So he descended to earth from above and transformed all who were evil or foolish into stones and animals. One man who had heard that he was coming decided to kill him. He sharpened his shell knives on a whet-stone. When Qā′is approached and saw him, he asked him what he was doing. The man answered, "I want to kill Qā′is when he arrives." "That is fine," the latter replied, "why don't you let me have a look at your knives?" He handed them over and Qā′is forced them into his forehead and transformed him into a deer. The bird, Sk·k·āk·,[5] was a medicine man. When Qā′is saw him, he had only to clap his hands and so transformed him into a bird.

---

1. "Sk·qōmic," anglicized as "Squamish," is Boas' rendering of sqxʷúʔmiš, the Native term referring to the aboriginal people living in the Squamish Valley, Howe Sound and Burrard Inlet areas; these people speak the Squamish Coast Salish language (Boas 1887e:map; 1887f:132, map; Barnett 1935–1936:4:101, 105, 119; 1955:31; Matthews 1955:33–34; Suttles 1990:453–455).

    In annotating this section, we have drawn upon our consultation in the 1970s–1980s with our Native Squamish colleague, Louis Miranda, Sr., whose assistance we gratefully acknowledge.

2. "Qā′is" is Boas' rendering of xays, the Squamish term for the Transformer(s), although the association of the Transformer(s) with the sun is not recorded elsewhere in the Squamish literature. Hill-Tout (1900:518 fn) stated: "The name Qais ... seems sometimes to be applied to the four brothers collectively and sometimes to the eldest only"—this is verified in contemporary collections of Squamish legends and stories.

3. Louis Miranda recognized "Qā′aqa" not as a Squamish word but as the Halkomelem term xɛ′ʔxɛ meaning 'sacred,' and pointed out that in Squamish mythology, what is deemed profound information is often given in the Halkomelem language.

4. "See the note on page 48" [Boas' original footnote]. Boas refers here to story 2 in Section IV of the *Sagen*, where he provides the Cowichan Halkomelem term " Stlā′lak·am" (sx̣'ɛ'lɛqəm) and comments that it "signifies something supernatural." This is the same term that Boas gives here in Squamish as "Slaā′lɛk·am" (sx̣'álqəm), where it also means 'supernatural power or being.'

5. "Sk·k·āk·" is Boas' rendering of the Squamish term sk̓ʷqaq which refers to the American Robin (*Turdus migratorius*).

After some time, the people became evil again. So Qā'is caused a dreadful fire which burned the earth completely. Only two men and two women escaped from the fire and a new tribe[6] descended from them.

People became evil a third time. So Qā'is caused a Great Flood. It began to rain and it rained without end. Only one man knew that the waters would cover all the land. He tied his canoe with a rope to Mount Ntck·ā'i (on the Squamish River)[7] and thus found his home again, after the Flood. The man said to his children, "From now on, always be sure to be good, otherwise Qā'is will surely destroy all of us."

Later, Qā'is sent smallpox and one winter sent a deep snow to the people as punishment for their wickedness. (Told by Chief Joseph).[8]

2. Raven

Raven had a brother, Seal. Raven had two children and Seal had one daughter. Once Raven went to Seal and found him sitting by the fire. He was holding up his hands and fat dripped down from them into a bowl. When the bowl was filled, he served it to Raven and gave him some dried salmon. When Raven had eaten his fill, he said to Seal, "Let your daughter come to my house; my children would like to play with her." Seal agreed and they left. On their way they passed a crabapple tree,[9] so Raven said to Seal Girl, "Just climb the tree and pick me some apples; they are very nice." Seal said that she couldn't climb, but Raven replied, "Just try it; I'll hold the trunk so that it won't sway." So Seal tried to climb up. Although she was awkward, she managed to get up safely and pick some apples. When she wanted to come down again, Raven called out, "There are such nice apples right at the top of the tree. Please pick them!" Seal crawled up and then Raven shook the tree until the poor girl fell down. She was so badly injured that she died on the spot. So Raven carried the body home and devoured it. A few days later, Raven's brother, Old Seal, came to inquire after his daughter. Raven said, "She is in the forest playing with my children." After some days, Seal came again to enquire. Raven said, "Don't be afraid;

---

6. Given as *Geschlecht* in the original *Sagen*; in this context, 'tribe' is the most appropriate translation.

7. "Ntck·ā'i" is nč'qaẏ ('dirty place'), the Squamish name for both Mount Garibaldi, the distinctive, high mountain located north from the town of Squamish, and the Cheekye (anglicized from nč'qaẏ) River which originates from this mountain. Mount Garibaldi is well known as the peak to which the Squamish tied their canoes during the Great Flood.

8. Chief Joseph mənátəltən, who was born *circa* 1825.

9. Given in the original *Sagen* as a mixed English-German term—"Crabapple"-*Baum* ('crabapple tree')—although the German term *Aepfel* 'apples' is used elsewhere throughout this same legend; likely this is wild crabapple (*Pyrus fusca*).

your daughter really enjoys playing with my children." But finally Seal found out, in spite of this, that Raven had killed and eaten the girl. Thereupon he became very sad and cried. (Told by a young man named Jack).[10]

3. K·a′lk·alo-itl[11]

K·a′lk·alo-itl was a huge, bad woman who lived in the forest and carried a basket on her back. Once many boys were swimming in the sea. They dried themselves on the beach in the sun and fell asleep. Then K·a′lk·alo-itl came along and stuffed them all into her basket. Among the boys there was one named T'ētk·ē′istEn (= always cutting).[12] T'ētk·ē′istEn had a knife in his hand. K·a′lk·alo-itl had caught him first of all and so he lay right down at the bottom of her basket. He cut the bottom out of the basket and threw out one boy after another until only a few remained inside. K·a′lk·alo-itl heard them fall, but thought that branches were crackling beneath her feet. She got home at last and then discovered that almost all the boys had escaped. So she became very angry. She took some pitch and smeared it on the boys' eyes. On T'ētk·ē′istEn's advice they closed their eyes tightly while she smeared the pitch on them. She then lit a huge fire and placed stones in it, with which she intended to cook the boys. When the pitch in the boys' eyes became warm, it melted, and they were able to see again. But K·a′lk·alo-itl didn't notice. Then T'ētk·ē′istEn asked K·a′lk·alo-itl to dance for them and she assented to his request. The boys beat time and when she was in the middle of the dance, T'ētk·ē′istEn pushed her into the flames and held her fast with a stick until she was burned to death. Then the boys went home.

4. The Woman and the Fish

A woman with beautiful white skin always bathed in the river in the mornings and afterwards warmed herself by the fire. One day, when she was bathing, many fish swam up, sucked themselves fast to her and scarcely allowed her to leave the water. This happened every time. Thus she caught countless fish without effort and carried them home to cook. Everybody was happy about it because she gave generous presents. Whenever she was in a canoe, the fish swam up and all she had to do was

---

10. We have not been able to determine the identity of this "young man named Jack."

11. This is qál'qaliɬ, the Squamish term for 'Cannibal Woman.'

12. The Squamish term transcribed here by Boas as "T'ētk·ē′istEn," and elsewhere by Hill-Tout (1900:546–548) as "Tētkē′tsEn," was provided as t'it'kíʔctn by Louis Miranda, both to Kuipers (1967:219–221, 228–229, 271) and to ourselves, although Boas remains the only source to give the translation 'always cutting.'

to thrust with a spear in order to catch ten of them at once. But finally, such schools of fish crowded under her canoe that she feared it would capsize. Consequently she returned home. When she went to bathe again, she rubbed herself with a magic substance in order to stop the fish from sucking themselves fast to her, but in vain. She also rubbed a magic substance on her canoe, but nevertheless so many fish sucked themselves fast to the canoe that they almost pulled it down. When she got home after this, she said, "I'm afraid that the fish will drown me yet. If they suck themselves fast to me again, I'll urinate on them, then they'll surely leave me be." When she bathed again, the fish came and tried to pull her down. So she made water and then the fish let her go. She reached the surface again and went home to warm herself. The following morning she anointed her body with a strong magic substance in order to keep the fish away. But when she stepped from the house to take her bath, a fire came down to the earth from the sun and killed her.

5. Sē′notlk·ē and Nuk·'ō′mak·ɛn[13]

An old man and his wife sat by the fire in their house while their son Nuk·'ō′mak·ɛn lay in bed with his wife, sleeping. Suddenly a dreadful noise was heard outside and a voice cried, "Ooh!" The old ones grew afraid, but Nuk·'ō′mak·ɛn did not wake up. The noise came closer and closer and trees could be heard falling, and then the old ones knew that the double-headed serpent,[14] Sē′notlk·ē, was coming. The parents tried to rouse their son, but he didn't stir. The mother hit him with a piece of fire-wood, but he didn't stir. At last she emptied a chamberpot over him and he woke up and heard the Sē′notlk·e. The man said to his wife, "I'll go and kill the monster. I'll be away for four years. Don't weep, but wait for me; I'll return."

He set out at daybreak. He took along his firedrill and a big stone knife. He soon found the serpent's track and followed it. When he had walked for some time he saw the monster. But he feared that he was not strong enough to withstand it. Therefore he bathed in a pond and then became so purified that the serpent was unable to scent him. He followed the serpent again and saw how a huge tree over which it crawled, broke under its weight, how fallen trees splintered under it, and how it churned up the earth deeply with its body. And he found the scales it had shed in many spots of

13. Boas' "Sē′notlk·ē" is sínuɫqaẏ, the Squamish name for the 'double-headed serpent.' However, the term "Nuk·'ō′mak·ɛn" is not now recognized and does not appear elsewhere in the literature. In most accounts of this legend, including variants recorded by Hill-Tout (1900:530–532), Matthews (1955:15), Barnett (1955:32), and Kuipers (1967:230–236), and by ourselves, from Louis Miranda and others, the name of the man who slays the double-headed serpent is xʷəč'tál.

14. "It had one head at the tail and one in front" [Boas' original footnote].

the track.[15] Along the way he saw many deer killed by the Sē'notlk·e, but he didn't eat them.

In the evening he lit a fire for himself and bathed again. The next day he followed the track again, when he saw many mountain goats which the serpent had killed. But he didn't eat their flesh. He followed the track for ten days without taking food. He bathed in each pond which he passed. Then he made two capes from soft, beaten inner cedar bark for himself. He put them on and followed the serpent again. Finally he reached a lake. He saw the serpent swimming in it. Its two heads were pointed forward, and when it moved, they crossed each other. So he grew afraid and resolved not to attack it yet, but to wait until he had become stronger. He climbed a tree in order to watch the serpent. When it crawled ashore, he followed its track. Then he found a magic herb which he rubbed on his body in order to become strong. When he caught up with the serpent again, it was swimming in a lake and he was still afraid of it. When it crawled on shore, he followed its track once more. He found a second magic herb and then bathed in a lake, staying in it for ten days without coming ashore. Now he was very strong. After he had lit a fire and had warmed himself by it, he followed the track of the Sē'notlk·e again. This time he found the serpent floating in a lake, asleep. But still he didn't dare attack it; instead, he rubbed himself with a third magic herb and bathed once more for ten days. Now when he followed it, he found ten mountain goats killed by the monster. He sheared their hair, made himself a loom and wove two large blankets which he draped around himself. When he had finished this, he continued his pursuit. Again he found the serpent in a pond where it was sleeping. So with the aid of his stone knife, he fashioned two huge spears of spruce-wood,[16] and also a swift canoe. He rushed upon the serpent and pierced each head with one of the spears. No sooner had he achieved this, than the water started to rise and the young man fell down dead. He remained dead for ten days, then came to life again. But in the meantime, salmon lice (?)[17] had gnawed at his face. When he awoke, he looked about for the serpent. But he didn't find it and noticed that the lake had dried up and that all that was left of the serpent was a row of bones and its tongues. He took the lower jaws and the tongues, hung them on himself and thenceforth became a great sorcerer. Thus he returned and took

---

15. Given in the original as *Spur* 'track, mark, or other evidence that something has gone past.'

16. *Fichtenholz* 'spruce-wood' in the original (although the term *Tannenholz* 'pine-wood' is given in the variant of this story identified as No. 5a in this section). One variant of this story that we have recorded among the Squamish refers to the spears being made of "spruce knots"; another variant we recorded refers to their being made of "pitch-wood."

17. Given in the original as *Lachsläuse* ('salmon lice') followed by a question mark; however, there is a parasite found on salmon that is known commonly as "salmon lice."

along all the skins of the mountain goats which the serpent had killed. He had followed the serpent for four years.

He walked along and at last saw a village. A boy saw him coming down from the mountain and called out to the people, "Oh, look, there is a stranger coming; let's see who it is." So all the men came out of the houses. But they had scarcely caught sight of him when they fell down dead because the magic emanating from the jaw and the tongue of the Sē′notlk·e was so strong. But Nuk·'ŏ′mak·ɛn became sad and thought, "What have I done that people die when they see me?" And he took a magic herb, rubbed it on them and thus revived them. So three of the men gave him their daughters as wives and presented him with many fur blankets[18] because they knew now that he was powerful.

Then Nuk·'ŏ′mak·ɛn wandered on, but everyone who looked at him had to die. He waved at the people from afar, indicating that they should get out of his way, but in vain! Anyone he waved at, died.

So he decided to bury the jaw and the tongue of the Sē′notlk·e. He went into the forest and placed them under the roots of a tree. Thereupon the tree fell down. He placed them under a rock, but it shattered. So he wrapped them in three blankets of mountain goat fur and hoisted these onto his back. He hoped that the magic would now be ineffective, but when he met people again, they fell down dead. So he sat down and cried. But, using his magic herbs, he revived everyone who he had killed, and in every village three men gave him their daughters as wives. Finally he rubbed his hands with a strong magic substance, and from then on, everyone whom he met stayed healthy.

He now had many wives and many woven blankets.[19] He loaded them into a canoe and returned home. When he had reached his home, he asked the people who had come down to the beach when they saw the canoe approaching, "Are my parents still alive?" "Yes," they answered, "they are still alive and healthy." He asked again, "And is my wife still alive?" They replied, "Yes, she is, and she has waited for you." So Nuk·'ŏ′mak·ɛn was glad. He went ashore and had all his belongings carried into the house.

After some time, the Qlu′mi[20] came to make war on the Sk·qŏ′mic. They raided them, killed many and carried others away as slaves. They went back in ten canoes,

---

18. Although Boas uses the German term *Mäntel* 'coats; capes' here, rather than *Decken* 'blankets,' we use the translation 'blankets' because in this area, blankets (specifically, mountain goat wool blankets) were items of wealth and symbols of status (see also the footnote that follows).

19. *Mäntel* 'capes' in the original, but as noted above, we use the translation 'blankets' because this is more likely a reference to mountain goat wool blankets.

20. This is xʷlə′miʔ, anglicized as "Lummi," the name of a Northern Straits Coast Salish group living in what is now northwestern Washington State, in the vicinity of Bellingham Bay and Hale Passage.

singing songs of victory. So Nuk·'ō′mak·ᴇn rushed after them. He held up the jaw and the tongue of the Sē′notlk·e and the Qlu′mi died. The Sk·qō′mic collected the bodies of their countrymen and Nuk·'ō′mak·ᴇn brought them back to life again.

5a. Sē′notlk·ē

An old man lived in a house with his son. The latter had just been married and was in bed with his wife. The old man got up early in the morning, while the young man and his wife slept on. Then he heard the Sē′notlk·e, which crawled down the mountain, crossed the river and crawled up again on the opposite side. He then woke his son by pouring a bucket of cold water over him, shouting, "Don't lie there so lazily, but rather go and kill the Sē′notlk·e." So the young man grew ashamed. He said to his wife, "I will pursue the Sē′notlk·e and will stay away for four days. Don't weep! Wait for me even if I should stay away for a long time." He left and followed the track of the Sē′notlk·e. He bathed in every pond that he passed, in order to make himself strong. It became winter and summer again and still he had not caught up to the Sē′notlk·e. At last, in the fourth winter, he saw in his dream the lake where the Sē′notlk·e dwelled and thus knew where he had to look for it. When he arrived at the lake, he saw the Sē′notlk·e on a rock in the middle, sunning itself. So he carved himself four spears from pine-wood[21] and made ropes from inner cedar bark, which he tied around his elbows and knees as protective charms. Then he hurled his spears and thus killed the Sē′notlk·e. When it died, he himself fell down as if dead. The lake rose and washed away his body, which then floated to and fro. After four days the lake started to recede again when the bird, Ā′qoē,[22] came flying past, dropped a bit of its excrement on the mouth of the dead man and called, "Arise!" The young man awoke at once. He saw that the lake had drained completely. Sē′notlk·e's corpse lay close to him. He stayed there a whole year, until all the flesh had decayed and only the bones were left. He hid them under his cape. Then he returned home and everyone who saw him, fell down dead. But he made them healthy again. His wife had taken another husband, but returned to him again.

---

21. Given as *Tannenholz* 'pine-wood' in the original (although it is given as *Fichtenholz* 'spruce-wood' in the initial version of this story that is identified as No. 5 in this section).

22. "Ā′qoē" appears to be Boas' rendering of ʔɛ′xə, the Halkomelem term for the Canada Goose (*Branta canadensis*), rather than ʔə′x, the Squamish term for this same species.

"On the south side of the fjord which forms the harbour of the city of Victoria on Vancouver Island, there is a roadway to the outlying reservation of the Songhees Indians, which I visited the same day when I arrived in Victoria. The Indian village consists of some large old houses and a few modern ones which were built in the urban style" (Boas 1891b:76). Old Songhees Village in Victoria Harbour, April 1874.

Royal British Columbia Museum, Victoria, B.C. PN8923 (Albert Maynard photo).

VII. LEGENDS OF THE LUKUNGUN

In his first few days in Victoria in September 1886, the novice Boas had difficulty finding a Lukungun mythteller on the Songhees Indian Reserve and we can sense his frustration in his letters home (Rohner 1969:21–23). Nor were the circumstances right for eliciting texts: the recent death of the Songhees chief's child had left the villagers in mourning; rumours of a potential railway line through their village caused the residents to be suspicious of Boas' presence; and to top it off, the Lukungun engaged in "sociable gatherings" that Boas viewed with some concern. To the description of Victoria in 1886 found in Rohner (1969:3) we can add Boas' (1891b:75–77) amplified German account ("A Visit in Victoria on Vancouver Island") where he comments that "The close vicinity of the city has had a very detrimental influence for the Songhees." Presumably all of these factors contributed to the paucity of stories in this section.

Herring fishing camp at Woods Landing, Constance Cove, Esquimalt *ca.* 1865.
Royal British Columbia Museum, Victoria, B.C. PN905 (Frederick Dally photo).

VII. Legends of the Lku'ñgEn[1]

1. MEnmā'ntauk·

There once was a tribe of people who all had heads of stone. Therefore they were called MEnmā'ntauk· (= Stoneheads).[2] They always made war upon their neighbours, killing the men and taking the women as slaves. Once they had taken a pregnant woman as a slave and she gave birth to a child in captivity. When the chief of the MEnmā'ntauk· learned this, he said, "Kill the child if it is a boy, but if it is a girl, let her live." The woman heard what the chief was saying. Her child was a boy, so she tied a knot around his penis and pulled it up to the back so that he would be taken for a girl. She only washed him at night when nobody observed her. Her ruse was successful. The child grew up quickly. When the child was one month old, the woman managed to escape into the forest. Nobody knew where she had gone. She thought, "It is better to die with my child in the forest instead of living always as slaves or being killed by the chief." She built a hut of bark in the woods and lived there for many years. The boy started walking early. His mother made a bow and

---

1. "Lku'ñgEn" is Boas' rendering of lək'ʷə'ŋən, anglicized as "Lukungun," the Native term referring collectively to several local groups who formerly occupied both shores of the southern entrance to Haro Strait, including the lands between Cordova Bay and Parry Bay on Vancouver Island, and, on the eastern side of the Strait, the lands from Open Bay on Henry Island to Eagle Cove on San Juan Island. Following the establishment of Fort Victoria in 1843, the Lukungun as a whole were generally identified as "Songhees" or "Songish," although these terms are the anglicizations of sčáŋəs, the name of the westernmost Lukungun local group. The Lukungun spoke a dialect of Northern Straits Coast Salish; other dialects of this language are or recently were spoken by the Saanich people on the Saanich Peninsula and adjacent islands, the Semiahmoo on the mainland around Semiahmoo Bay, the Lummi with their principal winter villages on Hale Passage near Bellingham, and the Samish in villages on Samish and Guemes Islands. The members of today's Esquimalt and Songhees Nations living on Indian Reserves in Esquimalt, adjacent to Victoria, are the descendants of the original Lukungun local groups (Boas 1887f; 1891d; Hill-Tout 1907; Duff 1969; Suttles 1951; 1990; 2001).

    While our annotating of this section is based primarily on the available literature, we also draw upon our 1971–1975 consultation with Christopher Paul, whose assistance we gratefully acknowledge.

2. Christopher Paul, who spoke both Saanich Northern Straits and Island Halkomelem, was told this story by his Cowichan grandfather who pointed out that these "Stonehead" people were said to have lived on Green Point, at the mouth of the north arm of the Cowichan River.

some arrows for him and he shot birds and brought them home. The mother was amazed how quickly he grew up. Soon he began hunting for bigger game and finally even shot deer. Now they had ample food supplies. She now named him K·'ē'sᴇk· (= tied one).[3] When he was an adult, he killed many birds, dried their skins and made a cape from them. He wanted to catch an eagle. To this end he took a heap of grass and went to a clearing. There he wrapped his body in inner cedar bark and lay down, stretching out his arms. Then he covered himself completely with grass. It wasn't long before an eagle swooped down on him. He caught it and killed it. One day he asked his mother, "How did it come about, Mother, that we live here all alone?" She answered, "Don't ask, my son," and began to weep. So he persisted and asked her again, "How did it come about, Mother, that we live here all alone?" But she gave him no answer. One day, he returned home from the hunt and said that he had seen people by the water. He asked his mother, "They make so much noise; why don't we go there and live with them?" "My son," the mother replied, "keep away from those people; they have heads of stone." But he continued, "How did it come about, Mother, that we live here all alone in the woods? The people down by the sea always play and have lots of fun." So she said, "My son, listen to what I will tell you. Do you know why we are living here all alone? All your relatives are dead; we are here all alone. Those people have killed them." He didn't answer and one day said, "Mother, I'll go to the sea and look at those people." He took his cape of bird skins; it was very beautiful and shiny. He went down to the sea. When the Mᴇnmā'ntauk· saw him, they were afraid because he looked as if he had supernatural powers. He returned to his mother and said, "I've seen those people." His mother warned him again of going to the sea. But he didn't listen to her. He went into the forest and made himself a club of oak. He tried it and it splintered. He tried clubs of all sorts of wood but they all splintered. At last he took wood from the yew (? tlink·'ätltc).[4] It did not splinter. When one day he heard them playing again, he put on his shiny cape, took his club and killed all the men. His cape made him invisible. Then he led the women away, went to his mother and said, "This land now belongs to us. I have killed all the Mᴇnmā'ntauk·."

3.   What Boas transcribes as "K·'ē'sᴇk·" is q̓íseq which means, literally, 'tied genitals'; this term is pronounced the same in both Island Halkomelem and Northern Straits.

4.   While Boas indicates doubt here, the Native word that he renders as "tlink·'ätltc" is ƛ'əŋ'q̓ɛ́łč which is the correct Northern Straits term for 'western yew' (*Taxus brevifolia*); the Island Halkomelem equivalent is təx̌ʷá?cəłp.

2. The Wives of the Stars

There was once a chief who had two daughters. During the summer the people moved to a camp where they fished for salmon. One day the girls went into the forest. At night they lay down among the trees and looked at the stars. The elder sister said, "I wish the big star up there (Jupiter) would be my husband." And the younger one said, "I wish the red star there (Mars) would be my husband." Then they fell asleep. When they awoke, they found themselves in a strange land. The stars had taken them into the sky. Now they saw that the stars were men. The shiny star's eyes were sick. And what they had wished for came to pass. The stars became their husbands. The following day their husbands told them to go out and collect onions.[5] But they forbade them to dig up the bulbs as is done on earth; instead, they were only allowed to cut off the stalks. To start with, the women obeyed, but one day the elder sister said, "I simply must eat an onion again." She dug one up and to their amazement they were looking down upon the earth through the hole. When they arrived home, they didn't say anything about this. They still went to the forest as before to gather onion stalks. But now they made a long rope there, without anyone knowing about it. When they thought that it was long enough, they made a big hole in the ground and the oldest daughter crawled down. She said to her sister, "You wait here. When I have arrived down there safely, I'll shake the rope; then follow me down. Otherwise assume that I've fallen into the sea." The younger sister then lowered the rope. At last the woman landed on Mount Ñgáʹk·un (some miles above the upper part of Victoria Harbour).[6] There, she walked back and forth over a long distance and pulled the rope to and fro. Thus she was able at last to shake it a little bit and her sister up in the sky felt some very weak movements. She tied the rope to a tree up there, clasped it with her hands and legs and climbed down. The elder sister sat down below and looked up. Finally she saw a small moving dot. It grew bigger and bigger and then she recognized her sister. Her legs had become quite crooked from climbing so long. She had scarcely arrived at the bottom, when the rope fell down. The people in the sky had missed the women and when they had discovered the rope, they cut it. Then the women went to their home. Their mother had quite forgotten them because they had been away for so long. Her hair had become grey and her eyes dim from weeping so much. They hid close to a pond. Soon, their youngest sister arrived to fetch water. Her hair was cropped because she

---

5.   The reference is to wild onions (*Allium cernuum* and *A. acuminatum*).

6.   What Boas transcribes here as "Ñgáʹk·un" is a Northern Straits term that is likely ŋeʹʔqən, possibly derived from sŋeʹnət 'rock; mountain,' or ŋeʹqə 'snow on ground.' This name, anglicized as "Knockan," is applied to Knockan Hill which is located just north of the upper end of Portage Inlet, about 3 miles (5 km) northwest from Victoria. In a variant of this legend recorded in the 1860s (Brown 1873:131–134), "Knochan" is said to mean 'coiled up,' but this does not appear to be linguistically supportable.

still mourned for her lost sisters. So they stroked her hair and immediately it became long again. The girl ran back and said, "My sisters are sitting out there by the pond." The old people said, "Don't be silly," and forbade her to say this. She went out once more and, after she had seen her sisters again, she ran back and repeated that her sisters were by the pond. When she said it for the third time, her mother beat her. So she went out again. Each time she came to the pond, her sisters stroked her hair and it became longer and longer. Then she ran back the fourth time, pointed to her long hair and said that her sisters had made it so long. So the old people thought that she might be telling the truth, after all. They went to the pond and found the women. The girls stroked their mother's hair and at once it became long and black again.

A young man who obeys the laws scrupulously, bathes frequently and has never touched a woman, is able to see the rope on Mount Ñgā′k·un. It is invisible for other people.

VIII. Legends of the Comox

Boas spent a substantial amount of time (12 November to 2 December 1886) with Comox people in their home village, with favourable results. "I have obtained two stories and am again very busy," Boas wrote in his diary the day after arrival (Rohner 1969:59). Presumably he was using Chinook Jargon at this point, but he was working up a vocabulary of the Comox language and within a few days he could announce that he had a text. On 19 November he writes, presumably of "Mary" the Native consultant named at the end of story 15: "I have found a Comox woman who dictates very well and am therefore taking the opportunity to learn Comox well" (Rohner 1969:62). By the end of his stay, Boas' knowledge of the Comox language has improved—he is able to follow conversations and speak a few phrases himself (Rohner 1969:67).

Boas' "Çal'ō'ltq Texts," part of the Comox manuscript materials held by the National Anthropological Archives of the Smithsonian Institution, indicate that the following *Sagen* stories may have been derived from the interlinear translations of the Comox language oral narratives, with some literary embellishment, or from other versions of the stories. Regardless of the parentage of the *Sagen* texts, Comox language versions exist for the following: No. 1, part 4; No. 4, parts 1, 2, 5, 8, 14, 15, 15b, 16; and No. 5, part 6. "Çal'ō'ltq Texts" (Boas n.d.2) also provides a lengthy version of No. 17, which is only referenced briefly in the *Sagen*. Several Comox stories printed in the *Sagen* have appeared in Boas' own English translation in "Myths and Legends of the Çatloltq of Vancouver Island." These stories are: No. 1, parts 1–7; No. 2; No. 3 (both versions); No. 4, parts 1–8 and 11–16; No. 7; and No. 9 (Boas 1888h:210–211; 366–373).

Comox Harbour Village, *ca.* 1870, showing both aboriginal and modern gabled-roof houses. The highest pole commemorates a high-status Comox man, his wife and daughter. It shows the three dressed in fine western clothes, and the man holding a carved wooden head in recognition of the day he beheaded eleven of his enemies. A flag with three streamers flies from the top. Cakes of berries dry in the sun on the wooden racks in the foreground.
Royal British Columbia Museum, Victoria, B.C. PN879 (Frederick Dally photo).

Village of x̣ʷəˀsam at Salmon River, 1881, with both Coast Salish and Kwakwaka'wakw (Southern Kwakiutl) style canoes pulled up on shore.
American Museum of Natural History Library, New York. Neg. No. 42272
(Edward Dossetter photo).

VIII. Legends of the Çatlōltq[1]

1. Kumsnō'otl (= our elder brother)[2]

1) Kumsnō'otl descended from the sky and wandered all over the world. On his

---

1. Boas uses the Native term "Catlo'ltq" to refer to the Coast Salish people referred to as either Island Comox or Comox, whose territory formerly extended along Vancouver Island's east coast between Salmon River and the vicinity of Kye Bay/Cape Lazo (just north from Comox Harbour), including the islands offshore. Descendants of these original Island Comox people presently live in the Comox Harbour village, which was originally in the territory of the Pentlatch Coast Salish (see Section XII). The few remaining Pentlatch became absorbed into the Island Comox who had been driven south from their own territory due to the southward expansion of the Lekwiltok that began in the mid-1700s or earlier (see Section XIV). Today, Lekwiltok people reside at the former Island Comox village sites of Cape Mudge and Campbell River, and the Comox Band has both Coast Salish and Lekwiltok affiliations. Speakers of Comox, together with Pentlatch and Sechelt, are classified linguistically as members of the Central division of the Salishan language family, and culturally comprise the Northern Coast Salish (Boas 1887a:230; 1887b:62–64; 1887e:map; 1887f:131–132, map; 1888:201; 1891d:608–609; Barnett 1955:24–25; Taylor and Duff 1956; Duff 1965; Kennedy and Bouchard 1983:16–27; 1990b:441; Mauzé 1984; 1992; Assu and Inglis 1989; Galois 1994).

    Comox is a Coast Salish language which has two main dialects, Island Comox and Mainland Comox (comprised of Sliammon, Klahoose, and Homalco), the latter spoken by people whose traditional lands extended along the mainland coast and offshore islands between Stillwater and the vicinity of Bute Inlet (see Sections IX and X). (The last fluent speaker of the Island Comox dialect, Mary Clifton, died in 1995.) Although the legends appearing in the following pages are from the Island Comox, it appears that at least one of Boas' storytellers was from the Mainland, as the Mainland Comox dialect has "θ" where Island Comox has "s"; this explains Boas' use of the term "Çatlōltq," that is, θáɫúɫtxʷ, the Mainland Comox pronunciation of the term referring to the Island Comox people, rather than "Sa'tlōtq", i.e. sáɫuɫtxʷ, the Island Comox pronunciation of this same term (where "s" is substituted for "ç" which is Boas' equivalent of "θ").

    In annotating this section, we have drawn upon our consultation in the 1970s–1980s with the following Comox-speaking people, all of whose assistance we gratefully acknowledge: Island Comox: Mary Clifton; Klahoose: Rose Mitchell, Bill Mitchell, and Jeannie Dominick; Homalco: Ambrose Wilson and Tommy Paul.

2. "Kumsnō'otl," said to mean 'our elder brother,' was identified elsewhere by Boas (1916:1019) as a Transformer figure. This Native term is not now known and is different than the word xáxgi·tən 'Transformer' used by the Comox-speaking people with whom we consulted.

travels he was accompanied by P'a, Raven,[3] by K·a'iq, Mink[4] and by Ts'ē'selētl (a colourful bird).[5] Once they came to a man called K·oā'lawāisit,[6] who knew that Kumsnō'otl would come to him, and who intended to kill him. To this end, he piled up a lot of resinous wood inside his house and invited Kumsnō'otl and P'a to a meal. When they were in the house, he set the pile alight, then seized Kumsnō'otl and flung him into the fire.[7] But the latter crawled into a log and caused it not to burn, even though all the wood around was in full blaze. Raven flew out of the smoke-hole. When the fire had burned down, Kumsnō'otl came out of the log. Kumsnō'otl took a magic substance and sprinkled it on K·oā'lawāisit; thereupon he was transformed into a stone.

2) And Kumsnō'otl walked on. Once he arrived at Qu'sam (Salmon River).[8] There he met a man called Çōçē'nēus,[9] whose whole body was covered with mouths. He laughed incessantly and made a noise as if hundreds of people were together. Kumsnō'otl said, "It is not good that you are so noisy," and transformed him into a stone which can still be seen today in Qu'sam.

3) And he wandered on. Soon he met a man called Kō'ma (a species of cod),[10] who was a mighty sorcerer.[11] Kumsnō'otl then said to his companions, "Let's not go any closer; I'm afraid of him." Thereupon Kō'ma laughed and called out, "Why are you afraid? Maybe because I am a powerful sorcerer? But I do harm to no one; I'm only happy that the weather is so nice." But Kumsnō'otl was afraid of him. Therefore he seized him and threw him into the water. He gave him a short tail and transformed him into a big fat fish, calling out, "Since you were a sorcerer, people shall use you

---

3.   What Boas transcribes as "P'a" is p̓ah, the Comox term for 'Raven' in mythology; the word for 'raven' in normal Comox speech is p̓úhu.

4.   The term transcribed by Boas as "K·a'iq" is the term qayx̱, the name for 'Mink' in Comox legends.

5.   This name of a "colourful bird" that is transcribed by Boas as "Ts'ē'selētl" is not now recognized, nor is what appears to be a variant of the same name, "Ts'i'tcilitl," given in story 11 of this same section.

6.   This term is not now recognized.

7.   Boas (1888h:202) states that both "Kumsnō'otl" and "P'a" were thrown into the fire.

8.   "Qu'sam" is Boas' rendering of the Comox term x̱ʷə'sam ('having fat or oil'), referring to a former Island Comox village site located at the mouth of the Salmon River on the east coast of Vancouver Island, near the community of Kelsey Bay (Kennedy and Bouchard 1990b:442–443).

9.   Boas (1916:596, 1019) translates "Çōçē'nēus" as 'mouth body'; here, it is given in the Mainland Comox, not Island Comox, dialect.

10.   The term transcribed by Boas as "Kō'ma" is kʷúma, the Comox term for ratfish (*Hydrolagus colliei*); the identification given by Boas (1888h:202) of this same fish as "*Gadus* sp." is incorrect.

11.   Given in the *Sagen* as *Zauberer* which means 'sorcerer.' Boas (1888h:202) also used the English term 'sorcerer' in his own translation of this legend, although in summarizing this same story elsewhere, he uses the English word 'shaman' (Boas 1916:1019).

henceforth to cure their illnesses." Therefore the fat of this fish is rendered and used as medicine.

4) And Kumsnō'otl went to K·'o'djomēn.[12] A woman sat there and sang to the nearby Mount Kō'kuanan,[13] "Oh, move to the side a bit so that I'll be able to look past you! My cheeks are sore from crying because I'm unable to look past you!" When Kumsnō'otl came, Mount Kō'kuanan grew ashamed and moved aside.

5) And he went on to a place where a monster in the shape of an octopus[14] lived in a lake and devoured anyone coming down to get water. Nobody dared to go down any more and the village's inhabitants died of thirst. Only one old man was resourceful. He went across to Mit'lnatc Island[15] every day and caught red snapper.[16] He rendered the fat and drank it. Thus it came about that he and his grandchild survived while everyone around died. When Kumsnō'otl arrived and noticed the misery of the villagers, he resolved to kill the monster. He told his companions to heat big flat stones. When the stones were hot, he put one on as a hat and with the others covered his body. Then he took a bucket in his hand, went down to the lake and splashed in the water, in order to attract the attention of the octopus. It wasn't long before it surfaced and stretched out its long arms in order to pull Kumsnō'otl down to its mouth. But as soon as it touched the glowing stones with its suction cups, these fell off. At last the monster even jumped onto Kumsnō'otl's head and nearly overcame him, but the glowing stone which he wore as a hat killed it. Then Kumsnō'otl cut the octopus up and flung the parts in all directions into the sea. He said, "You shall transform yourself into many octopuses and in future serve as food

---

12. "K·'o'djomēn" is q̓ʷújumin meaning 'defecation place,' the Island Comox pronunciation of the Comox term referring both to Little Bear River (now known as Pye Creek) and to Little Bear Bay, into which this creek enters; the creek and bay are situated on the east coast of Vancouver Island, about 28 miles (45 km) north from the town of Campbell River and opposite East Thurlow Island. The Mainland Comox pronunciation of this same place name is q̓ʷújúmin (see also story 12 of the present section).

13. Given in the manuscript version of this same story as "kōkuā'nan (hill? or mountain)" (Boas n.d.2) although neither this Island Comox term nor the location of this place (presumably, it is near Little Bear Bay) are now known.

14. *Tintenfisch* 'octopus; squid' in the original *Sagen*, but in this context it is clearly an octopus. Boas (1888h:202) uses the English term 'squid' in his own translation of this legend, but uses the term 'water monster' in his summary of this same tale (Boas 1916:1019).

15. "Mit'lnatc" is Boas' transcription of the Comox term məʼƛ'nəč 'calm back end' which is applied to Mitlenatch (anglicized from məʼƛ'nəč) Island, located in the Strait of Georgia between Shelter Point on the east side of Vancouver Island, and Hernando Island (Kennedy and Bouchard 1983:161–163).

16. Given in the *Sagen* as *rothen Schellfish* meaning literally 'red haddock,' but referring to the species known commonly as the 'red snapper' or 'yelloweye rockfish' (*Sebastes ruberrimus*). In his own translation of this story, Boas (1888h:202) uses the English term 'red cod.'

for people."[17] He threw the stomach onto the land, where it was transformed into a huge stone.[18] He plunged the head into the sea close to Cape Mudge,[19] where it creates the dangerous whirlpools and currents even today.

6) And Kumsnō'otl took a paint pot, painted all the people with bright colours, and then transformed them into birds. All the while P'a kept shouting, "Oh, that is beautiful; paint me too, but paint me really colourfully!" Finally Kumsnō'otl became exasperated at this and covered him all over with black paint. That is why the raven is black.

7) In the beginning the water always ran through Seymour Narrows[20] in the same direction. When Kumsnō'otl came there during his travels, he caused the current to run in opposite directions during ebb and flood-tides.

8) And Kumsnō'otl walked on and met a man called K·ē'u (Deer).[21] (This legend and the one of the origin of the Heron[22] who lived at Seymour Narrows are identical with the corresponding legends of the Nak·o'mgyilisala.)[23]

2. Pitch and the Sun[24]

A long time ago Pitch was a man called Mōmhānā'tc.[25] He was blind. Since he couldn't bear the warmth of the sun, he went out to catch red snapper at night. Consequently, in the morning, at daybreak, his wife called to him, "Come home quickly; the sun is rising." Thus he always returned home before it got warm. But

17. Boas' (1888h:203) own published translation of this story gives this passage as follows: "As you have eaten men, henceforth men shall eat you."

18. Known locally as the "Big Rock," on the beach near Willow Point, south of Campbell River; however, Comox-speaking storytellers in the 1970s told us that the "Big Rock" is actually the Whale who went ashore in the "Mink and the Whale" legend (see story 4, part 15b, of the present section); a photograph of this rock can be found in Kennedy and Bouchard (1983:106).

19. Cape Mudge is situated on the south end of Quadra Island, opposite Campbell River.

20. Seymour Narrows, between Vancouver Island and Quadra Island, is situated about 10 miles (16 km) north of Campbell River

21. The term "K·ē'u" is recognized as qiw, the name of 'Deer' in Comox mythology; the term *Hirsch*, ('deer') is used here in the original (see also story 8 in this section).

22. Appears as *Kranich* 'crane' in the original; the species is actually the Great Blue Heron (*Ardea herodias*) (see also story 3 in this section).

23. The corresponding legends of the Nakomgilisala (Boas' "Nak·o'mgyilisala") are in Section XIX, story 1, parts 23 and 25.

24. In his own translation of this story, Boas (1888h:204) uses the English term 'gum'; elsewhere he summarizes this story as "Sun Kills Little Pitch" (Boas 1916:1019).

25. What Boas transcribes here as "Mōmhānā'tc" is possibly mímkʷnač, the Comox name for the bird known as the Horned Grebe (*Podiceps auritus*); the normal Comox word for 'pitch,' is qʷáwił.

one day the woman slept in, and when she woke up she saw that it was bright daylight. Frightened, she ran down to the beach and called to her husband, "Come quickly; the sun is already high in the sky." He paddled as fast as he could, but it was too late! The sun shone down so hot on him that he melted before he arrived. Thereupon his two sons became sad and said to each other, "What are we to do? We will avenge our father." And they resolved to climb into the sky and kill the sun. They took their bows and arrows and went to the spot where the sun rises. There they shot at the sky. The first arrow stuck in the sky. The second hit the first and in this way they continued until a long chain had been formed which reached from the sky down to the earth. The elder brother shook it in order to see whether it was strong enough. He found the chain of arrows strong and both brothers climbed up along it. When they had reached the sky, they killed the sun with their arrows. Then they thought, "What should we do now?" And the older one said, "Let's become the sun." And he asked his younger brother where he wanted to go. The younger brother answered, "I want to go to the night; you go to the day," and thus it came to pass. The younger brother became the moon, and the elder, the sun.

3. Tlā′ik·[26]

Once there lived a chief up in the sky who was named Tlā′ik·. He had two beautiful daughters, and many young men came to court them. But Tlā′ik· would not tolerate their marrying and he killed all their suitors. In those days there lived here below a chief called Aiē′len (Good Weather),[27] who had two sons. In the mornings the boys were in the habit of going to the forest, and when their father asked them what they were doing there, they said that they wanted to light a big fire. But in reality they secretly looked for fern roots and ate them. At last they had eaten so many of them that fibrous roots grew out from between their fingers. Thereupon their father grew angry and shouted, "Don't waste your time with useless things; rather go and get the daughters of Tlā′ik·! Don't you know that all the young men are courting them?" The boys took their father's words to heart. They went out with their bows and arrows and began to shoot at the sky. When they had thus made a chain of arrows that reached from the sky down to the earth, the elder brother shook it in order to test whether it was strong enough. Since he found it strong, both brothers climbed up and crawled through a hole in the dome of the sky. They found a path up there and walked along it. And while they were thus walking they said to each other, "We

---

26.   What Boas transcribes here as "Tlā′ik·" is recognized as the character named x̣'ayk̓ʷ; Boas (1887c) elsewhere identifies this as "the sun legend."

27.   In the second version of this legend that follows, Boas identifies "Aiē′len" as "the name of the sun as a human."

will marry the daughters of Tlā'ik· and shame him." But Aiē'len wept because he believed his children were dead.

When the brothers had walked for a short way, they met a row of blind women sitting around a fire, cooking shoots (pE'k·cin).[28] One of them dished out the finished meal to all the others. Then the elder brother stepped on her cape and the younger one took all the full bowls from her hand and hid them in the fold of his cape. When she thought that she had distributed everything, she asked her companions, "Have all of you got your food?" But they replied, "No, you haven't given us anything yet." So she said, "Then someone must be here who has taken our food away." So they all called out with one voice, "Oh stranger, make us see; have pity on us!" The brothers chewed some roots and then spat on the eyes of the women. Thereupon they were able to see and flew away as ducks.[29] Only the one whose cape the elder brother held fast with his foot, couldn't escape. He said to her, "Tell us where Tlā'ik· lives. We want to marry his daughters." Duck replied, "Oh, Tlā'ik· is a very wicked man; he kills all the suitors of his daughters. If you want to carry through your intention, go and see your grandfather first; he will give you a magic substance so that you will be able to withstand Tlā'ik·."

The young men followed Duck's advice. They walked on and arrived at the house of their grandfather, Pā'cin (One-leg = Heron).[30] Because he was not at home, they went on to look for him. On their way they met a snake (not the Aihōs)[31] and took away its cape. Now when they saw their grandfather from far away standing by a creek, where he was fishing for salmon, they changed into salmon by putting on the cape of the snake. Then they swam to the spot where their grandfather was standing, harpoon in hand. When they came to him, they stopped swimming. As soon as he saw the two salmon close to him, he hurled his harpoon, hit both with one strike and pulled them ashore. But when he reached for his fish-club to kill the fish, they changed into his grandsons and laughed heartily because they had deceived One-leg in this way. "Oh, my grandsons," said One-leg, "where are you coming from? Where are you going?" "We want to marry the daughters of Tlā'ik·," they replied. "Then come along into my house first of all so that I may make you strong," said One-leg. He led the way and the young men followed. When they had arrived inside

---

28. The term for the "shoots" transcribed by Boas as "pE'k·cin" is pə'qšin, the Comox word for the plant known as 'sea milkwort' (*Glaux maritima*).

29. In contemporary Mainland Comox versions of this same legend, these birds are identified as Mallards (*Anas platyrhynchos*).

30. The term given here by Boas as "Pā'cin" is pá?šin which means literally 'one leg,' as Boas notes. While this is a descriptive name applied here to the Great Blue Heron, the usual Comox name for this bird is pal', and its mythological name is x^wiq.

31. Boas' "Aihōs" is ?áyhus, the Comox name for the 'double-headed serpent.'

the house he continued, "To start with, Tlā'ik· will offer you a porcupine as a seat. Sit down on this stone so that you will pass the test!" While he said this, he made them sit down on a slab of slate. Then their behinds were transformed into stone. Then he anointed their whole bodies with a magic herb and threw a black, hard stone (mE'sais, basalt?)[32] into the fire so that it glowed, pulled it out of the flames with tongs and put it into the young men's mouths. He had told them before to jump up quickly as soon as he released the stone. They obeyed, and so the stone fell right through them without doing them any harm. Then he gave a wedge to each of the young men and said, "The daughters of Tlā'ik· have teeth in their vaginas, just like in their mouths. With them they bite off your penises when you sleep with them; therefore take these wedges, let them bite onto these and then pull out their teeth." He told them the way to the well of Tlā'ik· and told them that they would find the girls there.

They arrived there safely and sat down on the branches of a tree which stood near the well. Soon the two girls stepped from the house and sang, "The sons of Tlēqē'len (Bad Weather) shall not become our husbands, but the sons of Aiē'len shall." The two young men were glad when they heard this. The following morning the two girls came to the well again to fetch water. When they bent down to the water, they saw the reflection of the young men and began to cry because they thought that they had drowned and were laying on the bottom of the water. So one of the young men spat into the water to attract their attention. Then they saw them among the branches of the tree and were glad that they were not in the water. The two young men jumped down. The older one took the elder girl, the younger one the younger girl, and they went into the house together. But while they were walking up to the house, they could hear the teeth grinding in the girls' vaginas.

They came into the house and there Tlā'ik· told them to sit on a porcupine. Since their behinds were of stone, they passed this test. Then he put the glowing stones into their mouths. They jumped up quickly as their grandfather had taught them and were not harmed. The girls were glad of this. When night fell the young men went with the girls to their chambers. But when they slept with them, they let them bite the wedges first and then pulled out the teeth. It is well that they did this, otherwise women would still have teeth in their vaginas today. When Tlā'ik· found the young men still alive in the morning, he grew angry and resolved to get rid of them in some other way. He had felled a tree and was busy splitting it up into boards. One day he asked his sons-in-law to come along and help him. They guessed his evil intentions and therefore first went into the forest to their

---

32. This stone is not identified, other than here, and the Native term "mE'sais" (presumably, "mə'says") is not now recognized. Boas omits the question mark in his 1888 publication of this story (Boas 1888h:206).

grandfather, T'amt'am (a bird)[33] and asked him for his cape. They also took red and white paint along. When they arrived at the felled tree, they saw that Tlā′ik· had already split it wide open with wedges. He was just driving in another wedge when all of a sudden he dropped his hammer,[34] which fell into the gaping tree. Then he asked the young men, "Oh, please crawl into the tree and fetch my hammer." They did so. But they were scarcely inside when Tlā′ik· knocked out the wedge and the tree snapped shut with great force. The young men both flew away as birds and left the red and white paint inside the tree. It oozed out of the crack like blood and brains and Tlā′ik· thought that he had finally killed his sons-in-law. But they had flown home and there had changed back to their normal shape. How Tlā′ik· marvelled when he saw them sitting safe and sound by the fire. He was full of shame.

And he pondered how he could kill his sons-in-law. Early in the morning he flung his dog into the sea and made it transform itself into a diver.[35] Then he called to his sons-in-law, "Get up and catch this bird." The brothers took bows and arrows, ran down to the shore and shot at the diver. They hit it many times, but the bird couldn't be killed and swam farther and farther away. Tlā′ik· said, "Oh, take my small canoe and go after it; surely you'll catch it easily." They did what Tlā′ik· had told them and pursued the bird, which lured them far from land. Then Tlā′ik· called the wind and caused a wild storm which was to swallow the canoe. But the young men started to sing and beat time on the gunwale. Thereupon it became good weather all around the canoe because they were the sons of Aiē′len. They went home, and, bad as the storm might rage, where their canoe was, the sea was calm.

The young men resolved to avenge themselves upon Tlā′ik·, should he try again to harm them. The following morning, Tlā′ik· called out to them, "Come, let's go and catch red snapper." So they went first to their grandfather, K·u′lk·uls (a small diver)[36] and borrowed his cape. They also took pitch along which they chewed on their way and formed into the shapes of whales, sharks and sea lions. When they had arrived at the fishing bar, Tlā′ik· set his line. So the young men thought, "Oh, if only the hook would catch on the bottom." They had hardly thought it when Tlā′ik·'s fishing gear caught on the ocean floor. At once they threw the kneaded shapes of

---

33. What Boas transcribes as "T'amt'am" is (s)t'ə′mt'əm, but this is not a Comox word; rather, it is the term for 'wren' (likely the Winter Wren, *Troglodytes troglodytes*) in the Sechelt language (the Sechelt are a closely-related Coast Salish group living immediately south of the Mainland Comox). Comox-speaking people point out that Wren speaks Sechelt in legends, so it is appropriate to find the Sechelt term here—the word for 'wren' in the Comox language is č′úč′u?.

34. *Hammer* 'hammer' in the original *Sagen*, and translated by Boas (1888h:207) as 'stone hammer'; very likely the reference is to a hand maul.

35. Boas uses the German term *Taucher* 'diver' in the *Sagen*; this term designates grebes and loons, both of which are found in this area.

36. Possibly a type of loon; the term Boas transcribes here as "K·u′lk·uls" is not now recognized.

pitch into the water. They transformed into real animals which all played around Tlā′ik·'s canoe. The young men jumped into the water as divers and swam home.

Tlā′ik· was so terrified by all this that his entrails fell out of his anus. He paddled home slowly. When his youngest son saw him, he called out, "Oh, what a lot of fish our father caught!" because he took the entrails laying in the bottom of the canoe to be fish. But Tlā′ik· moaned and groaned. So the two young men said to the boy, "Shoot at your father with your small arrows." The boy obeyed and, as soon as he had hit him, the entrails retracted into his body. But Tlā′ik· still felt very sick. He lay inside his house by the fire, which was burning very low because he had no more wood. So he sent his sons-in-law into the forest to get firewood. They obeyed and went to their grandfather, Woodpecker. They requested, "Order the bark to fall down." Woodpecker fulfilled their request and a large piece of bark fell to the ground. They carried it home and here broke it up into many pieces. They gave a small piece to the son of Tlā′ik· and said, "Take this to your father." The boy obeyed. But when Tlā′ik· saw the small piece of bark, he grew very angry, because he wanted to have a lot of wood in order to make a huge fire. The two men paid no attention to his scolding and continued to break up the bark. It became more and more and finally filled all the houses.

Then it occurred to Tlā′ik· that he would like to have cranberries although it was the middle of winter. The young men went to their grandfather (another aquatic bird)[37] and asked him to whistle. He fulfilled their request and when he whistled, all the bushes began to bud. When he continued whistling, they bloomed and at last bore fruit. The two then collected a small pailful and carried it home. There they ate to their hearts' delight. When Tlā′ik· saw this, he asked for some berries, too, and his sons-in-law gave him a small bowlful. As quickly as he might eat them, the bowl didn't get empty. In the end, he lost his patience and threw the bowl away. At once a cranberry bush sprouted from his navel.

Then Tlā′ik· demanded that his sons-in-law should catch Woodpecker for him. They went to their grandfather, Woodpecker, and while they carried him home, they whispered to him, "Peck out Tlā′ik·'s eyes, but before that, torture him." When they entered the house, Woodpecker hopped onto the belly of Tlā′ik· and pecked at him with his beak. Then he hopped up higher and higher, pecking all the while with his beak. At last he reached Tlā′ik·'s head. Tlā′ik· twisted his head to and fro in order to escape from Woodpecker, but in vain! Woodpecker pecked out the eyes of Tlā′ik·.

---

37. Throughout this region, it is salmonberries (*Rubus spectabilis*), not "cranberries" (mentioned in the preceding sentence of the original *Sagen*) that are believed to be ripened by the whistling of a bird, and the bird in question is not an "aquatic bird" (as Boas states here), but rather the Swainson's Thrush (*Hylocichla ustulata*), which is known as xʷət in the Comox language (see also story 11 of this section).

Then Tlā'ik· wanted to have the Aihōs, the double-headed serpent, in order to ruin the brothers. The younger one caught it, and, while he carried it home, whispered to it, "Devour Tlā'ik·." It obeyed. One head devoured him, starting from his head, and the other, starting from his behind. Thus he died. The brothers threw his corpse down to the earth.

Tlā'ik· (Second version)

Two young men, the sons of Aiē'len (Aiē'len is the name of the sun as a human),[38] went out in their canoe to catch birds. When they were far out to sea, they started to shoot their arrows at the sky, and didn't stop until a chain of arrows reached down to earth from the sky. Then the elder brother stood up in the canoe, shook the chain and found it strong. So he said to his brother, "I am going to climb into the sky now. Don't cry for me, but return home, sit down on the house roof and be cheerful and in good spirits." Then he began to climb, and the younger brother soon lost sight of him. He returned and said to his father, "I've lost my older brother. I don't know where he got to. He must be dead." Thereupon everybody who heard this, wept. But he went up onto the roof of the house and played there, because he knew that his brother was in the sky.

When the elder brother had reached the sky, he found a path which led through a beautiful, flat countryside. He saw smoke rising far in the distance. He walked towards it and met Octopus, who lay there cozily chewing pitch.[39] The young man requested, "Oh, give me some pitch." Octopus replied, "What do you want with it? You won't be able to use it for your teeth." But he requested again, "Oh, give me some pitch and your blanket."[40] Thereupon Octopus gave him both.

The young man walked on. Soon he again saw smoke rising far in the distance. When he came closer, he found a row of blind women sitting around a fire etc. (see above, page 65).[41] He asked the duck that was left behind, "Where does Tlā'ik· live? I want to marry his daughter." Duck said, "Just follow this path and you will get to

38. In his own translation, Boas (1888h:209) gives this as "the name of the sun when spoken of as a human being." In story 3 here in the *Sagen*, which is the first variant of the "Tlā'ik·" legend, Boas translates "Aiē'len" as 'good weather.'

39. Boas (1888h:209) translates this as 'gum,' and uses the term 'squid' rather than 'octopus.' It is a common Coast Salish belief that octopuses chew pitch.

40. Given in the original as *Mantel* 'cape; cloak; outer covering,' rather than *Decke* 'blanket'; however, the fact that Boas (1888h:209) used the English term 'blanket' in his own translation, suggests that 'blanket' would be the more appropriate translation here.

41. Boas' reference here is to the first version of the "Tlā'ik·" legend which begins on page 65 of the original *Sagen*.

a lake where the girls usually swim. Tlā'ik· has four daughters, but don't on any account take one of the three older ones for a wife, because their vaginas are set with teeth; instead, take the youngest."[42] So the young man was glad and walked on. Soon he met Woodpecker, who gave him the same information.

At last he arrived at the lake. So he wrapped himself in the octopus blanket[43] and assumed the shape of an octopus. Soon he heard the four girls coming, singing, "Oh, if only the son of the sun would come to marry me." Finally they arrived at the pond where the young man lay in the shape of an octopus. Right in front was Yini'sak· (from yi'nis, tooth),[44] the eldest of the girls. When she caught sight of the animal, she got a big shock and cried, "Hoo! What kind of animal is lying there?" The others came running to see it, too, and then they said to each other, "We will take him home with us as a slave. When father goes out to catch deer, he shall help him." Yini'sak· tried to lift him up, but the octopus stuck himself fast so that she was unable to move him. So she called the second sister, who also was unable to move him from the spot. The third one fared no better. But when the youngest one wanted to lift him, he let go and went along willingly. She carried him home and put him down in front of the door.

Then the girls ran into the house to their father and said, "Oh, father, we have found a slave for you in the forest." "Where is he?" he asked. "We've put him down outside the door," replied the girls. So Tlā'ik· had them bring the slave into the house. At first Yini'sak· went to get him. But Octopus stuck himself fast and didn't let himself be picked up. The second and third sisters were just as unable to lift him, but when the youngest one came, he let go willingly and let himself be carried into the house.

She put him down beside the fire. Then, when Tlā'ik· and his daughters were eating salmon, the girls flung fish bones to him. But he accepted food only from the youngest one. During the night, he crept unnoticed into the youngest daughter's chamber, dropped the octopus blanket and climbed into bed with her. So she saw that he was the shiny Sun. And he said, "I am the son of Aiē'len. I know that you are better than your sisters; that's why I want you for my wife. But from now on, don't throw food to me as to a dog, but give me my meal in a bowl." When day came, he again wrapped himself in the octopus blanket and lay down by the fire.

---

42. The passage that begins here as "don't on any account take" and ends "instead, take the youngest," appears in Boas' (1888h:209) own translation with several words (referring to "toothed vaginas") excised, as follows: "Mind that you do not marry any of the elder ones, * * * Marry the youngest one."

43. Boas (1888h:209) translates this as 'blanket of the squid.'

44. The literal meaning of this Comox term is 'toothed-genitals,' which is consistent with what Boas (1916:1020) subsequently translated as 'vagina dentata.'

Again Yini′sak· and her sisters threw fish bones to him. But he didn't pay any attention to them and instead turned at once towards the youngest of the sisters, who gave him good food in a bowl, as he had requested. At night he crept into the youngest sister's chamber again and dropped his blanket, which he put on again in the morning.

The following morning, the people decided to go hunting for deer and said to each other, "We will seat Octopus in the back of the canoe; he shall steer." They asked Yini′sak· to carry him into the canoe, but she was unable to lift him, just like the second and third sisters. But the youngest one carried him into the canoe. When they arrived at the spot where they intended to hunt deer, Tlā′ik· told him to guard the canoe and to watch that the rope which tied it to shore didn't break. Then they all went hunting and Octopus was left in the canoe. But he had Woodpecker hidden under his blanket and whispered to him, "Fly onto the treetops and warn Deer so that he will run away." Woodpecker obeyed and thus it came about that the hunters returned empty-handed. They returned home and the girls wanted to carry their steersman, Octopus, into the house. But none of them was able to, except the youngest. At night he went to her again and took off his blanket in her chamber.

The following day, the people went out again to hunt deer and took Octopus along as steersman. They left him behind again and he sent out Woodpecker to scatter the deer. He had scarcely flown off, when the young man dropped the octopus blanket and now sat upright in the stern of the canoe. He shone as brightly as the sun. Then Tlā′ik· and the rest of the hunters again returned empty-handed. When he saw Sun sitting in his canoe, he grew afraid. He called out, "I will give you my eldest daughter as a wife." In answer, the young man shook his shoulders and thereupon the canoe floated far away from the shore. So Tlā′ik· called, "Then I'll give you my second daughter as a wife." Again he shook his shoulders and the canoe floated still farther from shore. He didn't want to have the third daughter, either, but when Tlā′ik· offered him his youngest daughter, he shook himself and the canoe floated back to the shore. When they went to hunt deer again, he whispered to Woodpecker, "Call all the deer to the shore here." He obeyed. The deer came and fell over the steep cliffs of the shore so that they lay there dead. While all the other hunters hadn't caught a thing, his canoe was completely filled, and when they returned, he had already dressed his game.

But Yini′sak· would have liked very much to have the young man for her husband. She said to her mother, "Oh, look, Mother, isn't he just like the sun?" And she made her bed nicely in order to attract him. The second and third sisters did the same. But the youngest one didn't pay any attention to him at all. Then Yini′sak· and her two younger sisters invited him into the house, but he stayed in the canoe until the youngest one called him. Then he took her publicly for his wife.

But Tlā′ik· only kept brooding how he could kill his son-in-law. He went into the forest to split a tree, etc. (See p. 67.[45] A woodpecker then flies out of the tree and closely past Tlā′ik·'s eyes; this was the young man.)

He resolved to take revenge on Tlā′ik· and asked his wife, "Do you know of anything which Tlā′ik· fears?" She answered, "He is afraid of whales and similar huge fish."[46] The following day, Tlā′ik· and his son-in-law went out to catch red snapper. Then the young man chewed the pitch which Octopus had given him and spat it into the sea. It transformed at once into whales, etc. (see p. 68.[47] Then Tlā′ik· comes home ill. Woodpecker is supposed to heal him, but the young man whispers to Woodpecker, "Peck out his eyes" etc.)

4. Mink

1) K·ā′iq, Mink, wanted to take a wife. He went to Fog who was lying on the mountain and said, "Come, be my wife." She replied, "You can't become my husband; what are you going to do when I play with my sisters and dance around the mountain?" "Oh," said Mink, "I will play and dance with you." So Fog agreed and they became man and wife. One day, Fog began to play with her sisters and they flew around the mountain in a circle. Mink wanted to dance with them, so his wife and one of his sisters-in-law grasped his hands and danced around with him. Since he couldn't follow quickly enough, they tore out his hands. He fell to the ground and lay there as though dead.

2) Then K·ā′iq went to Eagle and said, "Come, be my wife." "You can't become my husband," Eagle Maiden replied. "What are you going to do when I catch salmon in the sea?" "Oh," said Mink, "I will go with you." Thereupon Eagle agreed and they became man and wife. One day they both were sitting in a tree, looking down into the water. They waited for the arrival of the salmon. K·ā′iq had donned Eagle's cape in order to be able to fly. Then his wife warned him, "When you see a salmon, don't dive down too quickly, but fly steadily, or else you will fall." Mink promised, but when he saw the first salmon, he forgot the warning and rushed at it greedily. So he fell, and lay on the ground as though dead.

3) Then K·ā′iq went to Pitch and wanted to take her for his wife. "You can't become my husband," said Pitch. "What are you going to do when the sun blazes down on us and I melt?" Mink replied, "Then I'll jump to and fro so that I won't stick to you."

---

45. Boas is referring here to the first version of this story, on page 67 of the original *Sagen*.

46. Given in the original as *ähnlichen grossen Fischen* 'similar huge fish' but translated elsewhere by Boas (1888h:211) as 'other large sea animals.'

47. Boas is referring here to the first version of this story, on page 68 of the original *Sagen*.

He took her for his wife and they lay down together on a board. In the beginning, K·ā′iq jumped to and fro, but in the end he grew tired and fell asleep. Now the sun began to blaze down on them. Pitch melted and K·ā′iq's back stuck fast to the board. So he grew ashamed. He ran into the forest in order to rub off the board on the trees, but it only stuck faster. An old man observed him there and asked what he was doing. So Mink told him his misfortune and the old one helped him to rid himself of the board.

4) Then K·ā′iq went to Kelp and said, "I want to have you for my wife." So she said, "What will you do when my hair drifts to and fro with the tides?" "Oh," replied Mink, "then I'll cling to it." Thereupon Kelp took him for her husband. Now when the flood-tide came in strongly, K·ā′iq held fast to his wife's hair. But it drifted up and down violently and finally pulled him under so that he almost drowned.

5) Then Mink went to the Whale lice[48] on the beach and wanted to have one for a wife. After a while he was angry with his wife and beat her about the face so that blood ran off his fingers. "There you are," he said then, "that serves you right; now your face is bleeding." The woman answered, "No, you are bleeding." "Where am I bleeding"? asked Mink. She replied, "Just look at your hand." So K·ā′iq turned his left hand back and forth and said, "I am not bleeding at all!" "No, the other hand, the one you hit me with," replied the woman. But K·ā′iq pretended that he couldn't find the blood and only looked at his left hand.

6) And Mink wanted to marry a beautiful white woman, etc. (See among the legends of the Tlatlasik·oala.)[49]

7) And Mink wanted to marry the wife of Otter.[50] (See among the legends of the Kwakiutl.)[51]

---

48. Given in the original as *Walfischläusen*—the literal meaning of this artificially-constructed German term is 'whale lice,' reflecting the storyteller's familiarity with the Comox belief that barnacles are a whale's lice. Mainland Comox accounts of this same Mink legend recorded in the 1970s also identify this wife as Barnacle (for example, see "Mink Marries Barnacle" in Kennedy and Bouchard 1983:94). Boas (1888h:367), in his own English translation of this same legend, refers to the entity that Mink marries on this occasion as "sharp-edged shells on the beach" which he identifies as *Saxidromus squalidus*, the *circa* 1890 identification of what is now known as *Saxidromus giganteus*, the butter clam. In Boas' (n.d.2) interlinear translation of another story (which appears in the *Sagen* as No. 4, part 16), the Comox term "sē′k̲'oaē̅" is translated first as 'whale louse,' which is crossed out and replaced with the term 'barnacle.' The term "sē′k̲'oaē̅" is not now recognized; the contemporary Comox word for 'barnacle' (*Balanus glandula*) is θ'úmaʔju.

49. See story 20 in Section XVIII.

50. Elsewhere, Boas (1887c) identifies this character as "sea otter," but here in the *Sagen* he uses the German term *Otter* 'any otter,' rather than *Seeotter* 'sea otter.'

51. See story 1, part 7 in Section XVII.

8) And Mink married Grizzly Bear. He always lay idly by the fire with his brother
and let his wife catch salmon and collect fish roe. But then when winter came, his
wife didn't want to give him anything to eat but roots. So K·ā'iq stole dried fish roe
from the box where it was kept and tied it to his arm. When Bear saw his arm, she
asked, "What happened there?" K·ā'iq answered, "I smashed my arm when I was
getting wood." When Bear again gave him only roots to eat, he nibbled the fish roe.
Bear could hear the fish roe crunching between his teeth and asked what he was
eating. In reply, K·ā'iq only said, "Oh, how tasty these roots are!" But in the middle
of winter, the woman didn't give K·ā'iq and his brother anything to eat any more and
K·ā'iq's brother nearly starved. So K·ā'iq said to his wife one day, "Our enemies are
going to come and attack us; let's take away our provisions." Bear Woman was
deceived and she loaded their canoe with salmon, fish roe and berries, and allowed
K·ā'iq and his brother to paddle away with it. She, herself, took her basket on her
back in order to search first for firewood. Then she followed the two. She hadn't
gone far when she saw salmon skins and sticks on which fish roe had been dried,
lying on the shore. Thereupon she became angry because now she knew that Mink
had lied to her. She pursued the fugitives and everywhere on the shore found salmon
skins and sticks on which on which fish roe had been dried. At last she got to
Taū'seman (not far from present-day Comox).[52] There she saw a big fire by which
Mink and his brother lay and slept. Mink noticed that Bear Woman was coming and
sprang up just in time and ran away, but she caught his brother and bit off his throat.
Then she pursued K·ā'iq. But he created a big river between himself and Bear
Woman, who thus couldn't reach him. Then he sat down and wept for his brother.
He said to a tree, "Oh, fall down and kill me! I would like to go to my brother." The
tree fell down at once and hit him straight in the face. But it was not able to kill him.
Then Mink begged a second tree. This one wasn't able to kill him either, and as
many trees as he asked, as many fell on him, but none were able to harm him.

9) A long time ago, women were able to take off their genitals; they grew onto their
bodies only after the deity was angry with them. When women went out to gather
berries in those days, they used to put their genitals in a box, which they tied up
tightly and put away. Once, when a number of women intended to go out, K·ā'iq
watched through a hole in the wall and saw how they took off their genitals and
packed them away. Among them there was a particularly beautiful white woman and
he wanted to get hold of her genitals. They had scarcely gone into the forest, when
he opened the box and threw everything out until he found the pretty woman's

52. What Boas transcribes here as "Taūseman" is táwusəman, meaning 'river along the beach,' the
Comox term for the place known as Little River, where the Comox-Powell River ferry landing is
presently located, about 5 miles (8 km) north from Comox Harbour (Kennedy and Bouchard
1983:169–170).

genitals. Then he threw the other genitals in again, tied up the box and went into his house. His heart was very glad. He lay down in bed and used the genitals to his heart's content. When he finally got up again, he saw that they had become very dirty. Therefore he washed them and dried them on the roof in the bright sunshine. Many girls were playing in the street and Mink first ran around among them, then ran back to the roof to see that nobody took the genitals away. He was very anxious that the genitals should become dry and clean again, because he expected the women to return at any moment. Lo, an eagle then flew over the house! It spied the genitals, swooped down upon them and carried them away in its claws. When K·ā′iq saw this he began singing, "Oh, Eagle, may your foot go to sleep." He beat time and had the girls join in. Thereupon Eagle's foot went to sleep and he dropped the genitals. K·ā′iq quickly picked them up but noticed that they had been badly scratched. He washed them quickly, dried them by the fire and threw them back again into the bottom of the box. Hardly had he tied up the box again, when the women returned, laughing and singing. And they said to each other, "Come, let's go and put our genitals back on." They did this. But when the pretty woman found hers in such terrible shape, she became sad and wept. She said, "Surely this is K·ā′iq's doing. Oh, if only he were dead."

10) On another occasion, some women were bathing in the river. K·ā′iq wanted to have one of them for himself and therefore changed into a trout which swam about close to the women. They attempted to catch the fish, but were unsuccessful. When the women stepped out of the water, K·ā′iq changed back into his real shape and hurried home, where he arrived before the women. When they told him that a nice trout had swum around so close to them, he said, "Oh, you could have caught it easily. All you had to do was sit with your legs apart." When the women bathed again on a different occasion, K·ā′iq swam up again in the shape of a trout. The women now did what he had told them. So he swam towards the beautiful woman and made her pregnant. She gave birth to a child after only a few days. All the women came and said to each other, "Whose child could it be?" Whereupon it cried out, "A! a! a! K·ā′iq is my father, K·ā′iq is my father." The child grew up quickly. The women carried it about in turn. As one of them held the child, it started to dirty her; but when she wanted to clean her clothing, she found it full of abalone shells.[53] When P'a, Raven, who was also in the house, saw this, he wanted to carry the child as well in order to get abalone shells, too, and shouted, "Give it to me; give it to me!" But another woman had a turn. When the child dirtied her, she received pure copper; thus it gave presents to all the women. But the last one whispered to the child, "When you get to P'a, don't give anything to him, but dirty him." And this is what

---

53. Given as *Haliotis-Schalen* ('haliotis-shells') in the *Sagen*, that is, abalone (*Haliotis kamtschatkana*) shells.

happened. So P'a called out, "K·a, k·a, k·a! Take him away from me!" Thereupon, all the people laughed at him.

11) K·ā′iq pretended to be ill and at last even to be dead. So the people said to each other, "Come, let's dig a hole and bury him." "No," cried dead K·ā′iq, "I don't want to lie in the ground because then the children will play above me." So the people said to each other, "Then we will suspend him in a tree." Again the dead one cried, "No, I don't want to hang in a tree; the children will throw stones at me there." He continued, "Take me to K·uē′mk·umēm Island[54] and leave me there." So the people built a funeral pyre[55] and put stones on it. The wife of K·ā′iq washed the corpse,[56] put it on the pyre in a box and then went away into Raccoon's house. Thereupon dead K·ā′iq called, "Wife, where have you gone?" When he noticed that Raccoon wanted to take his wife, he became jealous and sent a boy to her. He sent her a message that she should clean the house because he was going to return. Then he stepped out of the coffin and became alive again.

12) Once K·ā′iq was swimming in the river, when he saw a salmon which he would have liked to catch, but which was too quick for him. He went ashore and called to the salmon, "Please come to me; I want to play with you." The salmon came a bit closer. So K·ā′iq called out, "No, that isn't close enough; come quite close to the shore so that I'll be able to play with you." At last, after he had called it four times, the salmon came up very close and K·ā′iq killed it. He carried it home and roasted it by the fire. While he was sitting there roasting the salmon, he sang, "Who will eat its eyes? K·ā′iq will eat them. Who will eat its head?" K·ā′iq will eat it. Who will eat its roe? K·ā′iq will eat it." Finally he lay down and slept. Then Wolf came up and stole the salmon. But before he ran off, Wolf rubbed with the eyes, the head and the roe once over K·ā′iq's teeth. When K·ā′iq woke up and saw that his salmon had disappeared, he cried out "Who has stolen my salmon?" But when he picked his teeth and found salmon eggs in them, he said, "Ah, K·ā′iq must have eaten it, himself."

---

54. Boas' "K·uē′mk·umēm" is qʷíqʷəmqʷəmim, the Comox name of a tiny island known locally as "Mink's Graveyard" that is located at the southwest entrance to Whiterock Passage off the east side of Quadra Island (see Kennedy and Bouchard 1983:106–107 for a photograph of this island and a variant of this story).

55. Given as *Scheiterhaufen* 'funeral pyre' in the original *Sagen*.

56. Boas (1888h:368), in his own English translation of this legend, adds here, in brackets, some information that is not in the *Sagen*: "as it is the habit of the Çatloltq to do." While the Comox practice of washing the corpse, putting it into a mortuary box and placing it in a cave or rock crevasse on a nearby island is traditional in this area (Kennedy and Bouchard 1990b:448), the practice of cremation in former times was not known to the Comox-speaking people with whom we consulted.

13) After some time, a number of women passed by in their canoe. K·ā′iq called them over and asked, "Do you happen to know who stole the salmon of K·ā′iq?" They didn't know, but he climbed into their canoe and went along with them. After some time the women wanted to land, but K·ā′iq said, "No, go on for a little; I want to land at that point over there." But when they reached the point, he wanted to go on again and only on the fourth time did he allow them to land. By then they had arrived at the Wolves' place. He thought that they had stolen his salmon and therefore he wanted to visit them. When he got there, they played ball with his anus(?).[57] Each time when he tried to catch it, the Wolves struck it away. But at last he caught it and then ran away as fast as his legs would carry him. The Wolves pursued him, so K·ā′iq said to a fallen tree, "When the Wolves want to run around you, keep on putting yourself in their path, and if they want to jump over you, rise up." Thus it came about that the Wolves were not able to catch him.

14) K·ā′iq and his brother, Ā′las (Sea Cucumber)[58] went out one day to get wood. Soon they saw a log drifting in the water, so K·ā′iq said to Ā′las, "Change into a fish and lift the log from underneath." Ā′las didn't answer but jumped into the water without hesitation. Then K·ā′iq killed him and took him home as a fish to his grandmother to have him cooked. He said to her, "When you are eating the fish, don't throw any of the bones away but put them in a bowl." The grandmother did as she was told. In a short while she asked K·ā′iq, "Where is your brother, Ā′las?" K·ā′iq replied, "I believe he is with his lover, Pitch." When he had finished his meal, he took the bowl of fish-bones, went outside and sang, "Oh, grandmother doesn't know that she has eaten her grandson." He took the fish-bones to the spruce and covered them with pitch, into which he then stuck many multi-coloured pieces of wood. Then he threw them into the water and they were transformed into the sea cucumber. He took this to his grandmother, showed it to her and said, "Look, this is how your grandson comes back to us."

15) Once K·ā′iq watched the people fishing and they were all very successful. So he wanted to fish as well, but didn't have any bait. He went to his grandmother and said, "De-louse me." She replied, "Come put your head on my lap." K·ā′iq did so, and when she was de-lousing him, he cut off a piece from her genitals. Thereupon the grandmother transformed herself into a bird and flew away. But K·ā′iq rejoiced that he now had bait. He tied the piece of flesh on his line and started fishing. But no fish wanted to swallow the bait, although all the other fishermen had much success. K·ā′iq grew very angry at this and when a whale swam past, he called out

---

57. Later Boas (1916:706) identifies this as "musk bag."

58. Boas' "Ā′las" is ʔáʔləs, the Comox term for 'sea cucumber' (*Stichopus californnicus*). Elsewhere, Boas (1916:1020) identifies this character as "*Holothuria*," i.e. *Holothuroidea* which is the correct Latin term for the zoological class to which sea cucumbers belong.

to it, "Come and take my bait." Whale swam on. But when K·ā′iq had called him four times, Whale took the bait, after all. Then K·ā′iq tried to lift Whale from the water. But Whale was so heavy that the canoe sank. Thereupon Whale swallowed both the canoe and Mink.

(The same legend is told in the following version:)

15b) Once K·ā′iq went out to catch herring with a huge herring rake. But at the same time a whale was also out catching herring, scaring away all the herring from K·ā′iq's canoe. K·ā′iq grew angry at this. One time when Whale surfaced in order to blow, K·ā′iq called out, "Phew, Whale, how you stink!" He repeated this four times, whereupon Whale grew angry and swallowed K·ā′iq along with his canoe. Each time when Whale surfaced, K·ā′iq shouted from inside, "Oh know, you people, that Whale has swallowed me!" The fishermen heard it and then told each other that K·ā′iq had been swallowed by Whale. Whale continued to catch herring. So Mink lit himself a small fire inside Whale's stomach and dried the herring on a rack. Every time Whale surfaced, the fish fell off the rack. This angered Mink. In addition, it was very hot in Whale's stomach. K·ā′iq felt sick and pondered how he could get into the open again. He decided to kill Whale and cut his throat. So Whale died and soon drifted ashore close to a village.[59] As soon as the inhabitants saw Whale, they cut him up and lo! when they opened Whale's stomach, out sprang Mink. But Mink had lost all his hair in Whale's stomach.

16) Ā′c'icin, the son of Wolf, once went into the forest to catch deer, when he hurt his foot by stepping on a stick which was standing upright in the ground. He limped with difficulty down to the beach and sat down in order to wait for a canoe which could take him home. He saw K·ā′iq busy in the distance in his canoe, spearing fish. So Ā′c'icin called out, "Oh come, K·ā′iq, and take me home in your canoe." K·ā′iq heard him plainly but pretended that he hadn't noticed anything and calmly went on fishing. Only when Ā′c'icin had called to him four times did he look up and say, "Oh, did you call me? Wait, I'll come at once to take you in my canoe." Then he paddled over to him, prepared a comfortable place in the bow and placed a stick across the canoe, which was supposed to serve Wolf as a headrest. Then he carried Ā′c'icin down and laid him on the resting place. Since the stick didn't support his neck properly, K·ā′iq told Wolf to move up higher so that he could lie more comfortably. Then K·ā′iq spoke to him kindly and said, "Now sleep if you can. I will take you home." He covered him up, pushed off and paddled away. But K·ā′iq had

59. The Comox-speaking people with whom we consulted identified the place where Whale drifted ashore as the site of the well-known landmark called the "Big Rock," situated on the beach near Willow Point, south of Campbell River. Our Native consultants said that this Big Rock is Whale; for a variant of this "Mink and the Whale" legend and a photograph of the Big Rock, see Kennedy and Bouchard (1983:106–107) (see also story 1, part 5 of the present section).

only arranged him in this way because he wanted to kill him. His throat was supposed to lie exposed and high. When Ā'c'icin was fast asleep, K·ā'iq paddled ashore and carefully removed the cape from his face. He continued to sleep. So K·ā'iq cut his throat, took his cape and paddled home. There, he hung Wolf's cape over the fire to dry.[60] After some time, an old woman came into the house in order to barter K·ā'iq something. He told her to sit down by the fire and sang, "Look up and see what is hanging there." At first the woman didn't understand him, but finally she looked up and when she saw the pelt she realized that K·ā'iq had killed Ā'c'icin. She went to the chief of the Wolves and told him what she had seen. Thereupon he became angry. He resolved to kill K·ā'iq. He invited all the neighbours, among them also K·ā'iq, to a feast, and intended to slay him when he could. But K·ā'iq had a hunch what Wolf had up his sleeve. Therefore he called his grandmothers, Cockle, "Clams"[61] and Whale Louse,[62] and told them to dig themselves into the ashes by the fire in Wolf's house and to make water while K·ā'iq danced, so that steam would fill the house and he would be able to flee unseen. And he called to his grandmother, Snail, and said to her, "Lie down in front of the door so that everybody who comes out to pursue me will fall." And he called his grandmother, Mouse, and said to her, "Gnaw through the paddles in the canoes of the Wolves so that they won't be able to pursue me." They all obeyed him.

Now when the guards, who were stationed at Wolf's door, saw K·ā'iq coming, they called out, "Start to beat time, because the chief is coming." The singers inside the house started to beat time with their dancing sticks. K·ā'iq entered, went right around the fire and started to dance. When Wolf saw him, he bared his teeth. So K·ā'iq started to sing, "I have killed Ā'c'icin." Thereupon Wolf leaped at him in order to tear him to pieces. But at that very moment the shellfish extinguished the fire and K·ā'iq fled. Those who ran after him fell over Snail lying in front of the

---

60. The passage that begins here as "K·ā'iq paddled ashore" and ends "over the fire to dry" is given in Boas' (1888h:371) own English translation as follows: "κaiq made the shore, carefully he took the cover from the wolf's face and then cut his throat. When the wolf was dead, he took his blanket and returned home. Then he hung it over the fire in order to dry it." Although *Mantel* ('cape; cloak; outer covering') rather than *Decke* ('blanket') is used quite consistently throughout the original *Sagen*, Boas here provides the translation 'cover' in the first instance, and 'blanket' in the second.

61. Given in English as "Clams" (in double quotation marks) in the original *Sagen*; Boas (1888h:371) also uses the term "clams" in his own English translation of this legend.

62. Given in the original as *Walfischlaus*, an artificially-constructed German term meaning 'whale louse.' As previously discussed (see story 4, part 5), Boas (n.d.2) in his interlinear translation of this legend identifies one of these grandmothers as "sē'k̲'oaē," which he has translated first as 'whale louse,' and then crossed out and replaced with the translation 'barnacle.' This term, "sē'k̲'oaē," is not now recognized; the contemporary Comox word for 'barnacle' (*Balanus glandula*) is θ'úmaʔju.

door. And when they reached their canoes at last and grabbed the paddles, they broke because Mouse had gnawed them. Thus K·ā'iq escaped and sang, "I have killed him, the son of Wolf."

5. P'a, Raven

1) Once Ā'n'an (a small bird)[63] invited all the animals for a big feast. When they had all come, he carved a hook from wood and with it got a lot of mountain goat[64] fat out of his anus. He served it to his guests. Among them there was also P'a, Raven. He bragged, "Oh, I can do that, too. Come to my house; I will entertain you in the same way." The animals accepted his invitation and he carved a hook like Ā'n'an, and with it tried to get mountain goat fat out of his anus. But he only managed to tear his intestines, so that blood came streaming out. Thereupon the guests laughed at him. But P'a cried in pain, "Tsk·ān, tsk·ān, tsk·ān, tsk·ān!"

2) After this, Mā'melaquitsa[65] invited all the animals for a meal. He cut into his ankle, let fish eggs drip out of it into bowls held below, and served them to his guests. Again P'a bragged, "Oh, I can do that too!" He invited everybody and cut into his foot. But instead of fish eggs, black blood gushed out, and the guests laughed at him. But P'a cried in pain, "Tsk·ān, tsk·ān, tsk·ān, tsk·ān."

3) Then Seal invited all the animals. When they had arrived at his house he held his hands close to the fire and made oil drip out of them, which he served to the people with dried salmon. "Oh," bragged Raven, "I can do that too." But when he tried, he burned his hands so that big blisters formed, which burst, and from them water gushed. So Raven cried again in pain, "Tsk·ān, tsk·ān, tsk·ān, tsk·ān."

4) Raven and his sisters, Bluejay,[66] T'ets (Crow)[67] and Snail one day went out to gather berries, which they intended to take to their children who were staying with other people. When the canoe was full, they started off to where their children were.

---

63. Boas' "Ān'an" is ʔánʔan, the Comox name of a bird whose identity we have not been able to determine with certainty.

64. While mountain goats have never been found on Vancouver Island, they are widespread through the territory of the Mainland Comox.

65. What Boas transcribes as "Mā'melaquitsa" is derived from məlx̌ʷ, the Comox term for the bird known as the American Dipper (*Cinclus mexicanus*)—this bird's ability to produce fish eggs in the manner described here is widely believed throughout this region.

66. The bird that the storyteller refers to here is the Steller's jay (*Cyanocitta stelleri*), often called the "bluejay," and known as kʷíšk̓ʷiš in the Comox language.

67. "T'ets" is Boas' rendering of t'iθ' which is the Comox term for 'crow' in legends, although in the *Sagen* Boas identifies this bird by the German term *Dohle* 'jackdaw,' a species that does not occur in North America.

P'a sat in the stern and steered, but he kept looking at the berries, thinking, "How I would like to eat them!" He thought of a trick to send his sisters away and said, "I'm afraid that our enemies are going to come in their canoes and will raid us" etc. (see among the legends of the Bilqula.[68] He then relieves himself and makes his excrement shout. The sisters run into the forest; only Snail hides unseen close to the shore and observes him eating the berries. Then she points out to the returning sisters that his head and legs are smeared with cranberries, not blood.)

5) Once Raven took Seal for a wife. But she had a son. One day P'a went hunting with him and, when they had shot many deer, he let him eat to his heart's content. So the young man became thirsty and went to a spring to drink water. When he bent down, Raven took a stick and hit him across the neck, so that his neck broke. Then he lit a fire, roasted his stepson and ate him. He went back home and pretended to cry when he saw his wife. He called, "Tsk·ān, tsk·ān; your poor son has fallen into the water and drowned!" He sat down by the fire and reclined as though he were angry. All at once he had to burp because he had eaten too much oil and vomited straight into the fire, which flared up when the oil fell into it. Then the woman knew that P'a had killed and consumed her son. She grew angry and jumped into the sea. Since that time, seals have lived in the sea.

6) Raven was standing on the top of a rock sloping steeply to the sea and called out to Deer, "Come, let me smell your anus!" Deer came. So Raven made him turn around, and, after he had smelled him, he said, "Oh, you don't smell good; you have no fat at all. Run back into the forest." Then he called another Deer. This one was fat and smelled good. Therefore Raven made him sit down and said, "Let's swap stories of olden days! You start." "No," replied Deer, "you start." So Raven sang, "I have as many blankets to give away as there are needles on the trees." Then Deer began to sing, "I have as many blankets to give away as there is sand by the sea." Thereupon Raven became angry and said, "You are bragging far too much." While saying this, he pushed him, so that he fell off the rock. About this time, a few canoes had gone out to fish. They saw Deer fall down and came up in order to dress the welcome kill and to take it along. They left only the entrails behind. In the meantime Raven had tried in vain to find a path to the beach. When he arrived there at last he found that the deer had disappeared except for the entrails. So he became very sad.

7) P'a and his three sons, Watwitálksin (Sliding To and Fro in the Canoe), K·'aí'māmen (Devouring Everything in Camps) and Wī'woqōnats (Devouring Excrement on the Shore), went out one day in their canoe to shoot birds. Ha'iōm, Seagull,[69] had gone out in his canoe at the same time. P'a didn't get a single bird,

---

68.   Bella Coola (Nuxalk); see Section XXII of the *Sagen*, story 1, part 6.

69.   Boas' "Ha'iōm" is híyum̀, the Comox term referring to 'any seagull.'

while Seagull shot many by hitting them with his arrows as soon as they surfaced. Thereupon P'a became angry and wanted to provoke a quarrel with Ha'iōm. He said, "How on earth do you manage to catch so many birds, Ha'iōm?" Ha'iōm called out, "Leave me alone and go away!" P'a said, "My family is older than yours." Seagull replied, "That isn't true; mine is the older one!" When P'a stuck to his assertion, Ha'iōm said only, "Watch!" He took his cape of mountain goat skin and shook it, whereupon a dense fog developed. Ha'iōm went ashore, but P'a couldn't find his way back to the village and called, "Oh, Ha'iōm, your family is older than mine!" But Ha'iōm didn't answer. P'a and his sons became separated and reached the shore only after a long time. In Eō'miQ[70] he met Watwitálksin, who was wearing his hair very short. But he did not recognize him and said, "Why do you always run back and forth in front of me?"

8) Ya'qsenukomaē[71] had gone on a journey with his wife and two daughters and had left his small son, Alâ'tsenatc,[72] behind by himself. The latter went down to the river every day and caught trout, which he cooked. Just when he wanted to start his meal, Grizzly Bear came and looked in through the door. When she saw the boy she called out, "Alâ'tsenatc is cooking fish there!" Then she took them and ran away. Every time the boy caught trout, Bear came and took them away from him. Consequently the boy became very skinny from hunger and want.

Finally the father returned from his journey and when he heard from his son what had happened, he resolved to kill Bear. He made his wife and daughters hide and posted himself behind the door, armed with a bow and arrow. Then he had Alâ'tsenatc go down to the stream again, catch some trout and cook them. When the fish were almost done, Bear arrived, stood in the doorway and called out, "Alâ'tsenatc is cooking fish there!" and came into the house to take them away. Then she saw Ya'qsenukomaē standing behind the door with his bow. She became angry, ripped out his arm and ran away.

But Ya'qsenukomaē called together all the medicine men in the country and promised them his two daughters if they healed him. They danced and sang around his bed, but in vain! They were unable to heal him. At last P'a arrived to try his skill. When he heard what had happened, he went into the house of Grizzly Bear. He found only her daughters at home and asked them, "What does your mother do after

---

70. It cannot be said with certainty if Boas' transcription of "Eō'miQ" represents his attempt to render the Island Comox place name ʔáʔjumixʷ ('good land') or the Kwakwala pronunciation of this same name, which we have recorded as ʔíyumixʷ. This place name is applied to Deep Bay (and Mapleguard Point, adjacent to this bay), northwest from the community of Bowser on the eastern side of Vancouver Island.

71. This name is not now recognized.

72. This name is not now recognized.

she has eaten her fill?" The Bear daughters replied, "Then she sleeps and makes such a noise with her winds that all the boxes jump up high." Now P'a had found out what he wanted to know. He went away again and fished for red snapper. When his canoe was filled right up, he went back to the house of Bear and gave Old Bear, as well as the young ones, so much fish to eat that they were unable to move when they had eaten their fill. So they all lay down to sleep and soon the old one's winds started to make so much noise that the boxes in the house jumped up high. So P'a knew that she was fast asleep. He took Ya'qsenukomaē's arm, which hung above the fire to dry, and flew away with it. So the children shouted, "Mother, get up! P'a has stolen the arm of Ya'qsenukomaē." So the old one sprang up, roared in anger and pursued P'a by pushing over trees right and left. But P'a flew to and fro in a zig-zag flight, so that she was unable to catch him.

Then he put the dried arm into the water to soften it again. P'a now made the arm alive again so that it moved. Then he flew to the house of Ya'qsenukomaē and dropped the arm down on the roof. Then he went into the house and started singing. He made all the people assemble and sing with him and beat time. After he had been singing and dancing for a while, he sang, "The arm shall come into the house a little." Thereupon the hand of the sick man could be seen coming down through the smoke hole and moving its fingers. Then he spread out his cape and sang, "Fall down, arm, right into my cape." And this is what happened. Then he wrapped up the arm and put it on beneath Ya'qsenukomaē's cape. Then he said to the dog, "Go to my sister, Slug,[73] and whisper to her to come here and bring her magic substance along." So the dog went out and bawled at the top of his voice, "Come here, Slug, and bring your magic substance along." Slug arrived and crawled around the spot where the arm had been put on. The arm was as firm and healthy again as if it had never been torn off. Then P'a took the two girls for his wives and became a great chief.

9) Now P'a wanted to move to a different land with his wives. He loaded his canoe and steered, while the women paddled. After some time they met two canoes. There was a man in each one. They came up to P'a and manoeuvred their canoes in such a way that his lay between those of the strangers. Then they said to the women, "Please ask P'a whether he'd like to drink seal blood." P'a had the women answer that he didn't like it very much, but that he would accept some as a favour to the strangers. But this wasn't true, because he was burning with desire to drink the blood. The strangers gave him a full bowl. At first he licked a bit with one finger, then with two, then with three and finally drank fully from the bowl without putting

---

73. Given in the original as *Schnecke* meaning 'snail' or 'slug,' but very probably it is Slug in this context—slugs were formerly used by the Mainland Comox to heal severe cuts, which is in accord with Slug's role in this legend.

it down once. While P'a was thus occupied with the seal blood, the strangers took away his wives without his noticing it. When he had emptied the bowl and looked up, he saw the strangers' canoes far away and his wives in the two canoes. So he became angry and called out to them, "Let's find out who is the better man." They replied, "How can we find out?" "Let's see who can dive the longest," retorted Raven. The others agreed and let Raven dive first. He sprang into the water and only surfaced again after the sun had completed a long arc in the sky. Then he said, "I swam right to Mitlnatc."[74] Then the strangers dived. They also stayed under for a long time, and when they returned, they maintained that they had been past Mitlnatc. Then it was P'a's turn again and when he came back after a very long time he said that he had been in Agya'ik·sen[75] in the land of the Tlaā'men.[76] "Oh," shouted the strangers, "you are telling a lie; you couldn't have been that far. Dive once more or else we won't believe you." Raven did what they asked. Then they searched all the reefs and islands in the vicinity and finally found him quite close by, clinging to a rock and sticking his beak out of the water to breathe. So they became angry that he was cheating them and beat him to death. Thereupon he floated on the water like a piece of black coal.

10) P'a wanted to have mountain goat fat and said to the man who owned it, "Come let's play! Let's sit on top of our houses and fling mountain goat fat to each other." The man agreed. Raven pretended to fling the fat across, but in reality he threw only red snapper, while the other man really did throw fat. Thus he got what he wanted.

6. Origin of Frogs and Snakes

Once many women (frogs and snakes) went into the forest to gather berries. When they were tired, they lay down to sleep. Then K·ōl, Beaver,[77] came and wanted to

---

74. As noted earlier, this is Boas' transcription of the Comox term məʼx̣'nəč ('calm back end') which is applied to Mitlenatch Island, located in the Strait of Georgia between Shelter Point on the east side of Vancouver Island, and Hernando Island (Kennedy and Bouchard 1983:161–163).

75. "Agya'ik·sen" is Boas' rendering of the Comox term ʔáʔgəyqsn 'pointed nose,' referring to Harwood Island, near Powell River, which has been set aside as Sliammon Indian Reserve No. 2 (Kennedy and Bouchard 1983:164).

76. What Boas transcribes here as "Tlaā'men" is the Comox term ɬáʔamin, anglicized as "Sliammon," referring to the Mainland Comox group whose traditional territory comprised the mainland and also the offshore islands from the Stillwater area up to Desolation Sound, including the Powell River area (Kennedy and Bouchard 1990b:441–443, 451). (See Section X for a legend of the Sliammon.)

77. The term that Boas transcribes here as "K·ōl" 'beaver' is not now recognized—the only Comox term known for 'beaver' (*Castor canadensis*) is qʷúwət. Possibly "K·ōl" was the Comox term formerly used for 'Beaver' in legends.

sleep with Frog Woman. He wanted to crawl under her blanket, but she pushed him back. He tried four times without success to get close to her, then he went sadly home to his grandmother and wept, because Frog Woman didn't want anything to do with him. Grandmother sat with her back to the fire and warmed herself. When she heard K·ōl's complaint, she turned around and put her face towards the fire. Thereupon it began to rain. It rained and rained without end. The water rose in the forest and soon the frogs had to climb onto the fallen trees in order to escape. So K·ōl went back to the forest, believing that the frogs and snakes would be in dire straits because the water had already reached their last refuge. But they all sat there, singing while beating time, "Oh it is good; it is nice that it rains." So Beaver took a stick and lifted them out of the water by their feet. He changed some into frogs and the others into snakes.

7. Deer and the Wolves

Deer had killed the chief of the Wolves and taken his son as a slave. He tied together two canoes, put boards across and sang and danced on them, together with his child and his slave. Deer sang, "I have killed the chief of the Wolves." Then he tortured the slave and pushed him into the water, telling him to swim. The slave became angry and beat Deer's child. When it cried, Deer said, "My child shall become happy again and therefore I will cut off the head of my slave." And he did as he had said.

The Wolves heard him singing and resolved to avenge the death of their chief and his son. They set out to catch Deer. He escaped, but they reached his son and killed him. At last Deer climbed a tree to escape his pursuers. The Wolves sat down in a circle around the tree. They saw Deer's reflection in a puddle beneath the tree and thought that he was in the ground. So they all began to scrape with all their might to get to him. But a man who was passing by pointed out to them that Deer was sitting up in the tree. So the Wolves started to beat time and sing. The first one sang, "I will eat your ears." Deer, up in the tree, shook his head and replied, "Yes, you will eat them." The second one sang, "I will eat your nose." Again Deer shook his head and replied, "Yes, you will eat it." The third Wolf then sang, "I will eat your tongue," and the fourth, "I will eat your shoulders." The fifth wanted the ribs, the sixth the breastbone, the seventh the hips, the eighth the hooves, and the ninth the stomach. At last Deer was so angry that he fell from the tree. So the Wolves devoured him.

8. Deer Gets Fire

An old man had a daughter who owned a miraculous bow and arrow with which she could shoot anything she fancied. But she was lazy and always slept. Her father grew angry at this and said, "Don't sleep all the time, but take your bow and shoot into the ocean's navel so that we will get fire." The ocean's navel was a huge whirlpool in which rubbing sticks for firemaking were swirling around. The people in those days didn't have fire yet. So the girl took her bow, shot into the ocean's navel and the fire stick jumped ashore. Thereupon the old one was glad. He lit a big fire, and, because he wanted to keep the fire for himself, he built a house with a door which snapped open and closed like a snout and killed anyone trying to enter. But the people knew that he owned Fire and K·ē'u, Deer,[79] resolved to steal it for them. Deer took resinous wood, split it and put the slivers in his hair. Then he tied two canoes together, covered them with boards and danced and sang on them while he went to the old man's house. He sang, "Oh, I am going to fetch Fire." The old man's daughter heard him singing and said to her father, "Oh, let the stranger come into the house. He sings and dances so beautifully." Then K·ē'u landed and came up to the door, singing and dancing. He sprang towards the door and pretended to go into the house. So the door snapped shut and, when it opened again, he jumped into the house. There he sat down by the fire as if to dry himself and continued singing. At the same time, he let his head drop over the fire so that it became quite sooty and so that the wood sticking in his hair finally caught fire. Then he leaped outside, ran away and brought Fire to the people.

9. Grizzly Bear and Black Bear

One day Grizzly Bear said to Black Bear, "Come over here and delouse me." Black Bear did as she was told. But Grizzly Bear's lice were frogs. Black Bear caught them, threw them on the ground and they hopped away. Grizzly Bear heard the sound and asked, "What is falling to the ground and jumping about?" Black Bear answered, "Oh, it's small branches which are falling to the ground from the trees." But soon Grizzly Bear saw the frogs, became angry and killed Black Bear. Then she cut off Black Bear's breasts, cooked them and fed them to Black Bear's children. At once the children realized that Grizzly Bear had served them their mother's breasts. But they didn't say anything about it, and only asked, "Where is our mother?" Old Grizzly Bear answered, "She has gone to the forest and will probably come back tomorrow."

---

79. As noted earlier (see story 1, part 8 of this section), qiw is the Comox mythological term for 'Deer.'

Grizzly Bear went out after a while. So the little ones killed Grizzly Bear's children and placed their heads and forepaws in the storage boxes. Then they ran into the forest. When Grizzly Bear returned and saw her children at the boxes, she thought that they were stealing food and wanted to punish them. But when she came close, she saw that they were all dead. So she became angry and ran into the forest to look for the young bears. She found them sitting in a tree, and called to them in a friendly way, "Why don't you come home; your mother has returned." They called back from their tree, "Yes, we'll come. But first of all, lay down on the ground, open your mouth and nose wide and spread your legs apart; we want to give you something." Old Bear Woman did what they had told her. Thereupon the little ones threw down wood dust which fell into her eyes, mouth and other natural orifices. So she howled in pain and ran away, knocking down trees with her forepaws.

10. Tlṓ′menatsō[80]

Once a man said to Tlṓ′menatsō, "Come, let's go out together and hunt seals." Tlṓ′menatsō answered, "You go on ahead; I'll follow soon." The man went out and soon saw something which glowed like fire, swimming in the sea. It bobbed up and down but he was unable to reach it. After some time, Tlṓ′menatsō went out and he also saw the fire floating on the water. Then he recognized that it was the Aihōs (double-headed serpent). He paid no attention to his friend and didn't look out for seals, but pursued the Aihōs to K·ē′ik·oan[81] (an island of approximately three miles in length in the territory of the Tlaā′men). Here the Aihōs had its dwelling inside a cave. Tlṓ′menatsō caught up with it here and hit it with his fish spear. The spear had scarcely touched it when the hunter fell down as if dead and blood flowed from his mouth and nose. Thereupon the Aihōs gave him a piece of transparent stone[82] and led his soul through all the lands. Finally the Aihōs brought the soul back. Tlṓ′menatsō got up again and returned home. The following day he caught one seal,

---

80. The name transcribed by Boas as "Tlṓ′menatsō" is very likely the character whose Comox name is X̌′úmnaǰm (see Kennedy and Bouchard 1983:50–51 for another story of X̌′úmnaǰm, set on Cortes Island).

81. Mainland Comox people with whom we consulted explained that the serpent was trying to reach his cave at the place called x̌íx̌ax̌giɬ ('Indian doctors; shamans'), which is Hurtado Point located south from the community of Lund, and opposite Savary Island. However, the serpent was transformed before it reached home, and thus became the present Savary Island which is known as ʔáyhus ('double-headed serpent,' transcribed here by Boas as "Aihōs") (see also Kennedy and Bouchard 1983:164). Boas' K·ē′ik·oan is qíẏaqʷən, another word for Savary Island.

82. This "transparent stone" or crystal is likely xʷáṅi, a type of power that the Comox believe comes from a fallen star that is shiny on one side and on the other resembles a piece of bark (Kennedy and Bouchard 1983:50).

the next day two, then three and thus one more daily. They were given to him by the Aihōs.

11. Thunderbird

Ku'lten had a beautiful wife called Wa'qwaqolē.[83] Her skin was snowy white and her hair hung down to the ground. Qoā'tk·um, Thunderbird, had seen the woman once and decided to steal her. He asked his friends, Ts'i'tcilitl,[84] and Pal, Heron,[85] to aid him. They were willing and the three of them journeyed to the house of Ku'lten. They stepped inside the door and Wa'qwaqolē invited them to come right in. So they entered and sat down by the fire. But Qoā'tk·um wrapped up his head in his cape in order to hide his long nose. Then Wa'qwaqolē said to her husband, "Go to the forest and get me a salmonberry bush." He did what she had told him to do and brought her a bush. Wa'qwaqolē stuck it in the earth and began singing. Thereupon first leaves sprouted, then blossoms and, finally, berries. She picked them, put them in a bowl and served them to Qoā'tk·um. When he had eaten, he challenged Ku'lten to a contest. They stepped in front of the house and played with a disk which was wound with inner cedar bark. The four men arranged themselves standing in a row, with Qoā'tk·um at one end, Ts'i'tcilitl next to him, then Pal, and Ku'lten at the other end. First Qoā'tk·um threw his disk, which consisted of fire. His companions were unable to catch it, but Ku'lten did. Then Ts'i'tcilitl threw his disk, which consisted of fog. Neither Qoā'tk·um nor Pal caught it, but Ku'lten did. Thus Ku'lten had won both rounds. Thereupon Qoā'tk·um grew angry. He went into the house and sat down right on Wa'qwaqolē's cape. Then he called Storm, who blew the house to pieces. Only Wa'qwaqolē was left sitting, because Qoā'tk·um sat on her cape. Then Qoā'tk·um carried Wa'qwaqolē to his house.

---

83. This is another example of Kwakwaka'wakw (Southern Kwakiutl) influence on Comox culture. What Boas transcribes here as "Wa'qwaqolē" is the same term he transcribes among the Kwakwala-speaking tribes as "Waqwaqǒ'li" (see, for example, Section XVIII, story 1, part 17), and elsewhere as "wā'xwaxwEle" (Boas 1948:67)—these are all transcriptions of wáx̌ʷwax̌ʷəli, the Kwakwala term for the Swainson's Thrush (*Hylocichla ustulata*). The Comox name for this same species is x̌ʷət. As indicated in the present story, the Comox, together with other tribes throughout this region, believe that the Swainson's Thrush causes salmonberries to ripen (see also story 3 of this section; see story 12 for another example of a Kwakwala term used in Comox mythology).

84. What Boas transcribes here as "Ts'i'tcilitl" appears to be the same term he transcribes earlier in this section (see story 1, part 1) as "Ts'ē'selētl" and identifies as "a colourful bird." In any case, neither term is now recognized.

85. As we have noted, Boas' "Pal" is pal', the Comox term for the Great Blue Heron, although Boas gives the German term, *Kranich* 'crane,' here in the original *Sagen*.

But Ku'lten called all the people for a court assembly.[86] They were all assembled;
only chief T'ɛmt'ɛm (a bird)[87] was still missing. So Ku'lten sent him the following
message, "You are wise and know everything. Come and give your counsel as to
what we should do." Thereupon T'ɛmt'ɛm came and said, "Shall I tell you what I
have thought of in my heart? Let a trout swim to Qoā'tk·um to fight with him." So
Ku'lten went to Trout and borrowed his cape. The other people borrowed the capes
of other fish and they all swam to the house of Qoā'tk·um. K·ā'iq, Mink, had taken
the shape of spring salmon. They all went into Qoā'tk·um's fish trap and when he
went down to the stream in the morning, he found it filled right up. He went down
with Wa'qwaqolē, took out the fish and was happy about the good catch. He gave
the trout, which was especially beautiful, to his wife. She carried the fish into the
house and, after she had put the trout down by her feet, she began to split open the
other fish and dry them over the fire. Then she heard the trout talking to her, "When
you eat me, don't throw my bones away, but put them in a bowl and carry them to
the water." Wa'qwaqolē noted what the fish had said. Then she put the fish onto the
racks over the fire. But K·ā'iq jumped down every time when the woman put him
up, because he wanted to warm himself close to the fire. Then the woman ate the
trout, put the bones in a bowl and carried them to the water. She took a bath and
swam about in the sea. Qoā'tk·um watched her from the house and called out to her,
"Don't swim out so far." When they touched the water, the bones which the woman
had carried down, transformed into a trout again. Then all the fish laying on the
drying rack jumped down, revived and swam away. But the trout carried
Wa'qwaqolē home. There, the fish again assumed their normal shapes.

They met again and resolved to kill Qoā'tk·um. But they didn't know how to
carry out their intentions. Then wise T'emt'em said, "Don't you know that
Qoā'tk·um catches whales? Get hold of Whale's canoe and then attack him." Ku'lten
wanted to set out at once to borrow the canoe, but K·ā'iq shouted, "No, let me go."
Ku'lten agreed and K·ā'iq went to Whale. When he entered the house, he found Old
Whale lying by the fire, warming himself. K·ā'iq nudged him with his foot and said,
"Ku'lten is asking you for your canoe. Lend it to him." Whale answered, "If he
wants to have it, he'll have to send someone else for it instead of you. I won't give
it to you because you are full of silly pranks. You are going to break it." K·ā'iq
pretended to go back, but in reality only hid behind the door. After a while he came
back and said, "Oh, they are all too lazy and won't come. You'll just have to give it
to me." So Old Whale gave him a box in which he kept the canoe and said, "Now

---

86.   Given in the original *Sagen* as *Gerichtssitzung* 'court assembly.'

87.   As explained previously (see story 3 of this section), what Boas transcribes here as "T'ɛmt'ɛm"
      (and earlier, as "T'amt'am"), is (s)t'ə'mt'əm, the Sechelt term for what is likely the Winter
      Wren—the Comox name for this same species is č'úč'uʔ.

listen, don't open the box, otherwise I'll have to come out of the house at once and swim around outside." K·a̅′iq promised, but he was scarcely outside when he opened the box and a whale leaped out and swam about, blowing and diving. So K·a̅·iq pretended to be weeping and said, "I came ashore, when the box fell and broke." But he had opened it purposely in order to be able to go back in Whale's canoe. He brought the canoe to the shore where all the people were assembled, and on T'emt'em's advice, they all entered the canoe. They were led by Ku′lten, and he was followed by Bear, Wolf, Cougar and many other animals. They put a heavy piece of basalt into the bottom of the canoe and K·a̅′iq sat up ahead with a chisel in his hand. Thus they set out to fight Qoa̅′tk·um. The canoe had the appearance of a whale.

Early in the morning, Qoa̅′tk·um saw it floating in the sea in front of his house. So he called to his youngest adult son. "Get up, a whale is swimming here in front of our house." His son obeyed, put on his feather garment and flew off to catch the whale. He grasped it and lifted it up a little. Thereupon the piece of basalt rolled down into the tail and made it so heavy that he was unable to lift it higher. But K·a̅′iq slashed the bird's feet with his chisel, although all the other animals called to him to wait a bit longer. When Qoa̅′tk·um saw that his son was unable to lift the whale, he sent the next oldest son to help him, etc. (See Legends of the Nutka.)[88] … [89]At last the old one himself put on his feather garment to help his sons. But before he flew off, he said to his youngest child, who was still in its cradle, "Listen to my words. If I don't return, you will become the Thunderbird one day. Don't fly about all year to fill the earth with your voice, but only fly around in the summer and stay home in winter." Then Thunderbird flew off and he, too, was killed by the animals. So they returned home in good spirits. But since then, thunder is heard only in the summer.

12. T'E′cēk·[90]

There once were two men, K·o̅′k·ois (Copper)[91] and Tc'a̅′djas (Abalone Shell). The former had a son and the latter a daughter who was the lover of the son of K·o̅′k·ois. When she presented him with a son, the young man took her into his house. When the boy grew up, he always went out with his father to shoot birds, and finally the two men left their home and left the daughter of Tc'a̅′djas behind by herself. When the men didn't return at night, she cried a lot, wiped the tears from her face with some moss and cleaned her nose. Then she dropped the bunch of moss to the

---

88. See Section XIII, story 2, part 7.

89. Boas places these ellipses points here in the original *Sagen*.

90. The term transcribed by Boas as "T'E′cēk·" is the Comox term for 'mucus,' t'íšiqʷ.

91. What Boas transcribes here as "K·o̅′k·ois" is qʷíqʷʔis, the Comox term for 'copper.'

ground. After some time, she looked down and noticed that a human being was forming from her tears. At first it was very small, then it became bigger and bigger. Then she took it home as her child and called it T'ᴇ'cēk· (Mucus). The boy grew up very quickly and one day said to his mother, "I want to go and shoot birds." He had his mother make him a bow and some arrows, took her canoe and wanted to set out to hunt. Then she told him, "If you meet my husband and your elder brother and they want to take you along, tell them that you want to stay with me. You are my son only." T'ᴇ'cēk· promised. Not long after he had set out from his home, he saw a red glow in the distance. It emanated from a canoe and when he came closer he saw his mother's husband and his stepbrother. They demanded that he come to them, but he replied, "No, you are not my father; I don't want to go with you," and he returned home. There he saw his mother sitting at the shore, anxiously looking out for him. When she saw him coming she sang, "I see my child coming near." T'ᴇ'cēk· told what had happened to him and thereupon the woman told him how that man had abandoned her, continuing, "He is not your father, because you originated from my tears. I would have been very sad if you had left me."

In those days, in K·anis,[92] opposite K·'ō'djōmen[93] to the north of Seymour Narrows, there lived K·ōmō'k·oaē.[94] He used to stay on top of the mountain, in the shape of a grizzly bear. He had a big metal box there in which he kept coppers, earrings and other valuables. He rolled it down the mountain slope and if anyone came to steal the box, he pounced on him from above and killed him. T'ᴇ'cēk· heard about this and decided to steal the box. He went into the forest every day and bathed in a pond. This made him strong and he learned how to run fast and jump far. Finally he was able to jump from one end of a fallen spruce to the other. Then he tied together ten canoes and with them went to K·anis. When he heard the box come rumbling down the mountain, he sprang out in one leap, seized the box, and jumped in one leap back into the canoes, before Bear realized what had happened. Bear was unable to pursue him across the water and in anger pushed over trees right and left. But

92. Boas' "K·anis" is qáṅis, a Comox place name that is anglicized as "Kanish" and applies to the vicinity of Kanish Bay at the northwest end of Quadra Island.

93. As previously discussed (see story 1, part 4 of this section), what Boas transcribes here as "K·'ō'djōmēn" is q̇ʷújumin ('defecation place'), the Island Comox pronunciation of the Comox place name that refers both to Little Bear River (now known as Pye Creek) and to Little Bear Bay, into which this creek enters. The creek and bay are situated on the east coast of Vancouver Island, about 28 miles (45 km) north from the town of Campbell River and opposite East Thurlow Island.

94. Presumably what Boas transcribes here as "K·ō'mō'k·oaē" is the same Kwakwala term that he gives elsewhere (see, for example, Section XV, story 2) as "K·ōmō'k·oa," which is recognized by our Kwakwala-speaking consultants as q̇ʷúmugʷi, the sea-being whose name is derived from the Kwakwala term q̇ʷúmała 'wealth'—the same term is given in Boas (1948:362) as "q!ōmogweᵉ" and translated as 'a sea being' (see also story 11 of this section for another example of Kwakwala terminology in Comox mythology).

T'E'cēk· gave a great feast when he returned and became a powerful chief. Since that time, his family has worn the bear mask.

13. Ciā'tlk·am[95]

A long, long time ago Ciā'tlk·am descended from the sky. He wore the feather garment, Qoā'ēqoē,[96] and settled in Ñgā'içam (Cape Mudge).[97] He became the ancestor of the Çatlōltq. With him his sister, Tē'sitla,[98] arrived. She was so big that she needed two canoes to cross the sea. The brother and sister wandered through all the lands and visited the Nanaimo, Nī'ciatl,[99] Tlahū's[100] and many other tribes who all became their younger brothers.

---

95. Boas' "Ciā'tlk·am" is recognized as šáɬqəm, an Island Comox male ancestral name (Kennedy and Bouchard 1983:64) (see also the footnotes that follow).

96. "See Proceedings U.S. National Museum 1888 p. 213" [Boas' original footnote]. Boas' reference here is to his 1888 publication entitled "The Houses of the Kwakiutl Indians" (see Boas' Preface in the present Volume), where he describes the "Qoā'eqoē" as a "bird-like being that descended from the heavens and became the ancestor of the Çatlōltq [Island Comox]." What Boas transcribes as "Qoā'ēqoē" both in this article and here in the *Sagen* is the Comox term xʷáyxʷay, referring to the ceremonial mask and regalia used by certain members of some Coast Salish groups, including the Comox. A description and photo of this dance mask, together with a variant of this same story as told in the 1970s, can be found in Kennedy and Bouchard (1983:63–64).

97. "Ñgā'içam" is likely Boas' transcription of the Comox term kʷániwsam which means 'resting place' and refers to an area west of Campbell River that is known as Quinsam; "Quinsam," itself, is an anglicization of kʷə'nsam which is the Kwakwala pronunciation of this Comox term, kʷániwsam. A contemporary Island Comox account of this xʷáyxʷay mask landing at Quinsam has been recorded (see Kennedy and Bouchard 1983:63–64). Boas here in the *Sagen* mis-identifies the location of "Ñgā'içam" as "Cape Mudge" (located at the south end of Quadra Island, opposite Campbell River).

98. Boas' "Tē'sitla" is recognized as tísiƛ'a, an Island Comox female ancestral name (Kennedy and Bouchard 1983:64).

99. Presumably "Nī'ciatl" was a term that may have been used at one time by the Comox to refer to the Sechelt, a Coast Salish group closely related to the Comox and Pentlatch (the Sechelt people live mainly on the Sechelt Peninsula; formerly they also lived in Jervis Inlet and adjacent areas). However, as we have discussed elsewhere, the term used most often by the Comox, and others, to refer to the Sechelt is šíšáɬ (Kennedy and Bouchard 1990b:452). The possibility also exists that Boas simply mis-heard šíšáɬ as "Nī'ciatl."

100. What Boas transcribes here as "Tlahū's" is the Comox term ƛ'úhus (anglicized as "Klahoose") which refers to one of the groups comprising the Mainland Comox. Klahoose traditional territory was centred in the Toba Inlet/Toba River area but included East and West Redonda Islands, Read Island, and part of Cortes Island (Kennedy and Bouchard 1990b:441–443).

14. K·ōmō′k·oaē [101]

Two women, O′mak· and Kyē′ek·,[102] one day went to an island to look for shellfish. They started to quarrel there and Kyē′ek· stepped into the canoe and went far out to sea. So O′mak· called out, "Oh, don't leave me! Where are you going? Rather, come back to me." The other one answered, "Yes, I will if you tear up your cape into bits and throw them into the sea." O′mak· did what the other one had demanded. Then O′mak· called out again, "Oh, come to me and let me get into the canoe." Kyē′ek· called out, "First pull out your hair, then I'll come." Again O′mak· did what she demanded. Yet still Kyē′ek· didn't come, but demanded that the latter pull out her eyebrows and lashes, too. And then, when O′mak· stood there, naked and miserable, Kyē′ek· was glad. She called to the bird K·a′lk·uinas[103] to seize her enemy and went away. K·a′lk·uinas flew down and pecked at O′mak· a little, but didn't kill her.

The poor woman then lay down to sleep. Soon she heard someone say, "Wake up." She got up, but didn't see anyone and therefore lay down again and slept on. Soon she felt someone tugging at her foot, but still couldn't see anything. So she sat down and put her hands in front of her face, but peeped through her fingers. She saw a tiny mouse which kept calling her and tugging at her. She asked Mouse, "What do you want?" Mouse answered, "Come with me to the house of K·ōmō′k·oaē." She followed. Mouse slipped into the house first and called, "Come in, come in!" But a woman who was sitting in the rear of the house called, "Stay out, stay out; K·ōmō′k·oaē wants to harm you!" But O′mak· thought that there couldn't be anything worse than what had happened to her, so she followed Mouse. She sat down by the fire and saw the many, many children of K·ōmō′k·oaē sitting along the walls. In a short while, K·ōmō′k·oaē asked, "Who is that woman without hair?" Mouse replied, "She is O′mak·. Kyē′ek· has made her ugly." So K·ōmō′k·oaē gave her new, beautiful, long black hair, eyebrows and lashes, a cape and a dancing apron, and sent her back to the island.

A short while later, Kyē′ek· came there because she believed O′mak· to be dead. The latter hid when she saw her enemy coming, and Mouse whispered to her, "Now take revenge on her. When she comes ashore, cut the canoe loose and paddle away." Kyē′ek· went ashore to look for the corpse of O′mak·. So the latter leaped into the

---

101. As previously noted (see story 12 of this section), Boas' "K·ō′mō′k·oaē" is the Kwakwala term "K·ōmō′k·oa" which is recognized by our Kwakwala-speaking consultants as q̓ʷúmugʷi, the sea-being whose name is derived from the Kwakwala term q̓ʷúmała 'wealth.'

102. In Boas' (n.d.2) manuscript version of this story he identifies the two women (unnamed in that version) as "concubines."

103. Boas' "K·a′lk·uinas" is recognized as qʷəlq̓ʷí·nis, the Comox term for the bird known as the Turkey Vulture (*Cathartes aura*), although it is very unusual for this species to be mentioned in Northwest Coast mythology.

canoe, cut it loose and pushed off from the shore. Then she called out to Kyē′ek·, "Can you see how beautiful I've become? Do what I did and you will also become beautiful." Kyē′ek· followed her advice. She tore up her cape and her dancing apron and pulled out her hair, eyebrows and lashes. Then O′mak· called K·álk·uinas, who killed Kyē′ek·.

15. Alqs [104]

One day Alqs went out with his daughter to get wood. After some time they landed and the father said to the girl, "I'll tie up the canoe here. You stay and watch that it doesn't drift away. I'll go into the forest to fetch wood." He had scarcely gone when Wolf, Hak·hak·uā′tlsin,[105] son of SE′msāmām,[106] arrived and said to the girl, "Come ashore; I like you and you shall become my wife." She agreed and Wolf carried her away. When the father returned and found his daughter gone from the canoe, he became very sad and cried. He paddled home and left behind the wood which he had cut. "Oh," he thought, "who has killed my daughter?" He paddled everywhere and asked all the people, "Do you know who has stolen my daughter?" They all answered, "No, we don't know."

So Alqs looked for solitude. He went into the forest and wept and wept. He paddled up a river and arrived at a lake where the dead dwelt. He asked one of them, "Do you know where my child is?" He answered, "Go to our chief, Tlnā′naçegitl;[107] he will be able to give you information." Alqs went into the chief's house and found him; he was a big, old man with white hair, reclining in a chair, dozing. He asked him, "Do you know where my child is?" The chief replied, "I do know. The son of SE′msāmām has stolen her. Walk up that gently-sloping hill and you will find her. You will hear many people laughing up there; they are the young Wolves." Alqs followed his advice and went. Then he saw the Wolves playing ball. They had taken off their capes. He crept up and sat down beside the capes. When the Wolves caught sight of him, they were ashamed that he had seen them without clothes and hung their heads. Then one of them said, "I think he is the father of the woman Hak·hak·uā′tlsin has stolen," and they got up, took their capes and went to SE′msāmām. They told him, "The father of your daughter-in-law has come." "Let him enter," replied the chief. Then the Wolves invited Alqs to come in.

---

104. The term "Alqs" is not now recognized.

105. What Boas renders as "Hak·hak·uā′lsin" is not now recognized; the normal term for 'wolf' in the Comox language is x̣'áʔɬʔum.

106. This term is not now recognized.

107. This term, "Tlnā′naçegitl," is not now recognized.

When he had sat down by the fire, Se'msāmām sent out all his underlings to hunt. After a short while he called, "Ooh, all my children shall come back!" and the Wolves came running. One carried a deer, the second a seal, the third a dog, and every one had caught something. Hak·hak·uā'tlsin appeared last of all; he carried Papaā'k·ēn (the one-horned deer).[108] Se'msāmām asked him, "How did you catch the deer?" He replied, "I ran after it and caught up with it." Se'msāmām retorted, "I don't believe you, because you are not swift enough for it. I think you ran into each other at right angles." With this he cut the ropes binding the feet of Papaā'k·ēn; it ran away and the young Wolf pursued it. He stayed away a long time and Se'msāmām was already thinking that his son was unable to catch it. He said to Alqs, "That comes from eating too many salmon; now he can't run." But Hak·hak·uā'tlsin was ashamed that his father believed him incapable of catching up with the deer and now caught Sā'saak·ēn[109] (the deer with four antlers), which was much swifter, and carried it home. He threw it down by the fire and now Se'msāmām's heart was glad. He had the wolves heat up stones, dress the deer and cook it with red-hot stones. When it was done, they flung the meat to Alqs, saying, "Wolves don't eat cooked meat." He stayed with the wolves for four days, then they carried him back to his home. When he arrived there, he noticed that he had been away for four years. His wives had mourned for him as if he were dead and they were sitting weeping in front of the house just as he arrived. He was glad now because he knew that his daughter was alive and didn't suffer want. If the descendants of Alqs want to have a deer, they ask the wolves for one. They call the wolves their sons-in-law.

Once Alqs said to his people, "Come, let's go and see what the humans are doing." They stepped into Alqs' canoe, Cak·'āmōs (Elk-nose)[110] and went northward. After some time they reached a village. So they pulled the canoe ashore and laid down in ambush in the forest. Towards morning, a man arrived to cut wood. Alqs had him captured and caused one of his eyes to be put out. Then he released him again. He set the eye into the gunwale; he did the same wherever he went. The gunwale of his canoe was set closely with human eyes. At last he reached the west coast of Vancouver Island. There, a storm smashed his canoe. But he found another one, which was still being worked on, on the beach. When night came, he stole it and went on with his crew. At last they arrived in familiar surroundings and so knew that they were nearing their home. But, while they had set out towards the north, their return was from the south. When they were close to the village, Alqs shouted

---

108. This is the Comox term for a deer with one-point antlers; Boas' German equivalent, *einhörniger Hirsch* ('one horned deer'), implies a unicorn-like creature.

109. This is the Comox term for a deer with two-point antlers, not four.

110. Given in the original German as *Elchnase* 'elk-nose,' although the term "Cak·'āmōs" is not now recognized as the name for either elk or deer, or for any type of canoe.

loudly so that his friends would recognize him by his voice. He brought back four cedars which he used as posts in his house. His wives had waited patiently for him all these many years and he now took them back again. Then Alqs gave a big feast and danced with the Qoā'ēqoē.[111] (He was the seventh ancestor of "Mary," the informant.)

16. The Four Brothers

Once there were four brothers. The eldest of them went in to the forest to build a canoe. He asked his brothers to send food out to him so that he might work undisturbed. They promised, but though they went out daily to shoot seals, they didn't send any food to their brother. He grew angry at this, and one day when his son came out to him in the forest, he asked him, "Why don't your uncles send me any food? Haven't they caught anything?" His son answered, "They go out every day and catch seals." So the father said, "Now pay attention to what I'm going to do." He took his axe and carved a seal from cedar wood. Then he lit a fire and scorched its outside so that it looked black. Then he flung it into the sea and put it on a rock close to the shore. Then he said to his son, "Tonight when you get to the village, tell your uncles that there is a seal here." The boy obeyed. When the three brothers heard of the seal, they at once took their canoe and went out. They didn't see it at first, but when they had rounded the cliff and when the dark shape of the seal stood out against the bright evening sky, they noticed it. They approached carefully and harpooned it. Thereupon the seal jumped into the water and swam out to sea. It kept swimming for a long, long time. The brothers took turns holding onto the rope of the harpoon—one of them holding it with his hand—while the others slept. At last they had been led so far away that they saw nothing but sky and water all around and the nights were very long. Then the seal transformed into a piece of cedar wood again and so the brothers knew that their brother had taken his revenge in this way. They dislodged the harpoon and wanted to return, but they didn't know where their home was. Finally they believed they saw some land and steered towards it. When they came close they saw a low coast which looked black as coal. The youngest brother sprang onto the shore, but it disappeared at once. So he drowned. Thereupon the two survivors were very sad. They continued and came to a mountain with a huge cavern in it, through which the waters gushed with tremendous force. They went through and when they had arrived in open water again, they saw a big country in front of them. A village was there and smoke rose

---

111. As noted previously (see story 13 of this section), what Boas transcribes as "Qoā'ēqoē" is the Comox term x̌ʷáyx̌ʷay, referring to the ceremonial mask and regalia used by certain members of some Coast Salish groups, including the Comox.

from the houses. A woman saw the canoe arrive and came down to the beach to greet the strangers. She asked, "Where do you come from?" They answered, "We have come to see you." But they said this only to please her. "We have lost our youngest brother on the other side of the high mountain." The woman took pity on them and said, "Wait here, I'll bring you some salmon." She went into the house and there her husband demanded that she take Aihōs fat, which killed anyone who ate it, to the brothers. But the woman had taken a liking to the brothers. She pretended to take the Aihōs fat, but in reality hid it under her cape and took them salmon.

But the master of the house had a slave, Baqbakuālanusī́'uaē,[112] who had to guard the salmon weir for him. The corpses of drowned people used to catch in the salmon weir and he then devoured their eyes. In this way he had found the corpse of the youngest brother, ripped out its eyes and taken the body into the house. When the brothers saw it, they said to the woman, "Look, this is our brother! Bring him back to life again." The woman sent them to Baqbakuālanusī́'uaē in order to get back the eyes. The slave gave them the eyes and the master of the house put them back into the young man. Then he brought the young man back to life again.

But the man kept seals in his house like other people keep dogs. The brothers asked, "Where do you catch the seals?" He answered, "On a small island out in the ocean." So the brothers decided to go out and catch seals as well. They launched their canoe and set out.

When they approached the island, they saw a canoe on the ocean but there was nobody in it. After a while they observed a tiny man surface, put two halibut inside the canoe, then dive again. His name was Tcētciudjaī́'miQ.[113] The brothers paddled closer and took one fish from the canoe. In a little while, when the dwarf surfaced again and threw the halibut which he held in his hands into the canoe, he noticed at once that one of his fish had disappeared. So he stretched out his hand in all directions and then sniffed it; thus he scented the three brothers. But when they saw how small Tcētciudjaī́'miQ was, they decided to kill him. But he took all three of them by their hair, carried them into their canoe and took them home with him as slaves.

When they came to a headland, they saw a village full of dwarfs no bigger than Tcētciudjaī́'miQ. The latter shouted from far off to his fellow tribesmen that he had caught three big slaves. Thereupon they all rejoiced. He took them to his chief who said, "It is well that you have caught them; they shall help us fight the birds." It wasn't long before the birds came flying. The dwarfs fought them, but the birds shot

---

112. What Boas transcribes as "Baqbakuālanusī́'uaē" is not a Comox term; rather, it is the Kwakwala word bákʷbakʷalanukʷsiwi?, the name associated with a cannibal legend (see, for example, Section XV, story 9).

113. This is the Comox term meaning 'dwarf.'

at them with feathers and killed many. Then the three brothers arrived and killed the birds with heavy clubs. Those which they didn't kill flew away. Then the youngest brother pulled the feathers out of the bodies of the dead and lo, they came back to life again! The chief was very glad at this and permitted the young men to return home. He called a whale to serve as their canoe. When he arrived, the chief ordered him to dive and stay under water for a long time. But he surfaced very soon. So the chief called a second whale. But this one couldn't dive long enough, either, and only the fourth whale was good enough. So he told the brothers to enter and the whale took them back to their home. They arrived early in the morning. When a man stepped out of a house and saw the whale lying there, he called out, "Look, there's a dead whale on our beach." Thereupon the whale disappeared and the three brothers stood there in its place.

They went back to their house and invited everybody to a huge feast. Only the elder brother who had once made the magical seal didn't come because he was afraid of his brothers' revenge. They sent him the message, "Why don't you come to our feast? We want to give food to you, too." So he came with his wife and child. But while they gave everyone good food, they gave him Aihōs fat which they had received in the far-off lands. When he had eaten it, many sores erupted on his skin, and the same happened to his wife and child. They all died a miserable death.

17. The Jealous Husband (See Legends of the Nootka)[114]

The name of the youngest brother is T'ĕtk·ā'laiōsin

18. T'āl[115]

T'āl was a wicked cannibal woman. She used to sling a basket over her back and go out to catch humans. One day she found some girls swimming in a lake. She caught them, stuffed them into her basket and carried them home. She wanted to kill them, but they said, "First let us dance one more time around the fire." Then they took pitch and smeared it in the face of T'āl. They stoked the fire and started to sing while beating time, "Go towards the fire; come back from the fire." And the woman approached the fire and came back according to what they were singing. But then the pitch melted and glued up her eyes. When she was unable to see, the girls took a stick and pushed her into the fire. She shrieked, "Let me out, let me out!" and was

---

114. See Section XIII, story 17; the manuscript version of the present story is contained in Boas (n.d.2).

115. Boas' "T'āl" is t'al, the Comox name for the 'cannibal woman.'

only silent once she was dead. The sparks shooting from her ashes were transformed into mosquitoes.

19. Sētlā′natc and K·ātē′natc [116]

Sētlā′natc was jealous of his younger brother, K·ātē′natc, because he was always lucky hunting. In order to harm him, he said to his sister, Tᴇ′gya,[117] "Become your brother's lover." Now when K·ātē′natc was going out one day to hunt seals, Tᴇ′gya sat down on a flat spot on the beach and sang, "Oh, if only K·ātē′natc would come and sleep with me!" When K·ātē′natc heard the voice he paddled towards it. But he didn't recognize his sister and took her for his lover. Thus it came about that he returned home empty-handed. The following day he went out to catch birds. When he was far out, his sister sang, "Oh, if only I were a bird and he would shoot me!" When he heard the voice, he turned around at once and stayed with Tᴇ′gya. Thus he returned without game again. The following day he went even farther out to sea to harpoon dolphins,[118] when he heard Tᴇ′gya singing, "Oh, if only I were a whale and K·ātē′natc would kill me." When he heard her, he went to her at once and forgot the dolphins. But on the fourth day he went out so far that he didn't hear when his sister sang, "Oh, come K·ātē′natc, come to me!" Then he returned home with plenty of game. But there he found that his brother had taken all his land away from him and he became very sad.

The following day, Sētlā′natc said to him, "Come, let's go out to the island and get feathers in order to make arrows." They went out and, at the older brother's suggestion, K·ātē′natc went around the island in one direction, while the former wanted to go around in the opposite direction. But he had scarcely gone from sight, when Sētlā′natc stepped into his canoe and paddled back home. When K·ātē′natc then saw that he was left all alone on the small island, he became very sad. He sat down and pulled his cape over his head in order to sleep. He hadn't sat for long when he felt someone tugging his cape and calling, "K·ātē′natc; don't sleep any longer." He threw off his blanket. But since he didn't see anyone, he covered up his face again. Again he heard the same voice calling, "K·ātē′natc, don't sleep any longer," but couldn't see anyone. Only when he heard the voice for the fourth time did he see that a mouse was calling him. It said to him, "Beat me!" He did, and the mouse became as big as a dog. It said, "Beat me once more!" Thereupon it became

---

116. These names are not now recognized.

117. This is the Comox term tə′gə, referring to the Sandhill Crane (*Grus canadensis*).

118. The species most common in this area and the one that is identified by the Comox people is the harbour porpoise (*Phocaena vomerina*).

as big as a deer, and when he beat it for the third time, it grew as big as an elk and two big antlers grew from its head. It said, "I want to be your dog. Sit on my antlers and I will carry you back home." K·āté′natc obeyed and it swam back with him. It was a nice, clear day and Sētlā′natc saw his brother coming. So he tied all his dogs together and went out to catch the animal carrying K·āté′natc. When Sētlā′natc came close, he released the pack. But the animal pierced them one after the other and tossed them into the air. When all the dogs were dead, Sētlā′natc started to shoot his arrows at the monster. But they fell to the ground without harming it. Then it pierced Sētlā′natc, tossed him in the air and thus killed him.

IX. One Legend of the Klahoose

Writing to his parents from Vancouver Island on 16 November 1886, Boas described his good progress with the local Comox, and added that "the people here are well informed about the neighbouring tribes" (Rohner 1969:60). "Neighbouring tribes" in this part of the world meant those directly accessible by canoe across the waters of the Strait of Georgia, in this case the Klahoose of Cortez Island and the Toba Inlet region north of Powell River. Boas never visited these Mainland Comox people; he likely asked one of his Island Comox consultants to tell him a legend customarily thought of as Klahoose, or he may have found an appropriate potlatch guest.

The site of Quatam Bay (páɬx̣ən 'flat area') in Ramsay Arm, an area used traditionally by both the Klahoose and Homalco.

Photo by Dorothy Kennedy, June 1974.

IX. One Legend of the Tlahū́'s[1]

Tio'qtset

There once was a man called Tio'qtset who exerted magical power over seals. When he sat down on a cliff, the seals came swimming at once and he killed them with his arrows. His older brother, Qā'ik·,[2] then went out to take the seals home and his canoe was filled right up. Often Tio'qtset went out himself and caught as many seals with his harpoon as he was able to carry away. His friends were very glad that he had such power over the seals, because he supplied all of them with meat, and when all the provisions had been used up, he went out to catch more. Once he sat down on a cliff and started to shoot seals. When his brother had gone to fetch the dead seals, he jumped into the water in order to help him collect them. But a seal seized him and pulled him into the deep. When Qā'ik· came back, he searched for his younger brother in vain. He couldn't find him and finally returned home sadly. There he told them, "Oh, my brother, Tio'qtset, must have drowned. I left him in order to get his seals but was unable to find him again." So all the people went into the canoes to look for him. They went out in twenty canoes.

When they came to the cliffs, they saw Tio'qtset lying among the seals. They called to him, "Oh, come back home! We've come here to look for you." They paddled towards him. But when they came closer, he jumped into the water with the seals. They watched him swim away and surface once in a while in order to breathe. So they decided to return to the village to purify the house of Tio'qtset. They

---

1. What Boas transcribes here as "Tlahū́'s" is the Comox term x̌'úhus (referring to a type of sculpin), anglicized as "Klahoose," referring to one of the groups comprising the Mainland Comox. Klahoose traditional territory was centred in the Toba Inlet/Toba River area but included East and West Redonda Islands, Read Island, and part of Cortes Island (Kennedy and Bouchard 1990b:441–443, 451). The Klahoose, together with the Sliammon and Homalco, speak Mainland Comox, a dialect of the Comox Coast Salish language (see also the initial footnote to Section VIII of the present volume).

    In annotating this section, we have drawn upon our consultation in the 1970s–1980s with the following Klahoose people, all of whose assistance we gratefully acknowledge: Rose Mitchell; Bill Mitchell; and Jeannie Dominick.

2. Neither this name, "Qā'ik·," nor the name of his younger brother, given in the previous sentence here as "Tio'qtset," are now recognized.

believed that he would return then. They did it, and when it became dark he came back home. They saw him in the morning and were already rejoicing at his return. But when they approached him, he ran away and jumped into the water again.

So they went to the cliffs again in twenty canoes and found him lying among the seals. When they saw this they decided to turn back home because they knew that they wouldn't be able to catch him. But they thought that he might perhaps return if they also purified the beach and made it flat. They did this and saw him come again at night. He now had hair on his back and whiskers like the seals. In the morning he disappeared again in the water.

His friends went out in twenty canoes to look for him. They found him on the cliffs again. When the canoes came near he reared up and the people saw now that he was marked on his belly like a seal. So they wept because they believed that he had become a seal and would never return. Therefore they gave up trying any further to get him home.

But Qā′ik·, who was a mighty chief, didn't yet want to give him up for lost. He caught a huge whale and placed it on the beach in front of his house. He hid and waited for Tio′qtset to come near. And it wasn't long before he appeared. He came swimming up and seized the whale. So Qā′ik· sprang out and tried to hold him, but he was too strong. He twisted himself away and swam away with the whale. Then Qā′ik· wept because he hadn't caught his brother.

Then he made the people erect a pole and smeared it with a magical substance. He hoped that Tio′qtset would scent it and come up. He made four strong men lie in ambush, who were to hold Tio′qtset as soon as he arrived. When Tio′qtset approached, they jumped from their hiding place, but they were not able hold him, either. They wept, went back to Qā′ik·, and told him what had happened.

So Qā′ik· became sad and decided to go into the sea himself to search for Tio′qtset. He called all the people together and made them tie together two hundred capes to form a long rope. He tied the rope around himself and jumped into the water. He stayed far out in the sea for four days while the people held one end of the rope, then Tio′qtset came to him. Qā′ik· tried to hold him but after a long struggle he twisted away from him. So Qā′ik· returned sadly. He left the precious rope in the sea. He thought, "I have to give up trying to catch my brother because I am unable to do it." But one day Tio′qtset returned to the village quite unexpectedly. He had taken a wife among the seals and had a child by her. He brought both of them along and the people saw that his wife and child were snow-white. He went up and down the beach with them, but nobody tried to catch him. Only an old man stepped out of the house and called, "Tio′qtset, do come into the house! It is wicked of you that you always go back in the water again and stay with the seals." And Tio′qtset obeyed the call, went into the house with his wife and child and lay down in the bed which the people had arranged when they saw him coming, because they wanted him to feel comfortable. Nobody but a pure boy, who had never touched a woman yet, went into the house. Before they sent him in, they made him bathe so that he was completely purified. He said to Tio′qtset, "Oh, stay with us; don't go back into the water." But he received no answer. When the boy came out of the house again, he told the people that Tio′qtset had become so like a seal, that he wasn't even able to speak any more. The people said to each other, "Let's not go into the house, otherwise he'll run away, and let's not beat our dogs, else they might bark and scare him away." Already they were rejoicing that Tio′qtset would stay with them, when he came out of the house and jumped into the sea again. His wife and child followed him. The people hadn't seen him leave, but when they boy peeped into the house through a knot-hole, he saw that the bed was empty and that Tio′qtset had disappeared.

Then they laid down a row of long boards from the house to the beach and covered the whole floor of the house with planks. They coated them with a magical substance and posted two pure boys as watchmen. Then they called to Tio′qtset. He came and entered the house. When the watchmen saw that he had lain down in the bed, they informed the other people. These now sent the chaste boy into the house. He sat down by Tio′qtset and began to weep. Tio′qtset asked, "Why are you crying?" He answered, "I am crying because you are always leaving us in order to live in the sea." So Tio′qtset promised to stay in the village in the future and the boy was very glad about this. He told the other people that Tio′qtset wanted to stay there now. But they didn't trust him and sent ten people, who were to hold him, into the house. The ten men closed the door and sprinkled five magic substances into the fire, K·qmē′n (*Peucedanum leiocarpum* Nutl.),[3] SpótltEn, Ānō, Sqtsem, and TE′matl (the head fur of the mountain goat).[4] Then Qā′ik· entered the house and said to Tio′qtset, "Oh, stay with us." The latter answered, "I will stay here for three days, but on the fourth I'll go back into the sea." And this is what happened.

So Qā′ik· became angry and decided not to try to keep his brother back any more. But he was sad all the same about the loss of his brother and wept a lot. For twenty days Tio′qtset came home every night and slept there. But in the mornings he disappeared again into the sea. Then he said, "Stop grieving for me. I am living

3.   "K·qmē′n" is Boas' transcription of q̇ə′xəmin, the Comox term for the Indian consumption plant. The Latin identification given here by Boas—"(*Peucedanum leiocarpum* Nutl.)"—is correct for this species for the period *circa* 1890; the contemporary identification is *Lomatium nudicaule* (Pursh) Coult. & Rose. Some Klahoose people in the 1970s placed the seeds of this plant on a hot stove, to provide a pleasant aroma and as a "disinfectant."

4.   None of these terms ("SpótltEn," "Ānō," "Sqtsem," and "TE′matl") are now recognized.

happily with the seals down there in the water because it is more beautiful down below than here on earth with you." So his brother mourned no longer and the people paid no attention to him when they saw him on the cliffs, or in the water.

X. ONE LEGEND OF THE SLIAMMON

Boas never sought out the Sliammon on their home ground around Powell River. There may have been a Sliammon person visiting his fellow Comox-speakers in the Comox Harbour village on Vancouver Island, where several feasts took place during the three weeks Boas spent collecting stories there in November 1886 (Rohner 1969:58–67), or quite possibly he asked his Comox consultant for the origin legend known to belong to the Sliammon. While Boas voiced satisfaction with the quantity and quality of his work at Comox, his recording of a Sliammon story received no comment in his letters. In any case, that is what he got. It is still told as such today, although when given by a Mainland Comox person from across the Strait, it is generally lacking reference to the rapids near Cape Mudge.

Old Felix of Sliammon mending a salmon net, *ca.* 1925.
Powell River Museum, Powell River, B.C. Neg. No. 9052.

X. One Legend of the Tlaā′men[1]

Tlaō′k·ōk·t[2] once courted a girl who, however, rejected him. He was ashamed of this and went into the forest. He took a piece of pitch and chewed it, and when he spat it out, it transformed into a dog. Then he went back to the village and sat down by the fire, chewing the pitch and smacking his lips. So the girl who had formerly rejected him thought, "Oh, if only I had some of the pitch." She didn't like to ask for it, herself, but sent her sister to ask him for a piece of pitch. She went to Tlaō′k·ōk·t and made her wish known. But he refused, saying, "Your sister will only spit out the pitch. If she intends to swallow it, she may have some." The girl went back and delivered his message. So the sister sent him her promise that she wanted to swallow the pitch. Thereupon she received a piece and swallowed it. Around midnight she felt her body swelling and noticed that she was pregnant. On the following day, when her father noticed this, he grew ashamed. He became angry and resolved to abandon his daughter. He ordered his people to load the canoes and they took off on the following morning. And P'a, Raven,[3] extinguished all the fires. Only the grandmother of the girl, T'Ets, Crow,[4] took pity on her. She put a glowing coal in a shell and gave it to her secretly, etc. (See Legends of the Lekwiltok:[5] She then gave birth to seven dogs, one girl and six boys … The mother throws their capes

---

1. What Boas transcribes here as "Tlaā′men" is the Comox term łáʔamin, anglicized as "Sliammon," referring to one of the groups comprising the Mainland Comox. Sliammon traditional territory extended approximately from Stillwater up to Desolation Sound, including the Powell River area and offshore islands (Kennedy and Bouchard 1990b:441–443, 451). The Sliammon, together with the Klahoose and Homalco, speak Mainland Comox, a dialect of the Comox Coast Salish language (see also the initial footnote to Section VIII of the present volume).

    In annotating this section, we have drawn upon our consultation in the 1970s–1980s with the following Mainland Comox people: Klahoose: Rose Mitchell; Bill Mitchell; and Jeannie Dominick; Homalco: Ambrose Wilson and Tommy Paul.

2. The name Boas transcribes here as "Tlaō′k·ōk·t" is not now recognized. Elsewhere, Boas (1887c) gives the title of this legend as "Tlāōqoqt the ancestor of the Tlaā′men."

3. What Boas transcribes as "P'a" is p̓ah, the Comox term for 'Raven' in mythology.

4. "T'Ets" is Boas' rendering of t'iθ' which is the Comox term for 'Crow' in legends, although in the *Sagen* Boas identifies this bird by the German term *Dohle* 'jackdaw,' a species that does not occur in North America.

5. See Section XIV, story 4.

into the fire and thus the children become human forever.) The girl snatched her cape back from the fire, but it had already been burned except for one corner which she wrapped around her left hand. Then it became a dog's paw again. Then she said to her brothers and to her mother, "I will weave capes for all of you." The eldest son said, "I will hunt deer." The second wanted to hunt seals, the third, whales; in short, each one of them wanted to look after their mother. First, they made bows and arrows for themselves and shot many birds, from which the sister made a cape for the eldest brother. He put it on and went to hunt deer. Finally he grew tired and lay down on a small island in order to sleep. Then Sun descended from the sky and said to him, "Let us exchange our capes." This they did. Then Sun Man continued, "If you are hungry, dip the corner of the cape into the water and shake it a bit. Thereupon many salmon will come." Then he climbed back into the sky.

Now the woman and her seven children became very rich, and they had whales, seals, deer and fish.

One day, T'Ets came to her house to see how her granddaughter fared. The latter gave her lavish presents. She also gave her seal blubber to take along. When the old one returned, she sang, "When we abandoned her, she was poor, and now she has what her heart desires." When she arrived home, she roasted the blubber on the fire. Flea heard how it crackled and hopped near to see what was going on. The old one said, "Oh, the wood is crackling in the fire." In a short while, Flea heard the same noise. When he hopped close, he saw the piece of blubber. So T'Ets told Flea that she had visited her granddaughter, who was now very rich. Her father and all his people then returned to the daughter. When they arrived, P'a was the first to jump ashore. He ran into the nearest house and called out, "Oh, this is my house." "Go away," answered the young man, the son of the abandoned woman, who lived there. "You have no business being here." And wherever P'a went, he was sent away and he had nothing to eat but red snapper because the young people knew that he had extinguished the fires when the canoes had left their mother behind all alone. So P'a thought, "If they don't want to feed me, I'll catch herring." He made himself a herring rake and went out to fish. But the eldest of the brothers caused reefs to form just where he dipped his rake into the sea, and thus P'a came home empty handed. Since that time the sea to the north-east of Cape Mudge[6] has been full of reefs. The eldest of the brothers became the ancestor of the Tlaā′men.

---

6.   Boas appears to be in error when he speaks of the sea to the "north-east" of Cape Mudge. It is the narrow channel to the north*west* of Cape Mudge—i.e. Seymour Narrows, located between Quadra Island and Vancouver Island—that is particularly well known as a treacherous stretch of water.

XI. Legends of the Eiksen

There seems to be no compelling reason for separating these two legends from the bulk of the Island Comox stories in Section VIII. Boas nowhere explained why the Eiksen sub-group differed sufficiently from the other speakers of the original Comox Coast Salish language as to have these undistinguished stories identified with them. Possibly they were told to him by someone from Campbell River whose demeanor suggested that a separate section would be appropriate.

At the beginning of time, the x̣ʷáyx̣ʷay mask dropped down from the sky at Quinsam, near Campbell River, along with the First Ancestors, and from there spread to several families among the Island Comox who then also used the mask on grave posts such as the one seen here.
American Museum of Natural History Library, New York.
Neg. No. 31202 (R. Weber photo).

XI. Legends of the E′ek·sen[1]

1. K·atē′mōt[2]

K·atē′mōt once went into the forest and there bathed in a river which was flowing along in a deep chasm. After he had been in the water for a long time and had become completely pure, he could hear trees being pushed over in the forest. So he knew that the Aihōs[3] was approaching. K·atē′mōt took a piece of bark and flung it backwards over his shoulder. It hit the Aihōs, who was crawling through the forest, and wounded him. The Aihōs cried in pain and called out, "Oh, what has hurt me?" and hurried to his house. Thereupon K·atē′mōt returned home and lay down in bed. When he got up again he said, "I will visit the house of Aihōs." He launched his canoe and, with his brother, went out to Mitlnatc.[4] There he said to his brother, "I will now descend into the sea. Don't weep if I stay down there for a long time." Then he grasped a stalk of kelp bobbing up and down in the waves and climbed down along it. It reached to the roof of Aihōs' house. When he had reached the end of the kelp he jumped down onto the roof of the house and climbed down to the sea bottom. But Aihōs was lying sick by the fire inside the house and heard someone on his roof. So he said, "Surely K·atē′mōt is coming." K·atē′mōt met the son of Aihōs, who was chiselling a tree trunk in front of the house. But his chisel consisted of the

---

1. What Boas transcribes as "E′ek·sen" is ʔíʔiqsən, one of the named groups of the Island Comox who formerly lived in the vicinity of Campbell River. By the time of Boas' visit in 1886, the remaining people who regarded themselves as ʔíʔiqsən were living in the Comox Harbour village, together with other Comox-speaking people (Kennedy and Bouchard 1990b:450–451; see also the initial footnote to Section VIII).

    In annotating this section, we have drawn upon our consultation in the 1970s–1980s with the following Comox-speaking people, all of whose assistance we gratefully acknowledge: Island Comox: Mary Clifton; Klahoose: Rose Mitchell, Bill Mitchell, and Jeannie Dominick; Homalco: Ambrose Wilson and Tommy Paul.

2. This name is not now recognized.

3. This is ʔáyhus, the Comox term for the 'double-headed serpent.'

4. "Mitlnatc" is Boas' transcription of the Comox term məʔƛ̓nəč which means 'calm back end' and is applied to "Mitlenatch" (anglicized from məʔƛ̓nəč) Island, located in the Strait of Georgia between Shelter Point on the east side of Vancouver Island, and Hernando Island (Kennedy and Bouchard 1983:161–163).

end of the kelp which thus always bobbed up and down. Then K·atē′mōt entered the house, sat down close to the fire and placed his hands spread out forward in front of his mouth. When the sick Aihōs saw this, he cried out, "Oh, don't do that, we are afraid of you." K·atē′mōt now saw how all the fish were gathered around the Aihōs to try and heal him. But they were unsuccessful because the bark with which K·atē′mōt had hit him remained invisible to them. Then Aihōs asked him, "Are you a medicine man? I will pay you a lot if you heal me. Do you see this seal harpoon? You shall have it if you heal me." K·atē′mōt replied, "No, I don't want it," but in his heart he wished to have it very much. Then a small seagull flew into the house and hid. Aihōs offered it to him, but K·atē′mōt didn't want to take it, either, although in truth he wanted to have it. Then another bird came into the house and hid. K·atē′mōt didn't accept it either. Then the water rose and filled the whole house. Many rushes floated about on it. The water fell again and the rushes were left behind by the fire. K·atē′mōt didn't accept the rushes, either. Then Aihōs seized a man and cut off his head with a big knife. He carried the head into one corner of the house, put the body into the other, and then made the people sing and beat time. When they had beaten time three times, the head and body started to move. When they sang and beat time for the fourth time, the fingers started to move as well, and the head and body rushed together again. The Aihōs then rubbed the neck with a magic herb and the man was whole and healthy again. Then the Aihōˉs asked K·atē′mōt, "Do you want to have this skill?" The latter was satisfied with this and now pulled the piece of bark from the Aihōs' skin. At first he hid it in his palm while he sang, and then showed it to all the people. So the Aihōs became well again. He said then to K·atē′mōt, "When you return, go to the far side of Cape Mudge. There you'll find a beautiful flat country." K·atē′mōt returned to his home and floated in the sea like a drowned man. His hair was full of down feathers. The brother who had waited for him in the canoe saw him and took him ashore. Then he stood up and came back to life again. K·atē′mōt then said to his brother, "I will show you what I obtained down in the sea. Take this knife here and cut off my head. But don't cry. Then place my head on one side of the house and my body on the other, and then have all the people sing and beat time." But the brother was afraid and refused to cut off his head. So K·atē′mōt, himself, took a knife and cut off his head. Then the people began to sing and beat time. When they had beaten time three times, the head and body started to move; after the fourth song they rushed together again and K·atē′mōt stood up. At night he called all the people together in his house. He sang, danced and carried a rattle. After he had danced twice around the fire, the harpoon points which the Aihōs had offered to him, appeared. When he continued dancing, the seagull came and hid in the house. Then the other bird came and at last the whole house filled with water on which rushes were floating. Only a small spot near the fire remained dry. Then the water disappeared again and the rushes stayed behind. But all the people were ashamed because K·atē′mōt was so superior to them in his skills. Then he ordered his brother to cut off his head. Now the brother no longer refused because he knew K·atē′mōt's skill. When the people sang this time and he got up again, they grew so afraid that they ran away.

2. Kuta′qçut[5]

One of the descendants of K·atē′mōt was called Kuta′qçut. Once, deep in winter, he went on an elk hunt with his brother, but the hide of the elk which they were pursuing was so thick that their arrows bounced off without effect. They pursued the animal to a mountain, into which it suddenly disappeared. The mountain closed up behind it, so Kuta′qçut lit a fire in front of the mountain and lay down to sleep. When he woke up, two elk came out of the mountain and he killed them. The following day, three came out, then four, six, ten, and more every day. Then Kuta′qçut said to his brother, "Tear up your bowstring and put it on the ground." He obeyed and it grew warm; the grass rose and the bowstring, too, sprouted roots and grew into a bush. Thereupon the heart of Kuta′qçut grew glad. When the snow had melted, he tied up his hides and went back home. He asked his people to go to the mountain with him to get the hides. He cut them into the shape of whales, filled them with blankets, skins and coppers, and hung them up. The people wanted to have what was in the hides, so Kuta′qçut let them down and gave them to the people. But the hides were so heavy that they smothered the people.

---

5. This name is not now recognized.

XII. LEGENDS OF THE PENTLATCH

As story 4 indicates, the centre of Pentlatch territory on Vancouver Island was in Comox Harbour, but at the time of Boas' arrival there on 12 November 1886 the tribe was almost extinct through warfare and illness, with only two Pentlatch-speaking families here and one or more living further south (Boas 1887f:132; Rohner 1969:58–59, 62–63). Thus, Boas was very happy to have "the last of the tribe" available to him: "I immediately made friends with them and am now learning this newly discovered language" (Rohner 2969:59). His work with this family was interrupted by a feast which the Pentlatch—not exactly down and out—"had invited everyone to," but by 15 November Boas had "about four hundred words in both the Comox and Pentlatch languages ... I also got a story today." On 23 November he could report that he had "another long Pentlatch text" (Rohner 1969:59, 65).

Texts collected by Boas in the Pentlatch language, with interlinear English translation, are held by the National Anthropological Archives of the Smithsonian Institution (Boas n.d.6), and the American Philosophical Society Library has a preliminary working draft of these texts, with German interlinear translation (Boas n.d.5). For the *Sagen*, Boas chose to use not these sparse versions but more complete tellings of the same stories, likely from Chinook Jargon.

Boas met with Pentlatch people living in the Comox Harbour Village in November 1886, by-passing this other family of Pentlatch descendants living at Qualicum Beach who were photographed *ca.* 1900: (back) Qualicum Tom and his daughter Agnes Thomas; (front) Gertie Thomas, David Ford, Emily Thomas, Lily Thomas, Qualicum Annie, George Thomas.

Photo courtesy of Diana Recalma, Qualicum Beach, B.C.

XII. Legends of the Pe′ntlatc [1]

1. Kōaĭ′′min and Hḗ′k·ten [2]

A long, long time ago, two men, Kōaĭ′′min and Hḗ′k·ten, descended from the sky. They became the ancestors of the Pe′ntlatc. Once the sea receded far from its shore and the women went far out and filled their baskets with fish. The bottom of the sea remained dry for a long time. But Hḗ′k·ten was afraid that the water would rise that much higher later on. Therefore he made a long rope of cedar branches and tied together four canoes. At last the water really flowed back and began to flood the shore. So he tied the rope to a big rock in the mouth of the Pe′ntlatc River,[3] fastened the other end to the canoes, and the two chief families floated about on the rafts. The other people begged Hḗ′k·ten, "Oh, allow us to tie our canoes to your rope. We will give you our daughters as wives." But Hḗ′k·ten didn't allow it and pushed them

1. "Pe′ntlatc" is Boas' rendering of pə′nƛ̓ʼəč, anglicized as "Pentlatch," the indigenous name of a Coast Salish group on the east coast of Vancouver Island who spoke a language closely related to Comox and Sechelt. Pentlatch territory formerly extended from the vicinity of Parksville up to the Kye Bay area (north from Comox), including the nearby offshore islands (Boas 1887e:map; 1887f:132, map; Barnett 1955:23–24; Kennedy and Bouchard 1983:16–17; 1990b:441–443; Bouchard and Kennedy 1995). While the last known person who had any knowledge of the Pentlatch language, Joe Nimnim, died in 1940 (*Comox Argus* 1940), another person who may have had some knowledge of this language lived until the 1970s (Recalma-Clutesi 2001:pers. comm.) Some members of the present-day Qualicum Indian Band (Recalma-Clutesi 1992) and Comox Indian Band can trace ancestry to the original Pentlatch inhabitants of this region.

    In annotating this section, we have drawn upon our consultation in the 1970s–1980s with the following Comox-speaking people, all of whose assistance we gratefully acknowledge: Island Comox: Mary Clifton; Klahoose: Rose Mitchell, Bill Mitchell, and Jeannie Dominick; Homalco: Ambrose Wilson and Tommy Paul.

2. The Comox-speaking people with whom we consulted in the 1970s–1980s did not recognize either of these names, "Kōaĭ′′min" and "Hḗ′k·ten." However, in one of George Hunt's accounts of "Kwakiutl family histories" entitled "Marriage With the Comox," "Hēk!ŭtEn" (the same name transcribed here in the *Sagen* as "Hḗ′k·ten") was identified as follows: "The ancestors of the Comox lived at PEntlatch, and they had for their chief Hēk!ŭtEn," who married and had a son named "NEmnEmEm" (Boas 1921:2:951). This latter ancestral name, nə′mnəm?əm (anglicized as "Nimnim"), was held by the father of Joe Nimnim (see footnote above), the last known person who had any knowledge of the Pentlatch language.

3. Anglicized as the Puntledge River today.

away with poles. When the water receded, they alone found their home again, while all the others were scattered throughout the wide world. A whale remained stranded high up on the mountain near Pɛ'ntlatc Lake.⁴ The water up there froze and the whale was unable to get away again. The whale can still be seen there today and that is why the glacier in the Pɛ'ntlatc Valley⁵ is called K·onē'is.⁶

2. The Eight Brothers

Eight brothers went out to hunt mountain goats.⁷ When night fell they lit a fire and lay down to sleep. The following morning they saw some goats high up on the mountain, so they washed, ate their breakfast, took bows and arrows and pursued the goats. The eldest of the brothers said, "Let me shoot the goats. We'll meet again in that spot at the foot of the mountain." The brothers agreed, and the eldest climbed up the mountain, but on his way he found fern roots, ate them and thought no more about the mountain goats. Meanwhile, the brothers went to the rendezvous and were already looking forward to the goat fat. But when he brought nothing but the miserable fern roots, they grew angry and were ashamed of their brother. They took away his cape and tied him naked to a tree, where he was supposed to starve to death. They left him and when they arrived home they said, "Our eldest brother fell from the mountain and is lying there dead." But all the animals arrived to help the abandoned one. And an old woman who knew what the brothers had done put some fat into a small shell, and went to the spot where the young man was tied up. When she rubbed him with the fat, the ropes loosened and she untied them completely. So he went, caught many mountain goats and arrived back safely to his wife.

3. The Jealous Husband (See Legends of the Nootka)⁸

The name of the man killing his wife is QuakQū'kolatc⁹ here.

---

4. Now known as Comox Lake.
5. This area is now known as the Comox Valley and the glacier referred to here is known as the Comox Glacier.
6. "K·onē'is" is Boas' rendering of qʷənís, the term he identifies elsewhere (Boas n.d.6; [1886–1887]) as the Pentlatch word for 'whale' (the Comox term for 'whale' is qʷə'nis, with stress on the first syllable).
7. Mountain goats have never been found on Vancouver Island.
8. Presumably Boas is referring to story 17, "The Revenge of the Brothers," in Section XIII.
9. This name is not now recognized.

4. The Thunderbird

Two brothers went into the forest and stayed hidden there for a month. They bathed in a lake every day and then washed with fir boughs until they had become purified and had no human smell about them any more. Then they climbed up Mount Kulē'nas[10] (in the Pᴇ'ntlatc Valley)[11] and there found the house of the Thundergod, Wā'lek·um.[12] They stepped through the door and saw a woman sitting in the house. She invited them in and told them that her husband and his brother had flown out. Before they returned, she hid the visitors in a corner of the house. It wasn't long before the Thunderbirds flew up and alighted in front of the house. It sounded as if a tree were being blown down by a storm. When they entered the house they scented the visitors at once and asked the woman where she had hidden them. She called them out. Then the Thunderbirds took off their belts, which shone like fire and were made of Aihōs[13] skin, hung up their feather garments and assumed human shape.

Towards the end of summer, the Pᴇ'ntlatc tribe celebrated a feast (at the spot where the Comox shipyard is now situated),[14] when the Thunderbirds flew up and brought back the young men whom they had called Qū'mt'ik· and K·ā'penats.[15] The dancers could hear them call, "Hū, hū, hū, hū" (each time sung a fifth lower). So they tied two canoes together, placed boards across them and went out to look for the young men. But they saw nobody, although they reached the spot where the voice came from. Suddenly they heard something settle on the high prow of the canoe, but still could not see anything. So they returned to the village, purified the house, and then Qū'mt'ik· entered, danced with the Thunderbird mask and sang. He was the ancestor of the Qū'mt'ik· family. His daughter was called Siqsē'qawit.[16] His descendants are able to see the Thunderbird and, when there is a strong thunderstorm, they are able to persuade him to return to his home.

---

10. This term, "Kulē'nas," is not now recognized, nor is the location of the mountain that "Kulē'nas" referred to.

11. Now known as the Comox Valley.

12. What Boas transcribes as "Wā'lek·um" is not now recognized.

13. Boas ([1886–1887]) transcribes this Pentlach word as "Ai'hōs" and provides the translation 'fabulous doubleheaded snake.' This same term, ʔáyhus, is also in the Comox language, where it has the same meaning, 'double-headed serpent,' and also an association with power (see Kennedy and Bouchard 1983:90).

14. We have not been able to determine the exact location of the site where "the Comox shipyard" was located when Boas visited this area in 1886.

15. Neither of these two names, "Qū'mt'ik·" and "K·ā'penats," is now recognized.

16. The name Boas transcribes here as "Siqsē'qawit" is not now recognized.

XIII. Legends of the Nootka (Nuu-chah-nulth)

Boas did not get to the Nootka Sound tribes on the outer west coast of Vancouver Island, although George Hunt did gather stories here later, on Boas' behalf (see Hunt and Boas 1916). The stories given in this section of the *Sagen* were gathered during Boas' stay of 1–12 August 1889 in Port Alberni, at the head of a deep inlet that takes one far from the sea almost to the eastern side of the island. The Tseshaht, who speak the same language as the Natives of Nootka Sound, migrated from Barkley Sound up this channel, which event, writes Boas (1891d:584) in his report to the British Association for the Advancement of Science, "is said to be less than a century ago"; and it is possible that Boas received most if not all of these stories from a Tseshaht man. There are no details in the one published letter from Alberni (Rohner 1969:110), but in his BAAS report Boas (1891d:597) names as one of his helpers Tlutisim, "a man about thirty years old, belonging to the Netcimū'asath sept" of the Tseshaht. This young man had a fine sense of responsibility to family history. He told Boas about vision quests and about his great-grandfather's grandfather (five generations back), who "sat one night on his bed resting, but not sleeping, as hunters will do":

> At midnight he heard someone singing on the beach. He went out to see who was there, and discovered a number of Ya'ē—a fabulous people living in the woods—landing a sea-lion which they had caught. It is always a foreboding of good luck to see those people. The man ran down to the beach, cried 'hē,' and the Ya'ē were transformed into sea-foam. He gathered it carefully, and hid it. It became his charm, and henceforth he was a great and successful hunter (Boas 1891d:597).

This is a narrative from before the Tseshaht migration inland, and the whaling that figures conspicuously in many of the following stories indicates that the tribe still retained an interest in hearing about seagoing adventures. Thus we can take these stories as representative of all the indigenous peoples of Vancouver Island's west coast. To make the selection even more so, two stories from coastal tribes as such were included, a Nitinat (Ditidaht) tale (No. 17) and a Tokoā′ath (Toquaht) narrative (No. 2, part 8), presumably obtained from Tlutisim.

The one narrative that was likely told by someone else is No. 21 "The first Mohö′tl'ath," an origin story of one of the groups comprising the Opetchesaht, who were in the Alberni area before the Tseshaht came. The local version of this historic circumstance is given in story 23. The aboriginal tribe of women taking all the shellfish away from Alberni when they left is, of course, the stuff of myth. But the fact that the Opetchesaht originally spoke some dialect of Coast Salish (described by Boas as "the Nanaimo language") is in line with current linguistic thinking. This ancestral language difference, if nothing else, sets the Opetchesaht apart from the Tseshaht, and it would have been interesting to know if there were, in fact, stories besides No.21 from the Opetchesaht, but unfortunately Boas did not distinguish them for us.

Filleted salmon drying on rack near Port Alberni, no date.
Royal British Columbia Museum, Victoria, B.C. PN4740 (Chas. S. Sely photo).

Unidentified boys netting salmon from a westcoast-style canoe on the Somass River at Port Alberni, 1913.

Alberni Valley Museum Photograph Collection, Port Alberni, B.C. PN1898
(Leonard Frank photo).

XIII. LEGENDS OF THE NUTKA[1]

1. Kwē′kustEpsEp, the Transformers[2]

In the beginning only the Ky'äimi′mit,[3] birds and other animals, lived on earth. They knew that they would one day be transformed into people and real animals. Now when the rumour went round that two men, called Kwē′kustEpsEp (= the Transformers), had descended from the sky and were going to transform them, they called a council to talk the matter over. Ā′tucmit (= Son of Deer),[4] said, "When they come and want to transform me, I'll kill them. I'm not afraid." He picked up a pair of big mussel shells[5] and sharpened them on a stone at the seashore. He tested their

---

1. "Unless otherwise noted, the legends originate with the Ts'iciā́ath and Hopitcisā́ath" [Boas' original footnote]. The word that Boas transcribes here as "Nutka" is better known as "Nootka," a misleading term applied by early researchers to all the aboriginal people along the west coast of Vancouver Island between Cape Cook and Point no Point. Strictly speaking, "Nootka" (possibly from nu·tka· 'circling about') refers only to the Nootka Sound tribes. Since about 1980, the term "Nootka" has been replaced by the terms "Nuu-chah-nulth" (or, occasionally, "Westcoast"), referring collectively to the tribes between Cape Cook and Pachena Point, and "Ditidaht," referring collectively to the Nitinaht (Ditidaht) and Pacheedaht (Pachenaht) who speak a different language and whose territory is further south, between Pachena Point and Point No Point. The Nuu-chah-nulth speak a language that is now referred to either as Nuu-chah-nulth or Westcoast, and is classified as part of the Nootkan Branch of the Wakashan Language Family. Nitinaht or Ditidaht, a closely-related language spoken by the Ditidaht and Pacheedaht, is also part of this Nootkan Branch of Wakashan (Bouchard and Kennedy 1990; 1991a; Arima and Dewhirst 1990; Arima 1991; Thompson and Kinkade 1990). The dialect spoken by the Alberni area tribes, the Tseshaht (Boas' "Ts'iciā́ath") and the Opetchesaht ("Hopitcisā́ath"), differs in some respects from the other Nuu-chah-nulth tribes.

   In annotating this section, we have drawn upon our 1980s–1990s consultation with the following Nuu-chah-nulth people, whose assistance we gratefully acknowledge: Chief Adam Shewish; George Louie; Stanley Sam; and Peter Webster. Comparative Ditidaht information cited here has been provided by Carl Edgar, Sr. We also thank Denis St. Claire and John Dewhirst for comments they provided in 1977 concerning an earlier draft of this translated section.

2. This term, kʷik̓ʷistupsap, transcribed by Boas as "Kwē′kustEpsEp," is the name applied to the Transformer in several Nuu-chah-nulth dialects, but not in Tseshaht (Powell 1991:135).

3. The Nuu-chah-nulth people with whom we consulted translated this term as 'myth people.'

4. What Boas transcribes here as "Ā́tucmit" is ʕa·tušm̓it, the mythical term for 'deer' in the Tseshaht dialect; the equivalent term in other dialects of Nuu-chah-nulth is muwač̓mit.

5. Given in the original as *Muschelschalen* 'mussel shells'; the species referred to here is the California mussel (*Mytilus californianus*).

sharpness on his tongue and the scraped-off dust ran from his mouth down his chin. While he was thus engaged, he saw two people approach who looked just like his neighbours. They asked, "What are you doing there, Ā'tucmit?" He answered, "I'm making daggers for myself in order to kill them as soon as they come." "Who?" they queried. "The Transformers, when they actually do come," replied Deer. "You have chosen really nice shells. Let's have a look at them," they continued. When Ā'tucmit handed them over, they struck his forehead with them and shouted, "They shall always stay on your forehead—this one here and that one there! Now shake your head!" He had to obey. "Now once more," they called out. After he had shaken his head for the second time the shells were transformed into antlers. They then ordered him to prop his hands on the ground and smeared his rear end with the dust which he had ground off the shells. Then they told him to run into the woods and he became a deer. The Transformers then went to the village and transformed all the inhabitants into animals and birds. Land Otter had a long spear, Beaver had a long broad bone-knife and the Transformers made their tails from these.

When the animals had thus come into being, people came into the world, one couple in every village. The Transformers created them and said, "People shall speak different languages. Some tribes shall become powerful; others shall remain weak. We will give people everything they need—berries, shellfish and fish." When these had been created, the Transformers taught the people how to gather and catch them. They also taught them to pray to the sky and gave them healing herbs. That is why the chiefs nowadays pray to K·ā'otsē,[6] who lives in the sky, to make them rich, because this is what the Transformers taught them.

2. Kwo'tiath[7]

1) Kwo'tiath owned a certain stretch of the coast where he collected dead fish, which always drifted ashore. One day when he went down to the beach to collect fish, he found that they had all disappeared. The following morning he got up earlier, but again they had been taken away. No matter how early he got up, the

---

6. Boas' "K·ā'otsē," which he transcribes elsewhere as "Kā'tse" (Boas 1891d:595), is qa·ci, a term that our Nuu-chah-nulth consultants translated either as 'Provider' or 'pray for something.' According to Boas (1891d:595): "No offerings are made to Kā'tse; he is only prayed to." Drucker (1951:152, fn.31) referred to this same term, qa·ci, as "Quaw-autz (or like names)" while commenting that early historic accounts identified this as a single deity, dwelling above, about whom his aboriginal consultants in the mid-1930s knew nothing (see also story 11 of the present section).

7. The Nuu-chah-nulth people with whom we consulted explained that this character, kʷatya·t (Boas' "Kwo'tiath"), whose name is derived from the word meaning 'heavy,' was similar in nature to the trickster Mink, his cousin, but he had greater power to cause things to change.

thieves were always ahead of him. So he became angry and resolved to take revenge. He lay in wait and saw that Wolf was stealing his fish. Thus he called after him, "The next time when you come here, you must come to my house." When Wolf came along, Kwo'tiath invited him into the house. Wolf accepted the invitation and lay down by the fire. He rested his head on a neck-rest. Then Kwo'tiath stepped behind him as if he wanted to get something to eat, grasped his spear of yew-wood unnoticed, and killed Wolf by hitting him first in the neck and then in the body. After that he buried the corpse in the middle of the house. After a while two Wolves came to ask after their lost companion. Kwo'tiath lay by the fire and pretended to be sick. The Wolves asked, "Haven't you seen our chief?" Kwo'tiath replied, "No, I haven't seen anybody." He spoke slowly, as if with great effort and trouble. "I've been laying here for several days already and am unable to get up," he continued. When the Wolves had left, he made himself a comb and filled a fish-bladder with oil. Several days later, other Wolves came to him to enquire after their chief. Again they found him by the fire and he answered them, too, that he had been ill for a long time and unable to get up. After some time the Wolves came to him again and said, "Our friends say that our chief has been killed on this stretch of coast of yours." Then Kwo'tiath replied, "I'll try to find out." He made the Wolves, who by now had arrived in large numbers, form a circle. He hid the comb and the bladder of fish oil under his arms and began to dance in the centre of the circle, singing meanwhile: "Aqnī's, aqnī's, m m m m m m" (the latter sung very quickly). But after some time he began: "Aqnī's, aqnī's, ūq'uyēp'ā'tl, yak·syek·stekmū't k·oāqk·oayetsē'k· (I am the killer of the chief of the Wolves.)" Then he made a great bound and jumped out of the circle. The Wolves pursued him. So he stuck the comb into the ground behind himself and called out, "Become a mountain." And this is what happened. When the Wolves had bypassed the mountain and caught up to him again, he poured out some oil behind himself and transformed it into a lake. He made mountains and lakes behind himself four times like this and escaped safely. These mountains and lakes can still be seen today between Sproat Lake and the central part of Alberni Canal.

2) Kwo'tiath once went out in his canoe to catch halibut and red snapper.[8] Just when he was about to put out his lines, Shark swam around his canoe and drove away all the fish. Kwo'tiath became angry about this. He went ashore and made himself a harpoon of yew-wood in order to catch Shark, should he return. As soon as Kwo'tiath began fishing again, Shark appeared and Kwo'tiath hit him with his harpoon. Shark dived at once. Kwo'tiath returned home and set out the following morning to search for Shark. He went along the beach and after some time he saw

8.   Given in the original as *Schellfische* 'haddock,' the term Boas used to refer to the species available here on the west coast of Vancouver Island, the red snapper and yelloweye rockfish (*Sebastes spp.*), also known commonly as the "red cod," and called wa·n̓uɬ in the Nuu-chah-nulth language.

a village which he had never before noticed. He sat down close to it and now heard medicine men singing and dancing inside the house. During a pause in their song, Kwo'tiath shouted outside, imitating them, "Hōooo hǫ hǫ hǫ hǫ." After he had shouted like this four times, a woman heard him. She sent out a slave and had him ask whether the stranger was a shaman. The messenger went outside and said to Kwo'tiath, "One of our women is ill. Are you a shaman and can you heal her?" Kwo'tiath said he could and the slave led him into the house. Right away he saw his spear in the sick woman's back and thus knew that he was in the village of Sharks. But the Sharks were unable to see the weapon and believed instead that a big worm had crawled into the sick woman. Kwo'tiath now sang: "Wā wā oōctak·iǔ' tc'anēmō' koakoaqsē'e wā wā (Wā wā, the shaman doesn't see the stinging poison. Wā wā.)" So one of the relatives of the sick woman said, "If you make her better she will give you one of her daughters as a wife. Just look what beautiful white hair she has." So Kwo'tiath sang, "Ēǫ ēǫ ēǫ āqaniǔ'sa mēнmitlitsa'tk·ōs māǫmaa' ēǫ ēǫ ēǫ (Ēǫ ēǫ ēǫ. I can do it if you will give me both sisters; ēǫ ēǫ ēǫ.)" So the sick woman said, "Yes, you shall have both sisters if you make me better." So he grasped the spear and pulled it while continuing to sing. He tore it from the wound and flung it out of the house. The sick woman then said, "I feel that you have pulled out my sickness," and she recuperated quickly. Then he married the girls and took them home with him. But his penis was worn down on the rough skin of his wives and at last broke off completely. So he threw his penis ashore and called out, "This place shall henceforth be called Kyēky'ēqsā'a (Prickly Coast)."[9] It is situated a bit below Ikū.[10]

3) Once Kwo'tiath went to the Pitch Girls, I'ctēpas,[11] in order to sleep with them. He lay down between them and they embraced him. In the morning they woke him and said, "Go away!" When he wanted to rise he found that he was stuck fast and all the people laughed at him. He had to be freed from the bed by means of big wedges.

---

9. This name transcribed by Boas as "Ky'ēky'ēqsā'a," and literally translated as 'penises on shore,' applies to the area known locally as "Knob Point" that is situated near Chup Point on the east side of the entrance to Alberni Inlet. Very likely it is Knob Point that Boas (1891d:585) identifies elsewhere as "Vob Point" and gives as an example of a place where a rock "of singular shape" is used to mark a tribal boundary. One other source also identifies a tribal boundary in this area, but at nearby Chup Point (St. Claire 1991:124).

10. What Boas transcribes as "Ikū" is the place known as hikʷu·ɬ (anglicized as "Ecoole"), situated on the southeast shore of Seddall Island in Barkley Sound; it was the major village site of the hikʷu·ɬʔatḥ people and the place from which their tribal name was derived. The hikʷu·ɬʔatḥ are a Barkley Sound tribe whose territory included the area near the north side of the entrance to Alberni Inlet, and later the lower Somass River (St. Claire 1991:33–34).

11. This name appears to be derived from the word for pitch, ʔišči·p, in other dialects of Nuu-chah-nulth, but not in Tseshaht, where the term meaning pitch is ʔišʔaqƛ (Powell 1991:21).

4) A long time ago it was constantly windy and there was never any low tide. Consequently the Ky'äimi'mit were unable to dig for shellfish. Finally a chief called all his people to a council meeting. It was decided to go to the house of the Winds and to kill them. The canoes were launched and when the warriors approached the house of the Winds, they landed at the end of a point of land. The house of the Winds stood on a bay beyond this point of land. The chief ordered Loon to go around the point to have a look. But a terrible storm raged around it and he was unable to get past. Then he sent Sawbill[12] and he, too, had to turn back without success. Then the chief sent out "Winter Robin" (ī'tū)[13] and advised him to keep close to the shore since there was less wind there. The bird glided safely past the point of land, went to the house of the Winds and, through an opening, saw the Winds sitting asleep around the fire. So he went in and sat down with them by the fire to warm himself. Then his breast became full of red spots. He quite forgot to return to the people waiting for him. So the chief sent out Cormorant, but he was unable to fly past the point of land. Eagle (ts'ī'qōten)[14] and Osprey[15] couldn't do it either. Then the chief sent Kwo'tiath to Sardine[16] and ordered Kwo'tiath to deliver the message that Sardine should try and should keep close to the shore. Kwo'tiath went to Sardine, but instead of delivering the chief's message, he said, "Your eyes shall sit on your nose and not close to your gills," and ever since, the sardine's eyes have been close together. Kwo'tiath went back to the chief and pretended to have carried out the order. While the people were waiting for Sardine's return, they cooked a meal on the advice of Rocksnipe.[17] They gathered "barnacles"[18] and roasted them. While they were thus employed, the Sandpipers, who had also come along, made a lot of noise. The chief sent out Kwo'tiath to order them to be quiet.

---

12. In the original *Sagen*, the artificially constructed term "*Sägeschnabel*" (in double quotation marks) appears, followed by the English term (Sawbill) (in brackets). German dictionaries from this time give the terms *Sägeschnäbler* or *Sägetaucher* as referring to *Mergus merganser*, now known as the Common Merganser; "Sawbill duck" often refers to the Common Merganser or Red-breasted Merganser, and on the west coast of Vancouver Island, the storyteller could be referring to either.

13. Given in English as "winter robin" (in double quotation marks) in the original *Sagen*; what Boas transcribes here as "ī'tū" is ʔi·tu, the Nuu-chah-nulth term for the Varied Thrush (*Ixoreus naevius*).

14. Bald Eagle (*Haliaeetus leucocephalus*) is known as c̓ixʷatin (Boas' "ts'ī'qōten") in the Tseshaht dialect of Nuu-chah-nulth.

15. Osprey (*Pandion haliaetus*).

16. Likely the Pacific sardine, also known as pilchard (*Sardinops sagax*).

17. Appears in the original as *Strandschnepfe*, followed by the English term ("Rocksnipe") (in brackets and double quotation marks). *Strandschnepfe* means, literally, 'beach snipe;' possibly this is a Common Snipe or one of the dowitchers.

18. Given in English as "Barnacles" (with double quotation marks) in the original *Sagen*.

Kwo'tiath went, but told them to continue making a noise. Ever since, sandpipers always screech. When they had finished their meal and Sardine had still not returned, the chief said, "I fear we will have to turn back; we are unable to go around the point of land." Thereupon a man advised "Let's send Seagull." The others laughed and said, "What good would that do? How could he achieve what nobody else did with his weak eyes and broken arms?" Then they ridiculed Seagull, but finally sent him out after all. He flew off, soaring up and down and at last around the point of land. So they were all astonished. The wind had calmed as soon as he had glided past the point and now the rest of the canoes were able to follow. They landed close to the houses and hid their canoes in the woods. Heron and Kingfisher, who were the best lance throwers, were chosen to stand by the back door of the house of the Winds, and to strike down anyone trying to escape through it. Halibut and Skate were ordered to lie down in front of the main door. Then everybody rushed into the house with weapons drawn. When the Winds saw them coming, some of them ran out the back way but were struck down by Heron[19] and Kingfisher. Others escaped through the main door. They then stepped on Halibut, slipped and were pierced on Skate's stinger. Only Westwind offered resistance. Bear attacked Westwind yet was unable to overcome him. But when Wind saw at last that he would have to lose, he called out, "Spare my life! I will make good weather. There shall be only light breezes, and low and high tides shall change once a day so that you will be able to dig for shellfish." The people were still not content with this and threatened to kill him until he promised to let low and high tides change twice daily. Thereupon they left him in peace and returned to their home.

5) In "Hellgate"[20] in Barclay Sound[21] there lived a giant whale called Cicī'tlunak· (= devourer of canoes which are tied together).[22] Anyone who couldn't avoid passing this way would carefully keep close to the shore in order not to attract the monster's attention. One day the mother of Kwo'tiath went past in a small canoe. The canoe drifted away from the shore and thereupon Whale came at once and devoured it. When Kwo'tiath heard that Whale had devoured his mother, he resolved to take revenge. He cut long stakes, sharpened them at both ends and placed them across two canoes. Then he boiled water in a large box. He summoned

---

19. *Reiher*—the closest equivalent German term for the Great Blue Heron (*Ardea herodias*).

20. Boas gives the English name "Hellgate" (in double quotation marks) in the original *Sagen*. Hellgate is the English term applied locally to the rough waters of Barkley Sound in the narrows near Nahmint, and appears to be the same place referred to by Sapir and Swadesh (1939:35) as ƛukʷałċa 'bluffs standing big in the water.'

21. Appears as Barclay Sound, in English, in the original text; the contemporary spelling is Barkley Sound.

22. The name of this whale, transcribed by Boas as "Cicī'tlunak·," is not now recognized.

his three brothers, Ka′pkimis (p. 109),[23] T′ēʜtēiap′iʜiī′nε, and (?)[24] made them jump into the boiling water. They emerged unhurt and each one of them said when he came out, "I would be surprised if Whale's belly is as hot as this water." Then Kwo′tiath jumped in himself and emerged again unhurt. Then they went out to sea on the raft and sang: hĭʜnūsaā′ hāǫwa-ipcä′tl ökwitl cayak·atla′ watltck′ aktlā′k ts′ē′yup haǫaQtsē′yup.[25] When they had sung this twice, the water receded deeply, and Whale surfaced and swallowed the canoe. Kwo′tiath called to his brothers to steer straight down the throat. As soon as they had reached the stomach, they cut up Whale's intestines with shells and finally cut off its heart. Then it died. Soon it drifted ashore and when the Ky'äimi′mit found it, they wanted to slice it open. They prepared themselves quickly. Only Kuī′tcak (a small white fish),[26] didn't manage to get ready. He wanted to dress nicely and put his hair in a knot because he assumed that many people would gather there. Therefore he was late. The people also asked the shellfish Tl'ā′tckun[27] whether he wanted to come along. He answered that he was lame. So they offered to carry him to the beach in a basket. "No," said he, "I might fall through the weave and get lost." They offered to carry him on a mat. "No," said he, "I might fall off." So they left Tl'ā′tckun at home. Before they went down to the beach, Shellfish asked them to bring sinews back for him so that he could tie shut his door. The Ky'äimi′mit fulfilled his wish and ever since then Shellfish keeps his shells tightly closed. Then they went down to the beach, with Pāε′mε (Octopus)[28] in the lead. They cut Whale open and out came Kwo′tiath and his brothers. When they saw each other, they laughed at one another. T′ēʜtēiap′iʜi′nε had lost all his hair in Whale's belly; it had been that hot inside.

---

23. In the original *Sagen*, after the word Ka′pkimis, Boas refers to page 109 of the *Sagen* which is the story of "Ka′pkimis, a brother of Kwo′tiath." Golla (2000:167) found the name "Ka′pkimis" to be unanalyzable.

24. Boas' question mark may indicate either that the storyteller could not provide the fourth name or that the name was unintelligible to Boas.

25. A literal translation of the passage as given by Boas, "hihinusa· hawi·ʔipšiɫ u·kwi·ɫ sayaqač'a a·ƛa·k ċiyup," according to the Nuu-chah-nulth people we consulted, is: "[vocables] something comes to eat—make—far away—two—sealion sinew." This song is recorded in Sapir and Swadesh (1939:39) as: "Come up out of the water, you who are wont to swallow those that move past in a canoe, who have your intestines curled up behind you! Ha, ha, guts!"

26. The name transcribed by Boas as "Kuī′tcak" was recognized as the Nuu-chah-nulth name for striped seaperch (*Embiotoca lateralis*), xʷi·tčak.

27. The term transcribed by Boas as "Tl'ā′tckun" is the Nuu-chah-nulth term ƛ'učkʷin applied to the black turban snail (*Tegula funebralis*), which is not a bivalve, although the story speaks about a hinged two-shell shellfish, such as a clam or cockle.

28. What Boas transcribes as "Pāε′mε" is not the Nuu-chah-nulth term meaning 'octopus'; rather, this word is p̓aʕam which refers to the giant red or gumboot chiton (*Cryptochiton stelleri*) (Ellis and Swan 1981:38).

Until that time the Ky'äimi'mit hadn't had any intestines. They were made from the innards of this whale. (According to a different version they were made from kelp.)

6) In the beginning only the Wolves possessed Fire. The Ky'äimi'mit were anxious to get it. After they had already tried unsuccessfully many times, chief Tlehmamit, Woodpecker,[29] said to Ā'tucmit, Deer, "You go to the house of Wolf and dance. All of us will sing for you. Tie inner cedar bark to your tail and then when you turn towards the fire, the bark will ignite." Deer called out, "Patlitlka'na Tlehmamit!"[30] and ran away to the house of Wolf. There he danced until the bark on his tail caught fire. He wanted to leap out but the Wolves caught him before he was able to escape, and took the fire away from him. Then Tlehmamit sent out the bird, Tsatsī'skums[31] and said, "The whole tribe shall sing for you and you will get fire." Then all the Ky'äimi'mit went into the house of the Wolves, with Tlehmamit and Kwo'tiath in the lead. They sang before they entered:

Hā - yē   hā - yē   ä

(A fourth or octave lower.)

Inside the house they sang:

ā - atl - he ā - atl - hē na - na - hē' - wa Tsa-sis-kums.[32]

They danced around and the Wolves lay by the fire and watched. Some Birds danced up onto the roof-beams. The Wolves didn't notice because they were watching the dance down by the fire. Finally they came to the fire-drill which was being kept in the roof-beam. They took it, danced back and gave it to Tlehmamit and Kwo'tiath, while the others inside kept dancing until they had safely reached home.

---

29. Boas' "Tlehmamit" is x̣'iḥmaṁit, the Nuu-chah-nulth term referring not to "Woodpecker" but to the Common Flicker (*Colaptes spp.*) when a character in mythology.

30. The translation of this phrase is: "I'm going to get the fire, Flicker!"

31. What Boas transcribes as "Tsatsī'skums" is caci·skim, the name applied to the Song Sparrow (*Melospiza melodia*); Nuu-chah-nulth people say that this bird follows after wolves.

32. The translation of the song is: "We have it, we have it, Song Sparrow."

When Kwo'tiath got home he rubbed the fire-drill until sparks came out. He stuck the fire-drill on his cheek and burned it. Since then he has had a hole in his cheek. When the dancers knew that Kwo'tiath had arrived home they uttered a cry and flew away. Thus the Wolves lost Fire.

6b) A chief in Tokoā'ath[33] owned fire and eternal life. Tlehmamit, one of the chiefs of the Ky'äimi'mit, wanted to steal them. So all the animals went to the house of the chief and began to dance. Ā'tucmit, Deer, had tied some inner cedar bark to his calf. During the dance he stood close to Otter. The latter farted and the fart ignited and set alight the inner cedar bark on the calf of Deer. Then he ran outside and the people took the fire from him. But he had been slightly burned. Bear sprang onto the heavy crossbeam which carries the roof of the house, so that it split and the Ky'äimi'mit could see what was inside. In it they found the box with eternal life, but before they were able to grab hold of it, the chief snatched it away from them and moved away with all his belongings, eternal life and salmon. Since the Ky'äimi'mit didn't get eternal life, people have to die.

7) Thunderbird and Tlehmamit. Thunderbird wanted to play hoop[34] with Woodpecker.[35] He took along his three brothers as team mates. Tlehmamit had invited Kwo'tiath, Kingfisher and Heron as partners. On the one side, Thunderbird was team leader, on the other, Tlehmamit. (The team leader carries a small spear.) Kwo'tiath was Tlehmamit's hoop thrower. Kingfisher was the first catcher and Heron the second catcher. Thunderbird threw the hoop first and it rolled as fast as an arrow, but Kingfisher hit it all the same. Then Kwo'tiath threw. As soon as he had thrown the hoop, he clapped his hands and it grew so small that the Thunderbirds were unable to hit it. Then when they threw again, Kwo'tiath called out, "Become big!" and the hoop grew so big that Kingfisher and Heron were able to hit it very easily. So Thunderbird became angry. He began to clap his hands and to sing and at once there were flashes of lightning, thunder and rain. He thought that his opponents would thus be unable to see the hoop. Yet while Kingfisher missed sometimes, Heron was sure in his aim. At last Thunderbird gave up the game since he was unable to win and Tlehmamit invited him into his house for a meal. When they had sat down he told his wife Āwip'ā-i'k

---

33. "Tokoā'ath" is Boas' transcription of t'ukʷa·ʔatḥ (anglicized as "Toquaht") referring to the people residing in Toquart Bay, Mayne Bay and west Barkley Sound. They took their name from a summer village situated on the Ucluth Peninsula.

34. Boas (1916:1021) identifies this as the "hoop-rolling game," and elsewhere writes: "A favourite game is played with hoops, which are rolled over the ground. Then a spear is thrown at them, which must pass through the hoop " (Boas 1891d:590). This game is also described in Drucker (1951:447).

35. As previously noted, the term Boas glosses as "Woodpecker" and transcribes as "Tlehmamit" is ƛ'iḥmaṁit which is actually the name for the Common Flicker in mythology.

(Hummingbird?)[36] to prepare a meal. She took a small bowl and walked modestly and chastely behind Thunderbird to her boxes and sang, "Berries, berries." Thereupon the bowl filled up at once although it was right in the middle of winter. The Thunderbirds were very astonished when she served fresh berries to them. Their chief thought that she had given them very little and wanted to empty the bowl quickly. But they were unable to empty the bowl, eat as they might. Therefore, the second brother said to the eldest, "This is a precious woman and she is so beautiful. Let's abduct her. We are the strongest and we can do it." One of the Thunderbirds stood up and lightning flashed and it grew dark. They took the woman and flew away without anyone noticing. When it grew light again and Tlehmamit saw that his wife had disappeared, he became very sad. He called a council in which they discussed how to get her back again. Heron said, "Let's make a thick fog so that they will lose their way." But they had too big a head start and the fog didn't reach them. Then it was decided that Tlehmamit and Kwo'tiath should go together in a small canoe to the land of the Thunderbirds to find out if there would be an opportunity to recapture the woman. When they got there, they saw that she was guarded constantly by Thunderbird Girls and that they would have to outwit them. Woodpecker said, "I'll make a salmonberry bush; you change into a berry on it. When my wife comes to pick you, I'll carry her away." He made a nice even spot full of salmonberry bushes. Kwo'tiath transformed himself into an enormous berry. When the girls came with the woman, they suspected at once that the giant berry was dangerous and went away. So Tlehmamit called out, "You've done that badly. You should have become a small berry. Now change into a salmonberry bush, but don't become too big." Kwo'tiath didn't listen and transformed into a big trunk. When the girls saw it, they again knew immediately that danger threatened and went home. Again Tlehmamit called, "You've done that badly. You should have become a small bush. Now let us assume the shape of salmon and go into Thunderbird's weir." Again Kwo'tiath changed into a huge salmon (sätsup).[37] Woodpecker took on the shape of a beautiful small salmon-trout.[38] Thunderbird caught them and took them into the house. There Āwip'ā-i'k asked him for the salmon-trout and he gave it to her. The trout slipped from her hands to between her legs and whispered to her, "Keep all my bones and my skin and don't give a piece to anyone." The woman roasted the trout

---

36. Boas' use of a question mark here in the original *Sagen* suggests he was not certain of the identification of "Āwip'ā-i'k" as a "hummingbird." What Boas transcribes as "Āwip'ā-i'k" is recognized as the Nuu-chah-nulth term ʔawa·ʔayk, the word applied to the Swainson's Thrush (*Hylocichla ustulata*), a bird that the Nuu-chah-nulth and others associate with the ripening of salmonberries.

37. Boas' "sätsup" is sacup, the Nuu-chah-nulth term referring to a 'spawning red spring salmon.'

38. "Salmon-trout' is a folk name referring to steelhead (*Oncorhynchus mykiss*), known in the Nuu-chah-nulth language as qiẉaḥ.

and ate it all by herself. Another woman cut open the big salmon and hung it over a pole. But it broke under the weight and she had to get a new one that was stronger. Thunderbird told his wife to throw the trout bones into the river when she had finished her meal. When she had waded into the water up to her knees, he called to her not to go any farther, but the fish bones said, "Keep going," and when she stood in the water up to her waist, she suddenly sank. The fish bones had come to life again and the fish carried her away. At the same time Kwo'tiath broke the pole from which he hung, smashed up everything in the house and swam away as a salmon.

When they had arrived home again safely, they discussed how they might take revenge on the Thunderbirds. Kwo'tiath said to Tlehmamit, "Borrow the whale's canoe." The latter did. They all stepped into the canoe and, in the shape of a whale, went to the house of the Thunderbirds. One of the Thunderbirds was sitting in front of the house when they arrived and saw the whale bobbing up and down. He knocked on the house wall and called Nō'nup'itcmik (= Catcher of the Blowing One, of the whale). He put on his feather garment and swooped down on the whale and struck with his claws through the skin. So the ones inside the whale bound his feet so that he was unable to release them again. Then they slashed his feet. He became very weak through the loss of blood. Kwo'tiath then beat time on a stone which lay in the whale and said to it, "Become heavy! Become large!" and the whale pulled the Thunderbird into the depths. When the guard saw that Nō'nup'itcmik was unable to lift the whale, he called Nō'pitatcitl (= He Who Catches on the Water for the First Time) to aid him. He put on his feather garment and swooped down on the whale. His brother called to him, "Take care, the whale has supernatural powers. I am being held and something is cutting my feet." But he was not to be warned and he met with the same fate as his brother. The whale pulled them down into the water so that their wings got wet and they were unable to fly. So the guard called the eldest brother and said, "I've never seen anything like it. Go, and help your brothers!" They warned him to stay away, but he didn't listen and grasped the whale instead and lifted it a bit, but he was defeated by Kwo'tiath and his companions after all. Then the last of the Thunderbirds put on his feather garment and circled above the whale, but the three brothers begged him to stay away so that he would not share their fate. He obeyed them and flew away. Then Kwo'tiath made the stone inside the whale very heavy. The whale dived and drowned the three Thunderbirds. Then they went back home. When they reached the vicinity of Tokoath Point,[39] they landed

---

39. Given in English as Tokoath Point in the original *Sagen*. It has not been possible to confirm with certainty which point was referred to locally as "Tokoath Point." However, taking into consideration both the context of this story and the distribution of tribal territories in this area, it is possible that "Tokoath Point" was a reference to Lyall Point, located on the mainland of Vancouver Island between Mayne Bay and the entrance to Sechart Channel (see also the footnote that follows).

and Kwo'tiath transformed the canoe, and the birds who had set out in it against the Thunderbird, into rocks which can still be seen there today. He called the place Ehtŏ'pk·oa (= Whale Point).[40] Since then, there has been only one Thunderbird.

8) There once was a chief's wife who had no child but who wanted to have one very much. One day Kwo'tiath said to her, "If you want to have a child, you will be able to have one." The woman asked, "But how shall I go about it?" So Kwo'tiath filled a bucket with water, put it beside the woman and said, "Drink from this if you get thirsty tonight." When everyone was asleep, Kwo'tiath transformed himself into a tiny leaf and dropped into the bucket. When the woman became thirsty during the night she drank some of the water and swallowed the leaf. She tried to bring it up from her throat but was not able to do so; she had to swallow it. Then Kwo'tiath called in her belly, "Get big, Get big!" and she became pregnant. When the time of her confinement arrived, Kwo'tiath didn't want to be born like other children. Instead, he wanted to go straight through her belly and he caused her great pain. But he was born like other children after all. The whole tribe assembled then to see the new chief and everyone who saw him said, "He looks just like Kwo'tiath. He has a hole in his cheek just like him." The children always played with the chief's son and people couldn't admire him enough. The child grew surprisingly fast and soon began to laugh and play. So far his mother always kept him in the cradle, but one night he freed himself and ran away. When the chief's wife woke up in the morning she found that the child had disappeared and she cried a lot. She now knew that she had swallowed Kwo'tiath and had borne him again. She grew ashamed, and placed the cradle in a corner of the house and told the people that her child had died. But Kwo'tiath went home. He tied up his hair, scratched his face slightly and sang, "H, h, h, I wish I could see the wife of our chief now" (Tokoā'ath).[41]

9) During his journeys over the earth Kwo'tiath gave names to all the places.

3. The Raven Legend

1) Raven once said to Doe, Ā'tucᴇs:[42] "I'll go out and mourn for my dead relatives;

---

40.   Boas' "Ehtŏ'pk·oa" is recognized as ʔi·ḥtupqʷu·ʔa, derived from ʔi·ḥtu·p 'whale,' and thus the translation, 'whale point,' is confirmed. This point, located on the south end of the southernmost Stopper Island in Barkley Sound, is known locally in English as "Whale Point," and is situated not far from Lyall Point.

41.   As previously noted, "Tokoā'ath" is Boas' transcription of t'uk̓ʷa·ʔatḥ (anglicized as "Toquaht") referring to the people residing in Toquart Bay, Mayne Bay and west Barkley Sound.

42.   Boas uses here the usual Tseshaht dialect term for 'deer,' which he transcribes as "Ā'tucᴇs" (ʕa·tuš), rather than the mythical term for deer he uses in stories numbered 1, 2–6, 2–6b, and 6 in the present collection of "Nutka" legends. In the German original, Boas uses the German term for a female deer, even though elsewhere he paraphrases this story with the deer as a male (Boas 1916:1021).

won't you come along?" Ā′tucɛs replied, "I have no reason to mourn, my relatives are all well." Raven retorted, "That doesn't matter, we can mourn our great-grandparents." Doe finally agreed. They went to the top of a steep cliff and sat down close by the edge of the precipice. Raven said, "Let's sit in such a way that our tears will drop down." So they moved even closer to the edge. Then he began to lament. "Oh, my great-grandfather! You died long, long before I was born." Then Ā′tucɛs began to weep, but didn't say anything. Raven said, "You don't cry properly at all. Close your eyes and lift up your head in the proper way." Doe obeyed and closed her eyes. Thereupon Raven pushed her into the abyss, then flew down and devoured her.

2) Raven and a small bird lived in the same village. When the herring appeared in springtime, they both went fishing. Raven always caught plenty of fish while the small bird didn't catch anything and suffered great need. But Raven didn't come to his aid. The bird's children were very hungry. They went to Raven's house and peeped in through the knot-holes. When Raven saw them he showed them the fish mockingly and then poked a stick into their eyes through the knot-holes. So their father became very angry. He took his bow and arrow and went into the forest to try and hunt some game. He found a herd of elk and shot two big bucks. While he was skinning them, the Wolves passed by and asked, "How did you kill the elk?" He replied, "I think you killed them; I found them dead." Then they asked, "How are you going to carry them home?" "I'll carry them as well as I can. Do you want to help me?" retorted the bird. "Yes, we'll help you, poor fellow. Take the meat on your back!" "No, I can't, I'm too small." "Just try! You'll find it quite easy." So he tried. He took the fat and meat on his back; the Wolves said, "Light," and he was able to carry it home without trouble. Then he plugged up all the knot-holes and joints of his house and roasted the fat. Raven smelled it, went to the bird's house and asked, "What are you roasting?" The small bird didn't answer him. So Raven sent over his wife, Pā′c-hok,[43] with some herring. She placed the fish in a bowl, went to the bird's house and said, "Here is some herring for you." The bird didn't reply at all. So Pā′c-hok went back to her husband and said, "They didn't even open the door for me." So Raven went over with the herring himself, but the bird didn't answer him either. He got so angry at this that he gulped down the herring, bowl and all. Then he went home and lied to his wife that the bird had accepted the bowl and the herring. But he was jealous of his neighbour's luck and also went into the forest to shoot elk. Soon he met a herd and killed two big bucks. While he was skinning them, two Wolves came by and asked him, "How did you kill the elk?" "What do you think?" he cried in answer, "I killed them. I don't need anybody to help me!"

---

43. What Boas transcribes here as "Pā′c-hok" has been recorded in the Tseshaht dialect of Nuu-chah-nulth as pa·šḥuk, 'daughter of Squirrel' (Powell 1991:137).

and called the Wolves the worst names. "Well," they replied, "how will you carry home the meat and fat?" "I can carry it easily on my back," retorted Raven who picked it up and dragged it home with great trouble. Once there, he threw down the meat and fat outside the door. When he entered the house, his children asked, "Father, what did you catch?" "I got two elk," he replied, "they are outside the door." "Shouldn't we have some fat?" "Yes, go and get some. Put it on a stick and roast it at the fire just like the neighbours did. They roasted it on a stick and licked off the fat." The children and Pā́c-hok went outside to get the fat but didn't find anything. Raven sent them out again and when they still didn't find anything, he went out himself. Then he saw that the elk were transformed into rotted wood.

3) Bear invited Raven for a meal. He lit a big fire, put a bowl close beside it and held his hands above it. So fat[44] dripped from his hands into the bowl. Then he roasted salmon, which he served to Raven with the fat. After this Raven invited Bear. When the latter went to Raven's house, he laughed because he knew that he would try to imitate him. Raven made a big fire, placed a bowl close beside it and held his hands above it. He was waiting for fat to drip down, but nothing came out. He turned them and shook them, but no fat ran out. His hands were only burned black. Because of this Raven has black wings and feet.

4) Wosnḗ'p (a small bird)[45] once gave a feast and served salmon eggs to his guests. He had not invited Raven because he always ate so much. So Raven was very sad and nearly fainted with anger. He pulled his cape over his head and sat motionless by the fire in his house. Now when all the Ky'äimi'mit were gathered for their meal, Raven crept behind the house of Wosnḗ'p and called, "Hēyidḗ', yidḗ', yidḗ', all those who eat salmon eggs must die!" After he had chanted this twice, he ran back home. He had his wife, Pā́c-hok, quickly scatter ashes onto his cape so that nobody would be able to think that he had left the house. Wosnḗ'p sent someone out at once to investigate whether it was Raven who was calling out, because his tricks were known. The messenger went to Pā́c-hok and asked her, "Has your husband been outside just now?" "No," said she, "don't you see the ashes on his blanket?" Now when the messenger reported that Raven hadn't left the house, they believed that a ghost had uttered the cry. They sent for Raven to get his advice. The messenger said, "We heard a voice call behind the house: Hēyidḗ', yidḗ', yidḗ', all those who eat salmon eggs must die!" So Raven said, "When something like this happens, one has to move to a different village. Come, Pā́c-hok, pack our things." Thereupon the

---

44. *Fett*, meaning 'fat or grease,' in the original *Sagen*, although Boas (1916:1021) uses the English term 'oil' in identifying this motif.

45. What Boas transcribes as "Wosnḗ'p" is the Nuu-chah-nulth term wasni·p, applied to the American dipper (*Cinclus mexicanus*), a bird widely known in the mythology of this region for its ability to produce salmon eggs.

messenger ran back quickly and said, "Raven is moving away. Let's leave the eggs here and go along." In the meantime, Raven broke the thwarts in his canoe and was still busy mending them when the others pushed their canoes into the water. He said, "Go on ahead; I'll follow you." When everyone had left, he and his wife ate up the salmon eggs.

5) Once two women wanted to bring a box of berries to a friend in a distant village. Their friends didn't want to let them travel by themselves and asked Raven to escort them. He agreed and said, "It'll do me good to travel a bit." Then they put the box with berries into the middle of the canoe and set off. The women paddled and Raven steered. On the way, Raven became greedy for the berries and asked the women to give him some. They refused, so he thought of a ruse. When they had gone on a little he called, "There's a canoe coming. I can see that they are our enemies who want to kill us! Don't turn around but paddle as fast as you can. We are going to hide. They are already very close." The women were afraid and kept paddling without looking around. They landed and Raven had them hide themselves. As soon as they had gone he gobbled up all the berries. In between he kept shouting, "Oh, save me, save me!" and kept gobbling. When he had gobbled up everything he covered himself all over with juice, broke off a piece from the canoe, smashed the box and lay down. When the women returned they wanted to see his wounds, but he cried, "No, it'll only make the pain worse!" They turned around and carried Raven into the house. He was sick for several days on account of the many berries he had eaten.

6) Once Raven sent his wife to Skate in order to challenge him to a contest with spears. He wanted to kill him and eat his liver. Skate prepared for the duel and arrived. The combatants stood opposite each other. Raven gave Skate first throw. When the spear rushed towards him, Raven flew up and the weapon flew past between his legs. Then Raven threw and Skate at once turned his narrow side towards him. So Raven missed. He said, "You're not allowed to do that." Then Skate threw again and Raven flew up. Then Raven threw and Skate turned his narrow side towards him. But then Skate hit Raven and he flew off and cried in pain, "K·ātc, k·ātc."

7) Raven had two beautiful daughters and he desired to possess the most beautiful one. Consequently he pretended to be deathly ill. He said to the girl, "I will die now and won't be able to look after you any more. Should you fall ill one day, go into the forest where you will find a small red stick. Sit down on it and you will get better again." Then he pretended to die and let himself be buried. But when the people who had buried him had gone, he flew into the forest and buried himself under the leaves. He left only his penis sticking out. The girl soon got ill and followed her father's advice. When she came and sat down on him, he shouted, "This is fine, go on, go on! I am your father."

8) In olden times the Ky'äimi'mit held a council to decide where to place the genitals. Raven wanted them put on the forehead, but a chief called out, "No, they shall sit between the legs where they can't be seen."

9) In the beginning water was found only beneath the roots of trees. Anyone wanting to drink had to lick the roots. A mussel shell filled with water fetched a high price. Crow[46] wanted to bring the water to man, but Raven wouldn't allow it. But Crow paid no attention to him, stole the water, and then urinated while flying over the earth. Thus the rivers and lakes originated.

4. Mink

1) K·ā'yaq (or Tc'āstᴇ'mitmit), Mink,[47] wanted to swim with the two sisters Mâ'hentlis (= female Sawbill Ducks).[48] The girls allowed him to come along, and when they reached the pond, all three of them cast off their clothes and jumped into the water. Mink dived some distance from the girls and swam to and fro. Then the girls called out to him, "Come! Let's play together!" He came close and dived right in front of them. Then suddenly he swam under one of them and bit off her clitoris. The girl didn't say anything because she was ashamed, so she went ashore, put on her clothes and called her sister. But Mink cut himself a branch off a tree and put it on his head, sticking the clitoris, which he had bitten off, on the tip of it. The clitoris shook from side to side on his headgear when he went home. All the people were on the path when he got to the village. They asked him, "What do you have on your head?" He didn't answer and went home and stuck the branch into the wall.

2) Soon after this K·ā'yaq wanted to have two beautiful girls for himself. One day while they were making mats, he walked past them very closely. He had a piece of nice, white pitch in his mouth and was chewing it. He let a piece of it hang out of his mouth in order to make their mouths water. When they saw the nice pitch, they asked him for a bit. He gave a little to the eldest, who was also the prettiest. She became pregnant and gave birth to a child after a few days. Since nobody knew who the child's father was, the young woman's father invited all the people. He made her stand in the middle of the house and hold the child in her arms. His people, sitting along the sides of the house, were singing at the same time. One at a time, the men

---

46. Given in the original as *Dohle* 'jackdaw,' but it is actually 'crow' that is referred to here; the jackdaw is not found in North America.

47. What Boas transcribes as "K·ā'yaq" is qᴇyx̱ (or qayx̱), referring to 'mink' in legends, in several Coast Salish languages, including Halkomelem, Comox and Pentlatch; the equivalent Nuu-chah-nulth term is č'a·stimicṁit, which Boas transcribes here as "Tc'āstᴇ'mitmit."

48. What Boas transcribes as "Mâ'hentlis" is the Nuu-chah-nulth term ṁu·ḥanⱡas, applied to the mythical female Red-breasted Merganser (often referred to as "sawbill duck").

had to step up to the woman. The child didn't want to go to anyone until K·ā′yaq came; then it allowed him to take it in his arms at once. So the people knew that he was the father.

3) Once K·ā′yaq went for a walk and found a hornet's nest. He picked it up and wrapped it in his cape. He walked on and met a number of children at play. They asked him, "What do you have there, K·ā′yaq?" He replied, "I have salal berries." The children begged for some, but he answered that they were for his mother. But the children begged harder and ran after him when he went on. At last he gave in. He said, "Come here, sit down in a circle around me. Spread your legs wide and come up very close. When I open my cape reach inside as fast as you can." Then he shook out his cape. The children grabbed it and were stung cruelly. He had made them sit with spread legs so that their behinds and genitals especially were stung. He called, "Here are nice berries for you! Eat up! Enjoy them!"

5. Ka′pkimĭs (a brother of Kwo′tiath. See p. 100)[49]

There once was a woman who had a grandson called Ka′pkimĭs. One day, when she was weaving a mat on the house platform, she asked the boy to fetch her some water because she was thirsty. But he refused because he was busy making an arrow. She asked him again, and a third time, but he didn't fulfil her request. So she said, "If you don't go now to get me water, I will be transformed into a bluejay.[50] The boy only retorted, "I don't care," because he didn't believe her. Then she said for the fourth time, "Don't you want to go and get me water?" "No," said the boy, "I'm making arrows." Then she called, "Qwēc, Qwēc," and jumped off the platform, first onto a box, then onto a roof beam, and finally flew away as a bluejay. She flew from tree to tree and the boy ran after her in order to try and catch her again, but in vain. So he cried and sang on his return, "Oh, Grandmother, you will have all the tribes for companions." (i.e., in the future, all human beings will die.) When he had reached maturity, he invited all the tribes to a big potlatch. He had built a large house. All the birds, Goose,[51] Duck, Seagull, and all the others came. Elk came, also Bear and Octopus. Then he closed all the cracks and holes of the house, went to the door and displayed a big knife. Goose said, "Danger, danger!" But Duck, Bear and Elk called, "No danger for me." So Goose also called, "No, no danger. I can fly through the roof." Elk said, "I can leap over him," and so the birds flew away and

---

49. Boas refers here to page 100 of the original *Sagen* (story 2, part 5 of this section), which is a legend of Kwo′tiath and his brothers.

50. Steller's Jay (*Cyanocitta stellaeri*), known in the Nuu-chah-nulth language as xa·šxi·p.

51. Likely it is the Canada Goose (*Branta canadensis*) referred to here.

Elk and Bear sprang over him out of the door. Only Octopus was unable to flee. Ka'pkimĩs grabbed him by the hair and wanted to kill him. But he begged, "Don't kill me here, otherwise the people will say that your door is full of blood." The young man followed the advice and dragged him outside. When they got to the path, he wanted to kill him. But Octopus begged him, "Don't kill me here, otherwise people will say that the path in front of your house is full of blood." The young man dragged him to the beach, but when he wanted to kill him there, Octopus called out, "Don't kill me here, otherwise everyone will say that the beach in front of your house is full of blood. Kill me in the water." Ka'pkimĩs dragged him into the water. When he wanted to kill him then, Octopus called out, "No, go deeper into the water, otherwise people will say that the water in front of your house is full of blood." The young man pulled him farther into the water. When the water was as high as his neck, Octopus wrapped his arms around him and drowned him.

6. Deer and the Wolves

Deer once went fishing. While he was busy at it, he saw the heavily laden canoes of the Wolves pass by. The Wolves were about to move into a different village. When they were close to him, he shouted to them, "You travel on a fine day, you bone-noses, you eaters of raw meat!" The Wolves didn't understand what he said and called out, "What did you say, Ă'tucmit?"[52] He replied, "I spoke politely to you. I said: 'You travel on a fine day, you distinguished people'." When they had gone on a bit, he called out again, "You travel on a fine day, you bone-noses, you eaters of raw meat!" But this time they understood him, turned around and called out, "You are insulting us!" They beat him and made him a slave. Then they went to their village. They tied the wallboards to the frames of their houses and placed the roof boards on the roof beams. They took Ă'tucmit's canoe Hōpi'nuwuc (= small, round canoe) and flung it on top of the house. The canoe was round as a circle and had the property of moving all by itself. The chief of the Wolves said to Ă'tucmit, "When I go to bed you shall always sing to me." Ă'tucmit had hidden a shell-knife under his cape and when the chief retired, he sang: "Waĩ'tc, waĩ'tc, yū'i (Sleep, sleep, chief.)" So he fell asleep. During the following night, Ă'tucmit had to sing him to sleep again. He sang: "Waĩ'tc, waĩ'tc, yū'i," and when the chief was asleep, he cut off his head with his shell-knife. He ran outside with the head without anyone noticing, took his canoe from the roof, pushed it into the water and called out, "Go!" and it went off. He put the head into the bow of the canoe and sang: "Hōpatsianā', hōpat-sianā', hēiahsökmā' t'oqtsētakmū'tc hauĩtlukmū'tc k·oayatsēkmū't (the round thing

---

52. What Boas writes as "Ă'tucmit" is the Nuu-chah-nulth (Tseshaht) term for Deer in legends, ʕa·tušṁit.

up front in the canoe, the round thing up front in the canoe, here in the canoe is the head of the chief of the Wolves).” When the Wolves noticed in the early morning that their chief was dead, they called an assembly. They resolved to borrow fog magic from Ā́nusmit, the Heron.[53] When they had received it, they created a dense fog and Ā́tucmit lost his way. Without noticing, he returned to the land of the Wolves. When the canoe hit land he thought that he was in front of his own house and called to his wife Imā́aksā́, “Imā́aksā́ hīahsōkṓits kōatsōk·oä́ts Imā́aksā́ (Imā́aksā́, here is your chamberpot in here, Imā́aksā́).” Then he jumped out of the canoe. He grabbed a handful of sand and said, wondering, “The sand looks just the same as where I was yesterday.” When the Wolves heard him arrive, they ran down to the beach and tore him up. So he cried, “ Ā anasōkoapisamā́ k·ēnēk·ā́ts (Oh, leave the stomach in peace),” and therefore the Wolves left his stomach behind. Ever since then wolves kill deer but don’t touch their stomachs.

7. Tlōkoa′la Legends[54]

1) There once was a brave son of a chief who was called Hasā́k·utl (= Crab in the Face).[55] Summer and winter he went to the forest every day, bathed in a lake, rubbed himself with cedar branches and rolled about on sharp stones drawing blood, in order to become strong and brave. After he had thus obtained great power by lengthy adherence to these strict rules, he set out one day without anyone knowing it. He went to the beach and there found a seal. He cut it open along the belly, pulled off the skin and crawled inside it. He remained lying there on the beach waiting to see what would happen. The following morning he heard loud howling of Wolves. He wasn’t able to see anything because he was completely wrapped in the skin, but he heard everything that happened around him. He felt that the howling animals nudged him, picked him up and carried him away. The Wolves could feel him still breathing and said, “The seal must be supernatural. We’re not able to carry him.” Another one said, “I think he is still alive; let’s kill him!” In the meantime they had reached the spot where they usually killed all their game. There, many sharp needles were beside the path. He heard as one Wolf called to the other, “Let’s throw him onto the needles here.” When the wolf threw him down, he leaped across the needles

---

53. The term that Boas transcribed as “Ā́nusmit” is recognized as ʕanismit, the name applied to the Great Blue Heron in Nuu-chah-nulth mythology.

54. What Boas transcribes here as “Tlōkoa′la” is better known as ƛukʷana, more commonly referred to as the “Wolf Dance” ceremonial. This series of legends in the *Sagen* explains how certain families received ceremonial prerogatives performed during these dances. For descriptions of this ceremony, see Boas (1891d:599–604) and Drucker (1951:386–443).

55. Boas’ “Hasā́k·utl” is derived from the Nuu-chah-nulth word applied to ‘any crab,’ hasa·mac.

in one great bound. They tried to kill him like this four times, but did not succeed. So they said to each other, "Surely the seal has to be supernatural otherwise it would not have been able to escape the needles." They carried him farther. When they got home, one of the Wolf-chiefs had him cut open. At first they cut off his testicles. The chief's daughter took them and ate them. Then, when they cut open his belly, Hasā′k·utl sprang out, sat down and looked around him. Some of the Wolves fainted in fright when they saw him. But the girl cried out, "Phew! I've eaten the testicles of a man," and she vomited and brought them up again. But the chief of the Wolves sent out his messengers to invite all the Wolves, Raccoons and Otters. His messengers were the Wolves, Koaā′tlas (= Crackling Branch), K·ak·ā′tlqsit'as (= Settling Dirt in the Water), Astskwē′qapas (= Chips Flying Under the Blows of an Axe), and Ē′ik·atpas (= Falling Water).[56] They ran over the whole earth and invited all the Wolves, Raccoons and Otters. Soon, they assembled in the house of the chief. They placed the young man in the middle of the house and sat down all the way around him. They asked him, "What do you want here? Would you like to have this comb? If a woman combs her hair with it, her hair will get long at once." Hasā′k·utl didn't reply. Then they showed him magic herbs and asked him whether he'd like to have them. He didn't reply. Then they showed him the arrow of death (tci′tu) and said that if he pointed it towards anybody, that person would have to die at once. In order to demonstrate the power of the arrow, they pointed it towards the Wolves, who fell down as though dead. Then Hasā′k·utl said, "Yes, I came to obtain this." They gave him the arrow. When he touched it, he fainted and was only able to hold it on the fourth try. Then they placed him on a big box and taught him the Tlōkoa′la. The Raccoons and Otters started to shake rattles and to sing the Tlōkoa′la song. Then the Wolves around the house could be heard howling and inside everyone danced all the dances which today are performed by people. Hasā′k·utl gave some inner cedar bark dyed red to the chief of the Wolves. Thereupon they took him off the box and placed him beside the chief. Then the Wolves dragged in a dead person. They wrapped the corpse in a Wolf skin, laid it down by the fire and began singing, keeping time by beating on their sides and their haunches. Then the dead person rose and staggered around. But the longer they sang, the surer he stepped and finally he ran just like a Wolf. One of the Wolves gave him his cape and another one taught him to run. Then the chief said to Hasā′k·utl, "Now you see what becomes of the dead. We make Wolves of them." And he continued, "Know that this is the Tlōkoa′la. When you get home, teach the dance to the people. In future, when you move from one place to the other, always leave behind some inner cedar bark dyed red so that we will be able to fetch it for the Tlōkoa′la." Then they carried him back

---

56.   The names of the messengers refer to the quickness of their movements, and are generally given in order of their rapidity and rank (Sapir and Swadesh 1939:217, fn.110).

to his home. They ran around the village and sang Wolf songs. They forbade the young man to go immediately into the house but ordered him to prepare his friends. He called his friends and told them, "Go into your canoes and begin to sing. Thereupon many Wolves will come. When you see them, go farther away from the shore and come back only when they have gone. Then take a rope of inner cedar bark and catch me. Then I will teach the Tlōkoa'la to you." And he gave them the whistles which he had received from the Wolves. Everything happened as he had said. His friends went into their canoes, the Wolves arrived and, when they had run away again, they caught Hasā'k·utl and led him into the house. Then he sent everyone out of the house and said, "Come back when I call you. I want to show you what the Wolves have given to me." He sprinkled his hair with feathers and took the arrow of death. Then he called out, "Let everybody come and look at me!" He showed the arrow to them and they all fell down as though dead. He put down the weapon and they awoke again. He said, "All this the Wolves gave to me. My dance shall be passed on to my daughters and their husbands, and all their descendants shall own it."

2) A young man was always hunting whales without any success, while another one always came home with lots of prey. At last he lost his patience and said to his father, "If I come home again without any prey, you'll have to hold a Tlōkoa'la for me." Since he arrived home again empty-handed that night, his father sent out invitations for a Tlōkoa'la. He invited the Wolves to come and dance for the young man. Then the latter tried to imitate the dance, but made many mistakes. Finally he threw off the headband of red dyed inner cedar bark, put on his bear skin and ran into the woods. He crawled under a fallen trunk and met a Wolf right there. He fainted. When he came to again, he heard the singing of the Wolves. He stood up, received the song of the Wolves and went home. He had been in the woods for a long time. This was his song:

> Hēyōyā' häna yēā' tl'ēn'ēcinā'
> Nayiyā' nä tl'ē'nēcinā' nähayē'
> Ōyesē'imā' k'atsāyayua'p yātsōnōkoakā'otc nä k·oāyatsā'a yēk'a wäi'

(i.e.: When I run around in the morning, I always make it hail). He had been in the forest for a long time. From then on he always caught as many whales as he wished.

8. The Two Sisters

A woman was in the habit of scolding her two daughters a lot. At last they found their home unbearable and fled. They ran into the forest and there found two houses standing close together. The older sister went into one of the houses. The younger sister peeped through a crack into the other one and saw a woman sitting inside it. She went inside and then found that the woman was a figure carved from rotted wood. A short time afterwards someone entered the house and asked her who she was. She related that she had run away from her mother's scolding. So he said, "I want to marry you. Have you come here all by yourself?" She replied, "No, my sister came with me. She went into the house next door." The man answered, "I'm afraid your sister is dead. Cougar[57] and Raccoon live there and so far anyone entering there has been slain." He had scarcely said this when they heard someone running towards their house. It was the older sister who had luckily escaped. So he took both sisters as wives. He threw his wooden wife into the fire. After some time the oldest sister became pregnant and when her child was born, the younger one was also pregnant. The older one's child was a girl. When she had grown a bit, the father made her a bow and some arrows and taught her to shoot. He said, "Come here, my child!" took her on his knee and taught her his song. He was a great hunter. When he went to the beach, he always brought home several elk. He said, "When you grow up you shall be a great hunter despite any man." He went with her to a tree, put her on a branch and said, "If you want lots of game, you have to sing your song here four times. If you want less, sing it only twice." He left her there. When she had sung two songs, two elk came and fell down dead. When she sang on, four deer came and fell down dead. Her father then carried home the prey. He cooked the game and the sisters sang and danced in the house.

Once Raccoon heard the girl singing in the tree. He went to Cougar and said, "I hear a voice singing in the tree there." Cougar leaped from the house and also heard the song. He followed the voice, but when he reached the spot from where the voice appeared to come, it had stopped and nothing could be seen. So he ran back home and beat Raccoon. But the following day, Raccoon and Cougar heard the girl sing again. They followed the voice. When they reached the tree, the girl had just stopped singing but was still sitting in the tree. So Cougar climbed up a tree opposite and requested of the girl, "Teach me your song." She replied, "No, Father has forbidden me to sing more than four times." Cougar called, "Sing, or I will kill you!" She refused in spite of the threat, but at last had to give in. As soon as Cougar had learned the song, he killed her, took her heart from her corpse and buried her under the tree. Soon the father missed his daughter and the following morning he went out to look for her. He directed his steps towards the tree but didn't find her. He knew at once that Cougar had killed her. The following morning he went to the tree again and heard someone singing. At once he recognized the voice of Cougar, who was singing the song he had stolen from the girl. But the game didn't follow his call. The man stepped right under the tree without being noticed and shot straight through

57. Boas uses the German word *Panther* 'panther' here in the original; 'cougar' is the more appropriate translation. While there are no panthers in this area, some of the Nuu-chah-nulth people with whom we consulted spoke of a "large, fierce black cougar," which may be the animal of this story.

Cougar's heart. He found his daughter's corpse buried underneath the tree and saw that the heart had been ripped out, so he opened up Cougar and found the heart inside him. It was quite unharmed. He warmed it and put it back in its place. Then he gave breath back to his daughter; the heart started to beat again and she awoke to new life. Then he cut Cougar up, tore up his heart into small bits and scattered them to the four winds. But the sisters had become angry at everything that had happened and left the house with their children before he returned. When they arrived in their former home, they found no one there. Their relatives and fellow tribesmen had all moved away. They found a small trout, made a river and put the trout in it. It multiplied quickly and the trout in all rivers descend from it.

9. Ēi'scōitl (= All Pitch Inside)[58]

Once a group of children was playing on the beach as if they were grown-ups. They separated into several camps and gave a big feast. Only one girl didn't get anything, so she called out, "Why don't you give anything to me? If I don't get anything, I'll call the Woman of the Woods, Ēi'scōitl." Because the children didn't pay any attention to her, she called "Hitaqt'as'ä' Ēi'scōitl hitlahä' wĭkuap'ä't."[59] The bad woman rushed up at once. She had a big basket on her back, and she grabbed one child after the other, smeared their eyes with pitch, put them into the basket and carried them home. Only one of them got away and told those at home what had happened. Thereupon a young man went into the forest to look for the children. He followed the tracks of Ēi'scōitl and came to her house, where he hid in the branches of a tree which stood by her pond. Soon she came from the house to fetch water and when she bent over she saw the man's reflection. She thought it was her own reflection and said, "Am I not a beautiful woman?" and stroked her own cheeks. Then she looked up and saw a man sitting in the tree. She called to him, "Come down, I'd like to speak to you." When he came down she tried to stuff him into her basket but didn't succeed. Each time she put him in, he sprang out again. So she asked, "How did you become so powerful?" He replied, "I laid my head down on a big boulder and struck it with a rock. That's what has made me so powerful." She asked, "Can you make me powerful like that?" He refused at first but finally gave in and said, "If you insist, I'll do it. Look for a big, flat stone and lay your head

---

58.   According to Sapir and Swadesh (1939:222), the literal meaning of the name of this Pitch Woman (transcribed as "Ēi'scōitl" by Boas) is 'pitch about the inside walls of the house,' likely referring to the pitch which she had stuck on the walls of her house—Boas' "Ēi'scōitl" is ʔiʔi·šsuʔił (Powell 1991:135).

59.   The English translation is: "Come out of the bushes; I, ʔiʔi·šsuʔił, the one nobody likes, am here."

down on it." This she did, but when he was about to strike, she asked, "But are you really telling the truth?" "Yes, just close your eyes!" he replied, then beat her to death with the rock. Then he went into the house and found all the children stacked up on a platform. He poured oil into their eyes and this dissolved the pitch so that they were able to open their eyes again. She had already roasted one girl. He took the children home with him and the parents rejoiced when they saw them again.

10. The Children of the Dog

The daughter of a chief in Yē′kwis[60] had a handsome white dog whom she loved very much. One day she stroked him and said, "How handsome you are, my dog!" The dog wagged his tail at this. Once, at midnight, the girl felt someone creep into her bed, so she asked, "Who are you?" The man replied, "I am the one who you said was handsome." Thereupon she let him sleep with her. After some time she gave birth to ten children who all had the shape of dogs. So she realized that the white dog had slept with her. Her father killed the old dog. The father moved away with all his people and left the girl behind by herself. He had all the fires extinguished and the houses taken down before they left. But the girl's grandmother pitied her and told her that she had hidden some glowing coals in a shell for her. She had hidden some tinder (chewed fern roots) beside the shell. When they had gone, the girl went to the hiding place, took out the coals and made a fire for herself. She dug a cave in which she lived with the young dogs. She went down to the beach every day to dig for shellfish. One day she heard singing near the cave: "Tlah'ē′, tlah'ē′; ēk·ishmâ′ tcī̃takō̄′āmakō̄′ tlah'ē′, tlah'ē′ (i.e. Don't cry, don't cry; Mother is still there digging shellfish. Don't cry, don't cry.)" She was amazed and went to the cave in order to see who might be singing there. She didn't see anyone other than the puppies and didn't know who had been singing. The following day she went to the beach again and heard the same song, so she took off her clothes and draped them over her digging stick so that it looked as if she were digging shellfish, and stealthily crept back to the house. She peeped into the cave and saw her children playing about naked in human shape. The dog skins lay all in one heap. So she sprang inside, snatched all the garments and threw them into the fire. The children ran around crying because they were unable to become dogs again. They were all boys and had snowy white hair. They grew up quickly and when they were old enough to hunt, the mother made them bows and arrows and they began to shoot squirrels. Their mother sewed capes from the skins. Then they shot birds and their mother sewed

---

60. What Boas transcribes here as "Yē′kwis" is probably the place known as hi·kʷis (anglicized as "Ekwis"), Tseshaht Indian Reserve No. 8, located on the north shore of Sechart Channel, east from Lyall Point.

capes from the skins. Then they shot a raccoon. The mother skinned it and kept the sinews in order to make fish lines from them. When she had made many lines the boys went out to sea and caught halibut. From then on they had plenty to eat. The mother kept the strong sinews from the backs of the halibut and from them made a rope. She cut a strong fishing rod and sent her sons out again to fish. Thereupon they caught a whale, pulled it ashore and cut it up. She had a piece of the whale's skin brought to her and transformed it into a crow. She gave another piece of skin to the bird and made it fly to her grandmother. She said, "When you find an old weeping woman give her this skin and tell her: The sons of the girl whom you have abandoned killed this." Crow obeyed and gave the piece of skin to the old one. Thereupon she stopped crying. She showed the whale skin to her son and told him what Crow had said. The chief sent out a canoe to find out whether the report was true. When his messengers returned and reported what they had seen, the chief resolved to return to his daughter. They loaded their canoes and set out. When the boys saw them coming, they went down to the water and washed their hair. When they pulled their hair back and forth through the water a heavy wind came up, the canoes capsized and everybody drowned. The canoes and the people were transformed into many small islands which can still be seen today at the entrance to Barkley Sound.

11. Cī'ciklē

There once was a severe winter. It stormed, rained and snowed incessantly so that the people were unable to catch fish. They dug for shellfish and cooked them, but were unable to find enough and many starved to death. One man had dried a basket full of salmon roe in the summer and was now living on it. He ate one mouthful each morning and evening. He and his family, except for a small boy, went out every day to dig for shellfish. Before they left, the father forbade the boy to touch the salmon roe. The boy obeyed. All day long he lay on the beach and waited for his parents' return. When they came back late at night, they had found only a few shellfish. One day, when his parents had gone out again, the boy grew so hungry that he was unable to resist the temptation and took a mouthful of roe from the box. When the father noticed this, he beat the boy. The following day, the parents went out again and the boy wept from hunger. At last he fell asleep and when he woke up again, he saw a man approaching. The stranger came up to him and asked, "Why are you so sad?" The boy answered, "My parents have beaten me because I have touched the salmon roe. It is our only nourishment." The stranger asked, "Don't you have anything else? I don't believe it because you wouldn't be able to survive," and he ordered him to eat up everything. The stranger continued, "I will soon give you more." At first, the boy refused to eat, but the stranger forced him to. Then he said, "If your father beats you, come to the beach early in the morning. My name is Cī'ciklē.[61] Call and stretch out your hands. Stretch them up high and say: Give me what you have promised me." This is what happened. When the father came home and found that the boy had eaten the roe, he beat him until he was half dead. The boy went to the beach early in the morning. He prayed and at once many herring drifted ashore. Then he went to his father and said, "Come with your baskets! There are plenty of fish on the beach!"

12. Anthtine (= Made from Nasal Secretions)[62]

A chief had two daughters and ten sons. The girls went into the forest to bathe. One of them had just reached womanhood and wore the hair ornament[63] of young maidens. The other one was still a child. The older one tied up her braid and bead ornament and took off her cape. Then she stepped into the water. Suddenly she saw a man watching her from the bushes. She quickly threw her cape around herself but he was already upon her and carried her away. The abductor was the double-faced spirit of the forest, K·ōk·oā'tspatla. She shouted to her sister, "Run home and tell what has happened. I will break up my dentalia ornament[64] and drop the shells so that you will know where I have been carried." The man ran away with her and every ten paces she let drop a shell from her hair

---

61. There is some confusion concerning the term that Boas transcribes here as "Cī'ciklē." Boas makes reference to "Cī'ciklē" elsewhere, in his article "The Nootka," where he reports that "in a tradition of the Nootka it is stated that a boy prayed to a being in heaven Cī'ciklē," who, Boas adds, "is probably identical with" the deity known as "Kā'tse" (Boas 1891d:595). The tradition in question is the one referred to here, and "Kā'tse" is the same word that Boas transcribes as "K·ā'otsē" in story 1 of the present section, where we have transcribed this term as qa·ci and pointed out that contemporary Nuu-chah-nulth people translate it either as 'Provider' or 'pray for something.' However, some Nuu-chah-nulth recognize the term "Cī'ciklē" as šišikli, a pronunciation of the English term "Jesus Christ" that is influenced by the Nuu-chah-nulth language. Partial support for this latter derivation comes from a Chinook Jargon dictionary which translates "kli" as 'Christ' (Johnson 1978:290). Yet this information conflicts with Boas' statement in Section XXVI of the *Sagen* that "Cī'ciklē," as used by the Nootka, is derived from "Cikla," the name for the "Wanderer" used by the Chinook people of the Lower Columbia River.

62. Boas (1916:594) elsewhere refers to this as the "Mucus Boy" story; the term that Boas transcribes here in the *Sagen*, "Anthtine," is ʕintḥtin (Powell 1991:135).

63. *Perlenschmuck* 'bead ornament' (see also the footnote that follows).

64. *Dentalienschmuck* 'dentalia ornament' (but referred to as *Perlenschmuck* 'bead ornament' earlier in this same paragraph). In this area, hair ornaments varied in their degree of splendour depending upon the rank of the pubescent girl's family. Those of high class wore a long pendant of dentalia shells threaded on goat wool strands, whereas those of less status might be adorned with a hair ornament of less valuable materials (Drucker 1951:139).

ornament. But the way was long and she had run out of shells before they arrived. So she tore up her cape and dropped the pieces. When she had got to the end of them, too, they had reached the house of K·ōk·oā'tspatla. He held her captive there. She tried to escape many times but was unable because K·ōk·oā'tspatla had one face in front and one in the back and was watching her constantly. After some time she had a child by him. Her brothers set out to search for her. The eldest went first. He was shown the lake in which the sisters had bathed and then he followed the track. At last, after a long search, he reached the house. He found his sister and her child at home by themselves because K·ōk·oā'tspatla was out hunting. The sister called to him, "Flee as quickly as you can, because if my husband finds you, he will kill you." The child watched but didn't say anything. The young man obeyed. When K·ōk·oā'tspatla came home at night he called out, "I scent humans. Have your relatives been here?" The woman tried to dissuade him but he didn't believe her and followed the scent. Soon he saw the brother in flight. He caught up with him, tore him to pieces and put him on a platform in the house. After some time, the second and third brothers set out with bow and arrow to search for their sister. After wandering for a long time, they reached the house. They met their sister and her child at home by themselves, because K·ōk·oā'tspatla was out hunting. The sister begged them to flee as quickly as possible and showed them the dried-up corpse of their brother. So they fled. When K·ōk·oā'tspatla came home at night he called out, "I scent humans. Have your relatives been here?" Again the mother denied it, but the child told him that two of her brothers had been there. He at once threw down the game, which he still had on his back, and pursued them. He caught up with them, killed them and placed them beside the corpse of the eldest. In this way he killed the ten brothers who set out one after the other to free their sister. Not one of them was left.

The mother wept day and night about the loss of her children. Her tears and her mucus flowed to the ground. When she looked down one day, she saw that they moved and took on a human shape. She wrapped up the small creature in inner cedar bark and it became a child. She made a cradle for it and called the boy Anthtine. When he grew older and saw his parents always crying, he asked, "Why do you always cry, my parents? Why do you cut off your hair?" So the mother replied, "Oh, my child, I have lost all my sons and one daughter." Anthtine said, "Then let me go and find out what has become of my brothers." The mother begged him to stay, but he insisted on his plan. He went into the forest and after a long search found the house of his sister. There he saw the dried corpses of his brothers on the platform. The woman asked him, "Who are you?" "I am the son of your mother," he replied, "I want to kill your husband and bring you back. Tell me how I can get at him." The woman replied, "When he is asleep, his heart comes out of his chest, and if you hit that, he must die. Come back tonight! I will leave the door open so that you'll be able to come in unnoticed. But now flee! I fear that he will kill you beforehand like our brothers." The young man left. At night when K·ōk·oā′tspatla came home, his son called out at once, "Mother's brother was here!" So the old one threw down the deer which he carried on his back and pursued him. He had already come up to him and stretched out his hand to grab him, when Anthtine vanished. K·ōk·oā′tspatla turned back disappointed. He had scarcely turned around when he heard Anthtine running again and when he looked back he saw him. He pursued Anthtine further. But each time when he wanted to grab him, Anthtine vanished. Thus, Anthtine arrived back safely and K·ōk·oā′tspatla went home. When he got to his wife she was astonished that he hadn't killed her brother. But Anthtine said to his mother, "I've seen my sister and her husband. I will kill him." He took two bows and many arrows and went into the forest again. He hid until evening, after he had given his sister a sign of his presence. Then he peeped through a knot-hole in the house wall and saw the old one's heart come out. So he crept to the door which his sister had opened and shot him twice, straight through the heart. The sister told him to shoot the child, too, and he shot him. Then they returned home together.

In those days the sky was still close to the earth. Anthtine decided to go up there. He made himself many arrows—heaps and heaps of them—took a strong bow and shot up one arrow after the other. Slowly their number diminished and then he saw a thin, dark line in the sky. He continued shooting and the line came closer and closer until at last it reached the earth. Then he took a magic substance and coated the chain of arrows with it to make it firm. On the following day he began climbing up while constantly rubbing on the magic substance in front of himself. Finally he arrived on top and found a beautiful, large flat country and a path. He followed it and after some time saw smoke rising. He went towards it and found a house, where the Aini′mEk·as, Slug Women,[65] lived. He heard them talking, went inside and saw that they were roasting clover roots[66] on stones. Both of them were blind. He took the roots away from them when they wanted to eat. So they asked, "Is someone here?" "Yes," he answered, "it's me, Anthtine." "What do you want here?" "I want to marry the chief's daughter." "Do you really want to be killed? He murders all the suitors of his daughter." He didn't reply, but asked instead, "Are you blind? I will heal you." "If you do that, we will help you to obtain the chief's daughter." He made them sit down and then stuck his penis into their eyes. Thereupon they were able to

---

65. What Boas transcribes as "Aini′mEk·as" is the Nuu-chah-nulth term for a mythical female slug, derived from the usual term meaning 'slug,' ʕinmi. The German term *Schneckenfrauen* used here means 'snail or slug women'; Boas (1916:594, 1022) elsewhere uses the English term "snail women."

66. The rhizomes of wild clover (*Trifolium wormskjoldii*) were eaten by virtually all Coastal people in British Columbia, including the Nuu-chah-nulth and Ditidaht (Turner *et. al.* 1983:110).

see at once. Then the old women said, "First you will pass many rats, then many snakes. The rats will try to tear you to pieces; the snakes will threaten to devour you. After you have passed them safely, the door will bite you, and when you get inside, the fire will roast you, and on the ground and on the mats there are sharp needles which will pierce you." They taught him at once how he could overcome all these terrors, and gave him flat stones, fern roots, shellfish, and the slime of slugs. He thanked them and pursued his way. The path led through open country. Finally he came to a hill, behind which stood the chief's house. A guard sat outside the door and when he saw him come he called, "There's a stranger coming! Watch out!" Then Anthtine rubbed slug slime on himself and when the rats rushed upon him they were unable to get at him. They crawled over him four times but were unable to get at him. In the same way he got safely past the snakes. Thereupon the chief, who had come out, said, "He must be a powerful man. He passed safely by the rats and snakes. Will he also get through the door?" Then he went inside and sat down on his bed. Anthtine pretended to go in but, when he had arrived just in front of the door, he jumped back. It slammed together without doing him any harm. Then, just when it opened again, he leaped into the house. The chief greeted him and asked, "Do you want to marry my daughter?" "Yes," said Anthtine, "That's why I have come." So the chief bade him sit down beside him and made a great fire in order to burn him. But Anthtine secretly threw in shellfish which quenched the fire with their water. The chief tried to burn him four times, but without success. So he said, "You shall have my daughter. Sit down beside her." But she was sitting on a mat of spines and the backrest of the seat was covered with spines. So Anthtine put the stones beneath his feet, his behind and his back and pushed down the spines so that he was able to sit down without harm; and he took her for his wife. The old chief pondered how he could kill Anthtine. In front of his house he kept many fish, which killed anyone going into the water. He sent Anthtine out the following morning to get a log of driftwood, and when he had brought it, the old man began to split the wood and purposely let his stone hammer fall into the water. Then he asked Anthtine to dive for it and expected that the fish would devour him, but he came up again unharmed and gave the hammer back to the chief. Thereupon the latter was ashamed. The following day he invited his son-in-law to help him split a tree. When the tree had been split apart, he purposely dropped his hammer into it and asked Anthtine to get it out again. When the latter had crawled into the tree the old man knocked out the wedges, but Anthtine slipped away in time and escaped unhurt. So the old man realized that he was unable to harm him, and he gave him his daughter and allowed him to move down to earth. He ordered Anthtine to close his eyes and to open them only after some time. He did so, and when he opened his eyes, found himself home again.

13. The T'ātnōs'ēth (= Child-people)[67]

Once many women went out to dig for shellfish, which they dried. While they were digging for shellfish on the beach, their children ate up the dried ones. When the mothers saw this, they beat and scolded the children. Some others put excrement on each end of the sticks on which the shellfish were drying so that the boys should not pull them off. One chief's son who had been beaten by his mother called the children together the following day and said, "Do your mothers also scold and beat you all the time? Let's move away." Everybody except one agreed. The boys took two large canoes and the chief's son said, "Let's go to where there are many whales." They passed close by their mothers and sang: "Wīak·ītcamā′ wīak·ītcamā′ Eä′ne ä′tcim'ak tat'atnE ä′tcim'ak sesäwact ä′tcima'k tsuwä′tc hēhē′ hohō."[68] There were about one hundred children in the canoes. When the women saw and heard them, they laughed, because they did not believe that the children would really move away. The latter kept on singing: Ōtsatētlanā′, ōtsapētlanā′ hē′yes hē′itc noa′hnaha′ktlis hēyatnp manä′h hēhē′, hohō′! (There, where many whales come to the shore, we are going, we are going. There, where the whales shake their tails). They went away and were never seen again. They went to the country of Kwo′tiath and became the tribe of the T'ā′tnōs'ēth.

14. The Four Seal Hunters

Once upon a time there were four young men who went out to hunt seals. They came upon a group of seals and just when the harpooner wanted to hit a dark seal, the man in the middle of the canoe spied a spotted seal and shouted, "Hit that one!" The harpooner quickly changed aim and did as he had been told. He hit the seal and it started at once to pull the canoe along. It swam constantly in zig-zags and thus led the canoe farther and farther away from the shore without the hunters noticing it. At last one of them turned around and could see only the summits of the highest mountains rising from the sea like islands. So he shouted, "Let's take in the line, otherwise we'll get too far away from the coast." They pulled on the rope, but were unable to take it in. The seal continued swimming at the same speed. They tried to cut the rope, but this, too, proved impossible. They were also unable to cut off that part of the canoe where the line was tied. So they began to weep and thought that they would have to die. They saw nothing but sky and water. After they had drifted about for many days, they came to a spot where the ocean was covered in driftwood.

---

67. What Boas transcribes here as "T'ātnōs'ēth" is t'a·tnusʔatḥ, which does mean 'child-people.'

68. The translation of part of this song is recognized as " "We did something brave, isn't it so, us children ... "

This opened up in front of them and let them pass. Then they arrived at a dark spot which looked just like land. One of the young men jumped ashore but sank into the water because what they had taken for land was only floating stones. The survivors went on. They came to a spot where the ocean was covered with black coals, which looked like a long coast. After they had passed this, they came to a spot where the ocean was full of reeds. When they had continued for a few days, they spied land and the seal pulled them to the shore. As soon as it had reached land, it shook itself, took on the shape of a four-legged animal and ran towards a house close by. It had pulled the young men to the land of Kwo'tiath. Kwo'tiath came down to the beach and called out, "You men from the mainland, enter our house and visit us." They followed the invitation. Inside the house they saw an old woman, called Wēmōstcē'elak·sup, sitting near the door. She invited them to sit down beside her. She asked, "So you come from the mainland? The people here are different from you. They live on snakes and frogs. I have my own food here and will share it with you. If you eat frogs or snakes, you must die." Then the three went to Kwo'tiath, who lived in the back of the house. He bade them sit down. Soon young girls carrying covered baskets came in. They heated stones in order to cook the food in the baskets. Kwo'tiath said to the girls, "Now serve the food to us!" Thereupon they emptied the contents of the baskets, and frogs and snakes rolled out. When these hopped and crawled around, Kwo'tiath pushed them together with a stick and then cooked them. Then he served them to the three friends. They pretended to eat them, but in reality stuck them under their capes and ate salmon. Then Kwo'tiath said, "I will give good, sweet food to you every day." Then the seals, who were Kwo'tiath's dogs, came running. They were wounded and licked themselves. So Kwo'tiath said to them, "Ah, I see you've been to the mainland. You always get your wounds and illnesses there." When the strangers had finished their meal, Kwo'tiath led them out into the open. They noticed that there were no trees at all there. He led them to a small brook full of salmon and they saw copper fish traps there. They went back to the house and said to the child-people (see p. 119)[69] who lived there, "What an abundance of salmon in the brook!" "Yes," they replied, "but we are unable to catch them because we lack cedar wood. If you make a good trap for us we will be grateful and will send you back to your home." The young men constructed a salmon weir and caught many salmon. On the following day somebody said to Kwo'tiath, "Raven has found something on the beach and, when we checked, we found a human corpse." Then he asked the strangers whether they had lost one of their number on the journey. So they told him what had happened. They cried when they saw the corpse. Raven had pecked out one of its eyes. Kwo'tiath told them to

---

69. Boas' reference here is to page 119 of the *Sagen*, story 13 in this section, the T'ātnōs'eth or Child-People.

stop crying. He took the eye of a seal and fitted it into the socket. But it was too small. So he took the eye of a bigger seal and this fit. He blew into the dead man's throat and he awoke. Then he said, "Now go home, but don't stop on the way. You will go past the island of lice. Should you land there, the lice will devour you. In the same way, pass by the houses of Rainbow,[70] Se'tsup Salmon,[71] 'Dog Salmon,'[72] and "Cohoe Salmon"[73] without stopping." They followed the advice of Kwo'tiath. When they neared home, one of them said, "I'd like to know whether my wife has remained true to me or whether she has taken another husband." Three of the hunters said that their wives were very proper and would still be mourning. But the fourth said, "My wife is foolish. She surely married again long ago." When they reached land it turned out that only the last mentioned had remained true to her husband. All the others had married again.

15. The Dolphin Hunter[74] and the Seal Hunter

Once upon a time there were a dolphin hunter and a seal hunter. The former was jealous of the latter because he always brought home a great many seals, so he decided to lie in wait for him to find out how he hunted. He lay down in a hiding place and soon saw the canoe approach with the hunter and his sister sitting in it. He saw them land and observed how the man climbed a rock, while his sister stayed with the canoe. So he sneaked up, killed the sister and climbed after the brother. He came to the flat top of the rock and saw a hole with a rope hanging down inside it. The seal hunter had climbed down on it. So the pursuer rejoiced and thought, "You never wanted to tell me how you catch your seals. Now I'll take my revenge. You can stay with your seals." While he thought thus, he pulled up the rope. When the seal hunter intended to return and found that his rope had vanished, he became very sad and began to weep. When the seals came to the cave[75] to sleep at night, they said to each other, "The crying disturbs our sleep; let's send the stranger back." Then one

---

70. Given as *Regenbogen* 'rainbow' in the original German, although the context suggests that the storyteller actually meant steelhead, now classified as a type of salmon (*Oncorhynchus mykiss*), but formerly identified as rainbow trout or steelhead trout (*Salmo gairdneri*).

71. Given in the original as Se'tsup-*Lachs* which means 'Se'tsup-salmon'; what Boas transcribes as "Se'tsup" is sacup, the Nuu-chah-nulth term for a 'spawning red spring salmon.'

72. Given in English in the original as "Dog Salmon" (in double quotation marks); this is the species also known as chum salmon (*Oncorhynchus keta*).

73. Given in the original *Sagen*, in English, as "Cohoe Salmon" (in double quotation marks).

74. *Delphinjäger*—'dolphin hunter,' but should more accurately be called "porpoise hunter." The species known to the Nuu-chah-nulth people are the harbour porpoise and the Dall porpoise.

75. *Höhle*—'cave,' but in this instance the reference is to a seal rookery.

of them walked up to him and said, "We want to carry you back to your home. We are going to give you one of our skins. Put it on and you will become a seal." They gave him a magic substance and taught him how to use it to avenge himself on his enemy. Then he put on the skin and dived, upon which he became a young seal and swam to the village. There he heard all the people mourning his death. He played in the water in front of the village and thus lured out his enemy and his brother. He allowed himself to be hit, then daubed the rope with the medicine which he had received from the seals, so that it could not be torn or cut apart, and pulled them out to sea. When they had lost sight of land he surfaced and said, "Do you know who I am? I'm the one whose rope you pulled up. Now I am taking my revenge on you." He tipped the canoe over and swam back to the cave. The seals asked, "Have you seen your enemy?" "Yes," said he, "I've drowned him." They said, "We have helped you; from now on you must never again kill one of us." And they sent him home. There he told what had happened and then sang: "Yūkoā'atlEmō kwī̃sātāciä'tl yaā'nEtk·es tcī̃'misanup p'a'tuk t'ā'pak·anutl hē'tsuatk·mēk."

16. Aitck·ik·mik and Ītcā'yaptcitl

Once upon a time there were two chiefs, called Aitck·ik·mik (= Son of the Pointed Whale [fin whale])[76] and Ītcā'yaptcitl (always lifting Ītcā'yap),[77] who were jealous of each other. Ītcā'yaptcitl was a great whale hunter and had a large family. One day he found a huge whale floating dead on the sea. So he sent out canoes to take off the blubber. Aitck·ik·mik happened to be lying in bed asleep and didn't wake up when Ītcā'yaptcitl sent for him, so the latter sent for him once more, telling him to get up. He got up, took his knife and his cape and went into his canoe. None of his family accompanied him, while Ītcā'yaptcitl had many cousins and brothers with him. At last they arrived at the whale. They tied the canoes to its side and Ītcā'yaptcitl sent Aitck·ik·mik to the other side of the whale to take off the blubber, while he and his relatives took off the blubber on this side. While Aitck·ik·mik cut

---

76.   One of our Native consultants believed that Boas' "Aitck·ik·mik" was possibly the Nuu-chah-nulth term ʕičqimi·k, meaning 'person (whaler) who catches ʕičqi· whales.' We have been unable to confirm the species of whale referred to by the Nuu-chah-nulth term ʕičqi·, and possibly this is a special term used only in mythology. In the original *Sagen*, Boas provides, in square brackets, the German term *Finnwal* 'fin whale,' presumably with reference to the Common Finback Whale (*Balaenoptera physalus*), although this species has been identified by a different Nuu-chah-nulth term, k̓ʷučqi·. While finback whales are known to have been hunted occasionally by the closely-related Makah tribe on the Olympic Peninsula, conclusive information is not available as to what extent, if any, this species was taken by the Barkley Sound tribes.

77.   This meaning of the Nuu-chah-nulth term transcribed by Boas as "Ītcā'yapcitl" is confirmed as 'always lifting Ītcā'yap,' but it has not been possible to determine the meaning of "Ītcā'yap."

loose the blubber, they stealthily untied the canoes and went home. When Aitck·ik·mik had finished, he called across the whale, "I've finished, lift off the blubber!" No one answered. When he looked over the whale he saw the canoes far away. He begged, "Come back and save me!" Yet no one paid any attention to him and they went home. There they said to the friends of Aitck·ik·mik, "We have had bad luck. The whale was still alive. We threw our harpoon and it dived and the harpoon caught the foot of Aitck·ik·mik. That is how he lost his life." Thereupon his relatives began to weep.

When Aitck·ik·mik found himself abandoned, he cut a hole in the whale close to its back on the leeward side and crept in. He was very sad. A westerly wind came up and the whale drifted landwards. The waves broke over him in his hole. Suddenly he heard voices inside the whale which encouraged him and invited him to enter. They opened up a hole for him and he went inside. He now found that the whale was a canoe with many people in it. They said, "We will go ashore now where there is a flat, sandy beach." They started singing and the whale drifted ashore. On the beach they heard the Wild Man of the Woods, Ya'aē,[78] singing; he pulled the whale ashore and tied it to a yew tree. Then Aitck·ik·mik asked the people in the whale to make him powerful. They granted his request and he then hid in the woods in the vicinity of his village. He saw that his relatives had cut off their hair and that his house had been burned. They lived in a small, miserable hut. So he went to the creek where they always fetched water and sat down. Soon he saw his younger brother arrive. He threw small sticks at him to attract his attention. When he looked around he called out, "Come here, my brother! Or rather, wait, I'll come to you." He went to him and told him to tell their father that he had met Aitck·ik·mik in the water. The brother went home and told his father what he had experienced. The father replied, "Don't speak like that. You haven't seen him. He has died." The boy repeated, "No, I have seen him." The father said, "Perhaps it was his ghost." "No, it was really him," retorted the boy, but his father didn't believe him. So the boy went back to the creek and told his brother that his father wouldn't believe him. Aitck·ik·mik sent him back again and had him tell their father that he should keep open one corner of his hut and let the fire go out so that

---

78. Boas (1891d:597) elsewhere describes the "Ya'ē" (which he transcribes as "Ya'aē" in the *Sagen*) as "a fabulous people living in the woods." Drucker (1951:152) states they are a race of spirit beings, similar in form to humans, sometimes hairy, and with tufts of feathers in place of ears. They travel in a spirit canoe, and when they encounter humans, can bestow upon them special powers, ceremonial prerogatives and wealth. Our Nuu-chah-nulth consultants recognized "Ya'aē" as the term yaʕay, and commented that the female yaʕay, who travel in groups of ten, wear their hair braided with a substance that causes a pleasant perfume smell, and have a feather protruding upward from each braid.

he might come home without being noticed. The boy went back home and delivered the message. Thereupon his parents believed him and did what Aitck·ik·mik had asked. When Ītcā′yaptcitl didn't hear them weep during the night as they had usually done, he said, mockingly, "Aitck·ik·mik must have revived again because his parents are not weeping for him any more." The one believed to be dead came back at night and told his relatives how he would avenge himself. He coated the canoe of Ītcā′yaptcitl with a magical substance. Then he told his relatives to go out and search for the dead whale from which he had safely escaped. He described to them where they would find it. When they came home and told that they had found a beached whale, Ītcā′yaptcitl and his relatives wanted to go out and get it. They wanted to push their canoe into the water. But when Ītcā′yaptcitl tried to lift it, his leg went to sleep and he had to let it go again. This was the effect of the magic substance with which Aitck·ik·mik had coated the canoe. Try as often as he might, Ītcā′yaptcitl was unable to lift the canoe. So Aitck·ik·mik sprang from his hiding place and called out, "Look at me! Don't you know me? I am Aitck·ik·mik whom you tried to kill. You can count yourselves lucky if you should return to life as I did." He grabbed Ītcā′yaptcitl first with one hand by the knees and then with the other one by the chest and then tore him to pieces. Then he tore up his brothers and cousins. Aitck·ik·mik became a great whale hunter with whom nobody could compete.

17. The Revenge of the Brothers

Once upon a time there was a girl who had twenty brothers. Once a young man courted her. But she rejected him, although her brothers insisted that she should marry him. Finally she was forced to accept him, yet after the marriage she didn't allow her husband to touch her. Once a number of women asked her to come with them to the forest in order to peel inner cedar bark. Her husband went along to help them. Soon they found a nice cedar and peeled the trunk almost to the top. There the inner cedar bark stuck at a branch. The wife, who wanted to have the inner cedar bark badly, climbed up the side branches of the cedar to cut it off. Her husband followed her without her noticing. He took ropes of inner cedar bark along. When she reached the top of the tree he seized her and tied her up. The trunk of the cedar divided here and he tied one arm and one leg to each so that her arms and legs were spread far apart. Thereupon the women were frightened and ran home. But they didn't dare to say anything. The man climbed down again and cut all the branches off close to the trunk behind himself, so that it was impossible to climb the tree. The woman up in the tree sang: "Hanā′, hanā′, qaqatcē′ᴍ sik·saᴍâ′t hanā′ iātl ᴍāatsɴā′ hēnaᴍā′t atsɴā′ qaqatcē′ᴍ sik·saᴍâ′t hēē′, hēē′! Wē iēmetā′sōūtc qāqayó′tsek·tcē′ tlētlēmā′yatldē qaqatcē′M sik·saMâ′t hēē′, hēē′!"[79] (Oh, brothers! Yes, here I am up in the tree. Brothers, always when you went out to shoot birds, you had ten canoes. My brothers!) The brothers had just gone out in their ten canoes to shoot birds. One of them heard a noise and said, "Listen, what is that? Someone was singing. No, it isn't singing, it is crying." They listened. Another one said, "It comes from that mountain." Then they began to distinguish the words and said to each other, "That can only be our sister." They paddled in the direction of the voice and found their sister up in the tree. They tried to climb the tree one after the other but didn't succeed. When it was the youngest one's turn, the woman died. Foam came from her mouth and dripped down the tree. The youngest, whose turn it was now, licked off the foam and managed to get up. He untied the body and carried it down. Then they arranged her hair and sat her down in an upright position. The youngest called all his brothers and made them stand beside the body in order to see who resembled her most. He thought that the oldest, called Wo′tswin, looked most like her. He had beautiful, long, white hair. They braided his hair and gave him his sister's clothes. Then he went to the village. The man who had tied his wife to the tree was sitting in front of the house when the disguised man limped up. He said, "Here I am, your wife. But I will leave you now." The husband didn't reply because he was so surprised to see her again. When the brothers came back, they forced their sister—the disguised brother—to return to her husband. Wo′tswin had hidden a shell knife underneath his cape. The husband didn't suspect anything, but an old man who lived by the door looked upon the woman with suspicion and thought that she would take her revenge. But he didn't dare say anything. During the night, when husband and wife were in bed, the man embraced her and wanted to turn her around. But Wo′tswin said, "Leave me be today. I am ill and cannot spread my legs. Wait until I am better." So the former fell asleep. After a while Wo′tswin nudged him, and when he found that he was fast asleep, he cut his throat and ran away. The husband still rattled a few times in his throat and then died. The old man heard his rattle and called out, "Listen how he rattles, how his throat makes pEh. I knew that it wasn't the wife, but Wo′tswin, and he has avenged her death" (Nitinath).[80]

---

79. "N and M are *n* and *m* pronounced with half nasal closure, hence N between *n* and *d*; M between *m* and *p*" [Boas' original footnote]. Boas is describing here the manner of articulation of certain sounds in this song. The song indicates that while the story may have been associated with the "Nitinath" (Nitinaht or Ditidaht; see the footnote that follows), the storyteller spoke the Nuu-chah-nulth language, evident here by the replacement of Ditidaht " b" with Nuu-chah-nulth "m."

80. Boas indicates this is a "Nitinath" (Nitinaht or Ditidaht) story. What Boas transcribes here as "Nitinath" is the term ni·ti·nat, which is the Nuu-chah-nulth name for the Nitinat or Nitinaht, known today more commonly as Ditidaht (anglicized from di·ti·d?a·?tχ, the Ditidaht name for themselves, in their own language). The Ditidaht and their neighbours to the east, the Pacheedaht (Pacheenaht), speak the Ditidaht language. The traditional territory of these two groups extends along the west coast of Vancouver island from approximately Pachena Point to

18. The Girl and the Ghosts

Once upon a time there was an ill-tempered girl. When she was given food, she complained that it wasn't good enough, and nobody was able to satisfy her. One evening someone gave food to her parents and her, but she cried and wanted to have something better. When her parents had finished their meal and wanted to go to bed, she was still crying and didn't want to go to bed. Her mother said, "Come to bed, my child! I cannot give you what you ask for." Since she sat there obstinately, her parents finally went to bed by themselves and fell asleep. After a while the woman woke up. She called her daughter, but received no answer, so she got up and looked for the girl, yet was unable to find her. Then she woke up her husband and asked him whether he had seen their daughter. He also didn't know what had become of her, and all their searching was in vain. Suddenly they heard the girls voice calling deep under the ground, "Oh, give me good food, only a very small piece!" Thereupon the father called the whole tribe together and they considered what to do to get the girl back. They decided to dig after her. They dug ten deep holes, but were unable to reach her, so they gave up. When they had assembled for a council again, one of the men said, "The ghosts (of the dead) must have got her. You know, when a village is abandoned, the ghosts always come and look at the houses. Let's all move away! Two men shall hide, and when the ghosts come with the girl, they shall take her away from them." The people resolved to follow his advice. They loaded their canoes and set out. Two men hid on the roof-beam of a house and when it got dark, the ghosts appeared. They lit a fire and sang and danced. The girl sat among them and the ghosts sang magic incantations in order to change her, too, into a ghost, but these didn't bring the desired effect. Before the men could rush at the girl, they were scented by the ghosts, who vanished into the ground with the girl. So the two men went down to the river and washed themselves for four days. Then they returned to the house and hid again on the roof-beam. When it got dark, the ghosts came again to sing and to dance. This time they didn't scent the men, who rushed upon the girl and seized her before the ghosts were able to pull her down into the depths with them.

19. The Woman who Married her Cousin

Once upon a time there were two brothers. One of them had a daughter, the other one had a son. These were very much in love. The young man often took the girl

---

Point No Point. Elsewhere, Boas (1888c:53:20:316) presents a Ditidaht story that did not get into the *Sagen*. This story is about two brothers who visited Sun by shooting a chain of arrows from the earth up to the sky, and climbing up. Our Ditidaht consultant knew a variant of this Sun story, and identified the two people who visited Sun as ʕidititxti·dab ('Snot Man') and Wren.

along to the forest or into his canoe and they slept together. When the people found out at last, the two were ashamed. The young man went into the forest and remained there for a long time. He had his bow and arrow along and shot many ducks and divers.[81] At last he also shot a cormorant. The arrow smashed one wing of the bird, which thus wasn't able to fly well any longer. It ran and flew up a small river and the hunter followed. He shot it again and again but was unable to kill it and finally the bird vanished inside a cave. The young man went after it. Soon the cave opened and he reached a meadow where he found plenty of game. He turned back and stuck a stick right in front of the cave entrance in order to be able to find it again. He went home to his sweetheart and smiled at her. She asked, "Why do you smile? Have you seen something nice?" "Yes," he replied, "I want to take you along. We have nothing but scoldings and contempt here, so let's go away for a while." She consented and suggested that they should leave at night when all were asleep. She put on two capes; he took two bows and many arrows, two paddles and a light canoe. That is how they left. They went upriver to the spot where the young man had marked the entrance to the cave. They pulled the canoe inside and heaped up stones in front of the entrance. Then they went on and soon saw daylight again. They reached the plain full of grass which the young man had seen before. They built a small hut for themselves and the young man hunted all sorts of game: deer, elk, beaver, and especially bear. When they grew richer, they built a house and covered its walls with bear skins. In the course of time they had two sons. When these grew up, their father said to them, "I want to send you home, where I came from. I've lived in this country only for a short time." He described the way to them and they set out. The father had ordered them not to go into the houses right away, but to let themselves be seen first outside the village and to tell from where they came. They reached the village towards the evening and sat down outside it, and every time that they were seen they hid in the forest. At last they went to the house of their grandfather and sat down close by the door. The old man closed it and asked the two young people who they were and where they came from. So they told him that they were the sons of the escaped couple. Their grandfather called together all the people and they marvelled when they heard the story. The young people stayed there for two days, then they returned. They travelled at night so that nobody could find the way to their home. When they arrived at their parents, they told them that they had met with a friendly reception. So their parents resolved to go back, too. They loaded their canoe, left the cave, and went down the river. They had filled their canoe with many bear skins. When they got to their home village, the people said to each other, "There she is—

---

81. Given as *Taucher* in the original; although the literal translation of *Taucher* is 'diver,' dictionaries of this time period give both 'grebe' and 'loon' as possible meanings—the storyteller here is likely referring to the Western Grebe (*Aechmophorus occidentalis*), also known as the "helldiver."

she who has fled with her brother."[82] And one woman called out to her, "Just walk quickly, yes, just walk quickly, you fine woman who has taken her brother for her husband." She replied:

Tce-tcech - tā′-mah, tce-tcech - tā′-mah ö - ok· - tā′-mah tce-tce-ti - tā′- mah hā-

yuk· muts-mō - hā′-mak· ye-yeq - tā′-is tce-tcech - tā′- mah

(i.e., Yes, I have quick feet, my feet are nimble, since I have two hundred bear skins underneath my feet.)

20. K·atiniā′ak

There once was a famine which killed many people. Finally a chief killed all his cats (?)[83] since there was no food left at all, and invited his friends to eat cat meat with him. Ten chiefs accepted the invitation, but when they went home from the feast, they died as a consequence of eating the cat meat. In the village there also lived a poor slave called K·atiniā′ak, his sister Yaq'iē′sak·, and her husband. She said, "Let's move away from here to a river. Maybe we'll be able to catch fish there and survive on them." They moved and settled by a creek. K·atiniā′ak went out fishing and for several days caught large numbers of salmon. He said to his sister, "Now don't eat too much. You have starved for so long that now you'll get sick if you eat too much at once." She promised to take care, yet nevertheless ate so much that at last she burst and died. So the two men were left by themselves. K·atiniā′ak went fishing again and caught many salmon in a deep pool in the riverbed. He got so many that he threw them down beside himself to the right and left. He ate some of the salmon. Suddenly they changed into otters and ran away. Even the ones eaten by him changed into otters. His stomach swelled up. The otters tumbled around in his body and stuck their tails out of his anus. So his brother-in-law took a pointed pole and with it kneaded the belly of K·atiniā′ak until all the otters were dead. So the latter grew better again. When he went to the river again to catch salmon, there were none left. He looked up from the water and saw a long line of people pass by on the opposite bank. On their heads they all wore feathers which nodded to and fro as they

---

82. "Brother and cousin were indicated by the same word" [Boas' original footnote].

83. Boas' question mark here indicates his querying the mention of a domestic cat in a Nuu-chahnulth story.

were walking. Right in front there walked a very tall man; he was the chief of the Salmon. He was followed by large salmon, and the other species followed them in order of size. The small trout came last. Then the women and girls followed in the same order. By evening, the procession had passed. K·atiniā′ak followed them unobserved and finally saw a big house, which they entered. He crept behind the house and peeped through a knot-hole and he saw that it was completely dark inside. In a short while he heard someone say, "Let's open up the roof to let light into the house." When it grew light, he saw the men sitting in the back of the house on the platform, the women in front of them and the children down below on the ground. Two girls were singing the Ts'ē′k·a[84] in a corner of the house and then two men came jumping out from behind a partition of boards. They wore the big Hinkitsen[85] mask on their heads and moved their arms in wide circles on both sides of their bodies. After he had observed all this, he crept back. He went to his brother-in-law and said, "Let's return home now. It's time for the herring to spawn." He took along many salmon. When they arrived at their village, they saw a large amount of herring spawn there. It completely covered the corpses of the starved ones. K·atiniā′ak went to his chief, gave him the salmon and said to him, "Give all the survivors a feast with these salmon." This the chief did. When they had all assembled, K·atiniā′ak began to sing the song which he had secretly learned from the salmon. Since that time, the chief's family has owned the salmon song.

21. The First Mohö′tl'ath [86]

A father had two sons. One day they took their bows and arrows and went into the woods to shoot squirrels. Towards evening they heard the rushing of a river which they had never noticed before. When they approached it, they heard a noise as if many eagles were screaming. So the elder brother said to the younger one, "Let's turn back for now and go out early tomorrow morning to look at the river." They

---

84. Boas (1891d:596,598–599) transcribes this same term as "Tsā′yek·," which he identifies as a type of secret society, and Drucker (1951:215–218) refers to as a type of shamanistic group ritual—contemporary Nuu-chah-nulth people use the term či·qa· (Boas' "Tsā′yek·") to refer to a type of spirit song which is known as a "prayer song."

85. "Hinkitsen" is Boas' transcription of the Nuu-chah-nulth term hinki·cm which refers to a distinctive cedar headdress that is carved to represent a plumed sea serpent.

86. Boas presents here an Opetchesaht origin legend associated with the m̓u·ḥu·ɬʔatḥ (Boas' "Mohö′tl'ath"), one of the local groups (component groups). The fundamental social unit in this area was the local group or ʔu·štaqimɬ that centred on a group of chiefs who owned territorial rights and other privileges. Alliances of local groups formed tribes. Elsewhere Boas (1891d:584) uses the English term "sept" when referring to these local groups, and he lists the "Mö′hotl'ath" (transcribed as "Mohö′tl'ath" in the *Sagen*) as one of the "septs" of the Opetchesaht. The traditional territory of the m̓u·ḥu·ɬʔatḥ comprised Great Central Lake and the drainage systems of the Ash and Stamp Rivers (Sapir 1910–1914:xix:1).

returned home and told their father that they had heard many eagles by a river. They went to bed, but the elder brother was so impatient that he could not sleep. He woke his brother early in the morning and said, "Come, get up and let's go to the river." They paid no attention to the deer, elk and bear which they saw, but went straight down to the river. Then they heard the eagles and soon saw the river. They saw that the eagles were eating salmon. They went down to the bank and saw two girls who were building a salmon weir near a strong rapid, by driving poles into the cracks and holes of the rocky shore in order to brace their weir with them. These holes can still be seen today. When the weir was finished, the girls went away. The brothers followed them carefully at a distance in order not to be detected. Soon they saw smoke rising and noticed a house on the opposite bank at a narrow spot of the river. Here the girls entered. Soon they came out again and began to work on a dog hair blanket which was hanging across a pole on the shore. Each worked on one side of the blanket. The brothers crept down. The older one nudged the younger one and whispered, "I think this one here is the older one. I am going to take her; you take the younger one." Then they shot their arrows at the corresponding ends of the blanket. They went across the river and sat down beside the girls. These looked at each other and didn't know what to say. They went into the house. The brothers followed them and married them. Then the elder brother said, "I want to stay here. You go home and take your wife along." The younger one retorted, "No, I want to stay here. You go back." And this is what happened. They had many children. The older one became the ancestor of the Möhö'tl'ath; the younger one became the ancestor of the Ts'ōmā'as'ath.[87]

22. Tribal Legends of Some Local Groups[88] of the Ts'iciā'ath[89]

1) Ts'iciā'ath.[90] Two girls went out to get inner cedar bark and found a young wolf who was still blind. They killed it, tore it in two pieces and took one half home with

---

87. The c̓uma·ʕasʔatḥ (Boas' "Ts'ōmā'as'ath") and the m̓u·ḥu·ɬʔatḥ (Boas' Möhö'tl'ath) were identified by Boas (1891d:584) as two "septs" (local groups) of the Opetchesaht. The traditional territory of the c̓uma·ʕasʔatḥ included the Somass River and upper end of Alberni Inlet (St. Claire 1991:77–78).

88. *Stammessagen einiger Geschlechter*—literally 'tribal legends of some of the house/lineages,' although here the reference is to origin legends of the local groups (component groups). The local group is associated by Boas in the *Sagen* with the German term *Geschlecht* 'house; lineage,' although elsewhere Boas (1891d:584) uses the English term 'sept' when he refers to the local groups.

89. The traditional territory of the c̓iša·ʔatḥ, whose name is anglicized as "Tseshaht," which appears in the *Sagen* as "Ts'iciā'ath" and elsewhere in Boas (1891d:583–585) as "Ts'ēcā'ath," originally was limited to several islands in the southwestern portion of the Broken Group in outer Barkley Sound. But over time Tseshaht territory expanded to include all of the Broken Group Islands, most of the northern shore of Barkley Sound, the western half of the Deer Group, much of the inland area along Alberni Inlet, and the lower Somass River (St. Claire 1991:45).

90. The original local group of the c̓iša·ʔatḥ (Tseshaht; Boas' "Ts'ēcā'ath") from which the tribe as

them. It became a strong magic substance. Since then, the Ts'iciá'ath have danced like these girls did when they found the wolf.

2) Nɛc'á'ath.[91] A young man heard the blowing of a whale but was unable to find it, although he searched around very carefully. At last he went down to the beach. There he found a whale no bigger than his finger was long. He caught it and it became his talisman. Since then, his family has danced with the whale mask.

3) Tla'semĩesath.[92] A young man went into the forest and set himself a big fire on the beach far away from the village. Here he fell asleep. He woke up when he heard someone calling: ē, ē! He lifted his cape from his face and saw two girls who were warming themselves by the fire, first the front, then their backs. They wore long feathers on their heads and therefore were called Aia'tlk·ē (= Feather on Head). Therefore the Tla'semĩesath dance the Aia'tlk·e in the Tlokoala.[93]

4) Ha'mēyisath.[94] An orphan boy once went out to hunt sea otters. He had no relatives except for a little sister. Finally he saw a sea otter and shot it. His arrow hit it right in the belly, but didn't kill it and instead passed straight through it. After he had shot many arrows in vain, he aimed for the head and thus killed it. When he took it into the canoe he saw that there was an opening right through the belly of the animal, and that all his arrows had passed through it. From then on, he used the sea-otter mask in dancing.

5) K·utsɛmhaath.[95] Far from all settlements, in a spot never frequented by people, a man found a small spear belonging to the forest spirit Tcēnē'ath,[96] who has a red stripe running diagonally across his body. Consequently he and his family dance

---

a whole took its name; this local group, the čiša·ʔatḥ, derived its name from čiša·, the name of a village site on Benson Island in the Broken Group, north of Coaster Channel (St. Claire 1991:45–47).

91. The našʔasʔatḥ (Boas' "Nɛc'á'ath") were one of the local groups who became completely assimilated within the Tseshaht (St. Claire 1991:50–51).

92. The x̣'asimyisʔatḥ (Boas' "Tla'semĩesath"), like the našʔasʔatḥ, were another local group who became completely assimilated within the Tseshaht (St. Claire 1991:50).

93. See story 7 of this Nutka Section for an explanation of the Tlokoala dance ceremony.

94. Boas' "Ha'mēyisath" is recognized as ḥimayisʔatḥ, the name of a local group said to have originated as slaves to the original Tseshaht on Benson Island, who eventually rose above slave status but remained subordinate to the Tseshaht after they amalgamated with them (St. Claire 1991:141).

95. It appears that Boas is the only source who has identified this group, the "K·utsɛmhaath," a name possibly recognized as k̓ʷučimḥaʔatḥ that is noted here as a local group of the Tseshaht; elsewhere, in his listing of the Tseshaht local groups, Boas (1891d:584) transcribes their name as "Ku'tssɛmhaath."

96. The term transcribed by Boas as "Tcēnē'ath" is recognized by our Nuu-chah-nulth consultants as činiʔatḥ. Drucker (1951:152) describes these beings as "tall shaggy-haired red-skinned beings who pursued people with spears."

with the mask of the Tcēnē'ath, to which a spear has been fastened. They, too, wear a red stripe diagonally across their bodies.

6) Kuai'ath.[97] A man killed a whale and tied it to the shore. He made his daughter hold the line of the harpoon until his friends would arrive to cut up the whale. When he had left to call them, the whale revived. The girl didn't know what to do. She heard many people speaking and shouting inside the whale. But the whale did not swim away and stayed close to the shore instead. When her father returned, she told him what had happened. Consequently his family uses the mask of a whale and a man during dancing.

23. The Tribe of Women [98]

A long time ago only women lived in Alberni. Nobody knew where they had come from. At last they wandered eastward and took all the species of shellfish with them. Therefore there are no shellfish in Alberni to this day. The Ts'iciā'ath later moved from the outer coast up along the Alberni Canal and, at its upper end, met the Hōpitcisā'ath, who were speaking the Nanaimo language. The past generation still used the Nanaimo language just as much as the Nutka language.[99]

—In the beginning people paddled in such a way that they pulled the paddle's narrow edge through the water, until someone discovered that it was more efficient to push the water with the flat side. Since then, they have paddled as is done nowadays.

—In the beginning people used canoes made from pitch. They always poured water over them so that they wouldn't melt, and they went fishing only before sunrise.

---

97. As with the "K·utsɛmhaath" local group noted above, it appears that Boas is the only source to have identified the Kuai'ath (presumably kʷayiʔatḥ) as a local group of the Tseshaht; he also identifies the "Kuai'ath" as one of the Tseshaht local groups in his 1890 report (Boas 1891d:584).

98. The German term used here, *Weibervolk*, means literally 'womenfolk,' but is better translated in this context as 'tribe of women.'

99. Boas' reference to the "Nanaimo language" is to the Nanaimo dialect of Island Halkomelem Coast Salish. About two dozen words in this original language of the Opetchesaht were recorded by Edward Sapir (1910–1914) who commented at one point in his fieldnotes that the language was "about like Nanaimo," and in another part of these same notes stated that it was the "same as" Pentlatch (a now-extinct Coast Salish language formerly spoken between Parksville and Comox; see Section XII of the present volume). However, a linguistic review of these two dozen words indicates they are more like Halkomelem than Pentlatch.

—The Thunderbird uses a snake, Hahē′k·tōyek·,[100] for a belt. The snake's bones are a powerful magical substance.

—During an eclipse of the moon, the moon is seized by the door of the Sky Chief's[101] house. This door devours anyone entering the house.—

---

100. "Hahē′k·tōyek·." is Boas' transcription of the Nuu-chah-nulth term ḥiyiƛ'i·k 'lightning snake; sea serpent.' Elsewhere, Boas (1891d:596) states: "Thunder is produced by the flapping of the wings of the thunder-bird, Tū′tutc, the lightning by his belt, the snake Hahē′k·toyek·, which he casts down upon the earth. The fortunate finder of a bone of the Hahē′k·toyek· possesses one of the most powerful charms the natives know of."

101. The Sky Chief is one of four "chiefs" called upon by Nuu-chah-nulth people in prayers during their bathing rituals (Drucker 1951:152).

XIV. Legends of the Lekwiltok

The Lekwiltok were one of three tribes living in the Comox Harbour area of mid-Vancouver Island when Boas went there in November 1886. By that time, the few original inhabitants of this area, the Pentlatch, were amalgamated with the Comox who had originally lived farther north. The Lekwiltok had gradually moved southward over the previous few generations, displacing the Comox, and they had now worked out a delicate living arrangement. Though Boas observed the Lekwiltok and Comox feasting together, he noted that the two tribes "were formerly open enemies," and the picturesque Comox Harbour village remained physically divided. He wrote that the Lekwiltok were then living "in the first villages," while the Comox, who had "combined with" the Pentlatch, were living "in the last houses of the settlement." Nevertheless, the Comox Harbour tribes were "very friendly" to Boas, after he was introduced to them by a local settler (Rohner 1969:58–59). The myths and legends presented here come from the more recent arrivals to this area, the Lekwiltok; the Comox stories are presented separately as Sections VIII and XI, and the Pentlatch tales, as Section XII.

Potlatch "speaking posts" belonging to Major Dick (d. 1913) that came to Cape Mudge from Alert Bay as part of a dowry. Figure at left has a copper on its chest, showing that Major Dick owned a copper; the centre figure holds its stomach, showing that he gave feasts; and the right-hand figure calls out, showing that he called people to potlatches. While these stood formerly inside a house, they were in the Cape Mudge graveyard at the time this photo was taken.

Royal British Columbia Museum, Victoria, B.C. PN2349 (W.B. Anderson photo; no date).

XIV. Legends of the Lḗkwiltok·[1]

1. The Revenge of the Brothers

Once upon a time there was a man and a woman who lived in Tsa'wiloq.[2] One day the man said to his wife, "My dear, let's go to the forest to get pitch." The woman

---

1. "Lḗkwiltok·." is Boas' rendering of lígʷiɬdaʔxʷ (anglicized as "Lekwiltok") which designates the group of kʷákʷala-speaking tribes (see below) who originally lived in the Johnstone Strait region and spoke a dialect known as líq̓ʷala. Beginning in the mid-1700s or earlier, the Lekwiltok aggressively expanded southwards. By the mid-1800s, the Lekwiltok had displaced the Island Comox Coast Salish from almost all of their territory, which formerly extended along the east side of Vancouver Island from Salmon River in the northwest to the Kye Bay/Cape Lazo vicinity in the southeast, including the islands offshore. One result of this expansion was that many Island Comox place names throughout this region were either renamed or repronounced in the kʷákʷala language. Today, Lekwiltok people reside at the former Island Comox village sites of Cape Mudge and Campbell River, and the Comox Band has both Coast Salish and Lekwiltok affiliations (Boas 1887a:230; 1887b:62–64; 1887f:131–132, map; 1888h:201; 1891d:608–609; Barnett 1955:25; Taylor and Duff 1956; Duff 1965; Kennedy and Bouchard 1983:16–27; 1990b:441; Mauzé 1984; 1992; Assu and Inglis 1989; Galois 1994). The kʷákʷala language, identified by scholars for many years as the "Kwakiutl" language, is classified as part of the "Kwakiutlan" or Northern Branch of the Wakashan Language Family. A contemporary spelling of kʷákʷala is "Kwakwala" (or, "Kwak'wala"). The approximately 30 autonomous groups or "tribes" speaking this language throughout the region between Smith Sound and Cape Cook, on the shores of Queen Charlotte Strait, and eastward into Johnson Strait are known collectively as kʷákʷakǝw̓akʷ ('Kwakiutl-speaking people'); these groups were formerly referred to as the "Southern Kwakiutl." A contemporary spelling of kʷákʷakǝw̓akʷ is "Kwakwaka'wakw" (Boas [1925]; Codere 1990; Thompson and Kinkade 1990).

    Our annotation of this section was assisted greatly in the summer of 2001 by Kwakwala-speaking experts Chief Adam Dick and Dr. Daisy Sewid-Smith who are referred to here as "AD" and "DSS" respectively; we gratefully acknowledge their assistance. This annotation also draws upon our consultation in the 1970s–1980s with both Comox-speaking and Kwakwala-speaking people, all of whom we thank: Mary Clifton; Rose Mitchell; Bill Mitchell; Jeannie Dominick; Ambrose Wilson; and Tommy Paul (all speakers of Comox, although Mary Clifton spoke Kwakwala, as well); also, Lucy Hovell and Jim Henderson (speakers of Kwakwala).

2. Boas (1934:60) transcribes this same place name elsewhere as "tsa'wilax̣ᵘ" and describes it as "a pond near Puntlach," which is a reference to the lower Puntledge River area in the vicinity of Courtenay, in Comox Harbour. What Boas transcribes here in the *Sagen* as "Tsa'wiloq" is the same term written on an 1865 map of Comox as "Chaw-wil-ocq" (Comox District 1865) and applied to a prairie area located between what is known today as Portuguese Creek (formerly "Salmon Creek") and Finley Creek, adjacent to the Tsolum River near Courtenay. However, the Native term "Tsa'wiloq" was not recognized by either our Comox-speaking or our Kwakwala-speaking consultants.

followed her husband and after a long walk they reached a tall tree. The man climbed up and at the highest tip, found good pitch. When he had come down again, the woman asked him to give her a bit, but he told her to climb up herself. Reluctantly, she agreed. When she had climbed up a little and still not found any pitch, she called out to her husband, "Where did you find it?" "At the highest tip of the tree," he answered. When the woman continued to climb up the tree, the man followed her and with his axe, hacked off all the tree's branches close to the trunk, starting at the top, so that the woman was unable to come down again. When he arrived at the bottom again, he called out to his wife, "You have been unfaithful to me; your punishment will be to die on this tree." Having spoken, he went back to his house.

But the woman had four brothers who had gone out to shoot birds and fish, just about this time. Their sister, in the top of the tree, called out in her agony, "Come, oh brothers, save me!" It seemed to the youngest brother that he could hear his sister's voice, so he stopped paddling and listened. Then he heard plainly how she called out, "Come, oh brothers, save me!" He drew it to his brothers' attention but they were able to hear it only when the woman was calling out for the fourth time. The eldest said, "Let's quickly paddle there and look for our sister." This they did, and finally, after a long search, found the tree. The eldest tried to climb up, but was unsuccessful. The second and third didn't fare any better. At last the youngest ascended the tree, but their efforts had lasted so long that their sister had starved to death in the meantime. The young man sorrowfully brought down her body, and the brothers discussed among themselves how they should avenge their sister's death. They didn't doubt in the least that their brother-in-law had killed her. The youngest one said, "Let's strip off the skin from her head and put it on. Then we'll look like our sister." They did this. First the eldest put on the skin, her apron and cape, her hat and her arm and ankle ornaments. But he didn't quite resemble her. The second and third ones were likewise unable to assume her shape, but the youngest one resembled her completely when he had put on her skin and clothing. The brothers said to each other, "What shall we do now?" and the eldest sharpened his knife, gave it to the youngest and told him to kill their brother-in-law. He set out and when he came to his brother-in-law, he said, "I'm very tired; I almost starved in that tree." And the man replied, "I was angry with you, but since you have come back, everything will be forgotten." He asked his mother for roots and told his wife to prepare them. The disguised brother roasted the roots and then pounded them with a stone. The husband's small brother watched him and then ran to his mother and called out, "Oh, mother, just look! My sister-in-law there pounds like a strong man, not like a weak woman." But his mother forbade him such idle talk.

When night came the man went to bed with his supposed wife. He wanted to embrace her and turn her to him, but she said, "Oh, please let me be! I'm feeling very sick." But in reality the young man didn't want him to discover his knife. At midnight he pinched his brother-in-law in order to see whether he was fast asleep. Since the latter didn't budge, he pulled out his knife and cut off his head. Then he got up, smoothed out the blankets again and went away with the head.

Early in the morning the mother called her son, "Get up, it's bright daylight!" He didn't reply. So the old one sent her youngest son and told him to wake his brother. He nudged him, but he didn't move. The mother said, "Can you hear him breathing?" "No, I can't hear him," answered the little one. "Then pull his blanket away," called the mother, who was beginning to get impatient. The boy obeyed and then saw that he was without a head. But he was not yet old enough to understand that his brother was dead. He ran to his mother and called, "Oh mother, my brother doesn't have a head any more." The old one said, "Don't talk such nonsense." So the boy ran back, put his hand into the blood and showed it to his mother. This alarmed her, so she walked over and then saw that her son was dead. So she cried bitterly.

The four brothers buried their sister out in the forest.

2. The Four Siblings

Once upon a time there were three brothers and one sister. The latter was married to a man called Nāntsuwikyemaē.[3] He used to go to a lake with the brothers to catch beaver. After they had caught a number, they returned home and brought their wives the skins. Once Nāntsuwikyemaē caught only a few beaver. Consequently he thought that his wife was being unfaithful to him and decided to go back to find out whether his suspicion was based on fact. He arrived home early, unexpectedly, and found his wife sleeping with her lover, so he took his knife and cut off the latter's head, which he carried back to the lake. The woman was awakened by the streaming blood of her lover. She feared her husband's revenge and fled to her brothers after having thrown the corpse from the house. But the brothers didn't know who had killed the man. On the following evening, Nāntsuwikyemaē was singing in his house and one of the brothers sent over his son to see what he was doing. The boy went over and saw the head of the woman's lover there. Consequently all the people knew that he had been killed by Nāntsuwikyemaē. They intended to kill him, but he fled and hid in the forest, yet the brothers found him at last. He bade them come into

---

3. Boas' "Nāntsuwikyemaē" is possibly nánstuwiqami?, a Kwakwala term meaning 'the head of the grizzly bear,' referring to a character in a story obtained from the Oowekeeno people of the Rivers Inlet area (DSS).

his house and there served them food. Then he killed them and put their corpses into a box. He carried it in his canoe to a level spot and there put the box down. He built a burial house for them and purified and decorated the surroundings of the grave.

The sister discovered soon that her brothers were dead and she sat down by the grave and wept, "Oh, if only I were with my brothers!" She stayed there for three days. On the fourth day it suddenly grew light all around; someone patted her shoulder and asked her why she was crying. She didn't turn around. She felt someone pat her shoulder and ask her why she was crying a second and third time. But she turned around only when this happened for the fourth time and said, "Oh, my three brothers are buried here." The other one replied, "Don't weep. Take this magic substance; with it you will be able to recall your brothers to life. And take this poisonous herb; with its aid you will be able to find out who killed your brothers." Then she knew that the stranger who had come up to her so mysteriously, was K·ants'ŏ'ump.[4] And she became a shaman. She sang and flung the magic substance onto the grave; thereupon the three brothers arose and came out of the grave.

When they returned to the village, her husband gave a huge feast. He swept his house, lit a big fire and the woman danced at night. Then she threw the poisonous herb at the spectators and they all fell down dead. But she brought them back to life again with the healing magic substance. She did this four times, then she killed everyone present, for good, and did not bring them back to life again except for her brothers.

(The above legend is fairly obscure. The relationship of Nāntsuwikyemaē to the woman and to the brothers remains uncertain, especially. In the beginning of the story it seems that the youngest of the brothers is her lover, and elsewhere she appears clearly as his sister. The informant has lived on the Skeena river for awhile. Moreover, since the legend closely resembles the Tsimshian legend G·auŏ,[5] while diverging considerably from all other Kwakiutl legends, it can hardly be considered an authentic Kwakiutl legend.)

3. The Moon Man

Once there was famine in a village and all the supplies had been exhausted except for a box of dried fish eggs. The people lived on fern roots which they gathered labouriously in the forest and on which they survived wretchedly. A man and his

---

4. "K·ants'ŏ'ump is Boas' transcription of qəṅs ʔúmp which translates from Kwakwala as 'our Father,' referring to God (AD; DSS).

5. The reference is to story 6, "The family of G·auŏ," in Section XXIII of the *Sagen*.

wife had two sons whom they left at home while they went into the forest. They had strictly forbidden them to touch the fish eggs.

One day, when the parents were out, a man entered the house and said to the boys, "Why don't you eat the fish eggs; there's a whole box of them there." The boys replied, "No, we must not touch them; our parents have forbidden it." "Never mind," said the man, "just take as much as you want." Thereupon one of the boys was almost willing to do what the stranger had said, but the other boy warned him and said, "Our mother will beat us when she comes back and sees that we have taken her fish eggs." So the stranger disclosed his identity as the Moon Man and said, "Henceforth when you want to have food, ask me for it. I will replace a hundredfold the eggs you take from your parents." Thereupon the boys ate up all the fish eggs and the stranger went away.

The parents returned in a short while and when the mother discovered that the fish eggs were gone, she beat her children. They didn't say anything, but at midnight, when everybody was asleep, they went outside, looked up to the moon and said, "Oh, make us happy; you have promised it to us." When they had invoked the Moon Man like this four times, countless herring and all sorts of fish came swimming. They caught them, filled their capes with fish, and carried them to their parents' house. There they dropped the fish at their mother's feet and said, "Look, you were angry with us and punished us because we had eaten your fish eggs. This is how we repay you!" So she was glad and had them tell her where they obtained the fish, and soon all the people knew that they were rich. They came from everywhere to buy fish for bread, capes and skins. In this way the boys' father became a great chief.

4. The Children of the Dog

In Tsīkyā'les (= With Big Clams)[6] there lived a chief who had one daughter and a big dog. One night the girl took the dog along into her chamber. At midnight the father heard someone talking with his daughter and therefore he got up, went to her chamber and asked, "Who are you talking to?" "Oh, nobody," replied the daughter, "I only have my dog here." During the following two nights the same thing happened. So the man said to his wife, "Do you know that our daughter always has her dog with her at night?" She replied, "I have heard a story about a dog who slept

---

6. While Boas' "Tsīkyā'les" is very likely the Kwakwala term čík^walis meaning 'clam-steaming-on-beach place' (AD; DSS), neither our Kwakwala-speaking nor our Comox-speaking consultants knew which specific place was referred to in this legend. Boas (1934:59) later provided the transcription for this same place name as "dzē'k·alis," which he translated as 'clam digging on beach' although he did not indicate where this place was located.

with a woman at night and that she then gave birth to dogs. Possibly this is the same dog." The following day the man coated the dog with pitch and when he heard talking again in his daughter's room at night, he quietly opened the door, sprang inside and saw the dog lying with his daughter. The dog was unable to get up because it was stuck to the bed, and the father killed it right there.

The father was angry with his daughter and in the morning made all the people pack up their belongings and load the canoes. After all the fires had been extinguished they set out and left the girl behind by herself. Only her grandmother pitied her in her fate. She hid a glowing coal in a shell, put this into a hole and told the girl to take out the shell only when everyone had gone. She did what her grandmother had told her to do. She blew on the coal and lit a big fire for herself. She made a small hut for herself from branches and in a short while gave birth to ten young dogs. She collected shellfish in order to nourish them. To this end she lit a big fire on the beach at night in order to be able to see and search for shellfish. While she was thus occupied, she heard singing up at her house, "Tsī'kyala Iaia (Look for shellfish, Mother)." She hurried up but found only the young dogs. So she returned to her task and again heard them singing and beating time. So she took a pole, put it up on the beach and draped her clothes around it so that it looked as if someone was on the beach. Then she crept unnoticed into the forest and came up to the house from behind. She saw that her children had taken off the dog clothes and were singing and dancing. One boy stood guard in front of the door and watched the pole, which he took to be his mother. She quickly jumped into the house. She saw the dog skins hanging there, pulled them down and called out, "Why do you disguise yourselves as dogs when you are actually real people?" The skins of two of the children were hanging apart from the others. She was unable to seize them quickly enough to prevent two of the boys from slipping them on again. These two at once became dogs again.

At first the children remained silent, but soon the eldest said, "Let's talk to Iaia (he called his mother thus)." Then he said, "I will build a house for Iaia." The second, "I will build a canoe for her." The third, "I will catch whales for her." The fourth, "And I, halibut." The fifth, "And I, mountain goats." Each of them wanted to work for his mother. The woman went down to the beach again to look for shellfish, and when she returned, a big house was standing there. Two of her sons had gone out to hunt for whales and soon towed one of them behind their canoe. They had plenty to eat now.

But the woman's father was starving because the fish hadn't arrived. The woman thought of her grandmother who once had taken pity on her. She saw a Raven fly past and called out to him: "I wish you were a man!" He at once turned into one. She invited him into her house and gave him plenty of food. When he had eaten his fill, she said, "I would like to send my grandmother some blubber; will you take it to her?" Raven promised to do it. She tied four pieces of whale blubber to his back. He changed back into a bird and flew away. He came to the old woman who was just looking for shellfish on the beach. There he hopped about. The old one picked up a stone to throw at him, but he shouted, "Don't do that! Your granddaughter has sent me to bring this blubber to you." Then the old one saw the four big pieces of blubber on his back and took them from him. She hid the blubber underneath her cape and went into the house, where she sat down by a mat which she was making. While working, she often stealthily bit off a piece of blubber and her grandson, who was watching her, asked, "What are you eating there, Grandmother?" "Nothing," replied she, "I am only pretending to chew." The boy didn't believe her and watched closely. When she believed herself to be unobserved and took another bite, the boy said, "But you are eating, Grandmother." Again the old one denied it. But the small boy saw her taking a bite a third time and when he saw the same thing the fourth time, he went over to see what she was eating. The old one got angry at this and smacked his face with the blubber, while shouting at the same time, "My grand-daughter has sent this to me. She has plenty of food now." When the chief heard this, he decided to return to his daughter with all his people. But when the canoes approached, the sons of the dog and the woman waved the Death-Bringer Halaiu[7] towards them and the canoes began to roll. The occupants of the canoes trembled in fear and fright. Soon the canoes capsized and the people and canoes were changed into stones. Only the grandmother was saved.

5. Wḗk·aē (Ancestor legend of the Wī′wēak·em)[8]

Wḗk·aē came down to earth from the sky and built himself a house in T'e′kya.[9] He

---

7. Boas (1935:110) lists the occurrences of the "death-bringer," haláyu (transcribed here in the *Sagen* as "Halaiu") in Kwakiutl mytholgy, noting that it is seldom described and takes various forms, including a baton, arrow, or quartz, that when pointed at people or objects causes instant destruction.

8. Wɛ′qɛ (Boas' "Wḗk·aē") was the ancestral founder of the wíwɛqɛ (anglicized as "Weewiakay") and wíwɛqəm (Boas' "Wī′wēak·em," anglicized as "Weewiakum") subgroups or tribes of the Lekwiltok who in the early 19th century lived together at Topaze Harbour, north from Hardwicke Island. They subsequently separated; the Weewiakum occupied several sites in Loughborough Inlet, Cardero Channel and elsewhere before eventually settling at Campbell River, while the Weewiakay occupied several other sites (including Kanish Bay and Drew Harbour on Quadra Island) before settling finally at Cape Mudge (Duff 1965:87–92).

     Boas refers to this story, here in the original *Sagen*, as *Ahnensage* which means 'ancestor legend.'

9. Several of our Comox-speaking consultants identified the original Comox Coast Salish term for the Topaze Harbour area as t'íki which they translated as 'close one eye and squint.' What Boas

had three beautiful daughters who used to sit in front of the house, plaiting mats. Their faces were painted with red colour. One day, four young wolves ran up to them. The girls caught them and brought them into the house. They grew so fond of them that they took them into their beds at night. But the wolves raced around the house and so the sisters decided to let them loose again. They only kept the youngest wolf, whose fur had beautiful markings. Then the youngest girl dreamed of the wolves and in the morning said to her father, "I will take the young wolf back to his parents. Don't be afraid for me and don't weep for me. The wolves won't harm me." She took the young wolf into her arms and carried him to the house of the wolves. Thereupon these gave her the wolf head ornament and a rattle which was so big that it had to be carried by two people. They told her, "Your father will now become a great chief."

When the girl had returned, Wē′k·aē built a big house and decided to court the daughter of Kunkunqulikya, Thunderbird.[10] He journeyed to his house and asked for the girl's hand. Kunkunqulikya said, "First let's match our strength so that I'll be able to see whether you are strong and powerful." He told Wē′k·aē to sit down midway along the wall and then he made the waters of the sea rise higher and higher so that the house was completely filled. Wē′k·aē took a small piece of slate and pushed it against the ground and it grew with the rising water so that he was always sitting dry. So the Thunderbird saw that he had power and gave him his daughter. When Wē′k·aē returned, he painted the Thunderbird on his house.

Then he decided to take the daughter of the chief of the Awik′ē′noq[11] for his wife. Through this marriage he obtained the hā·mats'a[12] dance. The chief told him to call his first child Ts'ɛ′mk·oa.[13]

Then Wē′k·aē went to the Bilqula[14] to get a wife there. He found all the people

---

writes as "T'e′kya" is t'əká, the name by which Kwakwala-speakers know this same place—the Kwakwala form adopts the Comox term, switches the stress from the first to the second syllable, and changes the vowel qualities, resulting in a word that is identical to the Kwakwala term for 'dirt,' i.e. t'əká. Boas (1934:37, 56) later recorded this same place name as "T!ɛk·a′" and provided the translation 'soil.'

10. "Kunkunqulikya" is Boas' rendering of kʷə′nkʷənxʷəligɛ, the Kwakwala term for 'Thunderbird' (AD; DSS).

11. What Boas transcribes as "Awik′ē′noq" is ʔuwíkinuxʷ (anglicized as "Oowekeeno"), referring to the people of the Rivers Inlet area.

12. "Hā·mats'a" is Boas' transcription of hámaċa (anglicized as "hamatsa"), the Kwakwala term commonly translated as 'cannibal dancer; wild man'; DSS points out that the dancer is being captured so that the cannibalistic spirit can be exorcized from his body.

13. "Ts'ɛ′mk·oa" is the Kwakwala word c'ə́mq̓ʷəgaʔɬ which means 'sound made by swallowing something whole,' and is the name of a hámaċa (DSS).

14. Boas' "Bilqula" is bə′lxʷəla, anglicized as "Bella Coola," referring to the Bella Coola (Nuxalk) people of the central B.C. coast.

assembled in one house. Their faces were scratched and they wept because their salmon weir had been destroyed. Wē′k·aē laughed at their sorrows. He broke a giant tree in two and built a salmon weir for them. So they rejoiced and their chief gave him his daughter as a reward. He gave her many capes trimmed with abalone shells. Wē′k·aē grew angry that she wasn't given more and better things and he killed[15] this wife.

When he returned he purified and painted his house and gave a big feast.

---

15. DSS notes that what Boas translates here as 'killed' is the Kwakwala term wáyadixʔid which would be more appropriately translated as 'abandoned.'

XV. Legends of the Nimpkish

"This evening," Boas wrote of 20 October 1886, "the cannibal was explained to me. I have been looking for this for a long time but could never get it" (Rohner 1969:45). This was possibly story 9, and may indicate that some of the Nimpkish stories were collected during Boas' first visit to Alert Bay, 18–23 October 1886. Still, a Kwakiutl storyteller also narrated tales of the cannibal (Section XVII, Nos. 8 and 9) and, with representatives of so many neighbouring tribes attending the Alert Bay potlatches, it is likely that cannibal stories were recorded from both these groups at this time. During his second visit, 25 August to 3 September 1889, he "achieved good results" (Rohner 1969:111), but gives no details in his one published letter from that visit.

"Alert Bay is a well protected cove on a small island which is about two miles long. The settlement is stretched out along the flat shore and is much larger than the one at Newetti … The church is on this side of the woods at the west end of the settlement. Then come the Indian houses, which do not seem to have been much influenced by the mission" (Rohner 1969:43). Alert Bay, *ca.* 1888–89.

Potlatch in progress at Alert Bay, showing bales of blankets ready for distribution, *ca.* 1910.
American Museum of Natural History Library, New York.
Neg. No. 104464 (George Hunt photo).

Photo taken of house belonging to "Chief Klakwagila of Kingcome Inlet, B.C.," at Alert Bay, British Columbia, September 5, 1909. Sign above the camera-shy residents tells how the chief "Broke a Copper valued, 11500 blankets."

University of Washington Libraries, Seattle, Washington. MSCUA, NA2764
(John N. Cobb photo).

XV. Legends of the Nimkisch[1]

1. Ts'ētlwalak·amē
(Ancestor legend of the Ts'ēts'ētlwalak·amaē numaym)[2]

After the Flood the former people were transformed into animals and stones. When the waters had receded, the monster Nᴇmkyā′likyō (= Only One)[3] rose from the depths of the ocean. He looked like a huge halibut carrying a man on its narrow edge. He put him ashore at QulkH[4] and returned again to the deep. The man looked

---

1. What Boas transcribes here as "Nimkisch" is ṅə′mgis, the Kwakwala name referring to at least two subgroups or tribes in earlier times: the ṅə′mgis, anglicized as "Nimpkish"; and the ṅíʔnəlkinuxʷ (Boas' "Nē′nelky'ēnoq"), anglicized as "Ninelkaynuk." The traditional territories of both tribes were centred in the drainage system of the Nimpkish River; the Nimpkish occupied the lower portions of this drainage system and the Ninelkaynuk occupied the upper portions. It appears that the Ninelkaynuk amalgamated with the Nimpkish sometime in the early 1800s. They were joined by members of other tribes, some of whom settled at the mouth of the Nimpkish and some of whom moved instead to Alert Bay on Cormorant Island in the 1860s (Boas 1887f:130–131,map; 1897:331,333; 1934:maps 8,8a,9,11,12; Dawson 1888:72; Duff 1953–1954; 1965:31,37; Bouchard and Kennedy 1988b:98–102; Galois 1994:309–310). The Nimpkish are among the approximately 30 autonomous groups or "tribes" speaking the Kwakwala language and comprising the Kwakwaka'wakw (see also the initial footnote to Section XIV of the present volume).

   Our annotation of this section was assisted greatly in the summer of 2001 by Kwakwala-speaking experts Chief Adam Dick and Dr. Daisy Sewid-Smith, who are referred to here as "AD" and "DSS" respectively; we gratefully acknowledge their assistance. This annotation also draws upon our consultation in the 1980s with the following Kwakwala-speaking people, all of whom we thank: Willie Hunt; Maggie Frank; Cecil Wadhams; Charlie Matilpi; and Helen Knox.

2. Here in the original *Sagen*, Boas uses the German term *Geschlecht* to refer to the "numaym" which is an anglicization of the Kwakwala word nəmíṁa (loosely translated as 'one kind' or 'of one blood') denoting the descent-based groups comprising each Kwakwala-speaking tribe. As well, Boas uses here the term *Ahnensage* which means 'ancestor legend.'

   What Boas transcribes here as "Ts'ēts'ētlwalak·amaē" is ćićíɬwalaqami ('the famous ones'), one of the five numayms that Boas (1966:40) identified among the Nimpkish (DSS)—the ancestor transcribed here by Boas as "Ts'ētlwalak·amē" (ćíɬwalaqami) turns up at the beginning of the fourth paragraph of this same legend.

3. DSS confirms that nəṁxalagiyu (Boas' "Nemkyā′likyō") does translate as 'only one.'

4. "QulkH" is Boas' rendering of xʷəlkʷ 'criss-crossed logs,' the name applied to a village site situated at the mouth of the Nimpkish River (DSS; AD). Elsewhere, Boas (1934:36,78) identifies "xûlkᵘ" (xʷəlkʷ) as one of the places of origin for the Nimpkish people and provides the translation '(logs) placed crosswise.'

around on earth and saw nobody. Therefore he called himself Nᴇmōkyustâlis (= Having Come From the Earth as the Only One).[5] He had a son called Gyī′ī (= Chief).[6] They kept a fire going on the beach and were sitting beside it. Then one day K·'ā′nigyilak·[7] passed that way in his canoe and landed at Qulkʜ. He sat down by them at the fire in such a way that Nᴇmōkyustâlis and Gyī′ī were sitting on one side and he on the opposite. He wanted to test his strength with them, so he put some fish, which he had with him, by the fire and roasted it. Gyī′ī wished to eat some of this fish, so his father held his hand underneath it and caught the fat dripping down, which he gave to his son. K·'ā′nigyilak· took the fish, broke it and gave it to them to eat. He thought that they would die because it was sī′′siutl (the double-headed serpent),[8] but it didn't harm them. But Nᴇmōkyustâlis himself had sī′′siutl, which he roasted and gave to K·'ā′nigyilak· to eat. The latter was very surprised at this. Then K·'ā′nigyilak· tried to transform the two into ducks. He succeeded, but after a short while both became human again. They sat down by the fire again and K·'ā′nigyilak· now transformed them into two large mountains. These, too, soon regained their human shape. Then he transformed them into a pair of kingfishers. These, too, soon became human again. Nᴇmōkyustâlis also transformed K·'ā′nigyilak· three times, but was not able to prevent him from assuming his real shape again each time. When K·'ā′nigyilak· thus saw that he was unable to defeat them, he made friends with them and journeyed on.

Nᴇmōkyustâlis now assumed the name Guanā′lalis.[9] He reflected what to do if K·'ā′nigyilak· should return, and he decided not to take on human shape again, should he transform him again. At first he thought that he'd like to become a stone. But then it occurred to him that stones cracked. He thought that he'd like to become a tree, but then it occurred to him that trees fall and rot away. Then he thought that he'd like to become a river. K·'ā′nigyilak· was far away, but he heard all the thoughts of Guanā′lalis. He came back and, saying nothing, took the latter by the forehead, pushed him to the ground and then said, "Become a river as you have wished, and

---

5.   The name nəmúkʷustuʔlis (Boas' "Nemōkyustâlis") does translate as 'having come from the earth as the only one,' as Boas indicates here (AD; DSS).

6.   A better translation for the term gíɣa (Boas' "Gyī′ī") is 'a respected, high-born person' (AD; DSS).

7.   What Boas transcribes here as "K·'ā′nigyilak·" is q̓ániqiʔlakʷ 'the Transformer' (who is also known as hiɫatusəla) (AD; DSS); see Boas (1935:133–145) for a discussion of the Transformer's role in the mythological history of the Kwakwaka'wakw.

8.   AD and DSS confirm Boas' identification of the sísiyuƛ ("sī′′siutl") as 'double-headed serpent.'

9.   What Boas renders here as "Guanā′lalis" is gʷáṅalalis which is derived from gʷáṅa, the original Kwakwala name for the Nimpkish River. The term gʷáṅa, itself, is derived from the word gʷa, translated by AD and DSS as 'direction in which water is flowing,' and elsewhere by Boas (1934:68–69) as 'downriver' (see also the footnote that follows).

be full of fish!" He became the Guā'nē River[10] and therefore there are always all kinds of fish in it. Then K·'ā'nigyilak· gathered up all the shellfish, threw them away and said, "There shall be no shellfish here. The inhabitants of the neighbouring islands shall collect them and barter them here." Then he journeyed on.

Gyī'ī[11] (according to a different version the grandson of Guanā'lalis) wanted to marry the daughter of Tsāwatā'lalis,[12] who was one of the ancestors of the TsāwatEēnoq.[13] Guanā'lalis warned him by telling him that the former killed all the suitors of his daughter. But Gyī'ī insisted on the adventure, so his father let him go, but advised him to visit his aunts first. Gyī'ī set out on his journey to Tsawa'tē.[14] He was alone in the canoe, in which he carried along many gulls' wings and feathers. He didn't have to paddle because his canoe went by itself. He arrived at Gu'mpaq[15] at the entrance to Tsawa'tē. His aunt lived here. He landed and went inside the house to her, and after she had welcomed him, she asked where he was going. When he told her then that he wanted to marry the daughter of Tsāwatā'lalis, she warned him that the latter killed all his daughter's suitors. She gave him three slabs of stone, two to be tied under his feet and one to be fastened to his buttocks before he went into the house of Tsāwatā'lalis. And she gave him shellfish and instructed him how to use the stones and the shellfish. Gyī'ī thanked her and continued on his journey. On his way he met a man who asked him where he was going. Gyī'ī answered that he was going to marry the daughter of Tsāwatā'lalis. So the old man warned him. Gyī'ī gave him shellfish as thanks. The man then placed the shellfish on the beach and said, "There shall always be shellfish here. They shall multiply and serve as food for people." Gyī'ī

---

10. The Nimpkish River is known as gʷáńa (Boas' "Guā'nē"), derived from gʷa 'downriver' (Boas 1934:68–69; AD; DSS).

11. In this context, gíya (Boas' "Gyī'ī") is used as a term of endearment for someone not present (DSS).

12. Boas (1935:48) gives this name (transcribed in the present story as "Tsāwatā'lalis") for the ancestor of the G·ēxsEm numaym of the Tenaktak tribe in the upper Knight Inlet area who came to earth from the sky with his wife and house. AD knows this name as dzáwatalalis.

13. Boas' "TsāwatEēnoq" is the Kwakwala term dzawadɛ'ʔnuxʷ (anglicized as "Tsawatainuk"), the name for the Kingcome Inlet people. Although Boas indicates here that "Tsawatā'lalis" (dzáwata-lalis) was the ancestor of the Tsawatainuk, elsewhere he identifies Tsawatā'lalis as the ancestor of the "G·ēxsEm" numaym of the Tenaktak tribe (Boas 1910:455) in the upper Knight Inlet area, which is consistent with the history as known to AD and DSS.

14. What Boas transcribes here as "Tsawa'tē" is dzáwadi 'having eulachons,' a place at the mouth of the Klinaklini River at the upper end of Knight Inlet (AD; DSS; Boas 1934:23, 59).

15. Elsewhere, Boas identifies "gû'mbEx" (the place he transcribes here as "Gu'mpaq") as a site at the eastern end of Harbledown Island (Boas 1934:69; map 11:56), thereby suggesting that in the present sentence of the *Sagen* he is using "Tsawa'tē" (dzáwadi, a place at the upper end of Knight Inlet) in a more general sense to indicate all of Knight Inlet.

journeyed on. In K·o'āqEm[16] he met another man who asked him where he was going. Gyī'ī answered that he was going to marry the daughter of Tsāwatā'lalis. So the man warned him. Gyī'ī gave him shellfish as thanks. The man then placed the shellfish on the beach and said, "There shall always be shellfish here. They shall multiply and be poisonous and no one shall be able to eat them." Gyī'ī journeyed on. In Lālemaqä'es[17] he threw a piece of whale meat out of his canoe and it was transformed into a stone. The stone can still be seen there today. When he arrived at Ō'palis[18] he landed, hid his canoe in the forest and continued on foot along the shore. Soon he saw smoke rise up, so he went towards it and met four blind women, the Ducks. They were cooking tlEqsE'm[19] roots with the aid of hot stones. When Gyī'ī approached, one of the women scented him and said, "Gyī'ī must be close; I can smell him." When the roots were done, one of the women took them from the cooking box, intending to distribute them among her companions, but Gyī'ī took them away from her. They scolded and accused one another of stealing the bundles of roots. While they were thus fighting among themselves, Gyī'ī stepped up closely and said, "Grandmothers, are you blind? I am Gyī'ī." One of them replied, "So you are here after all? I can scent you." He asked, "Would you like to have your sight back?" So they shouted, "Yes, Gyī'ī, make us see!" He spat on their eyes and they were able to see again. Then they asked, "Where are you going?" He said that he wanted to marry the daughter of Tsāwatā'lalis. So the women said, "She always comes here about this time." When Gyī'ī heard this, he sat down and tied an octopus in front of his face so that he looked like an old man. Then when the girl came and saw him, she called out, "Ah, here is a slave for our father! He can watch his canoe!" Her brother, who was accompanying her, called out, "Oh no! How do you know that he is a slave? Perhaps he has supernatural powers!" But she paid no attention to her brother's words and called the old man, "Come slave! Sit down beside me!" He obeyed and she had him wash her back. Then she told him to go with her to the spot where she always dug for tlEqsE'm roots. Her brother said, "Don't take him along! Father is sure not to like it. You never get a husband because you talk to every

---

16. Boas (1934:75, map 16:44) elsewhere gives the translation 'hemlock on surface' for this place name, q̇ʷáqəm (given here in the *Sagen* as "K·o'āqEm"), situated south of Sim River near the head of Knight Inlet (AD; DSS).

17. Although Boas (1934:80) gives this as a place in Knight's Inlet, he does not note its location on his place names map. The name lálimaq?is (Boas' "Lālemaqä'es") is derived from lúʔlinuxʷ 'ghost' and appears to mean 'ghost on the beach' (AD).

18. Boas (1934:45, map 16:27) provides the transcription "ōbaᶜlis" for the place name ʔúbalis (given as "Ō'palis" in the present story), and identifies the site's location as a beach at the head end of Knight Inlet. The name translates as 'beach right at the end' (DSS).

19. What Boas renders here as "tlEqsE'm" here is λəxsə'm, the plant known as cinquefoil (*Potentilla pacifica*) (Turner and Bell 1973:189; AD).

stranger." She ignored the words of her brother and took the old man along. He asked her on their way, "What does your father say? Who are you supposed to marry?" She replied, "The man is called Gyĭ′ĭ. We don't know him; he lives far from here." So Gyĭ′ĭ took off the octopus mask and showed himself in his true form. The girl fainted because his face shone so brightly. When she came to again, he gave her some pitch to chew. Then he let her go on ahead and promised to follow her soon. When he saw that she had entered the house, he too went to the village. Gyĭ′ĭ knew that the door of the house of Tsāwatā′lalis killed any stranger who tried to enter, so he went towards as if he intended to enter but, when he was just in front of it, he sprang back and ran into the house when the door opened again. When Tsāwatā′lalis saw the stranger, he asked him what he wanted. Gyĭ′ĭ said, "I want to marry your daughter." So the old man invited him to sit down beside him. But there were pointed stones on the bottom and the back of the seat, and they killed anyone sitting down. Gyĭ′ĭ tied the flat stones, which he had obtained from his aunt, under his feet and on his behind and back, and with them crushed the pointed stones so that they didn't harm him. In front of the seat there was a big fire. Tsāwatā′lalis put on more wood in order to roast Gyĭ′ĭ. So the latter threw the shellfish which he had obtained from his aunt onto the fire one after the other, and they quenched it. Tsāwatā′lalis was amazed and said, "Now we know that you have supernatural powers." He served him food, bringing meat from the cache, roasting it and giving it to Gyĭ′ĭ in a bowl. It looked like salmon, but was sĭ′siutl.[20] Gyĭ′ĭ pretended to eat, yet in reality hid the meat underneath his cape. Tsāwatā′lalis waited for him to die; but since nothing happened, he served him food which looked like berries, though in reality was sĭ′siutl roe. Gyĭ′ĭ pretended to eat it, but hid it also beneath his cape. So Tsāwatā′lalis repeated, "You are more than human (an āu′mps,[21] a being imbued with supernatural powers) and shall have my daughter." Gyĭ′ĭ was with her for one night and she gave birth to a son in the morning. She had become pregnant already from the pitch which he had given to her. Tsāwatā′lalis said to Gyĭ′ĭ, "Let's go and get some wood for the child's cradle!" They journeyed to Mā′gyitānē,[22] cut down a cedar and began to split planks from it. While Tsāwatā′lalis was driving the wedges into the trunk, he dropped his hammer into the crack and asked Gyĭ′ĭ to get it out again. He crawled into the split trunk. He was hardly inside when the old man

---

20. Sísiyuⱡ 'double-headed serpent' (AD; DSS).

21. This is Ɂa?úms which means 'a person with extraordinary powers' (DSS).

22. While the term transcribed here as "Mā′gyitānē" was not recognized by AD or DSS, they did recognize an alternate transcription—"māgwɛt!anē (?)"—given elsewhere by Boas (1934:map 16:35, 52), as məq̓ʷət'áni 'burl on tree.' Boas' place-names map of upper Knight Inlet identifies two places by this name (one on the east side of the inlet, and the other on the left) (Boas 1934:map 16:35, 52); it is not clear from the *Sagen* which of these two places is referred to by this term.

knocked out the wedges so that the trunk snapped shut. He thought that he had killed Gyī'ī because he saw blood oozing from the crack, and called out, "You shall not marry my daughter. I have supernatural power, too, and am stronger than you." Gyī'ī had slipped from the tree in time and gone to the canoe unseen. The old man went down and to his amazement saw him laying in the bow of the canoe. Thus he said, "So you escaped from the tree unhurt. How glad I am! Just look at the tears which I have shed for you." Gyī'ī scarcely responded. He let his father-in-law paddle and, when they were far from shore, threw cedar needles into the water. They were transformed into herring which jumped into the old man's face, and whirlpools formed, which threatened to engulf the canoe. So Tsāwatā'lalis begged, "Oh, my son, stop it!" And Gyī'ī complied with his wish. After some time, Gyī'ī took some rotten wood and threw it into the water. It was transformed into four porpoises. Two were swimming on each side of the canoe. They began to jump over Tsāwatā'lalis and, at last, one of them jumped right against his chest and killed him. But when they reached shore, Gyī'ī called to his father-in-law, "Get up!" Tsāwatā'lalis rose, rubbed his eyes and said, "I've been asleep a long time." So he saw that Gyī'ī was stronger than he and left him in peace. Then Gyī'ī returned to QulkH.

After Guanā'lalis had been transformed into the river Guā'nē, Gyī'ī lived there. He had a son called Tsētlwalak·amē,[23] who was of gigantic height. His chest was four fathoms wide and when he went out in his canoe, he stood upright in its centre and propelled it like a sail. He had two wives: one called WāwanEmgyilaō'k·oa[24] was the daughter of the sun, the other, called Wilkuilatl,[25] was the daughter of Hawilkōlatl,[26] the ancestor of the TsāwatEēnoq.[27] He had a big house in QulkH and many slaves, whose names were Tlā'sōtlElāla,[28] Mā'muqsila,[29] Qē'uta,[30] Sikylā'litso,[31] Ō'tsuqumtsis.[32] One day all the men went out together in seven canoes to catch

23. This is číɫwalaqami which means 'the famous one' (DSS).

24. This name is recognized as wáwanəmgilaʔugʷa, meaning 'death-bringing woman' (DSS; AD).

25. This is wə'lkʷiʔlakʷ which translates as 'born to be a cedar tree' (DSS; AD).

26. Before číqimi went into the cedar tree, his name was hawə'lkʷiʔlakʷ (Boas' "Hawilkōlatl") which also means 'born to be a cedar tree' (DSS; AD).

27. DSS and AD associate these names with the Kwiksootainuk (see Section XVI), and not the Tsawatainuk.

28. DSS points out that this slave name, ƛ'ásutəlala (Boas' "Tlā'sōtlElāla") means 'going out to sea,' suggesting that this person had to go after seals and other food in the ocean for his master.

29. Recognized as the slave name mámuxʷsila which means 'person who cleans up human excrement and other dirt' (DSS; AD).

30. This slave name is possibly derived from xʷsíta referring to 'brushing the body during ritual bathing' (DSS).

31. The name səkalálicu (Boas' "Sikylā'litso") means 'harpooner' (DSS; AD).

32. What Boas transcribes as "Ō'tsuqumtsis" is údzaqəmdzis means 'person who is envied' (DSS; AD).

salmon. When the canoes were filled, they returned. Then the slaves said among themselves, "We'll give four canoe-loads to Wilkuilatl because she always gives us food, and three canoe-loads to the daughter of the sun." Tsētlwalak·amē heard what they were saying, but didn't comment. WāwanЕmgyilaõ′k·oa heard everything, although she was far away. When Tsētlwalak·amē came home, he saw that it was dark where WāwanЕmgyilaõ′k·oa was sitting, whereas it usually was always light around her. He sat by her and leaned his head on her bosom. Then he felt her tears falling on his face and saw that she was weeping blood, therefore he left her and went to his other wife. Thereupon WāwanЕmgyilaõ′k·oa cried even more and the house was filled with the water which flowed from her eyes. Then she transformed Tsētlwalak·amē and Wilkuilatl into ducks which were swimming about on the water. Soon they became human again and then Wilkuilatl in her turn transformed WāwanЕmgyilaõ′k·oa into a duck. After she had resumed her original shape again, she transformed her husband and Wilkuilatl into kingfishers, and then Wilkuilatl for her part did the same to her. WāwanЕmgyilaõ′k·oa then decided to return to her father. She was pregnant and said to her husband, "If you and your slaves had treated me as you should, I would have stayed here. I would have given you a child and it would have been immortal." Then she went to the beach and into the sea, over which she walked as if it were land. She walked towards the sunrise. When she came to Salmon River, she gave birth to a child. She threw it into the sea near Seymour Narrows, where it still causes the dangerous rapid Nōmaskyas[33] today.

Tsētlwalak·amē had a son by Wilkuilatl who was given the name Lalā′gyinis.[34] His son was K·′ōmнilā′gyilis.[35]

The posts of the house of Tsētlwalak·amē represented two Tsōnō′k·oa[36] which he had received from the father of Wilkuilatl. He also had a Tsōnō′k·oa mask. In the winter dance he used the wolf mask and sang, "You chiefs of other tribes are lying. You say that you dance like wolves, but I am the only one who has this dance."

---

33. "Nōmaskyas" is númaskas 'wonderful old man,' the Kwakwala name applied to the dangerous waters of Seymour Narrows (DSS; AD), situated north from Campbell River and about 35 miles (56 km) south of Salmon River, which is mentioned in the previous sentence of the *Sagen*. Elsewhere, Boas (1934:14, 64) noted that names for dangerous places like this one commonly contain the word "nō′mas" (númas) 'old man,' and he glossed this particular place name as 'real old man' (see also Section XIX, story 1, part 25 for another reference to Seymour Narrows).

34. Name not now recognized.

35. This is q̓ʷə′mxəlagəlis which means 'avalanche' (AD; DSS).

36. The dzúnuq̓ʷa is a mythological being, said to be large, stupid, sleepy, and with poor eye sight and hairy hands. The female members, who have pendulous breasts, occasionally visit the villages to steal fish and children, which they carry away in a large basket packed on their back. They are particularly fond of shellfish. In certain circumstances, these beings bestow wealth on select individuals (AD; DSS).

Tsētlwalak·amē heaped up a big mound of earth in QulkH[37] and on it built a house. Then he took Tlatlak·oaiyuk·oa,[38] the daughter of Tlāla′min (see page 145)[39] for his wife. His house was in Otsâ·lis[40] and was called Ku′mHelalitl.[41] It had doors in front and the back and Tlāla′min enslaved everyone who went through it. Tlāla′min's eldest son was called Ma′qolagyilis.[42] He built a house on an island in the middle of the river and called it Kyā′kyaqtla.[43] Once the river rose and destroyed the house and canoe of Ma′qolagyilis. This made him very sad. He went to his father and in the evening he sank suddenly into the ground beside the fire. His father dug after him, but didn't find him. Ma′qolagyilis reappeared from the ground in front of the house. The people caught him there, but he sank again. Thereupon the people wept. They were unable to find him again and thought that he was dead. Suddenly they heard something move and cry in the corner of the house. They made the fire blaze up high in order to see, and then discovered a human skull. It wept and cried, "Qiā′, qiā′, qiā′! I have lain in the water in the canoe and my flesh and my eyes have decayed. Where my eyes were once, there are deep caverns now."[44]

---

37. As previously noted, "QulkH" is Boas' rendering of x^{w}əlk^w 'criss-crossed logs,' the name applied to a village site situated at the mouth of the Nimpkish River (DSS; AD).

38. The woman's name λ′áλ′aq^{w}ay?ug^{w}a (Boas' "Tlatlak·oaiyuk·oa") translates as 'copper-woman' (DSS; AD).

39. Boas' reference is to the second story in this section in the original *Sagen* where he identifies this woman as an ancestor of a Nimpkish numaym.

40. The place known as "Ōstâ′lis" 'beach at small opening' is described elsewhere by Boas (1934:45, map 9:1) as a site located at the northern end of Anutz Lake, which is about a kilometre south from the southwestern end of Nimpkish Lake. Boas (1934:45) indicates that it is actually "Ōdzâ′ᶜlas," however, that form, "Otsâ·lis," is mentioned in the present story—this is udzú?las, meaning 'flat place' (AD), situated on the Nimpkish River near the outlet of Nimpkish Lake (Boas 1934: map 8:73). In another version of the story (Boas and Hunt 1902–1905:149), the place where this story occurred is confirmed as udzú?las.

41. Recognized by DSS as q̓^{w}ə′xəlalił which means 'avalanche inside a building.'

42. This name, máx^{w}əlagilas, translates as 'potlatching all over the land' (DSS).

43. AD and DSS recognize this place name (Boas' "Kyā′kyaqtla") as ƙáƙaxƛala. Elsewhere, Boas (1934:67; map 8:75) identifies the location of this place (whose name he glosses as 'crossed logs on top') on the east side of the Nimpkish River, downriver from the northern end of Nimpkish Lake.

44. The song sung by the skull is a lament for the loss of its former condition. A better translation for the song being sung in the Kwakwala language is: 'I was once the envy of the people, but now I sit here with caverns instead of eyes' (AD; DSS).

K·oā′k·oaqsānok·[45]

One of the descendants of K·ʼōmнilā′gyilis[46] was Hamā′lakyauaē.[47] He lived at the mouth of the Nimkisch River with his wife Ōmak·asemā′ē.[48] Once T′ē′sumgyilak·[49] came across from K·oaī′astEms,[50] attacked Hamā·ʼlakyauaē and abducted his women (see page 154).[51] The Nimkisch wanted to defend themselves but couldn't do anything against T′ē′sumgyilak· because he was made of stone. He killed many men and abducted their wives. Ōmak·asemā′ē and another of the abducted women were pregnant and T′ē′sumgyilak· ordered that their children should be killed if they turned out to be male. The other woman was confined first and gave birth to a son. To save him, she tied his penis back, and when T′ē′sumgyilak· came to see the child, he believed it to be a girl and let it live. He said, "Don't kill her, because when your daughter grows up she will collect shellfish for me." The two women then pondered how they might escape unseen from T′ē′sumgyilak·.

They managed to get away one night. They walked as far as their legs would carry them. Then they stopped by a small river and made a fire to warm themselves. They washed the boy in water so that he might become strong and called him Mōqsk·â′o (= With Tied Up Penis).[52] After they had walked for two days, Ōmak·asemā′ē gave birth to a son whom she called K·oā′k·oaqsānok·. She bathed him daily in cold water and therefore he quickly became strong and big. In the

---

45. AD and DSS recognize "K·oā′k·oaqsānok·" as q̓ʷáq̓ʷaqsanukʷ which means 'splitter'; this is also the translation provided for this term in Boas and Hunt (1902–1905:141) where it is explained that this character pulls apart the heads and bodies of his enemies (see also the footnote discussing this name in the second version of this story that follows in the present section.)

46. Recognized by DSS and AD as q̓ʷə′xəlagəlis which means 'avalanche outside on the land.'

47. Hámalakəwi (DSS; AD).

48. The term transcribed by Boas as "Ō′mak·asEmē" is ʔúʔmakasəmi 'noble woman' (AD; DSS).

49. Boas' "T′ē′sumgyilak·" is t′ísəmgiʔlakʷ which means 'born to be stone-bodied.' DSS and AD explain that when the boy was born he was called x̣ʼáx̣ʼaxʷas, and then later he was called t′ísəmgiʔlakʷ. Today, he is only known as t′ísəmgid 'stone body.'

50. What Boas transcribes here as "K·oaī′astEms" is gʷáyasdəms, the name of a village at Health Bay on Gilford Island. Prior to the mid-1800s, gʷáyasdəms was the main village of the Kwiksootainuk tribe whose traditional territory covered the area of Tribune Channel, most of Gilford Island, and some of the adjacent islands to the north and west (AD; DSS).

51. Boas' page reference is to the first paragraph of story 1 in Section XVI of the original *Sagen*; the character "t′ē′sumgyilak·" (t′ísəmgiʔlakʷ) also appears in that story.

52. The term given here as "Mōqsk·â′o" is múxʷsagu which means 'tied-up penis,' while a person in such a condition would be called múxʷsagaw̓akʷ 'person who has a tied-up penis' (DSS; AD).

meantime they had arrived at TetEk·'ā'niq[53] on Lake K·a'matsin[54] and there built
a house.

K·oā'k·oaqsānok· had grown up to be a strong boy, and one day was playing by
the river when he heard a terrible voice calling on the mountain, "O, o, hu, hu, hop."
So he ran to his mother and asked what the terrible voice was. She replied, "That is
the big Tsōnō'k·oa living in the lake up on the mountain. She kills anyone coming
near her." So K·oā'k·oaqsānok· said, "I want to go up the mountain and see her." His
mother begged him earnestly not to go and said, "Oh, don't go, otherwise my eyes
will never see you again." But K·oā'k·oaqsānok· was not to be detained because he
believed that he would be successful in this adventure. He went into the woods to
look for the Tsōnō'k·oa. So his mother's heart grew sad.

Having walked for some time he heard someone calling, "M! m!" and saw a man
standing by a tree trying to break it off. His name was Aq'a'lkos.[55] K·oā'k·oaqsānok·
crept up, grabbed him from behind and held him fast. So Aq'a'lkos called out, "Alas,
who has seized me from behind and has taken all my strength and power away from
me?" K·oā'k·oaqsānok· identified himself and told him that he had gone out to overcome Tsōnō'k·oa. So Aq'a'lkos asked, "Are you strong enough?" "I'm as strong as
you," he replied. "Then try to uproot that yew tree."[56] K·oā'k·oaqsānok· tried, but was
unsuccessful. So Aq'a'lkos said, "If you are unable to uproot the tree, you did not
get all my power." Then he sprinkled some water over him and made him try once
again. Since K·oā'k·oaqsānok· was still unable to uproot the tree, Aq'a'lkos breathed
into his mouth and then he uprooted the tree with his left hand. (According to a
different version, Aq'a'lkos dipped him into a river four times.)

Then he continued on his way upriver. When he had gone on a bit, he saw a sheet
of copper lying in the river. He took it and hid it in a hollow cedar because he
thought that if he were to take it along, and bring it back home, the people would
mock him. He went further upriver and arrived at a house, the roof of which was
supported by enormous posts. He didn't enter and take possession of it because he

---

53. Boas (1934:55, 56) gives the place name tətəq̓ánix̱ (transcribed here in the *Sagen* as
    "TetEk·'ā'niq") and says it is "far up Nimpkish Lake," but provides no map reference for its
    precise location. Moreover, no such name is indicated on Boas' (1934:map 8) mapping and
    detailed listing of Nimpkish Lake place names. AD recognizes this term as tətəq̓ánix̱ which he,
    too, describes as a place "somewhere on Nimpkish Lake." Later in this same story, Boas identifies
    this same place as "T'ɛ'tEk·'an."

54. What Boas transcribes as "K·a'matsin" is the name for Nimpkish Lake, which AD notes is
    possibly k̓ámacən, derived from k̓áma 'fingerlings.' This lake is known for its sockeye run (AD).

55. Name not now recognized.

56. Boas (1935:34) provides a footnote stating: "At this place it is said that he is to tear up a tree. This
    is undoubtedly a misunderstanding, since in all other cases the test is twisting of a tree. In S144
    [*Sagen*, p. 144] he is to break a yew tree."

thought that if he did, the people would mock him. He continued on his way and then met two men who were boasting to each other of their heroic deeds. One of them said, "I've killed thirty men in battle." K·oā′k·oaqsānok· was anxious to hear what they were talking about and crept up silently. He heard the other one reply, "I've killed only one man, but he was a great chief." Thereupon K·oā′k·oaqsānok· leapt out and called out, "What are you talking about?" So the two of them were transformed into stones, which he took along.

He continued on his way and at last arrived on the mountain summit. There he found a big, deep lake, on the shores of which he sat down. He threw the two stones into the lake and called, "Tsōnō′k·oa, come out of your house!" Thereupon the lake suddenly drained completely and then filled again. Then many sea lions appeared on the surface and vanished again. Then many sea otters appeared and vanished again. Then a canoe with three people in it appeared. He saw a bone arrow lying in the canoe and wished to have it, but he didn't know how to get it. Finally he cut his tongue and spat the running blood onto his hand. Then he went to a point of land, waded into the lake so that only his head protruded, and took the arrow from the canoe when it passed. Nobody noticed him. But if he hadn't cut his tongue, he surely would have died in the attempt. When the canoe had passed by, the steersman noticed him and saw that he held the arrow in his hand. So he said, "Take good care of the arrow. If you point it at a person, he will lose his mind, and if you shoot it at a crowd of people, they will all die at once." So K·oā′k·oaqsānok· thanked him and returned home. (According to a different version, he first saw a canoe in which a harpoon was laying; he didn't take it because he was afraid that people would scoff at him, and would believe that he was only a hunter and was unable to kill men. Then a second canoe arrived with two men in it. One of them held an arrow in his hand and they were pursuing a bear. K·oā′k·oaqsānok· asked, "How are you going to kill the bear? You don't have any bow." They told him to watch, and the man with the arrow pointed it towards the bear, which fell down dead at once. Then they presented him with the arrow and taught him its magical properties.) Then K·oā′k·oaqsānok· turned back towards home. When he walked downstream, he noticed that it was continuously darkest night. He then stayed overnight in the big house and broke up some of the roof-planks, with which he made a fire in order to light the house. He went on, but still it always stayed dark. Then he arrived at the hollow cedar in which he had hidden the copper. He took it out of the tree and at once it became day again. Therefore he left the copper where he had found it.

At last he arrived back home. One day he asked his mother whether she had any relatives and she now told him how T'ē′sumgyilak· had abducted her and had killed her relatives. So K·oā′k·oaqsānok· demanded to see his half-brothers and his father. The mother told him to make a small canoe, and when it was finished they began to go down the river. But the mother warned him of Ia'kHim[57] which lived in the river and killed anyone trying to get past them. They had been driven into the river during the time of the Great Flood and were left behind when the waters receded. She told him to let a big tree trunk drift down the river ahead of the canoe. K·oā'k·oaqsānok· followed her advice. When the tree trunk drifted past a Ia'kHim, it rose out of the water in the shape of a giant sea lion. So K·oā'k·oaqsānok· pointed his arrow at it, and it was transformed into stone at once. Then mother and son continued on safely. After some time they saw a dwarf sitting on the bank who covered his face with both hands and, shaking himself, shouted, "Tsi-tsi-tsi-tsi!" K·oā'k·oaqsānok· went up to him and asked him his name, but he was unable to speak.

They continued down the river and finally arrived in T'ε'tεk·'an, on the lake.[58] They saw smoke rising from a house. They landed and entered. Inside it there lived Tlē'semaē.[59] They invited him to come along, so he stepped into their canoe and the three of them journeyed on. After some time they arrived at another house, and from there took along AiHâk·alak·ε'ma.[60]

Then K·oā'k·oaqsānok· saw a man pursuing a bear on the opposite side of the lake. He paddled towards him in great haste in order to help him. But the man shouted, "Stop, I want to kill the bear." K·oā'k·oaqsānok· agreed and watched the hunt. But because the man was unable to catch up with the bear, he finally took out his arrow and pointed it towards the bear, which fell down at once and was transformed into stone. Then he paddled towards the shore and asked the stranger who he was. The latter answered, "I come from K·'ōkyes;[61] Hamā'lakyauaē[62] is my father." Consequently K·oā'k·oaqsānok· knew that he was his brother, Mōqsk·â'o. He made himself known to him and they all went on together.

---

57. What Boas transcribes here as "Ia'kHim" is yágim, the name of a sea-monster (DSS; AD). Curtis (1915:10:62) translates this as 'evil thing' and notes that it appears like a shark and waits for humans to capsize their canoes in stormy weather.

58. Boas' reference here to "T'ε'tεk·'an, on the lake" is the same place that he describes earlier in this same story as "Tεtεk·'ā'niq on Lake K·a'matsin." Both references are to Nimpkish Lake, and to a place that AD recognizes as tǝtǝq́ánix̣. As previously discussed, both Boas (1934:55, 56) and AD identify the location of this place as somewhere on Nimpkish Lake, although Boas' (1934:map 8) mapping and listing of Nimpkish Lake place names does not include tǝtǝq́ánix̣.

59. Name not now recognized.

60. The name that Boas transcribes here as "AiHâk·alak·ε'ma" is recognized by DSS as ʔíxalakami meaning 'head of something that is good.'

61. This name, q̓ʷǝgís, (Boas' "K·'ōkyes") which is anglicized as "Kokish" and means 'notched beach,' is applied to a small creek located in Beaver Cove, east from the mouth of the Nimpkish River (Boas and Hunt 1902–1905:137; Boas 1934:76, map 8:46; AD; DSS). See also the second version of this story that follows, where this place name is transcribed as "K·'ōkye" and tentatively identified as Beaver Cove.

62. This name is recognized as hámalakǝwi (AD; DSS).

Soon they arrived at Guā'mēla[63] on the K·'anis[64] River. There K·oā'k·oaqsānok· found his brother, T'ē'sumHstsāna,[65] whose right hand was made of stone. He smashed the canoe of K·oā'k·oaqsānok· with one strike and gave him a newer and bigger one. Then they all went downriver together and K·oā'k·oaqsānok· killed all the Ia'kHim with his arrow. The small islands of the Nā'nis[66] can still be seen in the river nowadays; they were the bears which were transformed into stones by K·oā'k·oaqsānok·.

At last they arrived in K·'ō'kyes and there found an old man busy repairing the door of one of the houses. It was Hamā'lakyauaē. But he didn't recognize his wife and sons when they went ashore and approached him. He asked Ōmak·asemā'ē, "Who are you and all those young men?" She replied, "Don't you recognize me, your wife, at all?" He recognized her and asked, "And did you marry that young man in the canoe?" "No, he is my son. Don't you remember that I was pregnant when Tlā'tlaqoas abducted me?"[67] Then the old man remembered everything again and his heart became glad.

The young people built themselves a house and a salmon weir. One day K·oā'k·oaqsānok· said to his father, "Tell me, where does our enemy T'ē'sumgyilak· live? I want to kill him." But Hamā'lakyauaē replied, "You won't be able to kill him. He is made of stone. Only his forehead, his nose and his throat are flesh." Once K·oā'k·oaqsānok· learned that T'ē'sumgyilak· was going to go to Mount Ts'i'lkyimpaē[68] in order to get goose-down for his mask, Qoēqoē,[69] which he wore in the winter dance. In order to

---

63. Boas (1934:69) lists this place name but provides no map reference.

64. This river is listed by Boas (1934:74) as a tributary of the Nimpkish, although he does not identify it on his maps.

65. What Boas transcribes here as "T'ē'sumHstsāna" is the name t'ísəmxċana meaning 'stone hand' (AD; DSS).

66. Boas (1934:64) translates this name as 'grizzly-bear water' and says it is a rock in the Nimpkish River, but does not provide a map reference. AD and DSS recognize Boas' "Nā'nis" as náʔnis, derived from nan, the Kwakwala term for 'grizzly bear.'

67. AD and DSS explain that ƛ'áƛ'axʷas (Boas' "Tlā'tlaqoas") was the earlier name of t'ísəmxċana 'stone hand' ("T'ē'sumHstsāna" in the previous paragraph) who was also known as t'ísəmgiʔlakʷ 'born to be stone-bodied.' This latter term, t'ísəmgiʔlakʷ (Boas' "T'ē'sumgyilak· ") is identified as the woman's abductor in the paragraph that follows. Today, he is only known as t'ísəmgid 'stone body' (DSS; AD).

68. In Boas and Hunt (1902–1905:151) the name of this mountain is given as "Feather-top Mountain." Boas (1934:61) states that although the mountain is said to be on Hē'łas, Triangle Island, it is probably mythological; there are no mountains on Triangle Island. The name is recognized as ċə'lkəmbaʔyi (Boas' "Ts'i'lkyimpaē" here in the *Sagen*) meaning 'feathers on the face' and identified as a mountain in the vicinity of the Nimpkish (AD; DSS).

69. Boas' "Qoē'qoē" is recognized as xʷíxʷi, the Kwakwala pronunciation of a Coast Salish term referring to a distinctive mask obtained from the Comox people (AD; DSS). Boas comments elsewhere that among the Kwakwaka'wakw, the xʷíxʷi dancer is distinguished by a painted mask with prominent eyes and tufts of feathers projecting from the top of the head-piece. The dancer carries

get there, he had to pass by Tlṓk·oē (Duvin Point),[70] so K·oā′k·oaqsānok· decided to ambush him there. He readied his canoe, and his brothers Mōqsk·â′o and T′ē′sumH-stsāna set out together with him, as well as Mamā′lakyus, Mā′maqsila, Qē′oten, Tlasō̄tletlelala, and the old man TlE′mkyēq.[71] They landed at Tlṓk·oē and awaited the return of T′ē′sumgyilak′. They could hear his companions singing already, and then they saw them, their hair covered with down. So K·oā′k·oaqsānok· pointed his arrow at them as they passed and lo, they all lost their minds and T′ē′sumgyilak′ fell over so that his canoe capsized when he fell. Then T′ē′sumHstsāna went out to the canoe and killed them all with his hand of stone. They cut off the heads and put them into their canoe, which was filled to the gunwale. Only T′ē′sumgyilak′ was still alive because he had sunk and they were unable to find his body. Therefore they left the old man TlE′mkyēq behind and pretended to paddle away. But they had told him to watch and to call them as soon as he spied T′ē′sumgyilak′ again. After a short time he shouted, "Come, help me! I've caught him!" They turned about at once but only saw the old man hacking with his stone axe at something which they couldn't recognize. T′ē′sumgyilak′ had crept out of the water at a crack in the rock. The old man had discovered him here and now hacked at his only vulnerable spot, his neck, until he had struck off his head. T′ē′sumgyilak′ resisted and with the movements of his body caused mighty waves. When the others arrived, the old man lifted the head up high and threw it into the canoe with the other heads. Then they also picked up the stone body and all the feathers which the latter had collected on Ts'i′lkyimpaē. When they arrived at QulkH,[72] they unloaded their canoe and went to the Mā′tsē[73] River to cut young trees. With these they staked out a square area and in it impaled the head of T′ē′sumgyilak′ on the highest pole. They heaped up the other heads around it and scattered the feathers in the river.

---

a rattle of strung shells, and therefore the dance is associated with earthquakes, and the dancer is believed to "shake the ground and to be a certain means of bringing back the hā′matsa who is being initiated" (Boas 1897:497).

70. This place name, given also as "L!ṓ′goᵋyo" 'bare in the middle' (Boas 1934:83, map 6:79), applies to Duval Point on the east side of Duval Island, situated at the entrance to Port Hardy. Boas errs in the *Sagen* in giving the English name of this place as "Duvan," but later corrects it in his list of geographical names (Boas 1934:84). This place name is recognized as ⋋úguʔyu 'bare in between' (AD; DSS).

71. These five names ("Mamā′lakyus, Mā′maqsila, Qē′oten, Tlasō̄tletlelala, and the old man TlE′mkyēq") are not now recognized.

72. As previously noted, "QulkH" is Boas' rendering of xʷəlkʷ 'criss-crossed logs,' the name applied to a village site situated at the mouth of the Nimpkish River (DSS; AD).

73. This name is given in Boas (1934:52) as "mā′ts!a" 'rock lengthwise current at hind end; or stripped rock' where it is indicated that it is just upstream from the mouth of the Nimpkish River (map 8:54, 8a:9). It was likely a creek that entered the Nimpkish River at this location. DSS and AD recognize this place name as máʔċa and confirm the translation 'stripped-off rock.'

The sister of K·oā'k·oaqsānok·, K·'ē'ʜoak·anak,[74] had married Nᴇ'lpē[75] from the tribe of the K·uē'qsōt'enoq. Her daughter was playing by the river and noticed feathers drifting down. So she called her mother and both of them went to see where the feathers were coming from. They came to the spot where their relatives' heads were. They screamed in terror and fled, pushing their canoe into the water and paddling back to their tribe. They rested for a bit in Paqulkʜ[76] and K·'ē'ʜoak·anak killed seals and salmon, with which she filled the canoe. Then they washed themselves and painted their faces red in order to hide the traces of their tears. Then they paddled on and finally arrived at K·oai'astᴇms.[77] But the people noticed, despite the paint, that they had been crying and asked, "Why have you been crying?" They replied, "We weren't crying, we were only laughing with pleasure to see you again." Then K·'ē'ʜoak·anak unloaded her canoe, had the seals carried into the house and presented one to each person. Then they all sat there and ate. Mother and daughter were sitting together and suddenly the daughter said, "Many feathers came floating down the river near Guā'nē." [78] Her mother reprimanded her for it because she didn't want her father to hear. She nudged the girl and said, "Don't torment my father." But he only sat and listened to the speeches of his friends. Soon the girl repeated, "Many feathers came floating down the river near Guā'nē." Again her mother told her to be quiet. But after she repeated it a third and fourth time, the old man's attention was attracted and he asked what the little one was saying. So K·'ē'ʜoak·anak said, "Oh, I forgot to tell you that wh K·oā'k·oaqsānok· has killed T'ē'sumgyilak·." The Kuē'qsōtēnoq refused to believe it until several slaves, who had been present and had escaped, verified the news. Thereupon many whose fathers and brothers had gone with T'ē'sumgyilak· died of fright.

But they still did not quite believe that K·oā'k·oaqsānok· had really killed him and paddled across the sea to satisfy themselves. K·oā'k·oaqsānok· saw them approaching and told his brothers to shoot at them with arrows of cedar wood. The arrows broke on their bodies. So the Kuē'qsōtēnoq laughed and said, "He couldn't

74. This name is recognized as q̓íax̣aq̓ənakʷ (DSS).

75. DSS points out that the man named nə'lbiʔ (Boas' "Nᴇ'lpē") , also known as ní?nəlbiʔ, was the ancestor of a numaym of the qʷíqʷsut'inux̣ʷ (Kwiksootainuk).

76. Elsewhere this place is given as "Dāg·ulkᵘ" (Boas and Hunt 1902–1905:155; Boas 1934:54, map 8:37). The place name dəgʷə'lkʷ (Boas' "Paqulkʜ" here in the *Sagen*) applies to the Green Islets situated off the mouth of the Nimpkish River and is derived from the Kwakwala term dúkʷała meaning 'strung out' (AD; DSS).

77. As previously noted earlier in this story, this is gʷáyasdəms, the name of a village at Health Bay on the west side of Gilford Island; prior to the mid-1800s, gʷáyasdəms was the main village of the Kwiksootainuk tribe.

78. The Nimpkish River, as previously mentioned, is known as gʷáṅa (Boas' "Guā'nē") which is derived from gʷa 'downriver' (Boas 1934:68–69; AD; DSS).

have killed T'ē'sumgyilak·." They paddled onward in order to kill K·oā'k·oaqsānok·. But when they were close to the shore, he merely pointed his arrow at them and they all lost their minds, and Tē'sumHstsāna killed them with his hand of stone. Then they tied the slain and the wounded onto planks and arranged these in a row which reached from QulkH to Ōtsâ'lis,[79] they had killed and captured that many. They then told a slave to pile up all the planks in one heap. But the slave whispered to the strongest of all the captives, "Try to break the rope with which you are tied." The latter began to move and broke the plan on which he lay. Then he slipped off the ropes and began to free his friends. But before he was able to set them all free, K·oā'k·oaqsānok· heard what was happening. He rushed up with his brothers and they killed all who hadn't fled. Then they cut up the bodies and threw the intestines into the water near Tsaimē'qotl.

Once one of the Kuē'qsōtēnoq wanted to marry a woman from the Lēkwiltok·[80] tribe and they brought a huge box full of coppers as a present for the woman's parents. So the Lēkwiltok· promised the whole box to anyone able to lift it. When K·oā'k·oaqsānok· heard this, he came down to the sea, lifted the box on his shoulders and carried it away. On his way he bumped into the corner of a house and stumbled. His youngest brother rushed up at once and supported him, otherwise he would have fallen. The brothers then went up the river and there built themselves a big house from poles. Then they invited all the neighbouring tribes to a great feast. K·oā'k·oaqsānok· stood on the beach and watched the strangers arrive. When he now saw a large, strong canoe which pleased him, he seized it and threw it onto his roof. Then he made everyone come into his house and entertained them. He started dancing while they sang for him and beat time. Suddenly he pulled out his arrow which he had kept hidden and pointed it all around at the guests. Thereupon they lost their minds and crowded out the door. But T'ē'sumHstsāna, who had stationed himself beside the door, now got up and killed them all. Only one old man and his son escaped, through a ruse. The old man shouted to T'ē'sumHstsāna, "I myself want to kill my son; don't kill him." As the young man was about to slip through the door, he grabbed him by his hair and pulled him back into a dark corner of the house. From there they both escaped. Then K·oā'k·oaqsānok· cut off the heads of the slain and fixed them to the front of his house.

79. That is, from the mouth of the Nimpkish River upstream to near the bridge situated below Nimpkish Lake.
80. Lekwiltok; see Section XIV.

K·oā′k·oaqsānok· (Second version)

Hamā′lakyauaē was one of the descendants of K·′ōmHilā′gyilis. He had a daughter called D'ātok·iū′nēk·a[81] who married T'ē′sumgyilak·, the chief of the Kuē′qsōt'ēnoq.[82] She visited her father often and brought along her son. Each time, Hamā′lakyauaē gave her many salmon, which she then brought home with her. The young men of the Nimkisch jeered at the boy because he was half Kuē′qsōt'ēnoq, and said to D'ātok·iū′nēk·a: "Just look at your son; green stuff[83] hangs from his mouth." They meant that he was always eating shellfish, while the Nimkisch had so much fish that they scorned shellfish, especially since there are none at the mouth of the Nimkisch River. But D'ātok·iū′nēk·a became angry and complained to her husband that the young men were jeering at her son. Thereupon T'ē′sumgyilak· called together all his people, the Kuē′qsōt'ēnoq, the Ts'ā′watEēnoq, the Qaquā′mis, the Lēkwiltok· and the Guauaē′noq.[84] They set off for QulkH and fought the Nimkisch. They defeated them and destroyed their houses. Hamā′lakyauaē escaped to Tawī′sē.[85] He had two wives, Ō′mak·asEmē and Mā′qulaok·.[86] The latter, who belonged to the Nē′nelky'ēnoq[87] tribe, fled upriver to her relatives. But Ō′mak·asEmē was enslaved by Wē′k·aē (see p. 133),[88] a chief of the Lē′kwiltok·. Both women were pregnant. Before Ō′mak·asEmē was confined, Wē′k·aē had ordered that her child should be killed if it turned out to be a son. When the child was born and Ō′mak·asEmē found that it was a boy, she tied back his penis with inner cedar bark. Consequently Wē′k·aē thought that the child was a girl and let it

---

81. What Boas renders as "D'ātok·iū′nēk·a" is a name recognized as dáduqʷiyaniga, meaning 'chosen woman' (AD; DSS).

82. "Kuē′qsōt'ēnoq" is Boas' transcription of the tribal name qʷíqʷsut'inuxʷ (DSS; AD), anglicized as "Kwiksootainuk."

83. The reference here is to the green-coloured intestines of the clam.

84. The tribal names that Boas transcribes here as "the Kuē′qsōt'ēnoq, the Ts'ā′watEēnoq, the Qaquā′mis, the Lēkwiltok· and the Guauaē′noq" are, respectively, qʷíqʷsut'inuxʷ (Kwiksootainuk), dzáwadɛʔinuxʷ (Tsawatainuk), haxʷáʔmis (Hahuamis), lígʷiɫdaʔxʷ (Lekwiltok), and gʷáwaʔɛnuxʷ (Gwawaenuk) (AD; DSS).

85. "Tawī′sē" is likely the place on the lower Nimpkish River identified elsewhere by Boas (1934: map 8:60) as "tEᶜwē′sēᶜ," which he glosses as 'attacking on beach (poling against strong tide?)' (Boas 1935:55). AD and DSS did not recognize this term.

86. The name Boas renders here as "Mā′qulaok·" appears to be the name máxʷəluʔugʷa 'potlatch woman' (DSS; AD).

87. What Boas writes as "Nē′nelky'ēnoq" is, as previously noted, the term ńíʔnəlkinuxʷ (anglicized as "Ninelkaynuk"), the name of one of the subgroups or tribes comprising the Nimpkish. The Ninelkaynuk occupied the upper portions of the Nimpkish River drainage system.

88. The *Sagen* page number refers to Section XIV, story 5, referring to Wɛ′qɛ (transcribed here as "Wē′k·aē") the ancestral founder of the wíwɛqɛ (anglicized as "Weewiakay") and wíwɛq̓əm (anglicized as "Weewiakum") subgroups or tribes of the Lekwiltok.

live. Ō′mak·asᴇmē lived by herself in a small hut back from the trail and nobody
paid any attention to her. So she decided to use the opportunity and flee. She arrived,
unnoticed, safely at K·′ōkye (Beaver Cove?)[89] and there built a house of branches
for herself. She bathed her son daily in cold water and therefore he grew up quickly.
When he was bigger, he made a fire-drill for his mother and lit a fire. Then he asked
her to make him arrows. When he had got them, he shot raccoons and minks and his
mother made capes from their skins. She now called him Mōqsk·â′o. Later he began
to shoot bears and elk and he started to catch salmon in the river. Ō′mak·asᴇmē was
always collecting fern roots, and one day she found a sī′siūtl scale. She put it on the
tips of her son's arrows and from then on he was able to kill any kind of game,
however big it might be.

Mā′qulaok·, who had fled to her relatives, also gave birth to a son. She lived high
up near the source of the river in TlaE′ns.[90] She bathed him in the river, which is so
cold here that the salmon die when they come up. Consequently he became stronger
than anyone among his people. He went to a spot where yew trees were growing and
tried to break them off. At his first attempt, he wasn't able to break them off straight
at the root. So he continued bathing in the river in order to get stronger, and at last
broke off the yew trees right at their roots. Then he went out to fight. In fighting, he
seized his enemies by the head and split them in two. Therefore he was called
K·oā′k·oaqsānok·, the Splitter.[91]

His mother and his sisters wept and lamented every morning. One day he
enquired about the reason and learned how they came to be there. So he became sad.
He wished to take revenge but didn't know how he would be able to do it. He went
to bed and stayed there for four days without food or drink. Then he got up, went to
a small lake with a flat shoreline and there sat down. After a short time he saw the
water rise. It reached his feet. But he remained sitting calmly, awaiting what was to
happen. Then a butterfly[92] flew out of the water. On its head it wore a ring of inner

89. "K·′ōkye" is the same place name transcribed by Boas as "K·′ōkyes" in the preceding version of
this same story in the present section. As has been noted, this place name is q̓ʷəgís, anglicized as
"kokish" and meaning 'notched beach,' applied to a small creek in Beaver Cove, just east from
the Nimpkish River mouth (AD; DSS; Boas and Hunt 1902–1905:137; Boas 1934:76, map 8:46).

90. Judging from the context of the story, the place that Boas transcribes as "TlaE′ns" is likely
situated on the uppermost Nimpkish River. AD recognizes this term as ɫəns, meaning 'difficult
terrain,' which he identifies as a place situated just upriver from the present-day Nimpkish River
bridge.

91. "Derivation possibly incorrect" [Boas' original footnote]. In a later published version of this story
(Boas and Hunt 1902–1905:141), this name which Boas renders here as "K·oā′k·oaqsānok·" is
transcribed as "K!wā′qaxsāno" and also translated as 'Splitter.' DSS and AD recognize this name
as q̓ʷáq̓ʷaqsanukʷ, derived from q̓ʷaxsʔə′nd 'to split' (DSS; AD). See also the discussion of this
name in the initial footnote to the preceding version of this story in the present section.

92. This is actually a moth, not a butterfly, in the story as it is known to DSS.

cedar bark dyed red. It was the Lâ'lēnoq (the ghost, the spirit of the departed).[93] It asked, "Would you like to have the Lōlō'tlalatl (= the dance of the Lâ'lēnoq)?"[94] and offered him its head-ornament. K·oā'k·oaqsānok· declined the offer. Thereupon the butterfly disappeared again into the water. In a short while the water began to rise again. Then a canoe rose to the surface; in it there was a two-pronged spear. The canoe said, "If you want to become a hunter, I will give the spear to you and you will be able to shoot anything." K·oā'k·oaqsānok· also declined this offer and the canoe submerged once more. The water rose again and a potlatch pole lifted up with many capes tied to it. It promised him that he would become the richest man, but he didn't accept this offer, either, and the pole submerged again. The water rose yet again and a copper emerged. K·oā'k·oaqsānok· took it and hid it, placing it with the decorated side downwards. The water rose yet again and four arrows appeared, which were Halaiu (death bringer).[95] They said, "Take us! Then you will be able to kill anyone, even people endowed with supernatural powers." He took them and hid them, too. When K·oā'k·oaqsānok· put the copper down, it had suddenly become dark. The earth was dark for ten days and no one knew the reason for this occurrence. When K·oā'k·oaqsānok· returned to TlaE'ns, the inhabitants of the village, which consisted of six houses, ran to him to ask him whether he knew why it was dark. K·oā'k·oaqsānok· had gone to bed, so his mother went and asked him. He replied, "I have found something; maybe that is the cause. Have your brothers split wood and make torches, then we will go there and see if that is the cause." The woman's brothers made ten big torches and then they all went to the pond. K·oā'k·oaqsānok· had them follow at some distance. Then he took the copper and tried to turn it over again, but it was so heavy that it slipped away four times. He succeeded only on the fifth attempt to turn it over, so that its painted (with a face) side faced up. Thereupon it became day again. They returned home again, having used up five torches on their way.

K·oā'k·oaqsānok· now asked his mother whether the ocean was nearby. She pointed down the river, but said that the way was far and dangerous because there were many Tsōnō'k·oa on the mountains and Ia'kнim in the river. But K·oā'k·oaqsānok· wasn't to be deterred and went downriver. He made a tree trunk drift ahead of his canoe and every time a monster rushed upon it, thinking that it was the canoe, he killed it with his Halaiu and transformed it into stone.

---

93. What Boas transcribes here as "Lâ'lēnoq" is lúʔlinux̌ʷ 'ghost' (DSS; AD).

94. DSS confirms that Boas' "Lōlō'tlalatl" is ləlútalał, the 'ghost dance' (DSS).

95. Haláyu 'death-bringer' (DSS).

Thus he arrived safely at the lake. He saw smoke rising in Tl'ē'sEmē,[96] which lay just opposite him. There he met an old man, whom he asked, "What is your name and to which tribe do you belong?" Thereupon the old man sat down, lifted up his hands and feet, and called out, "Tsī-tsī-tsī-tsī!" K·oā'k·oaqsānok· continued on his way. He arrived at Gyi'lbāla[97] and there met another old man who answered his question in the same fashion. He continued on his way and arrived at the River Wa'tsō[98] which flowed into the lake. While paddling along the shore he saw a big bear jump into the water. When he paddled towards it to kill it, a man called to him from the shore, "Leave it alone! It belongs to me. I want to kill it." Then he saw how the man pointed his arrow at the bear and how it fell down and was transformed into stone. This amazed K·oā'k·oaqsānok· because he had believed that he alone owned the Halaiu. He asked him who he was and to which tribe he belonged. So the man told him that his name was Mōqsk·â'o, that his father's name was Hamā'lakyauaē and that his mother was living in K·'ōkye. Thus K·oā'k·oaqsānok· recognized his brother. He told him that his own mother had fled to TlaE'ns. He took him into his canoe and continued on his way downriver. He had already taken two men into his canoe in Tl'ē'sEmē, so that they were now four. They arrived at the lower end of the lake and saw smoke rising from a house in K·'aui's.[99] They landed and went into the house, and inside it they found an old man, called Guā'milāla.[100] He asked them their names and their origin, and served them roasted salmon. He owned a beautiful canoe. Its bow and stern each had a wolf carved on it. The brothers said between themselves, "Let's ask whether he will lend his canoe to us." They asked the old man and he lent them his canoe and accompanied them. As before, they made a tree trunk float ahead of the canoe, and when any Ia'kHim rushed upon it, K·oā'k·oaqsānok· and Mōqsk·â'o pointed their arrows at them and transformed them

96. Boas (1934:28, map 8:107) elsewhere identifies "L!ä'sEmē" (the same place name transcribed here in the *Sagen* as "Tl'ē'sEmē") as a site on the southeast shore of Nimpkish Lake. This place name was not recognized by AD or DSS.

97. DSS recognizes "Gyi'lbāla" as gə'lbala, likely the same place name that Boas (1934:map 8:96) transcribes elsewhere as "g·î'ltbala," translates as 'long stretching point,' and situates on the west side of Nimpkish Lake, adjacent to the Kilpala River ("Kilpala" is an anglicization of gə'lbala). Presumably Boas' (1934:65) identification of "g·î'lbala" (without the "t" in "g·î'ltbala" that he gives elsewhere in his geographical names publication) as a place "on Nimkish River" is an error, because his accompanying map (Boas 1934:map 8) identifies no place by this name anywhere on the Nimpkish River.

98. This place name, "Wa'tsō," is given elsewhere by Boas (1934:42, map 8:100) as "wadzō" 'river on flat place' and identified as a small stream flowing into the east shore of Nimpkish Lake. DSS recognizes this place name as waʔdzú.

99. Recognized as q̓əwís by AD and DSS, referring to a site near the outlet of Nimpkish Lake identified by Boas (1934:75, map 8:84) as "q!äwēs" ("K·'aui's" in the *Sagen*) 'pond on beach.'

100. This name is not now recognized.

into stone. Thus they arrived safely at Tawī'sē[101] where Hamā'lakyauaē was living. They found him busy cutting stakes for his salmon weir. He had an ear pendant of abalone shells and wore feathers on his head. He didn't seem to notice them ... (Continuation as in the first version.)

2. Tlā'lamin
(Ancestor legend of the Tlā'tlElāmin, one of the numaym of the Nimkisch)[102]

Above the sun and the sky there lived a man called Tlā'lamin. He descended to the earth with his house and settled in NEk·ala',[103] above Lake Nimkisch. The clouds were the roof of his house and above them was the sun. The sun's rays were his cape and he wore a big hat. Therefore he was called T'ā'tEntsēt.[104] After some time he moved to Gy'ā'gyaqtlāla.[105] His house floated down the river and he anchored it there. Then he moved to Ōtsâ'lis.[106] His house stood on stilts in the water and his canoe lay under the house when not in use. The house was called Ku'mkumHalitl.[107] He had four slaves: Wā'watitla[108] Tlē'k·oatē,[109] Nā'lanuk· (Owner of Daylight),[110] and PEqpEwā'igyila,[111] who robbed all passing travellers of their canoes. Later, when the Great Flood came and killed all the people, Tlā'lamin returned to the sky and then

---

101. As previously noted, this village was located on the lower Nimpkish River.

102. Boas here uses the term *Ahnensage* 'ancestor legend' to describe this story. Elsewhere, Boas (1966:40) also lists this as one of the numaym of the Nimpkish. DSS notes that the ƛáƛ'aləmən (Boas' "Tlā'tlElāmin" in the *Sagen*) received their name from the man named ƛ'álamən ("Tlā'lamin"), and that the ƛáƛ'aləmən left Gold River, on the west side of Vancouver Island, and moved east to join the Nimpkish.

103. The place name transcribed here by Boas as "NEk·ala'" is recognized by DSS as nəkalá, possibly derived from the term nəká 'pit cooking.' Although Boas states here that nəkalá is "above Lake Nimkisch," it not among the place names that Boas (1934:map 12) gives elsewhere for sites on the uppermost Nimpkish River; moreover, Boas' (1934:63) map reference (i.e. map 17:20) for nəkalá ("NE'qǎla'" 'straight rock') is erroneous.

104. The name that Boas gives as "T'ā'tEntsēt" is recognized as t'át'ənsid (DSS).

105. This place name is recognized as gágaxƛala (DSS; AD).

106. Boas' "Ōtsâ'lis" is recognized by AD as udzú?las, situated slightly downstream from the outlet of Nimpkish Lake.

107. This name is recognized as q̓ʷə́mq̓ʷəmxəliɫ 'avalanche inside the house' (DSS).

108. This slave's name, given by Boas as "Wā'watitla," is recognized as wáwadiƛ'a meaning 'pulling canoes inside the house' (AD; DSS).

109. AD and DSS recognize this slave's name is ƛíqʷuwadi 'having many names.'

110. Recognized as nálanukʷ, which does mean 'owner of daylight' (AD; DSS).

111. This is recognized as the slave name pəqpəwáqila 'making kelp floats' and is derived from the term pəẃáq 'kelp float' (AD; DSS).

came back in the shape of the eagle, K·ō'los.[112] Therefore his family owns the K·ō'los crest and during potlatches uses the sun mask. He settled in Ōtsâ'lis again, assumed human shape and had a son called K·'ā'kyῑwē.[113] He moved down to QulkH at the mouth of the river. When K·'ā'kyῑwē grew up, his father sent him out to obtain supernatural powers (to obtain tlōkoa'la).[114] After he had fasted and bathed, he met the spirit of the sea, K·ōmō'k·oa,[115] who took him along down to the bottom of the sea, entertained him, and gave his house to him. Seagulls are sitting on its roof, a huge Tsōnō'k·oa stands in front of the house and carved men carry the roof-beams, which represent sea-lions. Inside the house, beside the door, stand two grizzly bears. When Tlā'lamin then wanted to dance, he had no one to sing for his dance. So he first invited his friend, Himgyῑ'ū,[116] then caught many seagulls in traps and transformed them into people. The family of the Tlā'tlElāmin descends from them. K·'ā'kyῑwē had a daughter called T'ā'kuisilaōk·oa.[117]

Tlā'lamin had a friend who belonged to the Salmon People. They visited each other from time to time. But Tlā'lamin was invisible to all the salmon, except his friend. Once the salmon asked his friend to sing a song of the humans. So Tlā'lamin accompanied him. The salmon heard him, but were unable to see him.

Ts'ētlwā'lak·amē[118] married Tlatlak·oai'ōk·oa,[119] one of the daughters of Tlā'lamin. Tlā'lamin had a son called Mā'qolagyilis,[120] who built a house on an island in the middle of the river and named it Kyā'kyaqtla.[121] Once the river rose and destroyed the house. So Mā'qolagyilis wept because he had lost his house and his canoe. He went to his father and at night suddenly sank into the ground beside the fire. His father dug after him, but was unable to find him. Mā'qolagyilis reappeared

---

112. Recognized as qʷúlus. DSS notes this refers to the 'small, gentle Thunderbird,' not the 'Eagle,' as Boas indicates here.

113. Possibly this name is k̓áqiwi 'a frontlet mask' (AD).

114. Boas' "tlōkoa'la" is λúqʷala which AD and DSS translate as 'gift from the supernatural.'

115. "K·ōmō'k·oa" is recognized by DSS and AD as q̓ʷúmugʷi, the sea-being whose name is derived from the Kwakwala term q̓ʷúmała 'wealth.'

116. Boas (1935:43) suggests that the name "X·ῑ'x·îmg·iu" (derived from the term he transcribes here as "Himgyῑ'ū") refers to a Nimpkish numaym. DSS and AD recognize this term as xíxəmgiyu.

117. This woman's name is recognized as λ̓áqʷusila?ugʷa (AD; DSS).

118. This is číłwalaqami 'the famous one,' whose name is applied to one of the five numayms of the Nimpkish (Boas 1966:40; DSS).

119. This name is recognized as λ̓áλ̓aqʷay?ugʷa 'copper woman' (AD; DSS).

120. What Boas renders as "Mā'qolagyilis" is recognized as the name máxʷəlagilis 'potlatching all over the land' (AD; DSS).

121. Boas' "Kyā'kyaqtla" is recognized by AD and DSS as k̓ák̓axλalis 'log brace on river.' Elsewhere, Boas (1934:67, map 8:75, 8a:28) translates this place name as 'crossed logs on top' and indicates its location on the Nimpkish River, just downstream from the outlet of Nimpkish Lake.

in front of the house. The people wanted to catch him there, but when they approached, he sank down again and was not to be found. So the people wept because they thought that he was dead. Suddenly they heard something move and cry in the corner of the house. They made the fire blaze up high in order to be able to see and then discovered a human skull. It wept and cried "Qiā′, qiā′, qiā′. I've lain in the water in the canoe and my eyes and my flesh are decayed. Where my eyes once were there are deep caverns now."[122]

3. Tribal legend of the Nē′nelky'ēnoq, one of the tribes of the Nimkisch[123]

The ancestor of the Nē′nelky'ēnoq was called Ō′meatlEmē.[124] He lived far above Lake Nimkisch in Nē′nelkyas.[125] Once his four slaves went out to hunt for elk. They saw an unusually large elk, and, when they pursued it, they suddenly saw at their feet the sea in the west. It was the first time that they had seen the ocean. So they broke off the hunt and returned home to report to their master what they had seen. When he heard their report, he prepared to go there. He wanted to see whether people were also living near the sea. He sprinkled his hair with feathers and put on his rings of red inner cedar bark. Starting from Was[126] Lake, he climbed to the top of the mountains and reached the Tā′sis[127] River which runs west. There he sat down and,

---

122. AD and DSS note that this song is sung as in the previous version, which states: "xiʔá, I was once the envy of the people, but now I sit here with caverns instead of eyes."

123. Boas uses the term *Stammsage* 'tribal legend' to describe this story here in the original *Sagen*. As has been discussed, what Boas writes as "Nē′nelky'ēnoq" is the term ńíʔnəlkinuxʷ (anglicized as "Ninelkaynuk"), the name of one of the subgroups or tribes comprising the Nimpkish. The Ninelkaynuk occupied the upper portions of the Nimpkish River drainage system. Boas (1966:40) also identifies the Ninelkaynuk as a numaym of the Nimpkish and glosses the name Ninelkaynuk as 'up-river people.'

124. DSS recognizes Boas' "Ō′meatlEmē" as ʔúʔmaƛəmɛ, and AD recognizes it as ʔúʔmagəmɛ—the meaning of both terms relates to a 'high-class noble person' (DSS; AD).

125. The place name rendered here by Boas as "Nē′nelkyas" is recognized as ńíʔnəlgas (AD; DSS), shown elsewhere by Boas (1934:64, map 12:34) as being on the uppermost Nimpkish River, east of Vernon Lake, and in the vicinity of Vernon Camp. Níʔnəlgas is the term from which the ńíʔnəlkinuxʷ ("Ninelkaynuk") take their tribal name.

126. Boas' "Was" is recognized by AD and DSS as waʔs. Elsewhere, Boas (1934:42, map 12:6) provides this name as "waᶜs," translates it as 'river on ground,' and indicates its location below the outlet of Woss (anglicized from waʔs) Lake.

127. Boas' "Tā′sis," anglicized as "Tahsis," refers to the Tahsis River that flows from near the upper end of Nimpkish Lake down into Tahsis Inlet on the west side of Vancouver Island. T'aši·s (Boas' "Tā′sis") means 'path; trail; road' in the language spoken by the Nuu-chah-nulth on Vancouver Island's west coast; elsewhere, Boas (1934:56, map 12:10) identifies "Tā′sis" as a "Nootka" (i.e. Nuu-chah-nulth) name meaning 'crossing place.'

after a little while, he saw a man approaching from the west. He was Qoi'nkulatl,[128] one of the ancestors of the Mâ'tsatq.[129] As soon as the latter had seen him, he turned back and told his friend that he had seen a shaman at the source of the T'ā'sis River. So they set out together to fetch him. They led him to the sea and brought him to the village in their canoes. There they asked him whether he would barter with them his rings of inner cedar bark. He consented, divided them into small pieces and bartered these for valuable skins. Then he returned to Nē'nelkyas with all his treasures which he hid in Hā'k·olis[130] near Was Lake. Then he gave a great feast for all the neighbouring tribes and assumed the name Mā'qolagyilis.

4. Quā'quas[131]
(Ancestor legend of the Gyī'gyilk·am numaym of the Nimkisch)[132]

At the time when Ts'ētlwā'lak·amē[133] lived in Ōtsâ'lis,[134] Quā'quas lived there as well. He felled big cedars and dragged them to the beach in order to build a house. Ts'ētlwā'lak·amē thought, "How will he go about erecting the tree trunks?" After a short while, Kunkunqulikya[135] arrived and sat down on the beach. So Quā'quas said, "I wish you were a man and would help me to build the house." Thereupon the former took off his bird's head, which was only a mask, became a man and built the house of Quā'quas. He became human in himself and built a house for himself, beside the one of Quā'quas. The Gyī'gyilk·am are descended from him and from Quā'quas.

---

128. This Nimpkish name is recognized as kʷə'nxʷəl'as, derived from the term for 'Thunderbird' (AD; DSS).

129. DSS points out that Boas' "Mâ'tsatq" is múwač̓ataq which is the Kwakwala pronunciation of "Mowachaht," the name of the Nuu-chah-nulth people residing on the west side of Vancouver Island in the Nootka Sound region.

130. This place name is recognized as háqʷulis, derived from háqʷuła, meaning 'two things up against one another' (DSS; AD). Boas (1934:47–48) gives this name for "two mountains close together on Lake Woss at the head of Nimpkish River."

131. This name is not now recognized.

132. "There were two divisions of the Gyī'gyilk·am: one of them traced its descent to Kunkunqulika, the other to Quā'quas" [Boas' original footnote]. Boas' "Gyī'gyilk·am" is gígilgəm (DSS; AD), said to mean 'the first ones' (Boas 1966:40). This story is identified by Boas here in the original as *Ahnensage* 'ancestor legend.'

133. This character is mentioned also in the last paragraph of story 2, "Tlā'lamin."

134. A place on the Nimpkish River near the outlet of Nimpkish Lake.

135. This character is kʷə'nkʷənxʷəligɛ, the largest of the Thunderbirds and very ferocious (DSS).

5. Ya'qstatl[136] (First version, told by a Tlatlasik·oala)[137]

A woman called Naualakusamā'k·a[138] lived near a lake. One day she heard a lot of noise in front of her house and soon saw a flock of geese settling down by the lake. So she called out, "Oh, come into my house. You shall be my children." Two of the geese accepted her invitation, took off their feather garments and transformed into humans. She called the two Ya'qstatl and Nau'alak·.[139] Once, when Ya'qstatl was sleeping with an open mouth, many frogs jumped into his mouth and then made an incessant noise in his belly. When he danced, the frogs came out of his mouth and jumped inside again as soon as he opened it. When Naualakusamā'k·a was cooking fish, the frogs came at once and gobbled everything up, so the mother abandoned her son. But Nau'alak· stayed with him and built him a small house. He caught salmon and cooked them for him, but the frogs again jumped out of the mouth of Ya'qstatl and gobbled everything up. So they both considered how they could get rid of the frogs and decided that Ya'qstatl should flee as soon as they came out again. Nau'alak· cooked a big meal of salmon and as soon as it was ready, the frogs came out and began to devour the fish. Then Ya'qstatl ran away, over valleys and mountains, so that the frogs were unable to reach him. At last he arrived at a pond and there bathed for a full day. Thereupon he was transformed back into a goose again and flew up to K·antsō'ump.[140] The latter gave him his daughter, Na'qnaikyem (= Great Light),[141] for a wife. After some time, Ya'qstatl wished to return to his home and told this to his wife. She asked her father to send Ya'qstatl back. K·antsō'ump agreed. He gave a pipe-whistle to Ya'qstatl and he returned to his home. He built himself a house and painted it. When he uses beautiful colours, it causes nice weather; when he uses ugly colours, it causes rain. K·antsō'ump had taught him the Hā'mats'a[142] mysteries and he was the first Hā'mats'a of his numaym.

But Nau'alak· caught many wolves for himself, which he transformed into humans. Starting from the lake, he wandered down along the Nimkisch River and met a beaver with a human face. So he said to him, "What do you look like? This

136. The name yák̓isǝla is derived from yák̓is 'having bad stuff in one's stomach' (DSS).
137. Stories of the Tlatlasikwala appear in Section XVIII.
138. The name Boas transcribes here as "Naualakusamā'k·a" is náwalakʷsǝmiga, derived from the term náwalakʷ 'supernatural' (DSS).
139. This Kwakwala term is recognized as náwalakʷ 'supernatural' (DSS).
140. AD and DSS use the term qǝns ʔúmp to mean 'Our Father,' referring to God.
141. What Boas transcribes as "Na'qnaikyem" is the name náxnagǝm (DSS).
142. Boas translates "Hā'mats'a" as 'cannibal.' Some Kwakwaka'wakw people say that there was no "Hā'mats'a" in the Nimpkish area before it was introduced by the Oowekeeno, although the Nimpkish had a dance known as hámsǝmc̓ǝs, which did not involve cannibalism (DSS; AD). See also story 9 in this section, "Cannibal at the North End of the World."

isn't right." He shook him and thus transformed him into a human. He cut off his tail and from it made a bowl. He continued down the river in his canoe and reached an island. But it sank at once when his canoe landed there. So he cut into his tongue, spat the blood into his hand and reached down into the water, where he found four shells. In one of them he found a copper. Then he said to Beaver, "Now paint the copper and make a dancing blanket and a dancing staff for me. From now on you shall be called Tlā′k·oagyila (= Copper Maker)."[143] He gave the dancing blanket which Beaver had made to Ya′qstatl, who wore it in the Hā′mats'a dance from then on. Then Nau′alak· and Ya′qstatl moved down to the sea together. On the way they met two ducks with human faces. Nau′alak· seized them, shook them and thus transformed them into humans. He ordered them to stay where he had met them. At last they arrived at the mouth of the river and there built a house for themselves. One day Nau′alak· heard a noise in the forest and went out to see the cause of it. He met a man there who was dancing with a neck ring and the Ts'ā′ek·umtl[144] mask. The man gave him the mask and ring and since then Nau′alak· has danced with the Ts'ā′ek·umtl mask (= mask of the Ts'ā′ēk·a, or of the secrets).

5a. Ya′qstatl (Second version, told by a Nimkisch)

A boy called Ya′qstatl ate a duck which transformed into a frog in his stomach. As soon as his mother cooked anything, frogs jumped out of his mouth and gobbled everything up. Therefore his parents decided to abandon him. They prepared everything for departure and one morning they loaded their canoe, pushed it into the water, and set off. But their youngest son jumped back ashore at the moment when they wanted to depart because he didn't want to leave his brother. The canoe drew away and the two brothers were left all alone. Ya′qstatl was unable to move because his stomach was full of frogs. He said to his little brother, "Can you go down to the river and catch us some salmon?" He replied, "You'd better crawl down yourself; I'm afraid that I am not yet knowledgeable enough." Therefore the elder brother crawled with difficulty down the slope, and the little one accompanied him. Ya′qstatl took bow and arrows and shot some salmon. When his little brother cut them open and roasted them, the frogs began to croak. Ya′qstatl said, "Now cook the fish quickly and put them into that box." He wrapped himself up tightly in his blanket until the little one was finished. Then he went to the box and the frogs jumped out of his mouth at once in order to devour the fish. He nearly choked to death when a big frog came up from his stomach. But as soon as all the frogs were out, the two

---

143. This name is recognized as ẋ′áqʷəgila 'copper maker' (AD).

144. What Boas transcribes here as "Ts'ā′ek·umtl" is číqəmł derived from číqa meaning 'actions carried out slowly and with a conscientious demeanor; sacred' (DSS; AD).

brothers ran away as fast as they could. The frogs, however, were soon through with the box of fish and pursued the brothers. So Ya'qstatl hung his inner cedar bark cape on a tree stump and they ran on. When the frogs saw the cape they thought that it was Ya'qstatl and jumped towards it. Thus the brothers escaped. At last they arrived at the island of Asī'wē,[145] where they built themselves a house and a salmon weir.

Then Ya'qstatl went down to the river and caught salmon, which his brother dried on a rack over the fire. In the evening he went down to the salmon weir again, having told his brother to guard the salmon.On his return in the morning, he was surprised to find that all the salmon had disappeared. He grew angry with his brother because he believed that he had eaten them all. His brother assured him that he hadn't eaten a single one and didn't know in what manner they had vanished. He promised, however, to stay awake the following night and to watch whether the thief would return. Yet he succumbed to his fatigue and, when he awoke the following morning, he found all the salmon gone again. Since he didn't fare any better the third night, Ya'qstatl himself resolved to watch. He hid in the back of the house, holding his bow and arrow ready to shoot the brazen intruder. When day dawned, he heard someone approach. Two huge hands parted the screen covering the door, and a long, gigantic arm stretched out, took the salmon from the drying rack and put them into a basket which the thief carried on her back. It was a Tsōnō'k·oa. Ya'qstatl notched his arrow, shot and hit her right in the breast. So she fled, cried loudly in pain and pushed over the mightiest trees in her path.

Ya'qstatl said to his brother, "I will follow the Tsōnō'k·oa and get my arrow back." He caught many salmon for his brother so that he would not suffer want during his absence, put on his neck ring, and then set off to pursue the Tsōnō'k·oa. He followed the fallen trees and finally arrived at a small lake. He bathed in the lake and then sat down on the shore. After some time a young girl came from the nearby house to fetch water. She was the daughter of the Tsōnō'k·oa, who was lying sick inside the house. Nobody knew what ailed her because the arrow with which Ya'qstatl had hit her was invisible to all eyes except his own. When the girl noticed the stranger by the lake and saw his neck ring of inner cedar bark, she knew that he was a shaman. She went up to him and implored him to enter the house to heal her mother. He followed her and at once saw his arrow stuck in the breasts of Tsōnō'k·oa. He asked what payment they were going to offer if he cured the woman, and was content only when they gave him the young girl for a wife and presented to him the water of life.[146] He remained there for four days and then returned with

---

145. AD and DSS recognize Boas' "Asī'wē" as ʔásiwi 'place above the rapids,' the location of an aboriginal fishery. Boas (1934:38, map 8a:16, 8:64) locates this place on the east side of the lower Nimpkish River.

146. The "water of life" is known as q̓ʷəlá ʔsta, derived from the Kwakwala term q̓ʷəlá 'alive' (AD; DSS).

his young wife to Asĭ'wē. There he found his brother dead. His bleached bones lay beside the fire site inside the house. He collected his brother's bones and found that they were all there, except for the clavicle. This he carved from wood and then sprinkled the bones with the water of life. Thereupon his brother rose up again and rubbed his eyes as if he had been asleep.

6. The Ātlâ'lēnoq (= Forest Dwellers)[147]

In the beginning, the earth was inhabited by the Ātlâ'lēnoq, the wolves, and there were no real humans. Later K·'ā'nigyilak[148] transformed the wolves into real humans. They had villages in Hā'tsatēlis,[149] on K·ā'lōkuis,[150] and in Mē'mkumlis.[151] Once the Ātlâ'lēnoq in Mē'mkumlis wanted to give a big dance. Four young people had hidden in the forest to prepare themselves for the dance. Then Tlē'selagyila (= Sun Maker),[152] Mink, came to Mē'mkumlis and killed the four young men hidden in the forest. He cut off their heads, carried them home and put them on the drying rack above the fire. After some time, a woman of the Ātlâ'lēnoq went to Tlē'selagyila to get fire. She saw the heads of her relatives drying above the fire and ran back and told what she had seen. So the Ātlâ'lēnoq became very sad and resolved to kill Tlē'selagyila. While they were holding a council to devise a plan of attack, Tlē'selagyila built himself a salmon weir in which he caught a sĭ'siutl. The Wolves pretended not to know anything about the murder of the four young people and made all the preparations for the dance, to which they also invited Tlē'selagyila in order to get him in their power. The latter went to the dance with his mother and they took hummingbird skins along. Then Tlē'selagyila entered the door, began to dance, and sang: "K·ap'amā'luq KHēH aqō nEk·amā'eaqs Ātlâ'lēnoq (i.e., KHēH

---

147. What Boas transcribes here as "Ātlâ'lēnoq" is ʔaᴋúl'inuxʷ which is the ceremonial name for 'wolf,' while the term that translates as 'forest dweller' is ʔaᴋaʔnəˊm (AD; DSS).

148. The Transformer, q̓ániqiʔlakʷ (AD; DSS).

149. AD and DSS recognize "Hā'tsatēlis" as xácistalis, derived from xáca?is 'low tide.' This is likely the place name translated by Boas (1934:77, map 14:77) as 'having great ebb tide' and located on the south side of Turnour Island near Nicolas Point.

150. Boas' "K·ā'lōkuis" is recognized as as qálugʷis 'bent beach,' applied to a village site on the south end of Turnour Island that was set aside as "Karlukwees" (anglicized from qálugʷis) IR No. 1 (AD; DSS; Boas 1934:73, map 14:75).

151. What Boas transcribes as "Mē'mkumlis" is recognized as mímkʷəmlis which means 'round things (islands) in front at beach' and refers to a village site on the west side of Village Island (DSS; AD; Boas 1934:51 map 11:65).

152. Although AD and DSS recognize Boas' "Tlē'selagyila" as ᴋ'ísəlagila, one of Mink's names in Kwakwaka'wakw mythology, and agree with his translation, 'sun maker,' they more commonly refer to Mink as ᴋ'ísəlagil'akʷ 'born to be the sun.'

[= Mink] took the middle of the Ātlâ'lēnoq face for a hat)."[153] At once everyone rushed at him in order to kill him. So Tlē'selagyila and his mother transformed into hummingbirds and flew away. When they had safely arrived in the open, they assumed their natural shape again. Tlē'selagyila put on the sī'siūtl as his head ornament, and everyone who saw it became transformed into sea foam. Then Tlē'selagyila fled in his canoe and the Ātlâ'lēnoq pursued him. When they got close, he lifted the sī'siūtl up high and the canoes were transformed into rocks. This is the origin of the many cliffs to the west of Mē'mkumlis (the village of the Mamalēlēk·ala).[154]

7. Ō'qsEm and Nūtlnutlili'kya[155]

Nūtlnutlili'kya lived in Gua'tsē,[156] close to QulkH. Tlā'k·oagyila[157] was a chief at Ōtsâ'lis.[158] Nūtlnutlili'kya invited him to a feast, during which he intended to kill him. Tlā'k·oagyila went down the river with his brothers and his son Ō'qsEm. They landed in Gua'tsē and the men went to the feast, while Ō'qsEm stayed in the canoe which they tied to the shore with a thick rope. When they had gone into the house, a small girl came down to Ō'qsEm. She pretended to relieve herself and said to Ō'qsEm, "Nūtlnutlili'kya wants to kill your father and your uncles and will not spare you either. Flee as soon as you hear noise in the house." While she was saying this, she cut with a shell knife the rope by which the canoe was tied to shore. Soon

---

153. The words of the song are known to AD and DSS as: qəpamál'uxʷ kɛ'ʔkax̣ λiλəwə́l'gamayax̣s ʔax̣úl'inəx̣ʷ, meaning 'q̓ánaqiʔlakʷ is wearing the heads of the Wolf princes.' The term that Boas transcribes as "Khēн" is kɛ'ʔkax̣ which is the shortened form of q̓ániqiʔlakʷ, 'the Transformer,' and not 'Mink,' as Boas indicates here (AD; DSS).

154. Boas' "Mamalēlēk·ala" is mámaliliqla (anglicized as "Mamalilikulla") which is the Kwakwala name applied to the people of Village Island and the adjacent islands. While their territory was centred on Village Island, the mámaliliqla are said to have originated in the Beaver Harbour area; they also lived in an area extending along the north shore of Knight Inlet as far as Matsiu Creek, as well as at a place near Turnour Island, and at White Beach, and at the end of Malcolm Island. The name of the village that Boas transcribes here as "Mē'mkumlis" is mímkʷəmlis, derived from məkʷə́'mliła meaning 'round object in front,' referring to the islets in front of this site at the southwest end of Village Island (DSS; AD).

155. This name that Boas has rendered as "Ō'qsEm" is recognized as ʔúxʷsəm 'having grey hair' (DSS). Likely the name given by Boas as "Nūtlnutlili'kya" is the name nułnul'ik'a, derived from nanúl'u meaning 'foolish' (DSS).

156. AD and DSS recognize "Gua'tsē" as gʷaʔdzí meaning 'north side.' Boas (1934:68 map 8:71) gives this same place name as "gwaʿᵋdzēᵋ" and shows its location on the Nimpkish River, downstream from the outlet of Nimpkish Lake, and close to "QulkH" (x̣ʷəlkʷ) at the mouth of the Nimpkish River .

157. "Tlā'k·oagyila" is x̣'áqʷəgila 'copper maker' (AD); see also story 5 in the present section.

158. This place name is recognized as udzúʔlas on the Nimpkish River (AD; DSS).

O'qsEm heard noise inside the house and fled as quickly as he was able. He got safely to Ōtsâ'lis and called to his mother and to the second wife of Tlā'k·oagyila, "Nūtlnutlili'kya has killed my father and my uncles. Let's flee!" They wandered upriver. Once, when O'qsEm had gone out to catch trout, enemy canoes came. They found nobody except for O'qsEm's brother, Wī'sekyē[159] (= Suckling), who was underage. They threw him into the water and destroyed the house. When O'qsEm and the women came home, they picked up the corpse and wandered through the forest to Beaver Cove.[160] O'qsEm had the body on his shoulder and was holding it by the feet. In this way the water ran out of Wī'sekyē's mouth and he came to life again. When they arrived in Beaver Cove, O'qsEm, who had no canoe, threw a tree trunk into the water in order to travel on it to his mother's relatives, the Tena'qtaq.[161] On their way they were met by their enemies in two big canoes. Some of them thought they could see people on the tree trunk, while others took them for sea lions. When they paddled towards them, O'qsEm made the women jump into the water and he himself swam about like a sea lion. In this way he deceived his enemies, who now paddled on. They went ashore to Wo'qtsat[162] and lit a fire. There O'qsEm found a chinook canoe[163] with oars, rope and all equipment. So he was glad. They went on and then arrived soon in Tena'qtaq. His uncles K·ō'tlk·oqstō[164] and Gy'ē'gyelaqstâ'la[165] lived here. The former always used to sit in front of the house in nice weather. He saw O'qsEm, and sent out his slaves to enquire who the stranger might be. When he heard that his sister had come with her son, he had the house of Gy'ē'gyelaqstâ'la cleaned and served food and drink and wanted to present him with capes and slaves. But O'qsEm said, "Don't give me riches. Give me weapons to kill my enemies." His uncle then offered him first a club of whale-bone, but finally gave him a huge stone axe. In order to test the weapon, they invited a number of people

159. This name that Boas has rendered as "Wī'sekyē" appears to be derived from the term wísa meaning 'boy' (AD; DSS).

160. Beaver Cove, situated east from the mouth of the Nimpkish River, is given in English in the original *Sagen*.

161. The term dənáxda?xʷ (Boas' "Tena'qtaq"), anglicized as "Tenaktak," refers to the people of Knight Inlet (AD; DSS).

162. While AD and DSS do not recognize this term, "Wo'qtsat," Boas (1934:44) applies it to an island situated "between Knight Inlet and Nimkish river" and glosses the name as 'having the howling of wolves.'

163. Given in the original *Sagen* as Chinook-*Boot* ('Chinook boat'), likely a reference to a type of large freight canoe.

164. This name "K·ō'tlk·oqstō" is not now recognized.

165. The name that Boas transcribes as "Gy'ē'gyelaqstâ'la" is possibly gígəlaxstula 'having eyes like a bear' (AD).

and entertained them. During the feast, first Gy'ē'gyelaqstâ'la killed his neighbour, then K·ō'tlk·oqstō seized the club, took a man by his hair and struck his eyes out.

When spring came, all the tribes gathered in Tsāwa'tē[166] to catch eulachon. Among the arrivals there was Wē'k·aē, the chief of the Wī'wēk·aē.[167] He had a beautiful daughter. Although many chiefs had courted her, he didn't think any of them good enough to be his son-in-law. Once Ō'qsEm went to the spot where the women were in the habit of digging roots. He had tied his hair together over his forehead and had sprinkled it with feathers so that he was quite unrecognizable. He sat down by the daughter of Wē'k·aē and said, "I know that many men want to marry you. Take me for your husband!" So the girl replied that no one was good enough for her father. Then he asked her for whom her father was saving her. So she replied, "For Ō'qsEm." When she had said this, he disclosed who he was and then she was very much ashamed. Then he married her and they had a son.

Then Ō'qsEm returned to Ōtsâ'lis with ten slaves, his wife and his child. The slaves paddled and he stood in the middle of the canoe with the axe in his hand. Thus he passed by the house of Nūtlnutlili'kya just when the latter was giving a feast. At just this time one of Nūtlnutlili'kya's slaves had run away. He escaped to Ō'qsEm and said; "My master always beats me, so I have run away. Let me stay with you!" Ō'qsEm replied, "No, go back!" We are going to kill Nūtlnutlili'kya. I will hide by the house and you shall call me when he happens to be quite defence-less." The slave agreed. Ō'qsEm hid. Towards noon, Nūtlnutlili'kya went to the river, first washed with urine, then bathed and dried himself by the fire. While he was sitting there, having his hair combed by his two wives, the slave called Ō'qsEm. He came and knocked Nūtlnutlili'kya down. The latter jumped up again, but Ō'qsEm broke his neck with a second blow. Then he killed all his relatives and abducted his wives.

---

166. What Boas transcribes here as "Tsawa'tē" is dzáwadi 'having eulachons,' a place at the mouth of the Klinaklini River at the upper end of Knight Inlet (AD; DSS; Boas 1934:23, 59).

167. Wε'qε (Boas' "Wē'k·aē") was the ancestral founder of the wíwεqε (Boas' "Wī'wēk·aē," anglicized as "Weewiakay"), one of the subgroups or tribes comprising the Lekwiltok. In the early 19th century the Weewiakay lived at Topaze Harbour, north from Hardwicke Island, but subsequently moved to several other places, including Kanish Bay and Drew Harbour, before settling finally at Cape Mudge on Quadra Island (Duff 1965:87–92). An account of wε'qε and the wíwεqε appears in Section XIV, story 5.

8. Mā'tEm[168]

In Pā'pēkyHin,[169] above Lake Nimkisch, there lived a young man called Mā'tEm. He always played with young people of his own age. One evening, when he had become very hungry, he took salmon eggs from a box and roasted them. When they burst, they spattered onto the back of his father, who was warming himself by the fire, and burned him. Thereupon he became angry and beat Mā'tEm with a stick. The boy became very sad and went into the forest. After he had wandered for a long time, he came to a spot where driftwood had formed a jam in the river. He wanted to die, and he jumped into the water above the jam, but reappeared again below it, unharmed. He got to a second jam and jumped into the water above it, but again resurfaced safely. Then he arrived at a steep rock. He climbed up and hurled himself down, but wasn't hurt. Then he climbed a high mountain and hurled himself down but remained quite unharmed. He went on and soon saw a mountain up ahead which shone like a light. It was the Nā'oalakoa rock,[170] where there was a constant rain of rock crystal. He picked up four pieces the length of a finger and stuck them into his hair in a row from the front to the back. He climbed up the mountain and became completely covered in rock crystal. He soon noticed that, through the rock crystal, he had acquired the ability to fly. Thereupon he flew all over the world. He thought that he was absent for four days, but it was four years. At last he flew back to his home. His relatives happened to be in Nē'nelkyas[171] and were working on the side of the lake by torch light, when he appeared in the shape of a snow-white eagle and caused rock-crystal to rain down. He alighted in a tree and sang:

---

168. Boas' own translation of this story (No. 8), as well as story 9, appears elsewhere (see Boas 1897:405–406, 411–412). In the 1897 translation of the present story, the young man is initially identified as "Ō'meaLEmaē" which is a name derived from the term for 'high-class noble person,' and recognized by DSS as ʔúʔmaλəmɛ, and by AD as ʔúʔmagəmɛ—the meaning of both terms relates to a 'high-class noble person.' DSS and AD point out that it is only after this young man obtains special powers that he becomes known by the name mádəm, which Boas gives here as "Mā'tEm" and uses as the title of this story. While the name "Ō'meaLEmaē" is not used in the present story, it does appear in story 3 of this section, where it is given as the name of the ancestor of the Ninelkaynuk, one of the subgroups or tribes comprising the Nimpkish.

169. AD and DSS believe that Boas' "Pā'pēkyHin" may be the term pápikəm but do not know where this place was located. Although Boas (1934:49, map 15:93) identifies "Pā'pēkyHin" as a "place above Nimkish Lake," he mistakenly shows its location as being in Call Inlet on the mainland; moreover, Boas does not indicate a place with this name on his maps of the Nimpkish Lake area.

170. The name is recognized as náwalak̓ʷa meaning 'supernatural on the rock' (AD; DSS).

171. The place name rendered here by Boas as "Nē'nelkyas" is recognized as níʔnəlgas (AD; DSS), and shown by Boas (1934:64, map 12:34) as being on the uppermost Nimpkish River, east of Vernon Lake, in the vicinity of Vernon Camp. Níʔnəlgas is the term from which the ńiʔnəlkinux̱ʷ (Boas' "Nē'nelky'ēnoq," anglicized as "Ninelkaynuk") take their name. The Ninelkaynuk are one of the subgroups or tribes comprising the Nimpkish (see also story 3 of the present section).

"Hā a   hā   a   hā a   hā   ha - nā   hā a a   nē."[172]

So the people knew that he had returned and that he had obtained supernatural powers. They bathed and went down to the beach. Each one carried a stick, to which he fixed crystal. But Mā′tEm could scent them and didn't allow himself to be caught. When darkness fell, the eagle circled above the houses and the people tried to catch him, but without success. A young man who formerly had always played with Mā′tEm wanted to catch him very badly. He succeeded in flinging a rope over the bird's head. The bird continued to fly around and the young man, who was now given the name Mā′taanoē,[173] followed him. He told the people to purify the house and erect a plank on the roof. When they had done so, Mā′tEm alighted on the plank. He flew up again three times, but came into the house the fourth time. Mā′taanoē remained his companion. The four following nights they danced the Tsētsā′ēk·a.[174]

Later Mā′tEm went out with his slaves to cut wood. Their canoe capsized on the way and he descended to Bēbenak·au′a (= Deepest).[175] He saw many dances there and Bēbenak·au′a gave him the Lōlō′tlalatl, the dance of the Lâ′lēnoq (ghosts of the departed),[176] and the name Lō′tlemāē.[177]

---

172. AD points out that Boas transcribed only the first line of the song, the entirety of which says: "I came to stand at the bottom of this mountain and it started to rain down crystals upon me. Crystals are coming down." The Kwakwala name of the mountain mentioned in the song is xʷíl′amagilis, derived from xʷíl′a 'crystal' (AD; DSS).

173. This name rendered by Boas as "Mā′taanoē" is recognized as mádanuwi, meaning 'mádəm with rope tied around his waist.' The mádəm dance continues to be performed by a Nimpkish dancer wearing a headdress adorned with spinning crystals. The man dances up a sloped plank while being held back by a rope tied around his waist (AD; DSS).

174. This is the Kwakwala name číčɛqa which is applied to the complicated series of ceremonials held in the winter including the initiation of young people into secret societies and feasting. During this season, certain beings, who reside during the summer in distant lands, come to the village. They capture and initiate humans of the tribe, and the object of the dance is to recapture those taken away and imbued with the qualities of the captors and restore them to human form (Boas 1966:173–174; DSS).

175. Bíbənagawɛ (Boas' "Bēbenak·au′a") 'the world beneath us' refers to the "underworld" (AD; DSS). The character obviously received the dances while there in the underworld and not from someone called by this name. In the stories of the Kwiksootainuk (see Section XVI) this chief is identified as "Satan."

176. The dance known as ləlúɫəlaɫ is derived from the term lúʔlinuxʷ 'ghost'; ghosts do not like to be called by the term lúʔlinuxʷ and prefer instead the name háyaɫilagas (AD; DSS).

177. This name is recognized as lúɫəmi (AD; DSS).

9. Baqbakuālanusī′uaē
(= He Who First Devoured Human Flesh At The River Mouth)[178]

Once upon a time there were two friends. One of them had gone into the forest to prepare for the Tsētsā′ēk·a, while the other one was still uninitiated. In spite of this he looked for his friend and, after four days, found him. When he returned he was asked by his father where he had been and he said that he had found his friend, who was preparing himself for the Tsētsā′ēk·a, in seclusion. So his father beat him and shouted, "Don't you know that this is forbidden? I am going to be killed because of you!" The young man became very sad. During the night he put on his abalone shell ornaments and went into the forest. He went upriver and washed with hemlock branches. The following morning he went on and washed again at night, when he heard the whistles of Baqbakuālanusī′uaē. At the end of the fourth day he arrived at a steep rock and lay down to sleep at its base. Early in the morning he saw how the rock opened and how Baqbakuālanusī′uaē came out. He hid and the latter flew away over him. He was completely covered in inner cedar bark dyed red.[179] He remained there for four nights. On the fifth morning he followed Baqbakuālanusī′uaē and saw how he took off his rings of inner cedar bark[180] by a pond and then swam in it. When he dived, the young man sprang out and put on the rings of Baqbakuālanusī′uaē. When the latter surfaced, he saw the young man and said, "You've done the right thing to put on those rings. I am now unable to kill you." He took him along to his house in the cliff. There he asked him what he would like to have of his, and the young man asked for the Hā′mats'a whistles, the death-bringer, the water of life, and a seal harpoon. Baqbakuālanusī′uaē kept him for four days; after that the young man was also able to fly. Then he told him to fly to the spot from where his father always had the water drawn. Soon his younger brother came along and then he realized that he hadn't been away for four days, but four years. He asked him, "Tell me, my brother, how is Father?" But the boy didn't recognize him and asked who he might be. Then he continued, "I am your older brother. Go and tell Father to purify the house." The boy went back, but when he delivered the message, he was beaten by his father who said, "My son has been dead for a long time. Don't speak about him." The boy ran back to the creek and complained to his brother that his father wouldn't

178. The original Kwakwala term transcribed by Boas as "Baqbakuālanusī′uaē" was pronounced bəkʷbákʷalanukʷsiwi, best translated as 'having a cannibal at the mouth of the river,' but in more recent times has been pronounced bákʷbakʷalanukʷsiwi (DSS).

179. AD and DSS question Boas' association of bákʷbakʷalanukʷsiwi with cedar bark here, as this material is used to pacify the spirit of the cannibal.

180. In the Nimpkish people's performance of the cannibal dance, a cedar bark ring is placed around the neck of the dancer to pacify him and rid him of his cannibalistic tendencies, after which he is reintegrated into human society (DSS).

believe him. So once again he sent him back with the same message. Then his father went out in person to convince himself. When the young man saw him he became wild. He flew across the river, tore corpses from the graves and devoured them. Baqbakuālanusī′uaē came and helped him. Then he went into his father's house and bit everyone he encountered.

The village of gʷáẏasdəms, Health Bay on Gilford Island, 1900. Painted house showing sculpin belonged to Chief Johnny Scow and to its left is house of Chief Sewid with double-headed serpent and mythical bird.

Royal British Columbia Museum, Victoria, B.C. PN235 (C. Newcombe photo).

XVI. LEGENDS OF THE KWIKSOOTAINUK

The Kwiksootainuk are the adjacent mainland tribe to the Alert Bay
Nimpkish and would be well represented at any of the numerous potlatches
held there. In fact, on both occasions when Boas stayed there, during the
time the *Sagen* stories were being obtained, a potlatch was in the offing
(Rohner 1969:44, 111). People "gaily painted" walked about the village and
from their houses could be heard "the muffled sound of a drum, hand-
clapping, and the monotonous song" (Rohner 1969:44). Boas found life in
Alert Bay tedious and complained to his wife that his existence was little
more than visiting, listening to stories, and then writing until his fingers
were stiff. While it is likely that he obtained these Kwiksootainuk tales
during his October 1886 visit to Alert Bay, especially considering he was
"always busy with something or other" (Rohner 1969:45), Boas left us with
no hints as to how, when, or from whom he obtained the rich stories
included here.

A dzúnuq̓ʷa figure standing in the village of gʷáẏasdəms, Gilford Island, *ca.* 1915.
Milwaukee Public Museum, Milwaukee, Wisconsin. Neg. No. 2536 (Samuel Barrett photo).

XVI. Legends of the Kuē′qsot′ēnoq[1]

1. Ancestor legend of the numaym Nē′·nelpaē [2]

Ts'ē′k·amē[3] had a wife called K·oā′k·wispālayūk·oa.[4] Her sons were Nɛ′lpē, G·ōlsɛlas and Pō′tlētē.[5] Ts'ē′k·amē had a salmon weir in Kwa'qulawat. Once, when K·oā′k·wispālayūk·oa was pregnant, Ts'ē′k·amē went in his canoe, to his weir, to see whether he had caught any fish.[6] He found the weir completely filled with salmon and among them there was the sī′siutl[7] as well. Ts'ē′k·amē was carrying the fish ashore when Pō′tlētē came running up with the news that his mother had given birth to a child. Ts'ē′k·amē asked, "Is it a boy or a girl?" When he heard that it was a boy,

---

1. "Kuē′qsot′ēnoq" is Boas' rendering of qʷíqʷsut'inuxʷ, anglicized as "Kwiksootainuk," the Kwakwala name for one of the Gilford Island tribes. This name, qʷíqʷsut'inuxʷ, has been translated as 'opposite shore people' (Curtis 1915:10:307) or 'people of the other side' (Boas 1966:40—this latter translation is preferred by DSS). Traditional Kwiksootainuk territory was centred in the Gilford Island/Tribune Channel area, but prior to the mid-1850s, the main Kwiksootainuk village was at gʷáẏasdəms, Health Bay on the west side of Gilford Island. As a result of a raid by the Bella Coola (Nuxalk) on gʷáẏasdəms village *circa* 1855–1858, most of the Kwiksootainuk population was killed, and the few Kwiksootainuk survivors went to live with the Mamalilikulla at this latter tribe's village of mímkʷəmlis on southwestern Village Island (Boas 1887a:227–228; 1887f:130–131, map; 1934:map 10:143; Curtis 1915:10:307; Duff 1965:17; Rohner 1967:30–40; Spradley 1969:32–35). The Kwiksootainuk are among the approximately 30 autonomous groups or "tribes" speaking the Kwakwala language and comprising the Kwakwaka'wakw (see also the initial footnote to Section XIV of the present volume).

    Our annotation of this section was assisted greatly in the summer of 2001 by two Kwakwala-speaking experts, Chief Adam Dick and Dr. Daisy Sewid-Smith, who are referred to here as "DSS" and "AD" respectively; we gratefully acknowledge their assistance.

2. This term is recognized as níʔnəlbiʔ meaning 'southern people' (DSS).

3. This name is recognized as ćiqamiʔ (DSS).

4. DSS does not recognize kʷákʷisp'alayugʷa ('urine-smelling woman') as the name of the wife; rather, DSS and AD know the wife's name as ćígiⱡil'akʷ ('born to be ćiqamiʔ').

5. These names are: nílbiʔ; gʷə'l'səl'as, meaning 'everyone who disembarks goes to your house'; and, púλidi 'guests never leave hungry' (DSS).

6. The weir was located in Shoal Harbour, called ʔápsəgiyu 'opposite side,' situated southwest of Echo Bay on the western side of Gilford Island (DSS; AD; Boas 1934: map 14:31).

7. Sísiyuλ (Boas' "sī′siutl"), the 'double-headed serpent,' can both harm people and bestow upon them great wealth and prestige (DSS; AD).

he killed the sī'siutl, had the boy brought to him and bathed him in the blood. Then the boy's skin turned to stone. The only spot where his father forgot to coat him was under the chin and the skin there remained soft. He was given the name Tlā'tlaqoas or T'ē'sumgyilak' (= Turned Into Stone)[8] and became quite invincible in war. Tlā'tlaqoas went out with one hundred men and defeated the TsāwatEēnoq.[9] On the way he saw the Thunderbird, Ts'ō'nE,[10] which he caught and carried into his canoe. Thereupon it started to rain and to hail and didn't stop until he had set the Thunderbird free again. When Tlā'tlaqoas returned home to K·oai·astEms,[11] he found that Ku'qagyila,[12] a Guau'aēnoq[13] chief, had abducted all the Kuē'qsŏt'ēnoq women. He set out in pursuit and, when his canoe got within sight, Kuē'qagyila tried to escape. He paddled so hard that his paddles broke. Thus Tlā'tlaqoas caught up with him easily and took all the abducted women away from him. This angered Kēqagyila. He took one of his broken paddles and hit against an island so hard with it that it broke into two parts. Because of this he is called Kuē'qagyila (Splitter).[14] And Tlā'tlaqoas made war on the Nimkisch. Their chief, Hamā'lakyauaē[15] (see page 138),[16] gave him his daughter, K·'ē'Hoak·anak,[17] in order to make peace. Tlā'tlaqoas gave her to his brother NE'lpē as a wife. He himself went to the Tlatlasik·oala[18] and

8. DSS and AD explain that when the boy was born he was called x̣'áx̣'ax̌ʷas (Boas' "Tlā'tlaqoas"), and then after he was bathed in blood he was called t'ísəmgi?l'akʷ (Boas' "T'ē'sumgyilak") which means 'born to be stone-bodied.' Today, he is only known as t'ísəmgid 'stone body' (DSS; AD).

9. Boas' "TsāwatEē'noq" is dzawadɛ'?nuxʷ (AD; DSS), anglicized as "Tsawatainuk," referring to the Kingcome Inlet people. The term dzawadɛ'?nuxʷ has been translated by Boas (1966:40) as 'people of olachen place,' and by Duff (1953–1954) as 'know how to handle eulachons.' Boas' (1887f) map centred Tsawatainuk territory in Kingcome Inlet but included much of Tribune Channel as well as the northern portion of Gilford Island.

10. DSS recognizes Boas' "Ts'ō'nE" as ćúna and observes that only the Knight's Inlet people (known as ?awíx̌la 'inside') use this term to refer to the Thunderbird.

11. "K·oai'astEms" is Boas' transcription of gʷáy̓asdəms; as previously noted, prior to the mid-1850s this was the main Kwiksootainuk village and was located at Health Bay on the west side of Gilford Island.

12. This name is recognized as kʷíx̣agila, derived from kʷíx̣?id 'to strike' (AD; DSS).

13. What Boas transcribes as "Guau'aēnoq" is gʷáwa?ɛnuxʷ (anglicized as "Gwawaenuk"), the name for the people of Drury Inlet, Grappler Sound, Mackenzie Sound, and Dixon Island (AD).

14. "Kuē'qagyila presumably stems from kuē'q'it 'splitting.' It probably means 'murderer' " [Boas' original footnote].

15. This name is recognized as hámalakiwi (DSS; AD).

16. This is a reference to page 138 of Section XV of the original Sagen, story 1, the subsection entitled "K·ā'k·oaqsānok·."

17. DSS recognizes this name as q̓íx̣aq̓ənakʷ, and adds that in the 20th century, people who always made trouble were called q̓íx̣aq̓ənakʷ.

18. The x̣'áx̣'asiqʷəla tribe; see Section XVIII.

took a wife from this tribe. Her father told him, "If you have a son, call him WēkyElā′lisEmēk·."[19]

NE′lpē and K·′ē′Hoak·anak had a son. Once, when they went across to QulkH[20] to visit Hamā·lakyauaē, the young Nimkisch people mocked this boy because he always ate shellfish while they ate salmon exclusively. They said, "Green stuff grows from your belly."[21] The small boy wept. Thereupon his mother grew angry, went back to K·oai′astEms and told what had occurred. So the Kuēqsōt′ēnoq made war on the Nimkisch.—

Once T′ē′sumgyilak· (as Tlā′tlaqoas will be called from here on) went to the Ts′E′ltsElkH country in order to gather feathers on Mount Ts′Elkyimpaē.[22] They stopped at a big river on their way. NEmō′kois,[23] an old man, lived there. He gave them a friendly reception. He had lots of provisions and served small bowls of meat and fat to his guests. Eat as they might, they were unable to empty them. So T′ē′sumgyilak· took the dishes away from the old man and put them in his canoe. NEmō′kois sat there quite calmly and didn't pay any attention to what they were doing. When the tide began to go out, the strangers wanted to set out but their canoe was stuck quite fast. So they realized that NEmō′kois was holding them back. They took the bowls back to him and he let them continue on their way. Then they went to Mount Ts′Elkyimpaē and fetched feathers which T′ē′sumgyilak· wanted to use in the Qoē′qoē dance.[24]

K·oā′k·oaqsānok· (see page 138)[25] knew that T′ē′sumgyilak· had gone to

---

19. This name is recognized as wíkəlalisəmi (DSS).

20. As has been noted, "QulkH" is Boas' rendering of xʷəlkʷ 'criss-crossed logs,' the name applied to a village site situated at the mouth of the Nimpkish River (DSS; AD). Elsewhere, Boas (1934:36,78) identifies "x̂ûlkᵘ" (x̂ʷəlkʷ) as one of the places of origin for the Nimpkish people and provides the translation '(logs) placed crosswise.'

21. The reference is to the intestine of a clam, which is green in colour.

22. Boas' "Ts′Elkyimpaē" is recognized by AD and DSS as the name of a mountain called c̓ə′lkəmbaʔi 'feathers on face,' derived from c̓ə′lc̓əlk 'feather' (Boas' "Ts′E′ltsElkH").

23. This name is recognized as nəmúkʷgʷis 'all alone on/in the land' (AD; DSS).

24. As previously noted, Boas' "Qoē′qoē" is recognized as x̂ʷíx̂ʷi, the Kwakwala pronunciation of a Coast Salish term referring to a distinctive mask obtained from the Comox people (AD; DSS). Boas comments elsewhere that among the Kwakwaka'wakw, the x̂ʷíx̂ʷi dancer is distinguished by a painted mask with prominent eyes and tufts of feathers projecting from the top of the head-piece. The dancer carries a rattle of strung shells, and therefore the dance is associated with earth-quakes, and the dancer is believed to "shake the ground and to be a certain means of bringing back the hā′matsa who is being initiated" (Boas 1897:497). AD and DSS add that among the Kwakwaka'wakw, the x̂ʷíx̂ʷi dancer is a clown with bulging eyes and a long tongue, and the words to the song sung for the mask make fun of its appearance.

25. AD and DSS recognize Boas' "K·oā′k·oaqsānok·" as q̓ʷáq̓ʷaqsanukʷ and confirm the English translation of this name that Boas and Hunt (1902–1905:141) provide elsewhere as 'Splitter'

Ts'ɛlkyimpaē and he decided to kill him. He asked his father Hamā′lakyauaē how best to attack him. The father warned him against this enterprise, but, since K·oā′k·oaqsānok· insisted on it, he told him that T'ē′sumgyilak‛ was vulnerable only at the throat and that he would have to pass Tlō′k·ōē (Duvin Point)[26] on his way back. K·oā′k·oaqsānok· then set out together with T'ē′tɛsumHstsāna[27] and took along many slaves. They hid their canoe behind the island and when the canoe of T'ē′sumgyilak‛ approached, he shot the hala′iu[28] at him. His own people trembled with fright when they saw T'ē′sumgyilak‛ approaching. But when K·oā′k·oaqsānok· shot the hala′iu, the enemies became crazy. He hit the throat of T'ē′sumgyilak‛, who fell overboard and capsized the canoe with his fall. Then T'ē′tɛsumHstsāna killed them all with his hands of stone. Even though they believed T'ē′sumgyilak‛ to be dead, they left an old man, called Qē′ūta,[29] as a guard on the island. Then they decapitated their enemies. Suddenly they heard the old man shout, "Ha, ha! I've got T'ē′sumgyilak‛!" and they saw him striking at something. T'ē′sumgyilak‛ had surfaced at the island and the old man had hacked through his throat. Then they put his head, too, into the canoe and went home. They strung the heads onto ropes which they pushed through the mouths and throats, sprinkled them with feathers and hung them up in MāsmEts'a.[30] Once K·‛ē′Hoak·anak came over to visit K·oā′k·oaqsānok·. When she got to the river, her child noticed feathers floating on it. The child drew this to her attention and then they saw the heads of the slain. They went back and cried a lot. But on their way they loaded their canoe with seals and salmon as if they had received them from the Nimkisch. When they arrived in K·oai′astEms, everyone asked them why they had been weeping. They replied, "We didn't weep; we laughed." Then when they were having their meal, her child said, "Hā′umats'a′[31]

(because this character pulls apart the heads and bodies of his enemies) (See also Section XV, where two variants of the "K·oā′k·oaqsānok·" legend are presented between stories No. 1 and No. 2).

26. This is actually Duval Point, situated at the entrance to Port Hardy. Boas errs in the *Sagen* in giving the English name of this place as "Duvan," but later corrects it in his list of geographical names (Boas 1934:84). The name is recognized as x̣'úguʔyu 'bare in between' (AD; DSS).

27. This name is t'ísəmxċana 'stone hand' (AD; DSS).

28. Boas' "hala′iu" is haláyu, the Kwakwala word for the 'death-bringer' (AD; DSS). As has previously been noted, Boas (1935:110) elsewhere comments that the 'death-bringer' takes various forms, including a baton, arrow, or quartz, that when pointed at people or objects causes instant destruction.

29. This name is recognized as x̣wəʔíta (DSS; AD).

30. This place name, "MāsmEts'a," is given elsewhere in Boas (1934:52) as "mā′ts!a" 'rock lengthwise current at hind end; or stripped rock' and its location is indicated just upstream from the mouth of the Nimpkish River (map 8:54, 8a:9). It was likely a creek that entered the Nimpkish River at this location. DSS and AD recognize this place name as máʔċa and confirm the translation 'stripped-off rock.'

31. Possibly haʔúm̀aċa (DSS).

(this is what the child called its grandfather), what do the feathers on the river mean?" The mother forbade it to speak, but the child soon repeated its question. So K·'ē′ḤOak·anak had to tell them that all the K·uē′qsōt'ēnoq had been killed. Thereupon the K·uē′qsōt'ēnoq and the Guau′aēnoq made war against the Nimkisch. When they approached the shore, K·oā·k·oaqsānok· waved the hala′iu towards them and they lost their minds. Then he captured them and tied them to planks which he put up in a long row. The ravens came to peck out their eyes and they were only able to blow at them to chase them away. At last two strong men, Quī′lisagyila,[32] a Guau′aēnoq, and Ts'â′kulis,[33] a K·uē·qsōt'ēnoq, broke their ropes, but before they were able to set everyone free, T'ē′tEsmḤstsāna came and killed them with his hands of stone.—

K·'ē′Ḥtlala,[34] the son of NE′lpē, lived in Qā′wakyis.[35] One day he went out in his canoe to hunt seals. NE·lpē waited in vain for his return. Finally he took to his canoe in order to search for his lost son. After a long search he saw a paddle floating on the water and he found the box and spear of K·'ē′Ḥtlala, but he didn't find his son. He searched in vain for five or ten days and all the people went along. So they believed that K·'ē′Ḥtlala was dead.

But he had descended to the bottom of the sea in his canoe. There he visited K·ōmō′k·oa[36] and obtained supernatural powers from him. They exchanged canoes and K·ōmō′k·oa presented him with a spear to hunt seals, sea otters, sea lions, and whales. He told him, "You will obtain many riches and will become a mighty chief. When you get back home, give a big feast and take the names Mā′qolagyilis[37] and Tlāk·oalitl (= Copper in the House).[38] He gave him many coppers and the dancing mask, Tsōnō′k·oa.[39] In addition he gave him three wooden kettles[40] which

---

32. This name is likely xʷílisagila (DSS).

33. This name is possibly čáqʷulis 'drifting away' (AD; DSS).

34. This name is recognized as q̓íx̣λala (DSS).

35. This place name is recognized as x̣áwagis 'place of loons,' applied to Simoon Sound, north of Echo Bay, on the west side of Gilford Island (AD).

36. This is q̓ʷúmugʷi, a Chief of the Sea, the most powerful being in the ocean who rules over all the underwater creatures, and is also referred to as "Wealthy One," and "Copper Maker." He bestows wealth and supernatural powers on selected individuals (DSS; AD).

37. Recognized as máxʷəlagilis 'potlatching all over the land' (DSS; AD)

38. This name is ƛ'áqʷaʔił 'copper in house' (DSS; AD).

39. The dzúnuq̓ʷa (Boas' "Tsōnō′k·oa") is a mythological being, said to be large, stupid, sleepy, and with poor eye sight and hairy hands. The female members, who have pendulous breasts, occasionally visit the villages to steal fish and children, which they carry away in a large basket packed on their back. They are particularly fond of shellfish. In certain circumstances, these beings bestow wealth on select individuals (AD; DSS).

40. The storyteller is referring to a large feast bowl, called łúq̓ʷa, carved to represent the dzúnuq̓ʷa and used on ceremonial occasions (DSS; AD).

represented the Tsōnō′k·oa, the Ak·ē·tl (= Open Mouth in the House)[41] and the monster, Ts′ē′kic.[42] He gave him a house with many platforms and told him to give skins to all the people and to dance the T′ā′ēk·āmē[43] in the winter dance. When he returned, he thought that he had been away for only two days. But in reality it had been two years. He returned to Kumkumleqa′tē[44] and gave a big feast.

1a. Tlā′tlaqoas

Tlā′tlaqoas built himself a salmon weir in Sikyamā′s.[45] The first day a silver salmon[46] was caught in it. During the night, Raven and a Tsōnō′k·oa came to steal it, but they were both caught in the trap. The following day, the K·′ōma (a legendary monster resembling the shark)[47] was caught in the weir. Tlā′tlaqoas tried to kill it by hitting it on the head, but before he succeeded, it killed many of his companions. When it was dead, Tlā′tlaqoas pulled it ashore and cut open its belly. Then he saw that its intestines were like fire. He cut them up and dried them. From then on he caught anything he wanted very easily.

One day he went out to harpoon salmon, he saw a small white fish and harpooned it swimming in the water. He wanted to drag it ashore, but found it too heavy. The small fish grew and grew and finally was as big as a whale. Then Tlā′tlaqoas knew that he had caught the sī′siutl. He cut his own tongue so that it bled and he spat on the fish. It assumed its real shape at once and Tlā′tlaqoas fell down as though dead when he saw it. The sī′siutl dived into the deeper water again by swimming as if it were paddling. Then the water began to rise. It reached Tlā′tlaqoas and continued rising up his body and finally swallowed him up completely. He awakened to new life on the bottom of the sea and there found himself surrounded by many sī′siutl people. They took him to their chief who was called Bē′benak·aua (= Deepest)[48] or

---

41. This name is ʔagíɫ (DSS; AD).

42. This name is likely číg{w}is 'seagull under the sea,' derived from cík{w}a 'seagull' (AD).

43. The name of this dance is not now recognized.

44. Boas (1934:69) elsewhere translates this name as 'having noise of thunder'; DSS and AD know this place name as k{w}ə′nk{w}ənligadi and confirm Boas' translation.

45. Likely this is the name that Boas (1934:57, map 10:137) gives elsewhere as "sEk·E′ma′as" 'place where sea beats against a point,' situated on the northwest end of Gilford Island near Cramer Passage—AD and DSS recognize this place name as səkəmás, meaning 'speared in face'.

46. Given in the original as "*Silberlachs*," meaning 'silver salmon'—silver salmon is a folk name for coho salmon (*Oncorhynchus kisutch*).

47. AD and DSS recognize Boas' "K·′ōma" as k̓{w}əmá, the Kwakwala term for 'bullhead.'

48. AD and DSS recognize "Bē′benak·aua" as bíbənagawɛ or bíbənagawalis which they translate as 'the world beneath us,' referring to the "underworld."

Sē′iten[49] and was living in a huge four-platform house. There Sē′iten gave him the small canoe, AitE′mk·aēk·,[50] which had its bow and stern in the shape of a sī′siutl-head. He had Tlā′tlaqoas anointed all over with fat, which made him as hard as stone. Only his forehead, his nose and his throat remained soft. Then he gave him the names T'ē′sumgyilak· (= Turned into Stone) and K·a·k·asuista′listā.[51] He gave him the death-bringer and then sent him back to Sikyamā′s. T'ē′sumgyilak· believed he had been down in the sea for one day, but in reality he had been away a year. When he arrived at the top, the canoe, AitE′mk·aēk·, grew to huge proportions and the fins of the sī′siutl-heads made it go all by itself.

---

49. Sɛ′dən is the Kwakwala pronunciation of "Satan" (DSS; AD).

50. This term is likely ʔaʔítəmkaʔakʷ 'able to go in either direction by itself' (AD; DSS).

51. These names are t'ísəmgil'akʷ 'born to be stone' and a name recognized as possibly kákasustalísta (AD; DSS).

"Then they returned wearing ornamented head bands and dressed in blankets with big neck rings around both shoulders and long strips of red cedar bark and white stripes in the middle" (Rohner 1969:188). Hamatsa dancers with group of women of the Koskimo tribe attending a feast at Fort Rupert, 25 November 1894.

National Anthropological Archives, Smithsonian Institution, Washington, DC
Neg. No. 3946 (O.C. Hastings photo).

XVII. LEGENDS OF THE KWAKIUTL

The Kwakiutl of Fort Rupert became important in Boas' later fieldwork through George Hunt, but these *Sagen* stories came from George Hunt's sister, who was married to Mr. Spencer, a cannery owner at Alert Bay, with whom Boas found lodgings during his first visit of October 1886. Having just stepped ashore after a horrendous small boat trip from the northern tip of Vancouver Island, Boas was handed his mail by Mr. Spencer, and introduced to his family: "I found his wife, whose mother was an Indian, to be very pleasant ... I spent the evening with the family. Mrs. Spencer was very gracious and told me many stories" (Rohner 1969:44). Boas got more stories from Mrs. Spencer subsequently, "the most valuable I received in Alert Bay" (Rohner 1969:46–47). But she was not the only Fort Rupert presence: "There are many Kwakiutl from Fort Rupert here," Boas wrote in a letter of 20 October 1886, "who have been invited to a large potlatch which is to take place soon." That morning he had run into some of them in the village when he went out "to find someone to tell me stories": "I collected two Kwakiutl family histories and then found a woman who related the heroic deeds of the Mink" (Rohner 1969:45). The latter would be the Mink cycle that leads off this section; the "family histories" could be any number of the stories here.

"Next the Koskimo brought blankets and gave them away with appropriate speeches, telling the Kwakiutl that they were nice people and open-handed, etc." (Rohner 1969:178). A composite photograph based on scenes photographed during Boas' own feast held at Fort Rupert, 28 November 1894.

National Anthropological Archives, Smithsonian Institution, Washington, DC
Neg. No. 44726 (O.C. Hastings photo).

XVII. Legends of the Kwā′kiūtl[1]

1. The Mink Legend

1) Once the people were teasing Mink by accusing him of having neither father nor mother. At this he wept and said, "Sun is my father. I will go up to him." But the people laughed at him and said, "How will you get there? The road to the sky is much too long." Mink ran to his uncle, YalamiHomī′k·ē[2] and asked him for his bow and arrows. When he had received them, he shot the first arrow. It hit the sky, the house of Sun. Then he shot the second arrow and it hit the notch of the first one and stuck in it. He continued in this way until a chain was formed which reached from the sky down to the earth. He climbed up along it and reached the house of Sun, where he sat down outside the door. Soon, Sun's slave came out, and when he saw

---

1. "Kwā′kiutl" is Boas' transcription of kʷáguʔł (commonly pronounced today as kʷágɔʔł), anglicized as "Kwakiutl" and meaning 'ancient smoke,' referring collectively to the Fort Rupert tribes, the composition of which has changed over time but includes the following: the wálas kʷágɔʔł 'great kʷágɔʔł'; the q̓ʷə′mk̓utʼis 'rich side'; q̓ʷúmuyuy 'rich in middle' (who became the kʷíxa); and the gʷítəla 'without knowledge, ignorant' (who became the kʷíx̣amut). These tribes were closely identified with each other, before they moved to Fort Rupert. Their winter villages were clustered within a few miles of each other around Turnour Island. They shared salmon fishing rights on the Nimpkish River, and owned eulachon fishing places at the head of Knight Inlet. The origin sites of most of their numayms were along the east coast of Vancouver Island. After the establishment of Fort Rupert in Beaver Harbour near Port Hardy in 1849, these four tribes moved their winter residences to the fort site. Kʷáguʔł territory was delineated along the east coast of Vancouver Island from the vicinity of Songhees Creek (about 5 miles, or 8 km., west from Hardy Bay) to the vicinity of the Nimpkish River, including Malcolm, Cormorant, and Hanson Islands, and portions of Turnour, Harbledown, and West and East Cracroft Islands (Boas 1887f:130–131, map; Curtis 1915:10:307–308; Duff 1965; Bouchard and Kennedy 1998b; Galois 1994). The Fort Rupert Kwakiutl are among the approximately 30 autonomous groups or "tribes" speaking the Kwakwala language and comprising the Kwakwaka'wakw (see also the initial footnote to Section XIV of the present volume).

   Our annotation of this section was assisted greatly in the summer of 2001 by two Kwakwala-speaking experts, Chief Adam Dick and Dr. Daisy Sewid-Smith, who are referred to here as "AD" and "DSS" respectively; we gratefully acknowledge their assistance. This annotation also draws upon our consultation in the 1980s with the following Kwakwala-speaking people, all of whom we thank: Willie Hunt, Maggie Frank, Cecil Wadhams, Charlie Matilpi, and Helen Knox.

2. Name not now recognized.

the boy sitting there, rushed back to his master and said, "Master, your child is sitting outside." So Sun was glad and told his slave to invite Mink inside. When he came in and had settled down by the fire, the old one said, "My heart is glad that you have come, my son. It is getting too hard for me to carry the sun every day because I am old and weak. From now on you shall carry it." He told Mink to bathe and gave him his ear ornament and his nose plug of shiny abalone shells. The father impressed on him not to walk too fast, so that he wouldn't burn the world. The following day he sent Mink out to carry the sun. The father sat in front of the house and watched his son, who obeyed his orders and was climbing slowly up the sky. Towards noon many clouds gathered and blocked Mink's way. He became impatient, pushed the clouds aside and began to run quickly.[3] Then his nose plug shone down upon the earth so bright and hot that the rocks cracked and the water began to boil. When his father saw this, he hurried up, snatched away Mink's nose plug and ear ornament and threw Mink into the sea. A woman who had gone out in her canoe found Mink swimming about on the sea. She took the small body into her canoe and said, "Poor thing, he must have been dead for a long time." Then Mink jumped up, rubbed his eyes and said, "Oh, I believe I have been asleep for a long time."

2) Mink set out to fight the Lâ'lēnoq (ghosts).[4] He crept into the house of their chief and stole his child from the cradle. When the chief of the Lâ'lēnoq noticed his loss, he pursued Mink, but caught up with him only when he had already reached his own house and locked it. Then he begged Mink, "Oh, give me back my child!" But Mink refused until the chief offered him fire as a substitute. This is how people obtained fire.

3) Wolf possessed the tides and kept the water always at the same level. Therefore Tlē'selagyila[5] set out to fight him. He defeated Wolf after a hard fight, cut off his tail, and brought it home with him. There he hung it up over the door. When he lowered it, the water fell and he was able to gather shellfish. When he pulled it up again, the water rose. This is how the tides originated.

4) Once Mink said to his mother, "I'd like to marry now. I will take Frog for a wife." His mother warned him, "Don't do it, or else your wife will make a noise in the house all night." But Mink didn't listen. He went to the Frogs and took one of them as a wife. All day long she was very quiet and, though he often begged her to speak,

---

3. These clouds are Mink's aunts, who his father advised him to treat patiently (DSS; AD).

4. "Lâ'lēnoq" is Boas' rendering of the Kwakwala term lúʔlinux̣ʷ meaning 'ghost' (DSS; AD).

5. "In myths Mink is called Tlē'selagyila = Sun Maker" [Boas' original footnote]. Although AD and DSS recognize this term provided by Boas, x̣'ísəlagila, and agree with his translation ('sun maker'), they more commonly refer to Mink as x̣'ísəlagil'ak̓ʷ 'born to be the sun.'

he was unable to make her talk. But when it grew dark, she began to call out and shout. Mink held his ears and eyes closed and at last died because of the noise made by his wife and her relatives. So the frogs threw him out of the house.

5) After some time, Mink woke up again. He ran to his mother and said, "Mother, I want to marry." She asked, "Who are you going to marry?" "I want to take Kelp for my wife," replied Mink. The mother warned him of Kelp, who submerged with each high tide. But Mink said that he would hold his breath and also submerge. He went to Kelp, presented her with his nose plug and took her for his wife. He said to his wife, "Now let's lie down." Mink embraced her and the flood tide began to run stronger. Then Mink said, "When you submerge, pay attention when I pinch you. I'll be losing my breath and you will have to let go of me." Kelp promised. The tide came in with full force and Kelp submerged. But she didn't let go when Mink pinched her, until she was certain that he was dead. Then she released him and his body drifted about on the waves. He was found there by the people and he woke again to new life. (The long fronds of the kelp are explained as the woman's hair. According to a different version, Mink called Kelp, who had become his wife, to him. Since she didn't come fast enough, he grew very angry and threw her into the sea. Since that time she has lain there with her long hair.)

6) But Mink still wasn't content and wanted to marry Stone (most likely obsidian), because she didn't talk much. One day he asked his wife, "What are you doing there?" She made no answer. Mink, who now grew angry, continued, "Answer me when I'm speaking to you." But stone stayed silent. Thereupon, Mink hit her so hard that his hand was bloodied. "There, you see," he said, "this is what it has come to. Now your face is bleeding." But in reality he had only hurt his own hand.

7) Mink once said to Otter, "I am angry with Hōstā'lakīmō (or Hō'stamitl)[6] and Lâ'lēnoq. Let's go and fight them." Otter agreed and they went out in their canoe. On the way, Mink saw sea urchins on the bottom of the sea, so he jumped into the water and brought some up into the canoe. When Mink was about to eat them all by himself, Otter said, "Why don't you give some of them to me, because I am your friend." Mink replied, "No, you know that when a person is angry with someone, he doesn't give any food away. If you want to have sea urchins, you'll have to dive for them yourself." Otter jumped into the water. While he was below, Mink took his spear and, when Otter came up again, he thrust it into his neck so that it came out again in his chest. Then Mink returned to the shore, relieved himself and transformed his excrement into a young man. Mink ordered him to tell everyone that he was the son of Hō'stamitl and that Mink had abducted him. In order to find out whether he had understood him, Mink asked, "Who are you?" He replied, "I've

---

7.   Name not now recognized.

been made from Mink's excrement." Mink said, "You mustn't say that; you have to say that you are the son of Hō′stamitl." Then when they came to the village, Mink began to shout and cry, and called out, "My friend had set fire to the house of Hō′stamitl and was killed by him." He went ashore with the young man and said that he was the son of Hō′stamitl whom he had enslaved. The people asked him who he might be. He told the truth, so they all became angry with Mink and called out, "What a liar you are! He is not your slave at all; rather, you have made him from your excrement!"

But Otter had a beautiful wife called K·'ōk·ōtsāsemā′lak·a (Merganser serrator).[7] She went down to the beach and there saw Mink. She said to him, "Tell me frankly how my husband lost his life." Mink replied, "Let's go into your house; I'll tell you there." Once inside, he said, "Make all the others leave; I'll have to tell it to you all by yourself." When they were all alone, Mink made her step behind a mat and there he said, "One hit him in the head, another one in the chest, another one in the belly." And he poked her in the corresponding places all the while. But suddenly he embraced her and called out, "No, I have killed him because I desired you for my wife." Then K·'ōk·ōtsāsemā′lak·a took him as her husband.

8) Once Mink's father-in-law went down to the beach and collected many sea urchins while Mink and his wife were still asleep. Then he called him and said that the sea urchins were ready. But Mink maintained that he didn't like to eat sea urchins, so the father-in-law invited all his neighbours to share the sea urchins with him. They all put on their ornaments for the coming feast and Mink also put on his feather head-ornament. Then he said to his wife, "Just see how your father has left the sea urchins in this dirt here! Take them outside the entrance; it's cleaner there." The woman obeyed. But before anyone realized what was happening, Mink ran outside and gobbled up all the sea urchins, at the same time soiling his beautiful feather head-ornament in the dirt. His father-in-law became angry and threw a stone at him because he was so ashamed of his son-in-law.

9) Mink travelled on, looking for a wife, when he was met by Salmon, whom he asked, "Do you want to become my wife?" Salmon consented and transformed into a woman. Once there was a great famine in the village because the salmon hadn't arrived. Salmon Woman[8] was sitting by the fire, picking her teeth. Then she had her husband fetch water and threw what she had found in her teeth into it. Lo and

---

7.   Boas provides the Latin identification (*circa* 1890) for the Red-breasted Merganser. AD recognizes the name of this 'female sawbill duck' (whose Latin identification is now *Mergus serrator*) as gʷəgʷɔ′c̓axsəmálaga.

8.   This character is known as məyúxʷana in legends. When salmon suddenly disappear from an area, the Kwakwaka'wakw say that they have gone to attend the wedding of the daughter of məyúxʷana (AD; DSS).

behold, it was transformed into a salmon! She said to Mink, "You cook it! I don't like it because it is just as if I were to cook my own flesh." When the salmon was done she let her husband eat it, but told him to fling the bones into the fire (as the Indians still do today).[9] Mink did what his wife had told him. Then he asked her, "How do you make salmon?" She didn't want to answer at first, but when he persisted she said, "Don't you know that I belong to the salmon tribe?" So he begged her to create salmon in the river along which the settlement was situated. At first she refused, but after pressing appeals from Mink, she went down to the river, and pulled her hair through the water four times against the current. Thereupon the river swarmed with salmon. Mink became a great chief. But his heart became overly proud now and one day he forgot himself so far as to beat his wife. So she said, "Don't do that again; you know that I come from a different tribe and will not tolerate it." Then Mink wanted to go outside, but several salmon hanging on the drying rack got caught in his hair. He pulled impatiently and they fell to the ground. This angered his wife because he was mistreating her tribe. She left the house and made the salmon follow her. She jumped into the river in front of them and transformed back into a salmon. So Mink was left without salmon and without a wife.

10) The legend how Mink wins the beautiful girl is identical to the one told of Raven below (See Legends of the Awiky'ē′noq.)[10]

2. The Sī′siutl[11]

Once several women went out fishing. Among the fish they caught there was a small fish with beautiful, shiny scales. And because they were very hungry, they cooked it. Only one among them didn't want to eat it, as she didn't know the fish. When the women had eaten the fish, their skin burst and they died. Only the one returned and told what had happened. But she had scarcely finished speaking when she too fell down dead. They had caught the sī′siutl and eaten it.

---

9. Some contemporary Kwakwaka'wakw return salmon bones to the water from which the fish was caught, in the belief that the salmon will be regenerated (AD).

10. The Oowekeeno people of Rivers Inlet; see Section XX, story 1, part 7.

11. 'Double-headed serpent,' sísiyuⱥ (AD; DSS).

3. Tlemạ′ē[12]
(See below among the Legends of the Tlatlasik·oala)[13]

The daughter of a chief was covered all over in boils and at last lost her mind. Thereupon all her relatives abandoned her and, when she regained consciousness, she found herself all alone with a dog. So she wept and scratched her boils so that blood flowed to the ground. Suddenly she noticed that a small hand was growing from her breast. When she looked down, it disappeared again at once. She closed her eyes and in a little while the hand reappeared, only to disappear again as soon as she looked down. This happened three times. So she thought, "I will keep my eyes closed and see what is going to happen." Then she felt how the hand grew out farther and farther and how, finally, a complete human came out. When it had come out entirely, she felt quite healthy again. She called him Tlemạ′ē. He grew up rapidly and said to his mother, "Come, let's go down to the river and build a house from branches." Then he made his mother make him a harpoon. When she gave it to him, he wanted to go down to the river to catch salmon. But there wasn't a single fish in the river. So Tlemạ′e took four pine needles. He threw the first of them into the river and said, "Become a silver salmon!" To the second one he said, "Become a dog salmon." He made a trout from the third one, and from the fourth a "humpback salmon."[14] Thus the river was filled with fish which he then caught (etc., see among the Legends of the Tlatlasik·oala.[15] Then he goes to the Tsonō′k·oa who, in addition to the death-bringer and the water of life, gives all her dancing regalia to him. Then he returns). Tlemạ′e believed that he had been with Tsonō′k·oa four days, but it had been four years in reality. He went back to his mother, but found only her bones because she had died long ago. So he sprinkled her with the water of life. She rubbed her eyes and got up as if she had been asleep for a long time.

After some time Tlemạ′e decided to travel all over the world. He saw seagulls swimming in the sea and called to them, "Where are you going?" They replied, "We're going far away." "Let me come along!" "No, our canoe is no good; its bow goes down too far." So Tlemạ′e called to the geese and asked them where they were going. The geese replied, "We are going to dig roots." "Let me come along." "No, our canoe is loaded too heavily." Then Tlemạ′e called the diver, Cormorant, who in answer to his question replied that he was going far away. "Let me come along." "No, my canoe goes down too far," was his reply. Neither the duck who was going

---

12. This Kwakwala term given by Boas as "Tlemạ′ē" is recognized by AD and DSS as ƛəmáʔi 'something coming from a scab,' derived from ƛəmá 'scab.'

13. See Legends of the Tlatlasikwala, Section XVIII, story 7.

14. Given in English as "Humpbacksalmon" in the original *Sagen*. This is the humpback or pink salmon (*Oncorhynchus gorbuscha*).

15. Tlatlasikwala; see Section XVIII.

to dig for roots,[16] nor the small duck (*Charitonetta albeola*, female)[17] who was moving far away, were able to take him along. Then he asked the Great Diver,[18] who was also travelling far away. He asked Tlema'e where he intended to go. He replied, "I want to visit Gyĭ′k·amē."[19] "What do you want there?" asked the bird. "I want to get a wife." "Fine, then come along with me." They had journeyed for a distance when Diver said, "We shall dive into the sea in a moment. Pinch me when you feel that you are about to suffocate, so that I will let you breathe." Tlema'e did as he was told by the bird and, when they had dived four times, they arrived in the land of Gyĭ′k·amē. They found a pond there and the bird told Tlema'e to hide himself in a hollow trunk. Then he flew away.

Soon the slave of Gyĭ′k·amē came and fetched the trunk in which Tlema'e was hidden, for firewood, and threw it down beside the fire. Gyĭ′k·amē had four daughters and Tlema'e was now able to hear how he scolded the youngest one because she still had no husband, saying to her, "I wish Tlema'e would come and get you." So Tlema'e crept secretly into her chamber. When the girl came in, he made himself known to her and she told him that Gyĭ′k·amē had often told her that he would come. The following morning she went down and told her father that Tlema'e had come and married her. He wouldn't believe it at first, until Tlema'e came down to the fire, himself. He stayed up there for four days, then he asked Gyĭ′k·amē, through his wife, to send him below again. He granted his request. He gave him the water of life and sent him back to earth. Again he found his mother dead and revived her with the water of life. But Tlema'e loved his second wife more than his first one. Therefore the daughter of Tsōnō′k·oa became jealous and wanted to test her strength with the second wife. First she changed her into the bird *Colpates caper saturator*.[20] Then the second wife changed her into a raven. And they tested their strength once more. The daughter of Tsonō′k·oa transformed the daughter of Gyĭ′k·amē into a woodpecker, which then devoured the house posts so that the roof fell in. Thereupon the latter transformed the former into a crow and both of them returned to their homes.

---

16. This duck is likely the Mallard duck (*Anas platyrhynchos*) known as ɫáɫku (AD).

17. Possibly this is the Bufflehead duck (*Bucephala albeola*), known as x̌úbi (AD).

18. This is possibly the Common Loon (*Gavia immer*) known as x̌áwi (AD).

19. Boas' "Gyĭ′k·amē" is the Kwakwala term gígame meaning 'chief; lord; leader' (DSS; AD).

20. This is the former Latin identification for the Common Flicker (*Colaptes cafer*).

4. Wa'walis

(For a more complete version of the legend, see the legends of the Hēiltsuk.[21] and the Bilqula.[22] Here, only the characteristic turns of the legend are given.)

Wa'walis believed that his wife was unfaithful to him. He wanted to find out whether his suspicion was based on fact and therefore said that he was going to be out hunting for a long time. But he came back after only two days and, at night, secretly crept up to his house. He scratched lightly at the wall where his bed was and then heard his wife saying to her lover, "Listen, there's a mouse. I wish it would gnaw at my husband's mask." So Wa'walis knew that his wife was being unfaithful to him. Around midnight he scratched again at the wall and nothing stirred. So he crept inside and cut off the lover's head. He took the head and fled.

After some time the small son of Wa'walis, who slept with them in the bed, felt the blood and started to cry. This awakened the woman's mother who called to her, "Your son is crying." She felt the blood of her lover and, still half asleep, said, "Oh, he's wet the bed." She nudged her lover and said, "Get up and take the boy out of the bed." But he didn't move. In a little while the child wept again and her mother called her again. So she got up and saw that her lover had been decapitated. She wrapped the corpse up in a bear skin and deposited it in front of the house where his parents were living.

Wa'walis returned after several days and he, as well as his wife, pretended that nothing had happened. He went up to the house and told her to get a basket of seal meat, which was standing in the canoe, and cook it. She obeyed, but when she took the meat out, she found her lover's head and shrieked. Thereupon Wa'walis beat her on the head with it and shouted, "That is why you are shrieking, because you can see the skull." Then everyone knew that he had killed the young man. They wanted to catch him, but he escaped. Now the villagers were afraid of him and dug a trench across the point where they were living. Then they pushed it away from the shore and ever since then, the place has been situated on an island in the middle of the sea. But Wa'walis impaled the heads of his enemy and of his wife in front of his house.

21. The Kwakwala name for the aboriginal people of the Bella Bella area is hítdzaqʷ; see Section XXI.
22. The name "Bilqula" refers to the Bella Coola (Nuxalk) people; see Section XXII.

5. ŌmeatlᴇmaꞋē[23]

ŌmeatlᴇmaꞋē had been sent out by his father to collect eggs. When he had filled his basket and was on his way back, he couldn't resist the temptation to eat some. His father noticed, and beat him when he came home. So ŌmeatlᴇmaꞋē ran into the forest. He bathed in all the rivers he came to and washed his cape. At last he came to a mountain and sat down on its summit. He had been sitting there for four days when he heard a whistling noise and a piece of rock crystal (which is used by shamans) fell against his head. In this way he obtained the ability to fly. But in reality he had been on the mountain for four years. He flew back home and alighted in the village path. The people tried to catch him there with big baskets, but were unsuccessful. At last they erected a plank on top of his house. He alighted on it and changed back into a man.

The following day he went out with some women to collect roots. He steered the canoe and when they were on their way back in the evening, he caused it to capsize. He sank into the sea and sank even deeper into the ocean floor. There he met many people, many of whom had no heads. They were dancing the TsētsāꞋēk·a[24] and promised him one of the rings of inner cedar bark and one of the designs which they used for painting themselves. First he saw the HámatsꞋa[25] dancing. The people asked him, "Would you like to have it?" He declined. Then he saw the Nūtlematl[26] dancing. He didn't take this one, either, but asked for the LolōꞋtlalatl, the dance of the lâlenoq,[27] and the spirits gave it to him. Then he rose up to the upper world again. When he got there, the people were sitting in his house, beating time. So he danced the LolōꞋtlalatl.

---

23. DSS recognizes Boas' "ŌꞋmeatlᴇmē" as ʔúʔmaλəmɛ, a term that AD pronounces as ʔúʔmagəmɛ—the meaning of both terms relates to a 'high-class noble person' (AD; DSS).

24. Boas' "TsētsāꞋēk·a" is ćíćɛqa 'winter dance' (AD; DSS) consisting of a complicated series of ceremonials held in the winter which include the initiation of young people into secret societies and feasting (Boas 1966:173–174; DSS).

25. DSS explains that while hámaċa (Boas' "HámatsꞋa") is known commonly as the "cannibal dancer," the dancer is being captured so that the cannibalistic spirit can be exorcized from his body.

26. Boas' term "Nūtlematl" is recognized as núɬəmaɬa, 'fool dancer.' At the beginning of the winter dance, a man wearing this big-nosed mask acts as a clown by pretending to be silly and throws around the mucus from his constantly-runny nose (AD).

27. The dance known as ləlúɬɬaɬ (Boas' "LolōꞋtlalatl") is derived from the Kwakwala term lúʔlinuxʷ 'ghost.' AD and DSS add that ghosts do not like to be called by the term lúʔlinuxʷ and prefer instead the name háyaɬilagas.

6. Qa'nalk·[28]

In Kwakiū'tis[29] (near Fort Rupert) there lived Qa'nalk·, who was descended from the Nak·o'mgyilisala[30] and the K·osk·ī'mō.[31] He had a wife called Nā'lagilikya[32] and a son called Nā'lak·anuk.[33] One day the boy went to play by the small river rushing past the house. While he was hopping about, four Wolves came suddenly from the forest and began to play with him, but in the process they tore his shirt and his cape. When he got home his mother asked him who had torn his clothes. He replied, "Eagles came and tore my shirt and cape." In the deep of the night, when everyone was asleep, the wolves came. They broke into the house, took the boy, who was sleeping between the parents, on their backs and ran away into the land of the wolves. The following morning the parents didn't know what had become of their son and thought that he was dead. But the wolves gave him the daughter of the chief of their tribe for a wife and he remained with them for two years. Then hair started to grow on his back, just where his wife always held him in her embrace.

He started to long for his parents. His wife knew his thoughts and asked her father, the chief of the wolves, to allow the young man to return to his home. She, herself, intended to remain with the wolves. The chief agreed and sent out his slave, NE'mtsaqtsis,[34] who consisted of only half of a body, in order to call together all the wolves. He was so fast that he had complied with the order before a stone, which had been hurled by the chief, hit the ground. When all the wolves had assembled, he told them to carry home the young man, whom he gave the name Nūn.[35] They obeyed. The young man stood on the back of the biggest of the wolves and they sang while they were taking him away at a quick trot, "We run and jump and carry our young brother, the young man. And Nūn is the name we have given to him."

---

28.   "Qa'nalk·" is recognized as gʷánəlkʷ (AD; DSS).

29.   Boas' "Kwakiū'tis" is gʷáƙudis, meaning 'downstream on opposite side of river' (DSS; AD).

30.   This refers to the nəqə'mgilisala, anglicized as "Nakomgilisala"; see Section XIX.

31.   What Boas transcribes here as "K·ōskī'mō" is gʷúsgimukʷ (AD; DSS), anglicized as "Koskimo," the name of the tribe who originated at the mouth of the Stranby River (also known as "Cache Creek") which empties into Shuttleworth Bight, west from Cape Sutil near the northern tip of Vancouver Island (Dawson 1888:68; Shotridge and Shotridge 1913:77; Curtis 1915:10:306; Wallas and Whitaker 1981:18–20,208; Wallas, in Galois 1994:367–371).

32.   This name is recognized as nálagiliga, derived from the word nála 'daylight' (AD; DSS) (see the footnote that follows).

33.   This name is nálagənakʷ, also derived from nála 'daylight' (AD; DSS) (see the footnote that precedes).

34.   AD and DSS know this character as nə'mċaxsis and explain that his name translates as 'one foot' (AD; DSS).

35.   Boas (1948:237) elsewhere provides this same transcription, "Nūn," and the translation 'myth name of wolf.'

When Nūn had returned to his father, the latter decided to go to Qō'yalis.[36] They met many enemies on their way, and the father didn't know what to do to escape them. But Nūn had only to rub his eyes and wave his hands in their direction, whereupon they fell asleep, and then they killed all of them. But they loaded their enemies' daughters into their canoe and took them along to Qō'yalis. The son of Nūn was called K·ak·ā'qoatEla.[37] When Nūn gave him his name, Nūn invited all the neighbours for a big feast and gave all his slaves to them. Then he returned home.

7. Kwu'lekum (= The Deaf One)[38]

Kwu'lekum was a chief in K·ā'lōkuis.[39] He was a miser and, when he was asked to give blankets away, pretended not to hear or else said, "No, first you have to give a potlatch, then I will hold one, too." So the other chiefs gave feasts in turn, but when Kwu'lekum's turn came, he refused; he gave no feast and distributed no blankets. Thereupon they all became angry and Chief K·ē'Hustâla (Deer)[40] took a copper, smashed it on the head of Kwu'lekum and thus killed him. In one of the dances a mask representing this chief is used. It is called Kwu'lekumqumtl.[41]

8. Baqbakuā'latlē (= He Who First Ate Humans on the Water)[42]

Once upon a time there was a woman who had married the water spirit, Baqbakuā'latlē, and was living with him in a lake. They had a son who was given his father's name. When he grew up he killed anyone he met, ripped out their eyes and roasted them in the ashes. When they burst, he was glad and shouted, "Ho! Ho! How the eyes are popping." Then he flung them into his basket. And he cut off the slain peoples' fingers, toes and ears and collected them in separate baskets. In this way he had killed everyone with the exception of his uncle and the latter's son. But he was also longing for their blood, and one evening he seized his spear and hurled it at his uncle, who was standing in a dark corner of the house. He missed and the

36. It is not clear what place Boas is referring to here as "Qō'yalis."

37. This name is not now recognized.

38. This is gʷə'lkʷəm 'deaf' (AD; DSS).

39. "K·ā'lōkuis" is Boas' rendering of qáluɡʷis (anglicized as "Karlukwees"), the name of a village on the south end of Turnour Island (Boas 1934:73 map 14:75; AD; DSS).

40. Boas' "K·ē'Hustâla" is gíxustula, a Kwakwala name for 'Deer' in legends (AD; DSS).

41. What Boas renders as "Kwu'lekumqumtl" is known to DSS as gʷə'lkʷəmgamł meaning 'deaf mask'; the mask worn by this individual has only one ear (DSS).

42. DSS translates the term bákʷbakʷalaƛɛ (Boas' "Baqbakuā'latlē") as 'he who eats humans on the water' (DSS).

uncle thereupon took his spear and thrust it into the left breast of Baqbakuā′latlē. He escaped, badly wounded. The uncle said to his wife, "You stay here; I will follow him and finish him off." He followed the trail of blood and finally arrived at a lake. There he found the young man about to die. Diver[43] was at his side, trying to heal him. The uncle walked up to him and said, "See, you wanted to kill me, but now you'll have to die yourself." While he was lifting his spear for the fatal thrust, the young man begged him for a short respite. He said, "Don't kill me yet; I want to give all my treasures to you first." He told him where he kept them hidden, then his uncle killed him and burned the corpse. When he blew into the ashes, these were transformed into mosquitoes. The finest ashes turned into the smallest flies ("sunflies"[44] and blackflies).[45]

9. BaqbakuālanuQsī′uaē
(= He Who First Ate Humans at the River Mouth)[46]

Once Nā′noak·aua (= Wisest)[47] went into the mountains to hunt for mountain goats. Suddenly he came to a house which he had never seen before. A woman called K·ōminâ′k·a[48] stood outside its door and called to him to enter. She was the daughter of the spirit of the mountains, K·ō′mō′k·oē, and her husband was the cannibal, BaqbakuālanuQsī′uaē. Nā′noak·aua was afraid to come any closer, but when she said, "Come here and I will delouse you," he approached and allowed her to take his head between her hands. But thereupon she pressed him to the ground and shouted, BaqbakuālanuQsī′uaē, come and devour him!" He tried vainly to get up. But when he heard the cannibal rushing up, bellowing loudly, he pulled free, but had to leave all his hair behind in the woman's hands. Then he ran as fast as his legs would carry him. BaqbakuālanuQsī′uaē pursued him, now above ground, now below ground. Thereupon Nā′noak·aua created a huge forest behind himself so that the cannibal

---

43. DSS notes this is more likely the Common Loon (*Gavia immer*) which is known as x̱áwi.

44. Given in quotation marks in English in the original *Sagen*. The insects into which the ashes transformed are all blood-sucking (DSS).

45. In a version of this story published by Boas (1888j:56) in "Songs and Dances of the Kwakiutl," he adds the following: "Then he went to search for his nephew's treasures, and when he found the baskets, filled with the ears, fingers, toes, and with the fried eyes, he became a cannibal himself."

46. DSS points out that the original Kwakwala term (Boas' "BaqbakuālanuQsī′uaē") was pronounced bəkʷbákʷalanukʷsiwi, best translated as 'having a cannibal at the mouth of the river,' but in more recent times has been pronounced bákʷbakʷalanukʷsiwiʔ.

47. The name nə′nwaqawi, transcribed here by Boas as "Nā′noak·aua," is derived from the Kwakwala term núgad 'wise' (AD; DSS).

48. Boas' "K·ōminâ′k·a" is recognized by AD and DSS as q̓ʷúminuwagas, the woman who assists the cannibal to get food.

was only able to follow very slowly. Nā'noak·aua arrived safely at home, but he had scarcely closed the door behind himself when BaqbakuālanuQsī'uaē arrived. Nā'noak·aua called to him, "Go and get your wife! I have four children whom I will give you to eat." He went to fetch his wife and in the meantime Nā'noak·aua dug a deep pit, made a fire in it, and threw stones on the fire. Then he killed a slave and cut him into pieces. He made his children hide outside the house and he covered the pit with boards which could be pulled away from outside.[49] When BaqbakuālanuQsī'uaē and K·ōminâ'k·a arrived, Nā'noak·aua made them sit down on the boards and then served to them the cut-up slave. Before the beginning of the meal, BaqbakuālanuQsī'uaē danced and his wife beat time. He danced in a squatting stance; his hands were trembling and he stretched his arms alternately right and left.[50] He was getting impatient to eat the slave. Then, on a given signal, the children pulled away the boards and man and wife fell into the fire and burned. The fire in the pit flamed up high and their fat sizzled. Nā'noak·aua blew into the ashes and they were transformed into mosquitoes.

10. MātE'm[51]

A young man was trifling away all his time with his lover, but in spite of his mother's urging, he wouldn't agree to marry her. Therefore his mother was angry with him. One evening he came home from his lover and asked his mother for something to eat. But she said, "Why don't you go where you've just come from and ask for food there? You won't get anything from me." So the young man became sad. He went to bed and stayed in it for four days, without food or drink. His mother grew afraid and begged him to get up, but he wouldn't listen to her. So she called her son's lover and asked her to use her influence on the young man to make him get up. But he didn't listen to the entreaties of his lover. At last, on the fourth day, he got up and went into the forest without knowing where he was going. He had lost his mind. Finally he came to a lake. He threw off his clothes, swam in the lake and dived. He stayed under for a long time. When he rose to the surface again, a totem

---

49. This chief's seat could be made to collapse so that the guests would fall back into the pit once the back board was pulled aside (DSS).

50. The storyteller describes the hand and body motions of a cannibal dancer.

51. Boas (1897:483–484) writes elsewhere that the "mātE'm" (mádəm) is a mythological bird who lives high in the mountains and bestows crystals as a gift that endows recipients with the ability to fly. The "mātE'm" dancer appears naked, except for a headdress of five pieces of wood covered with mica that is cut to resemble hexagonal prisms. While AD and DSS do not necessarily recognize mádəm as a bird, they do acknowledge it as the bringer of crystals that provide the ability to fly. A song describes how crystals fell from the mountain and hit a young man's head, giving him this power (AD; DSS).

pole rose up with him. So he said, "I don't want you." And he thought, "I will wander on now." He did so and after some time came to a lake again. He swam and dived again. He brought a seal harpoon up from this lake, but didn't take it either. He knew that the MātE'm, a beautiful bird, was living in the forest and he wanted to find it. He came to a third lake and, after he had bathed and dived in it, too, he knew that he would find the house of the bird. When he had put on his cape again he spied the bird, which now kept flying ahead of him. The man threw off his cape in order to be able to follow it more quickly, and finally the bird asked him, "What do you want from me?" The young man answered, "I searched for you. My mother mistreated me, so I am looking for your help." Thereupon the bird replied, "Do you see that mountain? My house is there. Let's climb up." He continued to fly on ahead and the young man followed him. On the mountain the bird MātE'm gave the rock-crystal and many beautiful things to him. The bird put the stone into the young man's joints and in this way he obtained the ability to fly. It sent him on to Mount Ts'E'lkyimpaē[52] to get bird feathers for himself. It was raining, snowing and hailing when the young man got there, but he carried on regardless. The people living there were keeping a big fire going in order to be able to see any stranger, so that they might catch him at once. But he managed to fly past without being seen, by virtue of the stone, and was able to obtain feathers. Then he had obtained the ability to transform himself into a bird. He now flew back to his home village. When his little brother saw the beautiful bird, he put out a snare to catch it. The bird slipped it on himself, because he wanted to be caught. He assumed human shape again. He had now become a mighty shaman. His father had his house swept and the young man danced in the evening. Then the bird MātE'm flew up and dropped down a totem pole which embedded itself in front of the house.

11. WalasnEmō'k·ois (= Great Only One)[53]

WalasnEmō'k·ois came down to earth from the sun and built himself a house in Tsā'qis (Fort Rupert).[54] Ōm'aqtā'latlē[55] was his son. He saw many seals and sea otters

---

52. DSS recognizes Boas' "Ts'E'lkyimpaē" as c̓ə'lkəmba?yi 'feathers on the face,' the name of a mountain located in the vicinity of the Nimpkish Valley.

53. This is wálas nəmúkʷg̊ʷis which means 'the great one who lives alone' (DSS).

54. The place name cáx̣is (given here by Boas as "Tsā'qis") is applied to the beach in front of Fort Rupert Indian Reserve No. 1 in Beaver Harbour. While Boas (1934:60, map 6:135) elsewhere transcribes the same term as "tsā'x̣is" and translates it as 'stream running on beach,' DSS and AD understand the name as referring to the small, shuffling step of the Long-billed Dowitcher (*Limnodromus scolopaceus*), known as c̓ásx̣əwiqʷ, that can frequently be seen in this area.

55. This name is ?úm̓ax̣t'alaλε (DSS; AD).

on K·'ā′msiqtlē (Shell Island),[56] so he took a driftwood tree trunk, which he used as a canoe and went over and caught them. Then he gave a big feast and gave everyone a gift of otter skins and seal oil. Then he went on to GyōkH[57] and ascended the river discharging there. He met there the spirit of the forest, Mā′kakyū,[58] who gave him a canoe. Then Ōm'aqtā′latlē turned east and, in the country of the Mamalēlēk·a′la,[59] met K·a′watilek·ala.[60] He invited him to come along to his home, the country of the TsāwatEē′noq.[61] Ōm'aqtā′latlē followed him and there was given Häaqk·olā′tlemak·a,[62] the daughter of K·a′watilek·ala, for his wife. His father-in-law gave him a big house. Its roof beams were double-headed serpents (sī′siutl). Then he moved with his wife to Gy'ā′k·a (near Fort Rupert)[63] and there built a house. The two posts in front of his house represent two men: Yē′k·'ent'Ek·a (Something that Speaks Inside)[64] and Wawēqēmitl (the Speaker).[65] The rear posts are also men: Lēqē′laqsta (the Boastful One)[66] and Hasak·awā′sui (He Who Tries to be Louder Than All Others).[67] The two

56. Boas' "K·'ā′msiqtlē" is recognized by AD and DSS as q̓ə́ndzəqλe 'chiton shells (plates) on top,' derived from q̓ánas 'chiton.' Elsewhere, Boas (1934:73, map 6:123, 6a:53) applies this name, "q!E′msex·La" 'shells on top,' to the islet known as Shell Island, in Beaver Harbour, adjacent to Fort Rupert.

57. The place name that Boas transcribes here as "GyōkH" is giyúx̣ʷ which applies to the stream that flows through "Keogh" (anglicized from giyúx̣ʷ) Indian Reserve No. 6, southeast of Beaver Harbour, near Fort Rupert (AD; DSS).

58. What Boas renders as "Mā′kakyū" is mákagiyu 'forest spirit' (AD; DSS).

59. Boas' "Ma′malelek·ala" is mámaliliqla, anglicized as "Mamalilikulla," referring to the people of Village Island and the adjacent islands who are said to have originated in the Beaver Harbour area. While mámaliliqla territory was centred on Village Island, they also lived in an area extending along the north shore of Knight Inlet as far as Matsiu Creek, as well as at a place near Turnour Island, and at White Beach, and at the end of Malcom Island (DSS; AD).

60. This is q̓áwadiliqəla which means 'the first born of the wolves' and is applied to a numaym of the Kingcome Inlet people (AD).

61. Boas' "TsāwatEē′noq" is dzawadeʼʔnux̣ʷ (AD; DSS), anglicized as "Tsawatainuk," referring to the Kingcome Inlet people. The term dzawadeʼʔnux̣ʷ has been translated by Boas (1966:40) as 'people of olachen place,' and by Duff (1953–1954) as 'know how to handle eulachons.' Boas' (1887f) map centred Tsawatainuk territory in Kingcome Inlet but included much of Tribune Channel as well as the northern portion of Gilford Island.

62. Possibly this term means 'leaning together' (DSS).

63. "Gy'ā′k·a," recognized as k̓áq̓a by AD and DSS, is likely the same place name given elsewhere as "k·!āq!a" 'logs laid crosswise on rock' by Boas (1934:67, map 6a:10), referring to a site on the east side of Beaver Harbour.

64. The term that Boas renders as "Yē′k·'ent'Ek·a" is recognized as yeʼq̓ənt'iq̓a by AD, who confirms Boas' translation 'Something that Speaks Inside.'

65. The name given by Boas as "Wawēqēmitl (the Speaker)" is not now recognized.

66. Boas' "Lēqē′laqsta (the Boastful One)" is not now recognized.

67. The name transcribed by Boas as "Hasak·awā′sui" is recognized as hásaqawasəwi by AD, who confirms Boas' translation 'He Who Tries to be Louder Than All Others.'

front posts support the longitudinal beams, which represent the sī′siutl, while the rear posts are covered with a cross-beam which represents a sī′siutl (or wolf ?). The door of the house is hinged at the top and anyone not running out quickly enough is killed by it. The dancing-mask of WalasnEmō′k·ois is a wolf worn on the head and called Ō′likyen.[68] The dance, given to him by K·a′watilek·ala is called Walas'aqā′ (something big given from above).[69] After he had completed the house, he gave a big feast and all the posts and beams became alive. The sī′siutl began to move their tongues and the men standing in the back of the house told them when a bad man entered. Then the sī′siutl killed him at once.

12. SE′ntlaē

SE′ntlaē, the sun,[70] descended to the earth in the shape of a bird, transformed into a man and built himself a house in Yik·'āmen.[71] From there he wandered to K·ō′moks,[72] then visited the Tlau′itsis,[73] the NE′mkic,[74] the Nā′k·oartok·,[75] and finally came to Tliksī′uaē [76] in the country of the Kwākiūtl, where he settled in

---

68. Boas' "Ō′likyen" is ʔulígən, the common Kwakwala name for 'wolf' (DSS; AD).

69. AD and DSS recognize Boas' "Walas'aqā′" as the dance known as wálas sáx̣aʔakʷ and confirm Boas' translation 'something big given from above.' An illustration of this dance appears in Boas (1897:476). The male dancers dress in blankets and wear headdresses representing the wolf. After making three circuits of the house, they squat down on hands and feet, imitating the motions of wolves (AD; DSS).

70. Sísənx̣̓i (given by Boas later in this same paragraph as "Sī′sintlē") is the name of the numaym founded by sə′nx̣̓i (Boas' "SE′ntlaē"), who came from the sun (DSS). Elsewhere, Boas (1897:330) gives sísənx̣̓i as the name for one of the numayms of the Kwakiutl of Fort Rupert.

71. Boas (1934:39, map 15:136) suggested elsewhere that "Yik·'āmen" might be a misprint for "x̣ēq!amen," the name applied to Blenkinsop Bay near Port Neville. This is confirmed by the fact that DSS knows Blenkinsop Bay as x̣íqaman (Boas' "x̣ēq!amen"), and by our own recording of this same place name in the 1970s–1980s as x̣íqamin with Mary Clifton (who spoke both Comox and Kwakwala), and as x̣íqam with Jim Henderson (who spoke Kwakwala). This latter term, x̣íqam, was also recorded as the name for Blenkinsop Bay by Wilson Duff (1953–1954) from Mungo Martin, a Kwakwala speaker—both Mungo Martin and Jim Henderson stated that x̣íqam was a Comox Coast Salish word.

72. Q̇ʷúmuʔqs (derived from q̇ʷúmuɬa 'wealth; plenty'), anglicized as "Comox," is the Kwakwala name for Comox Harbour (DSS; AD).

73. Boas' "Tlau′itsis" is the tribal name ɬáwičis, anglicized as "Tlawitsis" (DSS; AD) (see "One Legend of the Tlauitsis" at the end of the present section).

74. "NE′mkic" is the tribal name nə′mgis, anglicized as "Nimpkish" (DSS; AD) (see Section XV).

75. Boas' "Nā′k·oartok·" is the tribal name nák̓ʷaxdaʔx̣ʷ, anglicized as "Nakwaktak" (DSS; AD).

76. "Tliksī′uaē, clover roots at the mouth of a river" [Boas' original footnote]. DSS and AD recognize Boas' "Tliksī′uaē" as ƛəksíwi (anglicized as "Cluxewe") which is derived not from the term for 'clover roots' but from the Kwakwala word ƛəxsə′m 'cinquefoil; silverweed' (*Potentilla*

K·'ai'oq.[77] He took a wife from each tribe and his numaym has the name Sī'sintlē. He decided to stay in Tliksī'uaē and took a wife from the Kwā'kiūtl tribe. By her he had a son, called Tsqtsqâ'lis. Each side of his house has a big sun painted on it, while the posts of the house are men carrying suns. They were the slaves of SE'ntlae and are called Lōlō'qt'otpes.[78] The crossbeams above the posts also represent men; the longitudinal beams represent sea-lions. The steps to the house are three men, called Tlē'nonis.[79] In the winter dance the sī'sintle use the mask Tlē'selak·umtl, the sun mask;[80] in the dance yā'wiqa,[81] the dog mask, kuloqsâ',[82] who is supposed to have come down from the sky with SE'ntlaē (the name is supposed to mean: 'the sun shining red through the clouds'). The totem pole of the Sī'sintlē represents a number of coppers one above the other. Above them is a man called Lā'qt'otpes[83] (singular of Lōlō'qt'otpes; the name is supposed to signify: He who only gives to strangers), who is raising his arm for a speech; at the top is the sun mask encircled by rays.

13. Haialikyā'wē [84]

Haialikyā'wē was standing on a hill in Tliksī'uaē[85] where his house was. He was a mighty shaman and knew everything that would happen in the future. He said to his people, "Let us cover up our house because a great deluge will come and flood everything." The men followed his advice and covered the house. They had scarcely finished when the sea began to rise and covered all the lands, but they were sitting out of harm's way in their house. They lit a fire and the smoke rose up through the water. The flood covered the earth for one year. Then Haialikyā'wē sent his talisman

---

pacifica) (Turner and Bell 1973:189; DSS; AD). This name, ƛəksíwe, applies to the area at the mouth of the Cluxewe River which flows into Broughton Strait, west of Port McNeill (Boas 1934:81, map 8:26).

77. Name not now recognized.

78. Name not now recognized.

79. Name not now recognized.

80. DSS confirms that "Tlē'selak·umtl" is ƛ'ísəlagamł 'sun mask.'

81. Name not now recognized.

82. Name not now recognized.

83. Name not now recognized.

84. The name that Boas renders here as "Haialikyā'wē" is háyalik̓əwi, derived from hílika meaning 'to heal' (AD; DSS).

85. As previously noted, "Tliksī'uaë" is ƛəksíwi, referring to the area at the mouth of the Cluxewe River which flows into Broughton Strait, west of Port McNeill (Boas 1934:81, map 8, 26).

to Kuēkuaqā'oē (see Legends of the Awiky'ē'noq)[86] who had caused the flood, and asked him to make the waters recede again, promising to give him his daughter as a reward. Kuēkuaqā'oē made the waters recede and travelled in his sī'siutl-canoe to Haialikyā'wē. When he arrived and wanted to have the girl for his wife, Haialikyā'wē gave him a skull which was supposed to be his wife. But Kuēkuaqā'oē insisted on having the girl and in addition demanded the head-band of red inner cedar bark which Haialikyā'wē wore in the dance. At last Haialikyā'wē had to give him his daughter, and he gave one half of his head-band to him. When Kuēkuaqā'oē also demanded his canoe, he agreed, provided that he would get the sī'siutl-canoe in return. Thus they exchanged canoes. Kuēkuaqā'oē said, "Take care and use my canoe correctly, otherwise it will transform you." With this he left. The sī'siutl-canoe was made of copper. It went all by itself, without being paddled, over sea and land, and was collapsible. Haialikyā'wē thought, "I will cut it up and make coppers from it. But first I will see how it runs." He jumped in and called, "I want to go to Mount Ts'i'lkyimpaē (= Feathers on Top)." It is situated far to the north, and feathers and quartz, which are used by the shamans, are found here. His canoe went north for four days. Then it reached Mount Ts'i'lkyimpaē. Haialikyā'wē collected feathers and stones and returned home.

He saw many seals on his way. So he said to the canoe, "How can I kill the seals?" It replied, "Take feathers and throw them at them." Haialikyā'wē didn't believe that he would be able to kill them this way, but at last followed the canoe's advice. The feathers flew straight at the seals and killed enough of them to fill the canoe. He loaded the canoe and then called to it, "Start up!" But the canoe didn't budge from the spot. So Haialikyā'wē looked down at it and asked, "Why don't you start when I tell you to?" It replied, "For whom did you kill the seals?" He retorted, "For myself. I want to take them home." The canoe replied, "But no! You have to give them to me. My father always killed seals for me and fed them to me." "How shall I feed you?" "Just throw them overboard!" Haialikyā'wē obeyed and the canoe devoured all the seals. Then they went to Ts'āwa'tē (Olachen Place).[87] He didn't meet with a friendly reception here and therefore asked his canoe, "Can't you cause another flood?" It replied, "Yes, I can, because I am the power of Kuēkuaqā'oē, my father." And a new flood came, in which all the people perished except one who had climbed onto Mount Nō'lē.[88]

---

86. The Oowekeeno people, although the Kwakwaka'wakw refer to the Owekeeno as k̯ʷík̯ʷax̣awi, derived from the term k̯ʷíx̣a meaning 'to plan to do something' (DSS) (See Section XX, story 1, part 1).

87. What Boas transcribes here as "Ts'āwa'tē" is dzáwadi 'having eulachons,' a place at the mouth of the Klinaklini River at the upper end of Knight Inlet (AD; DSS; Boas 1934:23, 59). Boas uses the English spelling "olachen" here in the *Sagen*.

88. "Nō'lē" is recognized by AD and DSS as núla, which Boas (1934: map 5:92) elsewhere identifies as a mountain on the west side of Neroutsos Inlet in the Quatsino Sound area—likely this is a reference to Mount Clark.

Haialikyā'wē went on and arrived at GyīŌ'kH (= house, winter village, four kilometres east of Fort Rupert).[89] There he found a man on the beach who asked him his name. When he learned it, he said, "Haialikyā'wē is a shaman's name." "Yes, I am a shaman," replied Haialikyā'wē. "Then demonstrate your power and transform this stone into a salmon," said the man. Haialikyā'wē threw the stone into the water and it became a salmon right away. Then he asked the stranger, "Who are you? Are you a shaman?" "Yes," he retorted, "my name is Haialikyumgyilis,"[90] and, to demonstrate his power, he transformed Haialikyā'wē into a diver.[91] They both transformed each other into birds four times. Then Haialikyumgyilis said to Haialikyā'wē, "My friend, I can see that you are a shaman. Come into my house, I want to entertain you." They went inside. He took some fish from the box and roasted it beside the fire. It was very fat and looked good. Now Haialikyā'wē started to sing and sang about everything that was going to happen. Haialikyumgyilis then put the roasted fish into a bowl and served it to his guest. As soon as the guest touched it, all his limbs became distorted and he died. Thereupon his canoe went back to Kuēkuaqā'oē. Haialikyā'wē had known all this in advance.

14. Deer and Bear

Once BEtya', Deer,[92] married Nē'nEnk·as, Bear Woman.[93] They had one son called D'ā'pis[94] and several daughters. Once BEtya' and his son D'ā'pis went out to catch seals. They brought their catch home and cooked the seal-blood in a big wooden box. Then BEtya' gave the cooked blood to his daughters to eat and they all died of it. When Nē'nEnk·as came home and found all her children dead, she became angry. She pursued BEtya' and D'ā'pis, who fled, and, in her rage, she smashed everything in her way. At last they fled from the village. BEtya' and D'ā'pis escaped to the forest and asked all the trees, "Do your roots reach deep into the ground?" They all replied, "Go north, there you will find the yew-tree. Its roots go deep into the ground." So they both ran on toward the north. Finally they came to

---

89. As previously noted, the place name that Boas transcribes here as "GyŌkH" is giyúx̣ʷ which applies to the stream that flows through "Keogh" (anglicized from giyúx̣ʷ) Indian Reserve No. 6, southeast of Beaver Harbour, near Fort Rupert (AD; DSS).

90. This shaman's name, háyalikəmgilis, means 'healing all over the land' (AD; DSS).

91. Likely this is the Common Loon (*Gavia immer*), as that bird is associated with healing (AD; DSS).

92. This is an old term used for 'Deer' in Kwakwaka'wakw mythology (AD; DSS).

93. AD and DSS note that Grizzly Bear Woman was known as níʔnənga(s) (Boas' "Nē'nEnk·as").

94. This character, t'ápis, appears in other stories where it is identified as a deer, rather than the son of a deer and a bear (DSS; AD).

Ts'ōtlnaqsī'uaē,[95] where they found the yew tree and climbed up. Nē'nɛnk·as pursued the fugitives and asked all the trees where they had gone. But they didn't reply to her question and mocked Bear Woman. This made her furious and she pushed them over. At last she got to the yew-tree, and when this mocked her also, she wanted to push it over. But she didn't succeed because the tree was rooted too deeply in the ground. So she began digging in order to push it over and, when she was digging deeper, the hole filled with water. Then she saw the reflection of Bɛtya' and D'ā'pis and jumped into the water in order to kill them. Then Bɛtya' called the cold wind, Yu'yalanuk,[96] and the water froze at once and trapped Bear Woman. So Bɛtya' and D'ā'pis descended from the tree, heaped wood on top of Bear Woman, lit it, and that is how she lost her life.

One Legend of the Tlauitsis[97]

Nōmas (= Old One),[98] the brother of Ōmeatl,[99] invited him and all the neighbouring tribes for a huge feast (see Legends of the Tlatlasik·oala[100]). He served berries to them from a big carved spoon and danced at the same time with his elbows pressed to his sides and his fingers lifted up. Since the fire wasn't bright enough, he told Ōmeatl to pour oil into it, and now the fire flared up so high that it caught the roof. Nōmas made his guests go up and put the fire out. Then he made his brother throw two slaves into the fire. When they had been burned, he threw two large canoes, two coppers, ten marten skins, ten otter skins, and one hundred mountain goat skins, into the fire. Thus he became a great chief. Then he made Ōmeatl pour a bladder full of fish oil into the fire. The oil covered the floor of the house completely. It rose so much that the people were forced to swim in it. The fire caught the roof and many

---

95. This place is known as čúłnaqsiwi, derived from čúłna 'charcoal' (DSS; AD). Boas (1934:62; 1935:115) elsewhere identifies this site as "a mythical place to which all charcoal drifts."

96. Boas' "Yu'yalanuk" is yúyalanukʷ 'place of wind,' derived from yɔ'la 'wind' (AD; DSS).

97. What Boas transcribes here as "Tlau'itsis" is łáwičis, the name of a Kwakwala-speaking tribe that is anglicized as "Tlawitsis" and generally translated as 'the angry ones' (DSS; AD). The Tlawitsis originated in Hardy Bay and Beaver Harbour, but after the establishment of Fort Rupert in 1849, they moved to a village on Turnour Island, and subsequently Tlawitsis territory has been centred on Turnour Island and West Cracroft Island, and the islands in between (Boas 1887f:131,map; 1921:2:1386–1388; Dawson 1888:72; Curtis 1915:10:307; Duff 1953–1954; 1965; Bouchard and Kennedy 1998b:97–99).

98. Boas' "Nōmas" is númas 'old man,' referring to the one who made the first ceremonial songs for the Kwakwaka'wakw (DSS; AD).

99. The term Boas renders here as "Ōmeatl" is ʔúʔmeł, the Kwakwala name for 'Raven' in mythology, derived from ʔúʔma 'noble woman' (DSS; AD).

100. See Section XVIII, Legends of the Tlatlasikwala.

people perished. After the house had burned, Nōmas sat down and covered up his eyes in order to think. So Ōmeatl said to him, "Build yourself a new house and carve new posts from cedar-wood. Have four bears carry the roof-beams." Nōmas did as Ōmeatl counselled him. His sons were called TcimH, I′mk·oas, Ē′wak·itq, K·′ē′k·yena, and K·′ōmena′kula[101] (the last sentence appears to be doubtful).

Two Legends of the Ma′malelek·ala[102]

Wawikyustâ′lagyilitsuk (He Who is Hardly Able to Get Up)[103]

Wawikyustâ′lagyilitsuk, the son of chief K·′ōmgyila′gyilis[104] and his wife Tlatlak·oasilaō′k·oa, lived in Qē′kuikyen (Thompson Sound).[105] Once he went out to hunt for mountain goats. High up in the mountains he saw a young mountain goat and began to pursue it. After he had followed its track for a long time without catching up to it, he suddenly heard singing and found himself at the house of the mountain goats. They were singing in unison, and the young goat which had escaped him was dancing, her head ornamented with feathers. The man jumped out suddenly and called, "I am Wawikyustâ′lagyilitsuk," and took away her feathers. Thus he obtained supernatural powers. Then the goats taught him their dance, which moved to a rhythm of five beats to a bar. He tried the dance three times in vain, but danced it correctly on the fourth attempt. The mountain goats then told him that they were actually human and that they were wearing skins as clothing. They gave him a mountain goat skin and said, "If you turn this skin half around at the foot of Mount

---

101. Elsewhere, Boas (1910:486) gives only the name "Ts!â′mâ" as the offspring of "Nōmas." Of the five names given by Boas here in the *Sagen*—"TcimH," "I′mk·oas," "Ē′wak·itq," "K·′ē′k·yena," and "K·′ōmena′kula"—DSS and AD recognize yə́mgʷas (Boas' "I′mk·oas"), ǩíǩanɛ ("K·′ē′k·yena"), and q̓ʷúmənakʷəla ("K·′ōmena′kula"), although they do not recognize individuals of these names as the sons of númas ("Nōmas").

102. Boas "Ma′malelek·ala" is mámaliliqla (anglicized as "Mamalilikulla") which is the Kwakwala name applied to the people of Village Island and the adjacent islands. While their territory was centred on Village Island, the mámaliliqla are said to have originated in the Beaver Harbour area; they also lived in an area extending along the north shore of Knight Inlet as far as Matsiu Creek, as well as at a place near Turnour Island, and at White Beach, and at the end of Malcom Island (DSS; AD). DSS points out that the two legends told here are recognized as Kwiksootainuk stories that were likely told by people living among the Mamalilikulla people on Village Island (DSS).

103. The term given by Boas as "Wawikyustâ′lagyilitsuk" is the name wáwagustulagilicu, better translated as 'no one can jump as high' (DSS).

104. This name is q̓ʷúmxəlagilis 'his wealth tumbles all over' (AD; DSS).

105. Boas' "Qē′kuikyen" is known to AD and DSS as x̌əkʷíkən, referring to an area at the head of Thompson Sound, at the mouth of the "Kakweiken" (anglicized from x̌əkʷíkən) River.

K·ak·ō'lema (Quartzite)[106] you will get as many goats as you desire." Later, he went to the mountain three times, gave the skin a half turn and thereupon received many goats. But he wasn't content with this and turned the skin around completely the fourth time. Thereupon the mountain fell and killed him.

K·ō'stitses[107]

K·ōstitses also lived in Qē'kuikyen. Once he went to a lake with many beavers in it. He heard noise and singing there. He hid himself and then saw that the Beavers were building a house. He suddenly sprang from his hiding place, straight at the Beaver chief, and took away his skin. Thus he obtained supernatural powers. He built a house which was thirty fathoms long. The posts represented tsōno'k·oa.[108]

There was no door at the front, but there was one on each side. The longitudinal beams represented grizzly bears. Then he invited all the neighbouring tribes: the Nā'k·oartok·, Quaquā'mic, TsāwatEē'noq, Tlatlasik·oa'la, and NE'mkic,[109] and gave the beaver skins to all of them.

---

106. AD and DSS recognize Boas' "K·ak·ō'lema" as the mountain called x̌ax̌ʷíl'əma; Boas (1934:71, map 15:17) locates this mountain on the north side of the Kakweiken River which flows into the head of Thompson Sound.

107. Likely the name rendered here by Boas as "K·ōstitses" is gʷúsdidʒas meaning 'everyone disembarks in front of your house,' derived from the term gʷiyúɫəlas 'direction you are going' (DSS).

108. The Kwakwala term dʒúnuq̓ʷa (Boas' "tsōno'k·oa") refers to the 'cannibal woman' (AD; DSS).

109. These tribal names are: the nák̓ʷaxda?x̌ʷ (Nakwoktak); hax̌ʷá?mis (Hahuamis); dʒawadɛ'?nux̌ʷ (Tsawatainuk); x̓áx̓'əsiq̓ʷəla (Tlatlasikwala); and nə'mgis (Nimpkish) (AD; DSS).

XVIII. Legends of the Tlatlasikwala

"There is a totem pole in front of one of the houses which I am going to draw. It has been explained to me" (Rohner 1969:32). This is Boas writing of his first day in the field beyond Victoria, having alighted from the *Boskowitz* on 6 October 1886 at the Nahwitti village on Hope Island at the northernmost tip of Vancouver Island. The totem pole's history is given in story 2, part 4, and we should note, as a general preface to the stories of this section, what Boas admits as a difficulty in his footnote to story 2, part 6: "I must mention that this was my first attempt to collect legends and that communication was extraordinarily limited." Boas was using Chinook Jargon, but the chiefs who agreed to speak with him did not know this universal trade language of the coast and an interpreter was sometimes resorted to (Rohner 1969:33, 37). Boas' great skill at getting things on to paper in spite of difficulties is especially admirable here. For instance, the very first narrative in this section was obtained on a "miserable day": "The Natives held a big potlatch again. I was unable to get hold of anyone and had to snatch at whatever I could get. Late at night I did get something for which I have been searching—'The Birth of the Raven'" (Rohner 1969:38). This is ethnology at the point of exhaustion. Still, Boas' persistence paid off and his generous hosts provided him with "long, long stories from the two big chiefs" (Rohner 1969:34), stories so grand that their characters adorned the village houses and were enacted in dramatic dances performed for Boas' appreciation. Near the end of his visit he lamented: "I ... have not been here long enough to understand everything completely, but I have accomplished a good deal" (Rohner 1969:40).

The Nahwitti village of x̣ʷəˊmdasbɛ on Hope Island, 1884. Boas recorded the story (No.2, pt.4) of the house (far right) of kʷíx̣agila, the son of hádga, whose ancestors obtained the bear crests that appear on either side of the door. The sign on this house reads: "Boston—he is the head chief of the Newette (He is true and honest and he dont give no trouble to whiteman)." The second house from the right belonged to "Omatsems," and carries a sign that reads: "Cheap—he is one of the head chief—of all tribes in this country—whiteman can get information."

American Museum of Natural History Library, New York.
Neg./Trans. No. 42298 (Edward Dossetter photo).

XVIII. Legends of the Tlatlasik·oala[1]

1. Legends of Raven and Mink[2]

1) In Ts'ē'k·ōt[3] there lived a mighty chief. His wife was unfaithful to him and carried a child by her lover. When the chief discovered this he became furious and said, "Why do you cheat me so and dishonour me? Don't you know that I am a mighty chief? I will know how to save my honour." So the woman grew afraid and didn't dare to meet with her lover as before. But she thought of a ruse and told him, "I will

---

1. "Tlatlasik·oala" is Boas' rendering of x̱'áx̱'əsiqʷəla (anglicized as "Tlatlasikwala"), the name of one of the three tribes known collectively as the Nahwitti at the northernmost end of Vancouver Island and the adjacent islands offshore (see also Section XIX that follows). The term x̱'áx̱'əsiqʷəla, derived from x̱'ásakʷ 'ocean side,' has been translated as 'those of the ocean side' (Boas 1966:38) and as 'outside—or in front of one—on the ocean shore' (Curtis:1915:10:308). Tlatlasikwala territory, as identified by Boas (1887f:map) and Duff (1953–1954; 1965:59–60), extended along the north end of Vancouver Island, from Nissen Bight (near Cape Scott) eastward to the vicinity of Songhees Creek, about 5 miles (8 km) west from Hardy Bay, and included Hope, Nigei, Balaklava, Hurst, Bell, and Pine Islands offshore, as well as Shushartie Bay and Shuttleworth Bight. According to James Wallas' narrative (in Galois 1994:291–294), the first of the ancestors of the Tlatlasikwala lived at Bull Harbour on Hope Island. The main village of the Tlatlasikwala prior to the mid-1800s was situated at Nahwitti on Cape Sutil (Duff 1965:57) (See also the discussion of the Nakomgilisala in Section XIX).

    Our annotation of this section was assisted greatly in the summer of 2001 by Kwakwala-speaking experts Chief Adam Dick and Dr. Daisy Sewid-Smith who are referred to here as "AD" and "DSS" respectively; we gratefully acknowledge their assistance.

2. Boas (1888g:53) summarizes this legend which he says "originated among the Tsimshian and was later borrowed by the Kwakiutl."

3. There is some confusion concerning this place name. The term that Boas transcribes here as "Ts'ē'k·ōt" is the same word he gives elsewhere as "ts!ē'qōt (?)" (Boas 1934:62) and references both to this page of the *Sagen*, and to story 2 that follows (where "tsē'kuot," another variant of Ts'ē'k·ōt" or "ts!ē'qōt") is given as the name of "Birdhouse Island." AD recognizes neither the Kwakwala term "Ts'ē'k·ōt," nor the English name "Birdhouse Island." Boas (1934:62) gives another term referenced to this same page of the present story, and to story 2, as "ts!ē'gwadē" 'having birds or having clam eating.' However "ts!ē'gwadē" does not appear here, or in story 2, suggesting that Boas' "ts!ē'gwadē" is perhaps a variant of "Ts'ē'k·ōt." AD recognizes "ts!ē'gwadē" as ćígʷaći 'egg receptacle,' a place name referring to Egg Island, located near the entrance to Smith Inlet. Yet on Boas' place name maps of this area, "ts!ē'gwadē" is applied to Pine Island, located off the northeastern end of Vancouver Island—AD knows Pine Island only as diyáx̱.

pretend to be dead, then they will deposit me in a burial house and there you will be able to come and see me again." And she pretended to be dead. So her husband took her to a burial house which had been built in the chief's cemetery. When it grew dark, the lover went there, and the woman opened up the house for him. He left the house only at noon and the people saw him when he came out of the burial house. So they went to the chief and told him what they had seen. He didn't believe them at first, but then sent a slave to the burial house to look at the corpse. When he returned, he reported that the house had been broken open and that the woman was alive. Thereupon the chief became furious and decided to kill his wife. He went and stabbed her with a knife; then he took the child which she had by her lover and put it into the grave by its mother so that it might die.

But the child didn't die and instead grew up wonderfully quickly. Once many children from the village were playing with bows and arrows near the cemetery. Suddenly the woman's child came out of the burial house and took away one of the little ones' bow and arrows. Then he returned where he had come from. But the children became scared, ran to the chief and told him what they had seen. He sent out a slave again to see whether the children had told the truth. When the slave confirmed their report, he ordered the boy brought to him and adopted him as his son.

The boy made friends with one of the village boys and they spent days and nights together. One day the chief's son said to his playmate, "Will you come with me to K·ants'ō'ump?" Since he consented, they agreed to go into the forest early in the morning. There the chief's son first shot a (bird) Tlā'tsem,[4] and then a woodpecker. He skinned them both and gave one skin to his friend and kept the other for himself. Then they put them on and flew high up.

At last they arrived at Aikyatsaiensnā'laq, the sky.[5] They found a small pond there close by the house of K·ants'ō'ump and sat down on its banks. Soon the daughter of K·ants'ō'ump came out of the house to fetch water. When she saw the birds she threw stones at them to shoo them away. But they were tame and stayed there calmly. Then the girl caught the birds, hid them under her coat and took them secretly into the house with her. She brought the water to her father but kept the birds for herself and took them into her room. They were scarcely inside it, when the two threw off their bird-skins and she saw that they were young men. The chief's son took her for his wife.

K·ants'ō'ump heard them talking inside the room and asked his daughter who was with her. She replied, "There is a young man here who wants me for his wife."

---

4. Term not now recognized.

5. DSS and AD recognize Boas' "Aikyatsaiensnā'laq" as ʔíkistənsal'akʷ meaning 'place in the sky.'

Then K·ants'ō'ump told her to come to the fire with her husband. But she warned the latter, "Take care! The floor of our house is full of sharp needles; you'll die at once if they hurt your feet. I've had many husbands already and they all lost their lives this way." The young man demanded that she descend in front of him. But since she refused, he finally gathered courage, jumped down and went towards the fire, sliding his feet in such a way that they pushed the sharp needles down. Then his young wife and his friend came down as well and the woman embraced her husband joyfully because he had safely escaped the danger. And the woman bore him a son. But the child slipped from her hands and fell straight down into the sea.

Around this time the old chief, the young man's father, had just sent out a slave to get driftwood. He spied the child's small hands in the sea, took the child into his canoe and wrapped it up in his blanket. Thus he brought it home and gave it to the chief, who didn't know, of course, that the child was his grandson. He called for his sister and asked her to nurse the baby. But the child didn't accept the milk and grew up in one day. The chief wanted to feed him, but he refused all the food which they offered to him. The old man grew worried about it and had all the people called together in order to try whether they might be able to make the child eat. Among others, there came also an old man, and he advised the chief to have fish caught from the ocean. The chief sent out a slave right away, who soon returned home with several fish. The old man cut out their stomachs and gave these to the boy. He gobbled them up greedily and at once cried for more. The chief gave him a box full of berries; he gobbled them up and cried for more, and it wasn't long before he had eaten everything in the house. Then he called, "Don't you know me? I am O′meatl, Raven!" And he went outside and gobbled up everything in the whole village. So the people grew afraid. They moved away and left him behind by himself. When O′meatl didn't find anything to eat any more, he went into the forest to search for people.

2) Once he met a woman who was sitting in a tree gathering fruit. He asked her, "What kind of food do you have in your house?" She replied that she had all kinds. So he called to her to come down and told her that he wanted to have her for his mother. But the woman was Squirrel. When they got to the house, Raven gobbled everything up and then left her. He did the same to Eagle.

3) After some time, Raven met the Mink, Tlĕ′selagyila.[6] They made friends with each other and decided to wander over the earth together. They once met Whale. Raven hailed him, "Hi, we'd like to go over the water; won't you take us across?"

---

6. What Boas transcribes here as "Tlĕ′selagyila" is ƛ'ísəlagil'akʷ, meaning 'born to be the sun,' Mink's name in Kwakwaka'wakw mythology (DSS; AD). Boas uses the English word "Mink" (without quotation marks) here in the original *Sagen.*

Whale agreed, opened his mouth and they both crept in. After a short while Raven pinched Tlĕ′selagyila and he screamed. So Whale asked, "Why does the little one cry?" "Oh," replied O′meatl, "he is hungry." Whale said, "I have lots of meat; cut him off a piece." O′meatl cut off a piece and they both ate it up. In a short while he pinched Tlĕ′selagyila again so that he cried. When Whale asked what was happening now, and O′meatl said again that the little one was hungry, he permitted them to cut off more. He said, "Take as much as you want. Only don't cut my throat, because that would kill me." He had scarcely finished when O′meatl cut his throat. Whale still made a few convulsive movements and then died. His corpse floated ashore. But O′meatl and Tlĕ′selagyila were now in dire straits because they didn't know how to get out again. But soon a man found the whale, called his friends and they all began to cut it open. When they noticed that meat had been cut off everywhere, they marvelled. At last, when they opened up the stomach, Raven flew out and Mink sprang out. Then they knew that these two had eaten some of the whale. They took the meat and blubber ashore and cooked it.

4) But O′meatl wanted to have the blubber for himself and thought up a ruse how to get it. He transformed himself into an old, one-eyed woman. She relieved herself and then said to her excrements, "I'll go into the village. You shout 'hoo, hoo' in a moment!" Then she limped away. When she got to the village, she shouted at the top of her voice, "The enemies are coming! Enemies! Enemies! They will kill us all!" And the shouts of "Hoo, hoo!"—as from many people—could be heard, and the villagers were all afraid and ran away. This was what O′meatl had intended, and he now gobbled up the whale completely.

5) O′meatl came across some fishermen who were busy catching halibut. He jumped into the water without a moment's hesitation and gobbled up all the bait on the hooks. The fishermen thought that they had caught something when they saw their lines move. But when they found all their bait eaten away, they thought that a shark had done it. Their chief wanted to catch it and for this purpose took an especially long and strong line, onto which he tied a quill. When the people went out fishing again, O′meatl jumped into the sea again and ate the meat off all the hooks. Yet he was not able to bite through the quill. When the chief noticed that something was on his line, he pulled it up quickly. But O′meatl was unable to free himself and, although he beat his wings and resisted, he was pulled up to the surface. When he was almost up, he planted his feet against the bottom of the canoe. His nose broke off when the chief pulled hard. O′meatl fled into the nearby forest and transformed himself into an old woman again. He put on an artificial nose of wood, limped into the village and said to the first man he met, "I hear that the chief has caught a nose today. I'd like to see it." The man replied, "Then you'll have to go into the chief's house; that's where it is." The woman limped into the house of the chief and asked

him to show her the nose, which was hanging over the fire on a drying-rack. She pretended to be extremely astonished, but when the chief turned around for a moment, she took the nose, put it on herself and flew away through the smoke-hole in the shape of Raven. Oʹmeatl was nearly caught there, because the hole was so small that he was hardly able to squeeze through.

6) Once several women were looking for shellfish on the beach, so Tlēʹselagyila hid and sang, "Oh, if only your canoe would turn over!" He had scarcely finished the song when the canoe capsized and the women fell into the water. He jumped after them at once, took some pine pitch in his hand and glued up their genitals under the water. Then he went back home. The women reached the shore safely and then noticed that their genitals were glued together. They wept at this. When M'hāʹyus (Raccoon)[7] learned the cause of their complaint, he went to Tlēʹselagyila, told him what had happened and asked him whether he wasn't able to help them. "Oh, yes, I can," said Tlēʹselagyila. He took them into his house and relieved one after the other of the pitch. After a short time all these women became pregnant. One of them bore him a son.

7) Tlēʹselagyila wanted to move to another country with them. He joined two canoes with planks and set out on his journey in this craft. Suddenly Tlēʹselagyila said, "Oh, I've lost my nose ring; I can see it down there in the water." He jumped into the water. His wife looked after him and when she noticed that he had lied and wasn't looking for his nose ring, but was eating seals, she became angry and took off with the canoes. When Tlēʹselagyila came up again, he saw the canoe floating far, far away. So he called after his fleeing wife, "Throw me my bow and arrows!" She obeyed. Tlēʹselagyila took them and shot one arrow at the sky. It stuck fast up there. Then he took a second arrow, which hit the first and stuck to it. He continued thus until he had formed a chain of arrows which reached down from the sky to the earth. He shook the chain and found that it was strong enough to carry him. Then he climbed up and at last arrived in the sky. There he found his father, Amiaēʹqet (Sun),[8] who was sitting in front of the fire warming himself. He was old and weak and was very glad to see his son. He said, "It is good that you've come. Now you shall carry the sun in my stead." In the morning he gave him his nose ring (the sun) and impressed upon him to go neither too high nor too low, since otherwise it would get too cold or too hot on earth. Tlēʹselagyila promised to obey. Towards noon he bent low in order to look down. Thereupon it became hot on earth; the sea began to

---

7.   "M'hāʹyus" is Boas' rendering of máyus, the Kwakwala term for 'raccoon' (AD; DSS).

8.   The name that Boas transcribes here as "Amiaēʹqet" is the term ʔámyax̱id meaning 'praising' (AD; DSS). In story 10 of this section, Boas places the term "K·antsʹōʹump" (i.e. qəns ʔúmp 'our Father,' referring to God) in brackets following the name "Amiaēʹqet," rather than the word "Sun" as he has done here.

boil, the stones cracked and the forests burned up. When Amiaē'qet saw what his son was doing, he pursued him, seized him and tore him to pieces. Then he flung him down to earth, where he was found again as Mink.

8) But all the forests were burned up and only bare rocks formed the earth's surface. So Ō'meatl decided to create soil and shrubs. He went into his canoe, Tā'tatlta (= It Becomes Big),[9] and sent Loon down into the sea to get them. But he didn't find anything and drowned in the sea. Then he sent out Podiceps[10] and Harlequin Duck. Both of them drowned. Finally he sent out Oidemia deglandi,[11] who dived to the bottom of the sea and stayed there for a long time. At last he came up again with a fir bough, which Ō'meatl took and from it made mountains, soil and trees. He created a cedar tree and said, "You shall serve people for the building of their houses." And he created the fir tree and the hemlock tree, and all the other species of trees, and he made the sand on the beach.

9) In those days it was still dark on earth. So Ō'meatl decided to steal the sun.[12] To this end, he hid in a piece of driftwood and let himself be carried to the land of Nā'lanuk (= Owner of Daylight),[13] who kept the daylight. When Nā'lanuk saw the wood drift onto the beach, he said to his daughter, "Please go and bring the wood up to the house." She obeyed, but Ō'meatl, who was hidden inside it, took hold of her body. She took fright at this and threw the piece of wood far away, but he slipped into her and was born as a child after two days. The woman carried him about in her arms, and already that night he was able to speak. The boy wanted to play with the sun box and take it for a ride in a canoe. He kept crying until at last his grandfather gave him permission. Then he was glad. The canoe was tied to a peg, so he now made it rock until the water ran in, then he cut the rope which tied it to the land. He dipped his paddle three times into the water and thereupon the canoe went far away. Then he called, "Don't you know me? I am Ō'meatl." So Nā'lanuk warned him, "Don't open the chest. You know that it contains Daylight." But Ō'meatl had scarcely reached home when he opened the box and released Daylight. Still he didn't know how to make the night and therefore it stayed light all the time. So Nā'lanuk visited Ō'meatl and asked, "Why don't you cause it to be night also?" Ō'meatl admitted that he was unable to do it and then Nā'lanuk made day and night.

---

9. This term is possibly tátałta (AD).

10. This is the genus name for Horned Grebe. Boas uses the Latin form in the original *Sagen*.

11. Boas uses this older Latin identification in the original *Sagen* to refer to a species of Scoter, likely the White-winged Scoter (*Melanitta deglandi*).

12. What appears here as part 9 of story 1 was published earlier in German in *Globus* (Boas 1888c:53:8:124). Elsewhere, Boas (1935:138) provides a brief summary of the present story as the "Stealing of Daylight."

13. This Kwakwala term is nálanuk^w 'possessing daylight' (DSS).

10) Then Oʹmeatl wanted to get fresh water, which was closely guarded by one of his sisters.[14] He took ashes and sprinkled them onto his tongue so that his mouth became quite parched. Then he went to his sister and said, "Oh sister, let me drink water or else I'll die of thirst." The sister gave him a little, so he sprinkled ashes onto his tongue and said, "Look, I didn't get any, my mouth is still dry." The sister gave him a bit more, but cried at once, "Stop, you've got enough now!" But Oʹmeatl employed the same ruse again and again, until the container was quite empty. Then he ran out and his belly was full of water. So he thought, "Now I will take water to the people," and he flew across all the countries, passing water everywhere, and that is how the lakes and rivers originated.

11) Then Oʹmeatl wanted to have salmon and resolved to get them for himself. He didn't eat anything for days, but sat there, his head wrapped in his coat of bear skin, and thought. Then he made a decision; he carved a wooden fish, threw it into the water and ordered it to swim upriver. The fish became alive, but didn't go upriver as it had been told. Instead, it turned around at once and became a halibut. Then Raven took the blossom of the salmonberry, in order to make a salmon from it. It too became a fish, which he ordered to swim upriver. But it turned around soon, as well, and became a red snapper. So Oʹmeatl went to the graves and asked the dead, "Are there no twins among you?" He found a pair of twins, took the woman from the grave, infused life into her and married her. And they went home together. In the morning the woman said, "Get me some sea water so that I can wash." He brought her a shell filled with water. After she had washed in it, there was a salmon in it, which she told him to throw into the river. He gave the fish to his brother, Mēʹmkyulɛʹmpis,[15] who carried it to the river. The following morning the woman made her husband fetch sea water again. He brought a shellfull to her, and there were four salmon in it, after she had washed herself. These, also, he had to throw into the river. Thus the river was filled with salmon. When Oʹmeatl saw the countless fish, he ordered his slaves to build a salmon weir and caught many. Only K·ʹēʹHustäel, Deer,[16] didn't build the weir according to the instructions of Oʹmeatl, but made an angled dam of stones, so he caught only one fish. Oʹmeatl carried the caught salmon into the house and placed them on the rack over the fire in order to dry them. One evening when he wanted to go out, the salmon got caught in his hair. He became impatient and pulled so that all of them fell down. Then he cried, "How heavy the bodies of the dead (salmon) are!" Thereupon his wife was deeply insulted and returned at once to the grave. All the salmon vanished with her.

---

14. What is identified here as part 10 of story 1 was published earlier in German in *Globus* (Boas 1888c:53:8:124).

15. This name Boas transcribes as "Mēʹmkyulɛʹmpis" is recognized as mímkuləmbɛ (AD).

16. Boas' "K·ʹēʹHustäel" as gíxustula, a name for 'Deer' in Kwakwaka'wakw mythology (DSS; AD).

Then O'meatl regretted his vehemence. He covered his head in his bear skin and was very sad because he had lost his wife and the salmon.

12) And O'meatl pondered how he could obtain salmon again. At last he resolved to steal Mä'isila, the daughter of Mä, Salmon.[17] But she was married to Halqsēoa'lis (Delphinus Orca).[18] O'meatl boarded his canoe and dipped his paddle into the water twice. Thereupon the canoe went to the country of Mä all by itself. He disembarked and saw the slave of Mä, occupied felling a tree. O'meatl slipped into the tree unseen and bit off the tip of the wedge, which had been driven into the tree by the slave. The slave became angry and took a new wedge. O'meatl bit off this one, and the third and the fourth ones, as well. So the slave became sad and wept, and cried out, "Oh, my master will beat me because I have broken his wedges!" Then O'meatl came out of the tree, approached the slave as if he had just arrived and said, "Don't weep, I will help you." He took the wedges, held them to his mouth and in this way put the tips back on. Then he struck the tree one blow only, and it fell over and split into logs during its fall. Then he said to the slave, "Isn't this where Mä'isila lives? I'd like to have her for my wife. You must help me to get her." The slave promised to take him secretly into the house while Halqsēoa'lis was out hunting. He told him to hide in the canoe underneath the logs and paddled home. In the evening the slave and Mä'isila carried the wood into the house. O'meatl slipped into a log carried by the woman and put his arms around her on the way. Thereupon she took fright and threw the log away in terror. But since she couldn't see anyone, she thought that she might have been mistaken and picked it up again. But soon O'meatl put his arms around her again and she threw the piece of wood away once more. This happened four times, then she entered the house and O'meatl followed her unseen to her chamber. But when Halqsēoa'lis returned home from his hunt early in the morning, O'meatl took fright, put on his Raven garment and flew up onto the totem pole in front of the house.

There Halqsēoa'lis spied him and invited him to come down. O'meatl accepted the invitation. When he was sitting by the fire, Halqsēoa'lis asked him where he had come from. But he didn't reply to this question at all and instead said only, "What a fat belly you have; come here and let me make you slim and handsome." Halqsēoa'lis was afraid and at first didn't want to go over to him, but O'meatl knew how to speak so convincingly that at last he agreed. Thus O'meatl cut his belly open

---

17. The Tlatlasikwala people use the term mɛ (Boas' "Mä") to refer to 'any salmon,' and mɛ'ʔisila (Boas' "Mä'isila") for the 'chief of the salmon people.' The female form of this latter term is mɛ'ʔisilaga (DSS; AD).

18. This is the Latin identification of the species commonly known as the orca or killer whale. The Kwakwala name given here by Boas as "Halqsēoa'lis" is not now recognized.

and took out the stomach so that he died. He did the same to his three brothers who had returned with him from the hunt.

Then he took the young woman, put her into his canoe and went back home. Mä sent out all his canoes in pursuit of the robber, but they didn't catch him. When he was close to home, Oʹmeatl transformed all of them into salmon and assigned a river to each one. Thus it came about that there are salmon in all the waters nowadays. And Oʹmeatl taught the people to catch and dry salmon. A small fish called hanuq[19] was swimming close behind the canoe of Oʹmeatl when he was fleeing. Oʹmeatl pushed its eyes close together.

13) In those days there were no tides and the people were unable to gather shellfish on the beach. So Oʹmeatl resolved to make the tides. He went into the forest, lay down and pretended to be dead. Then Wolf came and wanted to eat him, but Oʹmeatl took hold of his tail (called Nūn in this context)[20] and bit it off. Filled with joy at the success of his ruse, he flew home with the tail, where he hung it over the fire to dry. Thereupon Wolf cried, "Don't put my tail by the fire; don't put my tail by the fire!" When it began to dry a bit, the sea receded four fathoms. But Oʹmeatl was not yet content and ordered his slave to lower the tail still more. The more they lowered it, the more the water fell and the sea became dry far out. Then the people went out and fetched what they needed, shellfish and fishes. Then Oʹmeatl made all kinds of berries and gave them to the people. They dried and ate them and their hearts were glad.

14) Once Octopus and Raven had a fight. Raven attempted to lift Octopus out of the water. But he was unsuccessful and Octopus, on the contrary, pulled him down into the water. Raven screamed, but Octopus didn't release him until he was almost dead, then he threw him ashore. All the animals saw him lying there. His belly moved only a little bit, otherwise he lay there as if dead. Octopus said, "You see, I am stronger than you!" And Raven begged him, "Leave me alone; I will be your slave!" And he gave his canoe and his house to Octopus. But Raven was derided by everyone.

15) One morning Oʹmeatl was sitting on the beach when he saw Salmon playing in the water right in front of him. So he called, "Oh friend, come and heal me! My back is sore; I am very ill!" Salmon swam up and asked how he could help him. Oʹmeatl replied, "If you jump over me once to the right and once to the left, I will become better." Salmon did what Oʹmeatl had asked. But Raven held a club in his hand and

---

19. The term that Boas gives here as "hanuq" is given elsewhere by Boas (1948:92) as "hāʹnŏ" where it is identified as the Koskimo name of a small fish that is called "hāʹlo" in other dialects of the Kwakwala language. Neither of these terms was recognized by AD.

20. The term that Boas renders here as "Nún" is given elsewhere by him as "nūn," which is glossed as 'the myth name of wolf' (Boas 1948:237).

killed him. Then he carried him home, cut him up and invited all the animals. He put Salmon into a big wooden box, poured water into it and threw glowing stones in to cook him. And the animals all sat around and were looking forward to the meal. At last the fish was done. O'meatl took a piece from the box, passed it to Squirrel and said, "Look, isn't this nice?" Just when Squirrel wanted to take the meat, he pulled it away. So Squirrel wept and rubbed her eyes. Raven said, "That's right; rub still a bit more!" And because Squirrel kept on crying and rubbing her eyes, O'meatl said, "Now you are beautiful, you shall always stay like this." She had almost rubbed away her eyebrows and the hair underneath her eyes. Then O'meatl turned to Thrush (Hesperocichla naevia),[21] who was beginning to get impatient. He said, "Don't sit so far away; come closer to the fire, I want to give salmon to you." Thrush obeyed and moved so close to the fire that his belly became completely black. Then Raven passed a piece of fish to Bluejay and wanted to pull it away again. But Bluejay was too nimble and caught it. At this O'meatl became so angry that he grabbed him by the hair and threw him out of the house. Ever since, bluejays have been crested.

16) After he had made fools of all the animals like this, he invited Cormorant and Bear to come fishing with him. He cut off a piece of Salmon's tail, used it for his bait and caught lots of halibut, while Cormorant caught only two and Bear none at all. So Bear asked, "What are you using for bait?" "Oh," said O'meatl, "I have cut off my testicles." Bear replied, "I don't believe that, because you would die if you did that." "Just look!" said O'meatl, and held a bit of salmon meat in front of himself so that it appeared as if he had really cut them off. Then Bear asked Cormorant to cut off his testicles, too, so that he might use them for bait. Cormorant fulfilled his request and thus Bear lost his life. Then O'meatl and Cormorant paddled to the shore and rendered his fat.

17) Another time the animals invited their friends in turn to a feast. Only O'meatl wasn't invited. First Kingfisher went to the river, harpooned a salmon and then invited everybody to share the salmon. When the stones had been heated and the salmon was cooking on them and everyone was still waiting for the meal, O'meatl appeared all of a sudden from beneath the ground and wanted to take the salmon away. But he was discovered by the animals and they pushed the stones aside and were just in time to prevent him from eating up the salmon. They pulled him out of the ground, beat him, stomped around on his body, and threw him out of the house. But he cried, "K·āq, k·āq, I will be your slave! Leave me be, leave me be! You are the chiefs and not I!"

---

21.   This bird is now known as the Varied Thrush (*Ixoreus naevius*).

Then Waqwaqŏ'li[22] entered the house and invited the assembled animals to eat. When they had all gathered he beat his behind four times, sat on the kettle and lo, it was filled with berries! He gave them to his friends to eat. Thereupon O'meatl said, "I can do that, too!" He invited all the animals for a feast. He sat down by the kettle and beat his behind four times. But the kettle filled with excrement and not with berries. So everyone present kicked him and he was nearly killed. But he cried, "Hä, hä, hä! Spare me, leave me be! I will be your slave! You shall be chiefs!"

After this, Squirrel invited all the animals for a feast and sent her friend Raccoon to O'meatl in order to invite him. At first he didn't want to come, but when he told him that Squirrel had many good things to eat, O'meatl came and peeped through a hole in the wall to see what there was. One of the animals standing by the door just then saw him there and called, "Look at our chief, O'meatl, standing outside!" So he hid, ran around the house and looked in from a different side. There one of the guests spied him, took a glowing coal, wrapped it in fat and threw it straight down O'meatl's throat. Thereupon he cried, "A! a! a!" and ran away.

Then Kilē'qoitsa (a river bird)[23] invited all the animals. When they were gathered, he cut his foot and behold, salmon eggs came out, which he collected in a dish. He served them to his guests. O'meatl thought that he could do that too, so he invited all the people and, while they were sitting expectantly before their dishes, he cut his foot with a stone. But only blood trickled out and he cried in pain. The animals kicked him and threw him out of the house. But he cried, "Hä, hä! Leave me alone! I will be your slave! You shall be chiefs!"

At last Seal invited the people for a feast. When they had all assembled, he held his hands close to the fire and let fat drip from them into the dishes. He served it to his guests. O'meatl again believed that he could do that just as well, but only burned his fingers and was mistreated by the animals.

18) One day O'meatl went out to gather berries with his four sisters. They went upriver in his canoe and it wasn't long before they had filled their box. Then O'meatl went ashore to relieve himself and said to his excrement, "Shout when I've gone away a bit!" Then he went on with his sisters. In a short while, loud shouting could be heard. So O'meatl said, "Oh, woe! Do you hear the shouting? They must be our enemies who are coming with many canoes to kill us. Go into the woods and hide; I will stay here and guard the canoe!" His sisters were scarcely out of sight when he gobbled up all the berries. The girls came back after some time. They saw O'meatl

---

22. What Boas transcribes as "Waqwaqŏ'li" is wáx̣ʷwax̣ʷəli, the Swainson's Thrush (AD), a bird that is commonly associated with the ripening of salmonberries throughout the Northwest Coast.

23. The Kwakwala term gilíx̣ʷiča (Boas' "Kilē'qoitsa") refers to the bird identified as the American Dipper (*Cinclus mexicanus*) (AD).

lying on his back in the canoe, and their box empty. So they asked what had happened. O′meatl replied, "Oh, the people have beaten me and eaten up all our berries!" But soon his sisters noticed that his tongue was quite black. They said, "How did your tongue become so black, and also your head? You have eaten our berries!" And they kicked him. So he called, "K·āk·, k·āk·! Leave me be, leave me be! I will be your slave!" And he flew into the forest and cleaned his tongue and head with sand. Then he flew back and said, "Look how unjustly you have accused me. I haven't eaten any berries." But they found some seeds still between his teeth. And they kicked him again until he was hardly able to move any more.

19) Once O′meatl pretended to be sick. His sister, Crow, who was a great healer, wasn't able to find out what was wrong with him. He cried, "Oh, I am ill; my stomach hurts terribly!" The sister scolded him off and reproached him that he was faking. But he sprang up, pretended that he had to run out urgently, and then soiled the threshold. So she had to clean the house again, and while she was thus occupied, O′meatl gobbled up all her shellfish. When the sister came back she shouted angrily, "O′meatl has gobbled up all my shellfish!" and she danced her magic dance. She scolded him and said, "Aren't you ashamed to be so greedy as to eat up everything?" But he only cried, "K·āk·, k·āk·!"

20) Once O′meatl was sitting by the fire opposite a wonderfully beautiful girl called K·ōk·ōtsaqsmā′lek·a (Merganser serrator).[24] Her skin was as white as snow. He would have liked to have had her for his wife, but she wouldn't have anything to do with him. So he thought up a ruse. He said to her, "You haven't had a bath for a long time; why don't you have one now?" She replied, "Alright, but make a fire for me." So she went into her room and washed herself all over. But O′meatl flew into the forest. He went to the cedar tree and asked it, "What do you do when people throw you into the fire?" The cedar answered, "Then I cry. The people call it crackling." Raven replied, "Then I cannot use you." He flew to the yellow cedar and asked it what it did when it was thrown into the fire. It replied, "I cry and jump up high!" So Raven answered, "That is fine. I will throw you into the fire and a beautiful girl will be sitting close to you. Jump straight into her lap and burn her." Raven carried the wood home, lit a fire and K·ōk·ōtsaqsmā′lek·a sat down beside it in order to dry herself. Then the wood jumped up high and burned her lap. Raven was in sympathy with her and said, "I know a good cure. Go into the woods and when you see a plant outside, a stalk without leaves which moves up and down, sit right on it and you will be cured at once." The girl followed his advice. She had scarcely left the house when Raven flew into the woods, hid under the leaves and left only his penis exposed. The

24. Boas' "K·ōk·ōtsaqsmā′lek·a" is recognized by AD as gʷəgʷɔ′ćaxsəmálaga 'female sawbill duck,' referring to the Red-breasted Merganser, whose Latin identification is now *Mergus serrator*.

girl arrived and did what Raven had told her. But then she noticed the glittering eyes of Ó′meatl and realized how he had cheated her. She seized him and beat him until he lay there as if dead.

21) Once Ó′meatl took a small splinter of wood and placed it between two pieces of cedar bark under a tree in the forest. Then he returned home. When he went to the forest again the following morning to see what had become of the wood, he found a small child lying between the pieces of bark. He bathed it in ice-cold water to make it grow quickly and then took two bigger pieces of bark, in which he wrapped it. Then he placed it underneath the tree again. When he looked at the child again the following morning, he found it considerably grown. He washed it again with cold water. Then he said to it, "Now jump so that I can see how strong you are!" The child jumped as high as the tallest spruce. Ó′meatl was glad and gave it the names K·ē′qenitl and Tlatlanäitl.[25] On the third day, he bathed it once more, and on the fourth he threw it into the water. Thereupon it became very strong. He told it to twist a big tree from the ground, and K·ē′qenitl succeeded with the first try. So Ó′meatl invited all the animals to match their strength with the young man. Among them there was also Kunkunquli′kya, Thunderbird.[26] He said to Ó′meatl, "Let's see how high K·ē′qenitl can jump." He jumped half the height of a cedar tree. So Kunkunquli′kya laughed and said, "He isn't strong." Ó′meatl exhorted the boy to gather all his strength. Thereupon he jumped over the cedar. And when he was just soaring above the cedar, Kunkunquli′kya seized him and flew away with him. So Ó′meatl grew sad. He went to bed and didn't want to get up again. But at last he resolved to take revenge. He took a mighty cedar and from it carved a whale.

22) Then he went to Pitch and said, "Come, let's go and catch halibut." Pitch didn't want to go and said that he had no hook. Ó′meatl promised to lend him his. Then he said that he had no line. Ó′meatl promised this to him as well. Pitch still didn't feel like going and said that he had no fish club and no cape. So Ó′meatl let him have his club and his bear skin and Pitch finally went along. There was warm sunshine. After some time Ó′meatl called him and said, "Friend Pitch, how are you?" "Hoo!" answered Pitch. In a little while Ó′meatl asked again, "Friend Pitch, how are you?" This time the "Hoo" sounded weaker, and when Ó′meatl asked for the fourth time he received no answer at all. So he paddled over to Pitch's canoe and found him completely melted. He then towed the canoe home and coated the wooden whale with the pitch. Then he told all the animals to go into its hollow body. He ordered Black Bear to sit in the head; Grizzly Bear was sitting in the back and Wolf in the

---

25. The first of these two names, "K·ē′qenitl," is not now recognized; the second, "Tlatlanäitl," is recognized as λáλanə?iɬ 'woodpecker' (AD).

26. The term kʷə′nkʷənxʷaligɛ (Boas' "Kunkunquli′kya") refers to the large, ferocious Thunderbird (AD; DSS).

tail. Then he ordered them to swim away in the whale. The carved animal didn't move quite like a whale, so O'meatl called them back and showed them how they had to move. Then he went inside, himself, and the whale swam to the coast where the house of Kunkunquli'kya stood. He was sitting in the front of the door when the whale arrived. So he sent out his youngest son, who was able to lift one whale, to catch it. He threw on his feather garment and went out in thundering flight. He swooped down on the whale, but was unable to lift it, and also to let go of it again, because he was stuck to the pitch. He hurt Tlē'selagyila (Mink)[27] with his talons and the latter screamed. So Duck took a stick and smashed his wings and Brown Bear ate his feet. So he lay on the sea with spread wings. And the old bird sent out his next son to help his brother. He was able to lift two whales. He swooped down on the whale and lifted it up so that it stood straight up. But Duck smashed his wings, too, and Bear ate his feet. So Kunkunquli'kya sent out his next son, who was able to lift three whales. He lifted the whale completely out of the water and O'meatl cried in fright. But Duck smashed his wings also, and Bear ate his feet. The eldest son and the old one didn't fare any better, even though they almost managed to carry the whale ashore. Only the youngest Thunderbird, still lying in its cradle, was left. So all the animals, and above all O'meatl, were glad that they had killed the Thunderbirds. They went into the house and fetched Tlatlanāitl and returned home with him in the whale.

23) O'meatl had a daughter called Hā'tak·a (Ā'tak·a [?] = Darling).[28] One day he told his sister, Crow, and Hā'tak·a to collect sea urchins. The two of them went down to the beach at low tide and soon had filled a basket with sea urchins. Crow carried them into the forest, broke them, and prepared them for a meal. Then she asked Hā'tak·a whether she wouldn't want to eat some. She replied that she didn't dare to have any because she was afraid of her father. But when Crow promised not to say anything, Hā'tak·a ate one sea urchin. She had hardly started to eat when Crow flew onto a log of driftwood and cried "K·āq, k·āq, k·āq, k·āq! Hā'tak·a is stealing sea urchins; Hā'tak·a is stealing sea urchins!" Hā'tak·a said, "Oh please, be quiet! I will

---

27. The term transcribed by Boas as "Tlē'selagyila" is ƛ'ísəlagil'a 'sun-maker,' but this is not the more commonly-used name for 'Mink' in Kwakwaka'wakw mythology, which is ƛ'ísəlagil'akʷ meaning 'born to be the sun' (AD; DSS).

28. This Kwakwala word, hádga—given here in the *Sagen* as "Hā'tak·a" or "Ā'tak·a"—can be translated as 'noble one' or used as a term of endearment; it is derived from háda which means 'having plentiful food' (DSS). Boas' use of square brackets and a question mark following the name "Ā'tak·a" in the *Sagen* indicates his uncertainty concerning the term's translation. This uncertainty is confirmed in his earlier publication (of what appears here as part 23, story 1) in German in the *Verhandlungen* (Boas 1888i:20:18–20), under the title "Omeatl and Hā'lāqa," where his transcription "Hā'lāqa" was clearly an error. (See also story 2 of the present section).

give my cape to you." But Crow was undeterred and kept shouting to all the people that Hā′tak·a was eating sea urchins. Again she begged her to be quiet and, as a reward, promised her own arm-rings of abalone shell. But a man had already heard what Crow had said and had told it to Ō′meatl. Thereupon the latter grew angry and ordered all the people to pack up, told them to extinguish the fires, and abandoned Hā′tak·a all by herself in the village. Only her grandmother took pity on her and secretly had given her a glowing coal concealed in a shell. Only one male dog and one female dog were left in the village. When the canoes were out of sight, Hā′tak·a lit a fire and built herself a hut from cedar branches. In it she lived with the two dogs. The following morning she sent them to the woods and told them to bring back pliant cedar branches. When they had brought these, Hā′tak·a made herself four round fish baskets. These she placed on the beach at low tide and, when the water receded again after the next high tide, she found plenty of fish in the baskets. But when she looked closer she saw a man in one of them. It was Aikyai′ālisānō, the son of K·omō′k·oa.[29] He came out of the basket carrying a small box. He said, "Take my little box and take it up to the house. I want to marry you!" But Hā′tak·a was unable to lift the box, so that he had to carry it up himself. He opened it in front of the house and behold, there was a whale inside! Then Aikyai′ālisānō built a big house of many platforms and married Hā′tak·a. He sent out the dogs to invite people to help him cut up the whale. The people arrived; he cut up the whale and rendered the blubber, which he kept in boxes. When some sea gulls flew over the house, Hā′tak·a called to one of them, tied some blubber to its back and told it to go to her grandmother, who once had taken pity on her. The sea gull flew away and came to the grandmother who was busy looking for shellfish on the beach. At that time there was famine in the village of Ō′meatl and there were only shellfish for food. The bird gave the meat to her and said, "This is sent to you by Hā′tak·a. But she doesn't want Ō′meatl to know about it, so eat it up right away out here." The old woman ate a piece and hid the rest underneath her cloak. Then she went home and sat down to her work. She was engaged in plaiting a mat. The piece of whale blubber was in front of her and she secretly took a bite of it from time to time. Ō′meatl noticed and went over to ask her what she was eating. She denied that she had anything, but soon Ō′meatl saw her taking a bite again. He jumped up and shouted, "I can see you eating!" At this she became angry and beat him about the face with the blubber, saying, "Hā′tak·a has sent this to me. She is married now and is very rich!" So Ō′meatl decided at once to return to her. But he didn't dare go back without a present. He went to Yā′k·olua Island[30] with his brothers Mē′mkyulEmpis and

29. The name for the son of q̓ʷúmugʷi (Boas' "K·omō′k·oa"), given here as "Aikyai′ālisānō," is not now recognized.

30. The Noble Islets in Goletas Channel are identified by Boas (1934:26, 40, map 6:66) as

HaiE′mkyētliqs[31] and there they collected shellfish. They brought these to Hā′tak·a. She didn't want to let her father into the house, but her husband ordered her to open the door. O′meatl and his brothers sat down by the fire and Hā′tak·a offered them a cup of whale oil. But O′meatl declined, saying, "I am a great chief; you'll have to give me more!" So Aikyai′ālisānō said to the cup, "When O′meatl drinks from you, you shall never get empty." Then O′meatl dipped salmon into the whale oil and enjoyed his meal. And the cup remained full all the time. Greedy O′meatl kept eating so that finally the whale oil ran straight through him. His winds made a frightful noise, but he excused himself by saying that he had a new cape of bearskin which crackled. But when he wouldn't stop at all and began soiling the house and his clothes, Hā′tak·a and Aikyai′ālisānō threw him out of the house.

24) O′meatl wept, went to bed and stayed there for four days. Then he loaded halibut and sea-otter skins into his canoe and took them and two slaves as presents to Hā′tak·a. She gave him two boxes full of oil in return. This made O′meatl glad and he took the oil home with him and there made many boxes from the two he had. He loaded them into his canoe and wanted to move to a different place. He was caught in a violent storm on his way, and his canoe capsized so that he lost all the whale oil. So he took a bowl and scooped up as much oil as possible floating on the sea. But it was only half a bowl full. He made as much from it, however, as he had before.

25) Then O′meatl built a big house for himself. He called two brown bears and told them to stand one on each side of the door to support the house. And he called Octopus, who had to hold the roof-beams together with his long arms. And he called Wolf, who had to support the walls. This was because he wanted to invite Metlā′lanuk, the Master of the Winds,[32] and all the animals. Therefore they had to support the house so that the Winds wouldn't blow it down. Metlā′lanuk came first and with him all the Winds. When the Westwind entered, it became warm, nice weather, but the Northwind brought ice. The house shook and trembled when the Winds came in, but the animals supported it well. Then Metlā′lanuk and the Winds sat down by the fire. They all had red eyes. Then NEmkyā′likyō,[33] the

---

"yā′q!alᶜwa," meaning 'place without landing.' AD confirms this term as yáqaləwa although he is uncertain which islets in this area are known by this name.

31. As noted previously, the first of these names, "Mē′mkyulEmpis," is recognized as mímkuləmbɛ, and the second, "HaiE′mkyētliqs," is recognized as hayə′mgəłəxs, meaning 'crosspiece in a canoe' (AD).

32. AD points out that məlálanukʷ (Boas' "Metlā′lanuk") means 'southeast wind,' which brings bad weather. The wind considered by AD to be the "Master of the Winds" is not məlálanukʷ, as Boas states here, but dzáqʷalanukʷ, the 'north wind' (see also story 4 in the present section).

33. Boas' "NEmkyā′likyō" is recognized by DSS and AD as nəm̓xalagiyu 'only one,' referring to a sea monster shaped like a "giant halibut," according to Boas, but said by AD to be like a large ocean ray (*Raja* spp.)

Iā'kнim[34] in the shape of a giant halibut, came (see Legends of the Nimpkish).[35] He was too big to enter the house and lay down outside the threshold; but he stuck his snout inside, opening it wide. And the sea monster Ts'ē'kis[36] came. He too had to stay outside the door because he was too big. And Beku's[37] came, the water spirit with long, loose hair, and Pâ'ē, the spirit of the sea with halibut eyes,[38] and Cod, Sturgeon, and the spirit of the Ts'ētsā'ēk·a,[39] who lives in the water and wears a head-ring of red inner cedar bark, all came. Then came Whale, a giant man with a big belly, who also was unable to get through the door, and Kyōkēkōnutlemā'la,[40] the whale with the sideways mouth, and Atsēk·ē',[41] the whale with the long flippers and feet, as well as T'ōto'sk·amis,[42] a third whale. Kunkunquli'kya[43] came flying down to the house and fire sparked from his eyes. He took off his feather garment and entered. Crane came, also Eagle, a big chief, and Owl, who is like a crazy person. All the birds came, and, last of all, Quail. He said, "That's enough; the house is filled." So Ō'meatl closed the door, put the oil on the fire and heated it. Then he put it into a big spoon and asked Metlā'lanuk whether he was able to drink the hot oil. He couldn't do it. But Ō'meatl emptied the spoon in one gulp, yet everything he drank ran out of his behind again just as quickly. Then he feasted all his guests with oil and fish.

26) Apart from Hā'tak·a, Ō'meatl had three other children, a son, Maqmalakyō'te, and two daughters Mamqemā'loq and Maqmalakyutai'oq.[44] The latter had a son called Wok·'ä's (Toad).[45] Once the sea began to stir in its depth; the water rose higher and higher and at last covered the house of Ō'meatl so that the smoke alone

---

34. What Boas transcribes here as "Iā'kнim" is yágim, 'sea-monster' (DSS; AD).

35. The reference is to Section XV, story 1.

36. The Kwakwala term that Boas transcribes here as "Ts'ē'kis" is čigis, 'an undersea bird' (AD; DSS).

37. Boas' term "Beku's" is recognized as bəgʷís, 'a water spirit' (DSS).

38. The term Boas gives as "Pâē" is p̓úy 'halibut' (DSS; AD).

39. Boas' "Ts'ētsā'ēk·a" is číceqa, the 'winter dance' that consists of a complicated series of ceremonials held in the winter, including feasting and initiating young people into secret societies (DSS; Boas 1966:173–174).

40. This is k̓úgʷikunuλəmala, meaning 'mouth on either side of face' (DSS; AD).

41. Term not now recognized.

42. Term not now recognized.

43. The term kʷə'nkʷənxʷaligɛ (Boas' "Kunkunquli'kya") refers to the large, ferocious 'Thunderbird' (AD; DSS).

44. The first of these three names, "Maqmalakyō'te," is recognized as maxmalák̓udi (derived from máxid 'the squirming motion of a swimming salmon'); the second name, "Mamqemā'loq," is not recognized; and the third name, "Maqmalakyutai'oq," is recognized as maxmalák̓udayugʷa, the female form of the first name, maxmalák̓udi (DSS; AD).

45. AD and DSS point out that the term wəq̓ís (Boas' "Wok·'ä's") refers to 'frog,' not 'toad.'

was able to escape through the roof. And on the flood waters there drifted a gigantic tree trunk with many people into his house. But they spoke a foreign language. And the Moon, Gyā'loyak·amē,[46] descended from the sky and came to Ō'meatl in order to ask him for water, because he had none himself. He gave Ō'meatl the snow in return.

27) Then Ō'meatl put on his Raven garment and flew to Tlā'laspaa (a small bay on Hope Island, just north of Qumta'spē).[47] From there he visited Haialikyā'wē, who was living on Tlalā'tē[48] River (in Hardy Bay). He entered his house and Haialikyā'wē asked him, "Are you K·'ōmk·'ōmkī'likya (Ō'meatl's second name)?" "Yes, I am," was the reply. Haialikyā'wē continued, "Are you strong and powerful?" "Yes, I am strong," replied K·'ōmk·'ōmkī'likya. In order to prove his strength, K·'ōmk·'ōmkī'likya pointed his index finger at Haialikyā'wē. It pierced his head. Then K·'ōmk·'ōmkī'likya made the sea rise above the house of Haialikyā'wē so that it was completely covered. Then he make the sea fall again and the shellfish stayed behind on the roof. Thereupon Haialikyā'wē picked one of them up and hurled it straight through the belly of his enemy, who tried to do the same in turn. But he didn't succeed in throwing the shellfish through Haialikyā'wē. It remained stuck in the centre of his belly. Then he made the River Tlalā'tē rise until it completely covered the house of Haialikyā'wē. The latter thereupon made his fire's smoke rise straight up through the water. Then he took the sī'siutl, the crest of his house, and threw it at K·'ōmk·'ōmkī'likya. Then K·'ōmk·'ōmkī'likya became angry and threw trees at the house of Haialikyā'wē. So the latter said, "This is enough. One day you will become as strong as I am, but for the time being I am still a bit more powerful." They became brothers and Haialikyā'wē gave his daughter, Tsā'ēk·is, to him for a wife. Then Ō'meatl built himself a house of many platforms.

2. Hā'tak·a

1) It has been told how Hā'tak·a, the daughter of Ō'meatl,[49] was abandoned by her father. The legend tells that once, when her periods were approaching, Ō'meatl had

---

46. The name gálugəmi means 'higher ranking than anyone' (AD; DSS).

47. The location of the place name given here as "Qumtáspē" is indicated by Boas (1934:78, map 3:7) on the south side of Hope Island. In this latter source, Boas translates this name as 'land otter place point.' AD recognizes this term as x̌ʷə'mdasbɛ 'place where there is otter,' derived from x̌ʷə'mdi 'otter.' A drawing of this village scene, with the parts of the village of "xumta'spē" (x̌ʷə'mdasbɛ) named, can be found in Boas (1897:391).

48. This place, known as ɫəl'ádi 'having a corpse,' is located just west of Hardy Bay at the mouth of Songhees Creek. The name refers to dead whales (Boas 1934:81, map 6:76; AD; DSS).

49. This is a reference to story 1, part 23 of the present section. As previously noted, Boas' "Ō'meatl" is ʔú?mɛɫ, the Kwakwala name for 'Raven' in mythology, derived from ʔú?ma 'noble

a dancing-platform built for Hā′tak·a which was supported by four bears. On its floor a giant halibut was painted, with a fire burning on its back. Hā′tak·a was standing on it in her ermine head-dress and danced the Nō′ntlem dance.[50] Suddenly she sank into the ground, but the head-dress remained on top. She had been transformed by her father into a whale (Delphinus orca).[51] And while all the villagers were asleep, she visited K·ōmō′k·oa at the bottom of the sea and fetched a house from him. When the people woke up the following morning, it stood in front of the row of houses in the village. Two eagles were sitting on it, and Hā′tak·a, with the ermine ornament on her head, was dancing in front of its door and calling "Hm! Hm!" to her dance.

Then she disappeared into the forest and visited BaqbakuālanuQsī′uae̅,[52] returning with the head of a man. She danced the Hā′mats'a dance and ate the human head. The people brought her back into the house with much trouble. Then her father killed a man and gave him to Hā′tak·a to eat. Then she went into her room and returned soon with a small staff in her hand and danced. She threw it at the spectators and these scratched their heads because the staff buzzed around them like a fly. Then they in turn threw the staff at Hā′tak·a and she scratched herself. At last she caught the staff and threw it up so high that it didn't come back. She took two rattles, shook them, and at once disappeared into the ground. She could be heard underneath all the houses shaking her rattles. The people dug after her in order to find her, but in vain. Finally she reappeared again in her own house and returned to her room.

TsEntsE′nk·atlaqs (O′meatl's brother)[53] and a woman were sleeping together four nights in a tree, while the dancing was going on in the house of Hā′tak·a. Each morning they cried "Hā!" up in the tree and the people didn't know who it was calling like that. On the fourth morning TsEntsE′nk·atlaqs poked his finger into the woman's vagina. At this she grew angry, and pushed him off the tree so that he lay there dead. The villagers found him, put him in a box, and buried him. Then they

---

woman' (DSS; AD). The term hádga (Boas' "Hā′tak·a") can be translated as 'noble one' or used as a term of endearment—hádga is derived from háda which means 'having plentiful food' (DSS).

50. AD recognizes "Nō′ntlem" as núnɬəm. Elsewhere, Boas explains that among the northern Kwakwaka'wakw tribes, there is a ceremony called "Nō′ntlem" (núnɬəm) which precedes the winter dance and is conceived as opposed to it; among the masks used in the "Nō′ntlem" are the killer whale, merman, and "K·ōmō′k·oa" [q̓ʷúmugʷi, a Sea-Being] (Boas 1966:400–401).

51. Orca or killer whale.

52. DSS points out that the original term was pronounced bəkʷbákʷalanukʷsiwi, best translated as 'having a cannibal at the mouth of the river,' but in more recent times has been pronounced bákʷbakʷalanukʷsiwi? (Boas' "BaqbakuālanuQsī′uae̅").

53. The name that Boas transcribes here as "TsEntsE′nk·atlaqs" is recognized as dzə′ndzənqaɬəxs 'stinging nettles in canoe' (AD; DSS).

went to search for the woman and, when they saw her naked belly in the tree, they grew ashamed. The dead man had risen again in the meantime, but his thoughts were full of murder and pillage. When the people returned from the forest, he killed twenty of them. When the hunters came back in the evening and were carrying the shot elk labouriously on their shoulders, he robbed them of the elk and took away their canoes. So the people decided to kill him. He was invited to a feast and was killed there. The corpse was cut up into pieces, which they threw into a box and carried to the burial ground. But the dead man transformed himself into a whale and lay down on the water. When the people spied it, they pulled it ashore, cut it up and at its meat. They all died from this, among them also Hā'tak·a. When she was dead, it stayed dark for four days. Only seven people hadn't taken part in the meal and remained healthy. They left the place of terror and moved to Wā'k·ama[54] and built a house there for themselves. Once a Tsōnō'k·oa came there and threw all of them into the big basket which she had on her back. But Tlā'lawitsē,[55] one of the seven, took a wedge and smashed her leg and she fell down. They crawled out of the sack, killed her and built a house on the very spot. They cut off her head, and her breasts, and nailed them to the house.

2) Not far from the house of Hā'tak·a there stood a hollow cedar tree. In front of it there was a small pond where she used to get her water. One day she drank from it and swallowed a cedar needle which had fallen into the water, and which she was unable to remove from her cup. This caused her to give birth to a child who was given the name Kuē'qagyila (= Murderer).[56] The grandfather, O'meatl, made a canoe for him which moved without oars. One day Kuē'qagyila and his playmates went in the canoe to Hauqsāā'o,[57] where they saw a salmon, which had been half eaten by a raven, on the beach. Only the head was left and was still moving. Kuē'qagyila took it into his canoe and then saw that it was a sī'siutl. It stretched out its fins and in this way propelled the canoe. Kuē'qagyila went on and caught a bear and a wolf, taking them both into his canoe. When he got to the land of the Guau'aēnoq,[58] he threw the bear ashore. That is why there are many bears there. He left the wolf with the

---

54. Boas' "Wā'k·ama" is wágəmi 'having a river flowing in front,' referring to the Koprino village situated on the east side of Nigei Island, that was set aside as Wakems Indian Reserve No. 6 (AD). Boas (1934:43, map 3:69) translates this name as 'river in front, i.e., chief river.'

55. Name not now recognized.

56. AD and DSS point out that the name kʷíx̱agila (Boas' "Kuē'qagyila") is translated as 'to strike someone with an instrument,' rather than 'murderer,' as Boas indicates here.

57. Name not now recognized.

58. Boas' "Guau'aēnoq" is the tribal name gʷáwaʔɛnuxʷ which means 'downstream (i.e. northern) people' (AD) and is anglicized as "Gwawaenuk." Both Curtis (1915:10:307) and Boas (1966:41) identify Drury Inlet as the former center of this tribe's traditional territory. Areas where the gʷáwaʔɛnuxʷ lived included Watson Island, Mackenzie Sound, Grappler Sound and Gilford Island (Duff 1965:12–13; AD).

Tlask·ēnoq (Ocean People)[59] and it became the ancestor of the countless wolves in that region. Finally he left the sī'siutl in Tsēk·tlisatl (Nutka) Sound.[60] This is why the tribe there often dances the sī'siutl dance.

3) Then Kuē'qagyila returned home and went to Yū'tlē (Cox Island)[61] to take a wife. Wa'qalala[62] and his daughter Hā'nēus[63] were living there. Wa'qalala had a totem pole covered with lice. The biggest one sat on top. He gave this one to Kuē'qagyila, who now became infested with lice. He went home and built a house on Mount Qusēla[64] where K·'ā'nigyilak·[65] (see Legends of the Nak·o'mgyilisala)[66] met him later. He lived at war with all his neighbours. Once he killed four people and cut off their heads, washing them in the River Ts'ōqumtā'as.[67] Another time he went out all by himself in his sī'siutl canoe to kill his enemy Halqalo'ē.[68] But he had so many friends that Kuē'qagyila had to retreat before them. He escaped from them by

---

59. The tribal name that Boas renders here as "Tlask·ēnoq" is recognized by AD as x̣'ásqinux̌ʷ (anglicized as "Klaskino"), derived from x̣'ásakʷ 'open ocean.' This name has been translated as 'people of the ocean' (Boas 1891d:605; 1966:38), or 'seaward-tribe' (Boas and Hunt 1902–1905: 358), or 'people that live at a place that is outside' (Wallas and Whitaker 1981:208). Klaskino traditional territory extended from the Brooks Peninsula (Cape Cook) north to an area that was approximately six miles (10 km) south of the entrance to Quatsino Sound, and included Klashkish and Klaskino Inlets and the creeks and rivers emptying into these inlets (Boas 1887f:map; Dawson 1888:70; Curtis 1915:10:306).

60. The name that Boas transcribes as "Tsēk·tlisatl," presumably referring to Nootka Sound, is not now recognized.

61. AD recognizes Boas' "yū'L!ē" as the place name yúx̌'ɛ. Elsewhere, Boas (1934:40, map 1:26) provides the transcription "yū'L!ē" and the translation 'landward on water' for this place, which he identifies as Cox Island situated west of Cape Scott at the northwestern tip of Vancouver Island.

62. Name not now recognized.

63. This name is recognized as háʔniyus (AD; DSS).

64. The term xʷəsəlá (Boas' "Qusēla") can be applied to any fortified site (AD; DSS). Boas (1934:77, map 3:11) indicated a place with this name on the south end of Vansittart Island. AD and DSS confirm this place name as xʷəsəlá and knew that it was situated somewhere on this island, but were unsure of its precise location.

65. What Boas renders as "K·'ā'nigyilak·" is q̓ániqiʔlakʷ, the 'Transformer' (DSS; AD).

66. "Nak·o'mgyilisala" is Boas' transcription of nəqə'mgəlisəla (anglicized as "Nakomgilisala"), referring to one of the three tribes known collectively as the Nahwitti at the northernmost end of Vancouver Island (see Section XIX, story 1).

67. AD recognizes cúxʷəmdas (Boas "Ts'ōqumtā'as"), 'place of washing the face,' as the name of a place just west of Boxer Point on the southeastern tip of Nigei Island. The same location for this named place is provided elsewhere by Boas (1934:62, map 6:145) who also gives the translation 'place of washing head.' Boas' suggestion here in the *Sagen* that the name applies to a "river" is supported by the fact that there is a stream indicated at this site on the topographical map of the area.

68. Name not now recognized.

disappearing inside Mount Qusēla, only reappearing at its summit. His enemies saw him there but were unable to reach him.

4) Once Kuē'qagyila descended into the ocean in order to ask K·ōmō'k·oa for a totem pole. He remained with him four days and was treated well and then sent back to the upper world with the totem pole. Then he erected the pole in front of his house. It depicted the Tsōnō'k·oa at the bottom, then two BEku's,[69] one of which has a split head and is upside down. Above them there can be seen the wolf, the beaver and at the very top the halibut.[70] When daylight came, the people saw the pole and Kuē'qagyila gave a big feast during which he danced the Nō'ntlem, disguised as a bear. He had many children: five daughters and three sons. The daughters were called: Hōyakitlanuk,[71] Pâogyilak·[72] (= Changed into a Halibut),[72] who was dancing as a Hā'mats'a, WawanEmgyīlaō'k·a,[73] Kēlpusla'yok·,[74] and Hōtlukuī'lak·a.[75] The boys were called: Ā'listalis,[76] Tsō'nok·oatsi[77] and Nank·omā'lis.[78] The first and the third were dancing disguised as bears, like their father, but Tsō'nok·oatsi wore the Tsōnō'k·oa mask. Hōtlukuī'lak·a had a son called Nai'nakus[79] who put up a new totem pole with great celebrations, to which all the neighbouring tribes were invited. WawanEmgyīlaō'k·a had a son called K·ayū'ya.[80] He built a house of ten platforms and carved a new totem pole. He carved himself a wooden figure which he called Hō'qk·oa (Grease Spitter).[81] He placed it inside his house close by the fire and,

---

69. This term is bək"ə's 'spirit of the forest' (DSS).

70. Boas (1935:2–3) indicates elsewhere that this describes the totem pole in front of the house in which the story was told, and comments: "I learned later that the carvings were a substitute for carved house dishes."

71. Name not now recognized.

72. Recognized as p̓úygil'ak" 'born to be a halibut' (DSS).

73. Boas' "WawanEmgyīlaō'k·a" is recognized as wáwanəmgila?úg"a 'warrior woman' (AD).

74. Recognized as ǩə'lbisilə?úg"a 'twisting cedar woman' (DSS; AD).

75. This name is recognized as húλik"ilaga 'listened-to woman,' derived from húλila 'listen' (DSS).

76. The name rendered here by Boas as "Ā'listalis" is recognized as ?áλistalis 'to come ashore to beach,' derived from the term ?áλista 'to come ashore' (AD; DSS).

77. Boas' "Tsō'nok·oatsi" is recognized as dzúnuq̓"adzi meaning 'dzúnuq̓"a (cannibal) woman' (AD; DSS).

78. This chief's name is recognized as nánqəma?lis 'grizzly-bear leader' (AD; DSS).

79. "Nai'nakus" is recognized as nε'?nag"as "place to go home to," derived from the Kwakwala term nε'?nak" 'go home' (DSS; AD).

80. This name is likely ǩεyúya, derived from the Kwakwala term ǩε 'carve' (DSS; AD).

81. Boas (1935:2) describes this as "a vomiting beam," which AD and DSS recognize as húq"a (Boas' "Hō'qk·oa" here in the Sagen) meaning 'grease-spitting.' When filled with eulachon oil and placed over a fire, the wooden beam "vomits" this oil, causing the fire to flare up (AD; DSS).

during feasts, he made it spit grease into the fire so that it burned brightly. From him descends the family of the Tlatlasik·oala chiefs. His son was Tlē′nemitenutl.[82]

5) Once Tlē′nemitenutl went out in his canoe to hunt for sea otters. Soon he saw a big halibut carrying fire on its back and thrust his harpoon at it. The harpoon struck and the fish pulled him out to sea. At last, after it had led him through all the world for four long years, it brought him ashore. A slave saw the canoe arrive and went to his chief Tā′ltam,[83] with whom he exchanged names, and returned to his home. There Whale once invited him to go out with him to hunt seals. Tlē′nemitenutl took along four canoes and filled them all. And Whale gave him all the seals which he had caught.

6) The son of Tlē′nemitenutl was K·ātsq (= Starfish),[84] who had a son called Nūtlustâ′lē. He begot NutsnutlEli′kya,[85] who erected a new totem pole. His son was called Nenâ′lēus.[86] He had a daughter called Hē′kyenitsenk·a,[87] who again erected a totem pole. Her son Nūtlustâ′lē also erected a totem pole. His son Ya′k·atenā′la[88] still lives today. He had a son called Nenâ′lēus, to whom he had given the pole. But when Nenâ′lēus died, his eldest daughter inherited it and the name now belongs to her widower, Ama′qulas.[89]

Ha′inakyalasō[90] was the son of Kuē′qagyila.[91] He built a house for himself on Tsē′kuot (= Birdhouse) Island[92] and there caught halibut and seals. His son was

---

82. The name rendered by Boas as "Tlē′nemitenutl" is recognized as x̓ínəmiƛnuƛ meaning 'place to get eulachon grease,' derived from x̓′ína 'eulachon grease' (DSS; AD).

83. This name is not now recognized.

84. Boas' "K·ātsq" is gádzəq meaning 'starfish' (DSS; AD).

85. What Boas gives as "NutsnutlEli′kya" is possibly the woman's name núɬnuɬiliga 'born to be stupid' (DSS; AD).

86. This name is recognized as n̓ən̓áliyus, derived from the Kwakwala term nála 'daylight' (AD; DSS).

87. Recognized as híkənidzəmga (DSS; AD).

88. The name rendered by Boas as "Ya′k·atenā′la" is likely yáqaɬʔənala, the personal name used by this whale that was given to the people (DSS; AD).

89. "The genealogy of this tribe appears quite uncertain. Above all it is debatable whether the eight children of Kuē′qagyila do not rather represent eight consecutive generations. I sometimes understood the one; sometimes the other. I obtained the following genealogy also in Qumta′spē, the village of the Tlatlasik·oa′la, from chief k·′ōmenak·o′lua. But I must mention that this was my first attempt to collect legends and that communication was extraordinarily limited" [Boas' original footnote]. The name that Boas renders here as "Ama′qulas" is recognized by DSS and AD as ʔamáxʷəlas 'place where you go to potlatch.'

90. "Ha′inakyalasō" is recognized as hínakəlasu 'words fail to describe your greatness,' derived from hínaxʔid 'make an attempt' (DSS; AD).

91. Boas' "Kuē′qagyila" (see part 2 of story 2 in this section) is the name kʷíx̣agila 'to strike someone with an instrument' (AD; DSS).

92. As we have discussed at length (see our footnote to the first line of story 1, part 1 of this section), the available data concerning this place name appear to be contradictory.

named Nai′nakuas.[93] He begot K·ayū′ya.[94] Around this time there was a huge flood which covered valleys and mountains. K·ayū′ya fastened his canoe to the summit of the highest mountain and thus stayed dry while all the surrounding mountains were covered by the water. In this way he escaped the flood. His son was named Tlē′nemitenutl (see above).[95] He became the father of K·oaqi′la.[96] His son was P′āts′s.[97]

3. K·oaqi′la

(I heard the following legend about K·oaqi′la[98] in Qumta′spē[99] from two chiefs. It is doubtful whether the hero K·oaqi′la is identical with the one mentioned above).

K·oaqi′la was a chief in Qumta′spē. He left there and moved to Tsūtsā′tsē[100] where he built a big house and lived in it with two slaves. He carved himself a giant spoon of cedar wood and invited all the neighbouring tribes to a big feast. He once saw many people climb down from the mountains and had them invited to his house. Among them there was also a woman who, shortly after her arrival, gave birth to a boy who was given the name Nikya′qa.[101] K·oaqi′la took her for his wife and they had a daughter, whom they called Tlalisilaō′k·oa.[102] K·oaqi′la now moved back to Qumta′spē. He had become chief of all those men and now made them build a big house, the posts of which were carved in the shape of sea-lions. He had a big cedar tree cut down and carved a totem pole. He made four men dig a deep hole in front of his house, then he killed two slaves and had them thrown into the pit. He erected the pole on their corpses.

---

93. The name that Boas transcribes as "Nai′nakuas" (as previously noted) is recognized as nɛ′ʔnagʷas 'place to go home to,' derived from nɛ′ʔnakʷ 'go home' (DSS; AD).

94. As we have previously noted, Boas' "K·ayū′ya" is likely kɛyúya, derived from the Kwakwala term k̓ɛ 'carve' (DSS; AD).

95. As noted above, what Boas renders as "Tlē′nemitenutl" is recognized as ƛ′ínəmiƛnuƛ meaning 'place to get eulachon grease,' derived from ƛ′ína 'eulachon grease' (DSS; AD).

96. DSS and AD recognize "K·oaqi′la" as qʷaʔxíla, a chief's name.

97. This name is recognized as p̓áċəs (AD; DSS).

98. As noted above, DSS and AD recognize "K·oaqi′la" as qʷaʔxíla, a chief's name.

99. Boas' "Qumta′spē" is x̣ʷə′mdasbɛ 'place where there is otter' (AD), a village located on the south side of Hope Island (see part 27 of story 1 in this section). A drawing of this village scene, with the parts of the village of "xumta′spē" (x̣ʷə′mdasbɛ) named, can be found elsewhere, in Boas (1897:391).

100. What Boas transcribes as "Tsūtsā′tsē" is recognized by AD and DSS as dzúdzadi 'having cockles' (derived from dzɔ′li 'cockle') which is anglicized as "Shushartie"—the name dzúdzadi is applied to a bay on the north end of Vancouver Island, across from Hope Island (AD; DSS).

101. Name not now recognized.

102. The name ƛ′áliƚilʔugʷa (Boas' "Tlalisilaō′k·oa") means 'finning whale woman,' derived from the term ƛ′áƚʔid 'finning' (DSS).

Now when Tlalisilao͗k·oa grew up to maidenhood and first came out of her room (after her first period), he invited all the neighbours to a big feast. He gave them five thousand otter skins and broke a copper. At last he died. After his death his daughter gave a big feast. She served the people food from the big spoon of K·oaqi′la, and then became chief. But in Qumta′spē there lived also another chief named K·ē′tsis[103] who wanted to have Tlalisilao͗k·oa for his wife. When he came to court her she shot him with her arrows. Then she left Qumta′spē, because she feared the revenge of his friends, and constructed herself a salmon weir on a river. There she was visited by a wolf who gave her the death-bringer, Halai′ū.[104] So she took courage again. She returned to Qumta′spē, hurled the Halai′ū. at the village and thus burned it. When she had killed her enemies this way, she went ashore and built herself a house, the door of which was always slamming open and shut.[105] She made her slaves catch many seals, poured the oil into her father's big spoon, and invited all the people to a big feast.

At last she died. So she was placed in a box which was weighed down with stones and thrown into the sea close to the island of Muqtsâ′lis.[106] There K·ōmō′k·oa found her. He brought her back to life, took her for his wife and sent her ashore again on a log of driftwood. After some time she gave birth to a son whom she named Nā′nakyimgyī′la.[107] He created many people from stones. As soon as he had sung his magic spell, the stones rose up in pairs—one man and one woman each time. He made his slaves shoot four deer and ate them, but he was still hungry. He cut off both hands of a man, but was still hungry after he had eaten them. Then he devoured ten halibut and four bears. He covered his face with a mask and began dancing, and the following morning, he sent the villagers a whale which drifted dead onto the beach.

When they were just about to begin cutting up the whale, Kunkunquli′kya[108] flew up and stole it. So Tlalisilao͗k·oa sent out Kutē′na (Glaucionetla langula Americana)[109] to fetch the whale back again. Kutē′na travelled accompanied by

---

103. The name "K·ē′tsis" is recognized as kíc̓əs (DSS; AD).

104. This is the haláyu 'death-bringer' (AD; DSS).

105. Such doors that automatically open and close were known to the Kwakwaka'wakw as kámaka-maq̓á?stu (AD; DSS).

106. AD and DSS believe this term is məxʷc̓úlis 'round object in bay,' although they do not know the location of this place (AD; DSS).

107. "Nā′nakyimgyī′la" is recognized as nánaqəmgil'akʷ 'doing the right thing' (DSS).

108. Boas' "Kunkunquli′kya" is kʷə′nkʷənxʷəligɛ, the Kwakwala name for the large, ferocious Thunderbird (AD; DSS).

109. What Boas gives here as "(Glaucionetla langula Americana)" is the duck now known as the Common Goldeneye (now identified as *Bucephala clangula*), known to AD as gʷədín (Boas' "Kutē′na").

many people and, after a long journey, arrived at the house of Kunkunquli′kya. He stood in front of the door and called, "Oh Kunkunquli′kya, come out!" He asked, "What do you want here?" "My chief has sent me to you." Finally Kunkunquli′kya was persuaded to come out and at once they all fell upon him, killed him and cut up his corpse. But they took the whale back home with them. On their way back Kutē′na saw many salmon swimming about in the water. He caught them and took them to Tlalisilaō′k·oa.

4. Kutē′na

1) At that time it was always windy and therefore Kutē′na decided to go to Metlā′lanuk[110] to obtain good weather. He arrived at his house and noticed that the door was wide open and that wind came blowing out of it with great strength. This was because Metlā′lanuk was sitting by the door and his winds escaped through it. Kutē′na first sent out Mink to close the door. But he only looked across the threshold and fell down as if dead, such was the stink caused by Metlā′lanuk. Then he sent out Raccoon, who didn't fare any better. The same fate befell Marten and Warbler. Eagle sank his sharp claws into Metlā′lanuk's behind, but then he also fell down. So Kutē′na ordered Halibut to lie down in front of the door and then called Metlā′lanuk. When he then came out of the house, he stepped on the slippery fish and fell to the ground. The animals seized him at once and carried him to the canoe. Because Kutē′na there threatened to have his head cut off, Metlā′lanuk promised to make good weather for a long time. Thereupon Kutē′na freed him again.

2) In those days there was no fire. Therefore Kutē′na sent out Lē′lek·oista[111] to fetch the fire, which was kept hidden by Natlibikā′q.[112] He took a glowing coal in his mouth and wanted to run away. But Natlibikā′q noticed it and asked, "What do you have in your mouth there?" Since he wasn't able to answer, he hit him on the mouth so that the fire fell out. Then Kutē′na sent out Deer. He stuck dry wood into his hair, ran to the house of Natlibikā′q and sang, standing outside the door, "I've come to get the fire! I've come to get the fire!" Then he entered, at first danced around the fire and finally put his head into it so that the wood caught fire. Then he ran away,

---

110. As we have discussed previously (see story 1, part 25, of this section), there is some confusion as to which wind is known as məɫálanuk[w] (Boas' "Metlā′lanuk"). While AD points out that he considers the "Master of the Winds" (Boas' terminology in story 1 above) to be dzáq̓[w]alanuk[w], the 'north wind,' Boas indicates this "Master" to be "Metlā′lanuk," which AD knows as məɫálanuk[w], the 'southeast wind' that brings bad weather.

111. Name not now recognized.

112. The name that Boas transcribes as "Natlibikā′q" is possibly derived from the Kwakwala term náƛ'ɛ 'wolverine' (AD).

but Natlibikā'q pursued him order to take the fire away from him again. Deer had planned for this emergency; when Natlibikā'q had almost caught up to him, he took some fat and threw it behind himself onto the ground. It changed at once into a large lake which forced the pursuer to make a big detour. But Natlibikā'q nevertheless kept up the pursuit. When he had almost caught up to Deer, the latter threw some hairs onto the ground behind himself. They changed at once to a thick forest of young trees, into which Natlibikā'q was unable to penetrate. He had to go around outside and thus Deer gained an advantage. But again his pursuer would almost have caught up to him if he hadn't thrown four stones behind himself, which changed into four high mountains. Before Natlibikā'q could surmount them, Deer had reached the house of Kutē'na. So Natlibikā'q was standing outside the door begging, "Oh, at least give me back half of my fire!" But Kutē'na didn't pay any attention to him and he had to turn back without success. Then Kutē'na gave the fire to the people.

5. Hē'likiligyala and Lōtlemā'k·a[113]

Hē'likiligyala[114] descended from the sky to the earth wearing a neck-ring of red inner cedar bark. He built himself a house and lit a fire in it. When the house was finished, a woman rose up from under the ground; she was named Lōtlemā'k·a. Hē'likiligyala said to her, "You shall stay here with me and be my sister." From then on the two of them lived in opposite corners of the house. One day, Hē'likiligyala asked his sister to come out into the open with him. He wanted to show his powers there. They sat down there on two big stones and he told Lōtlemā'k·a to bring him a big stone. Hē'likiligyala seized it and hurled it far away into a lake. But the stone soon surfaced again and then floated on the water. In the evening of the same day he invited many people for a feast. When they were all assembled, he and Lōtlemā'k·a danced. Hē'likiligyala danced first and Lōtlemā'k·a beat time for him. He carried a short staff which he soon flung into the air. He hit ten people with it and they were all killed by the stick. But the Guats'ē'noq[115] had heard of Hē'likiligyala's neck-ring

---

113. Elsewhere, Boas (1888j:62–63) identifies this as an ancestor story of a numaym of the Nakomgilisala, and therefore properly this belongs in the next Section (XIX). The story was obtained, Boas (1888j:61) reports, from "ĸalai'te, the chief of the Naĸomkilis [Nakomgilisala], a tribe of the Kwakiutl nation."

114. The name of this character, hílikiligəla (Boas' "Hē'likiligyala") is derived from hílixʔid 'healer' (AD; DSS).

115. Boas' "Guats'ē'noq" is recognized as gʷacínuxʷ (anglicized as "Quatsino"), which has been translated as 'people of the west' (Dawson 1888:68), 'northern people' (Curtis 1915:10:306), or 'people of the north country' (Duff 1965:63). The boundaries of Quatsino territory on Boas' (1887f) map encompassed the north side of outer Quatsino Sound, beginning at an area opposite

and wanted to have it. Therefore they went to his house in secret and arrived when he was asleep. A young man tried to sneak into the house in order to steal the neck-ring. But he scarcely opened the door when he fell down and an unknown power forced him to run screaming around the house without stopping. Thereupon Hē′likiligyala got up, stepped outside and said, "Why do you want to steal my neck-ring? Just ask me for it and I will give it to you." And they begged him, "Oh, heal the young man, don't let him die! We sent him to steal the ring." So Hē′likiligyala went back into the house, fetched the ring and gave it to the young man. Then he recovered his health and his heart was glad. And the Guats'ē′noq returned home. Since that time they dance the winter dance, Tsetsā′ek·a, during which the rings of red inner cedar bark are used. Then Lōtlemā′k·a began dancing and Hē′likiligyala beat time for her. She wore a stuffed mink head on her forehead and cried suddenly during the dance, "Mamamamamā′!" Thereupon Hē′likiligyala fell down dead. This had been caused by Lōtlemā′k·a. But soon he got up again and they exchanged roles; Hē′likiligyala danced and Lōtlemā′k·a beat time. Then he hurled his staff at her. At once blood began streaming from her mouth and she fell down dead. But Hē′likiligyala healed her again. Then he threw the staff up into the air so high that it didn't come back again.

Hē′likiligyala took a wife named Ts'ē′k·amē (Tsaēk·amē).[116] He had two daughters by her, Naualakoā′alis[117] and Ts'ē′k·amē. The latter became the wife of NEmō′k·ois,[118] the brother of K·′ā′nigyilak′.[119] They had a son named NEmōk·otsâ′lis.[120]

6. NōmasE′nqilis[121]

NōmasE′nqilis descended from the sky and built a house. There were two eagles sitting on his totem pole to watch over it. He had three children, the eldest being a

---

Cliffe Point and extending west to include all of Forward Inlet, Winter Harbour and Browning Inlet, and north along the Vancouver Island shore to the vicinity of Cape Palmerston—apparently this represented the extent of Quatsino territory after they had taken over most of the territory of another group, the Giopino of Forward Inlet (Dawson 1888:68; Duff 1965:65). According to Dawson (1885; 1888:67–68) the Quatsino originated in San Josef Bay and Sea Otter Cove.

116. While Boas' "Ts'ē′k·amē (Tsaēk·amē)" is likely číqəmi, DSS points out that the name číqəmi with which she is familiar is the name of a male ancestor of the Kwiksootainuk, and is not a woman's name.

117. This name is náwalakʷaʔlís meaning 'supernatural' (AD; DSS).

118. Recognized as nəmúgʷis (DSS).

119. The Transformer is recognized as a first ancestor among the Tlatlasikwala and other Kwakwaka'wakw groups in the north, but not among the Kwakwaka'wakw groups to the south (DSS; AD).

120. This name is recognized as nəmúkustuʔlis (AD; DSS).

121. Recognized as númasʔənx̣iʔlis which means 'old man among us' (DSS; AD).

girl who was given the name Aikyā'oēk·a (= Shining).[122] She was blind. Then
followed a son called Tlēqyā'ligyila,[123] and last, a daughter named Naqnaisilaō'k·oa.[124]

Once Aikyā'oēk·a wanted to go Yak·amā'lis (Hope Island)[125] to pick berries. She
left in a canoe with one of her slaves. Because they seemed to take a long time she
asked him, "Where are we? Shouldn't we be in Yak·amā'lis soon?" He replied, "I
don't know where we are; I can no longer see Yak·amā'lis, nor the eagles on your
totem pole." They travelled about for a long time without seeing land. At last an
island appeared far away and when they came closer the slave saw a house.
Tlā'k·oagyila (= Copper Maker)[126] lived here. When he saw the canoe, he invited the
two of them into his house. And he took Aikyā'oēk·a for his wife. NōmasE'nqilis
mourned his daughter as if she were dead. His heart was sad and he had his people
topple the totem pole and throw it into the sea. Then the tides carried it to
Yak·amā'lis and NōmasE'nqilis built himself a new house there. Aikyā'oēk·a gave
birth to two children, Tlā'k·oagyila and Tlāsutewa'lis.[127] One day she put them by the
fire and went to the beach to look for shellfish. The children were playing by the fire
and repeatedly fell on their grandmother's feet. At last she became impatient and
said, "Stop that! Don't disturb me all the time! I don't even know where your
mother comes from!" The boys became sad at this, and, when their mother had
returned, they asked her, "Mother, where is your native land? Grandmother says she
doesn't know where you come from." So the mother told them, "I went out far into
the sea with a slave and after long travels arrived here." Then the children said, "Oh,
make us glad! Let us go to our grandfather!" So she told them that his name was
NōmasE'nqilis and that he was a mighty chief. Their father gave his copper canoe to
them and their mother told them before their departure, "You will hear the eagles
screaming on our totem pole before you reach my home." They departed, and, after
a long journey, heard two eagles screaming, so they knew that they would reach the
house of NōmasE'nqilis. When they arrived, they gave many coppers to their grandfather, because their father had loaded their canoe with many coppers. The canoe,
the paddles and the bailer were of copper and NōmasE'nqilis was amazed when he
saw this. After some time the young men longed for their home and they asked their
grandfather to send them back. So he filled their canoe with fur blankets and they
returned home.

---

122. Boas' "Aikyā'oēk·a" is recognized as ʔaʔikiʔúgʷa meaning 'radiantly beautiful' (AD; DSS).
123. This name is recognized as ƛíqəlagila (DSS; AD).
124. What Boas transcribes as "Naqnaisilaō'k·oa" is possibly the name nánqnasilʔugʷa (AD).
125. Yíqamal'is (Boas' "Yak·amā'lis") is recognized as either a bay on the southeast end of Hope
    Island, opposite Kalect Island (AD), or as the name for the whole island, itself (Boas 1934:40).
126. This name is recognized as ƛ'áqʷagila 'copper maker' (AD; DSS).
127. Recognized as ƛ'ásutiwal'is 'ocean traveller' (AD; DSS).

When K·'ā'nigyilak' transformed NōmasE'nqilis into a stone (see Legends of the Nak·omgyilisala),[128] his son Tlēqya'ligyila moved to Qu'spalis.[129] He had one son named Tsē'selaso.[130] Tsē'selaso had three sons: Ō'maliqstē, Wa'lik·ona and Gya'lk·amistal.[131] One morning Ō'maliqstē became angry with the toads in the forest disturbing him every morning. He ordered them to be quiet and since then they don't call out any more.

Gya'lk·amistal carved himself a wooden human figure which he made come to life by pointing his finger at it and shouting at the same time. Then he went to BaqbakuālanuQsī'oaē, who lived in the River Malō'pa,[132] and became a Hā'mats'a. When he came back, he met Hā'k·oalatl[133] on the banks of the river, and killed him. He had a daughter named Tlō'nusiqtla,[134] who was taken as a wife by K·ā'qaitē,[135] the son of Hā'tak·a. He had two more children, called K·ōmenē'tē and Amā'qoagyila.[136]

7. TlEma'ē [137]

The daughter of a chief fell ill and her body was covered all over with boils. So her father decided to abandon her. He ordered everybody to pack their belongings and they loaded their canoes early in the morning and departed. The poor girl was left in the village all by herself. One day she scratched a boil on her right thigh so that the scab came off and lo, it was transformed at once into a boy! She suddenly felt healthy again, got up and put the child into a shell which she hid in a hollow tree. She went daily to look after the child and noticed that he grew rapidly. She gave him the name TlEma'ē (Boil) because he had been created from her boils. When the child had grown, he returned with the woman to the house. Then the boy put up a salmon weir in the river and had his mother make him a bow and four arrows. On the first day he trapped a salmon in the newly-erected weir. They opened it up and

---

128. The reference is to Section XIX, story 1, part 8.

129. The place name xʷəsbális (Boas' "Qu'spalis"), meaning 'fort at end of beach,' is applied to the Nahwitti Bar on the east side of the river mouth (AD; Boas 1934:77).

130. Name not now recognized.

131. These names—"Ō'maliqstē," "Wa'lik·ona," and "Gya'lk·amistal"—are not now recognized.

132. The name that Boas transcribes here as "Malō'pa" is identified elsewhere by him as the name for the Nahwitti River (Boas 1934:52).

133. Name not now recognized.

134. Name not now recognized.

135. Name not now recognized.

136. These names are not now recognized.

137. Boas subsequently identifies this character, "TlEma'ē," as "boil"; the name is recognized as λəmáʔi derived from λəmá 'scab' (AD; DSS).

suspended it over the fire so that it would dry there. Then they went back to the weir and found two salmon. But when they came back with them to the house, they saw that the first one had been stolen. They didn't know who the thief might be, because they hadn't seen anybody. The newly-caught salmon were stolen from them, too, while they went to the weir again, so TlEma'ē decided to watch and catch the thief. He hung the three salmon, which they had caught this time, over the fire, took his bow and the four arrows and hid inside the house while he sent his mother down to the salmon weir again. It wasn't long before he could hear a voice crying outside, "Hü! Hü!" And soon a Tsōnō'k·oa stepped in through the door. She was carrying a big basket on her back and stretched out her long arms to take the salmon and put them into it. She had giant breasts. Then TlEma'ē shot his arrows at her. The first hit her left breast, the second her right, the third her left side and the fourth her right side. Thereupon the Tsōnō'k·oa screamed in pain and ran away, beating around with her arms so that all the trees fell down. TlEma'ē pursued her by following the fallen trees and the trail of blood across four mountains and through four valleys. At last he came to a pond and there sat down to wait until someone should come. After he had sat there for a little while, Wälalitliloq,[138] the youngest daughter of the Tsōnō'k·oa, came with a container from the house to get water. TlEma'ē hailed her, "Hey! Who are you?" She was so surprised that she could only say, "O! O!" He asked again, "Who are you?" Then she replied, "I am getting water for my mother, who is very ill." "What is wrong with her?" enquired TlEma'ē. "She went out to get food for us and came back very ill. We don't know what is wrong with her." "I am a shaman," said TlEma'ē, "and am able to help her. Tell your mother that a doctor is sitting by the well, willing to help her." The daughter went quickly back to the house and then TlEma'ē was summoned. He saw the four arrows, which were invisible to all the others, at once, and promised to make the mother better. So she promised him her youngest daughter Wälalitliloq for his wife as a reward. Then he wrapped himself up in a cloak and had the places shown to him where the Tsōnō'k·oa had pains. Then he bent over her and pulled the arrows from her body with his teeth. The Tsōnō'k·oa cried in pain, "Ananā'!" But as soon as the arrows had been removed she was better again. She gave him her daughter for his wife, as a reward, and gave him the Nōntlemgyila (= Foolish-Maker)[139] and the death-bringer, Halai'ū. Then he returned to his mother.

The news that she had a handsome son had already reached the relatives of the abandoned woman. One morning she saw many canoes come. So the mother of

---

138. Boas' "Wälalitliloq" is possibly wílalitil'akʷ (AD).

139. What Boas has transcribed as "Nōntlemgyila" is the woman's dance known as the núłəmgila, a Kwakwala term derived from núłəmała 'foolish.' This dance is seldom performed today (AD; DSS).

TlEma'ē clapped her hands and sang while TlEma'ē let the arrivals see the Nōntlemgyila. He called one man ashore, who had always been friendly towards his mother, and then waved the Halai'ū towards the remaining canoes. Thereupon all the people in the canoes died. These burned and finally were transformed into stone.

Then TlEma'ē decided to marry the daughter of Eagle. He slipped into a log of driftwood and let himself be drifted in front of Eagle's house. When Eagle saw the piece of wood, he told his daughter SEpā'alē'tlilok·[140] to go down to the beach to get it. She obeyed, took the wood under her arm and went up to the house. On the way, TlEma'ē suddenly clasped her around the waist and, terrified, she threw the wood away. This happened four times. The fourth time TlEma'ē made himself known and said that he wanted to marry her. Then she threw the log onto the fire. It burned up and TlEma'ē, in the shape of a white flake of ash, flew unnoticed into her room and there made her his wife.

8. The Moon

Gyā'loyak·amē,[141] the Moon, came down to the earth and lived on Kaya'la Island.[142] He caught eagles, from whose beaks he made himself a rattle. He made a dancing hat from their lower mandibles. Thereupon he became strong and brave. Since he lived on the island all by himself, he transformed the seagulls sitting on the beach into people. They built him a big four-platform house and did all sorts of work for their chief. Once Gyā'loyak·amē was standing on a small point of land when suddenly the seas opened like jaws and a canoe came out of the crack. In it was a man called Waâ'yagyila.[143] He wore head and neck-rings of red inner cedar bark. He went up to Gyā'loyak·amē and gave him a huge stone which had been lying in the bottom of the canoe. Then he turned back and the sea closed again after him. Gyā'loyak·amē carried the stone home, but it was so heavy that ten of his slaves were unable to lift it.

Then Gyā'loyak·amē said to his slaves, "Let's go up to the lake behind our house. Wā'qaos[144] lives there and he also has a huge stone. We'll find out which one of us

---

140. Name not now recognized.

141. The name gálugəmi means 'higher-ranking than anyone' (DSS; AD).

142. What Boas transcribes here as "Kaya'la" is given elsewhere by him as "gǎɛyā'la" and translated as 'being across on rocks,' referring to a site on the southeastern portion of Hope Island (Boas 1934:71; map 3:10). AD, who knows this place as gayála 'crosswise on rocks,' points out that Boas incorrectly noted its location—gayála refers to the rock islet adjacent to the west side of the bay on southeastern Hope Island, opposite Kalect Island (AD).

143. Name not now recognized.

144. Likely wáqaʔas, derived from wáqís 'frog' (AD; DSS).

is the stronger." They went up the river and when they had got to Wā′qaos, Gyā′loyak·amē challenged him to a contest. He asked, "Can you lift my stone?" Wā′qaos replied, "Yes, I can, but can you lift mine?" Gyā′loyak·amē thought that he could do it. At the request of Wā′qaos he brought his stone and the former lifted it easily. But he was unable to lift the stone of Wā′qaos. So he said to him, "I see that you are stronger than I. You shall be my brother from now on." And from then on they lived in the house together and caught salmon in the river.

9. Moon Steals a Woman

A woman called Tspilk·ola′k·a[145] and her daughter, Tlaluakoagyilaka′sō,[146] were living together in Tlamnos.[147] The daughter was very beautiful and so the Moon Man resolved to steal her. He descended from the sky and asked Tspilk·ola′k·a for some water. She sent her daughter willingly to the well to get fresh water, but she had scarcely set foot out of the door when the Moon Man seized her and took her up into the sky with him. So Tspilk·ola′k·a became sad and moved to Nauê′tē.[148] After some time the Moon Man came down again and asked a woman for water. When Tspilk·ola′k·a heard him coming she warned the woman not to go outside because the Moon Man would take her with him. But she didn't listen to the advice and the Moon Man abducted her when she stepped out of the door. The girl with her container can still be seen in the moon today.

10. Apōtl

Once Baā′kumi[149] was standing in front of his house and saw a seal swimming in the water. So he said to his son Apōtl, "Go and shoot that seal." He obeyed. He took his harpoon, and, with two of his cousins, went into his canoe to pursue the seal. He paddled carefully up to it. When they had come close, Apōtl threw his harpoon and

---

145. Name not now recognized.

146. Name not now recognized.

147. Boas (1934:81) points out elsewhere that the name "Lᴇ′mwas" 'perch place' was erroneously given as "tlamnos" here in the *Sagen*. The location of the place that Boas transcribes as "Lᴇ′mwas" in his 1934 study is indicated on the west side of Hope Island, south of Mexicano Point (Boas 1934:map 3:31); AD confirms this location, and the Kwakwala name, x̌ámawaʔas (derived from x̌ámawa 'perch').

148. What Boas transcribes here as "Nauê′tē" is naẃídi (anglicized as "Nahwitti"), on Cape Sutil at the north end of Vancouver Island (DSS; AD).

149. Possibly the name that Boas renders here as "Baā′kumi" is the term bák̓ʷəmi 'a Native person who is not present' (DSS).

hit the seal, which swam away and towed the canoe far out to sea. They had almost lost sight of land when one of the cousins said to Apōtl, "Cut the harpoon line, otherwise we'll never return home." He took his knife and cut the line, but in vain, for the severed part sprang back and stuck fast to the canoe. Then they saw nothing but sky and water all around. They had drifted about for a long time when they saw a flat coast far away. When they got closer the steersman jumped ashore. But it turned out to be a mirage and he went under. Apōtl and his cousin were towed on irresistibly by the seal. They came to a spot where the sea was covered in black stones which looked like charcoal. These allowed them through. They got through a heap of piled up driftwood the same way. After some time they saw land with trees on it. The seal swam towards it and then they were so close to it that they were able to distinguish houses and people on it. When they reached the shore, the seal changed into a man. Apōtl had become very hungry and because he saw that one of the inhabitants had a lot of fish-oil, he intended to ask him for some oil and some fish. The transformed Seal said, "Ask that man for oil. He will give you some, but don't accept more than four mugs, then come back to the canoe." Apōtl obeyed. As soon as he set foot in the canoe, the man changed back into a seal and towed them along. After some time they arrived at the mouth of a river. There Salmon invited Apōtl and his cousin for a meal. Again the seal, who had changed into a man, warned the two of them not to help themselves more than four times, and they obeyed. Then they went on and visited Silver Salmon[150] and the fish hanū'n.[151] The latter said to Apōtl, "I'm not able to serve food to you but I will warn you of NEmō'k·oak·amē, who lives on that peninsula. He is a cannibal and the bones of the slain are heaped up round about." They went on and when Seal heard NEmō'k·oak·amē[152] calling, he swam away as quickly as possible. So the cannibal tore up a spruce tree and hurled it after the canoe. It nearly hit it and the seal hurried all the more to get away. So NEmō'k·oak·amē tore out a fir tree and tried to hit the canoe once more. He nearly hit it. The seal swam on. After some time they saw a canoe close to a small island. There was nobody in it, but they could see two halibut lying in the canoe. Apōtl took them and went to the island. Soon he saw a man named Gyingyinā'nimis (= Dwarf)[153] emerge from the sea, carrying in each hand a

---

150. Given in the original as *Silberlachs* 'silver salmon,' which is a folk name for coho salmon (*Oncorhynchus kisutch*).

151. AD recognizes "hanū'n" as hənúṅ, the Kwakwala term applied to pink or humpback salmon (*Oncorhynchus gorbuscha*).

152. The term given here by Boas as "Nemō'k·oak·amē" for this cannibal is likely nəmúkʷagamɛ, meaning 'only one doing something' (DSS; AD).

153. What Boas renders here as "Gyingyinā'nimis" 'dwarf,' is recognized by AD as gə'ngənanəṁis meaning 'children of the bottom of the sea.'

halibut. He noticed at once that his fish had vanished and called, "Oh, who has stolen my halibut?" Apōtl grew afraid and took the stolen fish back to him.

Seal swam on and at last they reached Amiaē'qet (K·ants'ō'ump). He gave one of his daughters to Apōtl for a wife and kept him in his house for four days. But in reality Apōtl and his cousin stayed there for four years. Then the two men longed for their home. Apōtl became sad, went to bed and didn't want to get up again. Finally he told his wife, after much questioning, that he would like to return, and she asked her father to fulfill Apōtl's request. Amiaē'qet complied with her wishes. He went to Apōtl and asked him whether he and his cousin had come by themselves. So Apōtl told him how his other cousin had lost his life. So Amiaē'qet took an eye from a box, tied a rope, which he gave to a slave to hold, around his middle, and dived into the sea. There he got the bones of the cousin, which he then put together. He put new eyes into him and then sprinkled him with the Water of Life. Thereupon he got up again. Then Amiaē'qet said to Apōtl and his cousin, "My house is in the extreme west; if you want to get back to your home, you have to journey always towards the rising sun." And he gave them a small a box, into which he put four sea otter skins as a parting present.

Long, long they journeyed towards the rising sun. Then they saw the mountains of their native land appearing on the horizon and found the whole country covered with snow sent by Amiaē'qet. Apōtl went to his father's house. To his surprise, there was nobody sitting in front of the door, and he saw that the house was very dirty. He entered and found his father Baā'kumi sitting by the fire. He hailed him, "Hey! I've returned from my travels, I, your son Apōtl!" The old man didn't believe him and replied, "You're lying; my son, Apōtl, went out to hunt a seal a long time ago and didn't come back." So Apōtl saw that he had become very old and he wept in sorrow. He said, "Don't you recognize me, Father? I am Apōtl, your son." Then Baā'kumi recognized him and his heart became glad. He took his dancing staff and started to sing because his son had returned. So Apōtl built a new house. He invited all the people and gave them generous presents from the small box that never grew empty, which had been given to him by Amiaē'qet.

11. Tikya'

Tikya' and his sisters Ts'ēqsâ'ke (Crow)[154] and Elk·sâ'yuk·a were living together in one house. One day Tikya' borrowed the cape of Ts'ēqsâ'ke and set out to visit a neighbouring village. But a cedar had recently fallen across the path. Tikya'

---

154. While the term given in the *Sagen* as "Ts'ēqsâ'ke" is recognized as the woman's name c̓áx̱siga, AD and DSS do not recognize it as a name for 'crow' (as Boas indicates here).

wrapped the cape closely around himself and tried to squeeze through. It tore and he turned back home. When his sister saw that her cape was torn, she grew angry and scolded her brother. He became sad and went to bed. He lay there for four days without eating. Then he got up, took a stick with which he beat time and sang, "My sisters are angry with me because I have torn their cape, but they will make a new one for me." They set to work at once and made him a new cape. As soon as he received it he set out anew and this time succeeded in pushing his way through under the cedar trunk. At last he arrived at the coast. He found a log of driftwood there in which he noticed a piece of iron (?).[155] The log was covered with slippery algae. He climbed onto it carefully, tore out the iron and sang, "I've never seen anything like this before. I will make an axe from the iron and no one else will have a tool to equal mine." He went on and arrived at a peninsula and there killed an otter with his iron. After he had wandered for some time he returned to his sisters. In answer to their questions he told them where he had been and what his adventures had been. Once he saw smoke rising from the roof of the house next door, where shellfish were cooked. He stepped up to the door, but nobody invited him in. So he said, "I'd like to eat shellfish with you," but nobody replied or invited him in. So he grew sad and lifted his dancing staff to beat time and sing. But the people thought that he wanted to kill them and they fled. He sang, "Everybody is angry with me. I would have liked to eat shellfish with them, but they didn't give me any, even when I asked them." And he went home with a heavy heart. There his sisters asked him to go to the forest with them to fetch cedar bark. He lost his way in the forest and only found it again after many detours near a big cedar tree. Then he sang, "Now I won't have to starve here in the forest. The birds won't come to eat me. My eyes won't fall from their sockets and I won't be transformed into a bear or wolf." At last he arrived safely home again.

Another time he went out to gather shellfish with his sisters. They embarked in their canoe and he steered while his sisters paddled. While they were gathering shellfish on the beach, he lay down in the canoe and awaited their return. He fell asleep and, when he turned around in his sleep, the canoe capsized. But he righted it in the water, got in and sang, "If I had drowned I would have become a huge whale or a fin whale and green algae would have grown on my body."

Once his sisters asked him to come with them to dig roots. They saw many plants growing at the edge of a steep rock and Tikya' climbed up to dig them. He threw the roots down from up above and his sisters down below gathered them into their baskets. When these were filled, they called to their brother to come down. So he tied his hands together with lichens and hurled himself from the rock. His sisters

---

155. Boas places brackets here in the *Sagen* to question the mention of iron in this story.

thought that he was dead. But he shook himself, stood up and sang, "Lâ′lenoq (the spirit of the dead) has killed me. Owl has killed me; he hoots all night long."

Unidentified Quatsino people cutting halibut for air-drying on the shore, Winter Harbour, *ca.* 1920.

XIX. Legends of the Nakomgilisala

Boas did not have to seek out the Nakomgilisala in their home territory at Cape Scott. They were among the local tribes who were visiting their neighbouring Nahwitti on Hope Island when Boas arrived there by boat in October 1886. "It is especially curious," he wrote in his diary for 12 October, "that myth cycles do not seem to be alike among the different tribes speaking the same language, although I am not sure how much of this may be due to my ignorance concerning the myths" (Rohner 1969:38). He had of course collected very little to compare these with, and adds forlornly, "At present I am quite confused ... " We might suspect this was Boas' puritanical response to the earthy antics of the Transformer, as related to him in a series of thirty-one brief episodes (No. 1, parts 1–31). Yet his method in the *Sagen* of presenting the texts pretty much as he got them ensures that readers get a similar sense of being in the field for the first time.

"Korpreno Tom," also known as "Sealing Tom," instructing a young boy in the use of a harpoon, Quatsino, *ca.* 1912.

Vancouver Public Library, Vancouver, B.C. No. 14059 (B.W. Leeson photo).

XIX. Legends of the Nak·o′mgyilisala[1]

1. The K·'ā′nigyilak· Legend[2]

1) K·'ā′nigyilak· and Nɛmō′k·ois (= Only One)[3] were the sons of K·ants'ōump (= Our Father).[4] A long, long time ago he sent both of them down to earth[5] where they were born again to a woman named Tsatsaquitela′k·a (= Eulachon Woman).[6] The twins grew up quickly. In those days there were no fish swimming in the sea or in the rivers and K·'ā′nigyilak· was anxious to see the waters alive with salmon and other fish. ButTsatsaquitela′k·a kept all the fish in her cape. K·'ā′nigyilak· asked her to lend it to him. When he had it, he went into the canoe with his brother and first they went upriver, then turned back and paddled out into the sea. Since they didn't find any fish anywhere, K·'ā′nigyilak· dipped one corner of his mother's cape into

---

1. "Nak·o′mgyilisala" is Boas' transcription of nəqə′mgəlisəla, anglicized as "Nakomgilisala," refer-ring to one of the three tribes known collectively as the Nahwitti at the northernmost end of Vancouver Island and the adjacent islands offshore (see also the preceding discussion of the Tlatlasikwala, Section XVIII). The term nəqə′mgəlisəla has been translated as 'always staying in their own country' (Boas 1966:38), 'those of the unprotected bay' (Curtis:1915:10:306), and 'always stay in the same place' (Wallas and Whitaker 1981:8). Boas' (1887f) map delineated Nakomgilisala territory between the Cape Palmerston area, about 13 miles (21 km) south from Cape Scott, and Nissen Bight, approximately 6 miles (10 km) northeast of Cape Scott. Duff (1965:61) estimated that it was in the mid-1850s, after a devastating raid by the Heiltsuk (Bella Bella) that the surviving Nakomgilisala joined with the Tlatlasikwala tribe living at the Nahwitti village on Cape Sutil which is about 18 miles (29 km) northeast from Cape Scott.

    Our annotation of this section was assisted greatly in the summer of 2001 by Kwakwala-speaking experts Chief Adam Dick and Dr. Daisy Sewid-Smith who are referred to here as "AD" and "DSS" respectively; we gratefully acknowledge their assistance.

2. What Boas transcribes as "K·'ā′nigyilak'" is q̓ániqi?l'akw, the name of the 'Transformer' who changed the world for the coming people (AD).

3. The term nəmúgʷis (Boas' "Nɛmō′k·ois") means 'a person who is left alone on the beach' (Wallas and Whitaker 1981:29); 'only one on the beach' (AD).'

4. AD and DSS use the term qəns ?úmp to mean 'Our Father,' referring to God.

5. Commenting on this incident of these two brothers descending from the sky, Robert Lowie (1908:116) wrote that Franz Boas told him "His recording it among the Newette resulted from a misunderstanding."

6. The term that Boas transcribes here as "Tsatsaquitela′k·" is the name dzádzaxʷitəyalaga 'eulachon woman' (AD).

the sea and lo, two salmon jumped out and swam away merrily! They multiplied rapidly and soon the river and sea were full of fish. But Tsatsaquitela′k·a became angry when she saw that K·'ā′nigyilak· had set the fish free. She left her children and went to the country of the salmon.

2) K·'ā′nigyilak· and Nᴇmō̄′k·ois went upriver to seek adventure. After they had journeyed for a while they saw a house. Heron[7] and his wife Woodpecker, who in those days were still human, lived here. The brothers landed and K·'ā′nigyilak· said to the man; "I will teach you how to construct a salmon weir." He showed him how to do it and Heron was glad to be able to get food so easily from then on. As a reward he adopted K·'ā′nigyilak· and Nᴇmō̄′k·ois as his children.

In the morning, Heron said to them; "I will go now with my wife to the salmon weir to see whether anything has been caught. You stay here. I will watch down by the water whether anyone comes here. If I see one of the bad people who live in the neighbourhood coming, I'll shout. Then hide in the forest so that you won't get caught." The two old ones left. But the woman was greedy and mean and didn't want to share with the children. So she said to her husband, "Should we find fish in the weir, shout before we get back. Then the children will run away and we'll be able to have the salmon for ourselves." And lo, they found one fish in the weir! They took it, went home and then the man shouted at the top of his voice. When K·'ā′nigyilak· and Nᴇmō̄′k·ois heard this, they hurriedly hid in the forest. The woman cleaned and cooked the fish and they enjoyed it. When the children dared to come out again at night the man told them, "It was good that you ran away. When I shouted this morning I saw two of our enemies coming towards the house. When I shout again tomorrow hide quickly again." But the woman said nothing and ate without stopping.

The following morning the two old ones went down to the river again to see whether any salmon had been caught. And lo, they found four fish! They carried them home and, when they were up close enough, the man shouted again. So K·'ā′nigyilak· said to his brother, "Let's find out who these bad people might be. Come, let's hide near the house and not go into the forest." They did what K·'ā′nigyilak· had suggested and thus saw that only the old man and his wife were coming and that they were carrying four heavy salmon into the house. They heard how the woman said to her husband, "Now make a fire quickly; let's eat before the children come back." The man obeyed and then they cooked the fish and began eating. Thereupon K·'ā′nigyilak· became furious. He took his bow and first shot the man, then the woman. Then he took their corpses and threw them up high, saying, "Now

---

7. Boas uses the German term *Reiher* 'heron' in the original; very likely the species referred to here is the Great Blue Heron.

fly away as birds." So the man was transformed into a heron, and the woman into a woodpecker.

3) And K·'ā'nigyilak· and Nɛmō'k·ois left the place and continued on their way. When they arrived at Tsā'mō (near Newette Bar),[8] they saw a marvellously beautiful fish swimming in the water, its body shining like light. K·'ā'nigyilak· took a stick and beat it. Thereupon the fish changed into a sī'siutl (the legendary fabulous double-headed serpent) which he killed. He pulled it ashore, cut it open and skinned it. From the skin he made himself a belt. And he took out its eyes, which he preserved carefully.

4) And the brothers continued on their way. Soon they came to Guā'nē (near Cape Scott).[9] There K·'ā'nigyilak· saw a mighty whale swimming in the sea and wanted to kill it. He asked Nɛmō'k·ois to lend him his sling. He put one of the sī'siutl-eyes into it as a projectile and when the whale came up again to breathe, he whirled the sling. The stone spun away and hit the whale, which died at once. K·'ā'nigyilak· killed four whales in this manner and they all drifted ashore the following morning in Pā'tsis.[10] He returned the sling to Nɛmō'k·ois, went down to the sea and lifted the whales by their tails. He carried them up this way into the country. Their backs and blow-holes can be seen there still today.

5) Then K·'ā'nigyilak· went into the forest, where he got a heap of small sticks from which he constructed two small houses. Then he took some water in his mouth and spat onto the houses, which suddenly expanded mightily. And he named the one house K·'oā'k·oakyiutelas (= So Big that the People on the Opposite Side Appear Small [??])[11] and the other one Yuibā'lagyilis (= Where the Wind is Blowing in From All Sides [??]).[12] He gave the second house to his brother and said to him, "I will

---

8. The Nahwitti Bar (referred to as "Tsā'mō" by Boas), at the mouth of the Nahwitti River on Vancouver Island, is located south from the west end of Hope Island. However, Boas did not identify a place called "Tsā'mō" on his place names map of the Nahwitti Bar area (Boas 1934:61, map 3). The term that Boas renders as "Tsā'mō" is possibly čámu, derived from čála 'tide' (AD).

9. What Boas transcribes here as "Guā'nē" is the same name he transcribes elsewhere as "k!wā'nē" and identifies as a place in Experiment Bight, located immediately east of the northern point of Cape Scott (Boas 1934:70, map 2:25). The name "Guā'nē" ("k!wā'nē") was given by the late James Wallas (in Galois 1994:287–288) as k̓ʷánɛʔ.

10. Boas' "Pā'tsis" is the name applied to Guise Bay at Cape Scott, which Boas (1934:22, map 2:30) transcribes elsewhere as "pātsx·ax·" and Dawson (1887a:map:site 6) gives as "Pā-tshih." AD believes he has heard this place name, p̓ádzis, but is uncertain as to its location.

11. The name that Boas transcribes as "K·'oā'k·oakyiutelas" is not now recognized (square-bracketed question marks are given in the original *Sagen* following this name).

12. The house name that Boas renders as "Yuibā'lagyilis" is recognized as yúbalagil'is 'wind blows on the land' (AD; DSS) (square-bracketed question marks are given in the original *Sagen* following this name).

leave now to travel around the world to get to know all the people. You stay here. If you are hungry, live on the whales. They will last until I return."

6) So they separated. After K·'ā'nigyilak· had wandered for some time, he arrived in a village where, to his astonishment, there was no smoke issuing from any of the houses. He went into every single house but saw no one. Finally, in the last house he found a man named Nau'etsâ[13] and his granddaughter, a small girl, who were the only inhabitants of the village. He asked, "Where are your fellow-villagers?" Nau'etsâ replied, "The monster Tsē'k·is,[14] which lives in that lake over there, has killed them all. As soon as anyone went down to fetch water, it appeared and devoured him. We are the lone survivors." K·'ā'nigyilak· stayed with Nau'etsâ and his granddaughter in their house. One day he said to the child, "Go down to the lake and get me some water." But the old man was violently opposed to this and didn't want to allow it. He cried, "No, she shall not, and must not, go! Tsē'k·is shall not rob me of the last of my children, too, and he will certainly devour her if she goes." But K·'ā'nigyilak· tried to calm him. He gave the pail to the child, tied the belt of sī'siutl-skin around her and told her to go. He followed her and saw how Tsē'k·is came and devoured the poor child. Then K·'ā'nigyilak· picked up a stick and sang, beating time on a stone, "Sī'siutl, become alive and kill him, wake up and kill him!" He had scarcely finished his song when the monster arose from the deep, writhing in agonies of death. It brought up all the bones of the people it had devoured. Then K·'ā'nigyilak· killed it with his arrows. He put the bones together again and sprinkled them with the Water of Life. Thereupon they got up, rubbing their eyes as if they had been asleep. They moved away from the place of disaster and became the ancestors of the K·ōskī'mō.[15]

7) And K·'ā'nigyilak· continued on his way. When he had travelled for a while he met Hē'likiligyala (= Healer, see Section XVIII, story 5)[16] who wore a neck-ring of red inner cedar bark. He was living in a house with his sister Lōtlemā'k·a (NŌtlEmā'k·a?).[17] When K·'ā'nigyilak· arrived, both of them were dancing. Hē'likili-

---

13. Boas' "Nau'etsâ" is possibly náwiċa 'person with supernatural powers' (AD; DSS).

14. What Boas renders here as "Tsē'k·is" is known to AD and DSS as ċígis, the name of a sea monster. Wallas and Whitaker (1991:18, 208) note that ċígis is translated as 'to lie on beach or in deep water looking up with a leer on face' and comment that ċígis is "like a giant bullhead with a long, long tongue."

15. What Boas transcribes here as "K·ōskī'mō" is gʷúsgimukʷ (AD; DSS), anglicized as "Koskimo," the name of the tribe who originated at the mouth of the Stranby River (also known as "Cache Creek") which empties into Shuttleworth Bight, west from Cape Sutil near the northern tip of Vancouver Island (Dawson 1888:68; Shotridge and Shotridge 1913:77; Curtis 1915:10:306; Wallas and Whitaker 1981:18–20,208; Wallas, in Galois 1994:367–371).

16. The name of this character, rendered by Boas as "Hē'likiligyala," is possibly hílikiligəla, derived from the term hílixʔid 'healer' (AD; DSS).

17. Boas provides the term "Lōtlemā'k·a," which is his rendering of the Kwakwala term lútəmaga

gyala was holding a stick in his hands, which he kept pressed together. When he blew on the stick it flew through the house towards his sister, who caught it. When K·'ā'nigyilak· saw this he grew afraid and crept secretly around the house before Hēlikiligyala had seen him.

8) And he continued on his way and came to Tsētsek·lā'sis (on Hope Island).[18] NōmasE'nQilis (= Oldest One on Earth)[19] lived here. He had a son named Tleqyā'ligyila[20] and a daughter named Aikyā'ōēk·a (= Shining, see Section XVIII, story 5).[21] NōmasE'nQilis knew that K·'ā'nigyilak· would come and said to his son, "K·'ā'nigyilak· will come soon, but stay calm; he will be afraid of you. Go to Qu'spalis (Newette Bar)[22] and wait for him. I will stay here." When K·'ā'nigyilak· saw NōmasE'nQilis he transformed him into a big stone, which is still on the beach today. His hair was transformed into grass and earth, which cover the upper part of the rock. Aikyā'ōēk·a had a house in Tsētsek·lā'sis with a totem pole standing in front. On it there were two eagles which screamed incessantly. K·'ā'nigyilak· pulled it up and threw it into the sea.

9) He continued on his way and came to QūtsEqstä'e (the burial place of the Newette).[23] There he met Ō'meatl (see Section XVIII, story 1, part 3),[24] who, when they saw him coming, simply pointed his index finger at K·'ā'nigyilak· and thus

---

meaning 'ghost-dance woman,' and then follows this with the term núłəmaga (Boas' "NōtlEmä'k·a) meaning 'clown-dance woman' (AD; DSS). His question marks following the second name seem to query whether the name of the sister, 'ghost-dance woman,' might be associated with the clown dance.

18. The place name given by Boas as "Tsētsek·lā'sis" is likely that which he applied to a site east of the Nahwitti River, across from Hope Island (Boas 1934:22, map 3, 92). The name cíłcəqalalis 'thimbleberry beach,' is derived from cəgəł 'thimbleberry, (*Rubus parviflorus*)' (DSS). Boas (1910:II:267) erroneously translated this same place name as 'red sand beach,' instead of "red-caps," the folk name for thimbleberries.

19. Boas' "NōmasE'nQilis" is the name númasənxa?l'is, 'the oldest man on earth,' derived from númas 'old man' (DSS; AD).

20. Name not now recognized.

21. What Boas has rendered "Aikyā'ōēk·a" is recognized as the name ?á?iki?ugʷa meaning 'beautifully-radiant' (DSS; AD). The reference to story 1 should actually read Section XVII, story 6.

22. Boas' "Qu'spalis" is xʷəsbális, 'fort at end of beach,' the name applied to "Newette Bar" located adjacent to the mouth of the Nahwitti River at the northern end of Vancouver Island (Boas 1934:77; AD).

23. What Boas transcribes here as "QūtsEqstä'e" is recognized by AD as xʷəc̓əx̣ste̓, derived from xʷəsəlá 'fortified.' AD recalls hearing this place name, but does not recall its location.

24. Boas' "Ōmeatl," is ?ú?mɛł, the Kwakwala name for 'Raven' in mythology, derived from ?ú?ma 'noble woman' (AD; DSS).

pierced his head. Then K·'ā'nigyilak· pointed his index finger at Oʹmeātl and pierced his head. So they were afraid of one another and went their separate ways.

10) And K·'ā'nigyilak· came to Qu'spalis, where Tlegyā'ligyila was waiting for him. He saw that the latter was dancing the Tsētsā'ēk·a (= Mysteries)[25] with his sister Naqnaisilaoʹk·oa (= Always Shining upon Earth).[26] So he grew afraid and went past.

11) And he met Nōʹmas (= Old One) (see Section XVII, appendix story) the ancestor of the Tlau'itsis (= Hot-tempered Ones).[27] Nōʹmas was the first man to have made fishing lines of kelp in order to catch halibut. Consequently the Tlau'itsis were also the first ones to employ such lines. K·'ā'nigyilak· became his friend and filled the rivers of his country with salmon.

12) He went on and met Kuē'qagyila (Murderer)[28] (see Section XVIII, story 2, part 2) whose house was on top of Mount Qusēla.[29] He saw him in the mask of the grizzly bear dancing the NōntlEm.[30] So he knew that he was strong and powerful.

13) And he went to Kwākiu'tis (the region of Fort Rupert),[31] where he found (see Section XVII, story 13) Haialikyā'wē[32] who lived in TlElā't (Hardy Bay).[33] He had the sī'siutl as his crest and during the dances wore the mask Hai'alikyamtl[34] and a

---

25. Boas refers to the winter dance complex known as číċɛqa (Boas' "Tsētsā'ēk·a") as 'mysteries,' likely referring to the initiation of young people into secret societies that is done during the winter dance season (Boas 1966:173–174; DSS).

26. This name rendered by Boas as "Naqnaisilaoʹk·oa" is recognized by AD as naqʷəqʷnasílə?ugʷa, derived from náqʷəla 'moonlight' (AD).

27. What Boas transcribes here as "Tlau'itsis" is łáwiċis, the name of a Kwakwala-speaking tribe that is anglicized as "Tlawitsis" and generally translated as 'the angry ones' (DSS; AD). The Tlawitsis originated in Hardy Bay and Beaver Harbour, but after Fort Rupert was established in 1849, they moved to a village on Turnour Island, and subsequently Tlawitsis territory has been centered on Turnour Island and West Cracroft Island, and the islands in between (Boas 1887f:131,map; 1921:2:1386–1388; Dawson 1888:72; Curtis 1915:10:307; Duff 1953–1954; 1965; Bouchard and Kennedy 1998b:97–99).

28. The name kʷíxagila means 'to strike someone with an instrument,' rather than 'murderer' (AD; DSS)

29. The term xʷəsəlá (Boas' "Qusēla") can be applied to any fortified site (AD); in this instance it is applied to Shushartie Saddle, situated between the Nahwitti and Shushartie rivers (Boas 1934:23).

30. Elsewhere, Boas (1966:400–401) explains that the northern Kwakwaka'wakw groups have a ceremony called "Nō'ntlem" which precedes the winter dance. AD recognizes the name of this dance as núnłəm and explains that this is the dance used during a girl's puberty ceremony.

31. Boas (1934:22, 69) gives this name elsewhere for "the region of Fort Rupert"—the term kʷáḵut'əs (Boas' "Kwākiu'tis") actually means 'where the kʷágu?ł live' (DSS; AD).

32. The term Boas renders as " Hai'alikyamtl" is háyaliḵəwi 'senior or head healer,' derived from hílika meaning 'to heal' (AD; DSS).

33. The name łəl'ádi (Boas' "TlElā't") applies to Hardy Bay and is translated as 'having dead whales' (DSS; AD; Boas 1934:22, 81, map 6:76). In part 14 below, Boas provides an alternate transcription, "Tlalā'etē," for this same place.

34. The term háyaliḵəmł 'healing mask,' derived from 'hílikəla 'healer,' is applied to a frontlet mask

headdress of ermine. They wanted to match their powers. First K·'ā′nigyilak· made the waters rise so that they covered the house completely. When they receded again he saw that Haialikyā′wē was sitting in the house alive and well. So he made them rise and fall once more, but Haialikyā′wē only blew and shook himself. The water could do him no harm. Then K·'ā′nigyilak· tried to burn him and his house. He piled up a big heap of logs in the middle of the house, set it alight and threw Haialikyā′wē in. He sank into the ground at once and reappeared again not far from the fire. The house didn't burn either, because the sī′siutl protected it. So K·'ā′nigyilak· realized that he was dealing with a powerful adversary and decided to make friends with him. He filled the river of TlElā′t with salmon, took Haialikyā′wē by the hand and said, "All this land shall be yours. You are a mighty magician. Keep on dancing your magic dance. Your descendants shall inherit your art and your dancing implements." And they called one another brother.

14) K·'ā′nigyilak· went on and arrived at Tlalā′etē.[35] There he met a big bird. When the bird saw him coming he took off his bird's garment and said, "Behold, I am Mā′tagyila!" (Ancestor of the Maa′mtagyila group of the Kuē′tela tribe).[36] So K·'ā′nigyilak· called him brother and created salmon for him in the River Ts'E′lqot (near the southern end of Hardy Bay).[37] Later Mā′tagyila moved to K·oā′tsē[38] and there built a house.

15) And K·'ā′nigyilak· visited mighty K·'ē′qtlala[39] and made friends with him. He met Hā′natlēnoq (= Archer, ancestor of one of the K·'ō′mōyuē numaym),[40] who nearly killed him with his arrows, Ts'E′nQk·aiō (ancestor of a Walaskwakiutl numaym with the identical name),[41] who was living in Tā′ek·otl,[42] and Lā′laqsEnt'aio

---

with an ermine headdress. The dance is called hílikəłał (DSS; AD).

35. This name, łəl'ádi (Boas' "Tlalā′etē") applies to Hardy Bay and is translated as 'having dead whales' (DSS; AD; Boas 1934:22, 81, map 6:76). In part 13 above, Boas provides an alternate transcription, "TlElā′t," for this same place.

36. The name mátagil'a, derived from mátaxs?alis 'to wander around,' refers to the First Ancestor of the ma?ámtagil'a, part of the gʷítəla subgroup of the kʷágu?ł (AD; DSS).

37. The place name that Boas transcribes here as "Ts'E′lqot" is the term cə́lgʷadi, meaning 'where the chum and pink salmon spawn' and is applied to a stream entering the south end of Hardy Bay (DSS; AD). The site's location is confirmed elsewhere by Boas (1934:23,61).

38. The site known as gʷá?dzí? (Boas' "K·oā′tsē") is situated at the southernmost end of Hardy Bay (Boas 1934:68, map 6:92; AD).

39. Boas' "K·'ē′qtlala" is the name ƙɛ′xλala, derived from ƙɛ′x 'carve' (AD; DSS).

40. Recognized as hánaƙ'ɛnuxʷ, an ancestor of a numaym of the q̓ʷúmuyuy ('rich ones') group of the kʷagu?ł (DSS; AD).

41. This is dzə́nqayu (or dzə́ndzənqayu), an ancestor of a numaym of the wálas kʷágu?ł (DSS).

42. The place called táyəgʷuł is situated at the south end of Beaver Harbour (AD; DSS; Boas 1934:23, 55, map 6:115).

(ancestor of a Kuē′tela numaym with the identical name),[43] as well as Sᴇ′ntlaē, the son of the Sun (ancestor of the Sī′sᴇntaē numaym of the Kuē′tela).[44]

16) He went on and came to E′lis (Cormorant Island)[45] where he visited Qutsetsâ′lis[46] and Iна′k·amē (Alert Bay Mission).[47]

17) Then he crossed over to Qulkн (at the mouth of the Nimpkish River).[48] There lived Guanā′lalis[49] (see Section XV, story 1), who had four beautiful daughters. The girls were swimming in the river when K·′ā′nigyilak· arrived. So he changed into an old man. When the girls saw him they called, "Oh, stay and wait until we come out of the water, then you shall wash our backs." He obeyed. When the eldest daughter had come out of the water he washed her back from top to bottom and then poked his index finger into her vagina. "Hoo," she cried, "what are you doing?" Then she went to her sisters and said, "Have your backs washed, you will see how nicely the old man does it!" The second and third went and K·′ā′nigyilak· did the same to them. But the youngest refused and didn't allow the old man to touch her. So K·′ā′nigyilak· assumed his real shape. When the girls saw this the youngest cried, "See, what did I tell you! If only you hadn't allowed the old man to touch you!" But he took the youngest for his wife.

The older sisters then went into the house to their father and said, "Father, your youngest daughter has got a husband. Purify your house to receive him!" So Guanā′lalis purified his whole house and invited K·′ā′nigyilak· in. He assigned a

---

43. Boas' "Lā′laqsᴇnt'aio" is recognized as ƛ′láksəndayu, a numaym of the ḵɛ′x̌ƛala group of the kʷáguɬ (AD; DSS).

44. Sə′nx̌'i, the ancestor of the sísəṅx̌'i numaym of the ḵɛ′x̌ƛala (DSS).

45. The name that Boas transcribes here as "E′lis" and elsewhere as "ᵉyîlē′s" is yəlís which means 'spread legs on beach (i.e. a bay bounded by two narrow points),' referring to Alert Bay. The name applies specifically to the beach on the south side of Cormorant Island, across from Port McNeill (Boas 1934:23, 40, map 8a:84; AD; DSS).

46. DSS and AD confirm Boas' "Qutsetsâ′lis" as x̌ʷədzədzɔ′ʔlis, and also confirm his translation, 'having great ebb tide,' although they do not know a place with this name anywhere on Cormorant Island (as suggested by this story). Boas elsewhere does not identify any place on Cormorant Island as x̌ʷədzədzɔ′ʔlis; rather, he identifies x̌ʷədzədzɔ′ʔlis only as a place on the south end of Turnour Island (Boas 1934:77; map 8a; map 14:77).

47. Boas (1934:41) gives the translation of this name as 'near face'; AD and DSS recognize this term (given in the present story as "Iна′k·amē") as ʔíxagamɛ, but do not know it as a place name. This is confirmed in Boas' (1934:map 8a) place names study, where no place by this name is identified on Cormorant Island—the name for the "old Alert Bay Mission" that is known to AD and DSS is ʔux̌ʷλaʔlís 'on the tip of the island.'

48. What Boas transcribes here as "Qulkн" is x̌ʷəlkʷ, meaning 'criss-crossed logs,' the name applied to a village site situated at the mouth of the Nimpkish River (DSS; AD).

49. The name gʷáṅalalis is derived from gʷáṅa, the original name of the Nimpkish River (AD) (see also the footnote that follows).

chamber to him, where he slept with his new wife. And the older sisters were sleeping in their chambers. The following morning all four women found that they were pregnant. But the wife of K·'ā′nigyilak· gave birth to a boy who grew up rapidly.

But Guanā′lalis was angry with his son-in-law because he had seduced all his daughters, and he decided to kill him. He said to him one day, "Come, let's go and split boards for a new house. I have selected a cedar tree, but am unable to cut it by myself." They took their hammers and wedges and went into the forest. Together they commenced to fell the mighty cedar and when they had done this, they began to split the tree. They had already driven their wedges deep into it and spread the one half of the tree far apart, when Guanā′lalis let his hammer drop on purpose deep into the gaping crack. He cried, "Oh, I've lost my hammer; won't you get it out for me?" K·'ā′nigyilak· crept into the crack willingly. Then Guanā′lalis knocked the spreading wedges out of the tree, which crashed together at once with great violence. And the old man called, "That serves you right K·'ā′nigyilak·! That is your reward for seducing my daughters!" But he had hardly finished speaking when he heard someone speak behind himself, "Guanā′lalis, here is your hammer." He turned around in terror and saw K·'ā′nigyilak· standing behind himself, unharmed. But he recovered quickly and said, "Oh, friend, I am so sorry; the wedges jumped out of the tree and I was sure that you were dead. My heart is glad that you escaped unharmed." K·'ā′nigyilak· didn't answer at all and both of them returned home. On their way K·'ā′nigyilak· picked two berries and threw each of them into a bowl when they had arrived home. His wife asked him, "Where did you find the berries?" He replied, "Where we cut down the cedar tree." He gave one bowl to his father-in-law and the other one to his wife and behold, both of them were filled with berries! Those which he had given to Guanā′lalis he had bewitched so that a tree grew out of his belly after he had eaten them. But later he made him better again.

After he had lived there for some time, he became sad and dejected. He lay down and stayed in bed for four days. Guanā′lalis tried to cheer him up, but he wouldn't listen to him. His wife asked him to get up and enquired whether he was ill. At last he said, "I am not ill but my heart longs for my brother. Stay here, my wife; I will come back to you."

18) After a long journey K·'ā′nigyilak· returned to Guā′nē,[50] where he once had left his brother. He saw no one outside. He entered the house and there saw him lying in bed. He called, but Nɛmō′k·ois didn't hear him. He wanted to shake him and then saw that he was already long dead. Only the bleached bones were under the blankets. So K·'ā′nigyilak· sprinkled him with the Water of Life and the dead man

---

50. "Guā′nē" is gʷáṅa, the Kwakwala name for the Nimpkish River, derived from gʷa which is translated elsewhere by Boas (1934:68–69) as 'downriver' and by AD and DSS as 'direction in which water is flowing.'

rose, rubbed his eyes and said, "Oh, I've slept such a long time!" K·'ā′nigyilak˙ replied, "You were not asleep! You've been dead and I have revived you!"

19) Then he carved four men from cedar wood and named them Tōqtoua′lis, K·apk·apā′lis, KH'ētok·â′lis, and Bēbekumlisi′la.[51] They became alive after two days.

20) In the far west there lived Hā′nitsum[52] who had a beautiful daughter named AiHtsumā′letlilok.[53] K·'ā′nigyilak˙ wanted to have her for his wife. He went into his canoe, K·ōk·ō′malis.[54] After long wandering, he reached the home of Hā′nitsum and found his house. There he married AiHtsumā′letlilok (= With Many Earrings of Abalone Shell) and returned with her to Guā′nē. After a while she gave birth to a boy, who was given the name Hā′nēus[55] and became a mighty chief.

21) And K·'ā′nigyilak˙ continued on his way. On his journey he met Mā′lēlek·ala,[56] whose whole body was diseased. K·'ā′nigyilak˙ passed his hand over his body and thus healed him. Then he gave him a totem pole and a house and filled the River Wēkyau′ayaas[57] for him with salmon.

22) And K·'ā′nigyilak˙ continued on his way. Finally he arrived in Comox. When he saw a canoe approaching there, he changed into an old man again and awaited the strangers' arrival. They caught sight of him and paddled to the shore. The chief asked, "Who are you and where do you come from?" K·'ā′nigyilak˙ replied, "Oh, I am a poor slave who has run away from his cruel master." "Then come with me to my house; I will be your master from now on." K·'ā′nigyilak˙ went into their canoe and they paddled home and he became the slave of the chief. He stayed inside the house, along with all the other slaves, throughout the winter. But when it grew warm again and when the chief had invited all the neighbouring tribes for a great feast, he sent out his slaves and many men of his tribe to get wood. The old slave into whom

---

51. The first and last of these names are possibly t'úqʷstəwalis (Boas' "Tōqtoua′lis") meaning 'narrow head' and bíbəkʷəmlisəla (Boas' "Bēbekumlisi′la") meaning 'not smiling' (DSS; AD).

52. This name that Boas transcribes as "Hā′nitsum" is possibly hánicəm.

53. This name rendered by Boas as "AiHtsumā′letlilok" is recognized as ʔaʔíxcəmaliłil'akʷ meaning 'born to be abalone shell woman' (DSS; AD).

54. Boas' name for this canoe, "K·ōk·ō′malis," is recognized by DSS and AD as qʷúqʷamalis, derived from qʷúqʷała 'tilted'; the canoe qʷúqʷamalis is mentioned again in part 25 of this same story.

55. This is the name hániyus, now anglicized as the surname "Hanuse" (DSS).

56. Boas' "Mā′lēlek·ala" is máliliqəla, the ancestor of the mámaliliqəla (anglicized as "Mamalilikulla") people of Village Island and the adjacent islands (DSS). The mámaliliqla are said to have originated in the Beaver Harbour area; they also lived in an area extending along the north shore of Knight Inlet as far as Matsiu Creek, as well as at a place near Turnour Island, and at White Beach, and at the end of Malcom Island (DSS; AD).

57. This is wákawayaʔas 'river running between hills,' a river which flows into the southwest end of Beaver Harbour (Boas 1934: 23, 43, map 6:113; AD).

K·'ā′nigyilak· had changed was too weak to cut trees and to carry wood. Therefore the chief let him bail water out of the canoe. He was so weak that five men had to lift him up and carry him to the canoe. Then they set out. When they arrived at the mouth of the river they landed and the twenty men in the party went into the woods to cut trees, while the old slave remained with the canoe to guard it. When they were all out of sight, K·'ā′nigyilak· went ashore, shook himself, stretched his limbs and thus assumed his real shape again.

He pulled the canoe ashore with one jerk. The day was bright and the sun shone hotly upon the earth. In order to preserve the canoe from the damaging effect of the sun, he flung a tree trunk into the water, so that the canoe was drenched all over with water, and then called for the branches of a tree to give it shade. They obeyed him and sheltered the canoe from the burning rays. Then he lay down to sleep.

After some time one of the young men came back to see whether the old slave was guarding the canoe properly. When he saw the strong man instead of the oldster and found the canoe pulled ashore, he was amazed and realized that K·'ā′nigyilak· had come to them in such a miserable shape. Soon the rest of the men came, carrying a tree laboriously on their shoulders to the canoe. They had to rest frequently because the trunk weighed heavily on their shoulders. When K·'ā′nigyilak· saw them he called, "Are you finished at last? I thought you would never come back." He moved his hand and the branches of the shade tree sprang back into their original position and he pushed the canoe back into the river. So all those who before had molested and teased him because of his weakness grew afraid. He went into the woods and met the men who had just put down the tree trunk in order to rest. He said, "Let me have a look at the trunk before you lift it again." And then he said to it, "Get up and follow me." And lo, the tree did what it was told! When K·'ā′nigyilak· and the tree came to the beach, he told it to split up into logs and to stow itself in the canoe. When the twenty men thereupon observed the tree crashing down and saw how it split into thousands of logs which stowed themselves, they grew very much afraid.

Now the canoe was heavily laden and they returned home. When the canoe had been beached, K·'ā′nigyilak· told the wood to go ashore and to stack itself in the house of the chief. It obeyed him and soon the logs were stacked high up to the roof. And he said to it further, "You shall avenge me for all the maltreatment which I had to endure here! Burn the house and all its inhabitants!"

Now when the chief was giving the feast and everyone was gathered for the meal, the wood ignited itself. Then the chief begged, "Oh, K·'ā′nigyilak·, spare us! Don't let the fire devour my house and I will give you my daughter for your wife!" The heart of K·'ā′nigyilak· grew glad at this and he made a downward motion with his hand and behold, the fire was extinguished! He stayed with his wife for four days, then he returned to Guā′nē.

23) And K·'ā′nigyilak· wandered on. Once he met an old man called Tlē′qēkyōtl[58] who was sharpening two shells on a whetstone. K·'ā′nigyilak· went up to him closely and asked him what he was doing. Then man turned around crossly and, without recognizing him, replied, "Hm! When K·'ā′nigyilak· comes here, I will hit him over the head with them and kill him." So K·'ā′nigyilak· said, "Oh, that's right! Let me have a look at your shells." Tlē′qēkyōtl first gave him one, and, when K·'ā′nigyilak· asked for it, also the other shell. Thereupon the latter drove one of them into his head on the right, the other one on the left, smeared his backside with dirt, and called, "So, now become a deer and run into the forest!" And this happened. The shells were changed into antlers and the deer are still black on their backside today.

24) K·'ā′nigyilak· went on and met a man who was busy painting a stick very carefully with black rings. He stepped up to him and asked, "What are you doing?" The man turned around and said, "When K·'ā′nigyilak· comes here I will kill him with this stick." He didn't recognize him either, and K·'ā′nigyilak· replied, "I don't know the man, but I'm sure that he deserves it. Let me have a look at your stick." The man handed it over, then K·'ā′nigyilak· made him get up and, taking him unawares, pushed the stick into his backside. Then he painted his mouth and back black and said, "From now on be a raccoon and live in the mountains!"

25) K·'ā′nigyilak· continued his travels and arrived at Ts'ā′lo (Seymour Narrows).[59] There he saw a man named K·oā′k·oa,[60] fishing with a salmon-harpoon. K·'ā′nigyilak· turned back before the man had seen him and considered how he could steal the harpoon. Finally he had thought of a way to accomplish this. He created a man whom he ordered to stand on a rock to watch what he was about to do. He changed into a salmon and asked him, "Do I look just like a salmon?" The man replied, "No, try once more." And K·'ā′nigyilak· transformed himself again and now had completely assumed the shape of a salmon which swims up the river in the springtime. Then he swam to Ts'ā′lo where K·oā′k·oa was standing, his harpoon in readiness to hit the first salmon to come. K·'ā′nigyilak· swam up to him and calmly played in the water right close to him. So K·oā′k·oa was glad, hurled the harpoon into his side and

58. This is λígiguł, a name for 'Deer' in Kwakwaka'wakw mythology (AD; DSS).

59. The name for Seymour Narrows (north from Campbell River) that Boas transcribes here as "Ts'ā′lo" is rendered elsewhere by him as "Ts!ā′la 'rapids' " (Boas 1934: 23, 61)—AD recognizes this term as čálu which he translates as 'strong tide.' Both AD and DSS more commonly refer to Seymour Narrows as cəčə′n 'narrows' (see also Section XV, story 1, for another reference to Seymour Narrows).

60. What Boas renders here as "K·oā′k·oa" is recognized by DSS and AD as qʷúqʷa.

wanted to pull him ashore. But the salmon braced himself against a stone and, when the man pulled in the harpoon line with all his strength, the tip broke off and the salmon swam away with it. Thus K·'a̅'nigyilak· had achieved his purpose.

But K·oa̅'k·oa was sad, and he went home and lay down. In the meantime K·'a̅'nigyilak· reassumed his true shape. He looked at the harpoon-tip joyfully and put it on his ear as an ornament. Then he went into his canoe, K·o̅k·o̅'malis,[61] again, created a steersman for himself, and went to the spot where the house of K·oa̅'k·oa stood. When they approached, the son of K·oa̅'k·oa, who happened to be playing in front of the house, saw the canoe and brought it to his father's attention, who told him to invite the arrivals. The boy went down to the beach and called, "Our chief asks you to come to his house; he wants to give a feast for you." K·'a̅'nigyilak· accepted the invitation; he landed and entered the house. There K·oa̅'k·oa showed him a seat by the fire and K·'a̅'nigyilak· sat down. He was vain about his ear ornament and turned his head to let it be seen. When K·oa̅'k·oa saw the harpoon-tips on the stranger's ears, he cried, "Where did you get your ear ornament?" K·'a̅'nigyilak· replied, "Oh, I've been wearing it already for years and years." But K·oa̅'k·oa shook his head and said hesitantly, "I don't know, I've lost something which looks exactly like your ear-ornament." He was convinced that he had stolen it from him and became very angry. He took a bone, split it up into tiny needles and stuck these into a salmon, which he served to K·'a̅'nigyilak·. When he began to eat, the sharp splinters stuck in his throat. He tried to spit them out but was unsuccessful; they only stuck faster in his throat, and blood came out of his mouth. So he said, "Why do you cheat me like this? You promised to give me a good meal and now you make me sick! If you rid me of the splinters of bone, I'll give you my ear-ornament." So Heron rejoiced. He shook K·'a̅'nigyilak· and the bones fell out of his throat. Then K·'a̅'nigyilak· took the harpoon-tips from his ears and pushed them onto the nose of K·oa̅'k·oa, calling, "So, this is where they shall stay for ever!" And he seized him, threw him into the air and he flew away as a heron.[62] K·'a̅'nigyilak· transformed his wife into a woodpecker.

26) And he continued on his way. After some time he met a man and a woman sitting opposite each other, with their arms raised high and nodding their heads. He

---

61. As previously noted, "K·o̅k·o̅'malis" is qʷúqʷamalis, derived from qʷúqʷała 'tilted' (DSS; AD); qʷúqʷamalis is the name for the Transformer's canoe that is mentioned both here and in part 20 of this same story.

62. Both here and earlier in this same paragraph, Boas uses the term *Kranich* 'crane' in the original. While this legend indicates that "K·oa̅'k·oa" is the Kwakwala name of the bird in question, neither AD nor DSS recognizes this term. We are providing the translation 'Heron' (likely, Great Blue Heron) in this particular context because this is the species that Boas most often refers to as *Kranich*—notwithstanding, Boas does use the German term *Reiher* 'heron' in part 2 of the present legend, but provides no corresponding Kwakwala term.

wanted to see what they were doing, paddled up closer and then saw that their genitals were on their foreheads and that they were copulating. So he said, "I'll have to put you in order," and made them look like other people. He said, "This is how you shall beget children in the future."

27) When he went on he heard a noise as if there were many people, but he couldn't see anyone at first. When he came to a point of land, he discovered a man who now rolled around on the ground, now jumped into the water and went back ashore again. His body was covered all over with mouths which all laughed and shouted at the same time. K·'ā'nigyilak· asked, "What are you doing?" But the man didn't answer and only kept on laughing and shouting so that K·'ā'nigyilak· had to cover his ears with his hands. At last it became too much for him and he passed his hand over the man's body. Thereupon the countless mouths disappeared and he became a normal man. K·'ā'nigyilak· named him Yā'k·'EntEmaks.[63]

28) He went on and came to a river. He found a house with an open door there and inside it saw four blind girls sitting around a fire, in which they were heating a stone in order to cook four roots in a wooden pot. When he approached, the eldest girl said, "I can scent K·'ā'nigyilak·; he can't be far away from us." But he crept secretly into the house and took away the four roots without being noticed. When the girls then wanted to throw the hot stone into the water, they found their roots gone and they said to each other, "Where have our roots gone?" So K·'ā'nigyilak· stepped up to them and said, "How did it happen that all of you are blind? I will heal you." And he took them separately by the hand and led them outside. He put some pitch into his mouth, chewed it and then spat it into their eyes. Thus they gained their sight. And he seized the girls by their legs and threw them into the air. Thereupon they were transformed into ducks.

29) And K·'ā'nigyilak· went on. After some time he met a canoe. A man and a woman were sitting in it, paddling as hard as they could. But they weren't holding the paddles in their hands; instead, the man had crossed his hands behind his back, the woman hers in front, and they had pushed the paddles beneath their arms. So K·'ā'nigyilak· taught them and showed them how to paddle.

30) In his further travels he came to Tsaue'te.[64] There he met a young man named Ts'ā'tso (a bird),[65] who owned a nice small spear. K·'ā'nigyilak· made a wager with him who would hit a target best with the spear and who would throw it the farthest.

---

63. Boas' "Yā'k·'EntEmaks" is recognized by AD as as yáḵəntəmak^w 'talking face.' AD adds that originally this man with all the mouths was called sə'msitək^w 'mouths all over body.'

64. What Boas transcribes as "Tsaue'te" is dzáwadi 'having eulachons,' a place at the mouth of the Klinaklini River at the upper end of Knight Inlet (AD; DSS; Boas 1934:23, 59).

65. Name not now recognized.

As a prize he gave his mother the cape of Tsatsaquitelā′k·a,[66] in which salmon were hidden. Ts′ā′tso won the wager and joyfully danced about in the cape of K·′ā′nigyilak·, singing, "Mother, you won't have to search for shellfish any more. From now on we will always have plenty of fish." He dipped one corner of the cape into the water and countless fish of all kinds jumped out of it. So K·′ā′nigyilak· said, "In future there shall always be plenty of fish here." This is how the abundance of fish at Tsaue′te originated.

31) The footprint of K·′ā′nigyilak· can still be seen today, pressed into the stone at Guā′nē.[67] It is two spans long and one span wide. He was able to step with one stride across to Hē′tlas Island.[68] His eyes are also petrified there. They look like the eyes of a salmon. If dirt is thrown into these eyes, a storm comes up and therefore they must not be touched. If anything is thrown into the right eye, the wind comes from the east; if anything is thrown into the left eye, the wind comes from the west. There is also a hole in Guā′nē into which K·′ā′nigyilak· once had thrown many people. Therefore it is still spitting blood today. Many people don't believe that the hole exists. In order to find out, one man once threw a candle into it, onto which he had carved many faces in order to be able to recognize it. After some time it was found again in Awī′kyēnoq.[69]

2. Le′laqa[70]

Two Eagles and their child once flew down from the sky to Qū′mqatē (Cape Scott).[71] There, they took off their feather garments and became human. The father was named Nā′laqōtau,[72] the mother Ank·â′layuk·oa,[73] and the son Le′laqa.[74] They built a house in Qū′mqatē and lived in it. One day Le′laqa went out in his canoe to hunt

---

66. Name not now recognized.

67. As previously discussed in association with part 4 of the present story, Boas' "Guā′nē" is k̄ʷánɛʔ, the name of a place in Experiment Bight which is located immediately east of the northern point of Cape Scott (Boas 1934:70, map 2:25; Wallas, in Galois 1994:287–288).

68. Hít̓aʔs (Boas' "Hē′tlas") is the name that refers to Triangle Island situated west of Cape Scott (AD; Boas 1934:23).While Boas translates this place name as 'far enough,' AD and DSS suggest that its meaning is derived from the term hít̓ała meaning 'place where everything is right.'

69. Oowekeeno; see Section XX.

70. Boas (1888j:61–62) includes a variant of this story which he obtained from "ᴋalai′te," a chief of the Nakomkilis.

71. AD recognizes Boas' "Qū′mqatē" as xʷə′mqadi, the name for Cape Scott.

72. Name not now recognized.

73. Name not now recognized.

74. Name not now recognized.

seals and saw some resting on a cliff. He paddled closer carefully and hit one with a sure throw of his harpoon. The seal jumped into the water at once and pulled the canoe far out into the sea. Then it changed into an enormous octopus which pulled the canoe under and killed Lē'laqa. But he awoke to new life, re-emerged and flew up to the sky as an eagle.

Since Lē'laqa didn't come back, his parents mourned for him because they thought that he was dead. They killed two slaves and coated the house-posts with their blood. They tied two others to the front of the house. Then suddenly they saw an eagle glide down from the sun onto their house and they recognized their son. He was carrying a small box in his claws. When he shook it, all sorts of things could be heard rattling inside it. Around his neck there was a ring of red inner cedar bark. Then he changed back again into a man and his parents' hearts were glad. They lit a big fire and he began to dance. He took many flutes from the box and imitated the voices of eagles with them. And he wore the big double mask Naqnakyak·umtl[75] (the inner mask represented a man, the outer one an eagle). After the dance he feasted all the people. He had a huge bowl representing an octopus, which always filled up with fish-oil without anyone pouring anything into it. Lē'laqa had a son who was given the name K·ak·â'lis.[76] He was the ancestor of the Nee'nsHa numaym (= Dirty Teeth).[77]

3. Nēmōk·otsâ'lis[78]

One morning, when Nēmōk·otsâ'lis was sitting in front of his house, he saw a beautiful white diver swimming close to the shore. So he said to K·'ē'qtlala, Ma'qmalakis and Woqsemā'qala,[79] "Shoot that bird!" K·'ē'qtlala took his bow, shot, and hit it right in the back. Then he called his brothers and told them to come into the canoe with him to pursue the bird, which was swimming away rapidly. When they came close, he aimed a second arrow at it and hit it again in the back. But since a third arrow didn't kill it, Ma'qmalakis advised his brother to tie a line to the arrow in order to pull it towards the canoe. K·'ē'qtlala followed the advice; he hit the bird, which then towed the canoe away behind itself. When they saw the land disappearing far away, Ma'qmalakis said to his brother, "Better cut the line; we're not able to

---

75. AD recognizes Boas' "Naqnakyak·umtl" as náxnagagəmł, derived from nála 'daylight.'

76. Name not now recognized.

77. The name of this numaym, "Nee'nsHa"—given elsewhere by Boas (1966:38) as NăE'nx·sa—is not recognized by AD or DSS.

78. Boas' "Nēmōk·otsâ'lis" is recognized by DSS as nəmúkʷustulis.

79. The first of these three names, "K·'ē'qtlala," is q̓íx̣ƛala (DSS).

catch the bird anyhow." K·'ē'qtlala tried to do so, but the line only fell down a bit lower and immediately stuck fast to the canoe again. They tried to cut the line four times, but they did not succeed in getting free of the bird.

They had long since lost sight of their home when they saw a dark strip appear far away. At first they took it for land, but saw soon that it was a dense mass of dark stones like charcoal which were floating on the water. They thought that the canoe wouldn't penetrate the densely packed mass, but lo, it opened up and then closed again after the bird had pulled them through! Then they came to a spot where drift-wood in tight packs covered the sea. Here, too, a passage opened up. Then they found themselves in front of a level beach. Already rejoicing at reaching land, they found that it was only pine needles. Then they arrived at a land where many seals were basking. Woqsemā'qala, who was steering, jumped ashore and lo, he vanished at once and sank into the depths! At last they arrived at a coast. Here the diver changed into a man and led the two brothers to the house of Kunkunquli'kya.[80] He said to him, "I have brought these brothers to you so that you will give your daughter to one of them for a wife." And Kunkunquli'kya gave his daughter Kōkōkua'k·s to K·'ē'qtlala.

When some time had passed, K·'ē'qtlala was longing for his father. He said to his wife, "Oh, I think that my father has died. I want to go back to my homeland." The woman asked her father for permission to move with K·'ē'qtlala to his homeland, and he gave her permission. He told the wind to carry back his daughter and the brothers. When they had travelled for some time, they came to the house of Grizzly Bear, a mighty chief. He invited them into his house and feasted them with salmon. The woman was carrying a basket, in which she kept a piece of whale-meat given to her by Kunkunquli'kya. Before they left Bear she put a small piece of salmon into the basket. They travelled on, following the course of the sun and came to the house of K·'ē'Hustäel, Deer.[81] He served fat to them and she also put a piece of it into her basket. They journeyed on and came to the house of Tlē'selagyila, Mink. He served shellfish to them and Kōkōkua'k·s put one of them into her basket. Then they came to the house of otter, Amaqama'kitla'seli (= Sitting on Top of the House ??).[82] They entered and saw many otters in the house. The chief invited them to sit down by the fire and then showed them a trap which had been built by his slaves. He requested K·'ē'qtlala to crawl into it to try it out. But he was afraid. So his wife whispered to him, "Just go inside! I will blow on the trap so that it won't be able to do you any

---

80. This is the large, ferocious Thunderbird, known as kʷə'nkʷənxʷəligɛ (AD; DSS).

81. Boas' "K·'ē'Hustäel" is recognized by DSS and AD as gíxustula, a name used for 'Deer' in legends.

82. Name not now recognized.

harm." Then K·'ē'qtlala went into the trap. Since his wife was blowing at it through her hollow hand, it couldn't shut. But he had scarcely jumped out, and his wife had hardly stopped blowing, when it banged shut with great force. Then K·'ē'qtlala called for his brother and for his wife to set the trap again and then they told Otter to go in. As soon as he was inside, it shut and killed him. They took his pelt and put it into the basket.

They journeyed on and finally came to a lake in which the monster Ts'ē'k·is[83] (see Section XIX, story 1, part 6) was living. The brothers didn't know how to get past, because the monster sat in their way and its mouth constantly snapped open and shut. Kōkōkua'k·s passed safely by because the monster could do her no harm. Then she called to the brothers, "Run forward quickly as soon as I shout, because then Ts'ē'k·is won't be able to harm you." She shouted when the monster just happened to have its jaws open wide and so it was unable to close them again. Thus the brothers passed safely through its wide-open mouth.

At last they arrived in Guā'nē, the destination of their journey. The Thunderbird had built a house there for his daughter and many eagles were sitting on its roof guarding it. During the night the wife said to her husband, "You must not sleep now because my father is going to come to give you whale meat." In the morning, when the man stepped outside, he saw a big whale lying there, which the Thunderbird had brought during the night. He became a great chief and from then on his slaves worked for him, while he did no more work. He invited all the neighbours; his wife took the whale-meat, the salmon, the deer fat, and the shellfish from the basket. It had multiplied so much that he was able to feast everybody. His slaves rendered the whale blubber and poured the oil into boxes. K·'ē'qtlala threw one box into the fire, making it flare up brightly. He emptied ten of them into the house, so that the people were swimming around in it.

---

83. What Boas renders here as "Tsē'k·is" is known to AD and DSS as čígis, the name of a sea monster. Wallas and Whitaker (1991:18, 208) note that čígis is translated as 'to lie on beach or in deep water looking up with a leer on face' and comment that čígis is "like a giant bullhead with a long, long tongue."

4. Ya′qstatl

The inhabitants of Qōyā′les[84] and Gyig·'ē′tlEm (near Dean Inlet)[85] were bitter enemies. Once the former raided the Gyig·'ē′tlEm village near Kimskuitq[86] and killed all the inhabitants except Tlēō′leqmut and his three sons. The eldest of them was named Ya′qstatl. The father wanted to make his sons strong so that they might withstand their enemies, and to this end dragged them behind his canoe around an island so that their backs were lacerated by sharp shells. No one but Ya′qstatl passed the test and Tlēō′leqmut took him back into the canoe after having dragged him around the island. Then they travelled to Qōyā′les to take revenge on their enemies. But in Ta′tsolis,[87] a wolf came into their camp at night, threw Ya′qstatl across his back and ran away with him. He put him down from time to time to see whether he was still breathing. When he had convinced himself, he threw him across his back again and ran on. At last he arrived in the country of the wolves. He threw Ya′qstatl down in front of the chief's door, assumed the form of a man, and whistled. Thereupon all the people came out of the houses to see what he had brought. But they took Ya′qstatl for a sea-otter, seized him by his arms and legs and carried him into the house, where they threw him onto a bench. They started to cut him up lengthwise, but when they had reached his belly, Ya′qstatl stood up and said, "Will you help me to take revenge on the men of Qōyā′les?" They promised him their help and asked, "What would you like from us? Do you want to have this wedge? With it you'll be able to construct canoes to reach them." Ya′qstatl didn't reply, but thought that he didn't want to have the wedge. Witlak·ā′latit,[88] the chief of the Wolves, read his thoughts. Then he asked, "Would you like to have this spear? With it you'll be able to kill four canoe loads of seals." Again Ya′qstatl thought that he didn't want to have the spear and Witlak·ā′latit heard his thoughts. So the Wolves

---

84. Qōyā′les, anglicized as "Hoyalas," is Boas' rendering of xʷúyalas, the name of one of the four groups known collectively as the Quatsino Sound Tribes of northwestern Vancouver Island, north from Cape Cook. The tribal designation xʷúyalas is said to be derived from the name of a place at the head of Rupert Arm. The Hoyalas disappeared as a distinct ethnic group around the mid-1700s and their territory was taken over by the Koskimo, another of the Quatsino Sound Tribes (Dawson 1888:70; Boas 1897:332; Curtis 1915:10:306; Malin 1961:16,112; Duff 1965:63–64; Galois 1994:55–56, 347–349, 351, 360–363).

85. This place name, rendered by Boas as "Gyig·'ē′tlEm" and said to refer to a place "near Dean Inlet," is transcribed elsewhere by Boas (1934:65) as "g·ī′k·!ēLEm," but we have not been able to confirm this Native term, or to determine what place it referred to.

86. Kimsquit, a Bella Coola (Nuxalk)-speaking group who lived in the Dean Channel area. See Section XXII for stories of these people.

87. The place name rendered by Boas as "Ta′tsolis" is transcribed elsewhere by him as "tatsō′lis," with a question mark following the name, which is identified only as 'a place in the Koskimo country' (Boas 1934:55).

88. Name not now recognized.

offered him the Water of Life and the death-bringer, halai'ū. This time he thought, "Yes, I'd like to have them." The chief gave both to him and then ordered the Wolves to devour Ya'qstatl. He was torn to pieces in a moment. The Wolves spat the devoured flesh out again and Witlak·ā'latit sprinkled it with the Water of Life. Thereupon Ya'qstatl arose again, safe and sound, and had become very strong. Then all the Wolves brought him to his homeland and he stood on the biggest one's back. Then he went on, together with his father and his brothers, to kill the inhabitants of Qōyā'les. He tried out the halai'u on the way. He waved it at a forest and the forest caught fire at once. When they came close to Qōyā'les, they saw the people approach in many canoes and Tlēō'leqmut then said to Ya'qstatl, "Point your halai'u at them, but don't kill them right away; only singe off their hair." Ya'qstatl did as he had been told. He waved the halai'u at them while his father and his brothers were singing and beating time. So their enemies jumped terrified into the water; their canoes burned up and they were transformed into stones.

Then Ya'qstatl wanted to fight the Kwā'kiutl. When he passed by Qumta'spē[89] the halai'u insisted on destroying the houses of this village, whose inhabitants were Ya'qstatl's friends. Therefore he threw it onto Hope Island and ever since there are many wolves there.

5. Kuni'Qua (KunkunQuli'kya)[90]

Once Kuni'Qua and Seagull were playing with hoops to see who could catch best. Seagull's hoop was fog, but Kuni'Qua's was fire, and because of this he was never able to catch the hoop of Seagull, while the latter hit his each time. After he had been defeated by Seagull four times, he grew so ashamed that he flew away and hid in the forest. Once K·'ō'toq (a bird) went into the forest and there met Kuni'Qua. When the latter looked at him with his fiery eyes, his own eyes became red.

Kuni'Qua wanted to have the red-winged Tlā'tsem[91] for his wife. He sat down on a tree close to her house and thought, "Oh, if only Tlā'tsem would go to relieve herself." He had scarcely thought this when she came out of the house. At once he swooped down on her and carried her away to his house. But she cried, "Oh, save me! Save me!" At once a big meeting was called in the village to discuss what to

---

89. The place name given here by Boas as "Qumta'spē" (and confirmed in Boas 1934:78) is recognized as x̣ʷə'mdasbɛ 'place where there is otter,' derived from x̣ʷə'mdi 'otter' (AD), situated on the southeast side of Hope Island, west of Nigei Island off the northern end of Vancouver Island.

90. These two terms, "Kuni'Qua" and "KunkunQuli'kya," are recognized respectively as kʷə'nxʷa 'thunder' and kʷə'nkʷənxʷəligɛ 'Thunderbird' (DSS; AD).

91. Possibly "Tlā'tsem" is a shortened form of the Kwakwala term λáλaniɫ, 'any woodpecker' (AD).

do. On the advice of Quail[92] it was decided to recapture Tlā′tsem again, while she was picking berries. Tlē′selagyila (Mink) was sent ahead to tell the woman that all her friends were hidden in the forest to abduct her. He met her in the forest gathering berries, and for joy she forgot to fill her basket and bring berries to her husband. He sent her out again the following day to pick berries and then the animals captured her.

So Kuni′Qua was very sad. He flew after his wife, sat down on a tree close to her house and thought, "Oh, if only Tlā′tsem would go out to fetch water." She took a pail at once and went to the water. So Kuni′Qua seized her and flew away with her. Again her friends discussed what to do, and on Quail's advice, they all changed into trout and swam about in front of Kuni′Qua's house. He caught one of the trout at once, namely the husband of Tlā′tsem, who then succeeded in getting his wife back.

Again Kuni′Qua flew after her, sat down on a tree close to the house and thought, "Oh, if only Tlā′tsem would come out of the house to pick berries." He had scarcely thought it, when she came and he abducted her a third time. Thereupon Tlā′tsem's husband became dejected. He went to bed and stayed there for four days. Then he got up, called together all of the animals and told them to carve a whale … (etc., see Section XX, story 2). Here the names of the Thunderbird's four children are: Maeā′musk·umnek·o′laps, Mosk·umnek·o′laps, Yutlusumnek·o′laps, and Matsemnek·o′laps;[93] he himself is called NEmskumnek·o′laps when he tries to lift the whale. Each time when one of the birds seizes the whale, Mouse gnaws his feet to pieces, Raccoon urinates into his eyes, Bear fractures his wings and Bekuē′as, Elk,[94] kills him.

6. Nā′k·oayē and Hī′qulatlit[95]

Once the men of Tlō′uqsEm[96] went out to catch halibut. When they came to the vicinity of Yū′tlē,[97] a heavy storm came up and all the canoes except two capsized.

---

92. Boas uses the German term *Wachtel* 'quail,' in the original, although quail are not indigenous to northern Vancouver Island. We do not know what species is actually referred to here.

93. These names appear to be: 'carrier of four whales'; 'carrier of three whales'; 'carrier of two whales'; and 'carrier of one whale' (DSS; AD).

94. The term that Boas uses here for 'elk,' "Bekuē′as," is not now recognized; DSS points out that the common Kwakwala word for 'elk' is ƛ'əwə′l's.

95. These names, "Nā′k·oayē" and "Hī′qulatlit," are not now recognized.

96. This place name, rendered here by Boas as "Tlō′uqsEm" is recognized as ƛ'úpəksəm, meaning 'looks like a root' (AD; Boas 1934:83)

97. The name yúƛ'ɛ (Boas' "Yū′tlē") is applied to Lantz Island, situated northwest of Cape Scott at the northwestern tip of Vancouver Island (Boas 1934: 40, map 1:17; AD).

Nā́k·oayē and Hī́qulatlit were in these two canoes. They saw four bird feathers floating on the water and, while the sea was wildly agitated all about, one stretch of five fathoms behind the canoes was as calm as in the finest weather. The feathers swam ahead of them and brought them safely to Cape Scott. The house of Nā́k·oayē was on Yū́tlē, and he returned there when the weather became better again. Then a Raven came down from the sun and settled right on the head of Nā́k·oayē.

Once Hī́qulatlit invited all the people for a feast. But in reality he had nothing to eat. He only wanted to see Nā́k·oayē dance. All the guests were sitting along the platform which runs all along the house, and they beat time while Nā́k·oayē was dancing. A big fire was burning in the middle of the house and Nā́k·oayē danced around it. Suddenly his mouth was filled with oil given to him by the Raven and he spat it into the fire, which flared up high. But he found that it was rancid. So he made the people beat time once again and kept on dancing. Then he had fresh oil in his mouth. First he spat it into the fire and then filled a big chest. Then he said, "Go to the beach tomorrow to see whether there is a dead whale there." They went down and found the whale. Raven had given it to them.

Then Nā́k·oayē called upon Hī́qulatlit to dance. He asked for a bowl filled with sea water, put some feathers on it and placed it in his room. That day it rained and stormed so hard that nobody was able to go out to hunt or fish. So Hī́qulatlit told everybody to go to sleep and behold, when they woke up it was the finest weather! He made everybody go out to catch the halibut and in a short time all the canoes were filled to the top. They took the fish ashore and went out again to catch more. And in the shortest time imaginable they had filled the canoes again. On top of this they found a whale killed for them by Nā́k·oayē. They rendered the blubber and then had a great supply of fish and oil. The following day Hī́qulatlit made the weather get bad again; but they didn't mind any more since they had provisions aplenty.

Then Nā́k·oayē returned to Yū́tlē. After two moons a chief in Qumtáspē invited him. He danced here, too, and spat fat into the fire. Before returning to Yū́tlē he promised here also that a whale would be on the beach the following morning. The villagers looked for the whale that next morning and went along the coast because they couldn't find it. They met Nā́k·oayē at Cape Scott. When they accused him of cheating them, he told them to come with him to Yū́tlē and said, "We will find the whale there for sure. But if it isn't there you shall tie a rope around my neck and kill me." They went to the Island of Yū́tlē and found the whale there indeed. The men of Qumtáspē cut it up, rendered the oil and returned home.

XX. Legends of the Oowekeeno

The Hamatsa mask story 14 is one of the first stories Boas heard on the North American continent. Arriving in Victoria on 18 September 1886 and six days later, having made the acquaintance of a Hudson Bay trader, Boas "got a wild dance story" from his wife, along with a lengthy explanation: "It relates to a mask which is in the Berlin Museum and the Museum in New York" (Rohner 1969:25). The next day, 25 September 1886, Boas wrote in his diary that he asked this woman, "a Wikiano Indian," to retell "the cannibal story I had got yesterday" in order to verify some of the parts that were not clear. Two days later the same Oowekeeno woman tells him "the story of the origin of the sun" (Rohner 1969:25, 27). This would be the first part of "The Raven Legend," the part Boas indicates as "Told by a young woman." Again, on 30 September: "I went to the Wika'no woman, who told me a strange story which almost sounds word for word like the story of Phaeton." This would be the second of the Mink stories given below. On the same day she also tells him "the story of the origin of mosquitoes." This would be story 8. The following day came "a story about the origin of the frogs," story 9 (Rohner 1969:29). The above are the tales Boas specifies, but on another occasion his Oowekeeno consultant greeted him with "an endlessly long tale": "Scarcely had she finished when she started on another" (Rohner 1969:27). This is a prolific lady. Story 10 was surely hers, and indeed, most of the rest. The only other story-teller cited is "an old Awi'ky'ēnoq Woman," to whom Boas attributes the alternate beginning of "The Raven Legend."

Rivers Inlet Village, showing spoon canoe (right) and northern style canoe on shore, *ca.*
1915.

Milwaukee Public Museum, Milwaukee, Wisconsin. Neg. No. 3296.

Pole belonging to the Johnson family of Rivers Inlet. Crest figures are from top to bottom: eagle; chief yáʔxci with his coppers; q̓ʷúmuk̓ʷa, the sea monster; whale; grizzly bear; and octopus. This pole now stands in Stanley Park, Vancouver, B.C.

American Museum of Natural History Library, New York.
Neg./Trans. No. 46064 (Harlan I. Smith photo).

XX. Legends of the Awi'ky'ēnoq[1]

1. The Raven Legend[2]

1) Once K·ants'ō'ump (= Our Father; the Deity)[3] sent Kya'lk·ɛmkyasō[4] down to earth. He reached Mount K·'oā'mu[5] and descended into the river valley, and the river

---

1. What Boas transcribes as "Awi'ky'ēnoq" is ʔuwíkinuxʷ (anglicized as "Oowekeeno" or "Owikeno"), referring to those people who, together with the Heiltsuk (Bella Bella) and the Haihais, are speakers of the Heiltsuk-Oowekyala language, which is part of the North Wakashan subgroup of the Wakashan Language Family. The language of the Oowekeeno is Oowekyala, and that of the Heiltsuk (Bella Bella) and Haihais is Heiltusk (see also Section XXI); the difference between these two languages is such that they approach mutual intelligibility. Traditional Oowekeeno territory centred in Rivers Inlet and Owikeno Lake. While the majority of Oowekeeno village sites were situated at the head of Rivers Inlet, on Wannock River, and around Owikeno Lake, the Oowekeeno owned resource sites down the inlet, on Calvert Island, and north along the mainland to the Koeye River/Koeye Lake area. In the earlier literature, the larger grouping called "Kwakiutl" included a subgrouping called the "Northern Kwakiutl" comprised of the Oowekeeno, Heiltsuk, and Haisla (Kitimat), but the Native people of this overall region, themselves, and recent scholars do not make such a subgrouping. The "Kwakiutl," as we have discussed previously, are but one of about thirty autonomous groups or tribes who speak the Kwakwala language and were formerly referred to collectively as the "Southern Kwakiutl," now known as the Kwakwaka'wakw (Olson 1954:213–215; Stevenson 1980; 1981; Lincoln and Rath 1980:2–4; Rath 1981:1:2–4; Hilton, Rath, and Windsor 1982:2–8; Hilton 1990:312–313, 321; Thompson and Kinkade 1990).

   Unless otherwise noted, the annotations appearing in this section are drawn from the work of David Stevenson, who in 1984 reviewed an earlier draft of this translation and commented on the Oowekyala terms, based on his research with the following Oowekeeno people: Hilda Smith; Roy Hanuse, Sr.; Norman Johnson, Sr.; Evelyn Windsor; Lucy Johnson; and John Johnson, Sr. We gratefully acknowledge the assistance provided by David Stevenson and his Oowekeeno consultants. Additional information concerning several Oowekyala terms was provided to us directly in September 2001 by Evelyn Windsor, a Native Oowekyala language expert; this information is specifically credited as "EW" in these annotations. We thank Evelyn Windsor, and we also thank Chief Adam Dick ("AD") for facilitating our discussions with Mrs. Windsor and for providing comparative Kwakwala data cited in the annotations of this section.

2. Part 1 of this Oowekeeno Raven legend was published earlier in German in the journal *Globus* (see Boas 1888c:53:8:123).

3. What Boas transcribes as "K·ants'ō'ump" is qənc ʔáump in Oowekyala, and translates literally as 'our Father.'

4. The name gálgəmkasʔu translates literally as 'great spiritual First One' and is used in stories to refer to the first Chief to descend from heaven at the beginning of time.

5. Boas' "K·'oā'mu" is kʷámʷa 'permanent seat' and is the Oowekyala name of the mountain behind

was rich with salmon. He sent four women into the forest to fetch cedar bark, and taught the people how to make nets. When the net was finished, he embarked in a canoe with the people and they began to catch salmon. In those days there was no sun; only the moon shone in the sky. The Raven, Hē′meskyas (= True Chief)[6] or Kuēkuaqā′oē (= Great Inventor),[7] knew that chief ME′nis[8] owned the sun, so he decided to steal it. He changed himself into a pine needle and dropped into the well where the eldest daughter of ME′nis, named Latāk·′ai′yuk·oa,[9] came for water daily. She scooped up water and Raven slipped into her container as a needle. But she blew the needle aside when she drank. Because this ruse had failed, Raven transformed himself into shiny berries and the girl noticed their reflections in the water. She desired to eat them, picked them and consumed them. Thereupon she gave birth four days later to a son, Hē′meskyas, who grew up rapidly and was able to speak from his first day. He played on the house floor and soon began to scream and scream and couldn't be calmed down. When his grandfather asked him, "What is it you want?" the boy answered, "Make a salmon weir for me; I want to have salmon." ME′nis fulfilled the boy's request, but still he cried and wept and wanted to have a bow and some arrows. The grandfather also fulfilled this request and made him a bow and four arrows. Then the boy calmed down. On the second day he was able to walk and he ran down to the water. On the third day he started to cry again and only calmed down after his grandfather had made a paddle for him, as he demanded. He went down to the water with it but soon came back screaming and wanting to go out on the water. So his mother asked ME′nis to make him a canoe. The grandfather fulfilled her request and made a canoe from the skin of sea-lions. So Hē′meskyas was glad, embarked in the canoe and played in it on the water. But he returned soon, crying, "I want to play with the small box there." The box was hanging from one of the roof beams of the house and the grandfather kept daylight in it.

So his mother scolded him and said, "You bad boy, you are not like other children, you want to have everything. You can't have this box." So the boy cried all the more and didn't calm down at all. At last the grandfather allowed his daughter to lower the box a bit so that his grandson might see it. But he wasn't content with

Oowekeeno Village, where the Oowekeeno people tied their canoes during the Great Flood, and where the first mythical eagle-like bird or qʷúlus sat. Elsewhere, Boas (1934:75) transcribes this same term as "q!wā′mo" (kʷám̓wa) which he identifies as a "mountain in Rivers Inlet country."

6. This is hímaskas?u, translated as 'mighty chief' (EW), and derived from hímas 'chief'; the term hímaskas?u is used by contemporary Oowekeeno people generally to refer to God.

7. "Kuēkuaqā′oē" is Boas rendering of kʷíkʷaxawa, the Oowekyala name for 'Raven' in mythology; EW notes that kʷíkʷaxawa is derived from kʷíxala 'ask somebody to do something.'

8. This name is məˈnˀʔis which means 'by oneself in space, the world, or the universe.'

9. Boas' "Latāk·′ai′yuk·oa" is possibly x̌′álagayugʷa—the meaning is not known with certainty. In story 5 of the present section, the same name is transcribed as "Lalak·′aiyuk·oa.'

this and finally forced them to allow him to play with the box. He took it into his canoe and paddled about with it on the water. But he soon returned to the house. The following day he cried again until he got the box. He placed it in the bow of his canoe and went far out to sea with it. There he opened it a bit. When his mother, who had been watching him, saw this, she called to ME'nis, "Oh, look what tricks he is up to!" When he opened the box still more, the sun escaped and lit the earth. (Told by a young woman).

1a) Once it was always dark. The sun couldn't be seen and the people, not knowing the reason, began to be afraid. They asked Kuēkuaqā'oē for advice and he told them that the chief, Nā'lak·amālis,[10] was holding the sun captive. The people asked him to go and free it, so Kuēkuaqā'oē set out with his sister Ai'Hts'umk·a[11] (see page 210)[12] and arrived at the house of Nā'lak·amālis. He told his sister to hide and changed himself into a berry for he wanted to let himself be swallowed by the daughter of Nā'lak·amālis, who was called Nā'la-itl (= Daylight in the House).[13] She didn't notice him, so he transformed himself into a pine needle and dropped into the water. (Then there follows the story as above.) Ai'Hts'umk·a cuts the rope tying the canoe to the shore. They both escape and then Kuēkuaqā'oē breaks open the box. (Told in Albert Bay[14] by an old Awi'ky'ēnoq woman.)

2) In the beginning there were no springs or creeks and the water was flowing out of reach beneath the tree roots. But an old man owned one container filled with clear water and Raven flew to him to steal it. He hid a piece of inner cedar bark under his wings and asked the old man for a drink of water. The old man allowed him to drink, but said, "Don't drink too much; I have only a little water myself." Raven drank. When the man called to him to stop, he furtively wiped his tongue with inner cedar bark and said, "Look, my tongue is still quite dry; I haven't had anything." So the old man allowed him to drink more. He tricked him like this four times; then the container was empty and Raven flew away. He let drops fall everywhere and from these the lakes and rivers formed. (Told by a young woman.)

3) Kuēkuaqā'oē arrived at Nō'qunts[15] (where he is said to have reached the earth first when he came down from the sky). In those days there were no salmon in the lakes

---

10. Boas' "Nā'lak·amālis" is ńá·lagəmalis 'chief of the weather,' derived from ńá·la meaning 'weather, cycles, or season.'

11. Likely Ɂáixċəmga, referring to the shine of an abalone shell.

12. This is a reference to page 210 of the original *Sagen*, where the same name, Ɂáixċəmga, appears in part 5 of this story, and Boas translates it as 'Shining, or Abalone Woman.'

13. This is ńá·laɁeiɬ, derived from ńá·la 'weather, cycles, or season'; EW gives the literal meaning of ńá·laɁeiɬ 'weather in house.'

14. Alert Bay.

15. What Boas transcribes as "Nō'qunts" is núxʷənc, the name of the village site located where the

and rivers and Kuēkuaqā'oē wished to have some. He went to the forest spirit, Mā'kyagyū,[16] who was a good carver and carpenter, and asked him for salmon. So Mā'kyagyū carved him four fishes (Quitlâ'la)[17] from cedar wood. Kuēkuaqā'oē threw them into the river and Mā'kyagyū caused them to swim upstream. Then Kuēkuaqā'oē caught them in a trap. Because Mā'kyagyū had carved them from cedar wood, their skins and bones were very hard and Kuēkuaqā'oē was not yet satisfied.

4) So he went to the graves and asked the dead, "Are there not any twins[18] buried here?" And he heard a voice answering from a grave, "I was formerly a salmon." He opened the grave and found the corpse of a woman in it. He bathed her in the Water of Life[19] and the woman rose and rubbed her eyes as if she had been asleep. Kuēkuaqā'oē took her home and said to her, "There are no salmon here; are you not able to obtain them?" So the woman asked for a mat and seagull feathers and swam about in the river. Everywhere she touched the water, salmon came into being. The woman was given the name Ōmagyī'ēk·a (= Highest Chieftainess).[20] Now Kuēkuaqā'oē caught plenty of salmon with his net and put them onto the drying racks inside the house. He carried firewood into the house and piled it up underneath the salmon in order to make a good fire. He bumped against the drying rack while doing this and the salmon got entangled in his hair. So he became angry, threw down the wood and called out, "Why do you always pull my hair?" Ōmagyī'ēk·a asked, "What are you saying?" Although Kuēkuaqā'oē replied, "Oh, nothing of importance," she knew at once that he had scolded the salmon and immediately became a dry corpse again.

5) So Kuēkuaqā'oē became sad, because along with Ōmagyī'ēk·a, all the salmon had also disappeared. He went into the forest early in the morning, stripped inner cedar bark off a tree and went back home. He had four sisters: Gy'ā'nauēk·a,[21] AiHts'umk·a (= Shining, or Abalone Woman),[22] Yā'lamēHumē'k·a,[23] and Ku'skus

---

"Neechanz" (an anglicization of núxʷənc) River flows into Owikeno Lake. This name is confirmed elsewhere in Boas (1934:65) where he identifies it only as "a village in Rivers Inlet." EW notes that núxʷənc is a very old term whose meaning is no longer known.

16. "Mā'kyagyū" is likely má·k̓iagiu, derived from k̓iá 'carve.'

17. This name is not now recognized.

18. "The Kwakiutl and the Awi'ky'ēnoq believe that twins were salmon before their birth and that they are able to become salmon again" [Boas' original footnote].

19. The Water of Life, known as q̓ʷəlásta, is owned by supernatural beings and bestowed as a gift to certain individuals. When sprinkled on a body, the water causes it to revive.

20. What Boas transcribes as "Ōmagyī'ēk·a" is derived from the Oowekyala term w̓ú·m̓aqs 'chief's wife.'

21. The meaning of this name, "Gy'ā'nauēk·a," given elsewhere by Boas (1932:6) as "k!ānawega," is not known with certainty.

22. As previously noted in story 1a of this section, this name is likely ʔáixc̓əmga, referring to the shine of an abalone shell.

23. The meaning of this name, "Yā'lamēHumē'k·a," given as Yā'lamēxumēga elsewhere in Boas

(= Bluejay).[24] And he had one brother: Na'noak·aoē (= Wisest).[25] He had his sisters make mats on which salmon were served and made himself a net. When everything was ready, he put the mats and the net into the canoe and went out to sea, far to the west, with AiHts'umk·a. Their canoe had the property of reaching any place, no matter how distant, in one day. After they had travelled for one day, they saw a black coast and found that they had reached the Salmon country. The chief Mä'isila (= Where There Are Many Salmon)[26] invited them into his house. Before they accepted the invitation, Kuēkuaqā'oē said to his sister, "In a little while, go along the beach and pretend that you are looking at canoes. Then drill holes in all the canoes." His sister did this. Then Mä'isila made his four daughters swim in the sea and they returned in a short time, each carrying in her hand a salmon which had been created while they were swimming. The wife of Mä'isila cooked them and the chief served them to his guests, ordering them to eat all the bones and not to throw anything into the fire under any circumstances. Suddenly the nose of one of the girls started to bleed and so they knew at once that Kuēkuaqā'oē had hidden a bone. They found the nasal bone of the salmon on the palate of Kuēkuaqā'oē and took it away from him. Immediately the girl's nose stopped bleeding. But Kuēkuaqā'oē pretended to be very angry, launched his canoe and wanted to depart. He had left one of his pretty mats behind on purpose, and Mä'isila sent word down to him that he should not forget it. But Kuēkuaqā'oē didn't want to return and therefore the chief sent down his daughter with the mat. The canoe was already far out in the water so that the girl had to wade into the sea up over her knees. Then when she stood beside the canoe, Kuēkuaqā'oē seized her, pulled her into the canoe and paddled away. When Mä'isila saw this he wanted to pursue the robber, but most of the canoes sank as soon as they had been launched, because AiHts'umk·a had drilled holes in them. But some canoes pursued them and nearly caught up with the fugitives, when Kuēkuaqā'oē threw into the water the mats which his sisters had made, and which the Salmon like so much. The Salmon picked them up and began to quarrel over who should have them. In the meantime he reached home. The Salmon made one more try to get her back, but were unsuccessful. Since that time there are many salmon in Wa'nuk (a place in Rivers Inlet; = With a River).[27]

(1932:6), is not known.

24. EW points out, and AD confirms, that kʷə'skʷəs (Boas' "Ku'skus") is the Kwakwala term for 'bluejay' i.e. the Steller's Jay (*Cyanocitta stelleri*)—the Oowekyala term for this same species is kʷáiga (EW).

25. Given in the *Sagen* as *Erzweise*, literally 'arch-wise'; likely "Na'noak·aoē" is related to the Oowekyala term nánuwaq̓ayu meaning 'wise.'

26. This is miyásila which means 'abundant with fish' and is the name for the Chief of the Salmon.

27. This name, wá·nukʷ, which literally means 'having a river' (EW), is applied to the Wannock River which drains Owikeno Lake into Rivers Inlet.

6) After some time Kuēkuaqā'oē gave the girl as a wife to the son of a chief of the Hēista-itq (one of the northernmost tribes of the Kwakiutl, near Skeena River).[28] After some time he made his sisters pick berries, which he wanted to give to the young woman as a present. When they had filled many boxes, they loaded his canoe and set out for the country of the Hēista-itq. On the way, Kuēkuaqā'oē became greedy and wanted to eat the berries. (There follows the story: Legends of the Bilqula[29] No. 6. He makes his excrement shout, "Many people are coming and want to fight with you!" Then he smears himself all over with the red juice of the berries in order to make his sisters believe that he is wounded. But they find out soon that nobody had been there and that he ate the berries).

7) Kuēkuaqā'oē married a widow who had a beautiful daughter. He built himself a house on Wī'k'etsē[30] Island (outside Rivers Inlet). Raven wanted to get the girl in his power and thought up a ruse. He made her take a bath. There follows the story: Legends of the Bilqula no.5. He takes wood from the yellow cedar, which burns her. Then he advises her to go to the forest and look for the medicine Lē'ʜlakis (Penis in the Forest).[31] Then she sits down on this and runs away when she discovers what has happened.

8) Then Kuēkuaqā'oē took a pair of mussel shells, gathered the secretion of the girl's vagina very carefully and put it inside. He placed the shells beneath a tree. He looked at the shell from time to time and soon found a small boy in it. He grew up in four days. Kuēkuaqā'oē gave him the name Ky'ĩō'tl[32] and took him along home. There he showed him to the girl and said, "Look, this is your brother." Then he built a canoe in the woods. When it was finished and he made ready to push it into the water, Ky'ĩō'tl asked to be allowed to come along. When they got there, they found a hat in the middle of the canoe and Kuēkuaqā'oē knew that it would be very dangerous to touch it, so he warned his son, but he didn't obey and put on the hat, which carried him up high at once. Thereupon Kuēkuaqā'oē sat down on the beach

---

28. What Boas transcribes as "Hēista-itq" is ʔísdáitx̣ʷ (Rath 1981:1:2) referring to the former Heiltsuk-speaking people of Dean Channel (Olson 1955:321); we have recorded the Bella Coola or Nuxalk name for these same people as istamx, although the Nuxalk term for the Dean Channel people is sucɬmx or, less commonly, nux̌'lmx (Kennedy and Bouchard 1990a:339). Thus Boas is wrong when he states here in the *Sagen* that the "Hēista-itq" (ʔísdáitx̣ʷ) lived "near Skeena River" (see also Section XXI).

29. Bella Coola or Nuxalk; see Section XXII.

30. While the term Boas transcribes here as "Wī'k'etsē" is not now recognized as an Oowekyala place name, it may be related to the term wík̓ʷa used by contemporary Oowekeeno people to refer to a fish camp on the south end of Calvert Island (off the entrance to Rivers Inlet).

31. This term is not now recognized.

32. This name is recognized as kíyuɬ and is associated with the Oowekyala term kíx̌ʷa meaning 'blond or reddish hair.'

close by his house and wept for four days. Suddenly he heard someone say behind him, "I am Ky'īṓtl; I have returned to you." He turned around, but didn't recognized the speaker and said, "You are not Ky'īṓtl; you have no hair, while his was very long. Your face, too, is quite different." The other one replied, "But it's me all the same. There is always a strong wind up there and that has changed me so. Please accept me! Believe me, I am your son!" He pleaded with him like this four times, but Kuēkuaqā'oē didn't believe him. So he said, "Because you won't recognize me, I will have to return to the sky and won't be able to come back. From now on, humans will die and after that won't be able to return." He flew up high and only then did Kuēkuaqā'oē recognize him. But now he wished to have him back in vain and stretched out his arms towards the sky. (See Section XXI, story 1, part 5).

9) From what had happened, Kuēkuaqā'oē deduced that K·Elēsiltsâ'ē,[33] a big Eagle, had brought the hat in order to abduct Ky'īṓtl, so he resolved to take revenge. He went to Mā'kyagyū[34] (see page 209)[35] and asked him to carve a huge whale. Mā'kyagyū granted his request, and when the whale was finished, Kuēkuaqā'oē coated it with pitch and threw it into the water. He himself, Halibut, Beaver, and Sea Otter went into the whale and he made it swim to Sā'lutsē (an island north of Malcolm Island in Queen Charlotte Sound),[36] where K·Elēsiltsâ'ē lived. K·Elēsiltsâ'ē happened to be sitting in front of his house and, when he saw the whale swimming up, he sent out his youngest son, NātlEmsk·EmEnkolā'k·amāē (= Catching One)[37] to catch it. He swooped down upon it, but the whale was too heavy for him and he wasn't able to free his talons from the pitch and thus was drowned. So Eagle sent out his next youngest son, Maē'matsEmEnkolā'k·amāē (= Catching Two),[38] who also drowned, even though he lifted the whale a little bit. Then Eagle's next son, Yū'tuqsEmEnkolā'k·amāē (= Catching Three)[39] flew out, who met with the same fate. So finally the eldest son of K·Elēsiltsâ'ē, Maē'musk·EmEnkolā'amāē (= Catching Four)[40] flew out. The old one called to him, "Seize the whale by its head, not by its

---

33. This name, "K·Elēsiltsâ'e," is not now recognized.

34. As previously noted, "Mā'kyagyū" is likely má·k̓iagu, derived from k̓iá 'carve.'

35. Boas' reference is to part 3 of the present story which appears on page 209 of the original *Sagen*.

36. Boas' "Sā'lutsē," said to refer to "an island north of Malcolm Island in Queen Charlotte Sound," is not now recognized. Boas (1934:57) elsewhere transcribes this term as "sā'lots!a," translates it as 'hazy on rock,' and identifies the place it refers to as the whole of "Blind Island" (it has not been possible to determine the location of "Blind Island").

37. This name is derived from the Kwakwala, not the Oowekyala, term for 'one.' The Oowekyala form of this name is m̓ím̓ənsgəm̓ənak̫ʷəla which means literally 'carrying one at a time.'

38. Recognized as máymałpənak̫ʷəlagəmi 'carrying two at a time.'

39. Recognized as yáyutx̫ʷsəmənk̫ʷəlagəmi 'carrying three at a time.'

40. Recognized as mámusgəm̓ənk̫ʷəlagəmi 'carrying four at a time.'

middle." He followed this counsel and seized the whale by its blowholes and lifted it up. There followed a lengthy and difficult struggle and, when the Eagle became tired, his father came up to help him. They were almost winning, when the whale gained the upper hand and plunged down into the depths with such force that he got stuck in the bottom of the sea. Beaver and Sea Otter had to get out and dig him loose again. Then they returned to the homeland of Kuēkuaqā'oē.

10) Once Kuēkuaqā'oē asked the Deer, Tlēk·Ewī'lak',[41] "When are you fattest?" He replied, "In summer when there are many berries." So when it became summer, Kuēkuaqā'oē said, "Come, let's weep together!" They went out, sat down on the edge of a precipice, and Kuēkuaqā'oē began, "A long time ago my father gave away as many blankets as there are tree-stumps all over the world." Then Tlēk·Ekwī'lak' sang; "A long time ago my father gave away as many blankets as there are leaves on the trees and shells on the beach." So Kuēkuaqā'oē shouted, "You are making fun of me! Your father has never done that." And he pushed him into the chasm, then carried him home and ate him up.

11) The older brothers of Stskin[42] went into the woods to hunt. But they returned without game and were very dejected because they had nothing to eat. So Stskin took his bow and arrows and went into the woods. Soon he noticed Grizzly Bear. Stskin sat down on a branch in front of Grizzly Bear and mocked him by saying, "Oh, how big your nose is!" At this Bear became angry and devoured him. But Stskin flew out of Bear's behind again, unharmed, and sat down once more on a branch and mocked him. Bear devoured him a second time, but Stskin again flew out of his behind. Bear devoured him a third and a fourth time. So Stskin broke up his bow inside Bear's stomach and made a firedrill from it. He used his rain cape for tinder and then lit a big fire in Bear's stomach. Then he again flew out of his behind. Bear first had to cough because the rising smoke irritated his throat. Then flames burst from all his natural orifices and he burned miserably. Then Stskin flew home and said to his mother, "Call all the people and let them go to the woods with me; I have killed a big bear." His mother didn't believe him and said, "You can't lie to me that you have caught something when your brothers came back empty-handed." So Stskin took a knife, flew into the woods and cut off Bear's nose; he took it to his mother and now she knew that little Stskin had killed Bear.

Many men then went with him into the woods to get Bear, among them Raven. They divided Bear up and found that he was very fat. So the greedy Raven wished to have all the fat for himself. He thought, "Oh, if only they would give me the fat

---

41. What Boas renders here as "Tlēk·Ewī'lak'" is λíqkʷilakʷ which literally means 'the one who is supposed to be brave' and is the Oowekyala term for 'Deer' in mythology.

42. This is c̓skn, the Oowekyala mythical name for 'Wren.'

to carry." He had scarcely thought it when the people said, "Raven shall carry the fat," and they tied it to his back. Soon he stayed behind and all the men had to wait for him. When they asked him why, he said that the fat was slipping from his back. So they tied it fast once more, but soon he lagged behind again. The men became impatient and told him to follow by himself. That is just what he had intended, and he now gobbled up all the fat. Then he hit his leg with a stone so that he was slightly hurt and flew home. "Oh," said he, "I nearly died. I've fallen off a steep mountain." But they didn't believe him because they knew his pranks and ruses. Raven had eaten too much and had to go out and relieve himself frequently. Matsilq,[43] the young son of K·atsi-tā′la,[44] followed him and saw that he didn't emit any excrement at all, but only fat. But still he kept calling, "Oh, I feel so sick! A hair has gotten into my anus." So Matsilq shouted, "He lies; there is only bear fat coming out!" So the people knew that Raven had stolen all the fat. But he also wanted to have the meat, which was being cooked in huge kettles. He went out, relieved himself and said to his excrement, "Shout in a moment: 'Oh, oh, many canoes are coming!'" They obeyed and all the men ran into the street to look for the canoes. In the meantime, Raven gobbled up all the meat.

2. Nōak·aua (= Wise One) and Masmasalā′niq[45]

After Raven had freed the sun, Nōak·aua and Masmasalā′niq descended from the sky in order to make everything beautiful and well.

Nōak·aua thought, "Oh, if only Masmasalā′niq would separate the land from the water." And Masmasalā′niq separated the land from the water. And Nōak·aua thought, "Oh, if only Masmasalā′niq would create the eulachon." And Masmasalā′niq created the fish rich in oil. Then Nōak·aua thought, "Oh, if only Masmasalā′niq would make a path leading up yonder mountain." And Masmasalā′niq made it. And again Nōak·aua thought, "Oh, if only Masmasalā′niq would make a cave in this mountain and would create many berries on its summit. Oh, if only he would carve people from cedar wood, men and women, and would

43. While "Matsilq" is not recognized by contemporary Oowekeeno people, Boas (1932:71) gives a very similar term that, among the neighbouring Bella Bella (Heiltsuk), refers to the son of Raven.

44. EW believes that what Boas renders here as "K·atsitā′la," is a Kwakwala term, qácistala; AD confirms the term is Kwakwala and agrees with the translation provided by EW ('walk around something') but is not aware of a story character with this name.

45. The first of these two names is nú·waqawa, derived from núwaqəla meaning 'old, mature or wise' and referring to the character's supernatural wisdom. The second name is that of an original ancestor of the Oowekeeno who initiated all arts, crafts and skills; the name as Boas gives it here, "Masmasalā′niq," appears to be the Bella Coola form, which we have recorded as masmasalanix̌ʷ 'supernatural carpenter' (see Section XXII, story 1, part 1)—the Oowekyala equivalent of this name is ṁásṁasalanuwa.

make canoes and paddles for them." And Masmasalā′niq executed all the thoughts of Nōak·aua. Again Nōak·aua thought, "Oh, if only Masmasalā′niq would make a box with four compartments for the dancing flutes." And Masmasalā′niq made one. He made a box with four compartments. He put the Hā′mat'sa[46] flute into the left front compartment, the Tsā′ek·a[47] or Tlōk·oa′la[48] flute into the right front one, the one of the Tlōola′qa[49] dance into the left back, and into the right back, the Mē′itla[50] whistles. Then Nōak·aua thought, "Oh, if only Masmasalā′niq would make a five-toned flute." And Masmasalā′niq made a flute with the voices of the k·ō′itsa,[51] t'ē′iqtlala,[52] kuai′ik·a (ducks),[53] ā′qaqōnē,[54] and the mouse. And Nōak·aua thought again, "Oh, if only Masmasalā′niq would make the dancing staff; oh, if only he would go into the forest to seek the cedar tree; oh, if only he would make the stone axe to cut down the cedar; if only he would make the box to store dried salmon. Oh, if only he would make the firedrill, so that the people would have fire, and if only he would look for the yellow cedar wood which has lain in the water for a long time, in order to set it alight by friction; oh, if only he would make the inner bark beater and would beat the inner cedar bark until it was soft enough to use for tinder." And Masmasalā′niq executed all the thoughts of Nōak·aua. Nōak·aua thought again, "Oh, if only Masmasalā′niq would make a net so that the people might catch fish." Masmasalā′niq tried, but without success. So he went to ask Spider to make a net for him. Spider granted his request. Spider also made the neck-ring of red inner cedar bark for the winter dance, and the basket, and taught Masmasalā′niq how to peel cedars. And Nōak·aua thought, "Oh, if only Masmasalā′niq would sharpen a bone to give to Spider in order to split the inner bark." And Masmasalā′niq sharpened the

---

46. This is the Oowekyala term hámaċa (translated by EW as 'look for food to eat') which designates the highest-ranking dance of the whole order of dances called the ċáiqa or "Shaman's series" (see also the footnote that follows).

47. Boas' "Tsā′ek·a" is ċáiqa, referring to the order of dances called the "Shaman's series." The name ċáiqa refers to the secrets learned by the initiates into the dances.

48. What Boas renders here as "Tlōk·oa′la" is ʎúgʷala, referring generally to the supernatural power possessed by the dancers of the ċáiqa series of dances (see the footnote above).

49. Boas' "Tlōola′qa" is ʎuwəl'áxa, referring to a series of dances that is separate from the ċáiqa series (see above). The ʎuwəl'áxa dances occurred after the ċáiqa season was completed and were more expressive of family crests and privileges.

50. The míʎa (Boas' "Mē′itla") is a dance of the ʎuwəl'áxa series (see above).

51. Recognized as gʷíʣa, the Oowekyala term for a small, wren-like bird that is brown and black in colour.

52. This term is not now recognized.

53. This is kʷáiga, the Oowekyala term for the Steller's Jay or "bluejay," and not "ducks" as Boas suggests here.

54. Boas' "ā′qaqōne" is ʔáxʷʔáxʷəni which refers to the Swainson's Thrush (*Hylocichla ustulata*). As discussed elsewhere in this section (see story 4, part 3), this bird is associated with the ripening of salmonberries.

bone and Spider made threads of inner bark. Then Nōak·aua thought, "Oh, if only Masmasalā′niq would make edible roots, houses, paintings, carvings, and masks." And Masmasalā′niq did so. When everything was done, Nōak·aua and Masmasalā′niq made a great noise in the sky and the people came to life. Then Nōak·aua told the people to marry and told them, "When you find no more berries at the foot of the mountain, use the path made by us. Ascend it and you will find many berries up there." The people obeyed.

Many young men were left without wives. Nōak·aua told them to climb up the mountain through the cave and to abduct the women who were picking berries up there. Then the young men ran up the mountain through the cave, but it was so low in many places that those running too wildly bashed their heads in and thus lost their lives. The rest appeared suddenly on top of the mountain, abducted the women picking berries and then rushed back through the cave. Those not running fast enough were killed by the men defending their women.

Then Nōak·aua thought, "Oh, if only Masmasalā′niq would teach the people to make traps with which they'll be able to catch raccoons." And Masmasalā′niq taught them how to catch bears and to make capes from their skins. He sent out four men, who were the first to catch bears, into the forest.

And Nōak·aua thought again, "Oh, if only Masmasalā′niq would get fire." But Masmasalā′niq was not able to do this. Therefore he first sent out Ermine to the house of the man who was guarding the fire. He took the fire stealthily in his mouth and wanted to run away, when the man asked, "Where are you going?" Ermine was unable to answer because he had the fire in his mouth, so the man gave him a mighty clout on the head and the fire fell to the ground. Because Ermine didn't have any success, Nōak·aua sent Deer. He went to Masmasalā′niq first of all in order to have his legs made slim and quick. And Nōak·aua thought, "If only Masmasalā′niq would stick fir wood[55] onto Deer's tail." And Masmasalā′niq stuck fir wood onto Deer's tail and he ran away on fleet feet. He came to the house where the fire was and danced around it while singing, "I would like to find the light." And he suddenly turned his backside towards the flames so that the wood in his tail caught fire and then he ran away. And the fire dropped to the ground everywhere and the people kept it carefully. Deer called to the wood by the wayside, "Hide the fire." It accepted the fire and since that time is combustible.

And Nōak·aua thought again, "Oh, if only Masmasalā′niq would make a whale of wood and would coat it with pitch." And Masmasalā′niq did so. For on a far mountain there lived the bird K·ani′sltsua[56] who was in the habit of abducting people. Nōak·aua wanted to catch him, so he made all the people go into the whale

---

55. Likely the reference here is to pitch wood, not fir wood.

56. What Boas transcribes as "K·ani′sltsua" is recognized as gənísəladzwis, a name for the Thunderbird.

and then Masmasalā′niq closed the whale and put it into the water. It swam to the house of K·ani′sltsua, who sent out his three sons Mēmensk·amE′nk·oa, MaimasemE′nk·oa and YaiutqsEmE′nk·oa one after the other to lift up the whale, but they all stuck fast to the pitch. The whale was too heavy for them and pulled them under, so K·ani′sltsua sent out his youngest son Mamosk·amE′nk·oa (the names signify: Lifting One, Two, Three, and Four). He rejoiced, put on his eagle garment and flew down to catch the whale. But he also stuck to it; the whale pulled him down and he lay on the water with broken wings. Finally K·ani′sltsua lost his life in the same manner.

And Nōak·aua thought, "When we've grown old we want to die." Masmasalā′niq wanted to live forever, but the small bird K·'oē′qtsa[57] wished very much for Nōak·aua and Masmasalā′niq to die. He said, "Where shall I live if you stay alive for ever? I want to build my nest in your grave and warm myself." Nōak·aua didn't know what to do and said to the Bird, "Agreed, we are going to die, but we will rise again after four days." But the Bird wasn't content with this; he wanted that they should die completely. So Nōak·aua and Masmasalā′niq resolved to die and then to return as children. They died and went up into the sky in order to see whether the people would mourn for them. From there they saw that all the people were lamenting and so Nōak·aua and Masmasalā′niq changed into droplets of blood which wafted down to earth with the wind. The women inhaled these in their sleep and consequently all gave birth to children. Thus Nōak·aua and Masmasalā′niq came back to earth.

3. Mink

1) Once Mink said to his mother, "I am hungry and would like to eat shellfish. I will fight Yā′ēqōēk·oa[58] (see page 232)[59] so that he will make low tides." He was a mighty chief living at the bottom of the sea. The mother allowed Mink to go and he swam out and attacked Yā′ēqōēk·oa. At last Mink managed to get the better of him and he held him under water until he began to lose his breath and cried, "Let me go and I will make the water recede so that you are able to gather shellfish." Mink was content with this. He let him go and swam back home. The sea receded a bit and he found one shellfish. When he came home, his mother asked, "Well, what have you found?" He showed the one shellfish to her and swam out again at once in order to

---

57. This bird name is not now recognized.

58. What Boas transcribes as "Yā′ēqōēk·oa" is recognized by EW as x̣áx̌ʷíyugʷa 'tides rising up and down.'

59. Boas' reference is to page 232 of the original *Sagen*, Section XX (Heiltsuk or Bella Bella), story 1, parts 3 and 4.

fight Yā'ēqōēk·oa once more. Again he defeated him and he made the water recede further and stay out longer. So Mink found six shellfish under the stones and took them to his mother. But he was still not content. Only after he had defeated the spirit of the sea four times was the sea made to recede far enough so that he got a basket full of shellfish. Then he was content. He let his mother taste the shellfish and they both ate their fill. Then he patted his stomach contentedly.

2) Once Mink played the hoop game with the ducks (kuaī'ik·a)[60] and won the game. Then they shot arrows at a stick to see who was the best shot. Here, too, he won. So they all fell upon him and broke his bow, but he defended himself and bit the ducks. Thereupon they said, "You have no father," in order to insult him. At this, Tlē'selagyila (= Sunmaker),[61] Mink, became sad and ran weeping to his mother to ask her whether it was true that he had no father. She consoled her son and said, "Just let them shout; your father is in the sky. His name is Toatusela'kilis[62] and he causes the sun to shine." So Mink resolved to visit him. He went to his uncle Hanatliaqtâ'o (i.e. Archer)[63] and had a new bow made for himself. When he had received it he shot an arrow at the sky and it stuck there. The second arrow stuck to the first and continuing thus he made a chain which reached from the sky down to the earth. Tlē'selagyila climbed up on it and finally reached the sky. He met the wife of Toatusela'kilis up there, for his father had married again. When she recognized Tlē'selagyila she said, "Your father will be very glad to see you. You can lead the sun now in his place." In the evening, when it grew dark, his father came home, and the woman said to him, "Your son has come and wants to stay with you. Let him lead the sun now in your place." Toatusela'kilis was very glad and awakened his son early in the morning. He gave his clothing to him and told him to rise slowly behind the mountains and warned him not to walk too quickly because then everything would burn up. Mink took his father's clothing and climbed up slowly as he had been told. But when it was almost noon, he became more impatient, began to run and thus set the whole world on fire. The world's inhabitants jumped into the water in order to escape from the flames, and here were transformed into real people (whereas they had been half animal before). But the woman in the sky called her husband and told him to throw Tlē'selagyila down to the earth before he burned everything. Toatusela'kilis hurried up, tore off Mink's clothes and threw him down

---

60. Recognized as kʷáiga, the Oowekyala term for the Steller's Jay or "bluejay," and not a reference to "ducks," as Boas suggests here.

61. "Tlē'selagyila" is recognized as a Kwakwala term, λ'ísəlagila, referring to 'Mink'—this is confirmed by AD, as is Boas' translation given here, 'sun-maker.'

62. This is the Oowekyala name tuátusəlagilis meaning 'walk around the sky.'

63. Recognized as hánaλ'qiyaxtua which means 'highest hunter,' derived from hánaλ 'use a bow and arrow.'

to the earth, saying, "If you had gone properly you could have led the sun for all time." Mink fell into the sea amongst many logs of driftwood. The people found him there and carried him home.

4. The Moon

1) Gyā'lōyak·amē (= First One)[64] was living with his father K·'ō'mHk·'ōmgyila.[65] One day he decided to go out in his canoe, so he pushed the canoe into the water and went far out to sea. There he met K·ōmō'k·oa[66] who tried to catch the canoe and its skipper. So Gyā'lōyak·amē ordered the canoe to rise up high and lo, it flew away like a bird! It climbed up higher and higher and finally struck the sky. There Gyā'lōyak·amē found a hole, stuck his head through it and asked, "Are there no people up here?" He heard someone answer, "Yes, we live here, the Wa'qsk·ᴇm (= Face on Both Sides),[67] but we are not happy because we have our mouths on the back of our necks." So Gyā'lōyak·amē said, "One day when I have a child, it shall be named after you." He went on in his canoe and after some time he saw a house below. The canoe at first circled above it, then went down lower and lower until it landed in front of the house at last. In the house there lived Tlā'k·oagyila (Copper Maker).[68] His wife was rocking her baby, who was crying constantly. In order to quieten it down she said, "Don't cry, or else Gyā'lōyak·amē will get you." The child went to sleep and the woman also laid down to rest. When everyone was asleep, Gyā'lōyak·amē crept into the house and stole the child out of the cradle. After some time the woman woke up and, when she continued to rock the cradle, she noticed that it was empty. So she shouted, "Tlā'k·oagyila, someone has stolen our child!" and then she wept bitterly. But Gyā'lōyak·amē came in at once and said to them; "Stop weeping; here is your child. I only wanted to learn his name." So the father was glad and said, "He is called Tlā'tlak·oasila (= Counting Copper).[69] When your sister has children, make her give this name to her elder son. The second child, a girl, shall be called Tlāk·oagyilaiō'k·oa (= Making Coppers),[70] the third, a boy,

---

64. Recognized as gáluẏagəmi 'first one to come out.'

65. Boas' "K·'ō'mHk·'ōmgyila" is likely q̓ʷúmq̓ʷumgila, a name that EW translates as 'made to be a prince.' What appears to be this same term is transcribed by Boas as "K·'ōmk·'ō'mgyila" in story 6 of the present section.

66. Boas' "K·ōmō'k·oa" is recognized as the name of the sea-being known as q̓ʷúmuk̓ʷa (EW).

67. Possibly this is the Oowekyala term ẇá·xsgəm 'facing both ways.'

68. Recognized as x̄'áqʷagila meaning 'copper maker.'

69. Boas' "Tlā'tlak·oasila" is x̄'áx̄'aqʷasila 'counting coppers.'

70. Recognized as the name x̄'áqʷagilaẏugʷa, the name of the daughter of x̄'áqʷagila ('copper maker').

Sēkyōk·oa′la (= Sounding Coppers),[71] and the last one, a girl, Tlā′k·oitl (= Copper in the House).[72] Now travel on to AiHts'umgyila (= Abalone Shell Worker)." Gyā′lōyak·amē went into his canoe and flew on. Soon he found the house of AiHts'umgyila. Again the canoe circled above it and descended slowly. Then Gyā′lōyak·amē stole a child from him, too, in order to learn its name. When he brought it back, AiHts'umgyila said, "When your sister has children, she shall call the eldest, a boy, after our son AiHts'umk·'ā′naq (= Cleaning Shells).[73] The next, a girl, shall be called AiHts'umk·a (= Shining),[74] the third, a boy, AiHts'umalitl (= Abalone in the House)[75] and the youngest, a girl, AiHts'umk·anlitl (= Box Full of Abalone Shells)."[76] Then Gyā′lōyak·amē returned to earth and told his sisters what he had experienced. He then rose up into the sky and became the moon.

2) A young girl was minding her brother while their mother was out catching eulachon.[77] Because the boy was crying incessantly, she wrapped him up in her cape, carried him up and down the street and gave him a small container to play with. Since he absolutely refused to stop crying, she threatened that the moon would get him. And, since he still wouldn't stop, she threatened him a second, third and fourth time. Thereupon Moon heard her. He descended to earth and grew enormous while coming down, and he took the boy up with him. The boy with the container in his hand can still be seen standing in the moon today.

3) A young man called Mē′itla[78] went up to the sky ten times in one year. The first time he found a seagull there and brought it back down with him. When he went up the second time he found a bird with a red beak, the third time the salmonberries,[79]

---

71. What Boas renders as "Sēkyōk·oa′la" is sík̓ugʷala which refers to a cane upon which hang several small coppers—the cane is carried by the cannibal woman and the coppers jangle as she walks about.

72. This is x̌’áqʷeiɫ 'copper in house.'

73. EW believes this name may be ʔáixc̓əmganuxʷ, 'having-abalone-shell woman.'

74. Recognized as the name ʔáixc̓əmga 'shining woman.'

75. What Boas transcribes as "AiHts'umalitl" is ʔáixc̓əmgaleiɫ 'abalone shell in the house' (see also the footnote that follows).

76. This is ʔáixc̓əmganeiɫ, the female form of the name ʔáixc̓əmaleiɫ ('abalone shell in the house') given in the preceding footnote.

77. While Boas provides this term in English as "olachen" here in the *Sagen*, we use the contemporary spelling "eulachon" for this fish (*Thaleichthys pacificus*).

78. As noted previously, m̓íx̌a (Boas' "Mē′itla") is a dance of the x̌uw̓əl'áx̌a series.

79. Boas provides the word "salmonberries" (in double quotation marks) in English here in the *Sagen*. As in other areas of the Northwest Coast, the ripening of salmonberries is commonly associated by the Oowekeeno with the Swainson's Thrush, known in Oowekyala as ʔáx̌ʷʔáx̌ʷəni (see also story 2 of the present section). We assume that the storyteller's reference here in the text to "a bird with a red beak" is a reference to the Swainson's Thrush.

then the diver[80] and the bird Qē'qēqē.[81] The sixth time he brought the bird AtE'mkuli[82] back down with him. But when he went up the tenth time, he found Nūsnū'selis, Moon,[83] and then returned no more. So his mother Tlēelaiak·s[84] and his father K·'ōmqtō'is[85] wept and lamented. At last they fell asleep. The mother saw a beautiful house in front of her in a dream, and when she awoke, she saw that it wasn't a mere dream; the house really stood close before her. She saw her son Mē'itla playing outside the house and she awakened her husband so that he could see him, too. When the father woke up, he also saw the house and the boy, and called, "There is our lost son!" They jumped up and ran towards the house, but it appeared to recede before them and they recognized at last that in reality it was far away, up in the sky. So they sat down and wept and sang, "Oh, our son is playing up there with Nūsnū'selis. He is staying in a strange country and will not come back to us again." While they were singing, their niece passed by and they told her that they had observed Mē'itla at play in the sky. She replied, "We will make your son appear again in a dance." The parents agreed; they let their niece, who was called K·'ōk·ōmē'tsemk·a,[86] dance in the shape of Mē'itla and gave his name to her.

5. Mē'maotlEmē[87]

On a hot summer's day four brothers went down to the sea to bathe. They found a tree trunk on the beach and laid down on it to sleep. While they were resting there the trunk began to drift and, when they woke up, they could no longer see land. They floated about for a long time and at last they saw a black line on the horizon. They came close and saw black coast. The youngest brother jumped from the log onto the beach, but behold, the land vanished and he was drowned! After some time they arrived at a similar land. The second youngest jumped from the log and he also drowned. The two surviving brothers drifted about on the log for a long time. Finally the second brother grew so tired that he was unable to hold on any longer

---

80. While Boas uses here the term German term *Taucher* 'diver,' which dictionaries of the time (*circa* 1890) translate as both 'grebe' and 'loon,' we are not certain which species of bird is referred to. Possibly it is the bird known in Oowekyala as q̇ʷúda, referring to some type of grebe.

81. The term that Boas transcribes as "Qē'qēqē" is not now recognized, although it may possibly be gilíx̣ʷiċa, the Oowekyala word for the bird known as the 'American Dipper' (*Cinclus mexicanus*).

82. This is ʔadə'mguli, 'Sandhill Crane' (*Grus canadensis*).

83. Recognized as n̓úsn̓usəlis, derived from n̓úsi, the Oowekyala term for 'moon.'

84. This name, "Tlēelaiak·s," is not now recognized.

85. EW believes this term, "K·'ōmqtō'is," is possibly q̇ʷúmx̣tuys 'protruding up the highest.'

86. This name, "K·'ōk·ōmē'tsemk·a," is not now recognized.

87. Name not now recognized.

and he, too, was drowned. Only the eldest was left, and after long wanderings he reached the country of chief Mᴇ′nis (see page 208)[88] at last. Here he found a river which flowed from a lake. He went up and sat down at the shore of the lake. In the evening, Lalak·'aiyuk·oa,[89] the daughter of Mᴇ′nis, came from the house to get water. When she saw the man, she asked him where he was from, and Mē′maotlᴇmē, for that was his name, told her of his fate, so she invited him to come to her father's house. He followed her inside and she offered him food from a big box. She took something, which he didn't recognize, out of it, mixed it with water and "crab-apples"[90] and served it to him. When Mē′maotlᴇme wanted to start eating he saw that they were human eyes and he refused to eat such food. After some time Mᴇ′nis happened to go into a room of his house, and when Mᴇ′nis opened the door, Mē′maotlᴇmē saw seals resting inside it. He said to Lalak·'aiyuk·oa, "Cook me some of that; it is what we eat in our country." The girl reported the guest's request to her father, who thereupon took a stick and killed one of the seals. The daughter cut it up and cooked it. But she found it distasteful that Mē′maotlᴇmē should eat such food, because the seals were their dogs.

And Mᴇ′nis gave his daughter to the guest for a wife. Not far from the house there was a fish-weir, and close to it there was erected a pole on which perched an eagle who called each time the weir was full of fish. Early in the morning, when Mē′maotlᴇme was still in bed, the eagle called out, so Lalak·'aiyuk·oa nudged her husband and said, "Go down to the weir and take out the salmon." Mē′maotlᴇmē went down and in the weir found his brothers' corpses. A raven had pecked out an eye from one of them. So he wept. When his wife heard him weeping, she got up, went to him and asked him the reason for his grief. When he showed the corpses of his brothers to her, she said, "Don't be sad, my father will resuscitate them." She fetched her father and he carried the corpses into the house. He took an eye from the box and put it into one of the brothers to replace the one which had been pecked out, then he shook the brothers and they became alive again.

One day one of the brothers was playing with a piece of cedar wood when Lalak·'aiyuk·oa reprimanded him for it, saying that the wood was very precious and that her father had to pay much for it. The man was astonished at this and told her that there were many cedar trees growing in his homeland. When Mᴇ′nis heard of

---

88. Boas' reference here is to story 1, part 1 of the present section, which is found on page 208 of the original *Sagen.*

89. This same name, "Lalak·'aiyuk·oa," is transcribed in story 1, part 1 of this section as "Latāk·'ai′yuk·oa"; both of these terms are variants of a name that is possibly ƛ'álagayugʷa, the meaning of which is not known with certainty.

90. Boas gives this term in English in the original *Sagen* as "crabapples" (with double quotation marks).

this through his daughter, he asked the brothers to visit their relatives and then to bring him back lots of cedar wood. But they had no canoe, so Me′nis gave them his skin-canoe and told them to embark. They were afraid to cross the sea in the skin-canoe, but Me′nis encouraged them. He gave them one of each of the different kinds of animals which he kept as dogs in the numerous rooms of his house. Among these was also a porcupine. He told them to embark. Lalak·′aiyuk·oa was going with them and said, "Always steer for the rising sun and keep the setting sun behind you, then you will reach your homeland."

They obeyed and after a long journey reached their native village. No one had seen the canoe arrive. The youngest brother jumped ashore and went to greet his father. But he didn't recognize him at first. Then he had his house purified and gave a big feast, and his sons gave him all sorts of animals as presents from Chief Me′nis. Then they asked all the people to go into the forest to get cedar bark which they wanted to bring as a present to Me′nis. They loaded a canoe built of cedar and went back. Lalak·′aiyuk·oa told them to steer for the setting sun and to keep the rising sun behind them. They obeyed and reached Me′nis safely after they had passed the two treacherous black islands. The daughter went to her father and told him that she had been treated well and generously. And the heart of Me′nis became glad when he saw the cedar bark, the canoe and all the things which were unknown to him. And he resolved to imitate everything.

6. K·′ōmk·′ō′mgyila[91]

K·′ōmk·′ō′mgyila, a chief of the Nō′quntsitq,[92] had the daughter of the Chief of the North for his wife. She was called Tlāk·oagyīlaō′k·oa (= Made of Copper), Tlā′k·uītl (= Copper in the House), K·′ak·′anqp′ā′lak·a (= Copper Smell),[93] and Tlā′k·oetlk·′e′naq.[94] Her father's name was Tlā′k·oagyila (= Copper Maker) and the country where he lived was called D′a′k·ō.[95] They had twin daughters and for a

---

91. What Boas transcribes here as "K·′ōmk·′ō′mgyila" appears to be the same term that he renders as "K·′ō′mHk·′ōmgyila" in story 4, part 1,of this section—both terms are likely q̓ʷúmq̓ʷumgila, a name that EW translates as 'made to be a prince.'

92. Boas' "Nō′quntsitq" refers to the people who lived at the village known as núxʷənc, located where the "Neechanz" (an anglicization of núxʷənc) River flows into Owikeno Lake (see also story 1, part 3 of this section).

93. This name is not now recognized.

94. This name is not now recognized.

95. This name, "D′a′k·ō," is not now recognized; Boas (1934:56) transcribes the same name elsewhere as "t!ä′qōᵉ" which he identifies as a "place in Rivers Inlet."

number of years lived quietly in Nō′quntsitq.[96] But then K·′ōmk·′ō′mgyila longed to
visit the chiefs of the other points of the compass and to see their countries. The
chief of the East is Ālagyilak·Emāē (= First of the Fur Capes). He decided to visit
him first. When they embarked in their canoe, his daughters refused to come along.
He asked, "How will you eat when we are gone?" They replied, "We are salmon.
When we swim in the water, many fishes will come."[97] At last K·′ōmk·′ō′mgyila left
his daughters behind and set out towards the east with his wife and four slaves. They
went up the River Nō′qunt[98] as far as it was navigable and then continued on foot
towards the east. Finally, after a long journey, they arrived at four lakes and saw a
big hole in the ground from which the sun rose each morning.

The wife of K·′ōmk·′ō′mgyila told him that they had arrived in the country of
Ālagyilak·Emāē.[99] Since they saw no one, K·′ōmk·′ō′mgyila called, "Doesn't anyone
live in this hole here?" Because there was no answer, he called again and again. But
only after he had called four times did Ālagyilak·Emāē appear. He had a face in front
and another in the back and a strip of hair across the middle of his head. He said,
"What do you want?" K·′ōmk·′ō′mgyila replied, "I want to marry your daughter."
The chief said, "What do you want with her? You can't marry her." But he retorted,
"Yes, I can marry her just as well as any other woman." Thereupon Ālagyilak·Emāē
went into the hole to fetch his daughter. She was called Ā′lagyilayūk·oa[100] (= Made
Fur Cape) and Ālagyimitl (= Fur Cape in the House). When he brought her,
K·′ōmk·′ō′mgyila saw that she was a tiny child, but Ālagyilak·Emāē forced him to
marry her and gave him many fur blankets and the Water of Life. After some time
K·′ōmk·′ō′mgyila travelled back to his homeland. So the chief said, "When you
have children, name them after my daughter and me." When the traveller then
reached home, he saw smoke coming from the roof and he found his daughters well
supplied with fish. Then he decided to visit his father-in-law, Tlā′k·oagyila, the

96. Boas here repeats the term he gave at the beginning of this paragraph, "Nō′quntsitq," which, as
discussed above, refers to the people of the village known as núxʷənc, located where the
Neechanz River flows into Owikeno Lake. The context suggests that Boas should have written
"Nō′qunts" here (his rendering of núxʷənc, the name of the village, itself—see story 1, part 3),
rather than "Nō′quntsitq.'

97. "The Kwakiutl believe that twins are transformed salmon and that they have power over fishes
(see the present section, story 1, part 4)" [Boas' original footnote].

98. What Boas renders here as "River Nō′qunt" is the same term he transcribes earlier in this section
(see story 1, part 3) as "Nō′qunts," i.e. núxʷənc, the name of the village site located where the
Neechanz River flows into Owikeno Lake. This river's name, "Neechanz," is an anglicization of
núxʷənc.

99. This man's name is recognized as Ɂálakilagəmi, likely derived from Ɂálakila 'tan or dress elk or
deer hides for use as a dancing cape' (see also the footnote that follows).

100. This is the female form of the name referred to in the preceding footnote.

Chief of the North. He loaded his canoe with many inner cedar bark nets and with dancing implements. Then they set out. Finally they reached a mountain which barred their way and K·'ōmk·'ō′mgyila didn't know how to continue. But his wife knew the route and she covered the canoe completely with fur capes so that no water could splash in. Then she made the canoe stop before a steep rock and wait till low tide. At that time a big cave became visible, leading through the whole mountain. They went through and on the other side saw the house of Tlā′k·oagyila. When the people saw them, they called to each other, "These must be powerful strangers who have come through the mountain." They didn't know that it was the canoe of the daughter of their chief. But when they came ashore, her father recognized her. He led them to the house and served a box of human eyes for them to eat. But the daughter said, "My husband doesn't eat this; give seal meat to him!" So the people killed some seals and gave them to him to eat. K·'ōmk·'ō′mgyila gave his father-in law the nets and the dancing ornaments which he had brought along. After some time they returned home again. Tlā′k·oagyila kept the canoe of his son-in-law and in return gave him a copper canoe which was shaped like a box and had a hole at each end. He filled the canoe with coppers and gave him the name Tlā′k·oagyila for his children.

He didn't visit Chief Gyō′gwisilāk·ᴇmāē (= First of the Shells)[101] of the South, nor AiHts'umgyīla (= Abalone Maker, or Who Makes It Shine) of the West.

7. K·ēk·tsumHskyā′na[102]

There once was a man who was called Apō′tl. One day he was invited to a feast and, when the meal was finished, he made a boy carry some of the leftover meal home to his wife and his four sons. The boy obeyed, and when the sons of Apō′tl, who had been resting in their beds, which were the boards along the side above the platform, saw the large bowl full of meat and berries, they got up and jumped down to eat. But their mother said, "This isn't for you. Apō′tl has sent the food for me. If you want some, go to K·ēk·tsumHskyā′na and get it from her." But K·ēk·tsumHskyā′na was a cannibal woman living in a far country, so the boys became sad and defiant. They went to bed again and stayed there for four days without food or drink. On the fourth day the villagers saw a beautiful bird (a swan?) swimming near the houses. The

---

101. Possibly kʷúgʷisilagəmi 'shiny shell face,' referring to the shine of the abalone shells.

102. This name is recognized as possibly qíkċəmxsḱana 'having hands as sharp as a knife'; in the first paragraph of this story, Boas describes qíkċəmxsḱana as "a cannibal woman living in a far country." Elsewhere, Boas (1888g:51–52) provides his own translated summary of this story, noting that he heard it "at Rivers Inlet from a wik'ē′nok," and adding that the story refers "to the Eskimo."

children tried to catch it, but couldn't get hold of it. When the sons of Apō´tl heard of this, they got up, took their bows and arrows out of a wooden box and climbed into their canoe. When they came close to the bird, they shot, and the arrow hit but didn't kill the bird. The bird swam away and the boys pursued it. They came close to it quite often and then shot at it with their arrows, but as often as they hit it, they were unable to kill it. In this way the bird lured them far out to sea. At last they did succeed in catching it. Thereupon they wanted to turn back home, but behold, there was nothing but sky and water around and even the summits of the highest mountains had vanished, so the boys didn't know where to turn. But this wasn't all; as soon as they had caught the bird, an icy wind began to blow and then they knew that the bird was the master of the winds. The sea began to freeze and they were able to pick a way through the blocks of ice only with much trouble. When they had wandered about like this for some time without really knowing where to turn, the paddle of one of the brothers broke; he became tired, fell asleep and finally perished with the cold and hunger. A short time after, the second brother's paddle broke; he also froze. So the two surviving brothers took the blankets of their dead brothers and wrapped themselves up in them, but at last the third one also died of hunger and cold. When the eldest then found himself all alone, he wrapped himself in the capes and wept bitterly. In a short while he began to doze off. But suddenly he jerked up because he felt that the canoe had hit land. He pushed his paddle into the water and struck the bottom. There wasn't a soul to be seen on the shore and so he was afraid to disembark. But finally he saw some footprints and then took heart, wrapped himself in his cape and followed the tracks, after he had pulled the canoe ashore. He hadn't gone far when he reached a village. He entered the first house and there found two boys. Since they didn't notice him he patted them on their shoulders. They turned around and asked, "Where do you come from?" When he had told them of his fate, they said, "This is the country of K·ēk·tsumнskyā´na. If you are brave and strong enough, kill her and take her daughter for your wife." So he replied, "Yes, I am brave and want to try it." Then the boys told him that many men had come already to marry the girl, but that all of them had been killed by K·ēk·tsumн-skyā´na. They asked, "Can you jump and run well? Otherwise she'll surely kill you." He replied that he could jump well. Meanwhile the men had come back from the hunt and he was given food. But his heart was sad because he was thinking of his dead brothers lying outside in the canoe. But an old woman consoled him by saying, "Cheer up; when you have killed K·ēk·tsumнskyā´na we will resuscitate them." They asked him whether he was brave and he replied that his sole desire was to kill her. The two boys whom he had met first told him to demonstrate whether he could jump and run, so he stepped outside the door and with one bound leaped the width of the house. But before he went away he made four small girls dig a deep pit close to the fire and he ordered the boys to boil a poison[103] and to keep it ready for the right time. Then he went to the house of K·ēk·tsumHskyā′na. He found the bird K·ak·ā′nis[104] posted as a guard outside the door. He wanted to raise the alarm, but the young man won him over by giving him a fish. Then he opened the door and found the bird T'āstumā′kua[105] posted as a guard inside. He gave him a fish, too, and thus won him over. Then he entered and saw the old woman asleep in her bed right by the door. And he observed that the sides of her hands were as sharp as knives. With them she killed anyone coming to her. Near the fire there was the daughter of K·ēk·tsumHskyā′na, and the young man went to her and asked her, "Will you be my wife, and is it alright with you if I kill your wicked mother?" She replied, "Yes, I have wanted to be married for a long time already, but she killed all my suitors. Now you kill her." She had already fallen in love with the young man and asked him anxiously, "But are you really strong enough?" When he reassured her, she said, "Then kill her now while she is still asleep; when she is awake you will surely succumb." So the young man leaped at the old woman and held her tightly in his arms. She woke up and cried out, "hr! hr! hr!" while flailing about with her sharp hands. But when she wanted to strike him, he jumped aside nimbly. At last he tied her up and carried her to the house where the villagers were anxiously waiting for the end of the fight. There he threw her into the pit and poured the poison on her so that she died.

The following day he said to the people, "Now climb down into the pit and get out the corpse." But they were all afraid and didn't dare to climb down, so he had a rope of inner cedar bark tied around his waist, climbed down himself and got out the corpse. Then he cut off her hands, hacked the rest of her body into pieces and threw them to the winds. They were transformed into the woodland flower K·ak·atsumalā′s.[106] But he kept the hands because they were potent magical charms. With the left hand he was able to harm his enemies; with the right one he could heal sick people and resuscitate the dead. He made a cut in the latter hand and made the clear liquid, which dripped out instead of blood, trickle onto his dead brothers. Thereupon they woke, rubbed their eyes as if they had been asleep for a long time, and entered the house. So all the people saw that he had resuscitated his brothers.

---

103. Ethnobotanist Brian Compton (1993:77–78, 119) suggests that this unidentified poison was likely Indian hellebore (*Veratrum viride*), known in Oowekyala as háuxʷsuli which is derived from the linguistic root meaning 'stinging; poisonous' (Lincoln and Rath 1980:407); this is an extremely powerful medicine that can be highly toxic if used incorrectly.

104. This is q̓áq̓anis 'Great Blue Heron' (*Ardea herodias*).

105. Recognized as t'ást'əmak̓ʷa 'Belted Kingfisher' (*Megaceryle alcyon*).

106. Compton (1993:119) was unable to identify the "woodland flower" that is transcribed here by Boas as "K·ak·atsumalā′s."

And there was also a chief there whose son had been killed by K·ēk·tsumHskyā'na and he said to the young man, "Oh, resuscitate my son, too." And all those whose sons or brothers had been killed by K·ēk·tsumHskyā'na, asked him to revive them again, so he went to her house and found the bones lying about like a heap of shells. He sprinkled them all with the liquid from the right hand and all those whose bones still had a bit of meat on them, rose again. He wasn't able to revive the others. Thus the young man became a big chief and took the daughter of K·ēk·tsumHskyā'na as his wife.

After some time his heart was longing for his homeland, so he loaded his canoe with all his belongings and his wife put her boxes full of blankets and meat in it. It was laden so heavily that his brothers doubted that it would be able to carry everything. Then when they wanted to set out, they didn't know in which direction their homeland lay, so the woman said, "Close your eyes and the canoe will go by itself." They did what she had told them, and when it grew dark the canoe hit land, and when they opened their eyes they saw that they had arrived in their homeland. But there was no light in their parents' house, as if no one was living there. So the eldest brother sent up his younger brothers to tell his mother to purify her house and to prepare it for the reception of her sons and her daughter-in-law. They obeyed. They went up, and when they opened the door they saw their father and mother sitting by a small fire, so they nudged them with their feet and said, "Get up and purify your house. Your children have returned and your eldest son has taken the daughter of K·ēk·tsumHskyā'na for his wife." But the old man didn't recognize them and replied, "Why do you address us with those words? We have lost our sons." They replied, "Don't you recognize us? We are your sons and are now back." So Apō'tl got up to welcome his children, but he was weak and it was difficult for him. He went to his brother's house and told him that his children had returned, and he split wood for the fire and soon all the villagers knew that the brothers had come back. These went down to the canoe and said sadly to the eldest brother, "Oh, you won't recognize our parents, they have grown that old." For the brothers had been away for years, although to them it seemed only days. When the house was purified, three men and one woman spread mats from the door down to the beach, accompanied those who had arrived, and carried their belongings from the canoe. Then everybody saw the young woman. She was very beautiful. Her hair was long and fell down over both her shoulders. Soon the whole cargo had been carried up to the house with the exception of a small box which no one could lift. When the young woman heard of this she sent the four brothers down to the beach, one after the other, to fetch the box, but not one of them was able to lift it, so she laughed and said, "How is it that nobody is able to lift my box? It is so small and light!" Then she went down to the canoe herself, picked up the box and carried it up to the house as if there was nothing in it. She opened the box and lo, in it there was whatever one's heart might desire: mountain goat fat, seals and whales. And from it she gave to all the people. It always remained full, however much she might take from the box. But the brothers were still sad because their parents were so old and weak, so the woman went to the beach and scooped up a bit of water in her small container. Then she undressed the old people and washed their entire bodies, whereupon they became as beautiful as they had been when they were young.

8. Baqbakualanusī'uaē
(= Who First Always Devoured Human Flesh at the River Mouth)[107]

A man named Nōak·aua[108] had four sons who once wanted to go hunting for mountain goats. Before they set out, their father warned them, saying, "If you see a house from which reddish smoke rises, don't go inside, because Baqbakualanusī'uaē, a bad man, lives there." The sons promised to heed his warning and went into the mountains. After some time they saw a house from which black smoke was rising. Black Bear was living here. When they had gone on a bit further, they came to a house from which white smoke was rising. Mountain Goat was living here. At last they came to the house about which their father had warned them, with reddish smoke rising from it. They stopped and said to each other, "We haven't found this house for nothing. Come, let's go inside and see who there is in it." This they did and met a woman rocking her child. Opposite her there sat a boy with an enormously big head. The four brothers went up to the fire and sat down on a box. While doing so the eldest hurt himself on a stick so that blood was flowing from his lower leg. Thereupon the boy with the big head nudged his mother and said, "Oh, mother, I would like to lick the blood." But the mother forbade it. The boy scratched his head and then started to lick the blood after all, after wiping it onto his fingers. So the eldest brother nudged the youngest one and said, "We should have obeyed our father." Meanwhile the boy started to lick the blood even more greedily. So the eldest brother gathered courage, took his bow and shot one arrow out through the door. Then he told the youngest to fetch the arrow back again. He went outside, but

---

107. Boas (1888j:53–55; 1897:400–401) elsewhere provides his own translation of this story. While Boas' transcriptions and translations of the term he gives here as "Baqbakualanusī'uaē" vary from one publication to another, the term commonly relates to the cannibalistic characteristics of this being. Thus, a well-known translation is 'cannibal at the north end of the world' (Boas 1948:114). A discussion of these variant translations appears in Hilton, Rath, and Windsor (1982:59–64) whose comprehensive linguistic research suggests the meaning of the name may be 'ever more perfect manifestation of the essence of becoming human.'

108. This name is recognized as núwaqawa, derived from the term meaning 'old, mature or wise.'

didn't come back and instead ran as fast as he could towards his home. Then the eldest took a second arrow, shot it out through the door and told the second brother to fetch it back again. He fled, too. When he shot the third arrow out through the door, the third brother escaped. Then the boy began to grow afraid. The old woman asked him, "Aren't your brothers coming back?" And he replied, "They've only gone to get my arrows back." Then he shot a fourth arrow, went out himself, and ran after his brothers. When the woman noticed that her guests weren't coming back, she stepped outside and called, "Come home, Baqbakuālanusī′uaē! I've let our good meal run away." Baqbakuālanusī′uaē heard her even though he was far away. He pursued them and shouted, "Ham, ham, ham! (Devour, devour, devour!)."[109] The four brothers heard his approach and ran as fast as their legs would carry them. The eldest brother had with him a whetstone, a comb, and fish oil which he used as hair oil. Baqbakuālanusī′uaē had nearly caught up with them, when the eldest brother put the whetstone down behind himself and lo, it changed into a mountain which forced the pursuer to make a great detour! But nevertheless he soon caught up to them, so the young man poured out the hair oil behind himself and it changed into a large lake. When Baqbakuālanusī′uaē had caught up with them again, the young man stuck the comb into the earth behind himself and it changed into a dense thicket of young trees around which the pursuer had to go. In the meantime the young men had arrived home safely. They knocked on the door and begged their father to open up quickly because the man he had warned them about was chasing them. Nōak·aua had hardly let them in and closed the door again when Baqbakuālanusī′uaē arrived and demanded to be let in. So Nōak·aua took a dog, cut it up and let the blood run into a dish. Then he let Baqbakuālanusī′uaē come to a small opening in the wall, handed the dish to him and said, "This is the blood of my sons. Take it and carry it to your wife." He took it. Then Tsō′ēnā,[110] the wife of Nōak·aua, dug a deep pit close to the fire and made the fire blaze up high. Then she placed stones in it, which quickly became red-hot. And they covered the hole by stretching out a hide. Soon Baqbakuālanusī′uaē, his wife and three children arrived in a canoe to visit Nōak·aua. He left the youngest child to guard the canoe, while the others came into the house with him. Tsō′ēnā made them sit down close to the fire so that their backs were turned towards the stretched-out hide concealing the pit. Then Baqbakuālanusī′uaē said to Nōak·aua, "You know how everything was in the beginning. Tell me about it." Nōak·aua replied, "I will tell you this:"

---

109. Hilton, Rath, and Windsor (1982:197–198) observe that the relation between the cry hayə́m (or hap) and "eating" seems to be "a linguistically unwarranted extrapolation from the cultural datum that a hámaċa dancer bites people or eats human flesh really ... "

110. This name is recognized as cwí?na, related to the term cúsa 'to dig.'

"What will I tell you now about the beginning of time, grandchildren? A long time ago a cloud hung over that mountain. Soon you will sleep."[111]

After he had twice sung this incantation, Baqbakuālanusī′uaē and his whole family were dozing off, and after he had sung it four times, they were fast asleep. Then Nōak·aua and Tsō′ēnā pulled away the back of the seat and they all fell into the hole. Then they threw the red-hot stones into the pit. Baqbakuālanusī′uaē could only cry twice more, "Ham, ham!" Then he was dead. After some time they pulled out their corpses with a rope. Then Nōak·aua cut them up into many pieces, scattered these over the earth and sang, "One day, Baqbakuālanusī′uaē, you will pursue people." Then they were transformed into mosquitoes.

9. The Ts'ilkigyila or Atsi[112]

Once a number of children were roasting salmon for themselves between heated stones. When they were done, they ate them up and then ran into the forest to play. Among them there was also a girl named TsumHqsta (Without Mouth).[113] She was running ahead, and the other children were calling to each other, "Which one of us, which one of us will catch TsumHqsta first?" They hadn't been running for long when they met Ts'ilkigyila who was carrying a big basket on her back. She grabbed TsumHqsta first and put her in it and then she put all the other children on top of her. But the girl happened to have a knife in her hand, with which she cut a slit in the basket and all the children fell out. But Ts'ilkigyila didn't notice and only said, "I think pine needles are falling to the ground." Only one small boy was unable to jump out of the hole because he was stuck in the basket. So Ts'ilkigyila carried him home. She put the basket down and was very surprised to find only the boy. She took him from the basket and put him down. Then he saw that there were many boxes of mountain goat fat in the house. Ts'ilkigyila then made the boy her slave. When she went out again, the boy looked around in the house and then noticed an old slave woman. Her names were K·'ō′k·oikya and Tlō′k·opak·titl.[114]

---

111. This verse and the one that appears in the next paragraph are presented as a song in Boas' (1888g:55) "Songs and Dances of the Kwakiutl."

112. The names that Boas transcribes here as "Ts'ilkigyila" or "Atsi" are, respectively, c̓ǝlkigila and ʔadzí (EW), both referring to the 'cannibal ogress,' described by Hilton, Rath, and Windsor (1982:83) as "a large hairy creature which walks erect and carries a basket on its back." The first term, c̓ǝlkigila, is derived from c̓ǝla meaning 'basket,' as the cannibal ogress carries upon her back a large basket in which she carries stolen children. The second term, ʔadzí, has a more general reference to all scary beings who reside in the woods.

113. Boas' "TsumHqsta" is cǝ′mkx̣ta· which EW translates as 'without teeth.'

114. EW recognizes Boas' "K·'ō′k·oikya" and "Tlō′k·opak·titl" respectively as the names qʷú·gʷiga 'hunchback' and ƛ̓ú·kʷu·p̓ax̣dił 'roots started to grow from sitting too long.'

Ts'ilkigyila had once stolen her in her basket, just like the boy now. The slave woman called him over and said to him, "When Ts'ilkigyila wants to give you food, don't take it, or else you will fare like me. Look, I ate her mountain goat fat and consequently grew fast to the ground." And she showed him then how a rope grew from her behind and branched out into the ground like a root. She continued, "Hide the food beneath your cape and only pretend to eat it." When Ts'ilkigyila returned she offered mountain goat fat to the boy and he followed the counsel of the slave woman and only pretended to eat it. In reality he hid the fat underneath his cape.

Then Ts'ilkigyila went out again to catch slaves. So the woman called the boy to her again and told him to go gather shellfish from the opposite side of the bay that stretched in front of the house. The boy obeyed. He brought the shellfish and the slave woman told him to cook them. After he had cleaned and chopped the shellfish he stuck their beards onto his fingertips like finger stalls. Then when they heard Ts'ilkigyila come back, the boy went outside and stretched out his fingertips towards her.[115] Thereupon she said, "What do you have on your fingers there? I've never seen anything like it and am afraid." K·'ō′k·oikya called to him, "Wave your fingers towards her and call 'Ai a tsai'!" The boy obeyed, so Ts'ilkigyila was very much afraid. And after he had moved his hands towards her four times, she fell down dead. K·'ō′k·oikya then told him to cut off the breasts and to cook them. She said, "When the four sons of Ts'ilkigyila return from their hunt, serve this dish to them. They will die from it."

They came back soon and asked for their mother. K·'ō′k·oikya[116] replied, "She will probably come back soon; she has gone out with her basket to catch slaves. In the meantime we have cooked for you; here is your meal." And the boy took the pot in which the breasts had been cooked and gave it to the sons. He took a spoonful and gave it to the eldest one. This one said, "This tastes just like the milk of our mother." Then he gave a spoonful to the second one. He tasted and said, "You're right, it tastes just like the milk of our mother." And the two youngest said the same after they had tasted it. The old slave woman told them to be quiet and to eat up. They obeyed; but after they had eaten everything they fell down dead. Then the boy wanted to free the slave woman, but as soon as he pulled a bit on the rope holding her to the ground, she experienced dreadful pains. He tried all day in vain to free her. When it grew dark he said, "I will go home so that I might get my friends to help me free you." But he was afraid that he would not be able to find the house of

115. Hilton, Rath, and Windsor (1982:84) comment as follows: "The action referred to is a hand gesture performed with clam siphons placed on the fingers. The motion of the siphons, which is meant to terrify the ʔadźí, is a complex series of finger flexes. It begins with flexing one finger on each hand simultaneously, then two fingers, three fingers, and finally all fingers."

116. As previously noted, this is qʷú·gʷiga 'hunchback.'

Ts'ilkigyila again, so the old slave woman tied a string around his middle and then let him go.[117] At last he got back to his parents. They had already mourned him for dead, and were very happy when their son returned safely and told them that all the Ts'ilkigyila were now dead. And he went on, "But in their house there is still the old slave woman K·'o̅'k·oikya. She has grown fast to the ground and can't get away. Come along with me, all of you, and help me to free her." They went after the boy who was following the rope. Everybody now grasped the rope by which the slave woman had grown fast. But when they pulled hard and it broke, the old woman died. The rope was like a blood vessel and the blood spurting out of it could not be stilled. Then the people cut up the body of Ts'ilkigyila into small pieces and scattered them in all directions. Then these were transformed into frogs.[118]

10. La'lqemitl[119]
(See legends of the Tsimschian)[120]

One day many women from Tsakoa'lo[121] went into the forest to pick berries. They scattered here and there, busily filling their baskets. One of these women was named La'lqemitl. While she was picking berries she looked only at the bushes and not at the ground and so it happened that she stepped four times in a row into the droppings of a Grizzly Bear. She grew impatient at this and cried, "Ugh, it is abominable how dirty the whole countryside is!"

Suddenly she noticed, not too far away, a handsome young man with a bear skin cape. He came up to La'lqemitl and said, "You are angry about the bear excrement; now let's see what you produce." La'lqemitl obeyed and sat down. But she reached secretly into her hair underneath her cape and pulled out a copper pin and put this beneath herself. Then she got up and said to the man, "Look, this is what I always produce." But Gya'lk·ɛm,[122] for that was the man's name, didn't believe her and

---

117. "I remained in doubt whether she didn't rather tie the string in order to force him to return" [Boas' original footnote].

118. "Ts'ilkigyila (the Tsono̅'k·oa of the Kwakiutl, the Snēnē̅'ik· of the Bilqula) appears in the dance Tloolā'qa (the Sisāū̅'k of the Bilqula). She carries a basket on her back into which she stuffs the children. A face is painted inside each of her hands. When she opens one of her eyes, light shines from it" [Boas' original footnote].

119. What Boas transcribes here as "La'lqemitl" is recognized by EW as the name lálkəmił.

120. See Section XXIII.

121. This Oowekeeno place name, c̓ág̓wala (Boas' "Tsakoa'lo"), anglicized as "Chuckwalla," is applied to a river that runs into the west side of Rivers Inlet, near its upper end; this same place name is transcribed as "Ts'ā̅'koala" in story 12 of the present section.

122. Boas' "Gya'lk·ɛm" is recognized by EW as gálgəm meaning 'first one.'

made her sit down again. The same thing happened again, and La'lqemitl was able to delude him four times; then he believed her. He was pleased and took her along to his home as his wife. Then he changed into a bear and the woman now knew that she had a bear for her husband. There was a big fire burning in the house, and when the bear was going out to catch salmon, he told his wife to fetch wood in the meantime. La'lqemitl obeyed and fetched good, dry wood for the fire. She threw the logs into the flames and soon her fire blazed brightly. In the evening, when her husband came back, he shook his fur, which was full of water, towards the fire, and so much water came out that the fire was extinguished. He became angry and said to La'lqemitl, "You always act as if you know everything, and can do anything, but you don't know a thing." Then he went out to fetch wood himself and collected soggy wood which had lain at the bottom of the creek for a long time. In addition he fetched a stone, from which he struck fire. Then he made a big fire and said to his wife, "Look, you'll have to take wood like this when you want to make a fire." When he then shook his wet cape towards the fire, it blazed up high. In the evening of the first day that La'lqemitl spent with the Bear, she gave birth to a son who was given the name Gyā'p'as (= Dry Wood).[123] In the evening of the second day she gave birth to a girl who was named Gya'lk·ᴇmk·a[124] after the father. In the evening of the third day she gave birth to a son who was given the name Ts'ē'mos (= Wet Wood)[125] and finally, in the evening of the fourth day, to a daughter, Gya'lk·a.[126] But the four days had in reality been four years.

Then La'lqemitl thought, "Oh, if only I were with my parents again to see how they are." Soon Gya'lk·ᴇm guessed her thoughts and said, "If you'd like to go and see your family I have no objections. Go to them and take your children along." Before she left he gave her his house and all its contents. Soon they came to the river where she had met the bear that time. The children, who looked like bears, saw salmon swimming in the water and said to each other, "Oh, let's go down to the river and catch salmon." The children went down to the river while the mother hid herself among the flowers growing on the shore.

But at that same time the brothers of La'lqemitl had come to the river to catch salmon. When their wives saw the bears playing by the river, they grew afraid. They ran away and told the brothers that there were four bears by the river. The men made ready at once to hunt them. They went upriver, but before they reached the bears,

---

123. Boas' rendering "Gyā'p'as" is recognized as gəṗás, and while it has not been possible to confirm Boas' translation, 'dry wood,' EW points out that the suffix -ṗás refers to 'plant.'

124. Boas' "Gya'lk·ᴇmk·a" is recognized by EW as gálgəmga.

125. The term that Boas transcribes as "Ts'ē'mos" and translates as 'wet wood' is not now recognized.

126. What Boas renders as "Gya'lk·a" is recognized by EW as gálaga 'first woman.'

La'lqemitl arose from the flowers and said, "Oh, don't hurt the bears, they are your nephews." And she told them everything that had happened to her since she was abducted by the bear. Then the brothers invited the young bears to come with them, but they were afraid and ran into the forest. La'lqemitl followed them and took off their bear skins and they were transformed into humans. Only the youngest daughter, Gya'lk·a, didn't want her skin to be taken off by her mother, and said to her, "Oh, Mother, first let me pick some berries." But she ran into the forest and didn't return. Then La'lqemitl came down to the creek with her three children and asked her brothers about her parents' health. They replied, "Oh, our parents have grown old and weak." And they cried when they saw the children of La'lqemitl. They took the children into their canoe and went home. But La'lqemitl stayed behind in order to fetch Bear's house out of the forest and placed it beside her father's house. When the canoe arrived, the children got out and went up to the house of their grandparents. There they stopped outside the door and said to each other, "How bad it smells in the house of our grandparents." The grandparents didn't know yet that their daughter La'lqemitl had come back. So the eldest of the brothers, Poē'tsit,[127] went up to them and told them how they had found La'lqemitl and her children, and that they had brought the children along in their canoe and that La'lqemitl would also arrive soon. Then the mother tried to get up in order to clean the house for the reception of those who were arriving. But she was so weak that she couldn't get up. Her neighbours helped her to put the house in order.

When La'lqemitl came back then and saw how weak her parents were, she became very sad. She made them come to the house of Bear, which now stood right beside the house of the old people. There she took a small mug full of water, undressed her parents and washed their whole bodies. Thereupon they became young and beautiful again. And she rejuvenated all the old people in this fashion. And in the house there were many boxes filled with good things: furs, salmon and mountain goat fat. She told her brother Poē'tsit to summon all the people and then gave them many presents. And as much as Poē'tsit might take from the boxes, they never became empty.

11. The Thunderbird

A chief owned twelve slaves who always had to cut firewood for him. Because he treated them cruelly, they conspired against him. Once, when he wanted to whip one of the slaves, they tied the chief with inner cedar bark ropes, carried him to a lonely island and there left him abandoned. There the chief wrapped himself up in his cape,

---

127. EW recognizes Boas' "Poē'tsit" as puát'it which means 'container of hunger.'

covered his face and wanted to die. He hadn't sat like this for very long when he felt someone tugging him. He didn't dare to get up and only peeped through a small hole in his cape. Then he saw that a mouse was sitting before him tugging at his cape. He straightened up and asked, "What do you want from me?" The mouse replied, "My chief Kunkunquli'kya[128] sends you the message to come to him. Follow me, but take care to jump quickly through the door, otherwise it will kill you." They set out together and soon arrived at the house of Kunkunquli'kya. The chief remembered the warning of the mouse and sprang through the door quickly, but it closed so rapidly that it still caught the skin of his heel. Kunkunquli'kya and his four daughters were sitting by the fire. Then the old one asked him, "Where did you come from and what do you want here?" Consequently the chief told him how he had whipped his slaves and that these had therefore abandoned him. The chief asked Kunkunquli'kya for assistance to return to his homeland again. Kunkunquli'kya promised to fulfill his request. That night, when everyone was asleep, the chief crept to the youngest daughter and wanted to have her for his wife. The old one heard talking in the daughter's room and made a fire to see what was going on. He saw the stranger with his daughter and she now told her father that he wanted to have her for his wife. Kunkunquli'kya told them to be patient until the following day. In the morning he gave the chief the Kunqumtl (i.e. the mask and the garment of Kuni'qua or Kunkunquli'kya, Thunderbird) and told him to try to fly. He obeyed, but at the first try fell to the ground. Kunkunquli'kya told him to try once more. This time he managed to fly halfway round the house. On the third try he managed to fly a bit farther and the fourth time he flew just as well as Kunkunquli'kya. Then the latter said to him, "Now you are able to fly all over the earth and I will give my daughter to you." One morning his wife said to him, "Come, let's catch a whale!" They put on the feather garments and flew out. When they saw a whale, the woman called to him, "Seize it by the head; I will grab its tail." That's how they caught the whale and carried it ashore. Then the woman made a hundred small baskets and in each of them put some whale meat, copper and the transparent stone Quē'la (= rock crystal, used by the shamans to harm their enemies). When all the baskets were filled, they flew to Awīky'ēnoq and sat down on a totem pole. There the chief saw that in his absence another man had married his wife. He grew angry, flew down and killed him. Then the birds took off their feather garments and entered the house. He shook the baskets and at once a huge whale lay on the beach. Many coppers lay in the house, and many stones (Quē'la). So then the people knew that their chief had returned.

---

128. "Kunkunquli'kya" is kʷə́nkʷənxʷəligɛ, a Kwakwala word for 'Thunderbird.'

12. Hāntl'ēkunas[129]

There once was an able, strong hunter with keen eyesight, who was good at hunting mountain goats and at harpooning seals. When he caught game, he always cut it up with shell knives and the blood always spurted into his face. He didn't mind it, but at last it caused him to go blind. Then he became very poor and his wife and his children had nothing to eat. He made them dig for roots and they lived on these. One morning his wife saw a big bear on the opposite side of the river. She told her husband, gave him a bow and arrow and aimed the arrow for him. Then she told him to shoot and he hit the bear and killed it. But his wife said, "You've missed," for she wanted to have the meat for herself. Then she went across, skinned the bear and roasted it without being noticed. She gave some to her children, but forbade them to give any to their father. She gave four pieces to each child. But one of the children, a boy, hid three pieces under his arm and took them to his father. He said, "This is from what you have killed. Take it and eat!" The old one asked, "So I've hit it after all?" "Yes, and Mother and my brothers are busy eating," replied the boy. Thereupon Hāntl'ēkunas became very sad. He said to his son, "If you are brave, lead me to the mountain where they used to make blind people see again in the old days." The boy took his father by the hand and led him up. In addition the old man carried a stick with which he felt the ground in front of himself so as not to miss the way. On top of the mountain there was a lake where they stopped and Hāntl'ēkunas sent his son back home and told him to expect him after four days. Then he swam in the lake and prayed to the Loon (Qā'oē),[130] "I am unfortunate. I am blind and my relatives have no compassion for me. Take pity on me." Then he heard Loon approach. It said, "Come, I will make you happy. Sit down on my back! I will dive with you and you will regain your sight. We'll have to stay under for a long time otherwise you won't get better, so try to stay under as long as possible. When you are unable to hold your breath any longer, scratch me and I will surface again." With this it dived. Hāntl'ēkunas lost his breath after only a short time and he scratched Loon. It said, "You'll have to stay under much longer! Press your mouth into my feathers then you will be able to stay longer." They dived again. After some time Hāntl'ēkunas scratched the Loon and when it surfaced he was able to see a weak glimmer of light. They dived for a third time. When they surfaced, his eyes were as good as they had been before. Loon asked him, "Are you able to see well now?" He replied, "Not quite as well as before," because he wanted to be able to see still better. So Loon dived once more with him and now his eyes had become much better than they had ever been. Then he went home. His wife had just gone out. He saw the skin of the

---

129. EW recognizes Boas' "Hāntl'ēkunas" as hánx̣'ikʷənas 'good with bow and arrow.'

130. While Boas in the original gives the German term *Gans* 'goose,' EW recognizes the Oowekyala term, Boas' "Qā'oē," as x̣áwi 'Common Loon' (*Gavia immer*).

bear which he had shot spread out in front of the door for drying. He grew furious and, when they returned, he shot his wife and his sons, except for the youngest who had brought him the meat.

Then he left his home and went to the country of the Hēiltsuk·.[131] There he met many people. A girl who had many brothers fell in love with him and he lived with her, but without marrying her. Her brothers became angry about this and resolved to kill him. One day they asked him to come with them to hunt sea-lions. Together they went to a cliff far out to sea which was difficult to reach because the sea bottom round about was overgrown with kelp. The canoes couldn't quite reach it. So they jumped into the water, swam to the island and killed the sea-lions with clubs. Then they divided them and began to load the canoe by swimming from the island to the canoe, thus carrying the meat to it. When Hāntl'ēkunas was busy on the island getting a load of meat ready, the brothers paddled away and left him behind. Only the youngest took pity on him and threw a fur cape to him. Hāntl'ēkunas grew dejected and was certain that he would die, and he sat down on the highest point of the cliff and wrapped himself up in his blanket. Then he heard a tiny voice call his name. He looked up but saw no one. He heard the same voice four times and the fourth time he saw a small man, who said, "My chief invites you to come to him." Hāntl'ēkunas asked for the name of the chief, who was called Amā'gyitläsela (= bird excrements).[132] He followed the little one, who led him into a cave in which there stood a house. Then Hāntl'ēkunas knew that he was with the chief of the Sea-Lions. He was cold and he sat down close to the fire. The chief entertained him and promised to send him back to his home. He sent for Seagull to borrow his canoe, but the people said that it was too slow. He sent for the bird Mātsēnē[133] but the people said, "His canoe always hits the rocks and splits." And he sent for Loon, but the people said that his canoe went down too deep. At last he sent for Sea-Lion, NE'msk·amisila (= First One),[134] and borrowed his canoe, a sea-lion skin. They tied Hāntl'ēkunas up in it and called the west wind, which carried him home quickly. When he got to the shore, he untied the sack, stepped out of it and hid it in the forest. In the evening he went to his sweetheart, who now had a child and was constantly weeping for him. Nobody was looking after her except her youngest brother. So Hāntl'ēkunas killed all her brothers, sparing only the youngest one, then he fled with

---

131. Heiltsuk or Bella Bella.

132. What Boas transcribes as "Amā'gyitläsela" is recognized by EW as the name ʔamá·kλiyasəlasu; elsewhere, Hilton, Rath, and Windsor (1982:131) translate the term as 'defecating on the roof' and note this person was a sea-lion chief.

133. The bird name that Boas transcribes here as "Mātsēnē" is not now recognized.

134. Boas' "NE'msk·amisila" is recognized by EW—and confirmed by AD—as a Kwakwala term, nə'msgəmisala, meaning 'only rock.'

his wife. The Hēiltsuk· pursued him, but he hid unnoticed in the forest and his pursuers paddled past without finding him. Then he went to Ts'ā'koala (in Rivers Inlet)[135] where he stayed for a few days. On the second day of his stay he took his dog along in his canoe and went to a steep mountain. He climbed up and found many mountain goats in a cave close to an abyss. So he set his inner cedar bark cape alight and threw it into the cave in order to force the goats out. As soon as they came out he pushed them into the abyss. Then he went back home and said to the people, "Let's go to dig roots!" He didn't tell them that he had killed many mountain goats. He guided the people to the abyss where all the mountain goats were. On their way they found two already in the sea and the people in the canoes were fighting about who should have them. So he said, "Stop quarrelling. We will find plenty of mountain goats soon." Then they loaded their canoes with his game and brought it home.

13. String Game[136]

Once upon a time there were many children who were busy playing making string figures on their fingers. Moon Man saw this and he came down to them and said, "It isn't right that you do nothing else but play at the string game. Rather, go and catch fish." Then he sang, "Many fishes are here." And at once swarms of herring came swimming and the children caught them.

14. Hāok·hāok·

A young man called K·'ō'mkīlikya[137] went into the forest once to get cedar bark. The spirit Hāok·hāok·[138] scented him there. He noticed that the boy was pure and good and therefore swooped down on him to abduct him. When K·'ō'mkīlikya heard the approach of the spirit who was coming in the shape of a giant crane,[139] he nearly lost

---

135. This same place name,"Ts'ā'koala," is transcribed as "Tsakoa'lo" earlier in the present section (story 10). As previously noted, "Chuckwalla," an anglicization of this name, c̓ág̓ʷala, is applied to a river that runs into the west side of Rivers Inlet near its head end.

136. The string game, also known as cat's cradle, was a favourite form of amusement among younger men and women in coastal villages prior to *circa* 1900. Anthropologist Julia Averkieva, who made a study of string figures in the winter of 1930, writes, "the figures represent both natural and artificial objects in a state of rest or motion. Each figure is named after an object which it seems to resemble" (Averkieva and Sherman 1992:3).

137. What Boas transcribes here as "K·'ō'mkīlikya" is likely q̓ʷúmxiliga.

138. EW recognizes the name of the spirit "Hāok·hāok·" as húhuqʷ. Elsewhere, Boas (1888j:57–58) provides his own translation of this story, which he describes as: "a tradition of the Wik'enoκ which treats of the initiation of a young cannibal by this being, the Hāoκhāoκ."

139. While Boas uses the term *Kranich* ('crane') here in the original, and also gives the English term

his breath for fright. He was hoping to overcome his fear by smoking a pipe, but in vain. He lost consciousness and lay there as if dead. Hāok·hāok· came up and, while the young man lay there unconscious, he infused him with his spirit.

When K·'ō'mkīlikya didn't come back, his friends went into the forest to look for him. Finally they found him laying there as if dead. They poured water into his face but he didn't wake up, so they carried him to the village and brought him to his father. When he saw his son laying there as if dead, his heart grew very sad, but soon he noticed that there was still a bit of breath in him and called the shaman and asked him to make his son better again. He consoled the father and ordered him to purify his house and to cover the floor with sand so that people could not walk on the old floor any more. He took the young man along into the forest and stayed there for four days. Then he came back. After four more days K·'ō'mkīlikya came back, too. But the shaman[140] had now given him the name K·oātlk·oā'oē.[141]

Then he sang about Hā'ok·hāok· and sprang up suddenly to devour his father sitting on the opposite side of the fire. He had the ring of inner cedar bark of the Hā'mats'a on his head. It slipped down right over his mouth so that, instead of biting his father, he bit a piece out of the ring. The people didn't know what to do in order to calm him down. His grandfather then took a big black cape and wrapped it around his head. He tore it, too, with his teeth. Then the people tied a rope around his mouth, but in vain; he bit through it. Then his father called upon all the neighbours for help, but no one was able to tame him. Everybody fled in terror from the house. They heard him singing on the inside and peeped through the cracks and knot-holes in the walls to see what he was doing. They saw him climb up the house posts and open up the roof. He wanted to pursue the people, so they posted two men as guards by the door and others were holding on to the roof so that he wasn't able to escape. Then they went inside and threw a bear skin over him. He crawled about on the ground under it and became so slippery that nobody could catch him. In the evening he became calm and lay so quietly that the people didn't know whether he was awake or asleep. Then they made a jacket of inner cedar bark in order to catch him and get him in their power, but when they tried to put it on him, he got away from them and was as wild as before. On the island of Nalkuitqoi'oas (Mackyol Island),[142]

'crane' in his own translation of this story (Boas 1888j:57), we are not certain which bird he is referring to. There are two birds that can be called "crane" in English—the Great Blue Heron (*Ardea herodias*) and the Sandhill Crane (*Grus canadensis*)—that have already been identified in the present section (see story 4, part 3, and story 7).

140. Given as *Schamane* 'shaman' in the original, although Boas (1888j:57) uses the term 'medicine-man' in his own translation of this story.

141. EW does not recognize the name that Boas transcribes as "K·oātlk·oā'oē."

142. The place name that Boas transcribes here as "Nalkuitqoi'oas," and elsewhere as "Nalkuitqoi'as"

women were busy cutting up salmon. He scented them and in his frenzy jumped into the water to devour them, but the women jumped into their canoe and paddled out to sea when they saw him coming.

At last K·oātlk·oā'oē came to again and said to his father, "When I fall into a frenzy again, don't defend yourself and I will do you no harm." After a short time he fell into another trance. He lay flat on the floor, with his face downwards. The neighbours threw a net of inner cedar bark over him to catch him and sometimes they succeeded in putting a foot on his neck but he always got away again. They held him by his long hair, winding it around their hands, but he got away neverthe-less and no one knew where he had gone. He ran around in the forest and the village and bit anyone he met. When he came to again, he asked his father to cook olachen[143] oil and to make him drink it during his next fit, then he would come to again. Once, when he fell into another one of his trances, he scented a canoe with fresh shellfish aboard even though it was still far away. He ran to the beach and, when the canoe landed, he devoured all the shellfish in it. After that he became calm again.

(This legend is represented in the Tsā'ēk·a dance.[144] A woman takes the part of Hāok·hāok·, the son of a powerful chief, that of K·'ōmkĭlikya. The dance is part of the Hā'mats'a ritual.)[145]

(Boas 1888j:58) or "nalkwitxoyas" (Boas 1934:64), is recognized tentatively by EW as nálgʷitkʷiwas. We have not been able to determine the location of Boas' "Mackyol" Island, said to be the island to which the name nálgʷitkʷiwas applies.

143. Eulachon.

144. EW points out that this is the dance series known as ċáiqa (Boas' "Tsā'ēk·a").

145. What Boas transcribes as "Hā'mats'a" is recognized by EW as hámaċa 'look for food to eat.'

XXI. Legends of the Heiltsuk (Bella Bella)

Boas intended to go to Bella Bella in July 1890, but missed the steamer north (Cole 1999:149). Where, then, did he pick up the stories in this section? Returning from Port Essington onboard the *Cariboo Fly* on 1 July 1888 Boas met "a Bella Bella who is willing to tell me things," so it may have been this opportunity when the texts were recorded, for he found him to be "pretty good" (Rohner 1969:95). The Oowekeeno wife of the Hudson Bay trader he met in Victoria in September 1886 certainly told him a great deal about the mythology of the Heiltsuk (Rohner 1969:25), a neighbouring tribe to her own. It is conceivable that there were Heiltsuk people at the Alert Bay potlatch of October 1886, but Boas does not single them out for mention. On board ship leaving Alert Bay was "a young girl from the Bella Bella mission" (Rohner 1969:48). Boas "taught her how to take down folktales, and she promised to collect some." There is no record that she did, but she probably told him something on the voyage itself. In short, these are stories picked up along the way.

Interior housepost showing bear figure, alongside covered canoe stern, Bella Bella, B.C., August 1897. *American Museum of Natural History Library, New York. Neg./Trans. No. 42854 (Harlan I. Smith photo).*

XXI. Legends of the Heiltsuk·[1]

1. The Raven Legend

1) We find here the same legend of the release of the sun by Raven as is found among the northern tribes. The name of the chief's daughter is Ky'ē′tētl.[2]

2) A long time ago the fresh water was owned by an old chief. Raven resolved to steal it. He tied a tube of sea-lion intestines around himself, keeping it hidden underneath his cape. He flew to the house of the chief and there assumed the shape of an old man. He entered and begged the chief and his wife for food and drink, pretending to be half-starved of hunger and thirst. The chief granted his request and told his wife to give him fish and berries. After the guest had finished eating, the chief allowed him to go to the bucket and drink the water which was kept in it. Raven put the container to his lips, but instead of drinking, he poured the water into the tube. Since he didn't put it down, the chief called, "What on earth are you doing? Where

---

1. What Boas transcribes as "Heiltsuk·" is híłdzaqw, anglicized as "Heiltsuk." These people are also referred to as "Bella Bella," which is an anglicization of pə′lbálá (the name of a place on Campbell Island), and are closely related to the "Haihais" (anglicized from x̣íx̣ís) or Klemtu people. The Heiltsuk, together with the Haihais and the Oowekeeno (see Section XX), are speakers of the Heiltsuk-Oowekyala language, part of the North Wakashan subgroup of the Wakashan Language Family. The language of the Heiltsuk (Bella Bella) and Haihais is Heiltsuk, and that of the Oowekeeno is Oowekyala; the difference between these two languages is such that they approach mutual intelligibility. The four principal Heiltsuk or Bella Bella tribal groups were: the q̓ʷúq̓ʷayáitx̣ʷ ("Kokyet") of the Spiller Channel/Ellerslie Lake area; the ʔuw̓íƛ̓ʼitx̣ʷ ("Uwitlit") of Roscoe Inlet; the ʔísdáitx̣ʷ ("Istait") of Dean Channel; and the ʔúyalitx̣ʷ ("Uyalit") of the Campbell Island/Hunter Island/Calvert Island region. Since about 1870, these tribal groups have lived together in the Bella Bella/McLaughlin Bay area on Campbell Island (Olson 1955:320–321; Lincoln and Rath 1980:2–4; Rath 1981:1:2–4, 458; Hilton, Rath, and Windsor 1982:2–8; Hilton 1990:312–313, 321; Thompson and Kinkade 1990).

    Our annotating of this Section is based primarily on the available literature, although we have also benefited greatly from the assistance in September 2001 of language specialist Evelyn Windsor (referred to here as "EW"), whose first language is Oowekyala but who also knows Heiltsuk. We thank Evelyn Windsor for her help, and we also thank Chief Adam Dick ("AD") for facilitating our discussions with Mrs. Windsor, and for providing comparative Kwakwala data cited in the annotations of this Section.

2. The name transcribed by Boas as "Ky'ē′tētl" is likely k̓ídił, meaning 'a chief's eldest daughter' both in Heiltsuk (EW) and in Kwakwala (AD).

do you manage to put all the water?" But Raven did not put the container down until he had emptied it completely. Then he assumed his true shape and flew away, crying, "K·ā, k·ā!" So the woman shouted, "So Raven has come after all and has stolen our water!" Raven flew all over the earth and dropped water everywhere, in some places much and in others little. This is why there are large and small rivers.

3) Yāēqoē'ok·oa[3] is a giant fish living in the depths of the ocean and guarding its waters. When he comes close to land, the waters rise.

4) Once Yāēqoē'ok·oa made the ocean recede and the bottom of the sea stayed dry for four days. Raven went to the sea with his sister, HalHa'[4] (the name of the Crow[5] in human shape), and they collected fish. Raven collected all the fish which looked beautiful, but HalHa' caught only "black cod"[6] although her brother advised her not to collect such ugly fish. Then, when the waters returned after four days, they went ashore and cooked their fish. When Raven tasted his, he found that they were very dry, while those of his sister were dripping with fat. So he started to devour the fish of HalHa', even though she told him not to, and to eat his own instead. At last he devoured everything his sister had caught, and then flew away. So she cried.

5) Raven had a child called Kyī'ōtl,[7] who had a shining white complexion and beautiful long hair (see p. 211).[8] One day both of them went out to collect firewood on an island. Raven went into the forest to gather wood while Kyī'ōtl remained in the canoe, when suddenly the Eagle, Kani'sltsua,[9] rushed up and abducted Kyī'ōtl. When Raven came back and found his child gone, he became very sad and began to weep. He asked the paddles and the thwarts, "Don't you know where my child is?" They were unable to answer. He asked all the parts of the canoe and at last the bow said, "Kani'sltsua has abducted her." He walked for four days looking for his daughter, weeping constantly, when suddenly Kyī'ōtl came back. She stepped behind her father and called to him. He turned, but did not recognize her because

---

3.   Boas' "Yāēqoē'ok·oa," is recognized by EW as ẏáxʷíẏugʷa 'tides rising up and down.'

4.   EW does not recognize the term transcribed as "HalHa'" by Boas, and points out that the normal word for 'crow' in Heiltsuk is k̓áka.

5.   In the original, Boas uses the German term *Dohle* 'jackdaw,' referring to a species not found in British Columbia. Very likely the bird referred to here is the Northwestern Crow (*Corvus caurinus*).

6.   Given in English as "black cod" (in double quotation marks) in the original *Sagen*. "Black cod" is a folkname for the sablefish (*Anoplopoma fimbria*), a deep-water fish found off the coast of B.C. and caught aboriginally by a few coastal tribes, including the Heiltsuk.

7.   This name transcribed by Boas as "Kyī'ōtl" is k̓íẏuɫ which means 'fair; blond' in Heiltsuk (EW).

8.   Boas' reference is to the original *Sagen*, Section XX, story 1, part 8.

9.   The name transcribed by Boas as "Kani'sltsua" is recognized by EW as k̓á·n̓ísəladzua 'soar in sky.'

her hair had fallen out. He said, "Don't mock me, I know that my child is dead. Your face is not my daughter's face, and your hair is not long like that of my daughter." She replied, "Yes, it's me, father! I was transformed like this up in the sky. There is always a strong wind blowing there and that has changed me so. If you don't recognize me now and take me home with you, I will return to the sky and never come back again." Raven did not reply at all. So Kyī´ōtl flew up to the sky again and only then did Raven recognize her. His daughter had begged him vainly for four days to recognize her. Ever since then, people do not come back to earth once they have died.

6) In the beginning the people did not know how to construct canoes. Raven was the first to practice this art. While he was engaged in building his canoe, all the people came to watch him. One day Deer also came, and Raven said, "Come closer, my friend. Sit down close beside me so that you'll be able to see what I am doing." Then he asked, "Tell me, at which season do you have the most fat?" Deer replied, "When the grass is long, I am fattest. I am fattest now." Thereupon Raven killed him with his club. Then he lit a big fire, right below the branches of a fallen tree beside which he was sitting, threw stones into the fire and cooked Deer. Then he stuck pieces of fat onto a stick, reclined luxuriously and began eating. He said to the tree, "See, you won't get any of the deer that I am eating here." He soon grew drowsy and fell asleep. While he lay there, the tree rolled onto Deer, grabbing him with its branches, and then ate him up. When Raven awoke, the whole deer had vanished.

7) Raven gave a feast once and had Mahai´us (human name of the raccoon)[10] dance and sing at the feast. While he was singing, Raven called, "Make your song longer! Make it longer!" Mahai´us grew angry at this. Then Raven took ashes and smeared it upon his forehead, and therefore the raccoon is grey.

8) Once Squirrel gave a feast. She relieved herself into a bowl and transformed her excrement into berries which she served to her guests. She sent two men to the chief, Raven, in order to invite him, as well. Raven replied, "I will come at once. I'll just relieve myself at the point of land there first." He went and defecated onto a board. Then he said to his excrement, "In a short while shout: 'Hō, hō! Your enemies are coming to kill you!'" Then he went into Squirrel's house where the meal was already underway. After a little while, one of the guests went outside and heard a voice shouting, "Hō, hō, your enemies are coming to kill you!" He quickly ran back into the house and called all of them outside. They came, and, while the house was empty, Raven gobbled up all the berries. But an old woman had stayed in the house without him knowing it and she called Squirrel, "Come, come! Raven has devoured

---

10.   The Heiltsuk name for raccoon (*Procyon lotor*) has been recorded as máyas (Kortlandt 1973).

484 / INDIAN MYTHS & LEGENDS FROM THE NORTH PACIFIC COAST OF AMERICA

all your berries." Raven said to her, "Be quiet and I will give you lots to eat." But because she kept on shouting, he flew away.

9) Raven once sat on top of a mountain near the Bella Coola River and saw many Half-People (i.e. half-animal half-human) in the valley. Among them he saw a woman whom he liked; her name was Hai′atlilak·s.[11] So he flew down and married her. They lived together for some time, but since she didn't bear any children, he left her again. He moved to the land of the Heiltsuk· and married Ts′ō′mk·lak·s[12] with whom he bore many children. Their eldest son was Ia′kis.[13] He painted some rocks in the vicinity of G·alts (Bella Bella)[14] with red paint and said, "When food is plentiful the colour shall be always bright red; when scarcity threatens, it shall appear dull." And even today it can still be seen by the colour whether the coming year will be good or bad.

10) Raven was sitting on the top of a tree at the mouth of the Skeena River; the Eagle Kyā′loyak·amē (= First One)[15] was sitting a little below him. One day he flew up and settled above Raven. The latter became angry at this and flew away. He finally came to Ky′imE′qk·[16] in the land of the Bilqula,[17] where Wēkyōyō′is[18] and his

---

11. The name transcribed by Boas as "Hai′atlilak·s" is recognized as háyáɫilaqs, derived from the term háyáɫila 'make beautiful' (EW). This woman appears also as the sister of "ču·əmqəlaqs" (Boas 1932:44).

12. "Many songs refer to Raven and this woman" [Boas' original footnote]. The name of this woman is recognized as cúmqlaqs 'totem pole woman' (EW). Olson (1955:332) presents a couple of stories about this woman whom he calls "Ts!u′mk!alakås" and notes: "To this day, the people of the Wolf sept of that village (and lineage) use this name. The mother's weeping song is used as a mourning song for persons of high rank." Louisa Morrison, a Heiltsuk consultant to Olson (1940:189–190), called this story "The Origin of the Heiltsuk or the Dog Children," and identified the woman as "Tsu′mkålaxs." According to Olson, her version explains that because the puppies mated, the Bella Bella people do not practise "clan exogamy."

13. The Heiltsuk term ẏágis meaning 'mythical monster of the sea' (EW) is transcribed by Olson (1955:332) as "Yai′kis."

14. EW recognizes Boas' "G·alts" as q̓əlc, the Heiltusk place name that Hilton (1990:313) identifies as the Bella Bella Reserve.

15. Olson (1955:330) transcribed this same name as "Gyĕloya′komih" and provided the translation 'just born' or 'just now become human.'

16. The place name transcribed by Boas as "Ky′imE′qk·" is k̓imxk̓ʷitx̱ʷ (anglicized as "Kimsquit"), the Heiltsuk name referring to the Bella Coola (Nuxalk)-speaking people who resided formerly at the mouth of the Dean River in Dean Channel. After about the early 1920s, the Kimsquit residents moved to the main Nuxalk village situated on the north shore of the Bella Coola River mouth (Kennedy and Bouchard 1990a:323, 338).

17. What Boas transcribes as "Bilqula" ("Bella Coola") is anglicized from the Heiltsuk term bə′lxʷəlá applied to the speakers of the Bella Coola language; the Bella Coola pronounce this same term as plxwla (Kennedy and Bouchard 1990a:338; see also Section XXI).

18. This name appears to be derived from the Heiltsuk term wikʷ 'eagle' (EW).

wife Āēqēlā′k·a[19] were living, who were always praying to Raven. So he settled down there.

2. Mink

Gyālastā′komē[20] was a boy who lived alone with his mother in a house. One day he asked his mother whether he had a father or not. She replied that his father was far away. So Gyālastā′komē began to weep and to cry, "I want to find my father." A woman who heard him weep gave him two stone axes and he hid them in his arm pits. A man called Hantlē′k· (= Archer)[21] gave bow and arrows to him. Gyālastā′komē shot one arrow against the sky and it stuck in the dome of the sky. He shot a second one which hit the notch of the first one, and in this way he continued until a chain had been formed which reached from the sky down to the earth. He shook it and found that it was strong enough to support him and so he climbed up. When he arrived in the sky he met his step-mother in front of her house door. She said, "Have you come at last?" "Yes," replied Gyālastā′komē, "I am searching for my father." "Good, then wait here," she replied, "he'll return tonight. He doesn't like to carry the daylight any more. You take his place!" In the evening, Sun, the father of Gyālastā′komē, came home. He was glad to see his son and told him to carry the sun in his place. He gave his clothing and his ornaments to him and impressed upon him, before he set out the following morning, not to walk too fast because otherwise the land would burn up and the sea would dry up. But Gyālastā′komē was disobedient. He became impatient, began to run, and it became so hot on earth that the rocks burst and the sea started to dry up. The shells on the bottom of the sea were burned quite black. Thereupon his father seized him and threw him down to earth, shouting, "You are fit for nothing; become a mink. Henceforth the people shall hunt you."

---

19. Not recognized by EW.

20. EW recognizes "Gyālastā′komē" as the Heiltsuk name gálástagəmi 'first into water'; Olson (1955:331) provides the translation 'rising of the sun.'

21. Boas' "Hantlē′k'" is the Heiltsuk term that is transcribed by Rath (1981:1:284) as haénlh'it and glossed as 'to fire an arrow from a bow.'

3. Wā′walis[22]

Close by G·alts (Bella Bella) there are two bays on a small island, which are called Wā′walitsēs[23] and Qunē′s,[24] separated only by a spit of land. At the first there lived a chief called Wā′walis; at the second, the chief Māk·oa′ns.[25] Wā′walis used to go out hunting seals with his slaves and he was a very successful hunter. Once, when he was out hunting, the son of Māk·oa′ns seduced his wife, and from that very moment on he found himself out of luck. He suspected that his wife was unfaithful, but wanted to make sure that his suspicion was founded on fact, and so returned home unexpectedly at night. He sneaked into the house without being noticed and crept up to his wife's room. There he listened at the wall and heard that his wife was talking to a man. He stole out again, sharpened his knife and came back at midnight. He carefully knocked at the wall to ascertain whether they were asleep, but he heard the woman say, "There is a mouse there." In a little while he knocked at the wall again and nothing stirred within, so he crept into the house and into the room, felt for the man's head, seized it by the hair and cut it off. Then he ran to the beach, jumped into his waiting canoe and rushed away.

In a short while the woman felt that her bed was wet. She said to her mother, "My child has wet the bed; you take it for a while." But when she looked around, she noticed that her bed was full of blood and that her lover's head had been cut off. She shrieked in terror. The son of Māk·oa′ns used to sit on a smooth rock at night, looking towards the east when the sun rose. He always sat there wrapped up in his cape, his chief's hat on his head. The woman carried the headless corpse to the rock, there wrapped it up in his cape and placed the hat on top so that it looked as if he were sleeping there.

The following morning the wife of Māk·oa′ns was surprised that her son didn't come for breakfast. When it was noon and he still hadn't come, she sent her youngest son to the rock to wake him up. The boy went there and shook his brother four times, "Get up! We've already eaten long ago!" Since he didn't budge, he ran back to his mother and said, "I can't wake my brother." The mother replied, "If he doesn't want to get up, take off his hat." The small boy ran back, took off his brother's hat and saw that his head was gone. So he shrieked loudly, ran down to the

---

22. This name appears to be wáwalis 'river bed; river banks,' derived from the term wa· 'river' (Kortlandt 1973:161).

23. What Boas transcribes as the place name "Wā′walitsēs" is recognized by EW as wáwaliƛis 'flowing on beach.'

24. This place name rendered by Boas as "Qunē′s" is recognized by EW as xʷənís 'hot spring on beach,' and appears to be applied to a site on Campbell Island in the vicinity of Bella Bella Indian Reserve No. 2.

25. EW recognizes Boas' "Māk·oa′ns" as mágʷəns.

beach and cried, "My brother's head is gone." When the people heard this, they scolded him and said, "Don't say such things!" and sent out two men to see what was going on. They found the body and carried it back to the house.

After some time Wā'walis returned from the hunt as if nothing had happened. He steered for the spit of land. The people called to him from a long distance, "Wā'walis! Don't lift up your paddles so high, because the son of our chief has been slain." Wā'walis pretended not to hear. His wife was fond of eating mountain goat fat and seal heads. He brought a basket of heads for her in his canoe, went up to the house and said, "Go down to the canoe and take from the basket what you like so much." The woman fetched the basket into the house, took one of the seal heads out and asked, "Is it this?" "No," replied Wā'walis, "it's right at the bottom." So she found her lover's head and cried out loudly in terror. But Wā'walis grabbed the head and beat her with it, saying, "Why don't you take it? Why are you afraid of it? You love him so much!" He beat her to death. Then he sliced open her belly and took out the kidneys which he hung up outside the door. Every time there is a new moon, they begin to bleed and this is why women menstruate.

Wā'walis had three sisters who were married to some people in the village of Māk·oa′ns. One day he presented them with rich provisions and went to them, with his three cousins, in order to eat. While they were sitting at their meal they were suddenly attacked by the people of Māk·oa′ns, who killed them. The murderers threw their bodies on the beach. Thereupon his three sisters wept. They left their husbands, went down to the beach, and mourned for the dead. They dug a pit to bury the bodies, and when they were tired out from digging, they sat down again and wept. When night fell, the sisters lay down to sleep beside the dead, but the youngest, who was very beautiful, was unable to sleep and only closed her eyes. Once, when she was blinking her eyes a little, she saw a man descending from the moon straight towards her. He had a completely white complexion and snow white hair. He was the son of Moon. He stepped up to her and nudged her, "Get up!" he said. She obeyed. "What are you doing here? Why are you weeping?" he continued. So the young woman said, "We are very unhappy. The people have slain our brother and our friends. We'd like to be dead with them." "I know," replied the son of Moon. "I saw that you were unhappy. Now stop weeping and wipe the blood from your faces."[26]

He passed his hand over her face and at once it became beautiful and white. In his right hand he carried a container filled with the Water of Life; in his left hand the death-bringer (iāHs'oā′m).[27] Then he told her to awaken her sisters, and made them

---

26. "When a close relative dies, the women lacerate their foreheads" [Boas' original footnote].

27. What Boas transcribes here as "iāHs'oā′m" is not recognized by EW, who agrees with Rath (1981:1:289) that the Heiltsuk term for 'death-bringer' is haláyu.

scratch the corpses from the earth. Then he poured some of the Water of Life into the mouths of the dead and blew on them four times. Thereupon they rose up and were alive again. He said, "I will now return to my father, the Moon. Let your youngest sister go along. She shall stay with me four days, then I will send her back to you." And he gave Wā'walis a small box, not longer than a finger, full of the Water of Life, and the death-bringer, and taught him how to use them. When he dripped the Water of Life into the mouth of a sick person, that person would get better. When he opened the box containing the death-bringer in the direction of his enemies, they would die. But he warned him not to look into the box himself. Then he said further, "When you pray to the moon, don't look at it but gaze at the ground." Then he placed the youngest sister onto his feet and flew up with her to the sky, circling higher and higher like an eagle. So Wā'walis, his cousins and his sisters prayed to the moon by gazing down at the ground.

Māk·oa'ns wanted to kill all the relatives of Wā'·walis, so he called together all the animals and made war on them. So Wā'·walis opened the box containing the death-bringer and all his enemies died, but his friends who had fallen in the fight were revived by him with the Water of Life. Then Māk·oa'ns called on the giant fish Yaēqoē'ok·oa (see p. 232)[28] to make the sea rise. Thereupon Wā'·walis dug a trench around his house, sharpened his knife and coated it with poison. Then, when the water rose up the trench, he cut with his knife along its banks and Yaēqoē'ok·oa had to fall back at once, and the water receded again. Yaēqoē'ok·oa tried to drown him six times, but he was unable to vanquish Wā'walis. So Māk·oa'ns gave up his attempts to kill him.

The sister who had been taken along into the sky by the Moon Man, stayed away four years, which only seemed like days to her. Once she sat on her bed and thought of her sisters. So her husband said, "Why are you sad? Do you think that your sisters are so far away? Just look down, they are quite near." With this he pulled the pillow aside and let her look down and she saw the whole world. Her husband outfitted a ship (not a canoe), made her embark and sent her back home. One morning the sisters heard a great noise and saw a ship arriving with their sister in it. She had become very beautiful, her skin was snow-white and her hair long and white like that of Moon Man. They unloaded the ship which was filled with riches. The Moon Man had also given her a drum and this made Wā'walis glad. He gave a great feast during which his sister told about the land in the moon. It never gets dark, and the people learned that the dead live there.

---

28. Boas' reference is to story 1, parts 3 and 4 in this Section.

Māk·oa′ns was so ashamed that he moved away to Awĩky'ēnoq.[29] He took along the body of his son, which was transformed there into a rock in the shape of a headless, crouching man. The head, a stone the size of a hut, was not far from it.

4. Masmasalā′niq[30]

A long time ago there were two brothers and their sister who lived in Rivers Inlet.[31] They owned a dog. In those days there were no fish yet and the people were always hungry. The brothers fashioned a small fish trap and put it into a small creek beside their house. Then a small fish came and got caught in it. The brothers saw the fish and took it from the trap, and the girl cut it open, dried it and then put it into a box. The following morning a bigger fish got caught in the trap and was prepared by the girl as well. The third day an even larger fish came and on the fourth, a salmon at last. One night the dog kept barking and the brothers and sister were unable to sleep, so the girl beat the dog with a stick and said, "What do you want? You'd better make the river bigger so that we'll be able to catch more fish." The dog ran out of the house and when they stepped out into the open the following morning, they saw a big river which they called Ky'ē′tēt.[32] They built huge salmon weirs and caught so much fish that their house was filled right up. The girl hung them on the roof beams to dry. When the eldest brother wanted to look at the fish in the morning, he found that they had all disappeared, but he didn't know who the thief was. He found his fish gone each morning on three successive days, so he said to his brother and sister, "You go to sleep! I will watch over the fish." He took his bow and arrows and hid. About midnight he saw Masmasalā′niq come. He was a huge man without a head whose eyes were on both sides of his chest. He shot four times at him, but he took the salmon nevertheless and ran away. The young man pursued him across three mountains and through three valleys. At last he saw the house of Masmasalā′niq standing on a plain by a lake. Masmasalā′niq ran inside. The young man had shot him many more times on the way, but had been unable to kill him.

---

29. Boas' "Awĩky'ēnoq" is a reference to the Oowekeeno tribe of the Rivers Inlet area.

30. The Heiltsuk equivalent of "Masmasalā′niq" is ṁásṁasalanuwa (EW). What Boas renders as "Masmasalā′niq" is the Bella Coola (Nuxalk) term for the 'supernatural carpenter' that we have recorded as masmasalanix̌ʷ (see Section XXII, story 1, part 1). Among the Heiltsuk, ṁásṁasalanuwa is the supernatural carpenter who is said to have established the arts of wood carving and painting.

31. Given in English as Rivers Inlet (without quotation marks) in the original *Sagen*.

32. This place, "Ky'ē′tēt" is identified as k̓ítit (Hilton 1990:313), a name glossed by Boas (1934:68) as 'grass body,' which is applied to the site of the Katit Reserve in Rivers Inlet.

He sat down on the shore of the lake and soon heard rattles and drums inside the house. Masmasalā'niq felt very ill and wanted to lie down but was unable because of the arrows in his body. But no one knew what was wrong with him because the arrows were invisible to him and his people. So they had summoned all the medicine men to cure him, but none were able to do it. After some time a man came from the house, and when he saw the stranger sitting by the shore, asked him, "Are you a medicine man?" When he said yes, he asked him, "Oh come and cure our chief." He went into the house and Masmasalā'niq promised him his daughter as a reward. The young man saw her sitting in the house and he found her delightful, so he put on his regalia and, unnoticed, pulled the arrows from the body of Masmasalā'niq. He pulled twice and thus removed all of them. Thereupon he was given the daughter of Masmasalā'niq for a wife. The chief invited him to stay for four days. But the four days were in reality four years. They had children together and at the end of the time the woman said, "Now let's go to your homeland. Go up that mountain, there are big cedars there. Cut one down and build a canoe." He obeyed but thought all the while, "How will the canoe get to the sea? There is no water hereabouts." At last he asked his wife and she said, "Don't worry about it. You will find out when the canoe is ready." When the canoe was ready, she took a small box and asked her friends to bring provisions for her. They did and she put everything into the small box; she put inside provisions which filled a whole house. Then she went to the canoe with her husband. She sat down in the bow and told her husband to sit in the stern and to look at the summit of the mountain. Then she passed water and from her urine a whole river came to be. Then she allowed her husband to turn around. She showed the river to him and said, "We'll go this way." Then he had to pull his blanket over his head so that he would not see how they were going to advance. The woman slapped the outside of the canoe with her hands and thereupon the paintings started to paddle. They soon reached his homeland and she allowed her husband to take the blanket from his face. He went ashore and saw that a couple of beams were all that was left of his house, and that his brothers and sisters were dead. He started to weep, but his wife said, "Don't weep! Take my box and my mat. Collect the bones of your brothers and sisters and of your dog and cover them with the mat." When he had done what she told him, she took her comb and scratched it four times across the mat. Thereupon his brother and sister and the dog got up, stretched and rubbed their eyes as if they had been asleep. When they had left the land of Masmasalā'niq the woman had warned her husband, "Don't ever scold our child, otherwise I'll become angry and do something which is very bad for us." For many years they lived happily and peacefully, but one day the child disturbed the man in his work and he scolded it. As soon as the woman heard this, she took the child, jumped into the canoe with him, slapped the outside of the canoe with her hands, and it carried them away.

5. K·ōmō′k·oa (= Rich One)[33]

Four young men went out in a canoe to hunt for seals. They stayed out overnight and anchored at the foot of a mountain. The anchor-stone fell right on the roof of the house of K·ōmō′k·oa. So he sent out his slave, Shark, to see who was there. He climbed up the anchor-rope and made a noise close to the canoe in order to scare away the people. The four men were kept awake by the noise, so they caught Shark, cut off his fins and threw him back into the water. He shouted, swam back to K·ōmō′k·oa and called out, "There are four people up there who have mutilated me." K·ōmō′k·oa said, "We will get them down when they are fast asleep." And he did what he had said. Soon one of the men woke up and noticed at once that he was in an unknown country. He thought that he was dreaming and bit his hand in order to wake himself up. Then he awakened the others and they discovered very soon that they were right in front of the house of K·ōmō′k·oa, who had them invited in. He placed them beside himself and said, "You shall stay with me for four days and you shall become my brothers." Then he invited all the people for a big feast. But an old woman, Mouse, warned the young men not to eat what K·ōmō′k·oa would serve to them, otherwise they'd never reach the upper world again. And she warned them of the sea monster Hā′nak·atsē.[34] So two of the men went outside and coated their canoe with a magic substance so that Hā′nak·atsē would be unable to devour it. K·ōmō′k·oa asked his guests, "Don't you have any mountain goat fat?" They gave a little to him. K·ōmō′k·oa divided it into four portions and threw it into the four corners of the house, which at once filled with mountain goat fat. Then they heard the noise of the arriving guests. All the fishes came and also the chief Yāēqoē·ok·oa who made the tides, and the house filled up with water. A huge whirlpool sprang up which nearly capsized the canoe, and the door to the room of K·ōmō′k·oa opened and shut like a maw and slurped up all the water. When the canoe got close to the door, the men threw poison into the water and thus escaped safely. The door was the monster Hā′nak·atsē. At last the men fell asleep and, when they awoke, they found themselves back on the surface of the water. K·ōmō′k·oa made three killer whales[35]

---

33. What Boas transcribes here as "K·ōmō′k·oa" is recognized by EW as the Heiltsuk name of the sea-being known as q̓ʷúmuk̓ʷa. While Boas provides here the translation 'rich one,' EW points out that q̓ʷúmuk̓ʷa is derived from q̓ʷúm which she translates as 'prince.' Elsewhere, Boas (1932:119, 124) records other Bella Bella texts in which this sea-being is identified as chief of all the sea creatures.

34. EW points out that the term Boas has transcribed as "Hā′nak·atsē" is the name of the fish known in the Heiltsuk language as hánagʷa and in English as the 'cabezon' (*Scorpaenichthys marmoratus*).

35. Given in the original as *Finwalen* which is an artificially-constructed term (comprised of English "fin" and German *Walen* 'whales') that Boas uses to indicate an orca or killer whale (*Delphinus orca*).

bring them back and fill their canoes with seals. They thought that they had been with K·ōmō′k·oa only four days, but in reality it had been four years. Their anchor-stone and anchor-rope were covered all over with seaweed. They took it ashore and from this originates all the seaweed.

6. The Mountain Lion

There once was a man in the K·ōk·aitq[36] tribe who lived with his wife and his brother. He was a successful hunter of mountain goats. His wife was always fasting and chewed only pitch while he was out hunting, and consequently he was always lucky. One time the brother went out hunting and stayed away for five days. Close by the house there stood a tree where the woman always got her pitch. She went there again this time, but Mountain Lion[37] was laying in wait for her and killed her. Then he put on her skin and went to the house in the form of the woman. Now when the man came home, his wife ate up everything that he had brought home. The man was very surprised that his wife had become so greedy all of a sudden. They went to bed, but at midnight Mountain Lion slipped out of the woman's skin and ran away. So the man knew what had happened. He pursued Mountain Lion and found his wife's bones underneath the tree. He killed Mountain Lion and then wept over the bones. Then an old woman, Mouse, who had been watching him, said, "Don't weep any more! I'll make her alive again." She went to the hot springs, Ēk·a′s,[38] and washed the bones in the water. Thereupon the wife came back to life again. The husband was very glad now. He went out hunting again. But one time he stayed away and his wife waited in vain for his return. So she sent out her brother-in-law to look for him. He didn't return, either. The woman was so afraid and worried that she couldn't sleep and at last went out herself to look for her husband. She took along two sticks which were coated with poison. When she was thus going up the mountain, she came to a fallen tree. She wanted to duck in order to crawl through under it, when

---

36. Boas' "K·ōk·aitq" is q̇ʷúqʷay̓aítx̌ʷ, anglicized as "Kokyet," which, as we have discussed, is the name of one of the four Heiltsuk tribal groups—the q̇ʷúqʷay̓aítx̌ʷ lived in the Spiller Channel/Ellerslie Lake area. According to Olson (1955:321), their name translates as 'calm water people.'

37. Mountain lion or cougar (*Felis concolor oregonensis*).

38. Boas (1934:41) elsewhere provides the transcription "ē′gäs" (equivalent to "Ēk·a′s" here in the *Sagen*) for what he describes as the "hot springs in Bella Bella," and notes that the name is derived from the word "ē′qa" meaning 'medicine' in Bella Bella and 'witchcraft' in Kwakwala. AD confirms that ʔíqa (Boas' "ē′qa") does mean 'witchcraft' in Kwakwala, and EW confirms that the same word means 'medicine' in Heiltsuk. Moreover, there is a place name known to EW as ʔígás (Boas' "ēəgäs" or "Ēk·a′s"), somewhere in the Bella Bella area, although EW is not certain of its exact location.

she saw a house. In it there were sitting her husband and her brother-in-law next to a woman. So she rejoiced and asked, "Why don't you come back to me?" They retorted, "This woman and her father keep us here by force." She hid until it grew dark. She saw how the chief offered the men human eyes to eat, but they only pretended to eat and in reality concealed the eyes beneath their capes. Mouse had counselled them to do this. After the meal the chief retired to sleep. His head always fell off when he was asleep. The woman seized it and coated the neck four times with poison; consequently the head and body could not grow together again and the chief thus lost his life. Mountain Lion had been the slave of this chief.

7. K·ōmā'nukula[39] and G·'ā'g·'apala'qsEm[40]

The first people in G·'ā'pa,[41] a village of the K·ōk·aitq,[42] were K·ōmā'nukula and his sister G·'ā'g·'apala'qsEm. They descended from the sky and with them there came two houses full of riches and many whistles for the Tsētsā'ēk·a.[43] A pole ornamented with the face of an eagle was standing in front of the house and a huge roof, which made an incessant noise, covered the smoke-hole. Inside, the house was decorated with representations of the bird āqaqonē'. The doors of the rooms represented the sea monster Hā'nak·atsē who always devours canoes. Game and fishes came to K·ōmā'nukula by themselves and many driftwood logs floated up by themselves. When they came to the shore they stood up and became people. Even to this day the K·ōk·aitq chiefs in G·'ā'pa utilize these same carvings with which the house of K·ōmā'nukula had been decorated.

   G·'ā'g·'apala'qsEm had one daughter, to whom she gave the dance Tlē'Htem'is[44] for the Tsētsā'ēk·a. Then the girl had to stay hidden for a long time in her chamber, which had been partitioned off for this purpose. Nobody knew what went on inside it. G·'ā'g·'apala'qsEm made a fire for her in there and the girl lay down and slept.

39. "The One Who Becomes Rich" [Boas' original footnote].

40. "G·'ā'pa—woman" [Boas' original footnote]. EW recognizes neither the term that Boas transcribes here as "G·'ā'g·'apala'qsEm", nor the word he gives as "G·'ā'pa" (but see the footnote that follows).

41. While EW does not recognize the name that Boas transcribes here as "G·'ā'pa," Olson (1955:321) has rendered this same name as "k!apa'h" and identified it as the name of a village situated at the southern tip of Yeo Island, between Spiller and Bullock Channels. This is the same place that Hilton (1990:313) transcribes as q̓ábá and identifies as the Kokyet Indian Reserve.

42. Boas' "K·ōk·aitq" is q̓ʷúqʷaẏaítx̌ʷ, anglicized as "Kokyet."

43. "The winter dance; literally: mysteries" [Boas' original footnote].

44. EW recognize Boas' "Tlē'Htem'is" as x̌'íx̣dəmís, possibly meaning 'place where sea lion goes,' but does not know a dance with this name.

Then she saw two beings, consisting only of heads, rise up beside the fire. They were called the Qā'uk·umā'las.[45] Thereupon she began to shake because of the sight of the spirits who made her Tlōkoa·la,[46] and who gave her the dance K·i'nk·la'tla.[47]

8. Baqbakuālanosī'uaē
(= He Who First Always Devoured Human Flesh at the Mouth of the River)[48]

A man called Nōak·au'a (= Wise One)[49] had two sons who used to go hunting mountain goats. One day they saw a house on a mountain with beautiful smoke coming from it. They entered and saw a woman and her child. She told them to wait until her husband's return. When they sat down one of the brothers hurt his foot, and the boy licked up the blood greedily. Then the brothers grew afraid and escaped. So the woman called for her husband, Baqbakuālanosī'uaē, shouting, "Two men were here and have fled. They are good food." The fugitives heard great noise and many whistles behind them and saw that Baqbakuālanosī'uaē was hard on their heels. They were carrying a stone, so they threw it behind them, beat time and sang, and it was transformed into a mountain. When Baqbakuālanosī'uaē had gone around the mountain and came close again, they broke up their arrows and threw them behind themselves. These were transformed into a dense forest. When their pursuer came up again, they threw their comb behind themselves and transformed it into a crabapple[50] thicket. Finally they poured out water behind themselves, which was transformed into a lake. Thus they reached the house of their father. They called to

---

45. EW does not recognize the name that Boas renders here as "Qā'uk·umā'las."

46. "The word Tlōkoa'la is almost untranslatable. It signifies finding something unexpectedly, as well as obtaining supernatural power by contact with spirits" [Boas' original footnote]. This term is recognized as λúgʷala; Hilton (1990:318) writes that the second series of dances, performed after the first was over, was called λuwəl'áxa 'coming down again.'

47. In describing her own initiation into this dance, Mrs. Moses Knight informed Olson (1955:337, 342) that the name of this dance translates as 'head against something.' Mrs. Sam Star provided Olson with the alternate translation 'whispered to by a spirit.'

48. The term that Boas transcribes as "Baqbakuālanosī'uaē" and translates here as 'He Who First Always Devoured Human Flesh at the Mouth of the River' has been commonly translated as 'cannibal at the north end of the world.' A discussion of the variant translations of this name appears in Hilton, Rath, and Windsor (1982:59–64) whose recent linguistic research suggests the meaning of the name may more correctly be: 'ever more perfect manifestation of the essence of becoming human.' While Boas' transcriptions and translations of the term he gives here as "Baqbakuālanosī'uaē" vary from one publication to another, the term commonly relates to the cannibalistic characteristics of this being (see also Section XX, story 8).

49. What Boas transcribes here as "Nōak·au'a" is given in Rath (1981:2:443) as núaqala 'to talk wisely (as elders).'

50. Given in English as "crabapple" (in double quotation marks) in the original *Sagen*.

him from far away, "Open up the door! Baqbakuālanosī'uaē is hard on our heels and wants to devour us." Nōak·au'a let them in and dug a deep hole, poured water into it and placed boards over it. Then when the cannibal arrived, Nōak·au'a invited him in to sit down and gave him a seat right above the pit. He promised him the flesh of his sons. All of a sudden he had the boards pulled away. Baqbakuālanosī'uaē fell into the pit; they threw red-hot stones into it and thus cooked him. They burned him to cinders, blew these into the air and transformed them into mosquitoes. (See a more complete version in the previous section.)

—A chief had two wives. Once one of them became angry, threw everything out of the house and ran away into the mountains. The chief and the other woman followed after her. When they grew tired, they sat down and were transformed into rocks there. The man, the wives and all their boxes and things can still be seen today.

—Tlā'tla[51] is a woman carrying on her back a basket in which she steals children. (See Legends of the Awīky'ēnoq.)[52]

—The human name of Deer is Tlēk·k·umē'[53] and Āsanōistē'sela[54] (= Torch [anō']⁵⁵ Bearer) because he stole fire with the aid of wood which he had tied to his tail.

---

51. The name x̱'áɫa (Boas' "Tlā'tla") is applied to the cannibal woman (EW).

52. Oowekeeno; see Section XX.

53. Deer is called ƛíqkʷəmi in Heiltsuk mythology (EW).

54. This alternate Heiltsuk name for 'Deer' in mythology, "Āsanōistē'sela," is recognized by EW as asánuwistisəla 'go around other side.'

55. Recognized by EW as anúy, the Heiltsuk term meaning 'torch.'

Looking eastward along the front of the q̓ʷumk̓ʷut's village at the mouth of the Bella Coola River, 1897. Group of Nuxalk (Bella Coola) people with a copper stand in front of Chief Adam King's "house of nusmata," with the peaked "house of nusq̓lst," belonging to the Clellamin family, behind them.

Canadian Museum of Civilization, Ottawa. Neg./Trans. No. 46917 (Ivor Fougner photo).

XXII. Legends of the Bella Coola (Nuxalk)

Boas' chief "Bilqula" (Bella Coola) consultant was a man named "Nuskelu´sta" who Boas first met in Berlin in 1885. Nuskelu´sta was one of the nine Bella Coola men who had been enlisted by the Norwegian Captain J. Adrian Jacobsen to come to Germany to give "ethnic exhibitions." Boas spent two weeks with these performers and learned enough to write a report for the Berlin *Tageblatt* of 25 January 1886 (Cole 1982:119), a short article on the Bella Coola language for *Science* (Boas 1886a), and another short article on Bella Coola language and ethnology for the *Verhandlungen der Berliner Gesellschaft für Anthropologie, Ethnologie und Urgeschichte* (Boas 1886b). It is to this latter article that Boas is referring in his footnote to story 1, part 4 of this section, and his comment reveals that through the medium of Chinook Jargon he collected several stories in Berlin.

There were actually two other Nuxalk men from the German group in Victoria when Boas arrived there in September 1886, but they were due to go north immediately (Rohner 1969:20–21). One stayed, and Boas made a start on gathering notes about masks and some of the area's mythology. Anyway, it was Nuskelu´sta Boas was really looking for. "This evening I saw the Bella Coola whom I have sought so long," Boas wrote on 2 October 1886. "He is quite intelligent. 'Auf Anhieb'[1] (as we used to say as students) he told me the story of the son of their highest being" (Rohner 1969:30). This would be the introduction to "The Raven Legend" attributed to Nuskelu´sta by name in the *Sagen*. In addition, stories 2, 15, 24, and 25 are listed as his.

Some of these stories would have been obtained during a later field season, in August 1890, in Ladner, where three Bella Coola, including one who had been in Germany, were working in the cannery (Rohner 1969:128).

---

1. This German expression means, colloquially, 'a quick study.'

After a few days Boas could report that he had "engaged one with whom I am making good progress" (Rohner 1969:130). Perhaps this is "Yākōtla's," Tom Henry, another of his Nuxalk friends from Germany, who is named as the source for stories 13, 21, and 23.

The remainder of the stories came from "a number of young women of the village of Sātsq on Deans Inlet" (Boas 1895d:31), a reference to the present Chatscah Reserve at the head end of Dean Channel. (Boas was never in Bella Coola until later; the women were living in Victoria.) "I visited the two Bella Coolas, who quite unexpectedly and without my asking told me the story of the origin on the salmon" (Rohner 1969:27). This would be story 16. The stories numbered 6, 9 and 10 came from the same source (Rohner 1969:30). Boas' mythtellers also gave him texts in the Bella Coola language, seven of which he published "along with an eighth from Nuskelu'sta" in "Salishan Texts" (Boas 1895d). These turn out to be truncated variants of *Sagen* stories: 1, part 1, second paragraph; 1, part 3; 1, part 11; 2, part 1; 5; 12; 14; and 16.

Nuxalk (Bella Coola) men poling a spoon canoe up the river in front of the q̓ʷumk̓ʷut's village at the mouth of the Bella Coola River, 1895.

British Columbia Archives, Victoria, B.C. No. G-00967.

Kimsquit village of nuẋ'l, 1881, showing the decorated house of aṅika.
American Museum of Natural History Library, New York. Neg./Trans. No. 32953
(Edward Dossetter photo).

XXII. Legends of the Bilqula[2]

1. The Raven Legend[3]

1) In the beginning there was no sun. A curtain was stretched between sky and earth, so that it was always dark down here. Raven wanted to free the sun, but was not able to do so. So he went to the deities Masmasalā′niq,[4] Yula′timōt (= Heron),[5]

---

2. What Boas transcribes as "Bilqula" is bə′lx^wəlá, a Heiltsuk (Bella Bella) term, anglicized as "Bella Coola," that is used to refer to the people now known as the "Nuxalk." This latter term, adapted from the word nuxalk, used by the Bella Coola to refer to the Bella Coola Valley in its entirety, has come into use since about 1980 to identify all those who speak the Bella Coola language. The Nuxalk or Bella Coola speak a Coast Salish language that is geographically isolated from the rest of the Salishan language family and forms a separate division within it. Nuxalk territory is surrounded on the south, west, and north by speakers of Wakashan languages, and on the east by speakers of Athapaskan languages. Nuxalk traditional territory extended from the head of South Bentinck Arm in the south to the headwaters of the Kimsquit River in the north, including the Bella Coola River and Dean River drainages in the east and reaching west to include North Bentinck Arm, Burke Channel, Labouchere Channel, and most of Dean Channel (Kennedy and Bouchard 1990a:323–325, 338–339).

   Most of our annotating of this section was undertaken in 1981 with the assistance of Margaret Siwallace, who was originally from Kimsquit (in Dean Channel) but spent the remainder of her life in the village at the mouth of the Bella Coola River. We gratefully acknowledge Margaret Siwallace's help. Our annotations also draw upon our consultation in the 1970s with the following Nuxalk people, all of whose assistance we also acknowledge with thanks: Agnes Edgar; Felicity Walkus; and Margaret Siwallace.

3. Boas' original shorthand version of this text is held by the American Philosophical Society Library (Item Pn 4.b 5; cited here as Boas 1890b), and his own English translation of parts 1 and 2 of this Raven legend appears in his 1891 report "The Bilqula" (Boas 1892a:420).

4. What Boas transcribes here as "Masmasalā′niq" is the Nuxalk term masmasalanix^w which refers collectively to the four brothers who were supernatural carpenters. McIlwraith (1948:I:39) reports that among the Kimsquit group of the Nuxalk, this name is applied to one of the supernatural carpenters, instead of the name "ma'apalitsak." See also Section XXI, story 4.

5. The name yulatimut (Boas' "Yula′timōt") means 'fix by rubbing over,' but contemporary Nuxalk people do not recognize it as a name for 'Heron' (which Boas gives as *Reiher* in the original German). McIlwraith's (1948:I:39) consultants stated that the name translates as 'he who completes any task with a single smoothing motion,' and was applied to the eldest and most powerful supernatural carpenter. Once this work was complete, yulatimut came to earth and married a Heiltsuk woman.

Matlapē'eqoek·,[6] and Itl'itlu'lak[7] (according to others, Matlapā'litsek·)[8] and asked them to free the sun. They tore open the curtain and the sun began to light the earth. But it did not shine clear and bright yet, but rather as through a dense mist. Raven flew into the sky through the tear made by the deities and there found an endless plain inhabited by the birds. Masmasalā'niq and his brothers wanted to paint them, but Raven demanded to be painted first. Yula'timōt painted him with bright colours but was unable to satisfy him. Then Masmasalā'niq painted him, but Raven disliked the new colours as much as the old ones. Thereupon Matlapē'eqoek· painted him first and then Itl'itlu'lak· but he wasn't satisfied by any of them. So Masmasalā'niq said, "Let's paint him black." They did this, but Raven called, "It doesn't matter that I'm ugly now. I will now fly down to earth and tease and torment the people." Then Masmasalā'niq threw Raven down to earth. Then the four deities painted all the birds and gave each one his song and his skills. They assigned them the seasons to sing in and those during which they should be quiet.

But Raven was not content with the sun because it shone so dimly and he decided to search for another one. He flew all over the world and at last came to the house of the chief Snq,[9] who owned the Nusqē'mta (= Place of Dawn).[10] This was a round box without a cover or a seam in which there was the sun. The chief kept it in his house where it hung from a roof beam. Raven knew that he was unable to get the box by force and so thought up a ruse. The chief had four daughters. The eldest one used to get water from a pond every morning. So Raven changed into a pine needle[11] and dropped into the container with which the girl drew the water. Then, when she drank the water, she swallowed the pine needle along with it. She became pregnant and gave birth to a boy. When he grew up he began to cry one day and couldn't be

---

6. The name of this character, maƛ'apali·xʷak, means 'two cuts.' McIlwraith (1948:I:39) also gave this name as one of the four supernatural carpenters and provided the translation 'he who completes any task with two strokes of his adze.'

7. This term, transcribed by Boas as "Itl'itlu'lak," is recognized as ʔiƛ'iƛ'iyuɬak, the name of the fourth and youngest supernatural carpenter. McIlwraith (1948:I:39) translates this name as 'he who completes any task in a single day.'

8. The name of this character, maƛ'apalitsak (Boas' "Matlapā'litsek·") means 'one chop.' McIlwraith (1948:I:39) also gave this as the name of one of the four carpenters; see also story 21 in the present section.

9. "Snq" is Boas' rendering of snx̱, the Nuxalk term meaning 'sun.'

10. Boas' "Nusqē'mta" is nusx̱imta, which does mean 'place of dawn,' as Boas notes here. Elsewhere, Boas (1895d:43) provides the transcription "nusxē'mtatx" which he glosses as 'having the daylight.' As the story explains, daylight was kept in a globe-like box.

11. Boas (1895d:42) calls this "qoa'ls" 'spike of fir,' which is recognized as the Nuxalk term qʷals meaning 'needle of Western hemlock (*Tsuga heterophylla*).'

calmed down. He cried for the Nusqē'mta. Because he refused to eat and cried incessantly, the old chief finally allowed him to play with it. With this he was content for the time being. But the following day he cried again until the chief allowed him to take the Nusqē'mta out of the house and to play with it in the lane. He had scarcely gone out when he broke the box. The sun leapt out and the boy flew away as Raven. (Told by Nuskelu'sta.)[12]

2) When the sun had been created in this way, Masmasalā'niq, Yula'timōt, Matlapē'eqoek·, and Itl'itlu'lak came down to earth and said, "Let's create man." Masmasalā'niq carved a human figure from wood, but was unable to bring it to life. Matlapē'eqoek· and Itl'itlu'lak also tried to carve human figures, but they were unable to bring them to life. Finally Yula'timōt carved a figure and made it come alive. Then he created one man and one woman in all the lands and they became the ancestors of all the tribes. Then Masmasalā'niq gave his skills to the people. He taught them how to build canoes,[13] how to catch fish, and how to erect houses. He created rivers so that the people would have water to drink and so that the fish were able to swim up these rivers. (Told by Nuskelu'sta.)

3) Then Masmasalā'niq carved a salmon, threw it into the water and told it to swim away.[14] But the salmon had no soul as yet and therefore was not able to swim. Because the four deities were unable to make a soul, they called Raven and told him to search for a soul for the salmon. So Raven launched his canoe Tupa'nkHtl[15] and went to the salmon with his four sisters, Tsuā'astɛlkHs (?),[16] StsuakHtɛlHs, Hilq, and Askyā'nik·s.[17] When they were almost at the house of the Salmon Chief, Raven

---

12. "Nuskelu'sta" was Boas' primary Native consultant from the Bella Coola Valley. A brief summary of a variant of this story (specifically, of story 1, part 1, paragraph 2), with the text in both Nuxalk and English, appears elsewhere in Boas (1895d:42).

13. In the *Sagen*, Boas provides the word "canoes" in English (without quotation marks).

14. Boas (1895d:40) provides a variant of this story elsewhere.

15. What Boas renders here as "Tupa'nkHtl" is given by McIlwraith (1948:II:408) as "Raven's self-moving canoe, Tobınkł."

16. The names of three of Raven's four younger sisters are also given in Boas (1895d:40) as "Stsuak·tɛ'laqs, X·īlx·, and Ask·anī'qs" (the same names given here in the *Sagen* as "StsuakHtɛlHs," "Hilq," and "Askyā'nik·s"), although no translations are provided. In addition to these three, the *Sagen* provides the name "Tsuā'astɛlkHs" which Boas follows with a questions mark, indicating his uncertainty about this name. McIlwraith (1948:II:408) records the names of the four Crow sisters as "Ḵäkämitł, Tcwa·st, Wılx, and Äsqänıks" and states: "They were non-marriageable female relatives, not his own sisters." Two of the four names given by McIlwraith correspond to those recorded by Boas. The Nuxalk people with whom we consulted in the 1970s identified three of the four "cousins" of Raven as: cwa·stalqs (Boas' "Tsuā'astɛlkHs (?)"; xalx (Boas' "Hilq"); and askaniqs (Boas' "Ask·anī'qs").

17. Contemporary Nuxalk people recognize this term, askaniqs (Boas' "Ask·anī'qs"), as a Heiltsuk (Bella Bella) name.

landed at a point and made his sisters hide in the forest. At night, when it grew dark, they crept secretly into the chief's village and drilled (gnawed?) holes into his canoe. Then they went back to their hide-out and next morning went to the village as if they had just arrived. The chief had them invited into his house and treated them generously. Then when they prepared to leave again, he furnished them with provisions for the journey. Raven asked him, "Let your daughter carry the provisions to my canoe; I will stow them there." Then he went down to the canoe. When the girl brought the provisions and stepped into the canoe, Raven called to his sisters to paddle away as fast as possible. In this way they abducted the girl. The chief wanted to pursue them. But when he launched his canoe it sank because its bottom was riddled with holes. So the fugitives arrived safely at Nutl'ᴇ'l[18] where they threw the girl into the river KH'lat.[19] Since that time there have been many salmon in the river.[20]

4) Masmasalā'niq knew that the deluge would come. So he tied the canoes of the Bilqula to Mount Nusk·'a'lst[21] to prevent them from drifting away. He told the people to lash the canoes together and to cover them with planks so that they would be able to get on them as soon as the waters began to rise. Because the canoes of the other peoples were not tied, they were scattered all over the world. The Heiltsuk·,[22] who had formerly lived inland, were driven to the sea coast. The interior Indians, who had formerly lived by the sea, were carried to the interior. When the waters subsided again, the rivers formed.[23]

---

18. The term that Boas has transcribed here as "Nutl'ᴇ'l" is recognized as nuχ'l 'canyon'; this place name is applied to the village site at the mouth of the Dean River (now identified as Kemsquit Indian Reserve No.1), as well as the canyon situated just over one mile (2 km) upstream.

19. What Boas has rendered as "KH'lat" is recognized as nuk̓lat 'steelhead place,' the name applied to the Dean River as a whole. In the version of this story told to Boas (1895d:40–41) by a young Kimsquit woman, salmon come to "Nuxa'lk·" (nuxalk) by which the storyteller is referring to the Bella Coola valley.

20. "This legend most likely consists of two fragments which the informant, not knowing them exactly, joined together. According to a fragment which I heard from another informant, the chief gave Raven salmon to eat. Raven then hid the soul—which is imagined as an egg-shaped body with its seat in the neck—beneath his tongue. But the chief noticed this and took it away from him again. But he succeeded in some way, but it was not told how the soul was received" [Boas' original footnote].

21. This distinctive mountain is known in the Nuxalk language as nusq̓lst (Boas' "Mount Nusk·'a'lst"); the same name is applied to a former village site located where the "Noosgulch" (anglicized from nusq̓lst) River, which originates from this mountain, meets the Bella Coola River. Nusq̓lst mountain, situated on the north side of the Bella Coola River, is the highest peak in the valley, and, as this story relates, is the peak to which the Bella Coola people (Boas' "Bilqula") tied their canoes during the Great Flood.

22. Heiltsuk or Bella Bella. See Section XXI.

23. "I formerly understood (Verh. 1886, p. 206) that Masmasalā'niq tied up the land and not the

5) Raven once sat by the fire and opposite him there sat a very beautiful girl with skin as white as snow. He would have liked to marry her, but she didn't want to have anything to do with him. So he thought up a ruse. He told her, "You haven't had a bath for a long time, why don't you have one now?" She replied, "Fine, if you will light a fire for me." Then she went into her room and washed her whole body. But Raven flew into the forest. He went to Cedar and asked, "What do you do when you are thrown into the fire?" Cedar replied, "I cry and the people call it crackling." "Then you are of no use to me," said Raven. He flew to Spruce and asked what it did when it was thrown into the fire. He replied, "I cry and jump up high." So Raven said, "That is just right. I will throw you into the fire and a beautiful girl will be sitting close to you. Jump right into her lap and burn her." Raven took the spruce home, lit a fire and the girl sat down close beside it to dry herself. Thereupon the spruce jumped up high, right into her lap and burned her. Raven was very sorry for her and said, "I know a good cure. Go into the forest and when you see a plant out there—a stem without leaves which moves up and down—sit right down on it and you will be better at once." The girl took his advice. She had scarcely left the house when Raven flew into the forest, hid beneath the leaves and let only his penis protrude. The girl came and did what Raven had told her. But then she noticed his eyes and knew that she had been cheated. She grabbed Raven and beat him until he lay there as if dead.

6) Once Raven said to his four sisters, "I hear that many blueberries are in the woods here. Let's paddle down there and gather some." They stepped into the canoe, Tudo'nkHtl, and went out. When the canoe was filled up with berries, they went to a level spot on the beach, cooked the berries in a huge cooking box and then filled their boxes with them. They loaded their canoe and paddled on. Suddenly Raven, who was steering, cried, "Sisters, I have to go ashore." They landed and he relieved himself. Then he said to his excrement, "When I have gone away a bit, shout winā'winā'!"[24] Then he went on with his sisters. In a short while the shout winā'winā'! was heard. So Raven said, "Oh, woe! Do you hear these cries? Those are our enemies who are coming in many canoes to kill us. You had better go into the forest and hide; I will stay here to watch the canoe." His sisters were scarcely

---

canoes. This was caused by the informant speaking Chinook and saying, 'Masmasalā'niq mamuk kau eli kopa lamotai,' Literally, 'Masmasalā'niq tied the land to the mountains.' But eli = land, here means the inhabitants of the country and not the land itself, so that the former version of the legend is incorrect" [Boas' original footnote]. Boas here refers to his article "Sprache der Bella-Coola-Indianer" published in the *Verhandlungen der Berliner Gesellschaft für Anthropologie, Ethnologie und Urgeschichte* 18:202–206 (cited in the present volume as Boas 1886b).

24. "Most likely the Kwakiutl word wina, war" [Boas' original footnote]. In fact, the same word, wina (Boas' "winā'" here in the *Sagen*), is used in the Nuxalk language with the same meaning, 'war; warrior.'

out of sight when he gobbled up all the berries. After some time the girls returned and found Raven lying on his back in the canoe and their boxes emptied. They asked what had happened. Raven replied, "Oh the people have beaten me and have eaten up all the berries." But his sisters soon noticed that his tongue was all black. They demanded, "How come your tongue is black, and also your head? You have eaten our berries!" And they kicked him. So he cried out "K·oā′q, k·oā′q!"

7) Raven flew on and saw a house floating on an arm of the inlet. A man called Yaii′ntsa,[25] who was fishing for halibut through a hole in the floor of the house, lived there. Raven went up to him and asked him for something to eat, so the man went to the hole, lowered his fishing line and caught a halibut. He cut it up, cooked a piece and gave it to Raven. Raven now thought that he would like to live in the house himself and he wanted to chase away Yaii′ntsa with a ruse. He said, "Your father is on the other side of the inlet." Yaii′ntsa replied, "I have neither father nor mother." But Raven insisted and said, "He ought to know. He told me that he was your father and that he would like to see you. I will take you across if you like." Yaii′ntsa asked, "But where is your canoe?" Raven replied, "Oh, I will carry you over on my back." Yaii′ntsa was afraid that Raven would drop him, but Raven reassured him and told him that he would fly very steadily. So Yaii′ntsa got on and Raven flew off. When he was a bit above the house, Raven began to shake and Yaii′ntsa grew afraid. Raven consoled him by saying, "Oh, that happens occasionally when I'm flying." But when he was right above the middle of the inlet, Raven threw Yaii′ntsa into the water and flew back to the house. Raven began fishing at once. When he pulled up the line he found no halibut on it but only a stick. At this he became angry and hit the stick. But Yaii′ntsa had hidden in it, and now crept out and drilled many holes into the house so that it filled with water. Raven was unable to get out and, when the water rose higher and higher, he at last stuck his beak through a tiny hole in the roof in order to get air. But Yaii′ntsa made the house sink completely. When he thought that Raven had drowned, he made it emerge again and opened the door. So Raven flew out and called, "K·oā′q, k·oā′q, k·oā′q." Yaii′ntsa didn't know to where he vanished.

8) Once Raven wanted to catch halibut. He went out fishing with Cormorant. The latter caught many big fish and threw them into the canoe, whereas Raven had caught only one tiny fish. So Raven became jealous and thought how he could take the catch of Cormorant away from him. He called to him, "I've caught so many fishes that my canoe is almost full." Cormorant asked, "What did you use for bait?" Raven replied, "I've cut off my tongue and put it on the hook." So Cormorant cut his tongue off, too, and became mute. Then Raven stole all his catch and, when they

---

25. This is the Nuxalk term for the teredo worm.

got ashore, pretended that he had caught everything, and poor Cormorant couldn't say a thing.

9) Once Raven and his sister were very hungry, so he went to Seal and begged him for some food. The latter complied with Raven's request. He held his hands close to the fire and let fat drip from them. He gave the fat and plenty of salmon to Raven and allowed him to carry it home to his sister.

10) AiHoa'qōnē (a small bird)[26] once wanted to feast Raven. He took a large bucket into the forest and chanted four times, "AiHoaqa'na qa'naqa'na," and the container filled with berries. He carried them home and served them to Raven, who gobbled up half and took the rest home to give to his sister. Raven thought that he would also be able to make berries in this fashion, so he took a container and went into the forest. But when he chanted, the container didn't fill with berries, but with excrement instead. When his sisters saw this they grew angry and beat him.

11) Deer had lost his child, who had been ripped apart by the wolves.[27] While Deer was sitting weeping on a mountain, Raven flew up and wanted to cry with him. Deer was glad that Raven showed compassion for him and asked him to sit down, but Raven only intended to kill and eat Deer. They were sitting next to each other on the mountain, right by the edge of a deep gorge, and Raven began weeping and chanting, "Oh, Deer, you have no meat at all on your legs." Deer grew angry and said: "I thought that you had come to weep with me, and now you taunt me!" Then he continued and chanted, "Oh, Raven, you have no meat at all on your feet." Raven became incensed at this and threw Deer off the rock. He rejoiced, flew down and ate Deer's hind-quarter. Then he flew to his sisters and said, "I have killed a big deer. Come along, we will carry it home."

12) Once K·'ō'tsikH,[28] Cougar, went into the mountains to hunt goats. He had his bow and arrow at the ready when he met the mountain spirit, Tō'alatlitl,[29] who asked him, "Whose bow and arrow are you carrying there?" K·'ō'tsikH replied, "They belong to Tō'alatlitl." The latter was glad about this and exchanged his weapons with K·'ō'tsikH. Since that time, Cougar catches mountain goats with ease. He feasted all the people with the exception of Raven, to whom he gave nothing. So Raven decided to hunt mountain goats by himself. He also met Tō'alatlitl and the latter

---

26. The Nuxalk term ʔixʔi·xʷni (Boas' "AiHoa'qōnē") is applied to the Swainson's Thrush (*Hylocichla ustulata*). Among the Nuxalk, as among many other Northwest Coast groups, the song of this bird is believed to cause the salmonberries to ripen.

27. A variant of this legend is provided elsewhere by Boas (1895d:41–42).

28. Although Boas identifies the Native term "K·'ō'tsikH" as *Panther* ('panther') in German, the Nuxalk people with whom we consulted recognized "K·'ō'tsikH" as qʷucik, the Nuxalk word for 'wolverine' (*Gulo gula*).

29. McIlwraith (1948:II:396) refers to this character as the 'supernatural hunter.'

enquired, pointing to the weapons of Raven, "To whom does this bow and arrow belong?" Raven replied, "To whom else but Raven?" At this Tō'alatlitl grew angry and left Raven. Thus it came about that he didn't kill a single goat. But he was ashamed to return home empty-handed, so he cut into his chest, took out some fat and put it on top of the quiver which he carried on his back; then he went home. There he bragged that he had killed many mountain goats and he gave his own fat, which he had caused to multiply, to his sisters. They took it and put it beside the fire. Thereupon Raven cried, "Oh, don't put the fat beside the fire, it hurts me!" When they paid no attention, he became ill; his intestines rumbled and he nearly died. Then K·'ō'tsikʜ gave food to Raven's sisters, but none to him. At this Raven grew incensed and said to K·'ō'tsikʜ, "Don't you know that the people want to kill you? You had better flee from here and stay away for good." K·'ō'tsikʜ took Raven's advice and the sisters became angry because their brother had robbed them of their provider.

13) Once Raven went fishing and soon a big fish (sāmtl)[30] took his bait. When he was putting it into his canoe, it was transformed into a woman. He married her and she promised to stay with him provided that he would never look at other women again. Raven kept his promise for four days. During this time he caught many salmon and dried them by the fire, but then he saw a pretty girl and began to look at her. His wife grew angry at this and went away with all the salmon. So Raven became very sad and wept.

14) Raven wanted to catch salmon but did not know the skill of net-making. Therefore he went to Spider and she taught him the skill.

2. Mink

1) Snq (or Tā'atau), Sun,[31] had a son called T'ŏt'k·oa'ya[32] who was living with his mother in a village. The boys of the village once made fun of him because he had no father, so he resolved to visit his father in the sky. He took his bow and arrows and shot one arrow at the sky, which stuck there. Then he shot a second arrow, which hit the first one's notch. He continued thus until a chain had formed, reaching from the sky down to earth. He shook it to test whether it was strong enough. When he found that he could dare attempt it, he climbed up. In the sky he found a house

---

30. This is the Nuxalk term samɬ meaning 'sockeye salmon.'

31. The usual Nuxalk term for 'sun' is snx̣ (Boas' "Snq"). Our Nuxalk consultants recognized the term ta·taw (Boas' "Tā'atau") as another name for aɬkʷntam, the creator of the world; both terms are used to translate the phrase "Our Father," when referring to God.

32. The term that Boas transcribes here as "T'ŏt'k·oa'ya" is identified elsewhere by Boas (1895d:42) as the name for Mink in Nuxalk mythology. "T'ŏt'k·oa'ya" is recognized as tut'kʷiya.

in which the wife of Snq was living. She welcomed him and said, "Your father will come home at night. He will be glad to see you." When Snq arrived, he greeted his son and said, "I am old. Henceforth you shall carry the sun in my stead. But pay attention, keep walking straight and don't bend down, otherwise the earth will burn up." T'ōt'k·oa'ya promised and in the morning walked slowly and quietly up the sky, but towards noon he bent down to have a look around at the earth. Thereupon it became very hot down there; the rocks burst open and the sea began to boil over, covering all the land. The people saved themselves in their canoes, but many perished and others were scattered. The mountain goats hid beneath stones; that is why they stayed white, while all the other animals were scorched. When Snq saw what T'ōt'k·oa'ya was doing, he seized him, tore him into pieces and threw them down to earth. There the pieces were transformed into minks.

2) Snq took a wife on earth and had a child with her which he called T'ōt'k·oa'ya. The people were mocking the child because his face was always dirty. The boy warned them, "Don't mock me, otherwise Snq, my father, will punish you." But the people didn't listen to him and didn't believe that Snq was his father. When they derided and teased him again, he said, "Now I will go to my father to take revenge on you. I will burn you all up." He began to climb up the eyelashes of Snq, which were the sun's rays, and thus reached the sky. He asked his father whether he could carry the sun in his stead. His father gave it to him and he climbed up in the morning, carrying the sun. Towards noon he made the sun hotter and hotter so that houses and trees started to burn. In the evening he returned to the village. He said to the people, "You see, I've burned your houses because you tormented me." But they did not believe him.

He had become more pure and more handsome now. He told the people, "If you torment me again I will go back to my father and burn all of you up." But the people decided to kill him. Since T'ōt'k·oa'ya noticed their intention, he climbed up to the sky again on his father's eyelashes. There he complained about the people, but Snq only said, "You are disliked because you are full of silly pranks." He let his son carry the sun again. And he caused it to become so hot on earth that everything burned up. The animals that didn't hide from the heat were singed all over. Bear pressed only his throat against a stone, consequently his whole fur became black, with the exception of this one spot. Ermine hid beneath a stone, but the tip of his tail stuck out and consequently is black. Mountain Goat crawled into a cave and therefore remained completely white.

But when Snq saw what his son was doing, he became angry and threw him down to earth. He transformed him into a mink. (Told by Nuskelu'sta from NuqalkH.)

3. The Man in the Moon

A man sent his wife into the forest every day to gather berries. One day, the Man in the Moon, Snq's son, saw her there. He took a liking to her and descended from the sky in order to stay with her. Then he returned to the sky. The woman returned home but had no berries because, instead of gathering, she had been with the Moon Man. When she now returned home daily without berries, although there were plenty growing in the forest, her husband became suspicious and decided to spy on her. He found her together with her lover. He stole back home unobserved and resolved to take his revenge. The following day he said to his wife, "You don't seem to find berries any more; I'll go myself this time to see whether there aren't any." So he put on his wife's hat and cape, concealing a knife under the cape, and went to the spot where the two usually met. It wasn't long before the Moon Man arrived. When the latter wanted to embrace him, he cut off his head with his knife. He carried it home and when his wife saw it she was terribly shocked and began to cry. He wanted to know who the man was and called all the people together to view the head, but nobody recognized it.

Then Snq descended to earth to search for his son. At last he came also to the man who had slain him and he asked, "Have you not seen my son?" The man replied, "No, I don't know him and have not seen him." Just then Snq spied his son's head which was hanging above the fire. He became very angry and made a huge fire on earth so that all the people perished. Only the lover of the Moon Man was spared. She fetched a container full of water from the river before it dried up, and with the water she caught many small fish (tutŏ́k·).[33] When everything had burned and when the rivers had dried up, she poured the water into the river, which then started to run again. The fish swam about in it and multiplied rapidly.

4. Kōlaiā́ns and Mak·'oā́ns

Once Kōlaiā́ns wanted to catch salmon. He made himself a rope from hair and fixed the hook, with which he intended to fish, to it. But Mak·'oā́ns wished to have the hook very much. He transformed himself into a salmon, swam upriver and bit off the hook and swam away with it. So Kōlaiā́ns went upriver to find his hook again. He hadn't gone far when he saw a big house. He opened the door a bit and saw Mak·'oā́ns sitting inside, beside a chest. He invited him to enter the house and to sit down beside him. Kōlaiā́ns accepted the invitation and then told him that he was out to look for his hook, which had been stolen. Mak·'oā́ns said, "I have heard nothing about your hook." But in a short while he opened the chest and showed the broken

---

33.   Boas' "tutŏ́k·" is recognized as the Nuxalk term tutup 'any trout.'

hook to him, asking whether he wanted to barter, so Kōlaiā′ns knew at once that he had stolen and broken it. But Mak·'oā′ns put the two pieces together again so that the hook was as good as new and gave it back to Kōlaiā′ns.

5. The Snēnē′ik·[34]

A man called Iā′lit[35] was once sitting by the fire together with his wife. The woman held their child in her lap and when it cried, she put it to her breast and suckled it. She looked up by chance and saw, above the smoke-hole on the roof, something white, which moved like a panting beast. She called for her husband and pointed it out to him. He took his bow and arrow and shot at it, and they saw something white falling down. When dawn came, the woman woke her husband and said, "Why don't you get up to see what you shot last night." He got up and saw a young Snēnē′ik· lying dead outside. His arrow had gone straight through its throat and it was as big as four buffalos.[36] So Iā′lit dug a deep pit, threw the Snēnē′ik· in and covered it over again with dirt. He left only the white throat uncovered. He didn't tell anyone that he had killed the monster. Then one day a group of men went upriver. They saw the old Snēnē′ik· sitting weeping on a large rock near Nutltlē′iq,[37] so they grew afraid and returned to Nuqa′lkʜ. When Iā′lit heard of their adventure, he went upriver with two friends in order to see the Snēnē′ik·. When they saw it on the boulder, the two friends turned back because they were afraid. But Iā′lit went on without fear. When he arrived at the boulder where the Snēnē′ik· was sitting, he pushed his canoe ashore, got up and leaned against the stone. Thereupon the Snēnē′ik· stopped crying and wiped its eyes. Iā′lit said, "My dear, I would like to help you. Tell me, why are you weeping so much?" The Snēnē′ik· replied, "Oh, I have lost my son. I don't know where he has gone and I'm afraid that he is dead." Then the Snēnē′ik· took a copper and gave it to Iā′lit, continuing, "Do you see the chief's house up on the mountain? It belongs to my son." Iā′lit replied, "I don't see anything." So the Snēnē′ik· passed its hands twice over his eyes and he then saw the beautifully-painted house. The Snēnē′ik· gave the house and everything in it to him

---

34. What Boas transcribes as "Snēnē′ik·" is recognized as the sniniq̇. Elsewhere, Boas (1895d:32–33) includes a translation of this story that he recorded in the Nuxalk language from a young Kimsquit woman.

35. Name not now recognized.

36. Given in the original as *Büffel* 'buffalo,' although this animal is not native to the Bella Coola Valley.

37. This name transcribed by Boas as "Nutltlē′iq" is recognized as nux̌'iɬi·x̌ʷ 'dry at the head' and is applied to the area just downstream from Burnt Bridge, at the east end of the Bella Coola Valley. The large rock located here is known locally as "the crying rock," because of the story of the sniniq̇.

and said, "When you get back to Nuqaʹlkʜ build four houses just like this." After the Snēnēʹik· had said this, it got up and wanted to go away. Iāʹlit asked, "Where are you going?" The Snēnēʹik· replied, "I am leaving this land and will go to Naus (near Fort Rupert)."[38] But Iāʹlit returned to Nuqaʹlkʜ. During the following four years he built four houses and carried everything from the house of Snēnēʹik· down to the sea, and he painted his houses just like the house of the Snēnēʹik· up on the mountain had been painted.

6. The Snēnēʹik·

One evening the daughter of a chief was weeping and wouldn't be calmed down, so her mother, a beautiful woman with long hair, said, "Lie down and be quiet or else the Snēnēʹik· will come and get you." At midnight, when everyone was asleep, the Snēnēʹik· appeared in the shape of an old woman. She came to the door and said to the child, "Come, I have dried salmon here for you. Take it and eat." But the child didn't come. So the old woman said, "Come, I have mountain goat fat here. Take it and eat." The child went to a knot-hole in the wall and said, "Hand it through here." The old woman came up and blew into the hole which immediately grew very large. She seized the child and stuffed her into a basket which she carried on her back. So the little one shouted, "Oh, Snēnēʹik· has put me into her basket!" The parents woke up; they lit a huge fire in order to be able to see and then pursued the Snēnēʹik·. But when they came close, she sank into the ground and thus they lost her track. So they returned home saddened. Snēnēʹik· arrived home at last and said to her slave woman, Nusk·ēeqtitlputsāʹaq,[39] "Look, I've found a sister for you." Snēnēʹik· had once stolen her, too, in her basket, just like this girl. The slave woman called her over and said, "When Snēnēʹik· wants to give food to you, don't take any, otherwise you will fare as I did. Look, I ate some of her mountain goat fat and consequently grew fast to the ground." She then showed her how a rope grew from her anus and branched out in the ground just like a root. She continued, "Hide the food beneath your cape and only pretend to eat." When Snēnēʹik· came back, she offered mountain goat fat to the girl, but she followed the slave woman's counsel and only pretended to eat. In reality she hid the fat beneath her cape. In a while the Snēnēʹik· heard a child crying and ran to get it. Before she left she told the girl to stay in the

---

38.   While our Nuxalk consultants said that naws (Boas' "Naus") is the name used both by the Nuxalk and by the Heiltsuk to refer to Knights Inlet, Boas (1898:70) states elsewhere that it "is near Kingcombe Inlet," and McIlwraith (1948:593) describes "Naos" as an "indeterminate locality in the distant east."

39.   The Nuxalk people with whom we consulted stated that the slave's name translates as 'roots from anus into ground.'

house because she wanted to bring her a sister. When the Snēnē′ik· was gone, the old slave woman called the child and said, "Take those eagle claws hanging there; put them on your fingers and wait outside for her to return." The girl did what she was told. She placed herself by the edge of a deep gorge which the Snēnē′ik· had to cross on a fallen tree trunk. When she had arrived at the middle of the trunk, the little girl raised her arms and opened and closed her hands and called out, "Sōk·ā′k·s k·amau (Open and close your eyes)."[40] The Snēnē′ik· called out, "Don't do that or else I will fall!" But the girl kept on moving her fingers until the Snēnē′ik· fell into the gorge. Then the slave woman lowered the girl down with a rope and had her cut off and cook the breasts of the Snēnē′ik·. She said, "When her four sons, the Wolves, get back home from hunting, serve this dish to them and they will die." Soon the young men arrived home. Their walking sticks could be heard hitting the ground from far away. They asked for their mother and Nusk·ēeqtitlputsā′aq replied, "She should come back soon. She went out with her basket to catch slaves. We have cooked for you in the meantime; here is your food." And the girl fetched the pot in which she had cooked the breasts, and served it to the sons. The milk, which had come out of the breasts during boiling, now floated on top. She took a spoonful and served it to the eldest son. He said, "This tastes just like our mother's milk." Then she gave a spoonful to the second. He tasted and said, "You're right, it tastes exactly like our mother's milk." And the two younger ones said the same after they had tasted. But the old slave woman told them to be quiet and eat up. They obeyed; but when they had finished they all fell down dead. When the four children of the Snēnē′ik·—four wolves—were dead, they threw the corpses down to the old one in the gorge. Then the slave woman said, "Give me a mountain goat skin." The girl obeyed and she pulled out her hair and made a thread. Then she filled a basket with meat and fat, tied the thread around the girl and told her to go home. She held on to the rope and said, "Tō′kyimq k·oastā′ (Become long, thread)." So the thread became longer and longer and followed the girl everywhere. At last the child arrived at her parents' house. Her mother was weeping inside. The small girl went to the outside of the house where the bed stood in which her mother slept, and knocked upon the wall. The mother heard the noise and sent out her youngest son to see who was there. When he saw his lost sister, he ran back and told his mother that she had returned. But she didn't believe him and said, "Don't talk nonsense; your sister has been dead for a long time." Since there was more knocking, she sent out her eldest son to look. He came back soon saying, "Yes, our sister is out there. She wants you to purify the house and to break through a door at the back; after that she will come inside." This time the mother believed the news. She purified the house and the girl entered, sat down by the fire and had a meal with her mother and brothers. Then she

---

40. Our Nuxalk consultants confirmed this translation, 'open and close your eyes.'

said to one of them, "Please fetch my box which is outside the door." He obeyed, but was unable to lift the box, although it was very small. All the people went out trying in turn to lift the box, but they were all unable to do it. So the girl went out herself and lifted the box by her little finger. She opened it up and gave presents to everyone. Then she said, "Tomorrow follow the rope to which I was tied into the forest. There you will find an old woman, who has grown fast to the ground. Please try to free her." The people did this. They found the old one and cut through the rope which kept her bound to the ground. Thereupon blood gushed out of it and she died.

According to a different version, the girl led the people to the house of the Snēnē'ik·. But they were afraid to cross the gorge on the tree trunk. Consequently she went into the house by herself and then brought them all the treasures of the Snēnē'ik·. She freed the old woman, who was then sent back to her home.

7. The Snēnē'ik·[41]

It once happened in the village of Stū'iн[42] that corpses were always being stolen from the graves and no one was able to find out who the robber was. There were two friends living in those days, one of whom said to the other, "I want to find out who is stealing the corpses. I will pretend to be dead. Wrap me up in a bear skin and pretend to bury me. Have the girls mourn over my body, then watch by my grave and see what happens." Then he pretended to be dead and let himself be buried. His friend built a fence around the grave and lay in wait. When it grew dark, a Snēnē'ik· came. She broke the fence, opened the grave and threw the supposed corpse into her basket. Thereupon the friend wept. He ran back to the village and shouted, "Snēnē'ik· has got my friend and I was unable to help him."

When the Snēnē'ik· had thrown the man into her basket, he opened his eyes in order to see where she was going. Where fallen trees were blocking her way she crawled through under them. He held fast to the branches and caused her to fall. She broke wind each time she fell. Snēnē'ik· soon thought that the man was possibly not dead at all. She took him from the basket, put him down and laid her hand on his chest. Thereupon he held his breath. When he was almost unable to hold it any longer, she took her hand back and threw him back into the basket in the belief that he was dead. This happened several times. At last the Snēnē'ik· arrived home. She threw the man down by the fire. Her child stepped up to the man, pulled his legs

41. This story also appears in Boas' (1890b) shorthand notes.

42. "Stū'iн," which Boas (1890b) elsewhere transcribes as "Stū'iн," is recognized as stwix, the Nuxalk name of a village site formerly situated far upstream on the Bella Coola River, near its confluence with the Atnarko and Talchako Rivers.

apart and said, pointing to his testicles, "I'll make myself an ear ornament from those." "Be quiet," replied the old Snēnē'ik·, "I'm afraid the man has supernatural powers; he has thrown me down several times." While the old one and her daughter were thus conversing, the man opened his eyes a tiny bit and spied a spear which had been an offering in one of the graves. The old Snēnē'ik· then sharpened her knife to cut the man open. She blew onto his throat as if she were blowing hairs aside and cut from his chin down to his chest. The blood spurted out and the old one cried, "Hoo!" But the man jumped up, grabbed the spear and ran outside. The Snēnē'ik· fell down in terror.

When she came to again, she ran from the house, and pursued the man. When she opened her eyes, fire flashed from them. This so frightened the man that he almost fell down. When the Snēnē'ik· had almost caught up with him, he jumped into the River Slā'ak·tl[43] and continued to swim for a stretch under water. The Snēnē'ik· was unable to swim and thus he gained on her. When the man grew tired he went ashore and ran on. Thereupon the Snēnē'ik· pursued him again and fire flashed from her eyes. When she had almost caught up with him, the man jumped into the water again. In this fashion he escaped her and arrived safely in Stū'iH and the Snēnē'ik· returned to her home.

The inhabitants of Stū'iH were assembled in the house of the remaining friend, and mourned the one who had disappeared. So the latter flung the spear into the house and called his friend by name. He jumped up and brought him inside, where he told of his adventures. He showed the spear to them and told them that many burial offerings were at the house of the Snēnē'ik·. So they called together all the men from the neighbouring villages and set out upriver to fight the Snēnē'ik·. But the skin of the Snēnē'ik· was as hard as stone and she was vulnerable only under her chin. Consequently the fight with her was a difficult undertaking. The men took along old fur capes and other discarded things, as well as inner cedar bark which had been used by women during their period and was saturated with blood.

When the Snēnē'ik· noticed that humans were coming to fight her, she retreated into her house. When the people had come close to the house, she merely looked out of the door and fire flashed from her eyes, and the people who saw this fell down unconscious. Then they heaped up all the old clothes in front of the door and burned them. They also threw burning rags onto the roof. The Snēnē'ik· tried to extinguish the fire, but was unable to do so. Then the men pushed the burning clothes into the door with long poles and the poisonous fumes finally suffocated her. When they noticed that she was dead, they extinguished the fire and entered the house. They

---

43. The storyteller is referring to the Atnarko village, known to the Nuxalk as sla·x̣ł (Boas' "Slā'ak·tl"), situated on the south side of the river at Stillwater in the upper Bella Coola Valley.

kicked the Snēnē′ik· and saw that she was quite dead. Thereupon they skinned her and the man who had been abducted by her took the skin for himself. They all took the grave goods of their dead and carried them back home.

8. NūnusōmikHēek·onE′m (= Sucking out Brains)[44]

Once upon a time there were five brothers. The older four went out every day to hunt for seals and left the youngest at home by himself. One morning he heard someone calling from the opposite side of the river. He went outside and saw an old woman who asked him to bring her across. The boy took his pole, jumped into the canoe, pushed it across the river and brought the old one across. Soon the people woke up and when they noticed the old woman in the house of the brothers, they asked where she had come from. The boy told them that he had brought her from the other side of the river early in the morning, in a canoe. When it grew dark and the people went to sleep, the old woman remained sitting quietly by the fire. Soon the people were asleep. Then her mouth began to grow and she stuck it into the ear of one of the sleepers, whose brains she sucked out. She was NūnusōmikHēek·onE′m, who sucked out people's brains. In this way she killed all the residents of one house, then those of another. The following morning the boy who had brought her woke up and was surprised that nobody was up yet. The old woman was still sitting quietly by the fire. He asked her, "Why aren't the people getting up?" He went out and found them all dead; only he was left alive. When the old woman heard what had happened, she said, "A great misfortune has happened," but remained sitting quietly by the fire.

The following morning the four hunters returned. Their canoe was deeply laden. The boy went down to the beach and told his brothers what had occurred. So they went into the house where the old one was sitting. They asked her what had happened but she only replied, "A great misfortune has happened." Then the brother told them in answer to their questions how he had found the old woman and had brought her into the house.

When night came, the old one said, "Go to sleep now; I'll watch that no harm will come to you." The brothers built a big fire and lay down to sleep. But the eldest had a supernatural helper and only pretended to be sleeping. Then the old woman made the fire small and extended her mouth in order to suck out the brains of the sleeping men. The eldest observed her and, when her mouth had nearly reached the ear of one of the brothers, he called them. They woke up and the old woman retracted her mouth. He called, "Now I know that the old woman has killed our fellow

---

44. Boas (1898:30) notes that this legend was collected in 1890; the original shorthand version of this text appears on pages 73–75 of Boas' (1890b) notebooks.

countrymen," then told what he had seen. But the old one said, "What do you want from me? I'm only an old, poor woman." But they took an axe, killed her and cut up the corpse into pieces. The eldest said, "Let us move away." They took the boards off their house, hacked them into pieces and set them on fire. Then they moved away and abandoned the boy who had brought the old woman into the village.

But the old woman was not dead and her body arose again, rejuvenated, and she pursued the brothers. When they saw her approach, they stopped. The eldest said, "Even though you have risen again, still I will kill you." They killed her again, cut her up and threw the pieces into the fire. Then they continued on their way because they were afraid that the old woman might rise again. While fleeing thus, they met Duck, who asked them why they were running away. So they told what had occurred. They enquired where they might find the house of Atlk'undā'm[45] and Duck showed them the way.

At last they came to the water. Because they were unable to cross and could hear the old woman approaching, they climbed up on a tree close by the shore. The old one arrived soon. She also was unable to cross the water and stopped underneath the tree. Then one of the men moved and she saw his reflection in the water. She believed that he was down below and jumped into the water in order to catch him. When she got ashore again, the second man laughed and moved a little bit. Thereupon she jumped into the water again. When she came out again, the third laughed and moved. The old one jumped into the water once again. So the eldest one said, "When she jumps into the water in order to catch me, I'll make the water freeze." He moved and the old one jumped into the water. Thereupon he waved his fur cape and the water froze immediately. Only the face of the old woman looked out from the ice and she begged, "Please set me free." But they continued their flight.

At last they arrived at the house of Atlk'undā'm. In front of it there sat an eagle, which was the totem pole[46] of the house. They asked to be let in and Atlk'undā'm said, "Be careful, don't all come in at once. Each time when the eagle opens his beak one of you must spring through quickly." They did what he told them to do. Then they told him what had occurred and asked for his help. Atlk'undā'm replied,

---

45. What Boas transcribes as "Atlk'undā'm" is aɬkʷntam, the name applied to the Supreme Deity who at the beginning of time created humankind in his house in the upper world and sent them down to populate the Nuxalk lands. The house belonging to aɬkʷntam, called the house of nusmata 'the place of myths,' is described by (McIlwraith 1948:I:35) as follows: "[It] contains a large number of rooms, in each of which a different set of Indians, with a different language, was manufactured; thus is explained the diversity of tongues among the people of British Columbia."

46. At this point in his original shorthand notes, Boas (1890b) provides the Nuxalk term "asḳai'atl" which McIlwraith (1948:580) transcribes as "äskaiätɬ" and translates as 'totem-pole, literally 'outside post.'

"The old one surely is my mother. She pursues the people constantly. She is certain to come here." He had hardly finished speaking when the old one was already knocking at the house outside. He opened and asked her, "What have you done? Have you killed people again? Do you think it would be nice if there were no more people?" Then he seized her, killed her and threw her into the fire. When she had been completely burned up he took her ashes, crumbled them and blew them up into the air, saying, "Become mosquitoes!" This is how mosquitoes came to be; they still put out their stingers today to suck blood as the old woman used to do.

Then the brothers wanted to gamble with Atlk'undā′m. They sat down outside the house and the three younger brothers played lahal[47] with him. In the meantime the eldest seduced his wife. Because of this, Atlk'undā′m had bad luck and lost his stake, the salmon. If this had not happened, mankind would not have any salmon.

And the woman gave some of her urine to the eldest of the brothers, saying, "You'll be able to resuscitate the dead if you drip some of my urine into their ears and noses."

Then the brothers returned home. They thought that they had been with Atlk'undā′m only for one day, but in reality it had been a whole year. When they arrived home they found their brother still alive. Then they resuscitated all their relatives. They didn't want to resuscitate the other people to begin with, but they did so in the end. Thereupon they were given rich gifts by all of them and became great chiefs.

9. Tl'ipā′atstitlā′na[48]

Once upon a time there was a man who was discontented with his wife and chased her away in order to take a new one. At this his sons grew very sad and ran away into the forest, never to return again. The eldest brother had taken along his bow and arrows and shot many tiny birds. He gave these to his brother and said, "You had better turn back home. I want to go far, far away and you wouldn't be able to walk as far. Take the birds and turn back." But the little one refused to leave his brother

---

47. A gambling game played between two sides in which the players guess in which hand their opponent holds a bone game-piece. Although this game is known commonly by the Chinook Jargon name "lahal," it is known to Nuxalk-speaking people as aɫiputnm.

48. McIlwraith (1948:II:624) describes this character as "one of the nine supernatural siblings, a woman who brings aid to those in sickness and is thus the initiator of shamans." Elsewhere, Boas (1892a:413) provides the transcription "Tl'ētsā′aplētlāna" (for the same woman's name he transcribes here in the *Sagen* as "Tl'ipā′atstitlā′na"), translates her name as 'the eater,' and notes that she "figures in several legends as stealing provisions and pursued by the people whom she has robbed."

and finally he agreed to take him along. They went far, far upriver. At last they saw a salmon weir and so the elder brother said to the younger one, "People must live here." The little one looked all around but couldn't find anybody and said to his brother, "No, there is nobody here. Someone passing by must have built the salmon weir. Let's stay here and build a house." When the house was finished the older brother went down to the salmon weir daily, while the younger one stayed up above and dried the fish. Now when the elder brother was down by the river, the little one suddenly heard a strange clacking up on the mountain. He looked up and saw a woman descending, whose hair and red cape were sprinkled with eagle down. She wore dancing bells on her feet and was constantly clacking with her mouth. Since she made straight for the house, the boy grew afraid and hid. He saw then how she opened the door, halted at the threshold and how her mouth suddenly grew gigantically long and how she devoured all the salmon on the drying racks. Then she went away again. When the older brother came up again, he was surprised that the little one had eaten so much, but he didn't say anything about it and his brother did-n't mention the woman's visit either. They shared a salmon which the elder one had brought and then lay down to sleep. On the following day the woman came back again and devoured all the salmon while the brother had gone down to the river. When he found all the salmon gone in the evening, he asked his brother, "Why do you eat so much?" He replied, "I haven't eaten a thing. Every day a woman comes here, stands by the door and then stretches her mouth out as far as the fire and devours all the salmon." Because the woman had returned again on the third day, the elder brother made up his mind to lie in wait for her. He went down to the river again in the morning, but returned at once without being noticed, took his bow and arrow, and hid in the house. It wasn't long and the woman arrived and began to devour the salmon. She wasn't through half of them when the young man shot her in her gigantic breast. She cried in pain and fled. The elder brother said to the little one, "I will pursue her. You stay here and use the fish sparingly so that they'll last until my return." Then he went away. The woman had lost down feathers on her path and blood marked her track which led from the earth up into the sky.

After the young man had walked for a while he passed by the house of Masmasalā'niq, who was wearing a big hat. He asked him, "Haven't you seen a sick woman pass here?" He replied, "Yes, I saw her. She is Tl'ipā'atstitlā'na, the daughter of Atlk'undā'm, and she seemed to be barely alive." The young man followed the track further and it led him right up into the sky. Finally he reached a small lake from which a river flowed and saw the house of Atlk'undā'm close by the shore. So he scattered eagle-down over his head, wrapped himself up in his cape and sat down by the lakeshore. He was a great sorcerer and had caused the arrow, with which he had hit Tl'ipā′atstitlā′na, to be invisible to everyone. He made the eagle-down on his head appear to envelop his head in smoke.

He hadn't sat there for long when the two daughters of Tl'ipā′atstitlā′na came from the house to fetch water. When they saw a man who was enveloped in a cloud of smoke sitting at the shore, they knew immediately that he must be a medicine man and so they ran back into the house to tell that he was sitting outside. The husband of Tl'ipā′atstitlā′na had already called all the medicine men to make his wife better, but not one had been able to do it. He had made his servant, Atlqulā′tenum,[49] stand by the door and call in the medicine men, one after the other. The Snēnē′ik·, Thunderbird, Crane,[50] Grizzly Bear and Black Bear had come, but not one of them was able to heal her.

So he sent for the stranger outside and promised him one of the four daughters of the sick woman for a wife, if he made her better. The people were sitting around the sick woman, but were unable to see the arrow. They chanted and employed drums and whistles, but she didn't get better. Then the young man said, "Give me a cedar cone." When he had got it, he broke it up and placed the scales singly in front of the drums which were standing to one side of the fire. When he then walked around the fire and sang, they began to drum. The woman was sitting at the opposite side of the fire. He now said, "Place mats over me and the sick woman." The people obeyed and he then pulled the arrow unseen from her breast, broke it up into many fragments so that he was able to hide it in his hand, and went outside. There he threw the arrow into the water and washed himself. The woman had become well again.

Now the people asked him which one of the four girls he was going to take. But they had already agreed amongst themselves that he should take the youngest one, who was a great sorceress. Because she was very pretty he actually chose her. Then they went down to earth together. When they reached the spot where the young man had left his brother, they found him dead and his body decomposed. Only the skeleton lay there, but it had one thigh bone missing, which had been carried away by the birds. It had seemed to the young man as if he had been in the sky for only one day, but in reality he had stayed there for one year. Then the woman took some Water of Life which she had brought with her from the sky and trickled some of it into her brother-in-law's nose, ear and mouth and washed his body with it.

---

49. "Atlqulā′tenum is represented by a red and green striped mask in the winter dance. The stripes run diagonally across the whole face from the upper left to the lower right; the dancer carries a similarly striped staff. His position is by the door and he is the herald of the dancers, as it were" [Boas' original footnote]. Contemporary Nuxalk people translate this name as 'come and sing.'

50. Given as *Kranich* 'crane' in the original, but in this context it is likely the Great Blue Heron (*Ardea herodias*), x̣aq̓ans, that is referred to; it is also possible, however, that the species in question may the Sandhill Crane (*Grus canadensis*), which is also found in this area.

Thereupon he rose as if he had merely slept. But from then on he limped because he lacked one bone.

The three of them then journeyed downriver until they reached the village of their father. A bit above it they met many people who were busy getting firewood. So the younger brother sent them back to the father to let him know that his sons had returned. And he had them tell him to purify his house, otherwise the young wife of his son would not come in. The people obeyed and the father had his house purified. Then he sent out two men to invite his sons to come.

But they sent him the following message, "First send away your new wife and take back our mother, then we will come." When their father had done what they requested, they entered the house.

In the course of time the wife of the elder brother gave birth to a child. She had impressed upon her husband not to laugh when he saw his former lover. One day she asked her husband to go down to the river to fetch some water. He did as she had asked. Down there he met his former lover and laughed because he was glad to see her again. When he took the container of water to his wife, the water had become blood-red, and by this she recognized that he had laughed when he had seen his lover. She went away and nobody knew where she had vanished.

10. The Origin of the Stars

A long time ago there lived a woman called Pakuā'na[51] who had a son called Stsk·ā'ak·a[52] (both are birds). They had a great store of dried salmon and when winter came the woman said to her son, "Place the salmon in the river and soak them." The boy obeyed. He took the fish to the river in the evening and covered them with heavy stones. When he went to the water in the morning to take them back, they had vanished. So he ran to his mother and cried, "Oh, mother, someone has stolen our salmon; I don't know who the thief might be." In the evening he again put dried salmon into the water and again they were stolen, even though he had covered them up with more stones this time. When the same thing happened the third night, he lay in wait to catch the thief. He hadn't been long in his hiding place when he saw Grizzly Bear come and pull out the fish from underneath the stones. So he jumped out and cried, "Tsk, Tsk! Why do you steal my

---

51. The term that Boas transcribes here as "Pakuā'na" and identifies as some type of bird was known to our Nuxalk consultants only as pakʷana, a word which they believed means 'big' in Heiltsuk, and which was applied to a Nuxalk village site in Kwatna Inlet and to the high mountain immediately to the northeast of the inlet (Kennedy and Bouchard 1990a:324–325).

52. Boas' "Stsk·ā'ak·" is scqa·xqa, the Nuxalk term for the bird known as the Winter Wren (*Troglodytes troglodytes*).

fish?" Bear replied, "Be quiet; I am big and you are small. I can swallow you up." With this he slurped up the little one through his nose, but Stsk·ā′ak·a flew straight through him and called mockingly, "Tsk, tsk! Here I am; your nose and your anus are just too big!" Bear swallowed him three times and each time he came out again at the back. Then Bear took two stoppers, swallowed the little one and stopped up his nose and anus so that he had him caught. So Stsk·ā′ak·a took his firedrill and lit a fire in Bear's stomach. When it was blazing high, he pushed out the plug from the anus and flew away. Bear roared, "The fire is burning me, extinguish it!" But Stsk·ā′ak·a retorted, "No, you'll have to die, because four times you wanted to devour me." Bear fell onto his back, lashed out with his paws a few times and then his belly burst open and he was dead. Many sparks flew out and were transformed into stars.

Then Stsk·ā′ak·a flew to his mother and said, "Soon Bear's friends will come to avenge his death." So Pakuā′na began to chant magic spells while beating time on a boulder on which they were sitting. The stone began to grow; it became bigger and bigger and at last turned into a gigantic mountain. They lit a fire on its summit and heated stones red-hot. Then when the forest animals stormed the mountain to avenge Bear's death, they rolled the red-hot stones down and killed their enemies. The stones nearly killed Grizzly Bear, Black Bear, the Snēnē′ik· and Wolf.

11. K·asā′na[53]

Once upon a time there was a man called K·asā′na who consisted only of half a body. He had only one leg, one arm, half a trunk, and half a head. He had his house in Kiltē′itl[54] and he killed many mountain goats. He carved himself a wife from gnarled wood and made a hat for her and called her K·ulE′ms. He fashioned her in a squatting position and placed her arms as if she were weaving a blanket. Then he placed her in front of a loom and put a blanket in her hands. He wanted to deceive

53. Our Nuxalk consultants knew this story of the 'half-of-a-man' named q̓asana (Boas' "K·asā′na") and associated it with a group of people of mixed Nuxalk and Heiltsuk ancestry who formerly lived in Dean Channel and were known as istamx in the Nuxalk language (as discussed in the initial footnote to Section XXI of the present volume, these same people, called ʔísdáitx̌ʷ in the Heiltsuk language, are considered one of the four principal tribal groups comprising the Heiltsuk). A version of this story recorded by Olson (1955:322) from Moses Knight, a Heiltsuk man, stated that "Ka′sana," whose name translates as 'half-man,' lived at the head of Cascade Inlet which is a northwesterly arm of Dean Channel (see also the footnote that follows, as well as story 21 of this section).

54. Boas' "Kiltē′itl" is kilti·ł, meaning 'bait,' the place name used by the Nuxalk to refer to Cascade Inlet, a long narrow inlet extending in a northwesterly direction off Dean Channel, in the territory of the istamx (see the footnote above).

the people and make them believe that he had a wife. In K·inā′at[55] near Tsainahat,[56] not far from Tᴏ̄ōnik· (Bella Bella)[57] there lived a chief in those days who had two daughters. He sent them over the mountain to Kiltē′itl and said to them, "K·asā′na has no wife; he will marry you." They obeyed and arrived at the house of K·asā′na when he just happened to be out hunting. So they peeped into the house through a knot-hole in order to see whether anyone was there. To their astonishment they saw a woman sitting by the loom. Since she didn't stir at all, they became even more astonished. They entered the house, the younger sister hiding timidly behind the older one. When they saw now that the woman did not pay any attention to them at all, they nudged her, and, when she paid no attention to this either, they grabbed her by the chin. Then they found out that she had been made from wood. They pulled off her hat and pushed her over. Then they hid. When K·asā′na came home and found the woman toppled over, he became angry and beat her, shouting, "If you're unable to remain sitting, I have no use for you." At this one of the girls had to laugh. K·asā′na found them and took both of them for wives. After some time both of them had children and so they wanted to return home. K·asā′na agreed to go with them and they all embarked in the canoe, went to K·inā′at, and the children played flutes in the canoe.

12. Wa′walis[58]

Once there was a man called Wa′walis. He ordered his slave one day to fetch firewood. But the slave replied, "No, I'm unable to get anything; I'm too tired." Wa′walis grew furious at this and beat him with a big piece of firewood. The slave cried in pain and called out, "Don't beat me so; you should beat your wife's lover instead." So Wa′walis stopped and said, "Stop crying! What's that you said there about my wife's lover?" So the slave replied, "The young man living in that house there is the lover of your wife." Wa′walis threatened to beat him if he didn't tell the truth, but the slave vouched for the truthfulness of his statements.

---

55. A Haihais village, known in the Heiltsuk language as qínát (Boas' "K·inā′at"), was situated at the head of Kynoch Inlet (Hilton 1990:313).

56. This name, anglicized as "China Hat," is used by the Nuxalk to refer to a place near Klemtu, located on Swindle Island in Haihais territory.

57. The Nuxalk refer to the Heiltsuk people by the term txʷunikʷ (Boas' "Tᴏ̄ōnik·") meaning 'outside,' or txʷunikʷmx, 'outside people.'

58. Contemporary Nuxalk people identify this as an istamx story (see footnote 53 of the present section). Boas (1895d:31, 33–39) provides a Nuxalk transcription and interlinear translation of a variant of this story, which he says was told by a young woman of the village situated at the mouth of the Kimsquit River on Dean Channel.

So Wa'walis decided to find out for himself whether his wife was unfaithful. He told her, "I'll go across the inlet today with the slave to hunt and to cut firewood. I'll be away for a few days." Then he went off with his slave. They collected some firewood and hunted seals, which they brought ashore and cooked, but when it grew dark, Wa'walis returned unnoticed to his house to see what his wife was doing. He ordered the slave to wait in the canoe and to be prepared to take off again immediately on his return. Wa'walis waved his dancing staff[59] in the direction of the village and all the people fell asleep. Then he went up to the house and scratched outside on the wall where his bed was situated. And he heard his wife say to her lover, "If only the mouse scratching there would devour the stomach of Wa'walis." This made Wa'walis angry for he now knew that the slave had spoken the truth, and he moved his staff in the direction of the house. The woman fell asleep at once and he entered, opened the bedroom door, and saw his wife in the arms of her lover. Wa'walis took his knife and cut off his head. The woman did not awaken but lay peacefully in the dead man's arms. Wa'walis carried the head down to the canoe and took off again.

Not long after he had left the house, his child, who was sleeping beside its mother, began to cry. The woman's mother, who was living with them in the house, heard the child and called to the young woman, "Hey, your child is crying." So she felt the blood of her lover and said, still half asleep, "Oh, the child has wet my bed." She nudged her lover and said, "Get up," but he didn't seem to hear her and lay still. The child kept on weeping and the woman's mother called to her again, "Look after your child, will you?" When she got up then, she saw her that her lover had been beheaded, so she took several bear skins, wrapped the corpse up in them and carried it from the house. She put it down in front of the door of his parents.

In the morning the young man's mother was astonished that he didn't get up. She had made breakfast and only the one man was missing, so she said to her youngest son, "Please go and see what your brother is doing. He should come for his meal." The little one went to look for him and found him in front of the door covered by the bear skins. He nudged him and said, "Mother says that you will have to get up and come for your meal." The sleeping man didn't budge. The boy went back into the house and told his mother that his older brother was asleep outside and didn't want to get up. The mother said, "Then pull away his blanket and he might get up." The boy went out and did what he had been told and he saw that his brother had been beheaded. He cried out in terror and shouted, "Oh, our brother doesn't have a head any more!" The mother didn't want to believe it, but convinced herself soon enough that her son was dead. She cried bitterly and all the people cried with her.

---

59.   Boas (1895d:34) elsewhere translates the original Nuxalk term as 'baton.'

About this time Wa'walis returned from his hunt. He had put the boiled seal meat into a basket which stood in the middle of the canoe. But he had placed the severed head right at the bottom. When he approached the shore, a man called to him, "Don't lift up your paddles, your relative is dead; someone has cut off his head." But Wa'walis paid no heed at all. He disembarked and carried the basket up to his wife and told her to prepare the seal and to invite all the people. He said, "I wonder whether you are going to like everything in that basket." The woman took out the meat and said with each piece she picked up, "I like this." "Just wait until you get to the bottom," replied Wa'walis. At last the woman saw the head. Wa'walis had spread its eyes open and placed it face up. She screamed in terror.

But Wa'walis seized the head by the hair and beat his wife about the face and genitals with it. Then he took his child in his arms and ran quickly down to the canoe. He shouted to his slave, "Now paddle with all your might; the people know now that I've killed the young man and they are sure to pursue us." They paddled as quickly as possible and the boy was sitting quietly in the middle of the canoe. When Wa'walis noticed that his pursuers were gaining on him, he made a big mountain behind himself, through which they were unable to follow. Then they continued at a slower pace and soon arrived in a village. Wa'walis was very surprised to see a little smoke come from only one of the houses, and he told his slave to watch the boy while he went up to look about.

He went into all the houses, but couldn't find anyone. At last he also went into the house from which the smoke came. There he found an old blind man and a girl, his daughter. The old man was cooking deer meat and the girl was busy in the back of the house plaiting a mat. Consequently she didn't notice the stranger entering. Wa'walis went up to the old man who was taking the deer meat from the cooking box and putting it into a bowl, and he took each single piece away from him as soon as it was in the bowl. So the old man said, "There must be somebody here who is taking away my meat." The daughter replied, "Where should anyone come from at this time?" But when she looked around she saw Wa'walis. The latter asked the old man, "Where are all the other people who have been living here?" He replied, "Oh, Sk'amtskʜ[60] came and devoured them when they were fetching water." Wa'walis enquired further, "Will you give me your daughter for a wife?" The other replied, "If you are able to give me back my sight, you shall have her." So Wa'walis spat into one of his eyes and he was able to see at once. The old man was very pleased and gave him his daughter for a wife, so Wa'walis spat also into his other eye and the old man who was now able to see again fully. Then Wa'walis brought up his child

---

60. The Nuxalk term sk̓amck (Boas' "Sk'amtskʜ") is applied to a supernatural creature (described as a "bad water monster") found living in the water; Boas (1916:1026) refers to it as a "water monster."

and his slave and they all ate the deer meat together. When they had finished, the child became very thirsty, and so Wa'walis sent down his slave to fetch water. He took his container, went to the mouth of the creek and Wa'walis followed him in order to see whether Sk'amtskʜ would get him. And Sk'amtskʜ came indeed, seized the slave and devoured him.

Wa'walis knew the monster now. He went down to the water and when it rushed at him to devour him, he only moved his staff in the direction of the animal and it lay there dead. Then he called his wife and made her cut the animal open. After that they pulled out all the dead from its belly. Wa'walis touched them with his staff and they became alive again. They stood up and rubbed their eyes as if they had been sleeping. Most of them had been swallowed in one gulp; these became completely healthy again. But others had their arms or legs bitten off; these remained cripples from then on. Then Wa'walis invited all of them into his house and gave them a feast. He went out in his canoe, caught seals and mountain goats and gave what he had caught to his new friends. Thus be became a great chief and built four houses. He always caught many seals and made his wife go down to the sea to wash out the intestines. She was no longer afraid to go down to the water, because Sk'amtskʜ was dead. One day she carried down a large bowl of intestines and began washing them. She saw a killer whale[61] swim up from afar, but carried on with her work undisturbed. But Whale came up, seized her and swam away with her. Thereupon the people called to Wa'walis, "Whale has stolen your wife!"

Wa'walis grabbed his paddle and went down to the beach with his slave. They launched their canoe and pursued Whale. When it dived and disappeared in the water with the woman, Wa'walis took a rope of cedar branches, held onto one end of it with his teeth and then had himself lowered to the bottom of the sea by the slave. He found a flat country down below and a different sun was shining there. He saw a path and followed it. Soon he met an old man with a big belly, whose name was Iʜēʹik·t (a species of fish).[62] He was busy splitting a tree with wedge and Wa'walis hid behind the tree and broke off the tip of the wedge. When the old man noticed that his wedge had been broken, he became angry and took another wedge. Wa'walis broke this one, too, and the old man started to cry. Then Wa'walis went up to the old man and asked him why he was weeping. He replied, "My master will

---

61. Given in the original as *Finwal*, an artificially-created term comprised of English "fin" and German *Wal* 'any whale,' and used by Boas to indicate an orca or killer whale (*Delphinus orca*); the Nuxalk term for 'killer whale' is syut. Elsewhere, Boas (1916:1026) also refers to this animal as a "killer whale."

62. Boas' "Iʜēʹik·t" is the Nuxalk term ʔixi·xʷ, referring to the 'red snapper' (*Sebastes ruberrimus*), also known as the "red cod," which is the English translation given elsewhere by Boas (1890b) for what he transcribes as "íḵīeq" (i.e. ʔixix·ʷ).

beat me because I have broken both his wedges here." So Wa′walis consoled him and promised to make the wedges new again. When he gave them to him newly sharpened, the old man was glad. Then Wa′walis enquired, "Have you seen a man carrying a woman past here?" He replied, "Yes, that was my master, Whale. He lives in the house to which I now have to carry this wood." So Wa′walis told him that the woman was his wife and that he had come to get her back again. The old man promised him his help and said, "I will now carry the wood into the house and light a big fire. Wait for me out here until tonight, when I will get water and pretend to stumble and extinguish the fire. Then everything will be filled with steam and smoke; you'll be able to get your wife unnoticed and carry her off." Everything happened as he planned; when the fire was extinguished, Wa′walis ran into the house, got his wife and ran back to the rope by which the slave had lowered him down. He shook it as a signal for the slave to pull him up, but since he didn't react, he climbed up to the surface with his wife. How surprised he was to find only the bleached bones of the slave in the canoe. Raven had carried away one of his knee-caps. Wa′walis had believed that he had been down in the sea for one day, but in reality it had been one year. Then Wa′walis resuscitated the slave, but he limped from then on because he lacked one knee-cap. Then the three of them returned safely to their village.

13. Astas[63]

There once was a man called Astas, who was always playing lahal,[64] and in the end lost everything he had, even his wife and his child. So he became very angry and went away and after a long journey he came to the house of the spirit of the mountain, Tō′alatl'itl,[65] who went out hunting mountain goats regularly. When he had killed a couple, he threw them across his shoulders and went home. There his wife dried and cooked them. Then he went to sleep and the following morning he would go out hunting again.

---

63. Elsewhere, Boas (1898:47) notes that "Astas" is the term used by the Carrier people to refer to Raven, their principal culture hero.

64. Given as "Lehal" (without quotation marks) in the original *Sagen*—as previously noted (see story 8 of the present section), this is the well-known Indian gambling game called "lahal" in Chinook Jargon.

65. Contemporary Nuxalk people explain that this is the spirit of the mountain goat who looks after both goats and hunters, but sometimes plays tricks on the latter. When this spirit appears before a hunter, it is always seen wearing a hat with a snake crawling around the lower brim. Boas (1898:45) adds that great hunters see this mountain spirit's hat, moccasins or mountain staff moving about.

One day, during his absence, Astas arrived at his house. He went to the woman and played with her, and she said, "I thank you; many strangers have been here, but not one of them has done me such good as you have. Therefore I will warn you. When my husband comes home he will tell you to fetch wood. Be very careful then, otherwise you'll fall off the mountain and lose your life." In a little while Tō′alatl'itl came home and sent Astas out to fetch wood. And he actually fell as foretold by the woman. But she had given him an amulet of bird feathers; this protected him. When Astas returned home unharmed, Tō′alatl'itl said, "Go up the mountain tomorrow. There are many mountain goats there and we will shoot them." They went out together the following morning, and when they saw several goats, Tō′alatl'itl called out, "Shoot them!" But Astas, who was a shaman, and knew that he wanted to kill him, replied, "No, I'll shoot goats later on." When Astas was on the mountain, Tō′alatl'itl sent the sisiutl, a giant serpent,[66] after him. It caused the rocks to slide into the valley where Astas was standing, but he was saved by his amulet. He floated down across the slide like a feather, stood up unharmed, and went home. He resolved to take revenge, and gave a magic substance to the woman, which warmed her internally. Then he sat down, fanned a bit with his cape, and an icy north wind sprang up which killed Tō′alatl'itl as well as the sisiutl. Then Astas took the woman and went away with her.

After some time he decided to go to Yula′timōt.[67] His wife said, "Do you know how to find him? When you get to his village you will see many people and they all wear beautiful clothes. Only one of them has a colourful cape which is red, black and white. That is Yula′timōt; walk straight towards him." Astas set out and wandered for a whole month, farther and farther. Then he reached a beautiful village. A man saw him arrive and called to his friends that a stranger was coming. So they all sprang up and ran outside to see him. Astas walked straight up to Yula′timōt, whom he recognized by his colourful cape. Yula′timōt invited him into his house and told him that he had just recently come down from the country in the sky because he hadn't liked the landscape there. He invited Astas to stay with him, led him into the house, and asked him, "What would you like to eat? Would you like to have salmon?" When Astas asked for some, Yula′timōt hid a small one in his hand and gambled for it with his guest. Astas soon guessed in which hand the salmon was concealed. Then Yula′timōt threw it into a bowl and the salmon became alive. In this

---

66. Boas' "sisiutl" is recognized as the Nuxalk term sisyuɫ, described by McIlwraith (1948:II:612) as a "supernatural creature somewhat resembling a double-headed salmon." Boas (1898:66) points out that it "has only one head; while among the Kwakiutl it is represented as having one head at each end, and one in the middle. The Bella Coola say that when first seen it is very small, but becomes larger and larger when being looked at."

67. The eldest of the supernatural carpenters whose Nuxalk name translates as 'fix by rubbing over.'

manner, Astas received many different kinds of salmon. Then Yula'timōt took a small stick and beat the salmon's face with it and it fell down dead at once. Then he cut it up into very small pieces, threw them into a big cooking box and cooked them. When the fish was done he distributed it among all those present and the tiny bits which he placed in the several bowls grew bigger and filled them right up. Then Yula'timōt took a beaver, showed it to Astas and asked him whether there were beavers in his homeland. Astas said no, and so Yula'timōt gave the beaver to him. He said, "When you come to a plain with a lake in it, throw the beaver into the water. Then if it dives four times, it will give birth to young ones there. Don't take those, but recapture only the old beaver and when you come to the next lake throw it into the water again." Then they continued gambling, hiding many different things and guessing in which hand they were hidden.[68] Astas was winning all the time and finally Yula'timōt lost even his blanket. After that he had nothing else to lose and sent Astas back to earth. When he arrived at a lake, he threw in the beaver, which dived four times and gave birth to young ones. Then Astas recaptured the beaver and journeyed on. He threw the beaver into each of the lakes that he passed, and it always dived four times. Therefore, nowadays there are beavers everywhere. At last he arrived at his wife's house; she had plenty of mountain goat fat and meat. Astas decided to return to his home after some time, and the woman put fat and meat into a small bag, which she gave him on his way.

After a long journey Astas arrived home. But he didn't go to the village immediately. Instead, he wrapped himself up in the cape which he had won from Yula'timōt and sat down by the pond where the girls were getting water. Soon the chief's daughter came down the path. She was surprised to see the stranger sitting immobile on the shore. She didn't recognize Astas, who had been away for a long time and who now was wearing the cape of Yula'timōt. She went back to the house and said to her sister, whose bed stood close to her own, "A stranger is sitting outside by the water." The sister didn't believe her and laughed, so the girl said, "Don't laugh! I have really seen him; why don't you go out and look for yourself?" The sister went out, but didn't see anyone because Astas had hidden. When the younger sister went out again, Astas reappeared from his hiding place. Then the sisters told their father what had occurred and he also went to the water to see the stranger. But Astas let himself be seen only by the girl. One morning she went out early and met him by the water. Then he said, "I know that your father is a great chief. Make him purify his house and invite all the people and I will come. I would like to have you for my wife, if you and your father are agreeable. I will give you great riches." The girl went back home and recounted what the stranger had said. So her father had the house purified and invited the whole tribe. Then Astas came. No

---

68. They are playing the lahal or bone game.

one recognized him. He opened his bag and took out plenty of mountain goat fat and meat, and had it distributed among the assembly. He didn't take any of it himself but asked for a bit of fish. At last, at the end of the feast, he made himself known to the people. The chief allowed him to sit down beside his daughter. Astas said to her, "Tonight, when it is dark, I will make the house beautiful." He had the chief take down the roof boards and, when it was dark and everyone was asleep, he opened his bag and took out a high, beautiful roof, that he placed onto the house. In the meantime Yula′timōt ornamented the house and carved the posts. Then when it became daylight and the people saw the house, they were very surprised. Then the chief invited all the tribes to a great feast and they came. During the feast Astas took all sorts of salmon from his bag, which was inexhaustible, and gave them to his father-in-law, who distributed them among the guests. Then Astas took two small salmon from the cape which he had won from Yula′timōt, and threw them into the river. They multiplied at once and since that time the river has been full of salmon. He built big houses and gave them to the chief and gave away everything which had been in his cape and bag. Yula′timōt grew angry at this and sent down Eagle to take everything back from Astas. Eagle obeyed and brought back the magic cape of Yula′timōt. (Told by Yākōtla′s[69] from Nuqa′lkʜ.)

14. The Visit in the Sky[70]

A young man[71] went out once in springtime down to the river in order to shoot birds. He built himself a small house[72] and shot the birds from there when they settled on the shore. He had a bow and an arrow to which a long rope made of women's hair[73] had been fixed. He shot the birds with this. But instead of taking them home, he skinned them and hid the skins close to his house. His father scolded him because he brought no birds home with him. The young man did this for four days, then he invited his younger brother to come along with him. He saw numerous tracks of birds on the shore and the young man then showed him the bird skins.

---

69. This is the Nuxalk name by which Tom Henry was known—he was the leader of the group of Natives from Bella Coola who Boas met in Berlin in the Fall of 1885, a year before he arrived on the Northwest Coast.

70. A shorthand version of this text can be found elsewhere in Boas (1890b), and a Nuxalk variant with interlinear translation can be found in Boas (1895d:47–48) where the story is called "The Ascent to Heaven."

71. Later in this same story (see paragraph 3 that follows), the young man is identified as "Mōk·oa′nts," a name transcribed elsewhere by Boas (1895d:47–48) as "Smōq′oā′ns."

72. Boas (1895d:47) calls this a "hunting hut."

73. Our Nuxalk consultants pointed out that this "hair" is actually pubic hair.

He lay down and covered himself with the bird skins. Then he gave his younger brother a short stick and told him to beat time with it on his body. He said to him, "You will see a big feather fly up to the sky. That is me. I want to see the country in the sky." The boy began to beat time and soon a big feather flew in wide circles towards the sky. Thereupon the boy started to weep because he believed that he had lost his brother. He went home, and his father asked him where his brother was, and the little one wept, but didn't give any answer. The father asked him for a second and a third time. When he asked him the fourth time, the boy replied, "My brother flew up to the sky in the shape of a big feather." His father didn't believe it at first. But the little one stuck to his statement. He showed his father the bird skins on the shore and since the young man couldn't be found, the boy was at last believed. The father carried the birds home, prepared a feast with their meat and invited the whole tribe. Then the boy told everything exactly as it had happened.

The elder brother arrived in the sky. There he found a path and followed it. After some time he saw a number of blind women sitting around a cooking box in which they were cooking roots (tqsōs).[74] They were Ducks.[75] He took one of the roots away from them and tasted it. Thereupon the women shouted, "I can smell Mōk·oa'nts, he must be here." The root made the saliva collect in his mouth. He spat into the eyes of one of the women and she could see again. So she cried aloud, "I can see!" The others shouted, "You're lying!" Mōk·oa'nts had hidden and now came out and spat into the eyes of another woman and she, too, could see. If Mōk·oa'nts hadn't done that, ducks would still be blind today. Then he rid them of their pungent smell. Then he threw them down to the earth and said, "Henceforth you shall serve as food for mankind."

Then Mōk·oa'nts went back home and arrived again on the river bank. His younger brother had constantly stayed around there, hoping to see his brother again. When he came back now he had become so handsome that his younger brother didn't recognize him. He asked, "Don't you know me?" And the little one replied, "No." "Don't you remember how I flew up into the sky? I am your brother and I have returned." Then they went to their father's house together. The boy went in by himself and said, "My brother has returned." His father threatened to beat him if he mentioned the dead man's name, but the boy continued, "Yes, he has come back,

---

74. What Boas renders here as "tqsōs" is t'x̌ʷsus, the Nuxalk name for wild clover roots (*Trifolium wormskjoldii*), an important vegetable for the Nuxalk that is dug in the early spring, or in the fall after the frost has killed the leaves. In Boas' (1890b) original shorthand version of this story, he writes "t'qsōs laqamus?", questioning whether this root might be camas (*Camassia quamash*).

75. Our Nuxalk consultants pointed out that both Canada Geese (*Branta canadensis*), known in Nuxalk as x̌ax̌aq̓, and Mallard ducks (*Anas platyrhynchos*), known as naxnx, are especially fond of wild clover roots (see the footnote above). Variants of this story mention both bird species.

and he is now very handsome. If you want to see him, come outside with me." The boy went back to his brother and asked him into the house. He replied, "Tell Father to purify the house." The boy went back and delivered the message. But the father still didn't believe him, but went out with him to see the stranger. He didn't recognize him at first, but the man said, "The sun has made me pure and handsome. I am your son who once flew up into the sky." So the father purified his house and invited all the people for a feast. The young man appeared and told what he had experienced. He asked the people to come down to the river with him the following day so that he could show them the supernatural powers which he had received from the sky. The next day they all went down to the shore and he caught ducks, as many as he wanted, with his bare hands. When the other people came near to them, they flew away. Then he feasted the people with the meat of the ducks which he had caught.

After some time he said to his brother, "Cover me up again with bird skins and beat time as before. I want to go back to the sky, but this time I will not come back again." He gave his name to his younger brother and flew up into the sky.

15. The Children of the Dog

1) A chief by the name of Ālk[76] had a dog with ugly bleary eyes. Once Ālk's daughter, who just then had her period and therefore wasn't allowed to leave her room, said, "Don't allow the dog into my room, because I don't like to see him while I am eating." When he ran in again, Ālk threw him out of the house and closed the door behind him. Night came and the girl lay down to sleep. Around midnight a man crept to her and lay down with her in bed. Since she was unable to see who it was, she put red paint on his head and back unnoticed in order to recognize him again the following morning. Now when her parents were getting up in the morning, they saw that their dog was covered all over in red paint. They cried, "Where could our dog have been? He's full of red paint." Thereupon the girl shrieked out loud because she knew now that the dog had slept with her. After some time she gave birth to five puppies, four male and one female. She hid them at first, but because they howled and whined, her parents soon discovered. When it became known that the chief's daughter had given birth to dogs, an old woman counselled the people to move away from the village and to abandon her. The chief followed her advice. He made the people load their canoes and extinguish the fire, and the whole tribe moved away with all their belongings. The chief's daughter and the five puppies stayed behind

---

76. Contemporary Nuxalk people use the term alkʷ (Boas' "Ālk") when referring to the person who acts as a messenger during a feast.

by themselves. Only her grandmother took pity on her in her plight. Before they left, she concealed a glowing piece of charcoal in a shell, placed it in a hiding place and told the girl to take out the shell only when the canoes were out of sight. She did what her grandmother had told her. When the canoes were out of sight, she blew onto the coals and made herself a big fire. She built a small hut from branches and collected shellfish on the beach, and lived on these with her children. One day, when she was busy on the beach, she heard the singing of children close by the house. She hurried up, but saw only the young dogs. She heard the singing on three consecutive days. When she came back to the house on the third day, she noticed the imprints of children's feet, so she decided to observe unnoticed on the following day to see which children were playing there. She went down to the beach and hung her hat and cape on the stick she used for digging shellfish, so that it looked like a person, then she crept up secretly to the house and saw that the dogs had thrown off their skins and were playing around as children. She quickly sprang from her hiding place, seized the skins and threw them into the fire. The girl's skin lay to one side and, before the mother was able to grab it, the girl had slipped back into it and was transformed into a dog.

The boys retained their human shape and their mother made bows and arrows for them. They soon learned how to hunt and fish. The girl, who stayed in the shape of a dog, sat down outside the door and sang, "My brothers, make a good house for our mother; catch halibut in the sea, mountain goats on the mountains and marten in the woods. Then our mother will make capes for you and I will accompany you when you go out hunting."

After some time the young woman's grandmother came back to see how she had fared. She concealed herself close to the hut and watched the young woman busily sewing capes from marten skins. She saw the four boys and rich supplies of halibut. The boys soon discovered her, led her into the house and the young woman gave her food. Then, when the old woman got ready to return to the tribe, the young woman gave her a piece of seal blubber, but ordered her to eat it by herself and not to share it with anyone. The old woman promised to obey. The tribe was suffering great want at that time, so when she returned and her daughter had nothing to eat, despite her promise she secretly gave her the piece of seal blubber that she had received as a present. Her daughter was so hungry that she tried to swallow the piece of blubber in one gulp. It got stuck in her throat and she began to choke. When Ālk heard this he asked the old woman, "What's wrong with your daughter? She is choking." The old woman said, "Oh, it's nothing." But Ālk could not be deterred; he put his finger in the girl's mouth and pulled out the piece of blubber. Then he forced the old woman to admit where she had got it. She told him that she had visited her grand-daughter who had four sons and one dog and was now very rich, so Ālk at once decided to return to her. He had the canoes loaded and the whole tribe set out, but when they neared the village, his daughter caused a storm that capsized all the canoes and the whole tribe lost their lives except for the old woman who had taken pity on the chief's daughter.

2) A chief had a beautiful daughter. Many men courted her but she didn't want to give herself to any of them. One night a man crept to her and was gone again in the morning, when dawn came. He came again many times. Since the girl didn't know who he was, she coated her hands with pitch and red paint and smeared the man all over with it. The following day she sat down in front of the door and watched which of the young men would have red paint on his fur cape. She saw no one, but towards noon she saw that her father's bleary-eyed old dog was covered all over in red paint and pitch. That night the man crept to her again, so she cut off some hairs from his fur cape and saw the next morning that they were dog hairs. So the girl knew that the dog had crept to her every night in human shape. Soon she became pregnant. When the people noticed this, they teased her father, who had before refused all the suitors.

When the time arrived, she gave birth to five puppies, four male and one female. The two midwives told of this event and her father ordered all the people to take down their houses and to abandon her. They obeyed, and all the provisions were packed and the fires extinguished. Only one old woman had pity on the poor mother and gave her some fire which she had wrapped up in an inner cedar bark cape.[77] When they had all left, the young woman built herself a small house of fir boughs and lit a fire. Her puppies grew up quickly.

She went down to the beach every day to dig for shellfish. She had no fur cape, but only a cape[78] of inner cedar bark. One day, when she returned, she saw many footprints of children near her house. She didn't know where they were coming from. The following day she saw many footprints by her house again, so she decided to see who it was who came to her house. She went down to the beach and draped her cape over the digging stick so that it looked as if someone was digging there, then she sneaked back to the house. There she saw four boys at play; their dog capes[79] were in one corner of the house. The girl sat outside the door in the shape of a she-dog and kept watch. The boys asked her, "Isn't mother coming back yet?" "No," replied the girl, "she's still at the beach digging shellfish." Then the woman jumped out, seized the boys' capes and burned them. She said, "Why did you

---

77. In the original *Sagen*, Boas uses the term *Kragen* which means 'collar,' but in his notes, Boas (1890b) provides the Nuxalk term "wa'qtsē cape," which McIlwraith (1948:II:627) transcribes as "wa·xsia" and glosses 'cape of yellow cedar bark.'

78. *Kragen* 'collar' in the original (see footnote above).

disguise yourselves? Because of you I've become unhappy. Formerly there were many people here but now I am alone. Now you shall look after me." So the she-dog said to her eldest brother, "You shall make planks for Mother and build her a house"; to the second, "You shall build canoes for mother"; to the third, "You shall hunt deer for her"; and to the fourth, "You shall catch fish for her." She added, "I will come hunting with you and will help all of you." The following day the eldest of the brothers made small planks and built a tiny house from them. The next day it had been transformed into a huge house with a beautifully ornamented front. He made four houses, one for each of the brothers. The second brother made good canoes, the third hunted deer and the fourth caught a big supply of halibut. The she-dog, who was called NuskH'ŏ'pElHinH,[80] helped her brothers.

One day three men from the tribe came to the village to see what had become of the abandoned woman. How they marvelled to see the houses and the canoes! When they disembarked they noticed that the houses were full of rich provisions. The woman gave them many gifts and they went back to their tribe. There, they told what they had seen. So the other people also went there and she gave them presents. She said, "All of you may come here. Only my parents and my brothers and sisters who abandoned me are not to come. If they land here, my children shall kill them."

If the woman hadn't taken away the children's fur capes, our women would still give birth to puppies today. (Nuskelu'sta.)

16. The Boy and Salmon[81]

There once was a widower who had one son. Finally he married again. One day, when he was giving his son a meal of seal meat, his wife, who was busy plaiting blankets of inner cedar bark, and who didn't like her step-son, became angry and scolded her husband for giving the boy too much to eat. The boy said to his father, "Your new wife always abuses me and begrudges me food; send her away or else I will go into the forest." Since the father kept the woman, the boy took his bow and arrows and went into the woods. He wandered long days and nights. Once, when he shot an arrow aimlessly, it hit the bones of a salmon lying on the banks of a creek, and they cried. The boy crept up to see who was there. When he came to the creek, the bones called out to him, "You can come out! Take us and throw us

---

79. Boas (1890b) in his notes adds "skin shirts" in English at this point in the story.

80. What Boas transcribes as "NuskH'ŏ'pElHinH" is recognized as nuskʷuplxmx which means 'one who knows how to track and can seize the right opportunity to act.'

81. Boas (1895d:43–47) provides a variant of this story in both Nuxalk and English.

into the creek." The boy obeyed and the bones were transformed into a fish. It said, "Look at me; do I look like a real salmon?" The boy thought that it was not yet quite like a salmon and, at the bidding of the fish, looked to see whether there were more bones on the banks. He found some and threw them into the water. But the fish still was not complete and he had found all the bones only after the fourth try. Soon the boy saw a canoe approaching and Salmon said, "Look, this is my canoe. Now close your eyes, step in and don't open them again before we reach land." The boy obeyed, and after some time they arrived in the country of the T'iнtla'la (a red-breasted bird),[82] whom Salmon didn't like, so they continued on their way. After some time they heard women singing in the forest. They were the AiHoa'qone[83] birds, whom Salmon didn't like, either, and so he went on. Then they came to the Sk·ol'aqlē'lits birds,[84] whom Salmon passed by, although they were very beautiful. At last they arrived at the K·oak·oā'oq (Partridges).[85] Here they landed, and the young man liked the women so much that he wanted to marry one of them. But Salmon warned him and said, "You will die if you marry one of these women." But the young man didn't listen to him and told him to come back again the following morning to see whether he was still alive. Salmon returned the next morning in his canoe and found the young man safe and sound. They continued on together and passed Dog Salmon,[86] who dirtied everything, T'li' (a big fish),[87] who made fun of them, Humpback Salmon,[88] and Sāmtl' (a river fish).[89]

---

82. "T'iнtla'la" is recognized as t'ixɬala, the Nuxalk term applied to the American Robin (*Turdus migratorius*).

83. As we have previously noted (see story 1, part 10, of this section), Boas' "AiHoa'qone" is ʔixʔi·x̌ʷni, the Nuxalk name for the Swainson's Thrush (*Hylocichla ustulata*). In Boas' (1890b) original shorthand notes, he mistakenly glosses this term as 'robin,' after crossing out the Nuxalk term that does mean 'robin' (see the footnote above) and replacing it with the form "aih'a'qone" (i.e. ʔixʔi·x̌ʷni).

84. Boas' "Sk·ol'aqlē'lits" was recognized by our Nuxalk consultants as skʷlxʷlilic, the name of a bird said to be a "wild canary." While the identification remains uncertain, this Nuxalk term does appear to include various flycatchers (*Empidonax spp.*)

85. Given in the original as *Rebhuhn* 'partridge,' although the partridge is not found in this area. The bird in question is identified by the storyteller as "K·oak·oā'oq," recognized by our Nuxalk consultants as qʷu·x̌ʷu·xʷ 'Trumpeter Swan' (*Olor buccinator*). Boas (1890b) on page 71 of his original shorthand notes provides the correct English translation, 'swan,' for this same Nuxalk term.

86. Appears in English in the original *Sagen* (see also the footnote that follows).

87. The Nuxalk term t'li (Boas' "T'li'") applies to the dog or chum salmon (*Oncorhynchus keta*); thus, Boas lists "dog salmon" twice.

88. Appears in English in the original *Sagen*.

89. Boas' "sāmtl'" is the Nuxalk term samɬ, referring to 'sockeye salmon' (*O. nerka*), although these salmon spend most of their life at sea, returning only to the river to spawn. In his original shorthand notes of this story, Boas (1890b) provides the English term "sockeye."

At last they arrived at the Silver Salmon.[90] There they saw four young girls bathing in a pond, while a small boy stood guard on shore to see that no one came. The young man asked to exchange clothes and then gave him his cape while he put on the boy's. The girls mistook him for the guard and called out to him to come into the water with them. But when he reached them, they saw that he was a stranger and ran away, frightened.

Salmon then went back with the young man to Sāmtl', where he took a wife, but he finally decided to return home. He took his wife into the canoe and the old Sāmtl' gave him many treasures on the way. He made all species of fish come into his canoe and then set out. T'li', who was always laughing, and Kн'ap'ai,[91] who dirtied the canoe, were sitting in the stern. But the fish had all assumed human shape. When he arrived at his father's house, he went up and said, "Father, purify your house so that it doesn't smell and my wife will be able to come in." His father was glad to see him because he had believed his son dead. It seemed to him that he had travelled with Salmon for two days, but it had been two years in reality. The father then purified his house and the son went straight into his father's salmon weir with his canoe. Then he told him, "Cut up white inner cedar bark and throw it into the water."[92] The father did this and at once they all were transformed into fish.

17. The Dead Man's Child

A man and his wife loved one another very much and promised each other to stay together if one of them should die. Now it happened that the man died and was carried to a burial hut, while the woman, weeping bitterly, went to her husband's corpse and lay down beside it to sleep. But in her dream she saw him alive. She stayed in the burial hut for eight days and conceived a child from her dead husband; the child was born after two weeks. Just about that time the women were going to the forest to collect berries. They heard the crying of a child and went to see who was there. They found the woman who held her child in her arms, wrapped in a cloth. She said, "Bring food for the dead because they are very hungry." So two women went back into the village and told what they had witnessed and all the people came out with them into the forest to bring food to the dead. Among them there was also the woman's father and mother. The old woman said, "Oh, let me see your child." But she replied, "No, I mustn't show it to you, because it isn't like other

---

90. Boas in the original *Sagen* uses the artificially-constructed term *Silberlachsen* 'silver salmon,' referring to coho (*O. kisutch*).

91. Recognized as kapʔay 'humpback salmon' (*Oncorhynchus gorbuscha*).

92. Our Nuxalk consultants pointed out that people pay respect to salmon by throwing into the water pieces of inner red cedar bark, as a gift to all species of salmon.

people." But when the old woman didn't stop begging, she finally gave it to her. But then she saw that the child consisted only of a head and had no body. She dropped it in terror. When the child touched the ground, it vanished into the earth and was seen no more.

18. The Girl Who Ran Away

Once upon a time there was a girl. Her brother was dead and her parents scolded and beat her all the time. So she cried day and night and at last ran away into the forest. She soon found a path there and followed it, and after some time she reached a house in which there lived an old woman who had a huge mouth and big hands and feet. When she saw the girl she invited her in and to her gave her own comb, her own basket, some fish oil, her own sharpening stone, and a needle used for splitting inner cedar bark. She told the girl to hide the presents under her cape. After some time the old woman's husband, Gnarled Root, came home from hunting. When he saw the girl he demanded that she delouse him. The girl obeyed and found that frogs were sitting in his hair like lice on a human head. She threw them into the basket given her by the old woman. Then Root ordered her to eat the frogs, but she deceived him by hiding them beneath her cape and picking her teeth with the inner cedar bark needle so that it sounded as if she were chewing. She deluded him like this four times. When the old man went out again to catch halibut, he told his chamber pot to call him if the girl should escape, for he intended to eat her up. He had hardly gone when the old woman filled the girl's basket with many things and told her to run away as fast as she was able, after having impressed upon her how to use the comb, the fish oil and the sharpening stone. The girl ran away and the chamber pot called out, "Qōla′, qōla′, qōla′, qōla′!" Gnarled Root came running at once and set out in pursuit of the escaped girl, who could hear him coming closer and closer. When he had almost caught up with her, she threw the sharpening stone behind herself, according to the old woman's instructions. It was transformed into a steep mountain which her pursuer had to go around. In that way, she gained an advantage. But soon Root came up again, so she threw the comb behind herself; it was transformed into a dense forest at once. Again she gained an advantage, but when the Gnarled Root had gone around the forest, he easily caught up with her again. The girl had then nearly reached home. When Root came up close, she poured out the fish oil. It was transformed into a lake over which a fog bank lay. Before her pursuer was able to go around it, she safely reached her father's house.

19. Tlā′lia

Once upon a time there was a man in Taleo′mн[93] (South Bentinck Arm) who wanted to marry, but not one among the women wanted to have him for a husband. So he decided to go into the forest. He wandered about for a long time. At last he arrived at the house of a great chief, who had a beautiful daughter called Tlā′lia[94] whose face was completely of copper. The chief said to him, "You have wandered about for a long time without finding a wife, so now I will give you my daughter, Tlā′lia." The stranger agreed and went with Tlā′lia into her room, where he saw that everything was made of copper. After some time he longed to be home again. Even before he expressed this wish, his wife knew what was on his mind. She asked her father's permission for her husband to leave and for her to accompany him. The chief gave his consent, made him rich presents of coppers, and gave his house to him. When the man and his wife then returned to Taleo′mн, they built a house like the chief's, and when the house was finished, Tlā′lia gave away many coppers. (After a note by Ph. Jakobsen.)[95]

20. K·ōmō′k·oa or Sky'amtsky[96]

K·ōmō′k·oa is a spirit of the sea, the father of the seals, who can often be seen on the beach. He takes the drowned ones with him. The son of K·ōmō′k·oa once said to Eagle, "Take me on your back and carry me all over the earth so that I might see whether there are more people here besides us." Eagle granted his wish and carried the young man through all the lands. So he saw that there were beings resembling humans everywhere, but he found that they were half human and half animal. In

---

93. Boas' "Taleo′mн" is talyumx which refers to all the people of South Bentick Arm, derived from the Nuxalk term talyu (anglicized as "Tallheo") which is applied to a former village site at the head of South Bentinck Arm, situated southwest of Bella Coola.

94. "Copper" [Boas' original footnote]. Our Nuxalk consultants confirmed this translation, 'copper.'

95. Philip [Fillip B.] Jacobsen is the Norwegian sea captain who in 1885 took nine Bella Coola men to Germany, resulting in Boas becoming acquainted with Northwest Coast aboriginal culture. Once Boas had reached Victoria in 1886, he asked a Nuxalk man returning to Bella Coola to take a letter to Jacobsen, presumably informing him of his arrival. On a later field trip, Boas met Jacobsen in Rivers Inlet. On 18 June 1888 he writes in his diary: "We had reached Rivers Inlet, where I hoped to see Jacobsen. I met him two hours ago and we were delighted to see each other again" (Rohner 1969:92).

96. "K·ōmō′k·oa = Rich One, a word in the Kwakiutl language" [Boas' original footnote]. Boas' "K·ōmō′k·oa" is recognized by our Nuxalk consultants as q̓ʷumuqʷa, the "head of the underwater kingdom." As we have noted previously, in association with story 12 of this section, the Nuxalk term skamck (Boas' "Sky'amtsky") is applied to a supernatural creature described by our Nuxalk consultants as a "bad water monster."

some places he found only two of these beings, in others he found large villages. When he returned, he told what he had seen. (After a note of Ph. Jakobsen.)

21. Ancestor Legends[97]

In the beginning, the salmon were unable to ascend the river near Nutl'ᴇ'l[98] because a tremendous mass of rocks lay in its course. At that time Snq[99] sent Nō'aktla[100] down to earth. He met Masmasalā'niq on the way, who gave him a canoe in which he went down the River ᴋʜlat[101] until he came to the rock barrier. At the same time Snq sent Qēmtsī'oa[102] down from the sky in the shape of an eagle. On his way to earth he also met Masmasalā'niq,[103] who gave him the eulachon.[104] He arrived at Kimskuitq[105] and wandered up along the inlet until he reached Nutl'ᴇ'l. He also found his way barred by the rock, over which the water flowed in a small trickle. So Nō'aktla, who was standing up above, called to Qēmtsī'oa, "Let's break up the rock so that the salmon will be able to ascend the river." There came Masmasalā'niq, Yulā'timōt, Matlapā'litsek·, and Matlapē'eqoek·[106] in order to try and break up the rock, but without success. So Nō'aktla called Crane,[107] who pecked in vain with his long beak at

---

97. Boas uses the German term *Ahnensagen* 'ancestor legends' in the original *Sagen*. This series of stories includes several First Ancestor legends of the Nuxalk, called in their language smayusta 'family history' (see Kennedy and Bouchard 1990a:329).

98. This name nuƛ'l (Boas' "Nutl'ᴇ'l") means 'canyon' and applies to the Dean River canyon.

99. 'Sun,' known in the Nuxalk language as snx̣ (Boas' "Snq").

100. "A Kwakiutl name meaning: Making Wise" [Boas' original footnote]. This name, "Nō'ak·īla," recognized by our Nuxalk consultants as nuwakila, refers to the First Ancestor of the people at Salmon House, a settlement on the upper Dean River. In another version of this story, Boas (1898:66) provides the transcription "Noak·ī'la."

101. The place name nuk̓lat (Boas' "ᴋʜlat") translates as 'steelhead place' and is applied generally to the Dean River, according to Nuxalk elders we consulted in the 1970s.

102. Ximcwa (Boas' "Qēmtsī'oa") came to earth in eagle form, landed on the mountain known as swak̓x in Kimsquit, and became one of the First Ancestors.

103. As we have noted (see story 1, part 1) what Boas transcribes here as "Masmasalā'niq" is the Nuxalk term masmasalanix̣ʷ which refers collectively to the four brothers who were supernatural carpenters.

104. Given as "olachen" in the original *Sagen*; the current spelling is "eulachon."

105. What Boas transcribes as "Kimskuitq" is k̓mxk̓ʷitx̣ʷ (anglicized as "Kimsquit"), the Heiltsuk name referring to the Nuxalk-speaking people who resided formerly at the mouth of the Dean River in Dean Channel. After about the early 1920s, the Kimsquit residents moved to the main Nuxalk village situated on the north shore of the Bella Coola River mouth (Kennedy and Bouchard 1990a:323, 338).

106. As mentioned previously (see story 1, part 1), these are the four supernatural carpenters.

107. Given in the original as *Kranich* 'crane'; this may be either the Great Blue Heron (*Ardea*

the rock. Sai'ōtl,[108] Thunderbird, met with just as little success. Then Nō'akīla sent one of his men to Atlkō[109] (a Hē'iltsuk village) where a mighty shaman by the name of Anōyastai'H[110] lived. He embarked in his canoe and went to Nutl'ɛ'l. He prodded with his spear at the rock, which broke up at once. Then the lake drained, the water ran into the sea and the salmon were able to swim upriver from then on.—

—At the same time that Qēmtsī'oa came down from the sky, Snq sent down four men and two women to Sātsk·[111] where they built houses by the Nutsk·oā'tl[112] River. Their names were Ot'oalo'stimōt,[113] Yaēlo'stimōt,[114] Tsītstsī'p,[115] Isyū'yōt,[116] and the latter's sisters, Kulai'yū[117] and Sqimā'na.[118] They carried the fire drill, and Brown Bear and Grizzly Bear. Yaēlo'stimōt married Isyū'yōt's sister, Kulai'yū. When Qēmtsī'oa learned that the people in Sātsk· had fire, he sent his sister out to bring fire to Nutl'ɛ'l. The chiefs of Nuqa'lkH and Taleo'mH also sent their sisters, who received the fire from Yaēlo'stimōt.—

—Snq sent down Isyū'yōt to Nuqa'lkH. After he had lived there for some time, he visited the Thunderbird, Sai'otl, who carried him all over the world. When they came to AskHlta,[119] a place above Nutl'ɛ'l, Isyū'yōt wanted to stay there. He built himself a canoe which he painted and carved beautifully, and which he called

---

herodias) or Sandhill Crane (*Grus canadensis*), as both species have been observed in the Bella Coola area, although Heron appears more commonly in coastal mythology.

108. Recognized as sʔayuł 'Thunderbird' by our Nuxalk consultants.

109. Boas' "Atlkō" is recognized as the Heiltsuk term Ɂałkʷu, referring to the area of the "Elcho" (anglicized from Ɂałkʷu) Reserve on the west side of Dean Channel.

110. What Boas transcribes here as "Anōyastai'H" was recognized by our Nuxalk consultants as the "Chief's name" of the person known as q̓asana 'half-of-a-man.' As we have noted concerning story 11 of the present section, the q̓asana story is associated with a group of people of mixed Nuxalk and Heiltsuk ancestry who formerly lived in Dean Channel.

111. This is sackʷ, the Nuxalk name applied to the Kimsquit River and the village at its mouth.

112. Possibly the term transcribed here by Boas as "Nutsk·oā'tl" is the old village site known to the Nuxalk people we interviewed in the 1970s as the place called nucqʷalst, situated a little over two miles (3.2 km) up the Dean River.

113. The translation of this name, which is recognized as Ɂut'walustimut, is 'made-larger fire.'

114. The translation of this name, yalustimut, is 'brightly-burning fire.'

115. This name is ciccip, referring to a 'huge supernatural eagle.'

116. What Boas renders here as "Isyū'yōt" is the name Ɂisyuyut, the meaning of which was not known to our Nuxalk consultants; it refers to a First Ancestor who descended from the sky to the Kimsquit River, wearing an eagle blanket (Boas 1898:65–67).

117. "A Kwakiutl name" [Boas' original footnote]. While our Nuxalk consultants did not know this name, they recognized it as a Kwakwala word.

118. Name not now recognized.

119. This is the Nuxalk name sʔałkłta that is applied to the place known locally in English as "Salmon House," situated on the upper Dean River.

K·ak·oā'osalotl.[120] In it he went downriver and met many chiefs in Nutl'ɛ'l and Ki'mkuitq. It is said that he kept the sun in the box, Nusqē'mta (see page 276),[121] and that he had a daughter called Sqēma'na[122] who was made pregnant by Raven, who, as her child, liberated the sun. (Told by Yākŏtla's from Nuqa'lkʜ.)—

—Tsāəeaqlitl[123] was chief in Sātsk·. Once he went up into the mountains in order to see the mountain spirit, Towa'latl'it,[124] who has a she-dog called Numā'ulaqsuts,[125] which he carries around in his arms and which catches mountain goats for him. At last Tsāəeaqlitl found the spirit and wanted to exchange clothes and weapons with him. But he didn't accept the proposal and only exchanged his dancing staff for that of the chief. Thus Tsāəeaqlitl gained power over the mountain goats and caught twenty each day. He called all the people together and gave a big feast for them. He had so much meat that he could fill two houses four times over. Then he built himself four big houses. His descendants are still living in Sātsk· today.—

—Ītliqua'ni[126] had a son who had a very fat belly. One day his mother sent the boy down to the salmon weir to get fish. The child waddled labouriously down the bank. Two other boys saw him go down. They threw him down on the bank, heaped sand over him and then hid themselves. Because the little one didn't come back, Ītliqua'ni went out to look for him. He found the two boys and asked them whether they had seen his son. At first they denied it, but then they freed the little one from the sand pile again.[127] (Told by Yākŏtla's from Nuqa'lkʜ.)—

---

120. Recognized as qʷaqʷawsalut 'merganser canoe,' derived from the Nuxalk term qʷaqʷaws 'merganser duck' (*Mergus merganser*).

121. Boas refers here to page 276 of the original *Sagen*, which is story 1 of the Tsimshian (Section XXIII), and more specifically is a reference to an incident of the Raven legend in which the sun is kept in a box in a chief's house.

122. The name Boas transcribes here as "Sqēma'na" is very likely the same name that he transcribes in the paragraph before this, as "Sqimā'na"; possibly this term is sximana.

123. Possibly ċayx̱lit.

124. As we have noted (in association with story 13 of this section), Boas' "Towa'latl'it" is recognized as the spirit of the mountain goat who looks after both goats and hunters, but sometimes plays tricks on the latter. When this spirit appears before a hunter, it is always seen wearing a hat with a snake crawling around the lower brim.

125. The translation of this dog's name is 'twenty-barks.'

126. Name not now recognized.

127. "When a chief is ill, and during burial feasts, songs are sung which have as a theme the ancestor legends of the family concerned. These legends are supposed to be recited at such occasions" [Boas' original footnote].

22. Anustsū'tsa

A young man married a beautiful girl. But his mother didn't like her daughter-in-law and one day gave her boiling water to drink. When she drank the first spoonful of it, she burned her mouth and was at once transformed into the bird, Anustsū'tsa (= Burned Beak).[128] Ever since she cries: "Anananatsutsatsē'!"

23. Deer

Once a chief invited all the people to a feast. When everyone was already there, Deer also arrived in his canoe, which he propelled with one paddle. The guard standing by the house door called, "A stranger is arriving." The chief had him called in. Deer entered and remained standing right beside the door. The chief enquired, "Can you dance?" "Yes," replied Deer, "if I have knives tied to my wrists, I can." So the chief had knives brought to him. Deer tied them to his wrists and began dancing. He sang at the same time, "Fall asleep, fall asleep!" He also sang to the children in the house, "Fall asleep, fall asleep!" While he was thus dancing, everyone fell fast asleep. If that hadn't happened, people wouldn't sleep nowadays. Then Deer took off his knives and cut the throat of each sleeper. He left only one man alive. (Told by Yākōtla's from Nuqa'lkн.)

24. Deer and the Wolves

Deer and his son went out one day to collect wood. Deer went into the forest and left his son behind in the canoe. Four Wolves came and asked the boy, "Where is your father?" "He's in the forest getting wood." Then the Wolves fingered the little one's fur and said, "You're bound to taste nice; we want to eat you up." Then they went away. When Deer came back from the forest, he asked his son, "Have you seen anyone?" "Yes," he replied, "four people came and said that my meat would taste nice." So Deer scolded the Wolves, who had hidden close by and heard everything. Then Deer and his son returned home.

The following day they went out again for wood. When the old one was in the forest again felling trees, the wolves came back and said, "Your father scolded us yesterday, so we are going to eat you up." With this they fell upon Young Deer and devoured him. When Old Deer came back and couldn't find his child, he cried. He threw his nasal secretion onto the paddle and asked it, "Where is my son?" It

---

128. The identity of this bird "that burnt its mouth" is now unknown—its name, ʔanusčuča (Boas' Anustsū'tsa"), is derived from the Nuxalk term ʔanana meaning 'it hurts.'

replied, "I don't know." He threw it onto the seat and asked it. It didn't know. He threw it onto all parts of the canoe but not one of them knew the answer. At last he threw it onto the bailer and asked it. The bailer replied, "The Wolves have devoured him because you scolded them yesterday."

So he resolved to take his revenge. He adorned his head with a ring of red inner cedar bark[129] and went to the Wolf village. When the Wolves saw him coming, they asked him, "Can you dance well?" "Yes," he replied, "go ahead and invite everybody." When all the people had assembled, he said, "I always dance with a big knife." One was given to him and then he began to dance, while singing, "Sleep, fall asleep." Thereupon all the spectators fell asleep. Only one old woman sitting in the back of the house stayed awake. Then, when he thought that everyone was asleep, he took his knife and cut off the sleeping people's heads. The old woman shouted, "Wake up! Deer is cutting off your heads!" And they woke up. Deer ran away and they all pursued him. Because he noticed his pursuers getting closer, he climbed a tree, and the people were unable to catch him. So they went back home and the old woman who had roused them taught them a magical song. Then they pursued Deer again. On the way they came to a fallen tree barring their way. They jumped across it and then found that they had forgotten the incantation. They returned home. The old woman taught them the song again. Then she enquired, "Did you jump over a fallen tree on your way? You mustn't do that. You must go around it, then you won't forget the song." They ran off again and finally arrived at the tree in which Deer was sitting. So they sang:

Stiti - кнtlak· ti - wa - tla [130]

i.e. I wish that your leg would fall down

So one leg of Deer after the other fell down and at last his whole body fell down. So they carried the meat home. They cut it up into small pieces and threw these from the house, saying, "You shall become a deer and serve as food for us." If they hadn't done that, there would be no deer nowadays. (Told by Nuskelu'sta.)

---

129. "It is the head ornament of the winter dancers" [Boas' original footnote].

130. The phrase presented here by Boas translates literally as 'drop down, one leg at a time.' The song as transcribed by Boas (1890b) in his notes contains two musical notes not included in the published version.

25. The Sorcerers

Once upon a time in K·oā'tlna,[131] there were four brothers, who were very bad. The youngest of them married a young girl. The men got hold of some old things of the young woman's brother, whom they wanted to kill. They took the things secretly into the forest, killed a wolf and put these things into its jaws, which they then tied up and placed in a box. Thereupon the brother of the woman died.

He was buried in the forest and the woman went to the grave every day to mourn, carrying her child on her back. One day when she was sitting there she heard two men come. She kept quiet and when they came close, she recognized her husband with one of his brothers. They broke open the grave and carried the corpse to their canoe, where the two older brothers had been keeping watch. The woman followed them. Their canoe left and she followed them in her small canoe. The men landed and, carrying the corpse into the forest, cut open the right side of the chest, took out pieces of flesh and cooked them, collecting the fat in a small bowl. Then they lay down to sleep. So the woman crept up and let the fat drip into their mouths. Thus the four brothers lost their lives. The woman returned to the village and told what had occurred.—(Told by Nuskelu'sta. This tale is not to be regarded as a legend but rather recounts the usual method of casting spells.)

—The Thunderbird lives in the mountains. The beating of his wings is the thunder. He makes lightning by beating together two pieces of quartz.—

—Raven is the grandfather of the Bilqula.—

---

131. This is the Nuxalk pronunciation of the place called kʷałna (Boas' "K·oā'tlna"), anglicized as "Kwatna," that is situated on the east shore of Kwatna Inlet, east of King Island.

XXIII. Legends of the Tsimshian

"My friend Mathew, the Tsimsian, came again this morning," Boas wrote in a diary-letter of 22 September 1886, "and told me a long story of the origin of the cannibal" (Rohner 1969:24). This must be story 17 of the present section, about the four kinds of winter dances. It is not a long story, but Boas had only been in the field three days, and thought it was. Boas had great hopes for Mathew; the first session on 21 September had been inspiring: "he is very intelligent and tells me more than I expected. He immediately recognized one of my drawings from New York and told me a long story that goes with it, first in Chinook and then in his own language" (Rohner 1969:22). This is probably the "Beheaded Raven" story, appended to story 1. It can be found in Tsimshian with an interlinear German translation in a manuscript held by the American Philosophical Society (Boas n.d.8) and was published by Schulenburg (1894:188–91). On 23 September Mathew told another "long story," which undoubtedly *was* long, as it took six hours to get it dictated (Rohner 1969:25). This presumably was story 15, the longest of the four attributed to this storyteller. (At the end of No. 18, Boas states that 15–18 "were told by Matthias, an Indian from Meqtlak'a'tla." The Matthias referred to here is likely the Mathew of the letters).

Things did not go well for Boas the following day; he "waited in vain for friend Mathew ... so far he has been the best one I have had" (Rohner 1969:25). Boas hoped to replace Mathew, but he did not find an alternate of that calibre, so the rest of the Tsimshian selection is something of a mixed bag, including many fragments and short pieces (Nos. 8–14). Mrs. Lawson, "the daughter of a Fort Simpson chief," provided the well-known Raven birth story. She is the spirited woman whose story is told by Thomas Crosby (1914:19–20) in *Up and Down the North Pacific Coast*. She likely gave Boas the three substantial traditional stories (Nos. 5–7). Or it may have been the "Tsimshian woman from whom I learned a great deal yesterday and today" in Victoria in June 1888, about whom Boas said nothing further (Rohner 1969:87). A Nisga'a fragment of the Raven legend was provided by Mrs. Spencer, and the missionary, William Duncan, described by Boas as "clever and ambitious," told some Raven tidbits (Rohner 1969:51).

One might have thought that Boas' stay in Port Essington on the Skeena River, 19–26 June 1888, would have produced stories, but apparently Boas chose to consult with the competent Mrs. Morrison mostly for grammar and vocabulary (Rohner 1969:93).

Painted housefront with Thunderbird desgn belonging to Chief Sgagweit of the Gitandau tribal group of Coast Tsimshian, Port Simpson, 1881.

National Archives of Canada, Ottawa. No. C-66431 (O.C. Hastings photo).

Eulachon strung on racks for air-drying at Mill Bay, near the mouth of the Nass River.
Canadian Museum of Civilization, Ottawa. Image No. 71-3096.

Unidentified men using elbow adzes to carve a dugout canoe on the beach at Metlakatla, B.C., *ca.* 1880.

Museum of Northern British Columbia, Prince Rupert, BC.

XXIII. Legends of the Tsimschian[1]

1. The Raven Legend

The wife of a chief laboured in childbirth, but died before she had given birth. When she was dead the chief said to his slave, "Let's deposit her corpse in a tree top." They placed the body in a chest, took it to a level spot near the mouth of the Nass River and tied it to the top of a tall cedar. This happened in the middle of winter, when the country was covered deeply in snow and it was bitterly cold. After the chief and his slaves had returned home, the child, a boy, was born to the dead woman. He stayed alive and fed himself on his mother's intestines. When spring came the boys who

---

1. The term Boas transcribes as "Tsimschian" is c̓msyan (literally, 'inside the Skeena River'), anglicized commonly as "Tsimshian" and referring to a group of linguistically and culturally-related peoples whose languages constitute the Tsimshian Language Family. The territory of the four major divisions, Nishga, Gitksan, Coast Tsimshian, and Southern Tsimshian, includes the Nass and Skeena Rivers and the islands between their estuaries, extending south to Milbanke Sound. The ten groups of Coast Tsimshian who had winter village on the lower Skeena River below its canyon, and later on the islands of Venn (Metlakatla) Pass were: Gilutsau; Ginadoiks; Ginakangeek; Gispakloats; Gitandau; Gitlan; Gitsees; Gitwilgyots; Gitwilkseba; and Gitzaklalth. After the Hudson's Bay Company established Fort Simpson (now Port Simpson) in 1834, nine of these ten groups moved to the area surrounding the fort. While the Coast Tsimshian language is comprised of an intergrading spread of dialects, a divergent southern dialect, Southern Tsimshian, may be considered a separate language. The Nass-Gitksan language is comprised of the mutually-intelligible dialects Nishga, Western Gitksan and Eastern Gitksan. There is, however, some evidence that Coast Tsimshian, Southern Tsimshian, Nishga and Gitksan could be considered four separate languages (Halpin and Seguin 1990:267–269, 282–283; Bouchard and Kennedy 1989; Rigsby 1989:245–247; Thompson and Kinkade 1990:31–33; Dunn 1995; Goddard 1996:322). The stories represented here, when localized, are from the Coast Tsimshian and Nishga areas. A contemporary transcription of the Native term for the Coast Tsimshian language is "Sm'algyax." The contemporary spelling of Nishga is "Nisga'a."

Our annotations for this section, when not drawn from the available literature or from our own Coast Tsimshian fieldwork in 1989, have been prepared on the basis of our consultation in August 2001 with the following Coast Tsimshian people of the Lax Kw'alaams (Port Simpson) community: John Alexcee (JA); Merle Alexcee (MA); James Bryant (JB); Eric Green (EG); Frieda Green (FG); Wilfred Knott (WK); Victoria Reece (VR). Terms known only to one or a few of these individuals have been marked with their initials; otherwise, the term was known commonly. We gratefully acknowledge the assistance that these people have provided. As well, we thank the Lax Kw'alaams Band Council for facilitating our interviews with members of their community at Port Simpson in August 2001.

had stayed in the village during winter began to play about in the forest. They took their bows and arrows and tried their skill at shooting. One day, when they were thus playing, a naked boy whose skin shone like fire suddenly appeared among them. He seized the arrows which they had shot and vanished so quickly that nobody knew where he had gone. The following day, when the boys were playing again, the stranger reappeared and took their arrows away. When the boys saw him, they were afraid and hid their heads under their capes. Only one of them dared to peep through a hole in his cape and saw that the shining boy came from the chest in the tree where the chief's wife had been deposited and that he returned there with the arrows.

The boys went home and told what had occurred. Their parents didn't believe them, but when the children persisted in their story, they sent a young man along with them into the forest and told them to continue with their game. The young man was supposed to report whether there was any truth to the children's story. The children had scarcely begun shooting when the shining boy came, took away the arrows and returned to his chest.

When the young man reported what he had observed, the chief called a council and it was resolved to try and catch the fiery boy. The people made a big bundle of arrows, placed it in the forest and, when the boy wanted to carry it away, they caught him and took him to the village.

The old chief, his father, had the door and the smoke-hole of the house closed up so that the boy was unable to escape and then bathed him in order to make him strong. This is when he saw that all his skin glowed like fire. Then he went out to see what had become of his wife and found her body completely dried up. The boy had lived on her intestines.

After two days the boy started to weep and wasn't to be consoled. He refused to accept food. The chief had all the children come to him and play with him, but he wasn't to be cheered up and continued weeping. At last a boy came to him who happened to chew pitch. When the little one saw this he asked him for some pitch and the boy gave it to him willingly. He didn't only chew it, but swallowed it, and was asking for more and more. The people gave their whole store of pitch to him and he ate it all up.

In the meantime he had grown bigger and bigger and soon learned to speak. The boy who had first given him pitch was his favourite playmate. One day they went out together to shoot birds. When they passed a tree with some pitch on it, he took it off and coated his body with it. After some time they each shot a woodpecker and the boy asked his friend whether he would come into the sky with him. The friend agreed and they put on the woodpecker skins, flew high up and finally reached a country far, far away from our earth. They saw a house, alighted not far from it and began to tap wood with their beaks. Two girls called KsEmtsiâ′lk (female kingfishers),[2] were living in the house. When they heard the noise, they called, "Is that you NEmōmhā́t" (=Gut Devourer)?[3] (NE'rEn nḗyadē NEmōmhā́t?). "Yes," he replied, "can you tell me where the hole in the sky is?" They replied, "It is too far for you, NEmōmhā́t!" (Wagai dâ nahā́unt, NEmōmhā́t!). The boys, who had taken off their bird garments, put them on again and flew on.

After some time they arrived at a different land and saw a house in which a girl called KsEmwuts'ḗen (Female Mouse)[4] was living. They heard her voice, "Q,Q," (drawn out for a long time), so they began to tap with their beaks on the wood and when KsEmwuts'ḗen heard them she said, "Come in, come in, NEmōmhā́t!" (Ts'ēn, ts'ēn,[5] NEmōmhā́t!). She wanted to offer him food, but he didn't want any because he was quite full with all the pitch that he had eaten. But his companion ate heartily. After he had eaten, NEmōmhā́t asked, "Where is the hole in the sky and how can I get through it?" She pointed the way to him and said, "The hole in the sky opens four times for a short spell. Count! Four times it closes." (Tqālpq tk·ā́parat Wulnak·'aq laqa! Lesqtlnā́t! Tqālpq wulEk·'āqt). And she told him how everything would come about and what would happen to them in the sky. The boys put on their bird garments and flew on. When they arrived at the hole in the sky, NEmōmhā́t said to his friend, "You know that I love you. I will try first to fly through the hole. Follow after me, but watch that you catch the right moment after it has slammed shut four times. I will wait for you on the other side."

When the hole opened for the fourth time, NEmōmhā́t flew through. But his friend didn't wait for the right moment and followed him at once. The hole closed before he was through and he was squashed. When NEmōmhā́t arrived in the sky he took off his cape and sat down to wait for his friend. But since he didn't arrive he perceived that he must have perished in the attempt to fly through the hole.

NEmōmhā́t found a path in the sky and followed it. In a short while he found a beautiful duck (mḗek·),[6] which he killed and skinned. He went on and at last arrived at a spring and sat down by it. He had been there for only a short time when a young

2. "KsEmtsiấlk" is Boas' rendering of ksmċi?ɔ́·lk, the Tsimshian term meaning 'female kingfisher' (*Megaceryle alcyon*).

3. The name "NEmōhā́t" (also given as "NEmōmhā́t" in this same story) is not now recognized, although it appears that this term is derived from ha·t 'intestines.' Boas (1902:9) translates the name of this character as 'Sucking-intestines.'

4. What Boas transcribes as "KsEmwuts'ḗen" is the Tsimshian term ksmwiċi·n 'female mouse.'

5. Boas' "ts'ēn" is recognized as the Tsimshian term ċe·n, meaning 'come in.'

6. "Mḗek·" was recognized by the people with whom we consulted as łkʷumí·k, the name applied to the Common Merganser or "Sawbill" duck (*Mergus merganser*) (JB; EG; WK), although Dunn (1995:73) gives this as mi'k (Boas' "Mḗek·"). Elsewhere, Boas (1916:971) describes this species as a 'brown-headed duck.'

girl, accompanied by a slave, came to fetch water. She was the daughter of the sun. He donned the duck skin and thus assumed the shape of a duck. When the girl came close and spied the beautiful bird, she tried to catch it. NEmōmhā't allowed himself to be captured willingly, without any attempt to fly away. The girl carried him beneath her cape into the house and to her chamber. At night she took him into her bed and clasped him in her arms. When she was fast asleep, NEmōmhā't cast off his bird garment and his true shape embraced the girl, who was dreaming that someone was caressing her. Then she awoke; she felt that his skin was very soft, answered his caresses and said nothing. In the morning NEmōmhā't gave some pitch to her and asked her to swallow it. She did and liked the taste of it because it was so sweet. Since the girl stayed late in bed the following morning, her father sent a slave girl to call her. She saw the young man lying by her, but was afraid to tell the chief what she had seen. So she went to the young girl's mother with the unexpected news. She was astonished and said, "Where can the young man have come from?" and told her husband. He sent for his daughter and the young man.

When the chief's daughter heard the message, she didn't dare to get up and said to NEmōmhā't, "I'm afraid my father will kill you." But in the end they had to obey and went down to the fire where the old chief was sitting. He bade the young man welcome and asked him to sit down. In a short while the chief's daughter noticed that she was pregnant. One night she said to her husband, "I have a pain in my stomach; come with me to the long trunk on the shore (the toilet)." She sat down and he held her. Then she gave birth to a child, which slipped from her grasp. It vanished and she was unable to find out where it had got to. It had fallen from the sky straight onto the earth, in fact onto some branches which were floating in the sea.

Just at this time the son of a chief in Meqtlak·qā'tla[7] had died and the chief had sent out four slaves, two men and two women, to fetch wood for the pyre on which the body was to be burned. When they were on their way to K·'atōʹo,[8] where they were supposed to cut wood, they heard the tiny voice of a child and found the son of NEmōmhā't, who was drifting about on the water. They took pity on him, took him into the canoe and one of the slaves wrapped him up in his cape. They returned back home, brought the child to their mistress and said, "You are very lucky. We have found a baby whom you can adopt in place of your own." So the woman got

---

7. Boas' "Meqtlak·qā'tla" is məqɬaxá·ɬa, anglicized as "Metlakatla," the name of a Coast Tsimshian community located on the north shore of the western end of Venn Pass, near Prince Rupert.

8. Boas' "K·'atōʹo" (spelled "K·'atōʹu" in story 15 of this section) is likely the Tsimshian term sqadɔ·' (JA), meaning 'sheltered; blocked off' (VR). Elsewhere, Boas refers to an event occurring "in the village Q!adū' in Metlakahtla" (Boas 1916:166). "Q!adū'" is likely the same term that Boas transcribes here as "K·'atōʹo."

up, sat down on a chair and had the child placed between her legs as if she had just given birth. His skin was snow-white.[9]

When the chief heard that a son was born to him, he gave a great feast. The child grew up, but once, in the winter, when the people had gone to the Nass River, he refused to eat. He only took deer and mountain goat fat into his mouth. He sat in a corner of the house and made himself arrows with which he intended to play. His grandfather became very anxious that he didn't want to eat anything, and invited all the people to a great feast, hoping that someone would be able to advise him how to persuade the boy to accept some food. When all the guests had assembled, he gave them a splendid meal. An old man happened to pass by and was invited as well, although nobody knew him. He was given a seat beside the boy, who had a piece of fat in his mouth, but couldn't be persuaded to swallow it. Suddenly the old man said, "I can make him eat." These words filled the old chief's heart with hope. The stranger asked for a bit of salmon and had it roasted by the fire. Then he took it, scratched some dirt off his body without being noticed and put it into the salmon. Then he wished that the boy would long for the piece of salmon in which the dirt was. He had scarcely thought the wish, when the boy asked for the piece of salmon and ate it as soon as it was given him. When the chief and his wife saw this, they were very happy and thanked the stranger, who rose at once and left the house. They didn't know that it was Laqaquwā'se whom they had entertained (the double-headed fish;[10] see Section IV, VI and following) and that he had done mischief.

After a short time the boy wanted more and in a few days devoured the complete winter stores of the group. Thereupon the chief and all his people abandoned him and he became Tqē'msem,[11] who in the shape of Raven wanders all over the earth. (Told by Mrs. Lawson, the daughter of a Fort Simpson chief.)

I heard a different version of the ending of this legend from an old woman in Port Essington:

"When the boy refused to eat, the chief sent to all the people to find out whether anyone knew of a way to persuade the boy to eat. Suddenly three big, dark men appeared and said to a slave, 'We want to see the son of the chief.' They were invited in; the fire was made to blaze and they were given seats. The boy was sitting close

---

9. "This part is not quite clear. It appears that the woman had given birth to a stillborn child and now took the other one to present it to the chief as her own" [Boas' original footnote].

10. Although Boas' "Laqaquwā'se" is not now recognized, the term is said to be derived from the word lagax, meaning 'at both ends' (MA; VR). Boas (1912:158–159) provides the transcription "lagaxwā'sga" and the translation 'Was-on-Each-Side,' with a footnote stating that "the Was is a monster."

11. "Tqē'msem" is txí·msəm, the name for Raven throughout Tsimshian mythology. Our Tsimshian-speaking consultants also referred to txí·msəm as 'giant,' as did Boas (1916:60).

by his father, who was very proud of him, but he obstinately refused to eat. The three strangers asked the slave, 'Why doesn't the boy eat anything?' He replied, 'His father is very sad about it. We don't know how to persuade him to eat.' 'We are able to heal him,' remarked the three men. 'If we chew what you intend to give him, he'll accept it.' The slave went to the chief and said, 'You are very lucky; the three strangers say that they are able to heal your son.' So the chief was glad and promised them a rich reward should they succeed. The strangers asked for salmon and for a clean spoon. One of them chewed the salmon and placed it in the spoon. Then he scratched some skin and dirt off his leg and mixed it into the food. When it was given to the boy he first ate a little, and then everything. Then the three strangers got up and left at once. A slave standing in the road saw them walk into the sea and assume the shape of Laqaquwā'se (see above).[12] Then the boy became so voracious that he devoured the complete winter stores in five days. In consequence he was abandoned."

I omit the legends of the liberation of the sun, water and fire, as well as the countless Tqē'msem legends which all agree with the corresponding Tlingit and Haida legends, and merely add a variant of the legend of the liberation of daylight. The daylight was in the chief's house in a box called ME,[13] which looked like a wasp's nest. Raven stole it in the often-told way and flew with it to the mouth of the Nass River where many people were busy fishing. He begged them for some fish. When they refused it to him four times, even though he had threatened to let it become day, he broke the box and day came. Then a strong east wind came up that drove the canoes to the river's mouth and Tqē'msem saw that the fishermen were huge toads which became transformed to stones which can still be seen in the mouth of the river today. (The above version is by a native of Meqtlak·qā'tla.)[14] The well-known missionary W. Duncan[15] told me the same tale in the following version: "In the beginning the frogs ruled the world and were living happily in the then reigning darkness. One day Tqē'msem arrived and asked them for something to eat. But they refused his request and said, 'You fool; we won't give anything to you.' So

12. The reference is to the 'double-headed fish' mentioned earlier in the story.

13. The term Boas transcribes here as "ME" for this box is transcribed elsewhere as "mā," where Boas (1916:61) notes that "Giant had known it before he descended to our world." Elsewhere, Boas (1902:21) provides the transcription "max." Our Tsimshian-speaking consultants recognized this term as hama·' meaning 'the cry of a baby,' and pointed out that this "box" resembled a balloon.

14. As previously noted in this same story, Boas' "Meqtlak·qā'tla" is məqɬaxá·ɬa, anglicized as "Metlakatla," the name of a Coast Tsimshian community located on the north shore of the western end of Venn Pass, near Prince Rupert.

15. On November 1, 1886, while still in Victoria, Boas wrote to his parents: "I also met Mr. Duncan, the missionary from Metlakatla ... Duncan has done a great deal for the Tsimshian Indians during the twenty years he has been here ... " (Rohner 1969:51).

Tqē'msem became angry and thought how he could avenge himself. He knew that the frogs were unable to bear Daylight; consequently, he went to steal Sun and Daylight. (Here follows the usual story.) Then he came back to the frogs and said, 'Give me something to eat. If you don't, I'll make Daylight immediately.' They laughed at him and said, 'Do you think that we don't know that a great chief has Daylight?" In order to convince them he made the light peep out a bit from underneath his wings. But the frogs thought he wanted to trick them and refused him the food. So he made the day and the frogs crawled back into the darkness."

I heard the following two legends also from Mr. Duncan: "Tqē'msem made himself a small man from a bit of inner cedar bark and took him along as a slave. He put two cockles into his ears and impressed upon the slave to say whenever they came to a village, 'Here comes the great chief with the abalone shells.' The slave promised. But when they came to a village he called, 'Here comes the great chief with the ornament of cockles.' Raven became angry and said, 'That's not what you are supposed to say. You have to call: Here comes the great chief with the abalone shell ornament.' But the slave kept calling, 'Here comes the great chief with the ornament of cockles.'"

"Then the chief of the village invited him and let him be asked, 'Would you like to have berries to eat?' Raven said to the slave, 'Say that the great chief wants to eat berries.' But he said, 'The great chief doesn't want to eat any berries,' so he got the berries which had been intended for Raven. Then the chief let Raven be asked, 'Would you like to eat salmon?' Again he ordered the slave to say, 'The great chief wants to eat salmon.' But the slave said, 'The great chief doesn't want to eat salmon.' Consequently Raven again received nothing while the slave ate so much that he was hardly able to walk."

For the following tale of the Nasqa'[16] I am indebted to Mrs. Spencer, a half-blood Indian from Albert Bay:[17] "Raven had caught a salmon and invited all the animals for a feast. He roasted the salmon and all the animals were sitting around the fire and were waiting greedily for the food. Raven became angry at this and told them to move farther away. But they paid no attention to him. So he grabbed one of the guests and held him close to the fire until one side of his face was completely red. Then he turned him and made the other side red. He flung him out of the house and transformed him into a bird with red cheeks.[18] Squirrel was so hungry that she cried

---

16. Boas' "Nasqa'" is "Nisga'a" (formerly often spelled "Nishga"), the name identifying the aboriginal people of the Nass River.

17. While Boas wrote "Albert Bay," he meant Alert Bay. Mrs. Spencer was the sister of George Hunt, Boas' native collaborator from Fort Rupert.

18. Presumably this is Northern Flicker (*Colaptes spp.*)

and rubbed her eyes. 'That's fine,' called Raven. 'Just keep on rubbing a bit,' and Squirrel lost her eyebrows. In addition Raven smeared her face with colour and then chased her into the forest. He let Cormorant taste some of the salmon and tore out his tongue when he stuck it out."

I here add a tale about Raven, although it doesn't seem to belong to the Tqḗ'msem cycle: A girl, the daughter of a chief, was weeping all day long. So her brother took his bow and arrows and shot a raven. He wounded him, caught him and took him to his sister to play with and she was glad. She carried the raven around the house. But one day, when she took him outside, he flew away. The girl was very sad at the loss and ran after the raven in order to recapture him. She pursued him for long days and at last arrived at the house of Raven's father. He enquired of his son, "Did you get the girl?" The son replied, "Yes, she is outside." So the father was glad and sent out his people to fetch the girl. When they brought her, he gave her to his son as a wife.

But the brother had followed his sister. He also arrived at Raven's house but was afraid to go inside. He only peeped in through a knot-hole and saw his sister. He waited outside for twenty days and then the girl came out of the house. When they saw each other, brother and sister burst into tears. The brother said, "Come, go away with me secretly." But she replied, "No, Raven will pursue us and will kill you." So the young man showed her his bow and arrow with which he intended to defend himself, but she said, "Go back and bring along all our people and you will be able to get me." The brother followed her counsel. He returned home and told his father that his sister had become Raven's wife and that he had been unable to liberate her all by himself.

So all the people went along with him to the house of Raven's father. They positioned themselves all around, and then the young man crept secretly inside and whispered to his sister, "Quick, come out of the house. All the people have come with me and they are going to tear the house down." So the woman went outside and took along her husband. Then the people tore down the house and killed Raven's father. They cut off his head and dried it and called it Wulbatlketl k·ā′aq (beheaded raven).[19] Then they spoke among themselves, "Let's kill young Raven as well," but his wife wouldn't have it and allowed her husband to fly away. All the ravens are descended from him.

---

19. The second of these two terms, "k·ā′aq," is recognized as ga·x̱ 'Raven'; the first term, "Wulbatlketl," is not now known.

2. Origin of People

Once upon a time, a rock near the Nass River and an elderberry bush were in labour at the same time. The bush gave birth to its children first. If the rock had been first, people would be immortal and their skin would be as hard as stone. But because the elderberry bush was first, they are mortal and their skin is soft. Only fingernails and toenails show how the skin would have become if the children of the rock had been born first.

3. Earth, Great Flood[20] and Sky

The earth is flat and round. It rests upon a pillar which is held by an old woman. When she moves there is an earthquake. In the beginning the earth was almost completely level; there were only small hills. In those days there was a village on the upper Skeena River in D'ᴇmlaq'ā'm[21] whose inhabitants were very wicked. They were singing and gambling all through the nights so that at last the sky grew angry and sent a Great Flood which covered the whole earth. By this Great Flood, the people were scattered all over the earth. When the waters had receded again, the people saw that mountains had arisen as we see them today. Some people say that the earth had been turned upside down at that time; recently, when coal was found in the Queen Charlotte Islands, an old woman said these were the fire pits of the people living before the earth was turned upside down.

Everyone wanting to go up to the sky has to pass through the house of the Moon. The chief of this house is called Haiatlilā'qs (Plague).[22] He is sitting in the back of the house and many pretty things are around him. On the west side of the house there live many ugly dwarfs called k·anā'ts (hermaphrodites).[23] As soon as a visitor appears at the door he has to call, "I wish to be made beautiful and healthy by Haiatlilā'qs." Thereupon the dwarfs call, "Come here! Come here!" When the stranger follows their invitation in the belief of obeying the summons of a chief, they kill him. The following tradition tells of this.

---

20. Boas in the original uses the German term *Sintfluth* for 'Great Flood.'

21. This legendary village (transcribed here by Boas as "D'ᴇmlaq'ā'm") on the upper Skeena River near Hazelton was made well-known to a larger population by Marius Barbeau (1928) as "Temlaham" or Prairie-Town. Boas (1916:394) calls this "the original home of the Tsimshian" and points out that most of the Tsimshian crests are said to have originated here.

22. Boas (1916:960) translates this term as 'spirit of pestilence.'

23. This term is not now recognized. Boas (1912:278) elsewhere provides the transcription "qanâ'ots" and the translation 'hermaphrodite, man acting like woman.'

4. The Visit to the Sky

Once upon a time, G·amdī̆gyētlnḗeq (Only Seeing Fire)[24] wanted to climb up to the sky. His friends didn't believe that he would be able to do it, so he said, "When I get to the sky you will see the sun stand still." He went to a small sandbar in the vicinity of Meqtlak·qā́tla and took along his bow and arrows and a strong rope; then he shot one arrow skywards. He saw it fly and finally strike the blue dome. He took a second arrow and aimed for the notch of the first one, hit it, and in this way continued to shoot until he had formed a chain which reached almost down to earth. Since he had used up all his arrows and there still remained a gap, he leaned his bow against the end of the chain. Then he climbed up. When he arrived at the house of the Moon, he stepped up to the door and called "I want to be made beautiful and healthy by Haiatlilā́qs." Thereupon the dwarfs called him. But he didn't look at them and went straight up to the chief, following the east side of the house, where he met with a pleasant reception. The sun stood still and so the people knew that G·amdī̆gyētlnḗeq was in the sky. The young man remained as a guest of Haiatlilā́qs for some time. The latter purified him first, by bathing and washing him. After the bath, scales fell from his body and he became as pure and white as snow. After some time he longed to be back on earth. Before he had said anything, Haiatlilā́qs had already heard his wish and promised to send him back. He said, "Behold what you shall teach the people when you get back to earth: I take pleasure in seeing men on earth, since otherwise there would be no one to pray to me and to worship me. I need your worship and rejoice in it, but if you go on doing evil, I will destroy you. Husband and wife shall be true to one another; you shall pray to me and you shall not look at the moon while sitting on the beach to relieve yourself. I take pleasure in your smoke. You shall not gamble and be noisy at night. If you continue doing what I forbid, I shall destroy you." Then he sent the young chief back. He pulled aside a board right in front of their seat and G·amdī̆gyētlnḗeq saw the whole earth in front of himself and the chain of arrows that he had climbed up. He climbed back down along it. When he arrived at the bottom and removed his bow, they all fell down. He went back to his homeland and taught the people what Haiatlilā́qs had told him.

5. Gualgabaʹqs (Fire Leggings)[25]

There once was a mighty chief who married a second wife in addition to his first one. His new wife belonged to a group living in a valley on the upper reaches of the

---

24. This term is not now recognized.

25. What Boas transcribes as "Gualgabaʹqs" is recognized as the term gʷalgəmṗáxs, meaning literally 'burning pants' (JA; MA; VR).

Skeena River. She had ten brothers and was very rich. One day her brothers came to visit her and brought rich presents for their brother-in-law: food, furs and other valuables. The chief's first wife was very jealous of the new wife and thought for a long time how she could bring it about that the chief would discard his second wife. One day the guests and the locals were playing with gambling sticks. One of the brothers had beautiful red paint with which he adorned his face while gambling, in order to tie luck to his side. The woman pretended that she wanted to have the paint very badly and sent a slave boy to the young man to ask for it. Even though he was not willing at first to part with his paint, he finally gave in to the repeated requests of the woman. After she had received the paint she pretended, on her husband's arrival, as if she was anxious to hide the leather bag in which the paint was kept. She intended to draw her husband's attention to the leather bag. When she had succeeded and the chief asked her who had given her the paint, she replied that it was a present from one of the guests. She did not tell him that she had asked for it. So the chief became jealous and killed the ten brothers. When the new wife had thus lost all her relatives and consequently there would be no more rich gifts from her, her husband neglected her and ceased to love her. She asked the people to carry the corpses of her brothers into the forest and to put them down in a row. She placed the gambling sticks beside them, gave them the inner cedar bark, which is used during the games to cover the sticks, as pillows and covered their faces with the mats on which they used to gamble. She went out every day to cry over the bodies. On her return the people laughed at her. They stretched ropes across her path so that she fell, and mistreated her in all sorts of ways. The chief had a big house with three platforms running all the way around. One time the people stretched a rope right across the door before she came in, so that she fell down the three steps. The chief's first wife now always pretended to be very fond of her and picked her up and seated her beside herself by the fire.

One day she had gone out again to weep over her brothers' corpses. When she started weeping she closed her eyes. She opened them again after some time and then saw a bolt of lightning flash right in front of her face. She was blinded. When she was able to see again, she saw a beautiful young man standing beside her, who enquired, "What are you doing here?" She replied, "Neqno'q,[26] you can see how miserably all my brothers lie here slain." He answered, "Yes, I have heard your laments and take pity on you, so have come to help you. Give me a pair of their

___
26. "Neqno'q denotes some intermediary between the deity and man" [Boas' original footnote]. Boas' "Neqno'q" is naxnɔ'x, a Tsimshian term that appears to have a wide range of meaning—while Dunn (1995:79) provides the translation 'a supernatural being,' Guedón (1984:139) opines that translating this term as 'supernatural' or 'spirit' does not adequately denote the concept embodied in it, and proposes that 'power' might be a more appropriate translation.

leggings." She obeyed. He shook them and threw them down in front of her feet. A mighty fire arose as soon as they fell down and she was very frightened. He continued, "Don't weep any longer. When you get home, don't walk along the wall as you have been doing since your brothers died, but walk straight up to your husband, shake the leggings and fling them in front of his feet. Then say: 'Behold here the leggings of those you killed.' You will see how amazed he will be, because a lightning bolt will strike in front of them. He will call together all his people to see the miracle. They will all come, with the exception of one who never believes anything, but he too will come at last. I will be with you by then. When he arrives, leave the house."

She did everything as he told her. Her husband was astonished when she walked straight towards him instead of creeping along the wall as she had been doing. But when the lightning bolt struck in front of him, he was very terrified. The news of the miracle spread rapidly through the village and its inhabitants didn't go to bed at all, but instead talked of it all night. Only Hōk·qsāug'am Neqno'q (the one not believing in Neqno'q) said, "That is quite impossible. It isn't true." Early in the morning the chief called all the people and they all came, except the nonbeliever. When he saw an old man go to the chief's house to see the miracle, he laughed at him and called, "Why don't you give the leggings to me?" He took them, put them on and jumped about crying, "Catch fire, catch fire! What nonsense!" But then Neqno'q caused him to go to the chief's house, too. When the woman saw him coming, she left the house. The nonbeliever took off the leggings and threw them to the ground. Thereupon a lightning bolt struck which set the house on fire and killed the whole tribe.

When the woman went back to the village, the Neqno'q had told her to return to the forest to the spot where her brothers' corpses were. When she arrived there, she saw him standing beside the bodies. He paced across them four times, forward and backward. Thereupon they returned to life. One after the other got up and rubbed his eyes as if he had been asleep. They returned home with their sister. There they had been believed dead and the people had cut off their hair and blackened their faces. But when they returned, they put on red paint again.

6. The Family of G·auō [27]

Once upon a time, there were two villages on the Nass River which were situated exactly opposite each other. In one of these villages there lived G·auō, who had four

---

27. Possibly this is the term gáwa (JB). Boas (1916:964) simply calls it 'a woman's name.' The G·auō story contains the "most definite statement of the origin of the exogamic groups," according to Boas (1916:524), although the pertinent passage is not included in the version presented here in the *Sagen*.

sons and one daughter. The four sons were very rich. They were outstanding
hunters and had abundant supplies of woodchuck skins. Each fall they went into
the valleys belonging to them in order to hunt for deer and beaver. After they had
been hunting for a month, their lodges were always full of skins. Then they
returned home, gave a feast to which they invited the chiefs from the opposite
village, and then went back to their valleys to continue hunting. One autumn,
three of the brothers were successful as always; their traps were always filled. But
the oldest brother didn't catch anything, although he had fasted as is prescribed
before going on the hunt. His wife had even fasted with him. They went to a different valley to see whether they would have more luck there. One day they found
many beaver dams in a lake there. But they were unable to reach them because the
water was so high. So they tried to dig through the dams. They made a hole from
the top down into one of them and the oldest brother crawled inside in order to
chase the beavers out, when suddenly the dam collapsed and buried him. The
brothers waited until the water of the lake had subsided and then searched for the
body. They found it. A trunk had pierced his heart and had gone through his body.
They carried the corpse back to the valley where they had been hunting first and
where their huts still stood. They discussed their misfortune and one of the
brothers said, "Surely our brother's wife has been unfaithful." They decided that
the youngest among them should go home, when nobody was expecting him, in
order to find out whether there were grounds for their suspicion. He left and
arrived at the village towards dusk, but stayed out of sight. Around midnight he
stole up unnoticed to the spot where the wife's bed was situated and listened outside at the wall. He heard her talking to someone, so he sneaked into the house
and went to his mother's bed. He nudged her and told her what had happened and
that they suspected that their sister-in-law must be unfaithful to their brother.
Thereupon his mother told him that a young man was always visiting her. She
started to lament and to weep, but her son ordered her to be quiet. But some
people had already woken up and asked her why she had wept. She replied, "I
dreamed that my eldest son had been killed by the beavers." The young man
returned to his brothers, but promised his mother that he would come back the
following night. He disguised himself so that he looked like his eldest brother and
tied leaves around his legs so that it looked as if they were swollen. He arrived in
the village late at night, supporting himself on a stick and groaning pitifully as if
he were barely able to walk. But his mother recognized his voice. He didn't go to
the big fire in the house but went to that of his mother instead, which was in a
corner, and lay down. The eldest brother's wife, who took him for her husband,
came up to look after him. But he didn't allow her to touch him and pretended that
it caused him too much pain. He was lying close by his mother's fire. A board had

been erected right in front of him so that nobody was able to see him, while he could observe the whole house. Late at night, at midnight, he saw a stranger enter the house, who walked straight towards his sister's bed. He was still lying by the fire, moaning and groaning. But when all was quiet he stood up, took off the dry leaves from his legs and lit a torch. He went to the bed of his sister-in-law and cut off the head of the man he found in her bed. Then he saw that he had killed the son of the chief of the village opposite. He ran from the house at once and took along the severed head.

When he had cut off the head, the blood flowed over the child who was sleeping with its mother in the bed. It woke up and began to weep and the grandmother asked her daughter, "Why is your child crying?" The woman woke up and, to her terror, found her lover's head cut off.

When the youngest brother arrived back in the valley where he had left his two brothers, he didn't say anything but he impaled the severed head above the corpse of his brother. The brothers had heard him return and one of them sent his son to him. He saw the impaled head and thus they learned what had occurred.

In the meantime, the chief of the second village was missing his son. He thought that he had broken through the ice on the river and sent out his slaves to look for him. Since no trace of him could be found, he suspected that his neighbours had killed him and, when the brothers had come back from their hunt, he resolved to find out whether his suspicion was founded on fact. He said to his people, "Let all your fires go out and tomorrow morning I will send over for some fire. This way we will find out whether my son has been murdered on the other side." His people obeyed. When smoke began to rise the next morning from the houses, he sent across a slave woman who asked for some fire. She was received well by G·auō's relatives and was invited to sit by the fire. A man threw a salmon bone at her and teased her by saying, "Your master must get up late, otherwise he would have sent someone over earlier to fetch fire." After the slave woman had eaten, they gave her fire and she left the house. On the threshold she noticed a dark stain and knew at once that it was blood. She stumbled purposely and fell in a way that her torch was extinguished. In this way she had the opportunity to enter the house again. She looked up above the bloodstain and discovered the dried head of her chief's son, which was hanging right above the door. She was given another firebrand and left, but when she reached some distance from the village, she threw away the torch and ran home as fast as she was able. Then the two parties prepared for war, because the brothers knew full well why the slave woman had been sent. The foes met in the middle of the ice-covered river and fought long and hard. The ice became red with blood and was covered with many corpses. At last the brothers and their people were defeated and killed and their village was burned. Old G·auō hid herself and her granddaughter in a well-covered pit. The flames were raging above them, but they remained unharmed. They heard the heavy beams falling and the death-shrieks of the burning and murdered people. When the fire had ceased raging and the enemies had gone away, they came out of their hiding-place. They left the cursed place and followed the path leading to the hunting grounds of the four brothers.

There they built a small hut from branches and lived in it. The girl was very beautiful and one day G·auō took her by the hand, stepped into the middle of the valley and called, "Who wants to marry G·auō's granddaughter?" After she had called this, a small bird flew up and said, "I want to marry her, G·auō." She asked, "What can you do, my son-in-law?" "I'm not able to do anything," he replied. "When an arrow passes close by, I am dead." "Then go away," she said, "you're of no use to me." She called again, "Who wants to marry G·auō's granddaughter?" A huge Deer came running and called, "I want to marry her, G·auō." "What can you do, my son-in-law?" "I'm able to excite a whole village. When I appear everybody reaches for his weapons to hunt me. When they have killed me, they fight for possession of me and kill one another." G·auō was almost inclined to accept him but then sent him away after all and called again, looking up at the sky, "Who wants to marry G·auō's granddaughter?" An old Grizzly Bear came and said, "I want to marry her, G·auō." "What can you do, my son-in-law?" "I am so strong and wild that I am a match for everybody. I tear off people's heads and devour them alive." She hesitated for a long time and nearly accepted him, but finally sent him away after all. She continued calling and all sorts of animals arrived and wanted to marry the girl, but she accepted none. At last, when she called again, a lightning bolt and thunderclap came. She was blinded and almost stunned, but continued to call and a second, third and fourth thunderbolt came. When she was able to see again, she saw a being, beautiful like a Neqno'q, with two great wings. He demanded, "Why are you calling?" She replied, "All my children and friends have been killed." And the Neqno'q said, "I know. My father has heard you and sends me to you." Then she knew that he had come down from the sky and gave her granddaughter to him. And the Neqno'q took the girl beneath one wing, the grandmother beneath the other, and flew to the summit of the highest mountain. Before he reached it, he flew to a steep cliff and tore out a huge block, thus creating a cave into which he put the old woman. He asked, "Are you comfortable there?" and closed the cave again with the block that he had torn out. G·auō called, "Oh, no, no! Take me out, take me out!" He did and flew on. After some time he settled in a yellow cedar, tore out a branch and placed G·auō in the resulting knot hole. He asked, "Are you comfortable there?" She said yes, so he replaced the branch and flew on. Since then, cedars groan when the wind moves them. Then he flew up into the sky and took the girl to his father. On the following day, they already had a son. The old man in the sky was delighted with his grandson whom he called LEqyē'wun.[28] He opened a small room in front of his seat where there was a cold spring, in which he bathed the child. After he had bathed him, he pulled him by the head and by the feet and in this way brought about that he grew quickly. The following day the woman gave birth to a girl who he called KsEmhamhē'm,[29] the day after that a boy, who received the name SisgEgō'osk,[30] then, the following day a girl, KsEmguds'aqda'la,[31] the day following, a boy, G·amt'asā'm,[32] and finally, a fourth boy. The old man bathed them all in the cold spring and then elongated them. He made a small war club for the eldest and a small house, on which he painted their crests, for each of them. To the eldest he gave the rainbow as crest, to the second the moon, to the third the stars, and to the fourth the (legendary) bird LEq'ô'm.[33] The houses stood opposite each other in pairs. Then he taught the boys to fight with clubs and made them practise constantly. He made gambling sticks for them and taught them to gamble. Then he made them quarrel while gambling and fight one another in order to make strong warriors of them. He made bows and arrows for them and let them fight with them. When one of them was hit by an arrow, the sisters came and sucked it out, saying, "It's only a thorn." The youngest of the brothers was completely made of stone. He watched while the others were shooting, using only his stone fists during the fights. When the boys had become proficient warriors, their grandfather sent them down to earth. He gave them a miraculous box, called Ts'ā'ō,[34] on their way and said, "If ever you get tired in combat and are afraid to be vanquished, open up this box, but aim the opening only towards your foes and never look inside it. Your enemies will fall down dead." Then he sent them down, one of them each night, to the spot where their uncle's village had stood.

---

28. Elsewhere, Boas (1912:213) provides the transcription "Ligi-yŭ'n?," with a question mark following the name. This term is possibly laχyewá·n, although the Tsimshian people with whom we consulted were uncertain.

29. Literally, 'female pigeon.' Boas (1916:964) translates this name as 'pigeon.' The Band-Tailed Pigeon (*Columba fasciata*) is found west of the Coast Range in British Columbia.

30. The term rendered by Boas as "SisgEgō'osk" may be sisgɔ'ʔɔsk, possibly meaning 'playing with toy canoe in water' (JA).

31. Boas (1902:224) elsewhere transcribes this woman's name as "KsEm-gwadẑîq-t'ē'lîx·" and provides the translation 'woman-excrements-grease.' In another publication, he provides the transcription "Gumdasŭ'mada?" although he queries the accuracy of the name (Boas 1912:213).

32. This name is not now recognized.

33. This name is not now recognized. Boas (1912:213) states that the carving was made of "the Lax-ōm in the form of a man."

34. The term transcribed by Boas as "Ts'ā'ō" is recognized as ċa·w 'inside (anything)' (JA). It is given elsewhere in Boas (1912:215) as "ts!uwa'n."

The other tribe was still living in their old village on the Nass and the people were as bad as ever. They gambled all night and transgressed the sky's commandments in every way. One night they heard a noise like the flight of birds. They laughed and mocked it, "The spirits of our enemies are around," but it was the first of the four houses that was coming down. The following morning it was very foggy and they were unable to see the opposite shore. They heard the noise four nights in a row and on the fourth morning the fog dispersed slowly. They saw the roofs of four houses where formerly the village of their enemies had been standing. The fog was still down over the doors. Then a girl came from the house and went down to the bank. They saw that she moved her hands as if she were picking berries and, while she was doing this, the fog disappeared completely. She had gathered it in her basket. When the people saw the houses they were very surprised. Some said that they were houses of spirits, and others wanted to go and see who lived there, but their friends warned them against this. After two days they observed people and took them for ghosts, but a young man took heart and went across to see who was living there. He entered the central house, in which the eldest brother was living, and saw that all four houses were connected inside by doors. He found the brothers at their meal. They had ample provisions and received the stranger kindly, inviting him to sit down and share their meal. He concealed several pieces of meat beneath his cape in order to show them to his friends, so that they could see that the strangers were not ghosts. When he left at last, the brothers invited him to come again. When he returned the following day, they invited him to a meal again. Then they asked, "Do you have good gamblers in your village? We would like a game with them." He replied, "Yes, there are many." When the people heard this and learned that the houses of the strangers were filled with food and skins, they were so anxious to go that they didn't even sleep but wanted to go at once. Yet in the end they sent over only two gamblers, namely their best, who were well received, and the brothers lost a lot to them. The gamblers were hardly able to carry back the amount of things they had won. Then all of them went over to play. The brothers lost constantly and finally had almost nothing left. The eldest said, "I have nothing left but my club; I will stake it." The people laughed at this and said, "The little club isn't worth anything; it wouldn't kill a fly." The oldest brother countered, "Shall I try to smash your foot with it?" The other replied, "Yes, go on." He cut the foot right off. Then they began to fight. The eldest brother killed the enemies with his club and, when they tried to escape from the house, they were killed near the door by the stone fist of the youngest. The enemies shot the brothers with arrows, but the sisters sucked them out of their bodies immediately. The battle lasted for some time and the brothers began to tire. They said to their enemies, as many as were left alive of them, "Let us make peace; and call all your other people so that we can become friends." They were glad to escape with their lives and called their relatives and friends from their village. When they were all together, the brothers opened the box, Ts'ā'ō, pointing the opening towards their enemies and turning their own backs on the box. They saw only that the lid was completely black on the inside. They pointed the box all around, every way their enemies were standing, and they fell down dead at once. Then they pointed it towards the enemy village and houses collapsed.

Then the brothers began to make war on all peoples and tribes[35] and took the box along on all their campaigns. Their sisters accompanied them in order to suck arrows from their wounds. After they had defeated all the Tsimschian tribes, they went north in order to make war on the peoples of that region. Since they were not content just to avenge their uncles' deaths, their grandfather grew angry and resolved to destroy them. He caused that on one of their expeditions they forgot the box, Ts'ā'ō. They were attacked by many enemies and were all killed. Their enemies severed their heads and impaled them on a long tree, but they were still able to speak. When they saw a raven coming to hack out their eyes, the head of the eldest brother said, "There comes a raven who wants to hack out my brother's eyes." Thereupon the raven took fright and flew away. Then the head said, "Now he's gone."

7. Asī'wa[36]

There once was a woman who had a daughter married to a man from a different group. It was winter and there was famine in both villages. So the mother thought, "I will visit my daughter; she won't be as poor as I am now," and she went down-river on the ice. She was unaware that there was want and need in her daughter's village as well. At the same time, the daughter decided to visit her mother because she hoped that she would be well provisioned, and went upriver on the ice. They had both left their homes on the same day and, when they had been on their way for two days, they saw one another and soon recognized each other. They knew at once that they both were in the same difficulty and began to weep. They embraced and decided to go to a nearby valley. While they were walking along, they saw some rosehips,[37] even though it was deepest winter. They were half rotten, but the women

---

35. Boas in the original uses the German term *Stämme* which means 'tribes; families; races; stocks; clans; household groups.'

36. Boas (1916:959) indicates that "Asī'wa" is a variant of the name "Asdi-wā'l"; another variant of this same name is given as "Asi-hwî'l" and translated as 'Going-across-the-mountains' in Boas' (1902:226) texts obtained from the Nisga'a. The first part of this name, "Asdi-wā'l," is from asdi-which means 'from the front to the middle of the house; to make a mistake' (Boas 1912:257; Dunn 1995:6–7). Boas (1912:257) also provides the translation 'by mistake.'

37. Boas (1912:73) identifies the berry as "hawberry," that is, the fruit of the black hawthorn (*Crataegus douglasii*). This shrub or low tree is a member of the Rose family. The berries are said

picked them, nevertheless, and divided them amongst themselves. They ate and swept the snow away from a spot where they intended to sleep. The daughter broke off twigs and branches from the trees and they erected a crude shelter. After a short time they heard a bird sing, "Hō, hō." They began to pray and sacrificed to him red paint, eagle feathers and inner cedar bark as it is used for dancing ornaments. They threw all this into the fire and prayed, "Feed us now, Hads'ena's." (= Luck, the name of a bird that is regarded as a heavenly messenger.)[38] Close to their camp there stood a tall hemlock tree. They peeled off the bark, beat it and ate it. They believed in the heavenly messenger and trusted that he would feed them. At night they lay down. The young woman woke up around midnight and found a man by her side who said, "You are doing the right thing. Continue to offer sacrifices when you hear the heavenly messenger. Tomorrow morning go down this valley and you will find another hemlock tree. Peel the bark off the tree." Then he vanished. The young woman went down the valley early in the morning and took along her stone axe. When she found the designated tree she began to peel the bark and found a dead partridge[39] under it. She was very happy, ran back to her mother, threw the bird down at her feet, but didn't say how she had received it. And her mother didn't ask. They killed the fowl since they didn't have a pot to cook it in. In the evening they heard the bird Hads'ena's again and they sacrificed and prayed anew. They gave it a part of the partridge. The young woman found an animal this way every day, and daily, a bigger one. At last she even found a mountain goat. They began to dry the meat that they were unable to consume; they made lodges from the skins and became very rich. Finally the young woman told her mother that a man who had given the animals to them had appeared to her nightly. After some time he showed himself to the mother, too, and married the young woman. His name was Hō,[40] and one night he told his wife that he, personally, was the bird to whom they had offered sacrifices and that he had taken pity on them. In a little while the woman gave birth to a boy. The father bathed the child daily and then stretched him by stepping on his feet and pulling him by the head. Consequently the boy grew up quickly and was soon able to walk. Then Hō went out hunting with him every day so that he would learn to look after his family. He taught him to obey the heavenly commandments, what he

---

to have a pleasant though sometimes bitter taste (Turner 1995:111).

38. In his telling of the story of Asdiwal, Tsimshian mythteller Henry Tate explains that this bird: "is like a robin, but it is not he. When somebody hears Hats!Enáʼs speak, he has good luck with whatever he wishes" (Boas 1912:73). The Tsimshian-speaking people with whom we consulted recognized "Hads'ena's" as haċná·s meaning 'luck.'

39. Given as *Rebhuhn* 'partridge' in the original *Sagen*, but likely it is a type of Grouse or Ptarmigan that is being referenced here.

40. Boas (1902:225) provides the transcription "HōʼuX" for the Nisga'a form of this name, which he translates as 'good luck.'

was allowed to eat and from what he had to abstain. When the boy had mastered the art of hunting, Hō told his wife to take him to his relatives, to give a feast and to make him choose a name. She complied and took all their belongings along to her mother's tribe. When their relatives saw them arrive, they were amazed because they had believed mother and daughter dead for a long time. She gave a great feast and saved all the people from starvation. She had her son take the name Asī'wa. Hō had vanished after he had sent his wife and his mother-in-law back to the village. In the course of time the boy became a mighty hunter, but he hunted only in the mountains and not on the sea. He killed a large number of moose[41] and mountain goats and became very rich. His mother cut ropes from the moose hides and sold them.[42] She was very rich and the young man invited his tribe and all the neighbouring tribes for a great feast during which he claimed to be the mightiest hunter on earth. During this feast his grandmother told of all her adventures. After the feast he took up hunting again and always showed compassion for the poor; he sold his catch cheaply and was loved by everyone. When he wanted to marry, he had to pay a high price before the girl's brothers gave their consent.[43] He gave them whole animals, not just pieces of the game.[44] He lived in the mountains with his wife and became very rich.

They had been married for one year when one day he saw a polar bear[45] near the Nass River, close to his house. He took his bow and arrows at once in order to kill it, but all his arrows shattered as soon as they hit the bear. But he was not discouraged and pursued the bear upriver with some of his men. Finally his companions turned back, one after the other. He saw the bear climb up a steep cliff where no one was able to follow, but he took off his snowshoes and climbed up by turning his toes outward.[46] When Asī'wa reached the summit at last, he saw a big house into which the bear, who had suddenly taken on human form, disappeared. He fell right through the door, he had become so tired from the long hunt. Asī'wa followed him and, when he stood by the door, he heard the chief say, "Come on in,

41. Given in the original as *Elenthiere* which literally means an 'elk or moose-like animal,' but in this area the species referred to is likely a moose (*Alces alces andersonsoni*).

42. "These ropes are used to tie up corpses in a bent position" [Boas' original footnote].

43. The reference is to the "bride price," paid by a young man to the family of his bride.

44. "This is looked upon as a great compliment" [Boas' original footnote].

45. In the original *Sagen*, Boas uses here the German word *Eisbär* 'polar bear'; later in this same paragraph he refers to it as a *weisser Bär* 'white bear.' The species in question is the Kermode bear (*Euarctos americanus kermodei*), which is a totally-white bear and is known in Tsimshian as mə'ksgmʔɔ'l, translated as 'white bear; Island white bear; cinnamon bear; polar bear.' Its Tsimshian name is derived from the term mɔks 'white' (Dunn 1995:74).

46. Boas (1916:794) footnotes his summary of this story: "It is evidently a misunderstanding that the text asserts that took he off his snowshoes in order to follow him."

my dear." He entered the house and saw that the bear that he had pursued was an old slave of the chief. The latter had heard of Asī'wa and had wished to see him in his house. To this end he had covered his slave with stones and sprinkled him with ashes so that he looked like a white bear.[47] The chief had a bear skin spread out and invited Asī'wa to sit down on it. He gave him his daughter for a wife and served him food. The following morning he said to his daughter, "My dear, have your husband bring me a mountain goat from the mountain behind our house. He is a great hunter and hasn't been out at all today." In the evening the young wife warned her husband. She said, "I am awfully sorry that my father is sending you to that mountain. I've had many husbands and my father sent them all onto that mountain and I was not allowed to warn them. But I love you and want to save you. Look at the foot of the mountain and you will see the bones of all my former husbands there." And she foretold him everything that was going to happen.

The following day Asī'wa took his bow and arrows, his staff, a collar, a mat which he tied around his body, his hat, and his snowshoes and began to ascend the mountain. He saw that it was very steep and consisted of bare, shiny mica, and was full of mountain goats.

As soon as he had left the house, the old chief had stones heated red-hot and, just when the hunter had reached the most dangerous part of the mountain, he had water poured onto the stones. A dense fog rose and soon reached the hunter, but he kept his wife's warning in mind and, as soon as he saw the fog rise, stuck his staff into a crevice of the rock, hung his mat and collar on it and crowned it with his hat so that it looked like a person. Then he fled from the dangerous spot and waited in a safe hiding-place until the fog had dissipated.

When the people in the valley saw the immobile human figure at the dangerous spot, they called to one another, "Look, Asī'wa is unable to move." They laughed at him and the old chief was very glad. Asī'wa remained in his hiding-place until everything was quiet again, then he came back without anyone hearing him. He had fetched his staff and had killed many mountain goats. He cut off their fat and tied it to his staff; he left the meat on the mountain. In the evening he entered the door suddenly, threw his staff with the fat down right in front of the chief and said, "Here is something for your enjoyment." So the old man grew ashamed. He was very angry but said not one word. Asī'wa went to his wife, who was very glad to have him back and who was proud that he had shown himself stronger than her father. After some time the chief, too, started to like him, but Asī'wa soon began to long

---

47. Given as *Weisser Bär* 'white bear' in the original *Sagen*. As we have previously noted, Boas refers to this animal at the beginning of this same paragraph as *Eisbär* 'polar bear'—both *weisser Bär* and *Eisbär* are references to the Kermode bear (*Euarctos americanus kermodei*) which is, in fact, a totally-white bear (see also story 8 and 17 of this section).

for his home. He didn't know how to get back and was very miserable. At last he talked about it with his wife and she told her father that her husband was homesick. The old man promised to send him back. Asī'wa fell asleep, and, when he woke up, he found himself at the foot of the mountain he had climbed when pursuing the Bear. He was sitting on the banks of the Nass River and his bow and arrows and his snowshoes lay beside him. He believed that he had been away for only a few days, but in reality it had been a whole year. Six brothers of the Gyitqā'tla[48] tribe who were on their way back from fishing eulachon found him there. They took him into their canoe and, when they heard that he was a skilful hunter, they wanted him to remain with them, and gave their only sister to him as a wife.

There were some rocks far out to sea which only the most courageous hunters dared to approach in order to hunt sea-lions. The brothers used to go hunting out there, each one in his own canoe. It had been so stormy for some time that they had been unable to get close to the rocks. When they went out again for the first time, Asī'wa, even though he had hunted only in the mountains so far, said, "Let me try this kind of hunting." He took his club, his bow and arrows, and his snowshoes. When they reached the rocks they found such a heavy surf that they were unable to land. So Asī'wa put on his snowshoes, took his club and bow and arrows and, when the canoe was hovering on the crest of a wave and he was able to see the rocks, he leaped in one jump onto the rock and clubbed and shot the sea-lions right and left. When the brothers saw this they grew jealous because, up to then, they had been the best huntsmen. They turned around and left him on the rocks to perish. Only the youngest took pity on him and stayed in the vicinity. He decided to watch and rescue him in case of need. When the water came up with the rising tide, Asī'wa soon noticed that it would cover the rocks. So he jammed his bow into a rock crevice, transformed himself into a bird and sat down on top of it. When the water rose higher, he fastened an arrow to the bow and sat down on the arrow. When the water continued rising he fastened a second arrow to the first and sat on it. He continued in this way until the rocks were dry again. Then he reassumed his real shape and lay down to sleep. All at once he heard someone say, "My grandfather invites you for a meal." He looked up but saw nobody and was just about to fall asleep again when he heard the same voice again. After he had heard it for a third time without seeing anyone, he peeped through a hole in his cape and saw a mouse. It hid in the sea-grass as soon as it had spoken. But he jumped up, ripped out the sea-grass and saw the entrance to a house. He entered and the chief invited him for a meal. There were many people ill in the house and nobody knew the cause of their illness. But Asī'wa saw at once that they had arrows stuck in their bodies and he promised to heal them.

48. Kitkatla, a settlement on the north coast of Dolphin Island near Prince Rupert. The Kitkatla are one of the tribal groups comprising the Coast Tsimshian.

He took a rattle, shook it over the sick people and pulled the arrows out unnoticed, thus healing them. They were the sea-lions which he had wounded. So the people took him for a great shaman. He stayed for a while but at last wished to return home. He became dejected and, when asked for the reason, said that he was homesick. The Sea-Lion chief promised to send him back and sent around to all his people for a canoe, but they were all damaged. But at last one was found which was in good shape. It was a sea-lion stomach. It was brought up to the house; the chief gave Asī'wa provisions for the journey and put him into the stomach, and he tied it up from the inside. But he had directed him before to call for a favourable wind as soon as the sack was tied and not to untie the stomach until he could hear the surf. He also asked him to tie the stomach up again when he had climbed out and to throw it into the water and to call the opposite wind. The stomach carried Asī'wa safely home, where he arrived towards evening. But he went up to the house only the following morning to see his wife again. He found her sitting with her child on her lap. He stepped up to her unnoticed and whispered, "I'm alive and have returned. It's me personally and not my spirit. Don't weep any longer; I will try to take revenge. Give me my axe, my carving knife and a bit of fat." She obeyed and he left her again. In the forest, close to a small lake, he carved a fin whale from elderberry wood. He threw the figure into the water and told it to swim but it sank because the wood was too heavy. Then he carved a killer whale from cedar wood but this was also too heavy. Finally he used the wood of the yellow cedar and it was right. He carved several figures of killer whales, coated them with fat and ordered them to swim. When he saw that they were swimming well, he called them back, "Gyē'gō, gyē'gō! (Come, come!)"[49] They came and he said to them, "Tomorrow you will see my brothers-in-law. Turn over their canoes, but spare the youngest one." When the six brothers went hunting the following day, the whales followed them. They saw them coming and got frightened. They hastened home as fast as they could but were overtaken and their canoes were capsized. But two whales stayed with the canoe of the youngest brother, protected it and brought him safely home. There he found Asī'wa who had come back and had told his wife everything that had happened. The youngest brother was afraid but grateful at the same time. They lived in peace from then on.

After a number of years, when the son of Asī'wa had grown up, the latter on one occasion longed to be back with the Sea-Lions who had entertained him so splendidly. The boy asked, "Why would you like to be back with them? What kind of food did they give you?" Asī'wa didn't want to tell him at first but when his son pressed him he said, "They gave me rock cod[50] and eulachon oil which tasted very

49. Part of this expression is recognized as the Tsimshian term ga 'come!' (JA).

50. Boas uses the term "rockcod" in English in the original *Sagen*.

nice." As soon as he had said this, he fell down dead and fish bones grew from his stomach. This happened because he told what had occurred at the Sea-Lions.

8. The Neqno'q[51]

There once was a widow of the Gyispaqlâ'ots tribe[52] who thought no man good enough for her daughter. She said to her, "If a man comes to your bed and wants to take you for a wife, feel the palms of his hands. If they are soft, reject him; if they are very rough, accept him." She wanted to have a skilful canoebuilder for a son-in-law. The daughter obeyed and rejected all suitors. One night a young man came to her bed. His hands were very rough so she accepted his suit, but he vanished early in the morning, before she had even seen him. When the mother got up and went outside, she found a huge halibut outside the house, even though it was in the middle of winter. The following night the young man returned, but again vanished before day-break. In the morning, the mother found a seal on the seashore in front of the house. They lived in this fashion for a long time. The young woman never saw her husband face to face, but each morning she found an animal on the shore; each day a bigger animal was left. Thus the widow grew rich. She was very anxious to see her son-in-law and one day waited on the beach until he arrived. Suddenly she saw a white bear (mɛco'l)[53] come out of the water. He carried a whale in each hand and placed them on the shore. As soon as he noticed that he was observed, he was transformed into a rock which can still be seen today. He was a Neqno'q of the sea.

9. The Visit in the Sky[54]

Three brothers once went hunting in the mountains. They lay down to sleep, and when they woke up they saw the stars so close that they were able to touch them. They found themselves on a flat rock high, high above the earth. They had no food or drink, so the eldest of the brothers said, "What are we to do? Let's cut ropes from

---

51. As we have noted in association with story 5 of the present section, Boas' "Neqno'q" is naxnɔ́x, a Tsimshian term that appears to have a wide range of meaning—'power' might be an appropriate translation. Boas (1916:192) translates this story elsewhere with the title "The Bear Who Married a Woman."

52. Gispakloats, one of the tribal groups comprising the Coast Tsimshian.

53. While Boas suggests here that "mɛco'l" is a Tsimshian term for 'white bear,' the contemporary term by which this 'white bear' is known is mə́ksgm?ól meaning 'cinnamon bear; white bear; Kermodi bear (*Euarctos americanus kermodii*); Indian white bear; polar bear,' derived from mɔks 'white' (Dunn 1995:74) (see also story 7 of this Section).

54. Boas (1916:344) elsewhere provides his own translation of this story, entitled "The Brothers Who Visited the Sky."

our mountain goat skins and climb down to earth." But the youngest said, "No, let's wait. Perhaps whoever brought us up here in our sleep will take us back again in our sleep, too." They took his advice and lay down again to sleep. Suddenly the youngest one heard a voice saying, "Take a round pebble in your mouth." It was the daughter of the sun speaking thus and he obeyed her order. When he woke up the following morning, he saw that his brothers were dead. He had seen in a dream that they had left him to try climbing down to earth. Since they hadn't prayed, they had lost their lives in the attempt. So the young man prayed to the sun, the moon and the stars. He wedged his arrow in a crevice of the rock, tied his rope to it and climbed down. He arrived down below, safe and sound.

10. The Land Otter

Anyone capsizing in a canoe is caught by the Otter people (wô′tsē)[55] and is transformed into an otter. There once was a man who maintained that he would never allow himself to be defeated by otters, should he capsize. One day, when he was out with his sister, his canoe capsized. He swam ashore and saw a fire which appeared to move away from him constantly. He didn't pursue it but lit his own fire, and, while he was sitting there warming his back, he heard a canoe arrive. He cast only a glance at it and looked back into the forest at once. The canoe landed but he didn't move and the crew came up to his fire. He rose at once, went down to the canoe and threw all the paddles into the fire. Thereupon they were all transformed into minks which cried pitifully. The people vanished and their canoe was now revealed in its true shape: an old trunk of driftwood. The Otters made another attempt to win him over in this way, but without success. One evening, when he lay by his fire, he heard a woman's voice calling him, "Don't be afraid, my dear. I am your friend. I have food for you here. Trust me." Immediately afterwards a woman stepped up to him and gave fish and seal meat to him. He was very hungry, but did not eat, although the voice addressed him by name and promised to bring him food regularly. She said, "Don't look around at me; look only at the bowls." So he looked her straight in the face and called, "Eat it yourself, you Otter." She continued begging him but he remained unmoved. He heard the voice every evening. On one occasion it seemed to him to be the voice of his sister who had drowned with him. He asked her and she replied, "Yes, I am the spirit of your sister." So he thought "I ought not to be afraid of my own sister," and accepted what she offered him. It did him no harm. Then he began to hunt seals, which he killed with a club, but he was still on his guard and feared the Otters. He was resolved at first to burn the paddles

---

55. This is the Tsimshian term ẃáča referring to 'land or river otter.'

and hack a hole into any canoe that might arrive. At last, after he had been away a full month, a real canoe came and took him back home. In this way he was rescued.

11. TsErEmsā′aks[56]

TsErEmsā′aks once went out hunting seals with his three brothers-in-law. They did not succeed in killing any, although they saw plenty. They stayed out for three days without catching anything. They became very tired on the evening of the third day and TsErEmsā′aks decided to drop anchor and rest overnight. They were just at the foot of a steep mountain. They tied a heavy stone to a rope of cedar branches, put it out as an anchor and lay down to sleep. But just at this spot there lived Nuguna′ks (a whale; this word signifies: "mistaken for water")[57] at the bottom of the sea. The stone fell onto the roof of his house and woke him from his slumber. So he said to his slave, Shark (Nō′tuk),[58] "Get up and see what causes this noise." The slave obeyed. He surfaced and saw the canoe whose anchor was right on the roof of the house. He returned to his master and reported what he had seen. Nuguna′ks sent him back and told him to order the four men to take away the anchor. The slave obeyed. He swam to the canoe and knocked on it. The man awoke from the noise and TsErEmsā′aks asked the man sitting in the bow, "What is making this noise?" The man looked down in the water and saw the fish knocking persistently against the canoe. He said, "It's a shark." TsErEmsā′aks replied, "Catch it and throw it far away." His brother-in-law did this and the fish swam back to his house. He said, "TsErEmsā′aks didn't understand me. They handled me roughly and threw me far away." So Nuguna′ks sent him up once more and he knocked on the canoe again in order to make himself understood. TsErEmsā′aks grew angry this time and said to his brother-in-law, "Catch the fish and kill it." The brother-in-law caught him, ripped off his frontal fins and threw him into the sea. So he cried pitifully, rushed back to Nuguna′ks and complained, "Oh, TsErEmsā′aks has ripped out my arms." Thereupon his master told him to lie down.

All was quiet now and the four men were asleep. But Nuguna′ks went out in the middle of the night, seized the canoe and pulled it down to the bottom of the sea. He put it down to the left of the entrance (on entering) but the four men slept on calmly. The man in the bow dreamed in the morning that it was raining because

---

56. Boas (1916:285) provides another transcription of this name as "Dzaam-sa′gîsk," with the translation 'Dragging Along Shore.' A precis of this "totem story of the whale gens" appears elsewhere (Boas 1890a:820).

57. What Boas transcribes here as "Nuguna′ks" is the term nagunáks, recognized as a chief's name in the Gilutsau tribe (JB).

58. Boas (1916:285) calls this slave "a blue cod."

there was water dripping continuously in his eyes. He woke up and saw the strange house. He thought that he was dreaming and rubbed his eyes, but when he opened them again, saw the house again and heard the people talking and the crackling of the fire, he was at a loss to know what had happened to him. He tried to rock the canoe but noticed that they were stuck, so he woke TsErEmsā'aks and called, "Look, someone has pulled us down into the water." Then all of them woke up and looked around in astonishment.

Nuguna'ks, however, was very glad that the people were with him. He made his slaves (the fishes) split wood and make a fire and had the house cleansed. Then he sent a slave to the men and invited them to come into the house. They entered and saw that it had many platforms. They were weeping in fear because they saw that the house was ornamented all over with fishes and that many terrible creatures were living in it. But Nuguna'ks invited them amicably to come closer and said to TsErEmsā'aks, "You shall be my brother." He gave his cape to him, which was made entirely from sea-grass, and invited him to stay there for two days. But TsErEmsā'aks wanted to give him a present in return and asked one of his brothers-in-law to get the box that was standing in the canoe and which contained mountain goat fat, paint and feathers for ornamenting the face. He gave it to Nuguna'ks who accepted it gratefully and multiplied the bit of fat and paint and the one feather until there was plenty. Then he invited all the chiefs living with him down in the sea for a great feast. They put on their dancing costumes and changed themselves into fish before they entered. Nuguna'ks presented each of them with mountain goat fat, paint and feathers, and then said to TsErEmsā'aks, "Now watch what is going to happen here." Suddenly the water flooded the house and the fish started dancing. Even TsErEmsā'aks' canoe and the stool on which he was sitting began to dance. When the dance was over, the water subsided again. Then Nuguna'ks and all the other chiefs gave presents to TsErEmsā'aks and ordered him to imitate in the upper world everything he had seen. In the evening the four men sat down again in the canoe and, when they were fast asleep, Nuguna'ks brought the canoe back to the surface of the water. Early in the morning, when the man in the bow woke up, he felt the canoe rocking on the water. He awoke his brothers and his brother-in-law and called, "Look what has happened to us." They all awoke. They saw that they were back on the surface of the water and sensed the rocking of the canoe. They looked about and saw that kelp and sea-grass had grown on their bodies, their clothes and on the canoe. They went back home and nobody there recognized them. They had been mourned as dead because they had been on the bottom of the sea for two years, not for two days.

TsɛrɛmsāꞋaks built a big house and decorated it just like that of NunaꞋks. Consequently the descendants of his sisters still use the house and dance ornaments today which he brought up with him from the bottom of the sea.

(Told by an old man from Meqtlak·qāꞋtla and a woman from Port Essington.)

12. Yaqagwonōꞌosk[59]

YaqagwonōꞋosk was the descendant of a man who had gone down to the bottom of the sea like TsɛrɛmsāꞋaks. He was a great chief and once upon a time invited all the other chiefs from all over the earth to a feast which was celebrated on the Nass River. All the sea monsters came and used killer whales for canoes. They were so numerous that the whole river was filled. They landed and went to the house of YaqagwonōꞋosk. Each time one of them opened the door, water gushed in. Each individual wore the clothes appropriate for him. The first to come was KuwâꞋk,[60] who was followed by TlkwatsꞋaꞋq, KntɛpwēꞋn, KtlkuoꞋl,[61] SpaedꞋanaꞋkt,[62] and KspahaꞋwatlk. The last-mentioned were very dangerous and killed all the people passing by their houses. The most dangerous monsters were sitting at the back of the house; the others along the platform all around the house. Then LakꞋanpɛtsēꞋqtl[63] arrived. He wore a head-ring made of branches given to him by passing travellers in order to gain his friendship. The WulnɛbālgꞋātlsoꞋks[64] and WudɛꞋanoꞋn (Big Hands)[65] arrived. YaqagwonōꞋosk gave everyone what they liked best: grease, tobacco, red paint, and eagle down. They all promised not to kill people any more in future and, after their return from the feast, moved away from the path taken by the canoe of men. YaqagwonōꞋosk imitated the clothing of all his guests and wore it. Consequently his family has all the sea monsters on their totem pole.

---

59. Name not now recognized. Boas (1916:414) states that the young man took "the name Y!aga-k!unēꞋsk, which 'staid among his relatives' in the Raven clan."

60. "This name and the ones following denote rapids and dangerous promontories" [Boas' original footnote]. The sea monster called "KuwâꞋk" was "very good to look at. He always smiled when looking around. He was bald-headed" (Boas 1916:276).

61. (Boas 1916:276) comments elsewhere that one of these individuals was called "K-łgu-âꞋl" ("KtlkuoꞋl" here in the *Sagen*) and that "his hat and his blanket were full of arrows."

62. An alternate transcription, "Spagait-an-āꞋ-tk," is provided by Boas (1916:276) who notes this was one of the two ugliest monsters.

63. Boas (1916:276) provides an alternate transcription "Lax-an-batsaꞋxł" and adds that he wore "a hat made of twisted cedar branches."

64. The translation 'Drift Log Enemy' is provided elsewhere by Boas (1916:276) .

65. Boas (1916:276) translates this as 'Long Hands.'

13. The Ancestor of a Family of the Raven Clan (Fragment)[66]

A man once went out in his canoe to hunt but didn't catch anything for three days. Then, on the fourth, he saw a big Raven, who flapped his wings and dived in and out of the ocean. He saw many people beneath his wings. When he returned home, he built a house and painted the sea raven (ts'Ema′ks)[67] on it.

14. The Ancestor of a Family of the Bear Clan (Fragment)[68]

A man once went up into the mountains to hunt mountain goats, when he met a Black Bear who took him along into his house. He taught him the skill of catching salmon and of canoe building. The man returned home after two years. When he arrived there, all the people were afraid of him because he looked like a bear, but one man captured him and brought him into the house. He no longer remembered how to speak and didn't want to eat cooked food, so he was rubbed with magic herbs and he became like a human again. Henceforth, when he was in trouble, he always went up to the mountain to his friend Bear, who always helped him. He caught salmon for him in the wintertime when nobody else was able to fish. He built a house and painted a bear on it. His sister wove the bear into his dancing cape. Consequently the descendants of his sister today have the bear as their crest.

15. Tsag·atilâ′o
(Tsag·a = opposite, di = together, lâ′ = to be on the water)[69]

Once upon a time there was a chief who had a beautiful daughter. In autumn, when the time to gather berries had arrived, she used to go with the other young girls into the forest to pick berries. One day she had thus gone out with her companions and

---

66. This ancestor legend appears elsewhere as "The Story of the Gunaxnēsemg·ád" (Boas 1912:147; 1916:285). Referring to this story, Boas notes that it contains four parts, and that the fourth part stands alone as a separate story in the *Sagen*. This would be story 15 here, "Tsag·atilâ′o," which Boas (1916:835) describes as "The origin of the crests of the Raven Clan." In the present German text, Boas uses the term *Geschlecht* for 'clan'; this same German term can also mean 'tribe; lineage; family; descent; and, race.'

67. Boas (1916:285, fn. 3) states "this is a personification of the snag," but we assume that "snag" is a typographical error for "shag," the local name for 'cormorant' (*Phalacrocorax pelagicus*). The term given here in the *Sagen* by Boas as "ts'Ema′ks" is recognized as cəmáks, meaning 'in the water' (JB), and is not the usual term for 'cormorant,' which is haẃts.

68. Elsewhere, Boas (1916:297) titles this "Story of the G·spawadwe′da," and summarizes it as the "Legend of the Bear Gens."

69. Boas (1912:156–157) provides the transcription "dzaga-di-lâ′" and the translation 'Floating-Across.'

they soon arrived at a spot where there were a lot of bear droppings. The chief's daughter tried to put her foot on a clean spot, but since it was dirty all over, she became cross and scolded the bears. Then the girls went on and found many berries. When it grew dark they went home with full baskets. On the way the straps on the basket of the chief's daughter broke and her berries fell on the ground. The other girls waited until she had collected the berries and had fixed her basket. But the straps broke again in a short time. Again the girls waited for her. They hadn't gone far when the straps broke a third time. But when it happened for the fourth time, the chief's daughter said, "Don't wait for me. It's almost dark. Rather go on home and ask my brothers to bring me another basket." So the girls went home and left her by herself in the forest. They went to the chief and said, "We've been waiting for your daughter for a long time. The straps of her basket are broken and she is unable to carry home her berries. Send your sons into the forest with a new basket to help her." At this the chief sent out his sons at once.

While the girl was waiting for her brothers in the forest, two handsome young men came to her and promised to guide her home. They carried her basket and walked rapidly on. It was very dark and they conducted the girl, without her noticing it, to the house of the bear chief. For the young men were the sons of the bear chief. He had heard her words when she was scolding the bears and had decided to get her in his power. He had caused the straps of her basket to break and then had sent out his sons to fetch her. When the bears saw them coming they reported it to the chief. He was glad and said, "She shall become the wife of my son."

Meanwhile the brothers searched the forest in vain for their sister and at last returned sadly home. The old chief sent out all the people to look for his daughter but they didn't find her. Then when it became winter, the brothers ate magic herbs for two months and paid strict attention to the rules governing their use so that they might be successful. They remained in their seclusion and consequently the herbs had the desired effect. Had they gone out amongst people they would have lost their mind.

The girl meanwhile lived amongst the bears. When winter had come, Mouse came to her one day and whispered to her, "Throw your earrings into the fire." She complied. Then Mouse told her to throw all her other ornaments into the fire and the chief's daughter obeyed. Then Mouse told her that the son of the bear chief was going to marry her and impressed upon her not to have intercourse with any other man under any circumstances because he was so jealous. And what Mouse had foretold, happened.

In the daytime the bears used to go to the river to catch salmon. The chief's son went as well and ordered his new wife to have a big fire, by which he would be able to dry himself, ready in the evening. So the woman collected good dry wood and had a bright fire ready for her husband when he arrived back from fishing. When the bears came back, they took off their wet capes and shook them out into the fires. While all the other fires only flamed higher, that of the chief's son's wife[70] went out. So her husband grew angry and said, "You pretend to know everything but you don't know a thing. Can't you find any better wood?" When the bears had gone out again to catch salmon the following day, the women told the newcomer that she had to make the fire with wet wood which had been in the river for a long time, then the flames would not go out when her husband shook out his fur. She followed their advice and in the evening when her husband shook out his cape, her fire, too, blazed up high.

One day Mouse came to the woman again and said, "Do you see that mountain? Your father's home is behind it. But know, if you want to escape, that you'll find a large lake on this side of the mountain. On the lake there lives a man called Tsag·atilâ'o who will possibly take you across." When the young woman heard this, she wished to escape, but didn't know how to go about it because the two sisters of her husband were watching her constantly. So she thought up a ruse.

One day she went out with her two sisters-in-law to get firewood. They collected great bundles and propped them up against a tree. Then the woman said to the girls, "I will help you to load." The girls sat down in front of the bundles in order to have them tied to their backs. But the woman tied the two girls to the tree without them noticing. Then she said to them, "Wait for a little while. I still want to get more wood." The girls promised to wait and then the woman ran away as fast as she could. When she didn't come back, her sisters-in-law realized that they had been tricked. They wanted to run after her but were unable to get up. They shouted at the top of their voices and, when the Bear Wives arrived, they told them what had happened. The Bear wives freed the girls by biting through the ropes with which they were tied up. Then all of them ran back to the village, called their husbands and they all pursued the fleeing woman.

She had arrived at the lake in the meantime and saw Tsag·atilâ'o on it in a copper canoe. The lake was so large that she was unable to go around it and she could already hear the bears coming from afar. She called, "Oh, Tsag·atilâ'o take pity on me. Take me into your canoe. You shall have all my father's treasures." But he didn't answer and only looked down into the water. The bears came closer and the woman called again, "Oh, Tsag·atilâ'o, take pity on me." But he did not answer. Then she heard the bears very close. So she wept in fear and said, "Take me into your canoe; you shall have all the treasures of my uncle, too." Still he did not reply and looked

---

70. While Boas refers to this woman as the chief's wife here in the original *Sagen*, the story makes it clear that it is the chief's son's wife, and therefore has been translated as such here.

down into the water without moving. The bears could already be seen approaching so the woman called, "Oh, Tsag·atilâ'o, take pity on me. Take me into your canoe and I will become your wife." Thereupon Tsag·atilâ'o was glad. He dipped his club into the water and at once the canoe went all by itself to the spot where the woman was standing. He took her into the canoe and pushed off again from the shore. The bears had arrived at the lake by then, and when they saw Tsag·atilâ'o and the woman together in the canoe, they grew angry. The chief's son called, "Tsag·atilâ'o, give me my wife back, or else I will kill you." Tsag·atilâ'o gave no reply, but he and his wife were happy together in the canoe. The bears threatened once more and, when Tsag·atilâ'o still paid no attention to them, they jumped into the water in order to attack the canoe. Thereupon Tsag·atilâ'o threw his club into the water; it became alive, swam towards the bears and bit through the throats of all of them except two who fled in time. At this Tsag·atilâ'o rejoiced.

He returned home in the evening. But he already had a wife called KsEmnâ'osō (Female Mountain Lion).[71] When she heard that her husband had taken a second wife, she thought, "I'll soon kill her." But Tsag·atilâ'o, who knew his first wife's evil heart, said to her, "I love the wife I brought home with me today and I don't want you to do her any harm." "Certainly," replied she, "she shall be my sister." Then Tsag·atilâ'o warned his new wife of KsEmnâ'osō; he said, "In the daytime I catch seals, mountain goats and bears. In the evening I bring my catch home and then KsEmnâ'osō eats everything. When you notice her eating, make sure that you close your eyes and don't look at her." The woman promised to obey. So Tsag·atilâ'o embarked in his canoe, which at once sank into the lake and re-emerged again in the ocean, where he killed many seals and completely filled his canoe. When the morning dawned he returned, and KsEmnâ'osō was glad. He gave all the seals to her. He didn't love her and gave her all his catch. But he loved his new wife and gave her nothing. When it grew dark, Tsag·atilâ'o went out again. Before he left, he impressed once more on his wife not to watch when the old woman was eating, and she promised to obey. When it was quite dark she heard KsEmnâ'osō eating. She was unable to resist the temptation and opened one eye a tiny bit. She saw that the other woman had a whole seal in her hand and was full up to her neck. The old woman knew at once that she was being watched, and she became incensed, jumped at her and bit through her throat.

When day dawned Tsag·atilâ'o came back from hunting. He asked for his new wife immediately upon his return. KsEmnâ'osō replied, "She is in bed, sleeping."

---

71. Dunn (1995:14) gives the term du·smgiłáwli which he translates as 'bobcat; cougar; lynx; mountain lion.' The term recorded here by Boas as "KsEmnâ'osō" is given elsewhere by Boas (1912:162–163) as "KsEm-nâ'sEr" and translated as 'Wolverine-Woman'; this term is recognized as ksmnɔ'·su, and the translation 'wolverine' is confirmed (WK).

Tsag·atilâ'o knew at once that she had killed her. When he found the body he became sad and started to weep. He said to KsEmnâ'osō, "You won't get any more meat from me." When it had grown dark, the old woman lay down to sleep, and, when she was fast asleep, fire flashed from her mouth and eyes. Thereupon Tsag·atilâ'o sent his club and had it bite through the old woman's throat. The club bit right through the neck so that the head fell to the ground. But after a very short time the severed parts flew together again. So Tsag·atilâ'o had the club tear off her head again and then he placed magic herbs on the wound which prevented the head and trunk from growing together again. Then he cut her open full length, took out her heart and carried it to the corpse of his wife. He swung it over the corpse four times and the young woman stood up and rubbed her eyes as if she had been asleep. At this Tsag·atilâ'o's heart became glad. Then they dismembered the old woman's body and buried the parts in different locations. Then Tsag·atilâ'o and his wife had no more worries. But soon the mountain lions, the children of KsEmnâ'osō, came to see their mother. They asked Tsag·atilâ'o, "Where is our mother?" He replied, "I don't know where she has gone." Then the mountain lions knew at once that she was dead. They searched for her body, carried the parts back to their home and wept together over the corpse of their mother. Then they resolved to avenge their mother's death and wanted to kill Tsag·atilâ'o. But he took refuge in his canoe and the animals had to turn back unsuccessfully.

After some time the woman gave birth to a son who was called Gunaqanē'sem-gyet.[72] As soon as he had been born, Tsag·atilâ'o carried him down to the water and bathed him. Then he lengthened him by pulling four times at his head and feet and then pressed him together again. In this way the child became as big as a young man. He taught hunting and fishing to him and the two of them always went out together. Once the young man asked where his grandfather lived, so the woman told him that his grandfather and his uncle were great chiefs and that they lived not far away. When Gunaqanē'semgyet heard this, he decided to visit his relatives. Tsag·atilâ'o was in agreement and gave his son the copper canoe, a club, bow and arrows, and a harpoon. He went up the mountain to get his skins which he had hidden there, and he gave his son round stones to take into his mouth and then to use them as projectiles, and taught him how to throw them. After he had carried all this to the beach he began loading the canoe. It was already quite full and he had only loaded the smallest portion of the things, so he pressed the cargo down with his hand and it became so small that he was able to add more. In this way he continued until everything had been packed. Then they launched the canoe and Gunaqanē'semgyet, his mother and a big slave called Hā'lus, given to them by Tsag·atilâ'o, set out. Hā'lus steered the canoe.

72. Name not now recognized.

After a long journey they arrived in the country of K·'atŏ'u,[73] where the young man's grandfather lived. The people saw the canoe approaching and asked the slave, "Who is in the canoe?" Hā'lus replied, "That woman is the daughter of your chief. She got lost in the forest a long time ago and is returning today with her son." At this the people nearly wept for joy. They said to Gunaqanē'semgyet, "Come, your uncle awaits you in his house. Stay with us and be our chief." They pulled the canoe ashore and began to unload it. They carried the things into the house of the old chief and it was quite filled. They carried much into the house of the young man's uncle and this, too, was quite filled. They unloaded so much from the canoe that all the houses of the village were filled. Now they had meat of seals, whales, sea-lions, bears, and skins from martens, sea otters and bears to their hearts' content.

When winter came there was great need in the village because no one was able to go out and hunt. Deep snow covered everything far and wide and it was impossible to gather firewood. So Gunaqanē'semgyet said to his slaves, "Let's go out to get meat and wood." In a short time they came to a rock with many seals on it. So the young chief asked, "Would you like to have seals? Close your eyes and hide in the bottom of the canoe and I will kill them." The slaves obeyed and Gunaqanē'semgyet took his club, threw it into the water and it swam towards the seals. It bit through their throats and returned to the canoe. Thereupon he told his slaves to get up again. They carried the seals to the shore and there cooked them. The young chief ordered them to eat everything up and not to take anything home with them. But one slave woman thought of her hungry child and hid a bit of seal meat beneath her cape.

When they had finished eating, they went on. Soon they saw a big tree and Gunaqanē'semgyet asked, "Would you like to have the tree for firewood?" The slaves replied, "Oh, chief, we'd like to have it very much but we are unable to cut it down." Again he ordered them to close their eyes and to hide in the bottom of the canoe. Then he took a stone from his mouth and flung it against the tree. It toppled over and broke up into many fragments. When the slaves then looked up again and saw the tree felled and split, they rejoiced. They loaded the canoe and, when it was full and there was still more wood left on the shore, Gunaqanē'semgyet pressed the cargo down so that there was room for more. Then they went back to their village. When they arrived there, all the people helped to carry the wood into their chief's house, but the slave woman who had the seal meat hidden beneath her cape went to her child, who lived in the house of the uncle of Gunaqanē'semgyet, and gave the

---

73. Boas transcribes this same place name earlier (see story 1) as "K·'atŏ'u." As we have discussed, what Boas renders as "K·'atŏ'o" or "K·'atŏ'u" is likely the Tsimshian term sqadɔ·' (JA), meaning 'sheltered; blocked off' (VR). Elsewhere, Boas refers to an event occurring "in the village Q!adū in Metlakahtla" (Boas 1916:166). Q!adū is likely the same term that воаs transcribes here as "K·'atŏ'u."

meat to it. Since the child was very hungry, it didn't spend any time chewing the meat, but swallowed it and the morsel stuck in its throat. Then the young chief's uncle noticed that the child was eating something, came up and took the morsel out of its mouth. Then he asked the slave woman where she had gotten the meat and she said, "Gunaqanē'semgyet killed many seals and toppled a big tree but he didn't allow us to see how he did it. All of us think that he is not really human but that he comes from the sky."

And the uncle of Gunaqanē'semgyet had two daughters, both of whom were very beautiful. The older one had already been married and the younger one was lame in one leg. Hā'lus soon noticed that Gunaqanē'semgyet was in love with the older of the two sisters, so he sneaked into her room at night and took her for his wife. When Gunaqanē'semgyet heard of this he became very sad, but his uncle consoled him and gave him his second daughter for a wife. The young man went with her to the pond where the people were getting their water and bathed her. Thereupon her lame leg healed and her hair, which had been red before, became black and very long. She was now outstandingly beautiful and Gunaqanē'semgyet went back home with her. When Hā'lus saw how beautiful the young woman had become, he grew very jealous, but her father presented many precious things to Gunaqanē'semgyet because he had made her so beautiful.

After some time Gunaqanē'semgyet thought, "Oh, if only Hā'lus would go out to fetch firewood." He had scarcely thought this when his uncle ordered Hā'lus to fetch firewood. He obeyed and went out with the other slaves to get wood. Gunaqanē'semgyet continued thinking, "Oh, if only Hā'lus would bring bad wood back with him." And this is what happened. Hā'lus brought home bad wood which smoked badly when it burned. And Gunaqanē'semgyet thought further, "Oh, if only the smoke would get into my mother-in-law's eye." This happened, too, and the mother-in-law went blind in one eye. He thought further, "Oh, if only my uncle would become angry and have the wood thrown out of the house." This wish too was granted. The following day he thought, "Oh, if only my father-in-law would send me out to fetch good firewood." That same morning his father-in-law rose early and told him to go out to get wood. Gunaqanē'semgyet took his canoe and went out with many slaves to fetch wood. He loaded the canoe with good dry wood and then pressed down the cargo with his hands so that there was room for still more. When the canoe was finally completely full, he returned. All the people helped him to carry up the wood, which filled his father-in-law's house completely.

After some time the people went to Tlō'sems (Nass)[74] in order to catch fish there. After a journey of six days they arrived at an island in the Nass. There

---

74. Boas' "Tlō'sems" is recognized as qlu·sims, the name applied to the Nass River.

Gunaqanē'semgyet said to the people, "Now let's find out who is stronger, Hā'lus or I." So the canoes stopped and the young chief continued, turning towards Hā'lus, "On the island there is a big stone. Let's aim at it and see who can smash it." Thereupon Hā'lus took a stone ball from his mouth and flung it against the stone, but the ball didn't smash it and instead bounded back with great force and hit his mother-in-law's mouth and made a great hole in her lower lip. So all the people laughed at Hā'lus. Then it was the turn of Gunaqanē'semgyet. He took a ball from his mouth and threw it against the stone and it knocked a hole through it. Thereupon all the people knew that he was very powerful.

They went farther up the river and came to a mountain on the summit of which there lay much copper. The people tried to get it but were unable to climb the mountain, so Gunaqanē'semgyet said, "Don't try in vain. We'll knock the copper down with stones, then you'll see who is stronger, Hā'lus or I." So the canoes stopped. Hā'lus threw first. He took a stone from his mouth and threw it but didn't even reach the summit of the mountain. The stone rolled down and fell into the water and all the people laughed at Hā'lus. Then Gunaqanē'semgyet took a stone from his mouth, hit the copper, and broke it up into many pieces. Thereupon two hermaphrodites got up in the canoe and said, "One piece of copper shall fly to the Skeena River, the other to Cassiar (on the Stikine River)." And that is what happened.

At last the canoes arrived at Tlō'sems. The fish were coming up the river very late and for a long time none were caught. So the people said to Hā'lus and Gunaqanē'semgyet, "Go down to the river and try to fish; we want to find out which one of you is the better man." The two of them went to their canoes and Hā'lus put his fishing rake[75] into the water first. He caught nothing but tree leaves. Then Hā'lus tried again to catch fish, but didn't get any. On the second try Gunaqanē'semgyet caught one fish, and, while he caught two on the third try, Hā'lus again caught nothing in his rake. The fourth time Gunaqanē'semgyet caught four fish and, because Hā'lus again caught nothing, he was so ashamed that he, as well as his wife, jumped into the water and drowned themselves. From then on many fish were caught.

In the fall the canoes returned to Meqtlak·qā'tla. One day the people saw a sea otter, but they did not succeed in catching it. So they asked Gunaqanē'semgyet to try his luck and he killed the animal. His wife dressed it and skinned it. Then she went down to the sea to wash it. It wasn't long before Gyileksets'a'ntk, Killer Whale,[76]

---

75. Presumably this is a herring rake, a fishing implement consisting of a long pole with teeth embedded on a flat end section on which the fish are impaled when the implement is raked through the water.

76. Boas (1912:183) elsewhere provides the transcription "G·îlks-ats!ā'ntk," and describes this character as the lead killer whale.

came swimming up and carried her away. The woman was afraid to fall into the sea and therefore held onto his back fins. Whale swam away with her before her husband could come to her aid.

But Gunaqanē′semgyet was in no hurry and repaired his canoe first, and then, with many slaves, pursued Whale. When they came to the Nass River he saw that Whale was diving to the bottom of the sea, so he threw a rope with a stone at its end into the sea and climbed down along it. On the bottom of the sea he found a path and soon saw many people who told him that Whale had passed that way with a woman. He walked on and everyone he asked gave him the same answer. At last he arrived at Killer Whale's house. He found a slave busily splitting wood in front of it, so Gunaqanē′semgyet hid himself. Suddenly the wedge with which the slave was splitting wood broke and the slave began to cry. Gunaqanē′semgyet stepped from his hiding place and asked the slave why he was crying. He replied, "Oh, my wedge is broken and if my master sees that he will become very angry." But Gunaqanē′semgyet consoled him and made the wedge whole again. Then he asked him, "Have you seen my wife?" The slave replied, "Yes, my master has stolen her, but I will help you to regain her. Tonight I will carry water to the house. When I get close to the fire I will pretend to stumble and will douse the fire. Then you must come and get your wife while it is dark in the house." And this is what did happen. Gunaqanē′semgyet seized his wife and ran back to the rope with her. Whale and all the people whom he had passed pursued him but didn't reach him. As soon as he shook the rope, the people in the canoe pulled him up quickly. But the whales had surfaced already and wanted to attack the canoe. Gunaqanē′semgyet scattered a magical substance onto the sea, which killed them all, and he reached his home safely.

16. Ts'ɛnslâ′ek· (Abandoned One)[77]

A long, long time ago, in the Gyitwulgyâ′ts tribe[78] there lived a boy whose father had been dead for a long time. His mother had four brothers, the eldest of whom was the tribe's chief. In the summer the tribe went up the Skeena River to fish. While all the people were busily catching salmon and preparing them, the boy paid not the slightest attention and played all the time with three young slaves.

---

77. Boas' "Ts'ɛnslâ′ek·" is c̓ənslɔ′·yk which means 'abandoned,' and is recognized today as a chief's name from Port Simpson.

78. What Boas transcribes here as "Gyitwulgyâ′ts" is recognized as Gitwilgyots, the name of one of the tribal groups comprising the Coast Tsimshian.

One evening, when the canoes were returning and everyone was busy unloading the canoes, splitting the salmon and drying them, his eldest uncle called him and asked him to help, but he disobeyed and continued playing. So the uncle said, "Look out, when winter comes and we won't be able to catch fish any more, you won't have anything to eat." When the second uncle came back from fishing, he also called the boy, but he did not obey him, and he obeyed just as little when the two youngest called him. When he saw a woman gutting the salmon, he stole the gills, called his three playmates and ran with them up a mountain where there were many eagles. He put up a trap and used the gills for bait. When the eagles saw them, they swooped down on them; the boy caught them and ripped out their wing feathers. He continued this every day; he went up the mountain early in the morning and only returned late at night. His poor mother had no one to help her dry salmon because her husband had been dead for a long time and she had only this one son. After some time the boy and his three playmates built a small house of cedar bark for themselves and made a hole in its roof. They put the fish gills on top of it. The eagles swooped down on them and the boy caught them and ripped out their wing feathers which he wanted to use for his arrows. At last he had two boxes full of feathers.

Meanwhile it had become autumn and the tribe went downriver again. It grew cold; snow covered the land far and wide and the provisions had been almost used up. The boy's mother had no more food left at all because she hadn't been able to dry sufficient salmon all by herself. So she went to her eldest brother and asked him to give her son some food. He refused at first and said, "Tell him to go to the eagles; he fed them in the summer, now they can feed him." After a while he appeared to take pity on the boy, and called him into his house. Then he told his wife to take a salmon from the box and cook it. The woman did what she was told. When the salmon was done she placed it in a bowl and handed this to the boy who had sat down by the fire. But just when he reached out with his hand and wanted to help himself, his uncle took the bowl away from him and said, "Go to the eagles; they will feed you," and then he ate the salmon himself. Then he said to his wife, "Go to the box and get ksĩ'ū (a kind of berry);[79] put them into a bowl and give them to my

79. The Tsimshian term that Boas transcribes here as "ksĩ'ū" and describes as "a kind of berry" is actually not a berry, but rather the 'inner cambium of Western hemlock,' well known as qsiw (Boas' "ksĩ'ū"). It is possible that Boas may have thought the name applied to a berry because a "berry plant" was obtained at the same time as hemlock bark, and was eaten with it, by both Coast Tsimshian and Nisga'a, while the people camped at the eulachon fisheries near the mouth of the Nass River (JB; EG). This other plant, known to our Tsimshian-speaking consultants as t'apya·'s, is described as having small, flat, green, rice-like "berries" (EG). This name actually refers to sedum (*Sedums divergens*), a plant with flat, berry-like leaves, which were picked along with the stalks in May from rock slides, and grew in abundance on lava (McNeary 1976:111; Turner 1995:35).

nephew." The woman did this. But just as the boy was reaching out for the berries, his uncle took them away from him and ate them himself. He said to the boy, "Go to the eagles; they will feed you." Then he had his wife take crabapples from the box, but again he took these away from him at once. So the boy became very sad and left the house. When the second uncle saw him, he too called him into the house. He also pretended to want to give him food, but tormented him just as the eldest brother had done. The third brother, too, invited him to eat with him, but took everything away just as he was reaching for it. At last the youngest brother also called the boy into the house. By this time he was very dejected and when the people saw him enter, they all wept. Then the uncle said to his wife, "Take some salmon from the box and cook it. I want to give something to eat to my nephew." The woman obeyed and when the salmon was done she placed it in a bowl and gave this to the boy. But he thought, "I won't even put my hand out for it; if I do, my uncle will only take the bowl away from me anyway." And he sat plunged in thought by the fire. The uncle said, "Help yourself and eat," but the boy did not want to help himself, and only when his uncle had asked him four times did he take the salmon. When he had eaten the salmon, his uncle had ksĭ'ū berries given to him. The woman poured the fruit into a bowl with water, mixed them with fat and gave them to the boy, who finished the dish. At last his uncle had crabapples[80] given to him. Then the boy was satisfied and went happily home.

But when his eldest uncle learned that he had been given food, he became very angry and decided to abandon the boy. In spring, shortly before the eulachon appeared on the coast, the chief one evening sent a slave to all the families and ordered them to get ready to leave next morning for the Nass River. They complied, packed their gear and prepared their canoes. When day dawned they launched them and the chief ordered, "Take all provisions and all the cedar bark and extinguish all the fires." The people obeyed. He wanted to leave his nephew and his young slave behind all by themselves, but the boy became aware of his evil intentions. Everyone was in the canoes, except the boy and one young slave. Then the chief sent for the boy and invited him to come into his canoe. But the boy knew that he would not allow him in, after all, and did not come. Nor did he follow the invitations of the second and third brothers. And the youngest did not even invite him since he knew full well that the chief would not allow him to take along his nephew. So he said to his wife, "Put some food and a fire drill into a bag and leave it behind for the boy." Then the canoes left and the boy and the slave were left behind alone.

So the boy decided to look after himself and his companion. He began to make himself strong and started to work. He built a small house and let the slave warm

---

80. Boas uses the English term "crabapple" here in the original *Sagen*.

himself by the fire inside while he remained outside. And he let the slave eat the dried fish left by his uncle, while he fasted. Early in the morning he sat down on the roof of the house and looked out to sea. He saw that the sea had gone out a long way and that on a promontory there, on a big rock, sat an eagle which screamed. So the boy said to the slave, "Go down to the beach, will you, and see why the eagle is screaming." The slave obeyed and saw a small fish beside the eagle on the beach. So he called, "Here is a fish," and carried it up to the house. He roasted and ate it; the boy didn't want to eat anything yet. The following morning he sat on the roof of the house again and looked out to sea. Again the eagle was sitting on the rock and screamed. The boy sent down the slave again and he found a flounder. He brought it up to the house and ate it. But the boy didn't want to have anything. This same day he built a bigger house and the following morning he again saw the eagle on the rock from the roof of this house. When the slave went down to it, he found a small halibut. He carried it up and said to the boy, "Now you have to eat something, too!" The boy agreed and had a small piece cut off for himself. He took it in his mouth, but didn't swallow it yet.

Next morning, when the eagle was screaming, the slave found a huge octopus and then a gigantic halibut. It was so big that he thought he wouldn't be able to carry it, but when he tried, he found that it was easily carried. The following morning the eagle screamed again and the slave found a big humpback,[81] then a seal, and at last even a sea-lion. The eagle did not come any longer from then on, but the boys found more food on the beach each day. The sea-lion was followed by many seals, then two, three, four sea-lions, and finally even a whale. They ran out of room to store all the food because their house was filled with meat and their boxes with blubber and oil. So the boy built four big houses on the spot where his uncles had been living, and a smaller one intended for his mother. All the houses were filled with provisions and there was so much on the beach that the stones could no longer be seen.

One day the boy caught a seagull. He skinned it and dried the gull skin. Then he put it on and thus transformed himself into a seagull. He said to the slave, "I will fly to the Nass to see what the people are doing there. You stay here and guard our houses." With this he flew away. When he had flown half a day, he spied the canoes of his countrymen who had gone out fishing. But they didn't catch anything because the fish were late and so there was great want amongst them. He flew about among the canoes in order to look for his youngest uncle who had been kind to him once. And he heard the people say amongst themselves, "What is that gull up to? It almost seems as if it wants to settle on our canoe." Finally he found his youngest uncle. He flew about and saw a fish in the water. He caught it, flew over his uncle's canoe and

---

81. The English term "humpback" appears here in the original *Sagen*.

dropped it right into it. Then he flew back home. One of the people, looking after the gull, saw his feet and called, "Look, the gull has human feet." When the boy arrived home, he took off the seagull garment and told the slave that he had found his countrymen, that they were in great need and that he had presented a fish to his youngest uncle.

The chief, who had left his nephew to starve, believed that he had died in the meantime and sent back two slaves and a slave woman to fetch his bones. They prepared for the journey early in the morning and arrived in the village after half a day. To their amazement they saw four big houses and a small one with rising smoke, and they asked each other, "Are many people living here?" The boy was sitting up on the roof just then, looking for the animals on the beach. When he saw the canoe arrive he called to his companion, "A canoe is coming; quick, give me my box with eagle feathers and my bow." He wanted to shoot the newcomers, but they called to him, "Are you still alive? Your eldest uncle has sent us to fetch your bones." He didn't want to give them permission to land, but since they saw the food on the shore, they begged him urgently and he finally allowed them to come up. They tied their canoes to the shore and the boy had fish and whale meat prepared for them. But he told them to eat everything up and to take nothing back with them. He also ordered them not to tell his uncle what they had seen. But the slave woman had left a child behind with the chief and concealed a piece of whale meat beneath her tiny cape in order to bring it back to the child. The following day the boy sent the three slaves back and told them to invite his youngest uncle to come. They set out at noon and arrived at the Nass in the evening. So the chief enquired, "What has happened with my nephew? Did you bring his bones?" They replied, "No, he is still alive and healthy." The chief could hardly believe this. The slave woman then went to her child and gave the piece of whale meat to it unnoticed. The child was so hungry that it wanted to swallow the whole piece at once, and it got stuck in its throat, causing it to cough. The chief's wife heard this and asked the slave woman, "What's wrong with your child?" She replied, "Oh, nothing, it has soiled its bed and cries." "No, it is coughing," retorted the chief's wife, and she made the fire blaze brightly, went over to the child and took the piece of whale meat from its mouth. She smelled it and noticed that it was whale meat, so she called, "Where did you get it?" The slave woman didn't want to answer, but the chief's wife told her husband and since he threatened to kill her, the slave woman told everything: how they had found the boy and that he had an abundance of provisions. So the chief was glad and issued orders to all the people to load up the canoes in order to return to the winter village. The canoes were loaded that very night and they set out early in the morning.

The chief had four daughters; the second and third brothers had three daughters each, and the youngest, two. The three older ones told their girls to dress nicely

because they wanted to give them to their nephew as wives, but the youngest didn't
do anything of the sort. When the canoes approached the village, they found that the
sea was completely covered in blubber. The chief's eldest daughter was so hungry
that she scooped it up in her hand and ate it. When they came closer, they saw the
boy sitting on the roof of one of the houses. They saw that there were four big houses and one small one. Then the chief stood up in his canoe and called, "I will give
you my four daughters as wives." And the second and third did likewise. But the
youngest brother said nothing. The boy threatened to shoot the three older ones. He
invited the youngest one to land and he took his daughters as his wives. Thereupon
the three older brothers became worried and implored their nephew to allow them
to land. At last he granted their wish. Then the boy gave a great potlatch and took
the name Ts'Enslâ'ek·.[82] He became a great chief among the Gyitwulgyâts.

17. Origin of the Wīhalai′t (The Great Dance)[83]

There once was a man who went hunting mountain goats. He met a white bear[84] up
in the mountains and pursued it. At last he got close and shot, hitting it in the side,
but the bear ran on and finally disappeared into a steep rock. It wasn't long before
a man stepped out of the mountain, went towards the hunter and called him in. He
found a big house inside the mountain. The man made him sit down on the right-
hand side of the house and then the hunter saw four groups of people and observed
what they were doing. The Mē′itla[85] were in one corner; in the second there were the
Nō′otlam,[86] who eat dogs; in the third there were the Wīhalai′t, who eat humans; in
the fourth there were the SEmhalai′t.[87] The first and the last mentioned were very
much afraid of the other two. The hunter remained in the house in the mountain for

82. This name is not now recognized.

83. Elsewhere, Boas (1886:63–64) provides a translation of this story. The term Boas transcribes in
the present story as "wīhalai′t" translates as 'great dancer' and, according to Guédon (1984:139),
refers to "the chief initiates or initiators of the secret societies." Our Tsimshian-speaking
consultants describe the wihaláyt (Boas' "wīhalai′t") as "the 'big dance' like the high chiefs used
to do" (see also footnote 87 below).

84. As noted previously (see stories No. 7 and 8 of this Section), the story-teller is referring to the
white-coloured Kermode bear.

85. This is the Tsimshian word meaning 'dancers,' and refers here to one of the dancing societies.

86. The Tsimshian dancing society known as the 'dog eaters.'

87. "SEmhalai′t means the ordinary dance; Wīhalai′t the great dance. The latter is called Ŏlala as
well. The three names Ŏlala, Nō′otlam and Mē′itla are words borrowed from Kwakiutl. The dance
and the attendant ceremonies apparently belonged only to the Kwakiutl originally, but have
spread to their neighbours in the course of time" [Boas' original footnote]. The term "SEmhalai′t"
can be translated as 'true or real halait' (Guédon 1984:139). Our Tsimshian-speaking consultants
note that the səmhaláyt (Boas' "SEmhalai′t") is a lower-ranked dance than the wihaláyt.

three days, but in reality it was three years. Then the man sent him back and told him to imitate all he had seen in the mountain. The hunter was escorted home by the white bear and deposited in the top of a tree, where the people discovered him. He slid down the tree on his back, rushed at a man and devoured him. He rushed at the next and tore him to pieces; he killed many people like this. But at last the men succeeded in subduing him and they cured him with magic herbs. When he was quite healed again, he taught them the dances of the four groups which he had seen in the mountain, and since then people eat dogs and tear humans to pieces.

18. The Six Hunters

Once upon a time six men went out hunting. They put their provisions into a small hut made of fir boughs. When they came back they discovered that a squirrel had stolen all of them, so they grew angry, caught the squirrel and threw it into the fire, with the result that its tail burned. Then they lay down to sleep. Next morning they discovered that they, as well as their six dogs, were in a deep pit from which they found it impossible to escape. Since they were very hungry, they killed one of the dogs and threw it into the fire in order to roast it, when all of a sudden they saw it standing at the rim of the pit, alive. When the men saw this, five of them flung themselves into the fire as well. Only one, the son of a chief, awaited his end patiently. Suddenly he saw the others standing at the rim of the pit and asked them to go home and ask his friends to help him out of the pit.

When it grew dark he lay down to sleep and he heard a tiny voice beside him and saw Mouse, who invited him to follow him. He got up and Mouse led him to a house where he found an old woman, Squirrel. She said, "It is well that you didn't fling yourself into the fire, otherwise you would have died. Your companions are all dead now. When you wake up tomorrow morning take the small path you will see, and avoid the wide one." When he awoke next morning, he found himself in the forest again and saw the bones of his companions by his side. He followed the narrow path and thus reached home again. When he recounted his adventures there, the people grew angry and resolved to kill the squirrels. They caught and killed all of them, except for one female. So she cried and called, "Your village shall burn down in four days time." And this is what happened; only the young chief's house was spared.

(Numbers 15 to 18 were told by Matthias, an Indian from Meqtlak·qā′tla)

19. Beaver and Porcupine

Beaver and Porcupine were good friends. Once they went into the forest together and Porcupine said to Beaver, "Climb up that tree." Beaver said that he wasn't able to climb. So Porcupine said, "I'm just as plump as you are; just look how I climb." Beaver allowed himself to be misled into imitating him. He got safely onto the tree but didn't know how to get down again, so Porcupine said to him, "Why don't you jump down as I do?" Since Beaver knew no other way out, he let himself fall and hurt himself considerably, while Porcupine laughed at him.

He pondered how he could obtain revenge, and after some time said to Porcupine, "Come, let's go to the lake and swim." Porcupine said, "I don't know how to swim." "Oh, that doesn't matter," replied Beaver, "I'll carry you. If you dive and lose your breath just scratch my back and I will return to the surface at once." At last Porcupine was talked into it and Beaver dived. Soon he was scratched and so he surfaced. But when they were in the middle of the lake, he submerged for a long time and paid no attention to Porcupine's scratching. He stayed down until Porcupine was almost dead. Then he carried him to a tree stump in the middle of the lake and swam back. When Porcupine woke up and found himself surrounded by water, he prayed to the Nass and Skeena Rivers to send frost so that the lake might freeze. The Rivers listened to his prayer: at first one star appeared, then a second one and the lake began to freeze. Porcupine tested whether the ice was thick enough, but broke through. So he continued to pray and at last the ice was strong enough so that he was able to return home.

XXIV. LEGENDS OF THE HAIDA

About his June 1888 Haida consultant Johnny Swan, Boas was far from his usual taciturn self. "The informant is a young, well-travelled man," says the headnote to story 1, part 3 of this section; but then, at the end of what he calls an "incorrect version" of a Raven episode, Boas feels bound to say that he found Swan unsuitable, for he "put on airs of being a great story-teller without knowing the exact contents." One might have wished that Boas had limited himself to photographing his informant's "handsome tattooing" (Rohner 1969:89–90, 97), and saved his illuminating comments for Native consultants he could praise, such as the Haida "who knows English well," whom he engaged in July 1888 (Rohner 1969:98). We know from other information that this helpful person was Johnny Wiha of Skidegate. Boas names him in his 1888 fieldnotes (Boas 1888f) and his 1889 report for the British Association for the Advancement of Science (Boas 1890a:867), where he indicates that Wĩha, with a Mrs. Franklin ("a half blood Indian, living in Victoria"), is the source for the linguistic section on the Haida language in that report. Wĩha is credited with story 1 (parts 2, 4, 5, 6, and 7) in the present section. The "old Kaigani" person mentioned in relation to story 1, parts 1 and 2, is not further identifiable.

Haida men exchanging news in the smokehouse at Jehloo Camp on the west side of the
Queen Charlotte Islands, B.C., 1897.
Royal British Columbia Museum, Victoria, B.C. PN366 (Rev. B.C. Freeman photo).

House-hole House in the village of q̇a·dasg̣u (Mathers Creek) was also known by the ceremonial name "Potlatch is Slowly Moving," implying that the house was so large that the potlatch was long. A description of the poles can be found in MacDonald (1983:89).

Royal British Columbia Museum, Victoria, B.C. PN342 (C. Newcombe photo).

XXIV. Legends of the Haida[1]

1. The Raven Legend

1) (Told by an old Kaigani.)[2] NEnkilstlas[3] had a sister who had many sons. He killed all his nephews by pressing them against the sharp, smoothed bone pieces with which his neck-ring was ornamented.[4] When all the boys were dead their father sent his wife back to NEnkilstlas, her brother. She was very sad at the loss of her children and went down to the seashore every day where she lay down on a rock and mourned bitterly. One day she heard someone say, "Get up!" But when she looked up there was nobody there, so she continued to weep and in a short while heard the

---

1. The Haida, who occupy British Columbia's Queen Charlotte Islands and part of southeastern Alaska in the vicinity of Hydaburg, are grouped linguistically into Northern Haida (Massett and Hydaburg) and Southern Haida (Skidegate) (Blackman 1990:240). While there has been considerable debate about the relationship between the Haida language and other languages, it is now generally accepted that Haida is a linguistic isolate that has no demonstrable genetic relationships with other languages (Levine 1979; Enrico 1989:225–226; Foster 1996:76–77). "Haida" is an anglicization of the Skidegate dialect term x̱ayda or x̱aydaga which originally meant 'person' (Levine 1977:30). Nowadays the Queen Charlotte Islands are commonly referred to as "Haida Gwaay" (formerly spelled "Haida Gwaii") which is loosely translated as 'islands of the people.'

   While our annotation of this section is based primarily on the available literature, we gratefully acknowledge the additional assistance provided to us by Robert Bringhurst in compiling these footnotes.

2. "Kaigani" is an anglicization of the Alaskan Haida term k̓ayk̓a·ni· referring to a place at the southern end of Dall Island in Alaska but said to refer in earlier times to Langara Island (off the northwestern tip of Graham Island) from which the Alaskan Haida people originated. The term "Kaigani" is used in a more general sense to refer to all the Alaskan Haida (Swanton 1905a:105, 281; Leer and Enrico, In, Blackman 1990:258).

3. In notes compiled from Johnny Wiha at Skidegate, Boas (1888f) identified this character as the uncle of Raven. Enrico (1995:19, fn.4) transcribes his name as naŋ kilsdla·s and says of him: "The old man and Raven would appear to have been two manifestations of the same spirit, and therefore belonged to the same lineage. This means the old man was Raven's paternal grandfather, if not his maternal uncle." Bringhurst (1999:236) transcribes this same name for Raven as Naŋ Kilsλas and provides the translation 'Voicehandler.' He also provides the etymology: naŋ = 'one'; kil = 'to speak'; sλa = 'to handle; manipulate'; -s = definitive nominalizing suffix (Bringhurst 2001:pers. comm.)

4. "The neck-rings of the shamans are set with such bone pieces" [Boas' original footnote].

same voice saying, "Get up!" Again she saw nobody. When she continued to mourn she heard the voice again for a third time. So she covered her face with her cape and peeped through a tiny hole. In a little while she saw a seagull come and heard it cry, "Get up!" So she quickly threw off her cape and called, "I've seen you." Thereupon Seagull said, "I've watched you mourning here already for a long time. Go down to the beach at low tide and search for four round stones, polished smoothly. Warm them over a fire and swallow them." The woman obeyed and after a short time gave birth to four boys. NEnkilstlas spared their lives. The children grew up quickly and soon the eldest asked his uncle to make him a bow and arrows and went out to shoot birds. One day he shot a duck and asked his mother to skin it. He kept its skin. When the boys grew up, their mother often told them of their brothers and how their uncle had killed them. They decided to take revenge. Gyīns:hā'noa,[5] the wife of NEnkilstlas, always kept a robin in each of her armpits.[6] Once when NEnkilstlas had gone out hunting, the boys teased and mocked his wife and when she wanted to beat them, the birds flew away from under her arms. NEnkilstlas returned at night and found that the birds had gone, so he grew angry and wanted to kill his nephews, but he soon noticed that he was no match for them. He went into the house, sat down opposite the door and put on his big hat, from which a stream of water started gushing into the house immediately. The oldest boy put on the duck skin and transformed himself into Yētl, Raven,[7] who flew skywards when the water rose. His mother put on the skin of a diver and swam away. The hat of NEnkilstlas grew correspondingly higher with the rising water. At last Yētl reached the sky and when the water rose still higher, he braced his feet against the hat, his beak against the sky, and so succeeded in drowning NEnkilstlas. He banished the wife of NEnkilstlas into the sea where she became a dangerous whirlpool.

2) (Told by Wīha,[8] a man from Skidegate.) NEnkilstlas had a sister called Cuva'c, (Loon). She had a son of about four who had grown up very rapidly. One day he asked his uncle to make him a bow and arrows, as well as copper arm rings. His uncle, who didn't like him, refused his request, but in the end the boy obtained what he wanted from another man. Then he went into the forest every morning to shoot

---

5. "Gyīns:hā'noa" is Boas' rendering of q̓in sga·nag°a·y 'summer spirit being' (Swanton 1908a:590; Bringhurst 1999:254–255; 2001:pers. comm.).

6. Bringhurst (2001:pers. comm.) points out that the birds living in the armpits of this myth creature are more likely flickers than robins (see also the footnotes that follow concerning the robin/flicker confusion in parts 2 and 8 of this story).

7. This is Boas' transcription of yɛł, the Northern (Masset) term for the Common Raven (*Corvus corax*) (Blackman 1979:45); this same term is used for 'raven' in Kaigani Haida, where it is pronounced yáł (Lawrence and Leer 1977:445), and in Tlingit, where it is pronounced yé·ł (Naish and Story 1963:22; De Laguna 1972:I:46; 1990:212).

8. Boas' (1888f) fieldnotes identify this man by his English name, Johnny Wiha.

birds. He made a cape from their skins and hid it in a hollow tree. Away from home the boy always assumed the form of a young man but when he returned home he was a small boy again, as before. One evening, when his uncle had gone out to hunt for seals, he stole unnoticed from his mother's bed, assumed the shape of a young man and crept to the wife of NEnkilstlas, lying down beside her in bed. She got a fright because the house door was locked and she hadn't heard anyone entering. She asked, "Who are you? Where do you come from?" He replied, "I am the nephew of NEnkilstlas." She didn't believe him and wanted to ascertain who he was, so she said, "Stay here; I'll just go outside and urinate." When she was outside, she ran at once to Cuva′c to see whether the child was there. She didn't find him there and now believed what the young man had told her. She returned to him and he requested her to meet with him in the forest on the following morning. He continued, "I'll go to my mother now so that she won't miss me when she awakes, but I'll meet you tomorrow morning." She promised to come and went into the forest early in the morning, but the boy slept until his mother woke him for breakfast. He said to her, "Before I eat I'll run into the forest to shoot a couple of birds. He ran to the forest and met his aunt there and showed her his cape of robin (= sk·ā′ltsit)[9] skins.

When the wife of NEnkilstlas came home she told Cuva′c everything that had happened, but Cuva′c didn't believe her and said, "I'm no fool. My son couldn't have been with you because he was in my bed all night." After some time the boy came back and brought three birds. So Cuva′c continued, "Just look how small he is. Surely you must be wrong." The wife of NEnkilstlas blushed in embarrassment. She went away and brought the cape of bird skins. When Cuva′c saw this, she believed her sister-in-law and said, "Make sure not to tell your husband anything, otherwise he will kill us all."

NEnkilstlas returned at night. He already knew that his wife had been unfaithful to him because he hadn't caught a single seal whereas normally his canoe always returned heavily laden. He asked her at once, "What have you done? You've been unfaithful to me." So she admitted that her nephew had been with her. Meanwhile the boy was running about in the house without a care, playing with his bow and arrows. NEnkilstlas was deeply insulted. He wanted to find out whether his wife had told the truth and therefore left as usual early the following morning, but instead of hunting he hid his canoe behind the closest headland and returned unnoticed. Then he saw how his nephew ran into the forest, there changed into a young man and then

---

9.   The bird referred to here is a flicker, not a robin (see also the preceding and following footnotes concerning the robin/flicker confusion in parts 1 and 8 of this story). "Sk·ā′ltsit" is Boas' transcription of sga·lc̓i·d which has been identified as the Skidegate dialect term for the Northern Flicker (*Colaptes auratus*) (Ellis 1991); the same Haida term for this bird was also recorded by Swanton (n.d.)

visited his wife. So he resolved to kill him. He put on his wooden hat and the water began to rise at once. The boy then put on his cape and flew out of the smoke-hole. The house was filled with water and at last it flooded the whole land. The boy flew up to the sky and pecked a hole through it. He found five skies, one above the other, each one like a village. When the water receded again he returned to the earth and then was Raven, K·oa'. Only two women had survived the deluge. The name of one of them was Squtlqodzā't (= Seafoam Woman).[10]

3) (Told by Johnny Swan, a man from the neighbourhood of Skidegate. The introduction, as in the Tsimshian legend, deals with Raven's birth and I did not write it down because it corresponded exactly with the latter. The informant is a young, well-travelled man and presumably told not only legends of his home but also those he heard among strangers.)

Raven was the grandson of Chief K·enk·[11] and as a small child didn't want to eat anything. When he had learned how to eat at last, his father invited all the people to a great feast. But Raven gobbled up everything and in ten days had devoured their entire winter supplies. When all the supplies were gone he even ate excrement. Then he went, in the shape of Raven, to his uncle NEnkilstlas and borrowed his canoe, Qōtlō',[12] and his hat. He beat the sides of the canoe and it swam at once all by itself to his father's house. There he put on the hat borrowed by him from NEnkilstlas and water poured out of it at once. Then K·enk· put on his hat, which grew longer and longer, so that his people were able to climb up on it in order to escape the water, but Raven smashed the hat to pieces so that the added wooden rings flew about. They were transformed into the islands at the entrance to the Skidegate Straits.[13] K·enk·, himself, became a mountain to the south of the straits.[14]

(The above legend, according to the storyteller's explanation, belongs to the inhabitants of the house Dā'tsdals [= Moving House][15] in his native village of

---

10. The term that Boas writes as "Squtlqodzā't" and translates as 'Seafoam Woman' is transcribed by Enrico (1995:5) as sguɫgu ja·d and translated as 'Foam-drift-ashore Woman.'

11. Boas' "K·enk·" is the name that Enrico (1995:49–59, 91–93, 102–105) transcribes as qiŋgi (see also footnote 14 below).

12. Boas' "Qōtlō'" is the term that Swanton (1905b:148) subsequently transcribed as "xōt-Lū" and identified as the 'hair-seal canoe' used by supernatural beings.

13. Skidegate Inlet, which separates Moresby and Graham Islands.

14. Enrico (1995:49) identifies qiŋgi (Boas' "K·enk·) as "the killerwhale spirit under a prominent mountain in Bigsby Inlet," which is located on the east side of Moresby Island, opposite Lyell Island. Additional information is provided by Swanton (1905b:148) who gives the translation of "Qi'ñgi" (qiŋgi) as 'looking-downward' "because this mountain ... hangs precipitously over the sea." The gloss 'always-looking-into-the-sea' is provided for "Kinggi Mountain" by local historian Kathleen Dalzell (1973:II:216), who adds that the mountain's location is on the north side of Bigsby Inlet.

15. Boas' "Dā'tsdals" can be analyzed as: da = 'housepit'; ċi = 'into'; dal = 'to move'; -s = definitive

K·atsk·ē′roē.[16] It is the house of the chief of the eagle moiety[17] and has three platforms circling it. The totem pole represents Mount K·ēnk·, the first chief of this lineage,[18] with a high hat and many rings on which people are climbing up. On top of the pole there sits the eagle "in order to watch over his lineage."[19] Inside the house there stand big carved beavers.)

There now follow the legends of the liberation of the sun, fire and fresh water as we learned them earlier, and in exactly the same form. I heard the following adventure, which I did not note down when I was amongst the Tlingit, although it can almost certainly be assumed that it is also known there.

4) K·oa′q, Raven,[20] came to the house of Woodpecker, who had a big supply of salmon spawn. He wanted to have it and, when it became dark, threw the boxes used for the storage of the spawn out of the house. How great was his disappointment when he saw the next morning that the house had vanished and the spawn was nothing but a bit of pitch in a hollow tree.

---

nominalizing suffix (Bringhurst 2001:pers. comm.; see also Bringhurst 1999:104–109); Swanton (1905a:283) notes the derivation is from "Da'as" which he translates as 'house-hole' and identifies as the newer house of the town chief at "t!anū'" (t'anu·, on the east shore of Tanu Island which is off from the east side of Moresby Island and north from Lyell Island). "House-hole House" is the term used for this same house by Macdonald (1983:93) who adds that it was on the site traditionally reserved for the town chief and was also known by several ceremonial names, including "Potlatch is Slowly Moving, implying that the house was so large that the potlatch was long." After 1885 the surviving residents of t'anu· moved *en masse* to the old village of q̓adasgu (Mathers or Church Creek) where they built a new town, before moving eventually to Skidegate (MacDonald 1983:89) (see also the footnote that follows).

16. "K·atsk·ē′roē" is the same place name that Chief Ninstints provided to Newcombe, and Swanton transcribed as "Q!ā′dso," located at the mouth of a stream of the same name situated on the north shore of Louise Island (off the east side of Moresby Island) and said to be "the first home of the family named from it" (Swanton 1905a:278). Enrico (1995:53, 137, 168, 211) transcribes this place name as q̓adasgu and notes that it is Mathers Creek, known locally as Church Creek, which flows northeast into Cumshewa Inlet from Louise Island; Bringhurst (1999:261, 314–315n 473) transcribes the same term as q̓a·dasgu.

17. *Phratrie* in the original *Sagen*, but refers to what is now called a "moiety." Blackman (1990:248) points out that "the Haida recognized a division of their society into moieties … Raven and Eagle, each composed of a number of lineages."

18. *Geschlecht*, although the contemporary usage in terms of Haida social organization is 'lineage' (see Blackman 1990:248).

19. *Geschlecht*, but the context suggests that 'lineage' might be the best translation here.

20. What Boas transcribes as "K·oa′q" is likely, as Bringhurst (2001:pers. comm) notes, the Coast Tsimshian term for 'raven,' which Dunn (1995:17) gives as ga·x̣. As previously noted, the term for 'raven' appears most often in Haida mythology as x̣uya· in the Skidegate dialect and yeł in the Masset dialect (see parts 1 and 2 of the present story).

5) He travelled on and took along Eagle as a companion. When they had travelled for some time they met an old man whose name was TciqusqānEg·oā′i (= Low Tide Man),[21] sitting in front of his house warming his back. Raven and Eagle wished to see the ocean fall and agreed on a plan: Eagle was supposed to stay outside while Raven went inside, hiding something rough beneath his cape. He sat down close to TciqusqānEg·oā′i and said, "Oh, how cold I am from catching sea-urchins." He had to repeat it four times before he managed to catch the old man's attention. Then the old man merely remarked, "Hah, Kitlkida′ñgit (Liar!)."[22] He was sitting there with his knees drawn up and thus keeping the water high. Nobody was able to get sea-urchins. Then Raven took the rough thing out from beneath his cape and rubbed it across TciqusqānEg·oā′i's back while saying, "Then what is this? Isn't it a sea-urchin shell?" The old man was so surprised that he stretched his legs and thereupon the water fell.

6) Eagle flew down to the beach at once and began catching "black cod" while Raven caught halibut and "red cod."[23] Then they lit a fire and roasted their fish. The fat of the "black cod" was dripping into the fire while Raven's fishes were quite dry and without juices. When Eagle began to eat, Raven asked him for a morsel and it tasted delicious. He said, "ts'ōk·agusqō′ga (that tastes marvellous!)," and asked for more, but Eagle refused to give him any more and so Raven resolved to obtain more through a ruse. He said to Eagle, "I will go and get some bark to carry my fish. Wait here. If a tree trunk with roots should come rolling down the mountain, look after it and grease it with fat from your fish." Eagle didn't reply and went on eating. When Raven had gone he stirred his fire and put two stones in it. He held two tongs in readiness to take them out again. It wasn't long before a big tree trunk with roots came rolling down the mountain. Eagle at once took the red-hot stones from the fire, hit the trunk with them, and cried, "Can you feel that?" Thereupon the trunk rolled away. Raven had assumed this shape in order to obtain possession of the fish oil. After some time he returned in his proper form but covered his face and kept it averted from Eagle. The latter enquired, "What has happened to your face?" Raven forced a laugh and said, "Oh, nothing, I only fell and hurt my face." "Let me see," replied Eagle, "I will heal it." When Raven removed his hands from his face, Eagle saw that it was all burned. Raven said, "It will get better if you rub it with some fish

---

21. Boas' "TciqusqānEg·oā′i" is ci·x̣ʷu· sga·nagʷa·y 'low tide spirit being' (Bringhurst 2001: pers. comm.) This name comes from the Skidegate Haida term ci·x̣ʷu·, translated as 'seafood (excluding fish)' and derived, itself, from the word ci·x̣ʷa· 'the tide is too low' (Ellis and Wilson 1981:xi).

22. What Boas renders as "Kitlkida′ñgit," may be the term kiɬgada·ŋgit, meaning 'little good-for-nothing liar' (Bringhurst 2001: pers. comm.)

23. Boas gives "black cod" and "red cod" in English (and in double quotation marks) in the original *Sagen*.

oil." Eagle took pity on him and gave him some oil to rub on his face, but Raven gobbled it all up. Eagle got so angry at this that he left him.

7) Raven travelled on and in his travels came to a place where children were playing ball with pieces of seal meat. Raven said, "Let me play with you." "No!" retorted the children, "you only want to steal our meat." Raven replied, "Never fear, my father and grandfather are out hunting and you are sure to win a lot from me." When the children heard this, they allowed him to play with them. He caught all their seal meat and put it in his sack.

   (Numbers 4, 5, 6 and 7 told by Wīha'.)

8) Raven wanted to get possession of a woman who was already married, so he decided to get her husband out of the way by a ruse. He went to an island belonging to himself and came back with the skin of a robin. Then he went to a spot where he was sure to meet the man, and carried the bird skin ostentatiously in order to attract his attention. He succeeded in this and the man said, "I've always wanted just such feathers, where did you get the bird skin?" Raven replied, "Yes, if you tie these feathers to your fish hook, you'll catch many fish. Here, I'll give one to you." The man was very glad and would have liked to get more feathers. So Raven continued, "There are many birds of this kind on my island. Let's go out to it tomorrow and shoot some." Then the man invited Raven to stay with him overnight and entertained him well. Thereupon Raven devoured all the stores of his host. They departed early in the morning. When they arrived at the island, Raven said, "I'll go ashore first to see where the birds are." His companion agreed; Raven went ashore and the man waited for his return. Raven picked some willow branches and transformed them into robins which he carried to the canoe. "Just look," he called, "how many birds I've caught." The man was all the more eager to go ashore, too, in order to try his luck. In the meantime Raven sat down in the back of the canoe as if he were waiting for him and pretended to fall asleep. He kept on thinking, "Oh, if only the wind would start to blow from the island against my canoe," and lo, soon a wind came up and blew the canoe away from the shore! Soon the man noticed this and called to Raven, "The canoe is drifting away; paddle back." But Raven pretended not to hear and, when he was far enough away, he paddled to the house of the man whom he had abandoned on the island. Before he reached it, he assumed the man's shape and sat down by the spring where the woman desired by him always got her water. It wasn't long before she came down to the water. Raven pretended not to see her and spoke to himself, "Oh, how badly Raven has treated me." Then he turned to the woman who took him for her husband and asked her for halibut and fish oil and stuffed himself until he could eat no more. Then he said to the woman, "Let's go to sleep now and I'll go on eating afterwards."

The man whom he had left to perish on the island was very sad. But suddenly he remembered his magical fish club and thought, "If only I had my fish club here." It appeared at once and carried him home. He sat down by the spring and when his wife went there to fetch water she heard everything that had happened. The rescued man still kept hidden, but told his wife to stop up all the cracks and splits in the house. When she had done this, he came in, caught Raven, who was unable to escape, and beat him almost to death. Then he threw him outside on the spot where everybody went to urinate. The woman went out to urinate next morning and sat right above Raven. So he called, "Your genitals are all red." When the man heard this he picked him up and again beat him almost to death. Then he threw him up into the branches and lit a big fire underneath him. He kept the fire going all day but Raven didn't die. When the man got up the following morning he saw Raven sitting unharmed by the fire. So he beat him almost to death again and threw him onto that spot on the beach used as a toilet, at the foot of a big stone. When the tide came in, the water washed Raven away. While thus floating about he thought, "Oh, if only my relatives would come and find me." What he wished for, happened. A canoe came with his relatives in it, and they picked him up. (Told by Johnny Swan.)

2. The Frog Woman

There once were ten young people who went out to catch salmon. Nine of them went ashore to fish while the tenth stayed behind in the canoe as guard. While he was sitting there looking down into the water in order to pass the time away, his hat, which was painted with cormorant figures, fell repeatedly into the water. He became angry, scolded the water and beat it with his hat. After some time his nine friends returned with plenty of salmon and they roasted them. Suddenly they saw a big frog hopping towards the fire. They scolded him, took a stick and threw him far away, but in a short time they saw him come back. So they threw him into the fire. How they marvelled when he didn't burn but only grew red-hot. At last he exploded and the burning logs scattered. The men heaped them up again but the frog soon exploded once more and again scattered the logs. This went on a third and a fourth time. Meanwhile the salmon had been roasted. They ate them and returned home. While they were paddling along the shore, they saw a completely red person running along the beach. It was Frog. He called them but they only mocked him. Now Frog Man grew angry and called, "When you get to that headland, you shall die one after the other. Only one of you shall stay alive in order to report your fate at home, then he shall also die." The young men continued to mock him, but when they reached the headland one of them dropped dead, and everything happened as Frog foretold. Only the steersman reached the shore, but he had scarcely told what had occurred when he, too, fell down dead. The people were very sad and scolded Frog. Next day they saw the reflection of a huge fire in the mountains and this appeared to come closer every day. They still went on scolding Frog and calling, "Why don't you burn our village?" On the sixth day the glow of a fire was seen on the sea; the water began to boil and soon the town was ablaze and all the inhabitants lost their lives.

While all this was happening, a girl who had just reached womanhood was locked up in a small hut, as demanded by custom. When the fire approached, she dug a pit and hid inside. The fire burned the whole village as well as her hut. But she remained unhurt. After some time Frog visited the village in the shape of an old woman wearing a giant hat which was painted all over with frogs. She called herself Tlkyānk·'ostā'n k'uns (= Frog Woman).[24] She was extremely old and supported herself on a stick. When she saw what she had done she cried sadly. She extended her finger and moved it about in a circle. Then she smelled it. She repeated this motion and then walked straight towards the girl's hiding place. She called, "Come on out. I have scented you." When the girl came she told her that she was Frog, that the young men had thrown her into the fire, and that in revenge she had destroyed the village and killed all its inhabitants. She took pity on the girl and led her into the forest … (Here the teller, an old Kaigani, didn't know the conclusion.) In the forest they met two men who were swimming in a pond. One of these was White Goose, who took the girl up into the sky and married her. Presumably the legend continues like the Tsimschian version.

---

24. "Tlkyānk·'ostā'n k'uns" is Boas' transcription of łḵan qu·st'a·n quns which translates as 'big crab-of-the-forest,' a literal translation of the Haida term for any species of frog or toad (Bringhurst 2001:pers. comm.)

Group of Chilkat Tlingit in ceremonial clothing displaying crests belonging to Tlingit clans and lineages, including painted hide tunics, Chilkat woven dance shirts and capes, and appliqué leggings. Klukwan, Alaska, *ca.* 1901.

National Anthropological Archives, Smithsonian Institution, Washington, DC.

Negative No. 42977-B.

XXV. Legends of the Tlingit

The parenthetical note at the end of story 6 indicates that all the "foregoing legends"—presumably all the stories of the Tlingit section except the last—were "told or translated by Mrs. Vine, a Stikine Indian married in Victoria." Mrs. Vine is also named as the source of the Tlingit linguistic section in Boas' 1889 report for the British Association for the Advancement of Science (Boas 1890a:856). Boas was introduced to Mrs. Vine by a Catholic priest in Victoria on 30 September 1886: "the Indian woman is married to a white man. She was very pleasant and helpful because of the manner of my introduction" (Rohner 1969:29). Boas wrote in his diary-letter of the day that he asked her only one question, "and the entire myth of the origin of the world descended on me" (Rohner 1969:29). This would be story 1, "The Raven Legend," which is given very amply here. On 28 October 1886, after a trip north, Boas looked up "the Tlingit lady," again accompanied by the priest; she "told me things all morning long" (Rohner 1969:50). When Boas returned to Victoria in June 1888 he went to see her several times (Rohner 1969:91, 96 and 98). She was obviously one of Boas' finest Native consultants. In addition, she translated stories provided by her Stikine Tlingit friends (Rohner 1969:90).

Most of these *Sagen* Tlingit stories were published earlier as "Einige Mythen der Tlingit" ("Some Myths of the Tlingit") (Boas 1888e:159–172). This collection consisted of stories that are identified in the present section as follows: The Raven legend (the first 15 parts of story 1); The Otter Tribe (story 4); Life After Death (most of story 3); The Europeans (a variant of story 6); and some ethnographic notes not published in the *Sagen*. Boas tells us in his introduction to "Einige Mythen der Tlingit" that the stories were collected in the Fall of 1886. He published much of the Tlingit story of Raven again, with comment, in another German journal, also in 1888 (see Boas 1888c:53(8):122, 124–126).

Seal skins drying at seal hunters' camp, south shore Yakutat Bay, Alaska, June 1899.
National Anthropological Archives, Smithsonian Institution, Washington, DC.
Negative No. 43547-E (A.K. Fisher photo).

XXV. Legends of the Tlingit[1]

1. The Raven Legend

1) A mighty chief was keeping Daylight, Sun and Moon in a box which he guarded carefully in his house. He knew that one day Yētl,[2] Raven, would arrive in the shape of a pine needle to rob him of them; and consequently he burned all the dried needles[3] around his house. But Raven wanted to liberate Daylight. He flew for long days on end trying to find the chief's house. When he had found it at last he sat down by the edge of a small pond and considered how he could get inside the house, which he did not dare to enter. Finally the chief's daughter came out of the house to fetch water from the pond. He said to her: "I want you for my wife, but your father must not hear of it because he won't allow strangers to enter his house." But she feared her father's wrath and rejected Raven's suit. Thereupon Yētl transformed himself into a pine needle and dropped into the pond. In a little while he thought: "Oh, if only the chief's daughter would come to fetch water." He had scarcely thought this when she took a bucket and prepared to go down to the pond. Her father said: "Why are you going when I have so many slaves who can get water for you?" "No," replied the daughter, "I want to go myself because they always bring me muddy water." She went to the pond and found many pine needles floating on the water. She pushed them carefully aside before drawing water. But one managed to

---

1. "Tlingit" is an anglicization of the Native name ɫi·ngít 'human being(s),' referring to the people who speak a language remotely related to Eyak-Athapaskan and live in the Alaska Panhandle and offshore islands region. Prior to the establishment of the Canada-United States border in 1906, Tlingit territory included part of northern British Columbia encompassing Dundas and Zayas Islands and the western shore of Portland Canal. The stories presented here are from the Coastal Tlingit, and not the Inland Tlingit of the Atlin and Teslin areas of British Columbia and the Yukon (De Laguna 1990:203,226; McClellan 1981:469).

    While our annotation of this section is based on the available literature, we thank Erna Gunther for comments she made on this section in March 1977, and Richard and Nora Dauenhauer for comments made in February 2002.

2. Boas' transcription "Yētl" is yé·ɫ, the Tlingit term for 'raven' (Swanton 1909:80ff.; Naish and Story 1963:22; De Laguna 1972:I:46; II:844 ff.; 1990:212; Dauenhauer and Dauenhauer 1990:519).

3. The German term used here is *Laub* which literally means 'leaves' but in this context subsumes 'leaves and needles.' As Erna Gunther (1977:pers. comm.) has pointed out, German literature omits the distinction between 'leaves' and 'needles.'

get into her bucket despite her caution. She tried to catch it to throw it out, but it always eluded her grasp. So she grew angry and drank the water with the needle in it. But this was Yētl. When she came back to the house and was asked by her father whether she had found clean water, she told him how a pine needle had constantly eluded her grasp and that she had at last swallowed it down. Consequently she became pregnant and, when after nine months her time had come, her father gave a great feast and told his daughter to prepare a bed of coppers[4] covered with beaver skins. But she was unable to give birth. So the chief ordered his slaves to fetch moss, and they obeyed. A bed of moss was prepared for his daughter and there she gave birth to a boy, who was none other than Yētl.

The boy grew up quickly and his grandfather loved him exceedingly. He gave the boy everything he wanted, even the most precious skins. But one day the boy cried incessantly and couldn't be calmed. He called, "I want the box hanging up in the roof beams." This was the box where the chief kept Daylight, Sun and Moon. His grandfather refused his request emphatically, so the boy wept until he was almost dead from crying, and his mother wept with him. Since the grandfather was afraid that his grandson might die from crying, he took the box down at last and let him look inside. So Yētl saw Daylight. Then the chief closed the box again and hung it in its former place. The boy started to weep again at once and thus finally forced the old man to take the box down again and to open it. He allowed him to peep through the newly opened crack and the boy called, "No, more! more!" and couldn't be calmed until the old man opened the box wider. But before he did this, he plugged up all the cracks and holes in the house, especially the smoke hole. Then he gave the box to the child to play with. He took great delight in it; he went around the house tossing it up like a ball. But soon he wanted to have the smoke hole opened up and, when the grandfather didn't agree immediately, he began crying again. Finally he opened the smoke hole a bit. "No, more, more!" cried the boy. When it was completely open at last, the boy changed into Raven, took the box beneath his wings and flew away.

2) And Raven flew to the people, who were fishing in the darkness, and said, "Oh, give me some fish." But the people mocked him and laughed at him. So he said: "Oh, take pity on me. Give me some fish and I will give you Daylight." The people laughed at this and said, "You don't know how to make daylight. We know you, Raven, you liar." He asked once more for some fish and when they refused again, he lifted up one wing a bit and let Moon shine out, so the people believed him and gave him some herring, which in those days didn't have any bones yet. But Raven

---

4.   This is not a copper bed, but rather stacks of coppers—wealth items on the Northwest Coast that are made into a bed covered with skins.

had become angry because the people hadn't believed him. So he stuffed the fish full of pine needles and, ever since, herring have had bones. Then he placed Sun and Daylight in the sky, divided Moon into two halves, set one half in the sky as the moon and had it alternately grow bigger or smaller. The other half he smashed into small pieces and made the stars from them, but when it grew day and the people saw each other, they ran away from each other. Some became fish, the others bears and wolves, and the third, birds. This is how all the creatures were created.

3) Once Raven was thirsty and wanted to drink water. He searched all over the earth but didn't find one drop. He knew, however, that K·anū́k, Petrel,[5] owned water. He was an old man and lived on Nēkyinō̄ (= Rock in the Open Sea),[6] an island between the mouth of the Stikine River and Sitka. He kept the water in a trough cut into the rock, which was closed by a stone on which the old man sat with closed eyes and legs drawn up. Yētl knew that he was awake when he had his eyes closed, and slept when they were open. In those days there were no tides yet, because the drawn-up legs of K·anū́k kept the water high. Yētl didn't want to have only fresh water but also the tides so that he would be able to catch sea creatures on the beach. Since K·anū́k didn't want to give them to the people voluntarily, Raven employed a ruse. He sat down close to K·anū́k, who sat there with closed eyes and said, "Ooh, how cold I am from catching sea urchins!" Since the old man didn't answer, Yētl repeated, "Ooh, how cold I am from catching sea urchins!" Thereupon K·anū́k, without moving, mumbled, "Hey, what fools these people are! Here I sit without moving my legs and consequently they are unable to catch sea-urchins. The water will fall only when I stretch my legs!" Raven replied, "If you don't believe me, just feel." And he rubbed the old man's back with something rough which felt just like sea urchin shells. K·anū́k was so astonished at this that he stretched his legs. Now the water receded far, far from the beach and Yētl caught halibut, shellfish and sea-urchins to his heart's content. Then he flew back to K·anū́k, sat down by him and thought, "Oh, if only K·anū́k would fall asleep." He sat by his side for days on end and thought always the same thing. Then at last the eyes of K·anū́k opened wide and he fell fast asleep. So Yētl took the lid off the stone trough and drank until he was completely full. Then he flew away. K·anū́k awakened at once. When he saw what had happened, he pursued Yētl, but he reached Ata (the headland closest to the

---

5. In the original *Sagen*, Boas identifies the bird "K·anū́k" as *Adler* meaning 'eagle'; however, the Tlingit term "K·anū́k" refers not to the eagle but to the petrel (*Oceanodroma furcata* or *O. leucorhoa*) that is referred to in Tlingit mythology as the "Keeper of Water" (Swanton 1909:4, 10, 83; De Laguna 1972:I:46: II:847).

6. What Boas transcribes here as "Nēkyinō̄" and translates as 'rock in the open sea' is transcribed by Swanton (1909:83) as "Dekī́-nū" and translated as 'fort-far-out.'

sea in the mouth of the Stikine River)[7] safely and there the path where he was pursued by K·anū´k can still be seen today in the broken rocks and trees.

4) In the beginning the people had no fire, but Yētl knew that it was guarded by K·'ōky, Snow Owl,[8] who lived far out in the ocean. He told all the people (who in those days still had the form of animals), in turn, to go and get Fire, but not one was successful. At last Deer, who in those days still had a long tail, said, "I will take pine wood and tie it to my tail. With it I'll get Fire." He did what he had said, ran to Snow Owl's house, danced around the fire and finally put his tail close to it. The wood ignited and he ran away. This is how his tail burned up so that ever since, deer has had only a stump for a tail.

5) In those days Raven was still white like the seagull. His wife was the daughter of a mighty chief, Woodpecker, who owned a great supply of pitch. Raven would really have liked to have some of it, so one day when all the Woodpeckers were playing in front of the house, he sneaked inside, dipped his finger into the red pitch and put it into his mouth. But his finger stuck fast and he was unable to take it out of his mouth again. When the Woodpeckers came home and saw that Raven had stolen pitch, they grabbed him, smoked him, threw him into a box, glued him with his back to the bottom of it, and smeared his eyes with pitch. Then they threw him into the sea. While drifting on the waves he called, "Oh save me, save me!" After he had been drifting thus for days he heard the cry of a Robber Seagull[9] overhead. Raven begged it to give him food and to release him, but all it did was to dirty him instead. At last, after he had been adrift on the water for a long time, a seagull took pity on him. It spat grease onto him; the pitch dissolved and he was able to open his eyes and move again. When he finally reached land he saw that he had become black all over.

6) He went on and came to a place where many halibut were being caught. The people received Yētl hospitably and entertained him well, but in spite of this he

---

7.   We have not been able to find independent confirmation of this Tlingit place name, "Ata," or its location.

8.   "K·'ōky" is Boas' rendering of the Tlingit term transcribed elsewhere as "k'ak'" and identified as the 'white owl' (Boas 1891e:180). But as Dauenhauer and Dauenhauer (2002:pers. comm.) point out, the identification of this bird has been a problem for many years. "K·'ōky" has been written as "kʷakʷ" by De Laguna (1972:I:47) and identified as the Snowy Owl (*Nyctea scandia*); Naish and Story (1963:21) provided the transcription q̇o·kʷ and the translation 'owl without ear tuffs.' The same bird's name was transcribed as "Gowkᵘ" and translated as 'owl' by Tlingit member William L. Paul on page 83 of an annotated copy of Swanton's (1909) publication of Tlingit texts held by the National Anthropological Archives (Ms. 4823). There it is noted that "Gowkᵘ" once had a fine beak, but after it got burnt while carrying Raven's fire, Owl's beak was replaced with an octopus sucker, and therefore is now small (the annotation indicates "Robert Zuboff 6/1/49" as the source of this information).

9.   Here in the original *Sagen* Boas uses the German term *Raubmöwe* which literally means 'robber seagull,' but throughout the rest of this same part of the Raven story, the word *Möwe* 'seagull' is used.

played a trick on them. When the men went out fishing and lowered their lines, Yētl dived and ate the octopus, used by them as bait, from their hooks. But he didn't dare to take real bites and only nibbled at the meat. After some time he became more daring, took a real bite and thus got caught on a line. He was pulled up in spite of all his resistance and at last braced himself against the bottom of the boat. The fishermen all pulled at the line together and thus ripped his nose off. So Yētl swam ashore, took a piece of bark to which he glued hair, and put this on in place of his nose. Then he transformed himself into an old man and went back to the village. When he came to the first house he was invited for a meal and one of the fishermen said, "Just think, old man, today we caught a nose." Yētl asked, "Where is it?" "Over there in the chief's house." Yētl went there to see the nose. He was also entertained in the chief's house. Soon he said, "Oh, I've heard that you caught a nose. Won't you show it to me?" He looked at it carefully and then said, "Don't keep it, otherwise many people will come to fight you." So the villagers got frightened and gave the nose to him willingly.

7) Yētl went on and found a raspberry bush. He shook it and thus transformed it into a man whom he called Kits'īno, who had to serve as his speaker.[10] They went on together and soon came to a village where large amounts of provisions were stored. The chief of the village invited Yētl for a meal and asked him what he would like to have. Yētl said to Kits'īno, "Say that I would like to have fish." But Kits'īno said, "The great chief doesn't want to eat." "Oh, don't say that," said Yētl. "Say that I would like to eat fish." But again Kits'īno said, "The great chief doesn't want to eat." Thus it came about that Raven remained hungry while all the others were eating and drinking.

8) They continued on their way and came to a village where there were great supplies of fish oil. Yētl said to Kits'īno, "We'll go to the chief's house and there some oil shall get into my eye. Then you will tell the people that I will die soon. When I have died, place me in a box and tell all the people to go away, but on no account let them take any fish oil along." The chief of the village entertained Yētl and Kits'īno and they all went to sleep, but during the night some fish oil spattered into an eye of Yētl and he grew ill. He kept rubbing his eye all day long and finally died. So Kits'īno sang mourning songs without end, put him into a small box and said to the people, "Tie the box up tightly now. I know that he is only pretending to be dead." They obeyed and suspended the box from the roof-beam. Then Kits'īno told the people to go away and forbade them to take fish oil along. He told them that they would be afflicted by illness and misfortune if they disobeyed. The people went

10. "A chief doesn't speak personally to people of the lower classes but keeps a slave who makes his wishes known" [Boas' original footnote].

away and Yētl and Kits'īno stayed behind by themselves. Raven wanted to come out of the box but found it tied fast. Kits'īno began to eat what he found and enjoyed it very much. Yētl heard him eating and jumped about angrily in the box, calling, "Don't eat everything up; don't eat everything up!" He jumped so much that finally the box fell to the ground where it tumbled about and splintered, but Kits'īno had eaten up all the oil meanwhile and left only some dry meat for Yētl.

9) Then Yētl made friends with Butterfly and together they wandered all over the earth. One day they came to a long inlet, which they wanted to cross, and after a long search Yētl found a giant kelp which stretched across like a bridge. He crossed the inlet on it but Butterfly was afraid to follow him. Raven, who had already reached the opposite side, called to him to cross on the kelp as he had done. But Butterfly called, "No, I'll fall into the water." "Stay calm," replied Raven, "you won't fall." When Butterfly stepped onto the bridge of kelp at last, Raven caused it to turn over. Butterfly drowned and his corpse drifted ashore. Yētl went to the beach, cut it open and ate the entrails, then he buried him under stones. After some time he returned to the grave, brought Butterfly back to life and said, "Oh, friend, I thought that you were lost. I've searched for you for a long time and here you are asleep."

10) Once Yētl allowed Whale to swallow him. He made himself at home in his stomach and lit a small fire. Whale asked him to be very careful and not to harm his heart, but Raven couldn't resist the temptation and pecked at it. Whale cried, "Oh!" because it hurt him, and asked Raven once more not to touch his heart. Yētl apologized and pretended that he had only pushed against it by accident, but soon he pecked at it again and this time bit into it heartily. So Whale died. Yētl didn't know how to get out again because the animal's mouth was closed tightly. He thought, "Oh, if only Whale would drift onto a flat beach." Soon he heard the breaking of the surf and felt Whale's body hit the stones of the beach, and he was glad. There was a village nearby and children were playing on the beach with bows and arrows. When they saw the whale, they ran home at once to call their parents, who then began to cut the blubber. While they were thus occupied they heard someone singing and shouting in the whale's belly, but couldn't imagine who that might be. So Yētl thought, "Oh, if only someone would make a cut straight down to me." He had scarcely thought this when his wish was fulfilled. A man cut a hole into the stomach and Yētl flew away immediately, crying, "Kolā', kolā', kolā'!"

11) Raven flew into the forest, dried himself with moss and picked moss from the trees which he glued to his head and face with pitch, so that it looked like grey hair. He took a stick and limped into the village in this disguise. All he met took him for an extremely old man. He entered a house, sat down by the fire and the people gave him some food. He heard them talking of a beached whale close to the village from whose stomach a raven had flown. He said, "Now I know for certain that your

enemies will come and kill all of you soon. Get everything ready; take to your canoes and leave the whale behind. Only thus will you be able to escape." The people took his advice. He, himself, went with one of the families into their old, decrepit canoe which had a hole in the bottom, temporarily stopped up with moss. When they were far from shore, he pulled out the wad of moss; the canoe sank and all its crew perished miserably. But he flew back to the village and devoured the whale and all the supplies stored in the village.

12) One day Yētl and his wife went out to get mussels. They had soon gathered a full load and took it home. The woman opened the mussels and ate them, but Raven sharpened the shells[11] on a stone. The people heard the noise but didn't know what it signified. When the mussels where sharp enough, Raven went to a big white rock, which in those days blocked the course of the Stikine River, and cut it right through the middle.[12]

13) Then Raven went upriver in his canoe until he found a house. He looked inside but couldn't see anyone. The house was inhabited by Shadows and Feathers that floated up and down in it. At first Raven was afraid, but when he saw the many halibut and the fat of deer and mountain goats stored in the boxes, he entered resolutely and cooked himself a meal of halibut with mountain goat fat. When it was ready he looked about for a bowl, but couldn't find one. When one of the Shadows brought him a bowl, Yētl was glad that he had found such good hosts. He ate until he could eat no more, then put the leftovers in a basket and went down to the canoe. He was on the point of leaving when it occurred to him that it would be a pity to leave behind so many good provisions in the boxes. He went back and fell upon the stores of Shadows and Feathers, but lo! they attacked him at once, beat him until he was unable to move and then threw him out of the house. When at last he collected himself and limped down to the canoe, he found it completely empty. He became sad, returned home and went to bed. His face and back were swollen from the blows he had received, but when he was asked what had happened to him he said that he had fallen off a rock.

14) Loon, Raven's sister, was married to Cormorant. One day Raven, Cormorant and his brother, Bear, went out to catch halibut. Cormorant and Bear were very skilful and caught plenty of fish, while Yētl caught none. So he grew jealous of his companions, and he said to Cormorant, "Just look, there is a big louse sitting on your head." He pretended to catch it and said, "It has bitten you; now you bite it

---

11. Boas uses the term *Schalen* 'shells' here in the original *Sagen*, and *Muscheln* 'shellfish; mussels' throughout the remainder of this story. The hard, sharp shells of California mussel (*Mytilus californianus*) were sought and used by the Tlingit as knives or scrapers (De Laguna 1972:55; Emmons 1991:211, 242).

12. Boas (1916:575) summarizes this story as "Raven cuts a canyon with a shell knife."

back. Stick your tongue out; I'll give it to you." Cormorant stuck his tongue out and Raven ripped it out. "Now speak," he called to him mockingly. But poor Cormorant could only say, "Wule, wule, wule." "That's fine," continued Raven, "that's how your uncles used to speak formerly." Then he made Bear fall on his knife, and Bear lost his life. Then he went ashore, took the fish that both of them had caught, and hid Bear's corpse. But first he cut out his bladder. When he came home accompanied by Cormorant, Loon asked, "Where is my brother-in-law Bear?" Yētl replied, "He's in the forest looking for roots." Thereupon Cormorant clapped his hands and said, "Wule, wule, wule!" He wanted to say that Yētl was lying, but was unable to make himself understood. His wife asked, "What are you saying? What has happened to you?" "I believe he has caught a cold," said Raven. "Just look how many halibut I've caught. There are so many that our canoe almost sank. Cut them open and clean them." Then he placed stones in the fire and cut open the back of Loon's hands so that the fat dripped out. And he took Bear's bladder, secretly wrapped one of the red-hot stones in it and swallowed it. Then he told his sister to do the same. But she hadn't seen that he had wrapped the stone and so ate a red-hot stone, which made her cry out in pain. Raven called to her, "Quick, drink water after it." She obeyed him and the water began to boil up at once, killing Loon. But Cormorant was told by Raven to stay on the beach. Ever since, Cormorant is found on the beach and his call is merely, "Wule, wule, wule."

15) Raven wanted to become chief and invited all the animals to a great feast. They all came, among them also Killer Whale who wore a hat with many adornments.[13] Raven served fish and fat to them. Suddenly he uttered a cry and they were all transformed into stones. The house and animals can still be seen today on the Stikine River.

16) Once Yētl met Tree Stump who was living by the seashore with his wife. The wife went down to the beach every morning and lured all the fishes to the shore with a magic chant. Then she caught as many as she and her husband needed for their daily sustenance. Yētl entered the house and enquired, "Are you in, Grandmother?" She invited him in and made him welcome. Next morning Yētl saw how the old woman lured the fish. When she was fast asleep in the night, he got up, put on her cape and sang the magic chant which he had learned from her, and danced to it as he had seen her dancing. Thereupon all the fish came and he caught them all. Only one of them was left in the water. When the woman called them the following morning, not a single one appeared because Raven hadn't left any, and so she and her husband were doomed to starve miserably.

---

13.   Gunther (1977: pers. comm.) has pointed out that among the Tlingit, each basketry ring on the top of a hat means that the owner has given a potlatch.

17) One day Yētl paid a visit to an old woman called K·āk·ak·atlak·ā'tcanuk.[14] He had a canoe full of seals which he had stolen and he said to her, "Grandmother, cook these seals for me." She promised to do so and, while she was tending the fire, she began to tell him a story. Yētl pretended to get drowsy and snored a bit. The old woman nudged him and said, "Come on and pay attention," but he didn't budge and pretended to be fast asleep. Thereupon the old woman, who was a witch, rubbed some inner cedar bark until it became soft, and took some sweat and dirt from the belly of Yētl. She wrapped it up in the bark and placed it in the shell of a whale louse. Yētl had carefully observed everything she did and, when the old woman was asleep, he got up and burned the cedar bark with the parts of his body wrapped up in it. Then he took another bundle of cedar bark, wrapped up some sweat and dirt in it, which he had taken from the old woman's belly, and placed it in the shell of the whale louse[15] from which he had taken the other bundle. The witch got up early in the morning when the tide was low. Yētl was awake, but pretended to be still asleep. She took the shell with the bundle of cedar bark in it, warmed it a bit over the fire and carried it down to the shore, where she put it down on the beach. Soon the rising water reached the shell, and the old woman started to scratch her belly. When the water covered the shell she felt very ill, and when it was high tide, she died. She had wanted to kill Yētl, but he knew her and killed her instead. When she was dead he ate up all the supplies which had been stored in her house.

18) And Yētl visited Tlēcauwā'k·ē (= One-Eyed One),[16] the one-eyed giant, in order to kill him. When he prepared for his journey, he took along one salmon eye, a big knife and the bird Ts'ɛrē'nē.[17] He met Tlēcauwā'k·e who was fishing not far from his house. Yētl said to him, "Tlēcauwā'k·e, let us see who is the better archer." The giant accepted the challenge and they agreed to try and reach the summit of a nearby mountain with their arrows. Yētl let the giant try first. He took two arrows, placed them on his bow one after the other and shot them, but not one of them reached the target. Then, when it was Yētl's turn to shoot, he took the bird Ts'ɛrē'nē which he had transformed into an arrow,[18] and whispered to it before he shot, "Fly, fly!" He shot the arrow and the bird flew up to the summit of the mountain. Thus Yētl had

---

14. Boas' "K·āk·ak·atlak·ā'tcanuk" is the same Tlingit term transcribed as "K!AgA'kqō cā'nAkᵘ" and translated as 'old Mole Woman' by Swanton (1909:96).

15. Given in the *Sagen* as *Walfischlaus*, literally 'whale louse.' Possibly the storyteller is referring to the barnacles that grow on whales.

16. Boas' "Tlēcauwā'k·e" is transcribed by Swanton (1909:95) as "Lēcawā'gi" 'man with one eye.'

17. "Ts'ɛrē'nē" is Boas' rendering of the Tlingit term for 'magpie' (*Pica pica hudsonia*), transcribed by Naish and Story (1963:21) as ćeginé, by de Laguna (1972:I:46–47, II:871) as "tšex̣ené" and by Swanton (1909:6) as "ts!ēgēnî'."

18. De Laguna (1972:I:46–47, II:871) notes that the Tlingit sometimes referred to the Magpie as "Raven's Arrow."

won the first contest. He said, "Let's exchange our bows. I'm your friend and you shall be able to shoot as well as I. Give me your bow in return." The giant was agreeable and they exchanged their bows. Then he continued, "Now let's exchange our eyes as well." "How are we going to do that?" asked Tlēcauwā'k·e. "Yes, it will be necessary," replied Yētl, "because without my eye you won't be able to use my bow." Then he pretended to take out his eye. He screwed up his eyelids and showed the salmon eye to the giant. He said, "See, it isn't hard to take the eye out of its socket." So the giant also tried to take his eye out, but without success. When Yētl saw this he said, "I see that you can't do it; let me do it for you," and he ripped out the giant's only eye. He stuck the salmon eye into the bleeding socket but it fell out again immediately. Then Yētl killed the blind giant and went into his house. There he met the wife of Tlēcauwā'k·e who asked him, "Have you seen my husband?" He replied, "Yes, I met him a short while ago." She invited him for a meal, but after some time, when her husband did not return, she suspected her guest of having killed him.[19] She said, "Now let us throw knives." They took their positions on opposite sides of the house and began throwing knives. The woman used a small, flat stone as a shield. She had the first throw. When the knife came flying towards him, Yētl assumed the shape of Raven, flew up high and the knife hurtled into the wall below him. Then he threw his knife and with his first try cut off the woman's legs. Then she threw again. Again Yētl, as Raven, flew up high and the knife missed him. With his second throw he hit the woman's neck and cut off her head.

19) Then Yētl paid a visit to the chief of the seals. He transformed himself into a woman and Mink into a child which he took into his arms.[20] He took the name Cā'wat kEtcē'k·qt'ē.[21] When the chief's son saw the woman, he fell in love with her and immediately married her. During the daytime the young man always went out hunting and when he came back at night to his canoe he was heavily laden with game. He went into the house and washed himself. One day, when he was going out hunting again, the woman followed him and pinched her child, Mink, a little, in order to make him cry. The child cried and she quickly ran back home. Her husband, who had heard the crying of the child, at once returned home. He said to his wife, "It seemed to me that I heard your child cry. So I've come back." At this she wept

---

19. Boas' ([1886–1888]) notes contain an English version of the remainder of this story told by his Native consultant, Mrs. Vine, a Stikine Tlingit woman.

20. This same story appears in English in Boas' ([1886–1888]) notes with Mrs. Vine, where the story begins: "He went on and visited the seal-men. He transformed himself into a woman and took the mink for child."

21. The name that Boas transcribes here as "Cā'wat kEtcē'k·qt'ē" is transcribed as "CāwA't kaLA'qdagê" by Swanton (1909:114–115). In Boas' ([1886–1888]) notes with Mrs. Vine, in English, this sentence reads: "He called him (self?) Cāwatketcē'k·qt'ē."

and said, "It is a sign that you will soon experience something sad." At night, when her husband was fast asleep, she pressed firmly against Mink's mouth and nose until he suffocated. Then she got up and began to weep, and when the people heard that the chief's son was dead, they all cried with her. She said, "Let's bury him behind that headland!" and they did so. Then she went to her husband's grave every day to mourn there. After some time, another man wanted to marry her and followed her unnoticed when she went to the grave. He saw her sitting close to the corpse and weeping "Gug'ē′, gug'ē′!" At each cry she pecked at the corpse and ate from it. When he saw this, he called all his friends. They caught Yētl and smoked him over the fire, where he received his black colour.

20) Yētl wanted to create men. He worked human shapes in stone, breathed on them, and the stones became alive, but soon died again. Then he made human shapes from earth, blew on them, and they became alive. But they soon died again, too. He carved men from wood and gave them life by breathing on them, but they, too, died soon. So he made human shapes from grass and blew on them. They became alive and became the ancestors of mankind. Consequently men come and go like the grass.

2. The World[22]

The earth is narrow and sharp like a knife. In the beginning, the world was standing upright and moved up and down in space. If it hadn't come to a standstill, all life would have been destroyed. All the animals tried one after the other to make it stand still, but without success. Ermine tried last of all. His tail touched the formless base above which the world was moving up and down and to which he wanted to fasten it with his tail. So its tip became black. Since the endeavours of the animals had been in vain, a female spirit (yēk)[23] made a try at last. She took some duck grease and smeared it onto her belly. Then she crawled under the earth. When it moved downwards now, her belly touched the base and stuck fast to it. That is how our earth is held fast in space. Consequently the spirit was named HāricanE′k'ō (= Old Woman Underneath Us). Occasionally Yētl pays her a visit and pulls on her. This causes earthquakes.[24]

---

22. Another version of this story is provided in English in Boas' ([1886–1888]) notes with Mrs. Vine.

23. Dauenhauer and Dauenhauer (1990:125) explain that yéik is the Tlingit word "for a disembodied spirit or supernatural power that reveals itself to a shaman and comes to the shaman as a helper." Later in this section, Boas refers to "yēk" (yéik) as a "guardian spirit" (see story 4, part 2).

24. Swanton (1908b:452) records several explanations for earthquakes, one of which describes how "Hayicā′nak!u," translated as 'Old-woman-underneath,' has charge of a post made from a beaver's foreleg, on which the world rests. When Raven tries to drive her away from this post, an earthquake occurs. Swanton's "Hayicā′nak!u" is the same term that Boas transcribes here in the *Sagen* as "HāricanE′k'ō" and translates as 'Old Woman Underneath Us.' Boas' ([1886–1888]) notes with Mrs. Vine confirm the translation 'the old woman under us.'

The earth itself is square. One corner points north, one south, one east, and one west. There is a huge hole in the northern corner through which, at low tide, the ocean's water plunges into the underworld, while it comes out of it again at high tide.

The sun and the moon are the "eyes of the sky." At the same time, the moon is the husband of the sun. During an eclipse of the sun, the wife is visiting her husband.

3. Life after Death

After death the soul lives in a country quite like ours. All those having died a violent death go to the sky where Tahī′t[25] reigns. All those who die in a sick-bed (including women dying during childbirth) go to a country on the opposite side of the rim of the earth. In the daytime the dead of both countries unite, to part again in the evening.

The souls dwelling with Tahī′t cause the northern lights. When it appears blood-red, they prepare for war. The milky way is a long tree trunk lying there, across which the fighting spirits (the rays of the northern light) jump back and forth. Tahī′t is master over men's destinies. He decides who shall fall in battle. When a child is born he decides whether it is going to be a boy or girl and whether the mother is going to die in childbirth.

This is where the following tale belongs: A shaman[26] had been ill for long years. When he sensed his end approaching, he asked his mother to look after his dog and then he died. His body was wrapped up in fur capes and on the fourth day he was buried in the burial place of the shamans, on a level plot of ground not far from the houses. His mother went out daily to the burial house and mourned him and burned food for him. One day the dog, who had run along, began barking and couldn't be calmed down. All at once she heard something moving in the grave and heard a moan as if someone were awakening. So she fled in terror and told the people what she had heard. They went to the grave, opened it and found that the man had returned to life. They took him home and gave him food. He felt all numb and slept

---

25. Concerning the fate of souls that travelled to a "happy country," Swanton (1908b:461) wrote that there was situated a house called 'Sleep house,' "tA hît" (transcribed here in the *Sagen* by Boas as "Tahī′t"), where people rested. Swanton added that "this seems to have been the name given by some Tlingit to the next higher region, otherwise known as kī′waA ('way up'), whither went those who died by violence."

26. Boas' earlier German publication of this story contains a description of a Tlingit shaman's training which includes the initiate being required to "tear out the tongue of an otter, a mink, a raven, an eagle, and a seagull, in that order" (Boas 1888e:172).

long and deeply. When he awakened again he felt a bit stronger and now said, "Mother, why didn't you give me food when I asked you for some? Weren't you able to understand me? I told you that I was hungry and nudged you. I wanted to nudge you on the right but couldn't. I always had to stand to your left. You didn't answer me and only touched the spot where I had nudged you and said, 'Oh, that's a bad omen.' When I saw you eating I asked you to share with me but you didn't, and without your permission I was unable to take any. You only said, 'The fire crackles,' throwing some of your food in the fire."[27]

"After I had died I felt no pain. I was sitting beside my body and watched how you prepared it for burial and painted my face with our crest. I heard you, Mother, mourning at my grave. I nudged you and told you that I wasn't dead, but you didn't hear me. After four days I felt as if there was neither day nor night. I saw you carrying my body away and was compelled to go along against my will. I asked all of you for food, but you threw it into the fire and then I felt satisfied. At last I thought that I must be dead after all since nobody heard me and the burned food satisfied my hunger. So I decided to go to the country of the souls and soon came to a crossroad. A well-travelled path led to one side; the path to the other side was hardly used. I chose the first. I wanted to be truly dead and I went on and on in order to reach the end of the road. Finally I arrived at a steep rock at the foot of which a river was flowing sluggishly. I saw a big village on the opposite bank and recognized many people. I saw my grandmother and my uncle who died long ago and many children whom I once tried to heal. But I also saw many whom I did not know. I called 'Oh, come and save me. Take me over to your side,' but they walked around as if they didn't hear me. I was overwhelmed by fatigue and lay down with the hard rock for my pillow. I slept well and on waking up didn't know how long I had slept. I stretched and yawned and the people in the village called, 'Someone is coming over there; let's bring him over.' A canoe came across the river and took me to the village where everyone greeted me amiably. I wanted to tell them about this life but they raised their hands in protest and said, 'Don't talk about it; they don't belong to us.' They gave me salmon and berries to eat, but everything tasted burned even though it looked good.[28] So I put it aside. They gave me water to drink. When I lifted it to my mouth I saw that it was quite green. It tasted bitter. They told me that the river I had crossed consisted of the tears of women weeping for their dead. Therefore you must not weep before your dead friend has crossed the river. Then I thought 'I came here to die, but the spirits are too badly off. I'd rather bear my

---

27. "The Tlingit believe that they hear the voices of the dead when fires crackle" [Boas' original footnote].

28. A feast known as "feeding the dead" was given to members of the opposite moiety from the deceased (De Laguna 1972:I:531).

mother's behaviour than stay here.' The spirits begged me to stay, but I didn't let them keep me. When I turned about, the river had vanished and the path on which I was walking was little used. I went on and on and saw many hands, which appeared to wave imploringly, growing out of the ground. I saw a great fire far away and behind it a curved sabre rotating rapidly. When I walked on I saw many eyes which were pointed at me, but I paid no attention to them because I wanted to die. And I went on and on. The fire was still before me. I reached it after a long, long journey and thought: 'What am I to do? My mother doesn't hear me and I don't want to return to the spirits. I want to die.' I stuck my head into the fire, right beneath the sword. All of a sudden I felt cold. I heard my dog barking and my mother weeping. I stretched, peeped through the wall of my burial house and saw you, Mother, running away. I called my dog and he bounded up to see me. Then you came and found me alive. Many would like to come back from the land of the spirits, but they are afraid of the hands, the eyes, and the fire. That is why that path is so little used."

A man called Ky'itl'a̅'c, who lived about seven generations ago, committed suicide. When he died he saw a ladder descending from the sky, and he went up. At the top of the ladder he came upon an old watchman who was completely black and who had curly hair (??).[29] He asked, "What do you want here?" When Ky'itl'a̅'c had told him that he had killed himself, the guard allowed him to enter. Soon he saw a big house with a kettle standing in front of it. He saw Tahi̅'t inside the house and was invited by him to enter. He summoned two of his people (they were called Kye̅wak·a̅'o̅)[30] and told them to show the whole country to him. They led him to the milky way and to a lake on which two white geese were swimming. They gave a small stone to him and told him to try hitting one of the geese. He did as they asked him and no sooner had he hit a goose than it began to sing. He had to laugh at this because its singing caused him the same sensation as if someone were tickling him. Then his companions asked him, "Would you like to see the daughters of Tahi̅'t?" When he expressed the wish, they opened a door in the clouds and he saw two beautiful young girls sitting behind the clouds. When he looked down to earth he saw the tree tops looking like the tips of needles. But he wanted to return to earth, so he pulled his cape over his head and hurled himself down. He arrived at the bottom unharmed and found himself at the foot of a tree when he awoke from the state of unconsciousness into which he had fallen. Soon he saw a small house, the door of which was closed with mats. He looked inside and heard the crying of a

29. Boas uses these double question marks in the text, presumably to question the curly nature of the man's hair.

30. What Boas transcribes as "Kye̅wak·a̅'o" is transcribed by Swanton (1908b:461) as "qi̅waqa̅'wo" in the expression "Ye̅ɬ qi̅waqa̅'wo," which Swanton translates as 'Raven's home' and describes as the place where a bad person goes after death, where Raven lives.

newborn child. He found himself inside the house. He, himself, was that child and when he grew up he told the people about Tahi̓'t. They had heard of him before, but only then did they hear more details about the upper world. Ky'itl'a̓'c also told that, up there, those whose heads had been cut off had their eyes between their shoulders.

A man called Gyinaskila'c didn't believe in Tahi̓'t. He said to the people, "Kill me. If I really go up to Tahi̓'t, I will throw four logs of wood from the sky." He was killed and after some time the four logs of wood fell from the sky. Thereupon the people knew that Gyinaskila'c was with Tahi̓'t.

4. The Kucta k·ā (Otter) Tribe[31]

1) Once upon a time a chief from the village of Tlokwan[32] went out to cut firewood. His canoe capsized and he drowned. After some time he woke up again and saw the Kucta k·ā (= Otter People) whom he followed. Thus he was changed into an Otter himself. He was anxious to return to his father's house, so he swam around near the shore as an Otter and was recognized by his father. He ordered his people to guard the animal, but they did not succeed in catching it. Then the old chief had a bright fire made inside the house and had the doors kept wide open. His son would have liked to run inside, but was unable because, as soon as he tried it, the Otters caused him to lose his senses. He ran back into the forest and finally hit his head against a tree and collapsed. Then he came back to his senses and he wept bitterly. He clasped the tree trunk tightly. The old chief's people had followed him into the forest and when they saw him now, they said, "Hold on to the trunk until we reach you." He tried, but the Otters soon forced him to let go again and he ran into the forest. The same thing happened the following three evenings. All his endeavours to return home were in vain. When it was almost spring again, the chief sent out all his people once more to search for his son.

---

31. Boas uses the German expression *Fischotter-Volk* 'otter tribe' as the title in the original German text, but uses *Fischotter-Mensch* 'otter people' in the third sentence of this same story. He also uses the English term 'land otter' elsewhere with reference to this same story (Boas 1916:862, 1028), which is consistent with Swanton's (1908b:456) and De Laguna's (1972:II:744ff.) translation, 'land otter,' referring to the Tlingit word kúšda (Boas' "Kucta"), the Pacific land otter (*Lutra canadensis pacifica*) (Naish and Story 1963:19; De Laguna 1972:I:38). The Tlingit greatly feared land otters as they believed they were lost or drowned persons who were turned into 'land otter men' "kucda/qa" (Boas' "Kucta k·ā") (Swanton 1908b:456–457; De Laguna 1972:I:38; II:744ff.)

32. "Tlokwan" is Boas' rendering of the term anglicized as "Klukwan," the name of a Chilkat Tlingit community located at the head end of Lynn Canal; the term has been transcribed by Swanton (1908b:397) as "Lāk"-ān" 'renowned town.' Thornton (1995:303) provides the transcription "ƛákʷa·n."

A poor old man lived in a village close by and went out daily to catch halibut. One evening, when the man had just gone out, the lost son of the chief came and peeped into the poor man's house through a narrow opening. When the women, who had remained home, caught sight of him, they fainted. But the boy soon ran away again into the forest. Next evening he came again, lifted up the mat and saw the poor people. This time they didn't faint at the sight of him and from then on he came every night. He sat down by the fire and told them everything he had seen at the Kucta k·ā—how they were living and what Mink, their slave, was doing. When the man returned late at night, the women told him that the son of the chief always came to them in the shape of an Otter and they decided to rescue him. The old man prepared a powerful magic substance by putting roots (devilstick)[33] and children's urine into a box and letting the mixture stand for three months. In the village there also lived a poor orphaned child who used to play with the Otter in front of a small house made of bark. One evening the women gave a small stick to this child and told him what to do with it. The child and the Otter took turns playing hide and seek with the stick. At last the child hid the stick way back in the house, as the women had told him to do. The Otter ran inside unsuspectingly to find the stick and the women rushed at him and tried to catch him, but without success. So they devised a different plan. They made strong ropes from inner cedar bark and dug a deep pit not too far from the house, and then drove four posts into the ground close to it. Again they let the orphan play with the Otter. They told him to arrange that the Otter would fall into the pit during their game. Four men, who had been digging the pit and who wanted to catch the boy, then pretended to go away and at once the chief's son, in the shape of the Otter, came back to the orphan. He concealed the stick and it wasn't long before the Otter fell into the pit during the game. At once the men and women, who had been hiding, came out and tied the Otter to the four posts with the ropes so that he was unable to move. Then they took pointed sticks and made cuts all over his body, into which they poured the strong magic substance prepared by the old man. Thereupon the Otter said, "Make my blood run freely, otherwise I won't be healed." They did what he asked and thus he became human again. But his lips were still swollen and he refused to put on a cape; there were fish-bones and sea-urchin spines in his teeth and fir branches on his feet. They continued treating him with the magic substance for half a month. During all this time he was not allowed to consume cooked food, or else he would have died. At the end of this period he asked the people to carry him to the town, but to refrain from telling his father who he was. When they arrived in the town together, nobody knew who he was. But when he spoke, an old man recognized his voice and said, "That is our chief's son." Then he went into his father's house and asked him to give rich presents to the poor man who had saved him.

---

33. Likely the Devil's Club plant (*Oplopanax horridus*).

Then he told the people what had happened to him, "My canoe capsized and I fell into the water. When I woke up again I found myself on the beach. I rubbed myself down with moss and, when I was dry again, wanted to go back home. Then I saw a big fire with all my relatives around it and I thought how lucky I was that they had just lit a big fire. I wanted to dry myself completely and walked towards the fire. I went on and on but was unable to reach the fire. While I followed it I bumped into a flounder who bit my big toe, at which I lost my senses. I hastened all over the earth and then knew that I had seen the fire of the Kucta k·ā. I went into the water with them and swam around with them. They have canoes which they use, but these are invisible to people. On land they take off their skin like a garment and dry it. Whosoever stays with them one year becomes an otter like them. His hands and feet shrink, his knees swell up, hair grows on his back, and he grows a tail. The Minks are the slaves of the Otters. They are a strange tribe. They look like children and do not eat any cooked food, because it causes them to die."

2) Ts'awi′nk· was a powerful shaman who healed all the sick. His guardian spirit (Yēk)[34] told him that the Kucta k·ā were coming to take him to the sick daughter of their chief. So he took his shaman's ornaments and placed them in a basket. And he took a bottle and filled it with his urine, which he had already kept for a long time. Then he closed the basket with a stick, concealed it beneath his cape and put all his dancing implements into a box which he had taken down to the beach. Then he said to the people: "When you see many Otters come, don't kill them. I will go with them to their country." But the people didn't believe that he really would go with the Otters into the sea. Soon the Otters arrived and asked him to come along to Cik·'ā′reta (a headland in the Sitka)[35] in order to heal their chief's daughter. He agreed and one of the Otters told him to lie flat on his back, but forbade him to look up. Then he noticed that he was in a canoe and that all the Otters had canoes. He heard the people paddling, but at the same time felt the kelp tugging at his hair. At last they arrived at Cik·'ā′reta and the Otter said to him, "Don't go where all the people are assembled, but go to the house which is deserted by everyone. There you will find the sick girl." When they arrived, Ts'awi′nk· saw all the Otter people standing in front of one house, while another house was all deserted. He went there, opened the door and saw the sick girl sitting by the fire. Immediately all the Otters came in and said, "Now we can see that you are a mighty shaman; you found our

---

34. As previously noted, what Boas transcribes as "yēk" (yéik) is the Tlingit word "for a disembodied spirit or supernatural power that reveals itself to a shaman and comes to the shaman as a helper" (Dauenhauer and Dauenhauer 1990:125). Earlier in this section, Boas refers to "yēk" as a "female spirit" (see story 2).

35. We have not been able to find independent confirmation of this Tlingit place name, "Cik·'ā′reta," or its location.

chief's daughter right away. Oh, heal her and we will give you our fur capes as a reward." Ts'awi'nk· went up to the girl and soon found that a harpoon was stuck in her side. He saw two magical fish lines in the house. The special feature of these lines was that a halibut hung on each one every morning. These he stipulated as his reward, but the Otters said, "We cannot give them to you because then we would starve. They nourish all of us." So Ts'awi'nk· refused to heal the girl and she grew worse and worse. When she was almost dead, the Otters at last promised the fish lines. Then he pulled out the harpoon and the girl became well again.

But the Otters didn't want to give the fishlines to Ts'awi'nk· and intended to kill him. When it grew dark they all lay down to sleep. Ts'awi'nk· took his basket for a pillow and wrapped his face in his cape. Then the Otters make a terrible stink in the house in order to choke Ts'awi'nk·. So he took the bottle of urine out of his basket and poured out a bit of the fluid. This gave off such a strong odour that the Otters ran from the house, snorting in order not to be suffocated. When the odour had subsided a bit, they came in once more and tried to kill Ts'awi'nk· with their foul odour, but he turned them out again with his fluid. So they saw that he was mightier than they and left him in peace. In the morning they gave him the fish lines and two daughters of their chief. They filled his box with many gifts and then placed him inside the stomach of a sea-lion, which was to take him home. But before that they impressed upon him not to think back to the land of Otters because then the Sea-lion would turn around immediately. He promised. But on the way he thought of the strange beings and the Sea-lion turned around at once. The Otters urged him once more not to think of their country before he had reached home, but he thought of the Otters again when the huts of his village were already in sight and thus he came back once again. He managed to get home safely on the fourth try and the Sea-lion flung him on shore there. The people heard a noise like dancing staffs and saw Ts'awi'nk· lying on the beach, covered with all the presents of the Otters. He got up and went into the house and all the presents were changed into gulls which flew away. He said to the people, "When I die, bury me on the beach, here where you found me." They followed his wish. He was buried there and all his descendants are buried on the same spot, one above the other.

5. Nānak·[36]

A long time ago Nānak· came here, accompanied by many Gyukk·oan (= Tribe of

---

36. "The Tlingit call the Russian merchant Baranoff, who made Southern Alaska a Russian colony, Nānak·. The following legend refers to the fights between Baranoff and the Tlingit. Baranoff later went back to Russia and the time of his absence is filled with his legendary travels" [Boas' original footnote]. Boas' own English translation of this "Nānak·" legend was published in 1905 (see Boas 1905b:159–161).

the Far Country, Alëuts)[37] who were his slaves. They landed in Tl'ēyak· (Sitka)[38] and he had a fort built by the Gyukk·oan. They erected a number of houses and surrounded these with a stockade. When everything was finished, Nānak· went back home and left his son behind as commander of the fort. He had a wife who always wore beautiful dresses. After some time quarrels arose between the son of Nānak· and our ancestors. They caught one of the Gyukk·oan, painted his face and then sent him back to the fort in order to mock Nānak·'s son. When he saw what our ancestors had done to his slave, he grew very angry. He gathered all his people and they went out to make war on our ancestors, who put on their armour, took their bows and arrows, spears and daggers, and a fierce battle began. But it wasn't long before most of the Gyukk·oan were slain and the survivors had been taken as slaves. Then our ancestors heaped wood shavings around the stockade and set the fort on fire. The son of Nānak· and his wife alone had been spared by our ancestors. But he was very dejected and walked slowly around the town, holding his wife in his arms. When he saw the houses being devoured by the flames he flung himself and his wife into the blaze. Thus he perished.[39]

Then our ancestors asked the Gyukk·oan, whom they had enslaved, "Where do the Russians build their forts?" The Gyukk·oan replied, "They erect their forts wherever they find good landing places." So our ancestors went to Kastahī'n (Sitka Town)[40] and built a stockaded fort. After several months Nānak· returned and when he heard what had occurred, he attacked our fort but was repulsed.

Then he made all the young men who had come with him embark and sailed off into the world to search for his son. He had a book along, which always spoke to him and advised him what to do. It said, "Tell your people to leave their wives at home, or else you will never find your son." Nānak· did what the book had advised him and forbade his men to take along their wives. Only one of them disobeyed. He was a young man very much in love with his wife; he concealed her in his storage box.

---

37. Some Tlingit people have pointed out that the southeastern Tlingit call the Aleuts "kiy'Ak-khwaan," said to be an attempt to say "Kayak-people" (De Laguna 1972:I:213).

38. Boas' "Tl'ēyak·" is likely the same village site name in the vicinity of Sitka that was transcribed by Swanton (1908b:397) as "ŁA'xq!uxo-ān" 'town-where-one-does-not-sleep-much.' In 1802, the Tlingit destroyed a fort that the Russians had established at Sitka in 1795 (De Laguna 1972:I:166–173).

39. Gunther (1977:pers. comm.) has pointed out that this incident and the story that follows, as described in the *Sagen*, are not historically correct. Indeed, Boas (1905b:157–163) elsewhere presents this "Nānak·" tale as an example of the "mythification of historical events."

40. Boas' "Kastahī'n" is transcribed by Swanton (1908a:397) as "Kastaxē'xda-ān." This same term is transcribed in Goldschmidt and Haas (1998:64) as "Kasdaxeixda.aan," based on information provided by George Lewis, a Sitka Tlingit man who applied this name to a village in Redoubt Bay that had nine tribal houses and was situated near the present city of Sitka.

After they had sailed for a long time they approached an unknown coast. Soon they saw a village and landed there. They went into some houses and found that they were inhabited exclusively by women. Not a single man was to be found in the village. Nānak·'s men wanted to marry the women, but they pointed to a huge trunk of driftwood lying on the beach and said, "Look at that log. He is our husband." At first, the Russians didn't believe them but when they inspected the log more closely, they noticed that all its branches had teeth. One of the sailors tried to get hold of a woman in spite of this, but they attacked him and nearly killed him.

Thereupon, Nānak· called all his people back on board ship and they sailed on. After many days and nights they saw another shore and saw a village in a small clearing. They landed and looked around but couldn't see a living being, but after some time they saw shadows floating up and down and feathers flying to and fro. At first they were afraid, but then they took heart and entered the houses. They found boxes filled with sea otter and seal skins, fish and deer fat. Since they saw nobody but the shadows and feathers, they decided to take away all these treasures. They took great bundles of skins from the boxes and wanted to carry them down to the beach when they were stopped by invisible hands which took the bundles away from them at the door. Thus they found out that the treasures must have an owner after all. But their greed exceeded their caution and they tried to carry the things away. At this they received a beating by invisible hands and reached their ship only with difficulty.

They sailed on and after many wanderings came to the land where the people were eating toads a span long. They sucked them dry and threw the skin away. The Russians were not able to get used to this diet, but since there was nothing else, they at least roasted the toads before eating them.

They journeyed on and soon came to that part of the earth where it is always dark. They sailed around in the dark for ten days. Fierce gales whipped up the sea into wild waves so that the foam struck the top of their mast. Nānak· was afraid that he might lose his ship and afraid that he and his crew might lose their lives. So he asked his book and it replied, "Don't be afraid. Keep to your course and tomorrow you will see your son." Nānak· obeyed and the next day reached the end of the earth. Far beyond he saw smoke rising up from the land of the dead, but he couldn't see his son. So he wept in sorrow. He went to his book and asked, "Oh, book, tell me why don't I see my son?" The book replied, "There is a woman on board ship, that is why you cannot see him." When Nānak· heard this he grew very angry. He called for his crew and threatened to kill the culprit. He searched the whole ship but didn't find anything. So he had all the trunks opened and when he found the woman, he had her head cut off and threw her into the water together with her husband.

He sailed on along the edge of the world. After some time he heard a terrible noise. He didn't know where it originated, but resolved to find out. Thus he arrived at that corner of the world where the waters of the ocean rush down into the lower world in a terrible whirlpool during low water, and from where they return in a few hours, thus causing high tide. When the ship approached this terrible place, it was almost drawn down into the whirlpool, but Nānak· dropped anchor and when the chain stretched too taut, he dropped a second and third anchor. After his ship had been secured in this manner, he tied a bucket to a long rope and flung it into the whirlpool from his ship's stern. He had to pay out many thousand fathoms of rope before the bucket reached the bottom of the sea. Then he pulled it up again and found a letter in it saying, "We who live here in the lower world are very happy that you have come at last. We have no drinking water; please give us some." Nānak· granted their wish and sent down a bucket full of water. When they pulled up the bucket, the water had gone but the bucket was full of money and there was a letter in it asking for more water and promising a good reward. Nānak· sent down water four times and each time they sent up the bucket filled with money.

After Nānak· had thus seen where the waters go at low tide, he came back here. But he had been away for so long that the crewmen who had left with him as young men, returned with grey hair.

6. The Europeans

When Cook visited the country of the Tlingit, his ship once was enveloped in fog.[41] The fog lifted suddenly and a chief caught sight of the ship. It was the first time that a Tlingit had seen a White. The chief went aboard and then returned home. He sat by the fire for four days without stirring and reflected on the unheard-of appearance. Then he told his tribe of the strange men coming out of the cloud of fog. Consequently Whites are still called Gutsk·nkoan, people of the clouds.[42] (The foregoing legends were told or translated by Mrs. Vine, a Stikine Indian married in Victoria.)

7. Kāts[43]

A man named Kāts once went out hunting with his dogs. He found a bear's den.

---

41. Captain James Cook, with the ships *Resolution* and *Discovery*, visited the Gulf of Alaska in May 1778.

42. Boas' "Gutsk·nkoan" is transcribed by De Laguna as "guṡ-k'iya-qwan" or "guṡ-k'ᴀ-qwan" ('people from the other side of the world,' literally 'cloud outside-of people') and described as the Tlingit name formerly applied to all White people. In more recent times, the name has been applied only to Russians, while other Whites, including Americans and Europeans, have been called "tłEd" 'snow' (De Laguna 1972:I:217).

43. "Kāts" is the term transcribed as "Kāts!" by Swanton (1908b:415) who also associates this name with

When his dogs disturbed the bear, he rushed from the den, seized the hunter and threw him to the She-Bear who had stayed in the den. She quickly dug a hole and hid the man in it. Then Bear came in again and, since he didn't find the hunter, asked his wife where he was. She replied, "You have given me only his gloves." The Bear said, "No, I can scent him; he is here." He searched for him a long time, even though his wife assured him that he was mistaken. His search was in vain. Next day he went hunting. When the rays of the sun shone into the den, the bear woman broke them into pieces and with these killed her husband.

Then she fetched the hunter from his hiding place and married him. They had three children. One day Kāts was longing for his home and as soon as the wish stirred in his heart the woman knew it and permitted him to visit his friends. But she warned him not to speak to his former wife but rather to think only of their children. She said, "If you smile at your former wife your children will fall sick. We are going to meet you from time to time on the flat beach here and you'll have to bring your children all the sea creatures you kill." Then she led him home.

During his absence his wife had taken another husband. The hunter built himself another house and on it painted the bear. He was now one of the most successful hunters. He killed many seals and caught plenty of halibut which he took to the pre-arranged spot and each time he came he saw an old She-Bear and four young ones coming down the mountain. His steersman was afraid when he saw them approach for the first time and he wanted to turn back. But Kāts jumped ashore and the She-Bear licked and hugged him. He lived this way for a long time and never looked at his former wife, but one day when he was going for water, he met her quite by accident. She placed her hand on his shoulder and so he smiled. She spoke to him in a friendly fashion but scolded the She-Bear. When Kāts then went to the Bears on the following day he saw that the young Bears' hair stood on end. Neither the old Bear nor the young ones glanced at him. So he said to his people, "Go home and tell them that the Bears will kill me because my former wife has scolded them," and he ordered them to turn back immediately. Then he jumped ashore and his eldest son struck him down at once. One tore off his arms, another one his legs and thus they killed him. But soon they were sorry that they had killed their father. They went back into the forest and sang mourning songs. The sisters of Kāts painted the Bear on their houses and carved it on their posts.[44]

---

the person through whom the Wolf clan emblem was received (see also the footnote that follows).

44. "Kāts" is associated with the Tlingit Wolf clan, the term for which is transcribed as "ka·gwa·nta·n" in De Laguna (1990:227) and "kā'gwAntān" in Swanton, who notes that these people " ... had bears' ears fastened to the sides of their heads and called them Kāts! after the name of the man through whom the right had been obtained. The kā'gwAntān of Chilkat have a shirt made out of grizzly-bear hide, which they wear in memory of this event" (Swanton 1908b:415).

XXVI. The Development of the Mythologies of the North Pacific Coast Indians[1]

A survey of the mythological material presented in this volume shows that particular myths enjoy a considerable distribution throughout the region under discussion. Since the population of the region belongs to quite a number of different linguistic groups it can safely be assumed that much borrowing has taken place. In the following pages I will attempt to show how such borrowings have influenced the development of the mythology.

With this end in view it seems advisable to briefly describe the distribution of languages and dialects in the region in question. Beginning from the south we find the following language families and dialects represented in our collection (map at the end of the book):[2]

FAMILY	DIALECT GROUP	DIALECT	DISTRIBUTION
I. Selisch	Inland Selisch	Shuswap	Southern interior of B.C. almost to the confluence of the Fraser and Thompson Rivers.
		Ntlakyapamuq	At the confluence of the Fraser and Thompson Rivers and in the Fraser Canyon.
	Coast Selisch	Cowitchin (Cowichan)	Fraser River Delta and the vicinity of Nanaimo and Cowichan on Vancouver Island.
		Lku'ñg·ɛn	Vicinity of Victoria, B.C.
		Sk·qṓ'mic	Burrard Inlet and Howe Sound.

---

1. Boas (1896:1–11) drew upon the analysis presented here for his article "The Growth of Indian Mythologies." Additional articles where some of Boas' ideas set out in the present Section are discussed include: "The Development of the Culture of North-west America" (Boas 1888b:194–196); "Die Mythologie der nordwest-amerikanischen Küstenvölker" ['The Mythology of the Northwest-American Coastal Peoples'] (Boas 1888c:53 (8):121–127; (10):153–157; (19):299–302; (20):315–319; 54 (1):10–14; (6):88–92; (9):141–144; (14):216–221); "Dissemination of Tales Among the Natives of North America" (Boas 1891a:13–20); "The Mythologies of the Indians" (Boas 1905:11:327–342; 1905:12:157–173); and, "Mythology and Folk-Tales of the North American Indians" (Boas 1914:374–410).

2. In this Section we retain Boas' original transcriptions of tribal names, as well as his original page references to the 1895 *Sagen* publication.

FAMILY	DIALECT GROUP	DIALECT	DISTRIBUTION
		Pɛ'ntlatc	Comox on Vancouver Island.
		Çatlō'ltq	Formerly north of Comox and on Valdes Island, now in Comox, Vancouver Island. The Tlahū's and Tlaā'men speak the same dialect.
II. Wakash	Nutka	Nutka	West Coast of Vancouver Island and Cape Flattery.
	Kwakiutl	Kwakiutl	Shores of Queen Charlotte Sound except the northern tip of Vancouver Island Tribes: Lē'kwiltok·, Nimpkisch, Kwakiutl, Tlauitsis, Mamalelek·ala.
		Newettee	The northern tip of Vancouver Island.
		Hē'iltsuk·	From Rivers Inlet to Milbank Sound. Tribes: Awī'ky'ēnoq and Hē'iltsuk·.
I. Selisch	Bilqula	Bilqula	Deans Inlet and Bentinck Arm.
III. Tsimschian	Tsimschian	Tsimschian	Skeena River.
IV. Haida	Haida	Haida	Queen Charlotte Islands.
V. Tlingit	Tlingit	Tlingit	Coast of Alaska to Yakutat.

In the discussion of the myths of these tribes it seems advisable to group together a number of tribes whose myths are very similar, while other tribes, which are distinguished by special characteristics, have to be detached from their language group. The following grouping appears to me to offer quite homogeneous groups of mythological material:

From here on referred to as:

1) Shuswap and Ntlakyapamuq . . . . Shuswap
2) Fraser River Delta . . . . Fraser River
3) Lku'ñgɛn, Cowitchin, Nanaimo, and Sk·qō'mic . . . . Coast Selisch
4) Pɛ'ntlatc and Çatlō'ltq . . . . Comox
5) Nutka . . . . Nutka
6) Lē'kwiltok·, Nimkisch, Kwakiutl, Tlauitsis, and Mamalelek·ala . . Kwakiutl
7) Tlatlasik·oala and Nak·omgyilisala . . . . Newettee
8) Awī'ky'ēnoq and Hē'iltsuk· . . . . Hē'iltsuk·
9) Bilqula . . . . Bilqula
10) Tsimschian . . . . Tsimschian
11) Tlingit . . . . Tlingit

The Haida had to be excluded from these considerations since the material at hand was too scanty.

For the sake of completeness it should be mentioned that Coast Selisch extends along the major part of the coast of the State of Washington, and that its southern neighbour is Chinook, which is situated along the Columbia River.

I will begin by setting forth the distribution of several groups of myths, starting with the Raven Legend. In the following table I have entered the various versions of this cycle, giving their respective page references. Krause means A. Krause *Die Tlinkit Indianer*.[3]

	Tlin.	Tsim.	Bil.	He.	New.	Kwa	Nut.	Com.	C.Sal.	Fra.
1. A woman gives birth to a son after swallowing stones. He defeats his uncle and becomes Raven.	K 254	-	-	-	-	-	-	-	-	-
2. A child of a dead woman flies to the sky and becomes the father of Raven.	-	272	-	-	170	-	-	-	-	-
3. Raven steals the sun.	311	276	242	208, 232	173	-	105	-	55	-
4. Transforms fishermen by liberating the light.	313	276	-	-	-	-	-	-	-	-
5. Steals freshwater.	313	276	-	209, 232	174	-	108	-	-	-
6. Loses his way in the fog.	K.260	P	-	-	-	-	-	77	-	-
7. Kills Bear and rips out Cormorant's tongue.	317	P	244	-	176	-	-	-	-	-
8. Steals bait from the rod of fishermen who then use rod to pull off his nose.	314	P	-	-	172	-	-	-	-	-
9. Induces Salmon to come close and then kills him.	K 264	277	-	-	176	-	-	73	-	-
10. Kills Pitch Man.	K 265	P	-	-	179	-	-	64	-	-
11. Sends people away on the pretext that enemies are approaching and then devours their food.	316	P	-	233	172	-	106	-	-	-
12. Transforms his guests.	317	277	-	233	176	-	-	-	57	-
13. Returns hospitality and is unable to serve his guests anything.	-	P	245	-	177	-	106	76	-	-

---

3. While Boas writes out "Krause" and "Present" in the following chart showing the location of specific motifs (which he identifies in this section as *Sagenelemente* or *Sagen-Elemente* 'myth/legend elements'), we are using "K" and "P" respectively. Presumably Boas was aware of the presence of these motifs in Tsimshian stories because of his field trip to the Nass River in September–October 1894 (Rohner 1969:311). The abbreviations used in tables appearing here are those defined by Boas later in this chapter: Shus. = Shuswap; C.Sal. = Coast Selisch; Fra. = Fraser River; Com. = Comox; Nut. = Nutka; Kwa. = Kwakiutl; New. = Newettee; He. = Hē'iltsuk·; Bil. = Bilqula; Tsim. = Tsimschian; Tlin. = Tlingit.

	Tlin.	Tsim.	Bil.	He.	New.	Kwa	Nut.	Com.	C.Sal.	Fra.
14. Raven's game is devoured while he isn't paying attention.	K.265	P	-	232	-	-	-	74	-	-
15. Raven, swallowed by Whale, kills him.	315	-	-	-	171	-	101	74	57	-
16. Deer gets Fire.	314	P	-	214, 241	187	-	102	80	-	-
17. Raven steals the herring from Gull, smears it over his canoe and goes to a fisherman. He pretends to have fish and thus causes the fisherman to distribute his.	K 263	P	-	-	P	-	-	-	-	-
18. He is cheated by his own slave.	315	276	-	-	-	159	-	72	-	-
19. He flings a companion from a bridge and then devours him.	315	P	-	-	-	-	-	-	-	-
20. He creates a canyon to drain water.	316	-	269	-	-	-	-	-	-	-
21. He visits the Shadows and Feathers.	316	P	-	-	-	-	-	-	-	-
22. He has a shooting match with his brother and uses birds for arrows.	318	P	-	-	-	-	-	-	-	-
23. He carves Salmon from wood.	-	-	242	209	174	-	-	-	-	-
24. He marries a dead twin.	-	-	-	209	174	-	-	-	-	-
25. He abducts the daughter of the Salmon Chief.	-	-	242	210	175	159	-	-	-	43
26. He steals his sister's berries.	-	-	244	210	177	-	107	76	-	-
27. He rapes a girl.	-	-	243	211	178	-	108	71	-	-
28. He sends Whale to Thunderbird who is drowned.	-	-	-	211	179	-	104	83	-	34
29. He kills Deer while mourning with him.	-	-	245	212, 233	-	-	105	77	-	-
30. He carves himself a son from wood.	-	-	-	211	179	-	-	-	-	-
Isolated Stories	6	5	4	1	6	-	(3)	-	-	-

The foregoing table shows with absolute clarity that the legend of Raven as shaper, not creator, of the world was originally limited to Tlingit and Tsimschian (and, it can be added, to Haida) and that its occurrence farther south is only fragmentary. Here the legend is preserved most completely in Newettee, but can be assumed to be present just as completely in Hē'iltsuk·, where my collection is less complete. The complete absence of this legend from Kwakiutl is based on the fact that Raven ranks as an ancestor of a tribe in the Newettee group and consequently is always told as belonging to that tribe and is known in its entirety to only its members. For this reason we have to regard Comox and Nutka as the southern neighbours of Newettee. And here it suddenly becomes evident that the number of known stories drops considerably at this point. While in Newettee there are still 13 stories present of the 18 common to Tlingit and Tsimschian in the northern cycle, we find only eight in Comox, six in Nutka, and only three tales have made it to Coast Selisch.

Furthermore, it can be seen that this group of tales occurs in Newettee in the same form in which it occurs in the northern region, so it can safely be inferred that the stories are completely identical, whereas, in contrast, we see already considerable modifications south of Newettee. Of the third tale (3) of the liberation of the sun by Raven, who transforms himself into a cedar needle, is swallowed by the daughter of Sun's owner, is reborn as a child, and then steals the sun which is kept locked up in a box, there remains in Nutka only the swallowing of a cedar needle which is reborn as a child, while Coast Selisch retains the more important element that Raven, by a ruse, forces the owner of daylight to release it from the box where he keeps it locked up. The same element, transferred to Jay, is still found with the Chehalis of Grey's Harbor (*Globus*, Vol. 65, No. 12).[4] Here, and in Newettee, Seagull is the owner of daylight. In the same way, the very complicated tale of the theft of freshwater (5) has been changed completely in Nutka, insofar as Crow steals the water against Raven's will and makes rivers and lakes with it. The adventure of Pitch Man (10), whom Raven has killed by the hot sun to later use the pitch, has been completely taken out of its context by the Comox, and appears in a new connection with the myth of the creation of sun and moon. The legends of how Raven's game is devoured while he is not watching (14) and how he is cheated by his slave do not occur anymore in the framework of the Raven cycle in the south, either.

The self-contained structure of the Raven Legend, as found in the region's north, and its gradual shrinking towards the south with simultaneous modification of the traits common to the north, prove that a gradual transmission of a legendary cycle from the north southward has taken place here, which essentially found its conclusion in Newettee; although, even from there, isolated traits, strongly modified, still penetrated southwards.

In Bilqula as well, Raven's adventures belonging to the northern cycle are considerably less in number than in Newettee. From these facts it can safely be deduced that the Raven cycle was diffused southward along the coast as a self-contained structure and gradually lost cohesion.

---

4. Boas' citation should read *Globus* Vol. 63, No. 12. These stories, along with those in parts 10 and 11 of Vol. 63, have recently been translated by Richard Bland and edited and annotated by Ann Simonds (see Boas 1999:85–104).

This does not, however, exclude the possibility of the cycle having adopted foreign elements, among others also those at home in southern British Columbia. Here, above all, the adventure (13) is to be mentioned where Raven returns hospitality and is unable to serve anything to his guests. Seal makes oil drip out of his hands for him, but when he tries to do the same he only burns his hands, and so on in this vein. This tale is found all over North America as a separate legend. Thus it is found in Chinook (F. Boas, *Chinook Texts*, Washington 1894, p. 178), in Omaha and Ponca (James Owen Dorsey, *The Cegiha Language*, Washington 1890, p. 557) actually identical in form to Chinook but in relation to different beings; in Ojibwa (H.R. Schoolcraft, *The Myth of Hiawatha*, Philadelphia 1856, p. 44), and in Micmac (Silas T. Rand, *Legends of the Micmacs*, London 1894, p. 302). I did not obtain this adventure at all in Tlingit and only in fragments with the other northern tribes, so it can be assumed that it was diffused from the south to the north. It is of interest to observe that here, too, the adventure is ascribed to the powerful Transformer who is also the Trickster at the same time. This is also the case in Micmac where it is Hare, in Ojibwa where it is Manabozho, and in Ponca where the corresponding Ictinike returns the hospitality. In Chinook the personality traits of Transformer and Trickster are separated, and here Bluejay plays the corresponding role in the tale under discussion. It can possibly be assumed that the myth, with an exchange of the principal role, has been transmitted from Chinook to Coast Selisch, and thus gradually reached the region of the Raven legend, into which it fitted quite well.

A second, far more important adventure, most likely originating in the south, is the introduction of the myth in Tsimschian (2) which differs radically from the form observed in Tlingit. The idea of a dead woman giving birth to live children, the flight up into the sky where the newcomer marries the sky chief's daughter and is then threatened and tested by his father-in-law, belongs entirely to the southern cycle. The separate elements of this tale are combined in a great number of variants as the following table will show.[5]

	Tsim.	Bil.	Newet.	New.	Kwa.	Nutka	Comox	Fra.	Shus.	Chin.
1. A young man flies into the sky.	273	263	-	170		117	65	38	17	-
2. There meets blind women.	-	263	-	-	135	117	66	38	18	-
3. Or other helpers.	273	-	-	-	-	-	66	-	18	-
4. Sits down by water. 4a. The door of the Chief's house snaps at him.	273	-	198	170	136	118	66	39	-	-
5. Is brought into the house by the chief's daughter. 5a. He forces his way into the house.	273	-	198	170	136	118	66	39	-	-

5. Boas provides two columns for the Newettee, listing the Tlatlasik·oala and Nak·o'mgyilisala separately.

	Tsim.	Bil.	Newet.	New.	Kwa.	Nutka	Comox	Fra.	Shus.	Chin.
6. Marries the chief's daughter.	273	-	198	171	136	118	66	39	-	34
7. Is placed on the spiky death-mat.	?	-	-	171	136	118	66	39	-	-
8. Caught in split tree.	-	-	198	-	136	118	67	39	-	34
9. Has to bring wild animals to his father-in-law.	-	-	-	-	-	-	68	39	-	34
10. Makes fish jump into father-in-law's face.	-	-	-	-	136	-	67	-	-	-

The persistent combination of the elements of this myth, which have no logical connection whatsoever, proves that the story must have been transmitted as a whole. It is quite possible that in Comox, where the myth is met with in the most complete form, individual traits were added later. But this possibility cannot efface the fact that the legend is a uniform complex, whose components are gradually disintegrating towards the north. This is corroborated by the fact that separate traits of the myth have been preserved as individual tales in the north. Thus the meeting with the blind ducks has been joined to the K·ā'nigyilak˙ cycle in Newettee (p. 202).

Another variant of the tale in which the man wants to regain his abducted wife can be found. He climbs down along a rope to the bottom of the sea, meets a slave splitting wood whose wedge he breaks without being noticed, then wins him over to his side by mending the wedge again. The slave then helps him to regain his wife. This tale is identical in Tsimschian (p. 300), Bilqula (p. 259) and Nanaimo (p. 56); in Newettee (p. 175) it is modified. Presumably it is a recent isolated acquisition by the Nanaimo.

Thus it follows that the structure of the legend used in Tsimschian to introduce the Raven cycle in this area most likely had its origin on Vancouver Island. But it has a much wider distribution throughout America. The introductory feature returns in Kiowa. Gatschet tells how the Sun's son supported himself on his mother's body and that an old woman captured him by making a target and arrows which the boy attempted to steal. This legend is evidently identical to the Tsimschian legend, but to date further links are lacking. The legend is also found in Micmac (Rand, pages 65, 290).

The group of tales from number 23 to number 30, limited to the area from Comox to Bilqula merits special consideration. The myth of the origin of the salmon is limited to Kwakiutl, Newettee, Hē'iltsuk· and Bilqula. In Kwakiutl it is ascribed to Mink, in Newettee to Raven, in Hē'iltsuk· to Kuēkuaqā'oē, who although not identical with Raven, nevertheless is closely related to him. In Bilqula the adventures are ascribed jointly to Masmasalā'niq and Raven. The tale of the killing of Thunderbird is centred even less upon Raven. A fragment of this myth is found in Fraser River where Woodpecker and Mink are the actors. The same applies to

Comox where the complete structure of the myth is found. In Nutka the adventure is ascribed to Kwotiath, to whom other features of the Raven and Mink legend have also been transferred. In Newettee they are ascribed to Raven and in Hē'iltsuk· to Kuēkuaqā'oe. In the less important adventure (27), too, the roles of Mink and Raven are interchanged. A survey of the Raven legend shows that Raven's essential attribute, which always comes to the fore, is his greed, while the cycle of the Mink legends is possessed of a very pronounced salacious[6] character. Consequently we will not be far wrong in regarding the salacious Raven legends, which are limited to the southern part of this area, as transferred Mink legends and, on the other hand, taking those Mink legends which have gluttony as their sole topic, for transferred Raven legends. I will return to this later on.

It appears that such transfers from extraneous legendary cycles into the Raven cycle have been strongest in Newettee and Hē'iltsuk·, and I believe that the transfer took place originally in Newettee because here Raven is the ancestor of a lineage, and this brings about the concentration of very many exploits around him.

In this respect one of the individual stories which has no analogue on the coast of British Columbia is of special interest. The Newettee tell that after the burning of the world, bare rock formed the earth's surface, and that Raven made the animals dive in order to get soil and leaves from the bottom of the water. After many vain attempts, Duck at last succeeded in reaching the bottom and bringing up a branch from which Raven formed mountains, earth and trees (p. 173). A look at this legend's distribution proves that it must have been diffused from the Mississippi basin across the Rocky Mountains. In the region of the Great Lakes the legend in question is the common myth of the Deluge: A number of animals escape drowning in a canoe or on a raft, and some of them dive in order to bring up soil. After several vain attempts Muskrat succeeds in bringing up some mud which is enlarged by magic and then forms the new world. Petitot has reported several versions of this tale from the Mackenzie basin (E. Petitot, *Traditions Indiennes du Canada Nord Ouest*, Paris 1886, pp. 147, 318, 473). It is known to the Ojibwa and Ottawa (cf. Schoolcraft, *op. cit.* page 39). James Owen Dorsey communicated to me a number of years ago that he had found the myth with tribes belonging to the Sioux linguistic group and that the Rev. W. Hamilton has recorded a version with the Iowa, who also belong to this linguistic family. Zeisberger has heard this myth from the Delaware on the Atlantic coast and Mr. Mooney communicated a version to me which had been told to him by the Cherokee. Since this myth has a variant form I will briefly describe it here. In the beginning all the animals were in the sky and there was

---

6.   Although Boas uses the term *erotisch* 'erotic' here in the original *Sagen*, 'salacious' is a more
      appropriate English term to use in this context.

nothing but water down here. At last a small Water Beetle and a Spider came down from the sky. They dived to the bottom and brought up some mud from which the world was made. The Buzzard flew down when the earth was still soft and made the mountains with the beating of his wings.

The Iroquois have a closely related myth: A woman fell down from the sky into the sea which covered the whole world. Thereupon a Turtle rose. The woman remained on its back until an animal brought up some mud from which the world was made. No trace of this myth is to be found in the southern part of North America, nor in the Atlantic provinces of Canada. It is found again, however, in three locations on the Pacific coast. The Yocut[7] in southern California recount that the world was once covered in water. In those days there lived one Hawk, one Crow and one Duck. Duck dived and came up dead, but brought a bit of mud along. So Hawk and Crow each took half of this mud and from it made the mountains. This form of the legend is reminiscent of the Cherokee myth. Farther to the north I found the legend with the Molalla and the Chinook. Here Beaver causes a flood, the animals seek refuge in canoes and Muskrat succeeds in bringing up earth (*Globus*, Vol. 65, No.12). Consequently it is evident that the myth in question originates in the region of the Great Lakes. From there to the Chinook it is Muskrat who succeeds in reaching the bottom. The action has been transferred to other animals only at the extreme periphery of the area of distribution. I will prove later in more detail that many eastern myths have reached the Pacific coast along the Columbia River. Here it will suffice to point out that the myth is an extraneous element which in Newettee has been woven into the Raven legend.

Thus we see that on the southern coast of British Columbia the Raven legend has assimilated extraneous elements and loses unity. We observe moreover that the legends of this cycle contrast with other mythological tales in the same region, especially with the Mink legend and the K·á′nigyilak′ legend. The concept of the liberation of sun and daylight is not easily reconciled with the myths of the chief in the sky who carries the sun. This group of myths is absent from the Tlingit and Tsimschian so their mythology bears a far more unified character.

From all this I deduce that the Raven cycle developed originally with the Tlingit or Tsimschian and from there spread south and was absorbed by the mythology of the southern tribes.

Unfortunately we are unable to trace the diffusion of the cycle northwards. There are only hints with the Athapaskan tribes of Alaska and it appears unlikely to me that very distinct traces will be found with the Eskimo. Only one myth, which I

7. Yokuts, the name applied to a group of tribes in the San Joaquin River valley and western slopes of the Sierra Nevada mountains in California.

obtained from an Eskimo born in Port Clarence, Alaska, is worth mentioning (*Journal of American Folklore*, 1894, p. 206): Once upon a time the sun vanished and the people went out to get it back. After some adventures which have no bearing on our discussion, they met counsellors who told them where the sun was. At last they came to a house. One of the men crawled in and saw a young woman and her parents inside the house. In each corner there was a ball under the roof, a big one on the right and on the left, a small one. The man got possession of the big ball, the people tore it up and it became light again. I believe that this myth undoubtedly is connected with that of the theft of the sun.

If we turn to the Mink legend now, a brief comparison shows that all the essential features of this legend, unless borrowed from the Raven cycle, are limited to the Kwakiutl and their neighbours as the following table shows:

	Bil.	Hē'iltsuk	New.	Kwa.	Nutka	Comox	C.Sel.	Fra.
1. Mink ascends into the sky on a chain of arrows, visits his father and carries the sun for him. Since he burns the world, he is flung down.	246	215, 234	172	157	-	-	-	-
2. Obtains the fire from the ghosts.	-	-	-	158	-	-	54	43
3. Kills the son of the chief of the Wolves.	-	-	-	150	98	75	-	-
4. Attacks bathing women.	-	-	172	-	108	73	-	26
5. Marries plants and animals.	-	-	-	158	100	71	-	44
6. Has himself buried.	-	-	-	P	-	73	-	33
7. Kills Otter to obtain his wife.	-	-	-	158	-	72	-	-
8. Seduces a girl to go into the forest with him and to sit down on him under the pretext that he is a healing herb.	243	211	178	160	108	71	-	-
9. Goes to Thunderbird to steal his wife.	-	210, 211	179	104	-	82	-	34

Since this group of legends among the Selischan tribes is found only with the neighbours of the Kwakiutl and, in contrast, appears to be preserved far less completely with the related tribes on Puget Sound, I am inclined to interpret it as one that originated from the Kwakiutl. This applies especially to the most important feature of the myth: the ascent to the sky on a chain of arrows; the burning of the world caused by Mink; and his fall from the sky.

The ascent to the sky is a myth occurring very frequently in America, but ascent with the aid of a chain of arrows appears to be limited to our area. The above-mentioned version of the myth is found only in Kwakiutl, Newettee, Hē'iltsuk· and Bilqula. In Tsimschian we find the chain of arrows in a rather unimportant myth

(278); otherwise the visitors fly up as birds or are brought up by spirits. In Nutka the chain of arrows is a feature added to the tale in which the young man wants to marry the daughter of the heavenly chief (117). This also applies to Comox (65) and, much farther to the south, to Cathlamet on the Columbia River (*Globus*, Vol. 65, No. 12). On the Fraser River and with the Ntlakyapamuq (17 & 31) the feature has been added to the war against the inhabitants of the sky, which belongs to an eastern group of myths. With the Tillamook the myth is also found as an individual feature. So the only doubt remaining is whether the tale had originated with the Kwakiutl or slightly farther south on the Pacific coast. The salacious segments of the Mink legend are so characteristic that we have to regard them as homogeneous, as well. The legend numbered 27 in the Raven cycle, where Raven rapes a girl, fits much better into this legendary cycle and most likely has been transferred from it into the Raven cycle. The tale how Raven was swallowed by Whale and then killed him, on the other hand, most likely has been transferred from the Raven cycle to the Mink cycle (Newettee, p. 171; Comox, p. 75).

Another important cycle of legends in the area under discussion comprises the Wanderer legends, which are also developed most strongly in the south and terminate in Newettee, yielding to the Raven legend from there on. No sharply-defined home could be found for this legend because it is common to the whole continent and exhibits an infinity of variants. However, the Raven legend discussed above has to be regarded as a peculiar arrangement of this group, whose home could be determined with much certainty. While Raven is essentially a shaper of the world, the Wanderer in the south appears distinctly as cultural deity and, in addition, as creator of animals and strangely-formed rocks. Thus we find him with the Chinook, on the Fraser River, the Coast Selisch, Comox, Nutka, Kwakiutl, and Newettee. The Masmasalā'niq myth of the Bilqula has to be added here as well, in spite of its peculiar features.

But what gives the Wanderer legend its character in this area is the strict division of the cultural deity and the trickster. Neither Cikla of the Chinook, nor Qäls of the Coast Selisch, Kumsnō'otl of the Comox, the two Wanderers of the Nutka, or K·'ā'nigyilak· of the Newettee perpetrates tricks in addition to their cultural mission, as is done by Raven in northern British Columbia, by Glooscap with the Micmac, by Manabozho with the Ojibwa, by Napi with the Blackfeet, by Coyote with the tribes of the southern Rockies, or by "Boatman" with the Northern Athapascens. These tricks are not absent by any means, but have been transferred to different animals or other beings: to Bluejay with the Chinook; to Mink and Raven with the Coast Selisch, Comox and Newettee; to Kwotiath, Mink and Raven with the Nutka. The Shuswap have not made the division so strictly and through their influence the picture on the Fraser River is not quite as clear as with the rest of the coastal tribes.

The strictest division appears with the Coast Selisch and the Bilqula. The Coast Selisch from Puget Sound have not made the division either.

The most common features of this legend are the following:

Transformation of Deer.	(Chinook, p. 20; Coast Selisch, p. 56; Comox, p. 64; Nutka, p. 98; Newettee, p. 200.)
Contest between the Wanderer and a second Wanderer or a powerful chief.	(Chinook, p. 21; Shuswap, p. 16; Fraser River, p. 21; Coast Selisch, p. 47; Newettee, p. 196.)
Gives man his present shape, especially by situating the genitals.	(Fraser River, p. 23; Comox, p. 72; Nutka, p. 108; Newettee, p. 202.)
Transforms humans into strangely-shaped rocks.	(Shuswap, pp. 16, 19; Coast Selisch, pp. 46, 56; Comox, p. 63; Newettee, p. 193.)

The structure of the legend varies considerably, but several types can be distinguished clearly. The Wanderers of the Chinook, Nutka and Newettee appear as twins of supernatural origin. The Cĭ'ciklē legend of the Nutka (p. 115), which is closely related to the K·'ā'nigyilak˙ legend (p. 194), insofar as both appear as bringer of herring and eulachon respectively, must be included here in any event. I have no doubt that Cĭ'cikle is derived from the Chinook name for the Wanderer, Cikla. Cikla is a dual form and indicates that the Wanderer is a duality. Nutka, by reduplication, forms the plural Cĭ'cikle from it, which signifies two or several Cikla.[8]

The peculiarly rich development of the myth with the Kwakiutl, which is characterized by Wanderer's meeting with the separate numaym ancestors, has its origin most likely in the Kwakiutl's numaym organization. The crests and privileges of the numaym almost without exception are authenticated by the fact that they were granted by Wanderer who either had a contest with an ancestor or married his

---

8. Boas' certainty notwithstanding, the available data concerning "Cĭ'ciklē" are confusing. Boas made reference to "Cĭ'cikle" in his article on the Nootka, where he wrote that "in a tradition of the Nootka it is stated that a boy prayed to a being in heaven Cĭ'cikle," who, he added, "is probably identical with" the deity known as "Kā'tse" (Boas 1891d:595). "Kā'tse" is the same term that Boas transcribes as "K·ā'otsē" in story 1 of the Nutka (Nuu-chah-nulth) section in the *Sagen*, where we have transcribed this term as qa·ci and noted that contemporary Nuu-chah-nulth people translate it either as 'Provider' or 'pray for something.' However, we also note (in story 11 of the Nutka section) that some Nuu-chah-nulth recognize "Cĭ'cikle" as šišikli which is a "Nuu-chah-nulth-ized" pronunciation of the English term "Jesus Christ." Partial support for this latter derivation comes from a Chinook Jargon dictionary which translates "kli" as 'Christ' (Johnson 1978:290). This information conflicts with Boas' statement in the present discussion that "Cĭ'cikle," as used by the Nutka, is derived from "Cikla," the name for the 'Wanderer' used by the Chinook people of the Lower Columbia River.

daughter. This is also the most likely reason for many myths from other cycles being woven into the Wanderer legend, especially the marriage with the following tests (pp. 198, 199).

The second group of the Wanderer legend is distinguished by the fact that four brothers always appear together. This version is peculiar to the Shuswap and Bilqula, but has also spread to the tribes along the lower Fraser River.

We can see from these examples that the regions of the myths have had a strong influence on each other. I will now attempt to demonstrate, through a statistical arrangement of the diffusion of the myth elements, that the transfer of myths, which could be clearly proven in these separate cases, has occurred everywhere, and will seek to ascertain the paths along which these transfers have taken place. At the end of this study the legendary elements are given on which the study is based. To begin with I have compiled the number of features of myths which are common to different tribes. I have included the Chinook, the northern Athapascens, the Ponca, and the Micmac, about whom there are relatively complete collections extant. Of these the Chinook border directly onto our region, while the Athapascens represent the Mackenzie Basin, the Ponca, the Mississippi Basin, and the Micmac the farthest-north Atlantic coast.

Number of Myth Elements Common to Different Tribes

	Tlin.	Tsim,	Bil.	He.	New.	Kwa.	Nutka	Com.	Fra.	C.Sal.	Shus.	Chin.	Ponca	Mic.	Ath.
Tlingit	48	20	8	6	11	4	7	9	5	3	3	4	1	1	5
Tsimschian	20	135	16	22	23	15	11	20	8	8	4	10	5	8	6
Bilqula	8	16	117	26	24	22	23	25	14	13	8	12	7	8	14
Hě'iltsuk·	6	22	26	118	33	19	20	21	6	8	5	12	9	7	12
Newettee	11	23	24	33	166	25	34	39	21	11	11	15	8	11	11
Kwakiutl	4	15	22	19	25	147	24	32	17	10	7	9	8	7	9
Nutka	7	11	23	20	34	24	127	37	20	10	8	19	12	7	8
Comox	9	20	25	21	39	32	37	158	26	12	11	23	10	12	12
Fraser River	5	8	14	6	21	17	20	26	106	8	11	13	3	5	6
Coast Selisch	3	8	13	8	11	10	10	12	8	60	6	6	2	4	3
Shuswap	3	4	8	5	11	7	8	11	11	6	72	9	8	5	8
Chinook	4	10	12	12	15	9	19	23	13	6	9	-	16	20	10
Ponca	1	5	7	9	8	8	12	10	3	2	8	16	-	-	-
Micmac	1	8	8	7	11	7	7	12	5	4	5	20	-	-	-
Athapascen	5	6	14	12	11	9	8	12	6	3	8	10	-	-	-

Obviously this table does not give the correct proportions since the collections are not exhaustive. I have now assumed that the number of common features would increase proportionally with greater amounts of material, and furthermore, that the same amount of material would be available from all tribes. In this, double versions in each separate collection must of course be counted only as one. According to this, including the Tlingit collection by Krause (*op. cit.*), I have compiled the following contributions:

Tlingit	17 pages	Nutka	31 pages
Tsimschian	38 pages	Comox	34 pages
Bilqula	30 pages	Fraser River	27 pages
Hē′iltsuk·	30 pages	Coast Selisch	17 pages
Newettee	38 pages	Shuswap	17 pages
Kwakiutl	40 pages		

Even the above assumption is not quite correct, since the number of new elements will increase only slowly with growing amounts of material, once the essential myths have been collected. But since the Tlingit, Coast Selisch and Shuswap material is rather incomplete, I do not think that I made much of an error in the above assumption. In any case, an error in this instance compensates for those in the first compilation. In the first case, tribes with scanty material would be credited with too few common features, and in the second case, with too many. Thus we can safely assume that the results in both cases are correct. I have assumed the maximum amount of 40 occurrences only with the tribes where the collections were very voluminous, namely Kwakiutl, Chinook, Ponca, Micmac, and Athapascen, because above this limit the increase of elements proves to be very slight. The computation in the case of the Tlingit, for instance, is carried out as follows: The number of the elements common with other tribes is divided by the number of pages of the respective tribes' myths. This result is multiplied by 100, yielding the amount of common elements for 17 occurrences in Tlingit and 100 occurrences of every other tribe. But since a change in the amount of the Tlingit material also influences the amount of common elements, this latest result has to be computed for 100 occurrences of Tlingit material, dividing by 17 and multiplying by 100.

Number of Myth Elements Common to Different Tribes
With Equal Numbers of Pages of Material Extant

	Tlin.	Tsim.	Bil.	He.	New.	Kwa.	Nutka	Com.	Fra.	C.Sal.	Shus.	Chin.	Ponca	Mic.	Atha.
Tlingit	282	30	15	12	17	6	13	15	11	10	10	6	2	2	7
Tsimschian	30	356	13	20	17	10	9	15	8	12	6	7	3	5	4
Bilqula	15	13	390	28	21	19	25	25	17	26	16	10	6	7	12
Hē′iltsuk·	12	20	28	393	30	16	22	21	8	15	10	10	8	6	10
Newettee	17	17	21	30	437	17	29	30	20	17	17	10	5	7	7
Kwakiutl	6	10	19	16	17	367	20	25	16	14	10	6	5	5	6
Nutka	13	9	25	22	29	20	410	35	24	19	15	15	10	6	7
Comox	15	15	25	21	30	25	35	465	28	20	19	17	7	8	9
Fraser River	11	8	17	8	20	16	24	28	393	17	24	12	3	5	6
Coast Selisch	10	12	26	15	17	14	19	20	17	353	21	9	3	6	4
Shuswap	10	6	16	10	17	10	15	19	24	21	424	13	12	7	12
Chinook	6	7	10	10	10	6	15	17	12	9	13	-	10	13	6
Ponca	2	3	6	8	5	5	10	7	3	3	12	10	-	-	-
Micmac	2	5	7	6	7	5	6	8	5	6	7	13	-	-	-
Athapascen	7	4	12	10	7	6	7	9	6	4	12	6	-	-	-

To begin with, the tables quite generally show that very pronounced borrowing between neighbouring tribes must have occurred everywhere. This is expressed by the decreasing amounts with increasing distance between the areas compared. This can be observed in every row, but in order to appreciate the numbers properly it must be realized that some tribes have several neighbours. Thus the Newettee are neighbours to the Nutka, the Kwakiutl and the Hē'iltsuk·; the Comox are neighbours to the Kwakiutl, the Coast Selisch and to the tribes along the Lower Fraser River.

Then a number of peculiarities have to be pointed out. Looking at the groupings which show the distribution with the Comox, the tribes of the Fraser River, the Coast Selisch, and the Shuswap, it becomes evident in all cases that the number of elements common with these tribes is appreciably greater with the Bilqula than with the neighbours. This irregularity is so pronounced that it can not be missed. We know that the Bilqula belong linguistically to the Selisch family to which all the tribes mentioned belong, and that their language is related especially to the coast dialects. For this reason we have to assume that the Bilqula still possess a portion of their myths from the time when they were united with the other Selisch tribes.

Furthermore, the tables show distinctly that the northern cycle has had a strong influence on tribes as far as, and including, the Comox, while its influence wanes very quickly farther south. Conversely, the influence of the southern cycle on the northern region can also be traced in our tables. But here the Bilqula have to be excluded for the reasons mentioned, because they have retained many elements belonging to the Selisch tribes of the south. The Shuswap have hardly any contact with the cycles of the coast, except with their neighbours on the Lower Fraser River. With the Tsimschian and Tlingit, only very slight points of contact with the south are to be found. For the rest of the Selisch tribes, contact towards the north essentially comes to an end with the Newettee. The Kwakiutl have close contacts as far as the Hē'iltsuk·. The Chinook, finally, have generally only slight contact with the tribes of British Columbia, but it becomes evident that the contacts on the one hand extend along the coast to the Nutka and Newettee, and on the other hand reach the Comox.

With the Micmac and Ponca cycles it becomes marked very clearly that essentially they reached the coast along the Columbia River, transmitted by the Chinook, while the Athapaskens influenced their immediate neighbours, the Shuswap and Bilqula and, through transmission by the latter, the Hē'iltsuk·.

Finally I would like to discuss the number of contacts of each separate group with the other groups. It is no surprise that the number is only slight with the groups living on the outer periphery of the area, while the tribes situated in the centre of the area show a greater number of contacts. But it is precisely in the centre of the area where a very peculiar deviation is found, namely the Kwakiutl, who share only a very small number of elements with the other tribes, while on the other hand having many exclusively for themselves, so that they appear as the most original tribe among their neighbours.

In our consideration so far, only common features have been counted, so that the same elements are repeated quite often in the tables. The total of legends or features found with more than one tribe on the Pacific coast between Columbia River and southern Alaska comes to 174. The amounts for the separate tribes are as follows:

Tlingit	25	Fraser River	46
Tsimschian	54	Coast Selisch	27
Bilqula	59	Shuswap	24
Hē'iltsuk·	59	Chinook	52
Newettee	74	Ponca	27
Kwakiutl	50	Micmac	31
Nutka	64	Athapasken	33
Comox	82		

Assuming as before, that the number of elements with each tribe would increase proportionally with the material, and computing it for 40 pages of material for each tribe, we find the following amounts:

Tlingit	59	Kwakiutl	50	Shuswap	56
Tsimschian	57	Nutka	83	Chinook	52
Bilqula	78	Comox	96	Ponca	27
Hē'iltsuk·	78	Fraser River	68	Micmac	31
Newettee	78	Coast Selisch	64	Athapasken	33

These two tables agree in showing that the Comox have the most mixed mythology. They are followed by the Nutka, the Newettee, Bilqula, and Hē'iltsuk· in this order. However, for the Tlingit, Coast Selisch and Shuswap, for whom the available material was scantiest, the connections are reduced considerably. The numbers are lowest for the Chinook, Kwakiutl, Shuswap, and Tsimschian.

The first general table of the distribution of common elements shows that the heaviest borrowing always took place between neighbours. In order to investigate how far the myths of a group have been influenced by tribes living further removed, we will exclude those elements common only to one tribe and its immediate neighbours, because these show up local transfer vis à vis the general distribution. The following tribes are neighbours:

Tlingit and Tsimschian.
Tsimschian and Tlingit, Hē'iltsuk·.
Bilqula and Hē'iltsuk·.
Hē'iltsuk· and Tsimschian, Bilqula, Newettee.

Newettee and Hē′iltsuk·, Nutka, Kwakiutl, Comox.
Kwakiutl and Newettee, Comox.
Nutka and Newettee, Coast Selisch, Comox.
Comox and Newettee, Kwakiutl, Coast Selisch, Fraser River, Nutka.
Fraser River and Coast Selisch, Comox, Shuswap, Nutka.
Coast Selisch and Comox, Fraser River, Nutka.
Shuswap and Fraser River.

Two points in this compilation need to be explained. First, the adding of the Comox to the Newettee's neighbours, even though the Kwakiutl are between them, stems from the fact that the legends of the Newettee are mostly known to the Kwakiutl and are only ascribed to families of the former. Therefore very many legends pass over the Kwakiutl and are common to the Newettee and Comox. For this reason they must be regarded as neighbours. Second, I have listed the Nutka and Comox as neighbours even though they have no more contact now. The reason for this is also the fact that they share a great number of legends which are common to them, not through transmission by the Newettee, and which do not appear elsewhere, as well as the other fact that the Chinook share a lot of material with these two tribes alone. This can be explained only by assuming that the two tribes were formerly in close contact. For this reason I have listed both as neighbours here. The review yields the following result:

Number of myths and elements common to tribes which are not neighbours:

Tlingit	19	Kwakiutl	48	Shuswap	20
Tsimschian	42	Nutka	54	Chinook	52
Bilqula	53	Comox	57	Ponca	27
Hē′iltsuk·	46	Fraser River	38	Micmac	31
Newettee	57	Coast Selisch	24	Athapasken	33

Or, according to the same computation as above:

Tlingit	45	Kwakiutl	48	Shuswap	47
Tsimschian	44	Nutka	70	Chinook	52
Bilqula	71	Comox	67	Ponca	27
Hē′iltsuk·	61	Fraser River	56	Micmac	31
Newettee	60	Coast Selisch	56	Athapasken	33

From this it is apparent again that the Bilqula, Comox and Nutka represent the most strongly mixed types while the Shuswap and Chinook in the south and the Tlingit and the Tsimschian in the north exert less influence on the other tribes. In addition it becomes evident in all tables that the Kwakiutl form the exception because they have little in common with the other tribes.

Finally, I will employ yet another method to test the relations of each region. I have added all the features which I extracted from the total material and have computed for each tribe the percentage of the total of features in relation to those it has in common with other tribes. With this method the arbitrariness of the equalization applied above is avoided. This yields the following results:

	Total Elements	Common features % in all tribes	Common features % with other tribes excluding neighbours
Tsimschian	135	40	31
Bilqula	117	50	45
Hē′iltsuk·	118	48	38
Newettee	166	43	34
Kwakiutl	147	34	33
Nutka	127	48	43
Comox	158	51	37
Fraser River	106	43	37
Coast Selisch	60	42	38
Shuswap	72	33	29

In spite of some slight variations in the arrangement, the results in both methods turn out to be very similar. The differences are mainly restricted to those groups where there is little material available. Here the material of the Bilqula shows up to be the most mixed. The Comox, Nutka and Hē′iltsuk· follow. The result obtained for the Coast Selisch most likely is doubtful since their material doesn't lend itself to comparison. This also applies to the Tlingit, whom I have omitted from the table for that reason. The Shuswap, Kwakiutl and Tsimschian have the least elements in common with their neighbouring tribes. The results arrived at by such different means prove conclusively:

1) That the Shuswap or, as we may say generally, the Selisch tribes of the interior, in their mythologies, had only slight contact with the coastal tribes.

2) That the Tsimschian essentially have influenced only their immediate neighbours and otherwise have had only very little influence on the development of the mythologies of the coast.

3) That the Kwakiutl have preserved a great independence from their neighbouring tribes.

In addition it has to be assumed that in all instances where numerous transmissions have taken place only with the neighbouring tribes and where distant cycles have remained untouched, the contact is not very old, especially in cases where the total number of contacts with other tribes is small. This applies especially to the case of the Tsimschian who have numerous contacts with their immediate neighbours while their relations are slightly lesser to the south. Furthermore, since the independent elements of the Tsimschian myths contrast strongly with all the other cycles and have the character of myths of an interior tribe, I judge them to be recent intruders on the Pacific coast. Without having more comprehensive materials of the Tlingit and Haida, one cannot assess their relations with the Tsimschian. The great amount of features limited to the Hē'iltsuk· and their neighbours can be ascribed to the transfer of features from Tsimschian myths, as well as to the intrusion of the peculiarly-developed myths of the Bilqula, and to the Athapasken myths transmitted by the latter.

Farther in the south, a distinct division occurs with the Comox, where the northern elements cease almost completely. Linguistically the Comox belong to the Coast Selisch, but they are culturally far more related to the Kwakiutl tribes than to their southern neighbours who are related to them linguistically. I believe that new displacements have occurred here which possibly are connected with the profusion of dialects in the region and the separation of the Bilqula from the Coast Selisch. For linguistic reasons we have to assume that the Bilqula and the Coast Selisch were formerly united. They share many words in common with all Selisch languages, as well as the occurrences of the pronominal gender and the distinction of local conditions, i.e., presence or absence.

I have previously pointed out that the Bilqula are still closely related with the Southern Selisch tribes through their myths. This would hardly be the case if the division were very old. In addition it becomes evident that the Comox, who up to the end of the past century were limited to the islands north of the Gulf of Georgia, exhibit close relations with the Nutka and Chinook.[9] The close relation of the Comox with the Nutka can scarcely be understood without assuming a recent displacement. It has not occurred through transmission by the Newettee, since the Comox and Nutka have much in common which the Newettee lack. It is possible, however, that this connection, seemingly so hard to comprehend, might be cleared up very simply once the myths of the Coast Selisch are better known. This much is certain, however, that the southern and northern cycles merge with the Comox and that the northern ones come to an abrupt end with them, so that it must be assumed that they have not yet had time to spread farther to the south. At the Fraser River, finally, we observe the encroachment of the cycle belonging to the interior British Columbia plateau. Hence we can summarize up as follows:

9.   See Section VIII, fn 1, for a discussion of the southern movement of the Comox.

1) The Tsimschian turn out to be recent intruders on the coast.

2) The Coast Selisch must have experienced strong displacements recently which brought the Bilqula north and probably led the tribes living south of the Comox into their present sites.

3) The Chinook have exercised a strong influence along the coast on the Nutka and Comox, and indirectly on the Newettee.

4) The myths of the Algonquin and Sioux have reached the coast along the Columbia River. The influence of the Algonquin can be termed strong while that of the Sioux seems to be less.

5) The myths of the Athapasken have reached the coast essentially through transmission by the Shuswap and the Bilqula.

The mythologies of the North Pacific coast discussed here could easily be summarized in a few short words, but I will limit myself to those groups with which we are better acquainted. The Tsimschian, apart from the Raven legend, have no well-defined animal legend in which only animals appear as actors. All their tales treat of human conditions, mostly of episodes where unfortunates were helped by supernatural beings, and also the way in which ancestors of certain families[10] obtained their crests or other privileges, as well as abductions by animals or spirits and visits to them.

With the Kwakiutl we find the animal myth represented by the Mink cycle and the Wanderer cycle. Apart from that, the animal myth recedes even further into the background than with the Tsimschian. In its stead the mythology is dominated by ancestor legends which deal with the descent of the several numaym. With the Kwakiutl it becomes very clear that the numaym, as with the Selischan tribes, was originally a local group. The inhabitants of a village derive their descent from one mythological ancestor, who in turn comes from the sky, the earth or the ocean.

In the course of time there developed from these local groups, by consolidation, the tribes and their subdivisions. Since each lineage traced back its crest and its privileges to the mythical ancestor, the number of such legends grew very large. This might be the reason why the Kwakiutl legends occupy such an isolated position in the whole area. This tendency in the formation of legends is strengthened even more by the development of the secret societies belonging to the numaym's privileges, and whose origin is always traced back to the ancestor legends. The common American idea of the acquisition of a manitou[11] is shaped in such a way that the individual cannot obtain just any manitou, but only the one hereditary in the

---

10. Boas uses the term *Familien* here in the original *Sagen*.

11. Given as *Manitu* here in the original *Sagen*.

family. With this the tale of its acquisition moves into the realm of the tribal mythology. The family manitou becomes the lineage totem or the protector of that secret society belonging to the family or tribe. Because of this, almost each one of the Kwakiutl legends deals with the acquisition of magic powers and belongs to certain numaym or societies. The Tsimschian only have four clans which, however, are subdivided, but their appearance is not nearly as clear, although their existence is indicated. The number of tales of the acquisition of crests is not small with them either. It also has to be regarded as a development of the idea of the hereditary manitou, even though the idea of the divine origin of the ancestors, so characteristic for the Kwakiutl, is completely lacking. In this respect the Hē′iltsuk· are far closer to the Tsimschian than to the linguistically-related Kwakiutl. I regard this as a later influence through the totems of the north, especially since the totems of the Hē′iltsuk· vary so much. Their legends of the secret societies and tales of acquisition of supernatural powers, in contrast, are very close to those of the Kwakiutl. It has been explained above that the Bilqula took several Selisch legends north with them. But their whole system is under the spell of the Kwakiutl mythology. The lineage division, their privileges, as well as their secret societies are almost exactly like those of the Kwakiutl. The roots of this similar development become apparent in the fact that many of the actors bear Kwakiutl names. The beautiful arrangement of the creation myth, dealing with the divine brothers who descend to earth and appear as cultural deities, is their own. Woven into it are the Raven legend from the north and the Mink legend from the south. In addition, the influence of Athapasken myths can be clearly demonstrated.

I pass over the Comox and the Nutka since we have recognized both their myths as strong mixtures of northern and southern elements.

Turning to the Coast Selisch we find the same preponderance of ancestor legends as with the Kwakiutl, but the totemic aspect of the legends, as well as the references to secret societies, are almost completely lacking. As mentioned above, they also share with the Kwakiutl the strict separation of the Wanderer as cultural deity and as fool who tricks everyone and is frequently tricked himself. As far as can be judged by the scanty material, the animal myths are more pronounced with them.

These get the upper hand completely with the Shuswap and the Chinook and everything else recedes into the background. Both most likely share a close connection with the Coyote cycle of the Shoshones.

Finally I would like to look more closely at the relations with the tribes of North America dwelling farther away. In connection with the discussion of the Raven legend it became apparent that relations exist with the farthest Atlantic coast as well as the distant southwest. I pointed out that the Wanderer legend is distributed all over America in endless repetitions with countless variations; the statistical breakdown yielded many relations to the Mississippi basin and to the farthest east, with the strongest links tied along the Columbia River. May I be permitted to illustrate this diffusion of myths across the whole continent with a few more examples.

The tale of the woman giving birth to dogs is found very frequently on the Pacific coast (Fraser River, p. 25; Comox, p. 93; Nutka, p. 114; Kwakiutl, p. 132; Bilqula, p. 263; Tlingit, Krause p. 269). Its content briefly is as follows: A woman marries a dog and gives birth to a number of puppies. Her tribe abandons her and she goes out each day in search of food. She finds tracks of children upon her return but can only see her puppies. At last she sees from a hiding place that the puppies throw off their skins as soon they think themselves unobserved. She takes away the skins and burns them and the children become human. They become the ancestors of a tribe. Petitot (*op. cit.* p. 311) heard the tale from the Dogrib Indians on Great Slave Lake and a similar one from the Hare Indians on Great Bear Lake (p. 314). We find a similar tale with the Eskimo of Greenland and Hudson Bay. A woman marries a dog and has ten young ones. Her father abandons her and kills the dog. She sends five of her children inland, where they become the ancestors of beings half-dog and half-human, the other five became the ancestors of the Whites. (F. Boas, The Central Eskimo, *Annual Reports Bureau of Ethnology*, p. 630.) The Greenland version differs only slightly from the one given here. (Rink, *Tales and Traditions of the Eskimo*, p. 471). Murdoch has collected a fragment of the myth at Point Barrow and I have heard a fragment of it from Eskimos from Port Clarence, Alaska. The myth of beings half-dog and half-human which here is connected with it, can be found also with all the Athapasken tribes as well as the Eskimo. Hence this myth is identical no doubt, and can be found from Greenland across all of northwestern America to Oregon.

A second tale, also common to the Eskimo and to the south of the North Pacific coast, tells of the restoration of a blind boy who is maltreated by his mother but whose sister gives him food. Once a bear came to the hut. The mother aimed the arrow and the boy shot the bear. The meat served as food for the mother and daughter; however she told her son that he had missed the bear. In springtime a goose flew over the hut and invited the boy to follow. The bird reached a pond and dived three times with the boy, who thus regained his sight and avenged himself on his mother (Hē′iltsuk·, p. 229; Loucheux [Petitot, *op. cit.* p. 84]; Hare Indians [Petitot, *op. cit.*, p. 226]; F. Boas, The Central Eskimo, p. 625; Greenland [Rink, *op. cit.*, p. 99]). Consequently these two myths share exactly the same area of distribution from Greenland across the Athapasken northwest to the North Pacific coast.

The myth of the two girls who lie down in the forest, see two stars which they wish to have for their husbands, and, on awakening, find themselves in the sky, has an extraordinarily-wide distribution. A shiny star proved to be a beautiful man, a small star an old man. We find the myth with the Micmac, the Kwapa, Kiowa, the Lku′ngEn, and the Alaskan Athapasken, where I collected it in 1894. I referred already above to the birth of a son to a dead woman, who feeds on the body of his mother and then becomes the great Wanderer. We find the myth with the Tsimschian, the Newettee, the Micmac, and the Kiowa. A compilation of those features common to east and west results in the following:

In common with the:	Micmac	19 myth elements[12] (of 31)
″ ″	Ponca	11 myth elements (of 27)
″ ″	Athapasken	25 myth elements (of 33)
In common with the:	Micmac and Ponca	4 myth elements
″ ″	Micmac and Athapasken	4 myth elements
″ ″	Ponca and Athapasken	5 myth elements
″ ″	Micmac, Ponca & Athapasken	2 myth elements

The myth elements are found in the final list, but perhaps I am permitted to emphasize some of the more important ones.[13]

COMMON TO THE PACIFIC COAST AND MICMAC

A canoe is guided back by a dog given to the traveller beyond the ocean. After the return of the traveller the dog vanishes and returns to his home.

Dogs of finger length are carried by a hunter. They grow big as soon as they are needed.

Contest between the supernatural dogs of two powerful men.

A child is born after its mother's death. It sustains itself on her entrails and is later caught (see above).

Children abducted by a being carrying a basket on its back into which the children are stuffed.

Tests. Getting animals for father-in-law which are supposed to tear to pieces the person who brought them, but instead attack the father-in-law.

Burning of a culprit in his own house which is filled with wood. The culprit is lulled to sleep, the house locked and then set alight.

Diving competition. One of the divers hides on the beach until the opponent resurfaces.

In addition, Nos.15, 48, 63, 75, 82, 87, 111, 145, 146, 161, 178.

---

12. *Sagenelemente*, literally: 'myth element.'

13. "The numbers relate to the list at the end" [Boas' original footnote].

Common to the Pacific Coast and Ponca

Luring of game by the song of a woman who then is placed in a tree and gets killed by a mountain lion[14] which has learned her song.

Excrements call as if enemies were coming, in order to frighten villagers.

Animals appear as companions and each one proclaims its abilities. Successively stronger ones appear (No. 40).

Confession of a murder during a dance before the assembled tribe of the victim.

Fish bones or bones thrown into the water to revive again.

Trunk of a game animal carried home by an old woman who on the way uses it to cohabit.

Dancer kills spectators after having put them to sleep.

Killing of a monster. The murderer pretends to have become strong and handsome by being beaten on the head with a stone.

In addition, Nos. 21, 26, 143, 158, 188.

Common to the Pacific Coast and Athapasken.

Painting of birds, especially Raven.

Beaver and Porcupine separate.

A blind person regains sight through diving with a goose.

Origin of mosquitoes, flies, and frogs from the body of a monster.

Earth kept upright by a pole. No. 37.

Dog fathers children who are born as puppies and later assume human shape.

Bones of dead person carried away so that its body is incomplete after resuscitation.

Theft of a fisherman's harpoon by a man who transforms himself into a salmon, allows himself to be hit in this shape, and steals the harpoon.

Diving by animals in order to find dirt.

Curtain drawn over the earth during creation.

In addition, Nos. 14, 28, 30, 44, 69, 78, 100, 106, 112, 120, 128, 147, 166, 195, 213.

Common to the Pacific Coast, Micmac and Ponca.

Imitation of hosts who serve food to their guests by supernatural means.

Birds get their necks wrung during a dance. They are made to dance with closed eyes.

---

14.   Given as *Panther* here in the original *Sagen*.

In addition, Nos. 109, 176.

COMMON TO THE PACIFIC COAST, MICMAC AND ATHAPASKEN

Giants fight each other. When one is on the point of losing, he is helped by a human who cuts the foot tendon of the other giant.

Ferryman brings an escapee across the river and makes the pursuer drown.

Lice of bear or monster are frogs, mice or weasels.

Stones are being changed into their shape by the Transformer.

COMMON TO THE PACIFIC COAST, PONCA AND ATHAPASKEN.

Tree, from which an arrow is supposed to be fetched, grows up high and thus carries the arrow's owner into the sky.

Food of the inhabitants of beyond the ocean consists of human eyes, snakes, frogs and the like.

Young eagles are killed by a man who was carried into their nest.

Devouring of an enemy by an animal which is then killed by him.

In addition, No. 93.

COMMON TO THE PACIFIC COAST, MICMAC, PONCA AND ATHAPASKEN

Marriage to the stars. Two girls wish for stars as their husbands and are carried into the sky.

Never-empty bowls.

It is very striking that a few traits which constantly re-occur in these myths can hardly have any basis in the Indian way of life. Foremost among them is the scene where the newcomer to the village sits down by a pond and is found by girls drawing water. The villages are hardly ever near ponds but always along small brooks from which the water is drawn, so that the whole scene does not agree with actual circumstances, especially in the case where the reflection of the newcomer is seen and the stranger is mourned as drowned. To me this is proof that such traits are borrowed.

Another peculiar occurrence is the way in which the person returning is seen. Usually he hides in the forest and allows himself to be seen by one person but hides from another, or he is found by a blind boy. But in all cases he is invisible to some of the villagers. I take this as a rationalizing interpretation of the newcomer's ability to become invisible, retained from the olden days or possibly borrowed from extraneous myths which, in the course of time, have become reshaped in this way. The ability to become invisible, except for a few examples, is lacking from the mythology of the North Pacific coast.

In my opinion there is no doubt that in this area are to be found not only borrowings from all over America, but that the Old World, too, has supplied relatively much material which has been assimilated into the myths. Reading the accounts by Steller of Kamchatka, for instance, the similarity becomes apparent at once. The number of complicated fairy tales found in Eastern Asia and Western America is great, but only a few of them crossed the Rocky Mountains to the east. They are limited to the region between southern Alaska and the Columbia River.

One of the most remarkable is the story of the cannibal who pursues children, the so-called magic flight. Castrèn (*Ethnologische Vorlesungen*, p. 165) has noted the following Samoyed tale: Two sisters were escaping from a cannibal pursuing them. One of the girls threw a whetstone over her shoulder which was transformed into a gorge which blocked the cannibal. But at last he succeeded in crossing it. So she threw a flint over her shoulder which was transformed into a mountain, and at last a comb which was transformed into a thicket. I have noted the tale which corresponds precisely in the following list under the entry "Magic Flight." On the Pacific coast the articles thrown over the shoulder are mostly a whetstone which turns into a mountain, a bottle of oil which turns into a lake, and a comb which turns into a thicket.

In a series of Aino[15] tales published by Basil Hall Chamberlin in the *Folk Lore Journal* of 1888, four or five (Nos. 6, 21, 27, 33, 36) are found which are very similar to tales from the North Pacific coast.

Another peculiar similarity is found in the following myth which is diffused from Japan to the Sunda Islands and Micronesia. I will give the version communicated by J. Kubary from the Pelew Islands (A. Bastian, *Allerlei aus Volks- und Menschenkunde*). A young man had lost his hook to a fish which had bitten through his line. He dived for it and on the bottom of the sea came to a pond and sat down on its shore. A girl came out to fetch water for a sick woman. He was called in and healed her, while all her friends were unable to see the hook which had caused the illness. The parallels to this story have been noted in the following list under the title "Human projectile, invisible to spirits." Particularly in this cycle there occurs an incident which is highly unlikely in the Indian way of life; a stranger sits down by a pond and is seen there. I have referred to this above.

I have to leave a more thorough comparison of the myths of America with those of East Asia to the experts of the last-mentioned region. But the number of similar myths is so great and, above all, strictly limited to the area of Oregon, Washington

---

15. More commonly spelled "Ainu" in English today.

and British Columbia, without crossing the mountains to the east, that I am convinced of an immigration of fairy tales here.

Hence the final result of this study shows that we have to look upon the mythology of each separate tribe as a fusion of materials of diverse origin. This material is arranged by each tribe according to its predisposition, its social facilities and the older conceptions which govern its line of thought. This obviates once and for all the justification of attempts to explain the myths of primitive races from natural events or to see in them the results of observations of nature. It is not to be doubted that the appearance of the sun, of the animal world and the roaring sea has strongly stimulated the imagination of the primitive races, otherwise we would not find sun and animal myths everywhere. But the special forms in which we find them today are the result of a long historical evolution far antedated by the "elementary idea." In order to recognize these elementary conceptions it is necessary to interpret not the myths found now, but to detach the changes brought about by historical, social and geographical causes, and thus to go back to the simplest and most general concepts.

Today nobody ought to doubt that there are elementary ideas, that the human spirit has brought forth certain cycles of ideas again and again and still does so. But nobody ought to doubt either that there has always been borrowing and transmission of ideas, that ideas take root in foreign soil and either develop independently or perish and are preserved for a long time in strange fragments. But nobody is able to say where the border is between what is developed originally from human spirituality and what requires an outside stimulus for its formation. Thus it follows that we can hope to arrive at fruitful results only by minutely investigating the historical development of known cycles and then to take the common developmental traits as the basis for comparison. The expression of the elementary idea in the *Völkergedanken*, i.e., the form that the elementary idea takes in specific instances as a result of historical events, social conditions and geographical environment, gives us—as has been demonstrated so often by Bastian—the comparative material from which we may hope to prove the laws of the psychic development of man. But in order to arrive at an understanding of specific phenomena, the cultural level of the people concerned has to be investigated closely with regard to that of the neighbouring people, since without this investigation an understanding of the development of that particular conception of the world is out of the question. Thus it will become necessary in further investigations to deal with self-contained areas and to employ strictly geographical methods in these areas. An irregular comparison cannot lead to anything since the material has to be looked at in its geographical and historical context.

But just as we must not presuppose a connection between similar phenomena in regions far away from each other without being able to demonstrate the missing links, we must also not presuppose that the same ideas develop independently everywhere. For this is precisely one of the fundamental problems in ethnology, to demonstrate the limits of the development deeply established in the human spirit. In order to explore these limits we require thorough studies based on geographical and historical methods.

In the following list only myths common to several tribes have been given. I have employed the following abbreviations: Cathl. = Cathlamet; Shus. = Shuswap; C.Sel. = Coast Selisch; Fra. = Fraser River; Com. = Comox; Nut. = Nutka; Kwa. = Kwakiutl; New. = Newettee; He. = Hĕ′iltsuk·; Bil. = Bilqula; Tsim. = Tsimschian; Tlin. = Tlingit. The numbers accompanying the entries for the Micmac, Ponca and Athapasken (Loucheux, Hare Indians, Dogrib, Slave, and Chippewayan) refer to the works by Rand, Dorsey and Petitot cited above.

1) Fall from a mountain avoided through the help of supernatural powers. Bil., p. 260; Tsim., p. 287.

2) Anus used as a toy and thus spoiled. Cathl.; Com., p. 74.

3) Ancestors descend from the sky. C.Sal., p. 47; Com., p. 95; Kwa., p. 166; He., p. 24; Bil., p. 269.

4) Anchor of a canoe drops onto the house of the chief of the ocean who fetches down those inside the canoe. He., p. 238; Tsim., p. 288.

5) Luring of game by the song of a woman who is placed in a tree. Nut., p. 113; Ponca, p. 82.

6) Extinguishing of a fire in order to abduct a woman in the ensuing dark. Fra., p. 43 ; C.Sel., p. 56; Bil., p. 260; Tsim., p. 300.

7) Tree, from which an arrow is supposed to be fetched, grows up high and thus carries the arrow's owner into the sky. Shus., p. 17; Ponca, p. 607; Hare, p. 127; Chip., p. 355.

8) Raven kills his companion and eats him. Tsim.; Tlin., p. 315.

9) Companion created by a man who wants to carry out a fraud with his aid, but the companion thwarts his plans by telling the truth. Com., p. 72; Kwa., p. 159; Tsim., p. 277; Tlin., p. 314.

10) Burial of Mink. Fra., p. 33; Com., p. 73; Kwa.

11) Painting of the birds. Cathl.; Com., p. 64; Bil., p. 241; Chip., p. 350.

12) Landslide caused in order to destroy enemy. Shus., pp. 3, 16; Bil., p. 260.

13) Bribing of a guard at the door in order to gain access to an enemy's house. C.Sel., p. 54; He., p. 221.

14) Punished or insulted boy goes into the forest where he obtains supernatural powers. Kwa., pp. 151, 162; Bil., pp. 253, 266; Hare, p. 224.

15) Visitor is told to go to the smallest hut in the village first. Chinook, p. 35; Micmac, p. 336.

16) Game of a hunter is devoured while he is asleep. Shus., p. 7; Com., p. 74; He., p. 232; Kr.; Tlin., p. 265; Ponca, pp. 68, 566.

17) Fugitive throws decaying wood or prickles from a tree at the pursuer waiting below. Cathl.; Fra., p. 32; Com., p. 81.

18) House is inhabited by invisible shadows. Chin., p. 181; Tsim.; Tlin. p. 316.

19) Beaver causes flood by weeping in jealousy. Cathl.; Fra., p. 35; Com., p. 79.

20) Beaver and Porcupine separate. Tsim., p. 305; TsEtsa'ut; Hare, p. 234.

21) Food is taken away from blind women. They smell the thief, who gives them sight. Shus., p. 17; Fra., p. 38; C.Sel., p. 55; Com., p. 65; Nutka, p. 118; Kwa., p. 136; New., p. 202; Bil., p. 263; Ponca, p. 204 (Invisible one burns the thunderers' cheeks.)

22) Blind man gains sight by diving with a goose. He., p. 229; Loucheux, p. 84; Hare, p. 226; Boas, *Central Eskimo*, p. 625; Greenland; Rink, *Tales and Traditions of the Eskimo*, p. 99.

23) Canoe goes by itself. Kwa., pp. 135, 167; New., pp. 175, 184; He., p. 238.

24) Canoe guided back by a dog given to the travellers beyond the ocean. After the travellers' return the dog vanishes and returns home. Chin., p. 54; Micmac, p. 146.

25) Theft of berries which Raven takes from his sisters. Com., p. 76; Nut., p. 107; New., p. 178; He., p. 210; Bil., p. 244.

26) Theft; drying fish are stolen by a bear or spirit which is then shot and pursued. Com., p. 78; Kwa., p. 149; New., p. 189; He., p. 237; Bil., pp. 254, 256; Ponca, p. 216.

27) Theft noticed by an onlooker who at first allows himself to be bribed, but then gives away the thief after all. Cathl.; New., p. 180.

28) Thunderbird causes the thunder. All tribes. Hare, p. 283.

29) Double-headed serpent. Fra., p. 41; C.Sel., p. 58; Com., p. 81; Kwa., *passim*; New., p. 195; Tsim., p. 276.

30) Canoes and paddles gnawed through in order to forestall pursuit. He., p. 210; Bil., p. 242; Dogrib p. 330; Chippewayan, p. 375.

31) Tides caused by lifting and lowering of Wolf's tail. Kwa., p. 158; New., p. 175.
Mouse invites someone who is threatened. See warning.

32) Fugitive climbs a tree; is induced to come down by magic or kills pursuers by magic. Com., p. 80; (Nutka, p. 110); Kwa., p. 168; Bil., p. 270.

33) Abduction of a woman by Thunderbird, fetched back by animals who change into fish. Fra., p. 34; Com., p. 82; Nutka, p. 103; New., p. 206.

34) Abduction of a man by the wolves. Com., p. 86; Nutka, pp. 110, 112; Kwa., p. 163; New., p. 205.

35) Creation of mosquitoes, flies, and frogs from the body of a witch or a spirit. Com., p. 89; Kwa., pp. 164, 165; He., pp. 222, 224, 226; Bil., p. 253; Chippewayan, p. 410.

36) Earth burned because the bearer of the sun came too low. Kwa., p. 157; New., p. 173; He., pp. 216, 234; Bil., p. 246.

37) Earth supported by a pole. Tsim., p. 278; Tlin., p. 320; Hare, p. 256.

38) Speaking excrements. Chinook, p. 101; New., p. 177.

39) Excrements shout that enemies are coming in order to frighten people. Nut. p. 106; New., p. 172; He., pp. 213, 233; Ponca, p. 19.

40) Skills of animals who appear as companions or suitors. Successively stronger heroes appear. Tsim., p. 283; Ponca, p. 272.

41) Ferryman brings a fugitive across and makes the pursuer drown. Chinook, p. 32; Fra., p. 32; Micmac, pp. 164, 312; Chippewayan, p. 409.

42) Ferryman brings a fugitive across on the condition that she marries him or his child. Chinook, p. 32; Tsim., p. 295.

43) Boy who is supposed to bathe in order to obtain his guardian spirit eats bracken roots. C. Sel., p. 51; Com., pp. 65, 96. Skin of a slain friend discovered in enemy's house. See Kopf.

44) Rock rises suddenly beneath travellers who then escape from it through magic. Tsim., p. 290; Hare, p. 207.

45) Rock pecked through by a bird so that a gorge results. Bil., p. 269; Tsim; Tlin., p. 316.

46) Rooted woman. New.; He., p. 225; Bil., p. 249.

47) Fat, made to drip from hands, is served to guests. Chinook, p. 181; Com., p. 76; Nut., p. 106; New., p. 177; Bil., p. 245; Ponca; Micmac.

48) Fire left behind by someone taking pity on an abandoned person. Chinook, p. 51; Shus., p. 10, Fra., p. 20; C.Sel., p. 52; Com., p. 93; Nut. p. 114; Kwa.,

p. 132; New., p. 180; Bil., p. 264; Tsim., p. 301; Krause p. 269; Tlin.; Micmac, p. 46.

49) Ermine attempts to get fire. New., p. 187; He., p. 214.

50) Deer gets fire. Com., p. 80; Nut., p. 102; New., p. 187; He., pp. 214, 341; Tsim.; Tlin., p. 314.

51) Fire obtained from the ghosts in exchange for their abducted child. Fra., p. 43; C.Sel. p. 54; Kwa., p. 158.

52) Fingers being wiggled frighten an enemy so that he falls into a chasm. He., p. 225; Bil., p. 249.

53) Fish obtained from their original owner by a visitor who had coated his canoe with fish scales and pretended that it had been full of fish so that their owner gets disgusted owning them. Tillamook; New.; Tsim.; Krause, p. 263; Tlin.

54) Escape from a witch's basket. Chinook, p. 110; C.Sel. p. 57; He., p. 221.

55) Magic flight. Nut. p. 99; Kwa., p. 164; He., p 224, 240; Bil., p. 268.

56) Deluge cannot harm Wanderer when he puts on his beaverskin cap. Shus., p. 16; Fra., p. 23.

57) Deluge survived by tying up canoes to a mountain. C.Sel., p. 57; Com., p. 95; Bil., p. 243; Tsim., p. 278. Deluge. After the deluge, animals dive for dirt, see diving. Woman abducted by Thunderbird is brought back; see abduction.

58) Guests are transformed, taunted or killed during feast. C.Sel. p. 57; New., p. 177; He., p. 233; Tsim., p. 277.

59) Way to the land of the spirits marked by decaying wedge, see murder.

60) Sexual organs placed in their proper locations. Fra., p. 23; (Com., p. 72); Nut., p. 108; New., p. 302.

61) Sexual organs of bathing women are attacked by their lovers who swim up to them unnoticed (often in the guise of fish). Fra., p. 26; Com., p. 73; Nut., p. 108; New., p. 172.

62) Bear abducts a woman who has scolded and insulted him. He., p. 226; Tsim., p. 294; Krause p. 271; Tlin.

63) Human projectile invisible to spirits. Com., p. 94; Nut., p. 102; Kwal, p. 149; New., p. 190; He., p. 238; Bil., p. 254; Tsim., p. 289; Micmac, p. 87.

64) Hunter's weapon claimed by another one. One hunter gives in and is rewarded while a second one does not give in and is punished. C.Sel., p. 46; Nut., p. 106; Bil., p. 245.

65) Wolves prove their speed in a contest. Com., p. 86; Nut., p. 111.

66) Murder confessed during a dance before the whole tribe. Shus.; Com., p. 76; Kwa., p. 150; Ponca, p. 19.

67) Fish bones. A shaman causes fish bones or splinters to stick in his enemy's throat. Fra., p. 39; New., p. 201.

68) Fish bones, thrown into the water, become alive again. Fra., p. 27; Nut., p. 104; He., p. 210; Bil., p. 266; Ponca, p. 557 (beaver bones).

69) Half man. Bil., p. 256; Chippewayan, p. 363.

70) Herring sent to a boy who had stolen his parents' last fish eggs on the orders of Moon Man. C.Sel., p. 52; Nut., p. 115; Kwa., p. 162.

71) Harpoon line is stuck to a canoe and cannot be thrown off. Nut., p. 119; New., pp. 191, 203.

72) Pitch man exposed to the hot sun until he dies. Com., p. 64; New., p. 179; Tsim.; Krause, p. 265; Tlin.

73) Models of houses transformed into real houses. New., p. 196; Bil., p. 265; Tsim., p. 284.

74) Domestic animals of the tribe beyond the ocean are sea animals. Com., p. 88; Nut., p. 120.

75) Marriage of a girl or man to a stick which becomes alive. Chinook, p. 194; Micmac, p. 321.

76) Marriage with stars. Two girls wish to have stars for their husbands and are carried into the sky. C.Sel., p. 62; Micmac, pp. 160, 308; TsEtsa'ut; Kwapa.

77) Marriage of Mink to animals and plants. Fra., p. 44; Com., p. 71; Nut., p. 100; Kwa., p. 158.

78) Visitors to the sky are let down in baskets. Shus., p. 18; Fra., p. 40; Chippewayan, p. 358 (on a rope).

79) Visit to the sky by boys who have assumed the shape of birds. Fra., p. 38; Kwa., p. 147; New., p. 170; Tsim., p. 273.

80) Climbed up to the sky by means of a chain of arrows. Tillamook; Cathlamet; Shus., p. 17; Fra. p. 31; Com., pp. 64, 65; Nut., p. 117; Kwa., p. 157; New., p. 173; He., pp. 215, 234; Bil., p. 246; Tsim., p. 278.

81) Origin of Deer through transformation of a man who intends to kill the Transformer. Chinook, p. 20; C.Sel., pp. 46, 56; Com., p. 66; Nut., p. 98; New., p. 200.

82) Cave, leading through a mountain, is traversed in a canoe. Com., p. 88; He., p. 219; Micmac, p. 275.

83) Wooden woman, which a man tries to make alive in order to marry her, is burned by a woman visitor. C.Sel. p. 49; Nut., p. 112; Kwa.; Bil., p. 257.

84) Salmon carved from wood are animated but turn out to be no good. New., p. 174; He., p. 209; Bil., p. 242.

85) Dog fathers children who are born as puppies but later assume human shape. Cathl.; Fra., p. 25; Com., p. 93; Nut., p. 114; Kwa., p. 132; Bil., p. 263; Krause, p. 269; Tlin.; Dogrib p. 314.

86) Finger-long dogs carried by a hunter grow big as soon as they are needed. Tsim.; Micmac, p. 286.

87) Years appear as days to a traveller. Com., p. 87; Kwa., p. 153; New., p. 192; He., pp. 237, 238; Bil., p. 260; Tsim., p. 292; Micmac, p. 95.

88) Only the youngest daughter is able to lead a stranger into house. Chinook, p. 85; Com., p. 69.

89) Cold summoned. Fra., p. 21; Kwa., p. 168; Bil., pp. 2532, 260.

90) Combat of two giants. One of them is being killed by a human who severs his foot-tendons; see giants.

91) Combat of the supernatural dogs belonging to two heroes. Chinook, p. 21; Micmac, p. 4.

92) Tip of a wedge bitten off surreptitiously and then put on again in order to obtain the user's good will. C.Sel., p. 56; New., p. 175; Bil., p. 259; Tsim., p. 300.

93) Creation of a child from bodily secretions or splinters. Fra., p. 28; Com., p. 84; Nut., p. 116; Kwa., p. 160; New., pp. 179, 189; He., p. 211; Ponca,, p. 224; Hare, p. 187.

94) Child born after its mother's death, grows up in the grave and is caught. New., p. 170; Tsim., p. 272; Micmac, pp. 65, 290; Kiowa.

95) Children ask for berries and instead are given a basket full of hornets which sting them. Tillamook; Nut., p. 109.

96) Children abducted by a being which carries a basket on its back into which it stuffs the children. Chinook, p. 110; C.Sel., pp. 49, 57; Com., p. 89; He., pp. 224, 241; Bil., p. 249; Micmac, p. 183.

97) Bones of someone dead carried away so that the individual is not quite complete when resuscitated. Kwa., p. 149; Bil., pp. 255, 260; Loucheux, p. 37.

98) Bone breaks, thereby causing the owner's corresponding bone to break at the same time. Chinook, p. 189; Kwa.; Bil., p. 266.

99) Coal accumulated on the ocean. Com., p. 88; Nut., p. 119; New., pp. 192, 204; He., p. 217.

100) Head or skin of a slain friend discovered in the house of the enemy. Com., p. 75; Kwa., p. 150; Tsim., p. 282; Hare, p. 241.

101) Head and trunk grow together again until the severed neck is coated with poison. He., p. 240; Tsim., p. 296.

102) Trial of strength between two heroes who attempt to kill or transform each other. Shus., p. 16; Fra., p. 21; C.Sel., p. 47; Kwa., pp. 134, 137, 161, 168; New., pp. 182, 188, 196.

103) Salmon is invited to play and then is killed. Com., p. 73; New., p. 176; Tsim., p. 277; Krause, p. 264; Tlin.

104) Salmon originating from abduction of the Salmon Chief's daughter. Fra., p. 43; Kwa., p. 159; New., p. 175; He., p. 210; Bil., pp. 242, 246.

105) Monster's lice are frogs, mice, weasels, etc. Com., p. 81; Bil., p. 268; Micmac, pp. 272, 286; Loucheux, p. 65; Greenland (Rink, *Tales and Traditions of the Eskimo*).

106) Meat or skins become alive and run away. Cathl., p. 192; Hare, p. 223.

107) Lover marked with soot or paint by girl in order to recognize him. Fra., pp. 27, 37, 41; Bil., p. 263; Krause, p. 270; Tlin.; Central Eskimo (Boas, *The Central Eskimo*, p. 597); Greenland (Rink, *op. cit.*, p. 236).

108) Hole in the house floor of the Sky Chief. He., p. 237; Tsim., p. 279.

109) Someone powerful assumes the shape of someone weak. Chinook, pp. 78, 85; Com., p. 69; Kwa., p. 136; New., pp. 198, 199; Micmac, pp. 78, 337; Ponca, pp. 174, 606.

110) Male children killed right after birth. Cathl.; C.Sel., p. 61; Kwa., p. 138.

111) Man who is repulsive to girls is made handsome and consequently pursued by the girls but rejects them. Shus., p. 14; Micmac, p. 97.

112) Man in the Moon explained as human fetched up to the moon. Shus., p. 15; New., p. 191; He., p. 217; Loucheux, p. 69.

113) Coat containing all the fish dipped into the water so that they are freed. Shus., p. 17; Fra., p. 20; Com., p. 93; New., p. 194; Bil., p. 262.

114) Man is murdered in order to obtain his wife. Com., p. 72; Kwa., p. 158.

115) Murder of Deer who had been invited to mourn. Com., p. 72; Nut., p. 105; He., pp. 212, 233; Bil., p. 245.

116) Murderer pointed out by inanimate objects which were present at the murder. Way to the land of spirits indicated by a decaying wedge. Chinook, p. 168; He., p. 233; Bil., p. 271.

117) Imitation of hosts who feed their guests in a supernatural manner. Chinook, p. 178; Com., p. 76; Nut., p. 106; New., p. 177; Bil., p. 245; Tsim.; Micmac, pp. 300, 302; Ponca, p. 557.

118) Food of the inhabitants of the country beyond the ocean consists of human eyes, snakes, toads, etc. Chinook, p. 54; Com., p. 88; Nut., p. 120; (Kwa., p. 164); He., pp. 218, 220, 240; Ponca, p. 187; Loucheux p. 31; Chippewayan, p. 399.

119) Nose ripped off when a thief eats the bait from a hook. New., p. 172; Tlin., p. 314.

120) Noses of Lynx or Coyote given their present shape. Tillamook; Hare, p. 217.

121) Fog created in order to make Raven lose his way. Com., p. 77; Tsim.; Krause; Tlin., p. 260.

122) Netmaking learned from Spider. He., pp. 208, 213; Bil., p. 246.

123) Rape of a girl who is misled into sitting down on a plant which in reality is a penis. Com., p. 71; Nut., p. 108; Kwa., p. 160; New., p. 178, He., p. 211; Bil., p. 243.

124) Otter tribe takes in drowned people. Tsim., p. 290; Tlin., p. 322.

125) Tests. Split tree into which a hammer has been dropped crashes shut when the man to be tested intends to get it. Chinook, p. 34; Fra., p. 39; Com., pp. 67, 70; Nut., p. 118; Kwa., p. 136; New., p. 198; Krause, p. 256; Tlin.

126) Tests. A man is tested by having to go into a sweat-house which is then overheated. Cathl.; Chinook, p. 58; Ponca, p. 160.

127) Tests. Animals fetched for father-in-law which are supposed to tear the bringer to pieces, but instead attack the father-in-law. Cathl.; Chinook, p. 33; Fra., p. 39, Com., pp. 68, 70; Micmac, p. 12.

128) Raven assumes the shape of a bird whenever threatened by danger and flies off cawing. New., p. 177; Hare, p. 152.

129) Revenge taken with the aid of an artificial seal which the enemy attempts to kill. Com., p. 87; Tsim., p. 289.

130) Theft of a fisherman's harpoon by a man who transforms himself into a salmon and in this shape allows himself to be caught and then steals the

harpoon. Shus., pp. 13, 16; Fra., p. 23; Com., pp. 64, 66; New., p. 201; Bil., p. 248; Loucheux p. 33.

131) Abduction of a woman by killerwhale. Fetched back by her husband who descends to the bottom of the sea. C.Sel., p. 55; Bil., p. 259; Tsim., p. 299; C. Sel., p. 55; Bil.; p. 259.

132) Games with magic hoops (fog and fire). Com., p. 82; Nut., p. 103; New., p. 206.

133) Giants fight against each other. When one has almost been defeated, a human helps him and cuts the tendons of the other giant. (Cathl.); Micmac, p. 196; Tsɛtsā'ut.

134) Rolling hoop transformed into a buffalo. Kootenay; Ponca, p. 605.

135) Robin, sent out as scout, sits down by the fire instead of bringing back information; consequently his breast becomes red. Cathl.; Nut., p. 100.

136) Teaching of paddling. Nut., p. 128; New., p. 202.

137) Trunk of a game animal carried home by an old woman who uses it on the way to cohabit. Chinook, p. 119; Ponca, p. 22.

138) Woman's song conjures up berries in a bowl. Fra., p. 34; Nut., p. 103; Bil., p. 245.

139) Box with the Death-Bringer. He., p. 236; Tsim., p. 284.

140) Ornaments thrown into the fire on Mouse's orders. (He., p. 239); Tsim., p. 294.

141) Snapping door which doesn't admit strangers. Com., p. 81; Nut., p. 118; Kwa., pp. 136, 166; New., p. 186; He., pp. 228, 239; Bil., p. 253; Tsim., p. 274.

142) Never-empty bowls. Cathl.; Shus., p. 4; Nut., p. 103; Kwa., p. 154; New., p. 181; He., pp. 223, 227; Micmac, p. 24; Ponca, pp. 138, 139; Chippewayan, p. 369.

143) Someone weak says that he has killed a big animal. His grandmother doesn't believe him. Chinook, p. 119; Ponca, p. 25.

144) Pregnancy caused by chewing pitch. Com., p. 92; Nut., p. 108; Kwa., p. 136; New., p. 172; Tsim, p. 274.

145) Father-in-law tries to kill his son-in-law. Cathl.; Chinook, p. 33; Fra., p. 39; Com., p. 70; Nut., p. 118; Kwa., p. 136; New., pp. 171, 198; Tsim., p. 274; Micmac, p. 90.

146) Soul put aside so that it cannot be hurt. Tillamook; Cathl.; Micmac, p. 245.

147) Theft of the sun by Raven who, in the guise of a cedar needle, makes the owner's daughter pregnant and is borne by her; then he obtains the sun to play with by crying loudly and stealing it. Chehalis, *Globus* Vol. 65, No. 12; C.Sel., p. 55 (Gull keeps Daylight in a box); Nut., p. 105 (impregnated by a cedar needle); New., p. 184 (impregnated by a cedar needle); He., p. 208 (impregnated by a cedar needle); New., p. 173; Bil., p. 242; Tsim., p. 276; Tlin., p. 311; Hare, p. 145 (Child obtains toy it wants by crying loudly).

148) Sun hung up in his house by the bearer of the sun. Cathl.; Shus., p. 15.

149) Reflection seen in the water mistaken for the real person. Com., p. 66; Nut., p. 114; Kwa., p. 168; Bil., p. 253.

150) Gambler who always loses becomes successful through supernatural help. Chinook, p. 220; Shus., p. 14.

151) Spikes on the floor or the seat of the house which are supposed to kill the guest are pushed down. Fra., p. 39; Com., p. 66; Nut., pp. 111, 118; Kwa., p. 136; New., p. 171.

152) Splinter remains stuck in throat; see fish bones. [No. 67].

153) Rocks are beings who were given this shape by the Transformer. Shus., pp. 4, 17; Fra., p. 28; C.Sel., pp. 45, 56; Com., p. 63.; New., p. 196; Micmac, p. 236; (Hare, p. 167).

154) Creation of freshwater. Nut., p. 108; New., p. 174; He., pp. 209, 232; Tsim.; Tlin., p. 313.

155) Dancer kills spectators after having put them to sleep. Nut., p. 110; Bil., p. 270; Ponca, p. 108.

156) Diving of animals in order to search for soil. Cathl.; New., p. 173; Hare, p. 147.

157) Animals guard an entrance and kill intruders. Chinook, p. 56; Fra., p. 32.

158) Spirits present animals for food, bigger ones each day. Chinook, p. 52; (He., p. 237); Tsim., pp. 290, 302; Ponca, p. 174.

159) Daughter, offered as wife to someone insulted, is rejected. Chinook, p. 54; Fra., p. 20; Com., p. 70; Tsim., p. 304.

160) Daughter of a spirit given away as wife in return for healing of the spirit. New., p. 190; He., p. 238; Bil., p. 255.

161) Resuscitated person rubs eyes as after sleep. Cathl.; Shus., p. 5; Kwa., pp. 149, 157; New., pp. 196, 199; He., pp. 209, 222, 238; Tsim., p. 281; Micmac, p. 275.

162) Dead relatives resuscitated while the survivor mourns over the bodies. He., p. 236; Tsim., p. 280.

163) Killing of young eagles by human who has been carried to their nest. Shus., p. 4; Ponca; Hare, p. 144; Dogrib, p. 323.

164) Killing of an enemy woman's children who then are propped up in various poses as deception. Cathl.; Com., p. 81; Klamath.

165) Killing of a woman's lover by her husband who catches them in the act. Kwa., p. 162; He., p. 234; Bil., p. 257; Tsim., p. 281.

166) Killing of a woman's lover by her husband who disguises himself in her clothes. Bil., p. 247; Chippewayan, p. 407; see the previous entry. [No. 165].

167) Killing of Seal after a feast. C.Sel., p. 57; Com., p. 77.

168) Killing of the Wolf Chief's son. Com., p. 75; Nut., p. 98; Kwa., p. 150.

169) Killing by a ruse. Someone weaker persuades a powerful enemy to put his head onto a stone and allow himself to be struck with a second stone. Cathl.; Nut., p. 114; Ponca, p. 30.

170) Killing. Mink kills his brother. Fra., p. 35; Com., p. 74.

171) Monster abducts a girl who is then looked for by her brothers. Chinook, p. 17; Nut., pp. 116 (124); He., p. 223.

172) Monster invited by a boy who had been left alone by his brothers. Chinook, p. 31; Bil., p. 252.

173) Bad luck in hunting caused by unfaithful wife. Kwa., p. 130; Tsim., p. 281.

174) Unfaithful wife impaled on tree-top. Her brothers avenge her death. Fra., p. 22; Com., pp. 89, 96; Nut., p. 123; Kwa., p. 129; (see also previous entry).

175) Father takes child into his arms and is recognized as father of illegitimate child by his behaviour. Shus., p. 9; Nut., p. 108.

176) Prohibition to visit certain localities near habitation because they bring bad luck. Cathl.; Chinook, pp. 189, 194; Micmac, p. 84; Ponca, p. 217.

177) Burning of an evil-doer in his own house which is filled with wood. The evil-doer is put to sleep, the house locked and set alight. Chinook, p. 18; Micmac, p. 67.

178) Pursuer detained by throwing objects belonging to his child in his way. He., p. 210; Micmac, p. 56.

179) Pursuit of an animal until home is gone from sight. Fra. p. 30; Com., p. 87; Nut., p. 119; New., pp. 185, 191, 203; He., pp. 217, 220.

180) Mocking of a murder victim's relatives. The murdered man then comes back and takes revenge. Chinook, p. 132; Nut., p. 122.

181) Gluing shut of eyes with resin. Shus., pp. 7, 17; C.Sel., p. 57; Com., p. 89; Nut., p. 114.

182) Abandoning of a man on a rock or island where he is invited and saved by a being. Chinook, p. 131; He., p. 230; Tsim., p. 288.

183) Abandoning of a man while he walks around an island. Chinook, p. 131; Com., p. 90.

184) Lost man who had drowned on a journey across the ocean is found again beyond the sea and is revived. Nut., p. 120; New., p. 192; He., p. 218.

185) An enemy is devoured by an animal and then kills it. Chinook, p. 119; Shus., p. 3; C.Sel., p. 51; Com., p. 74; Nut., p. 101; New., p. 171; He., p. 212; Bil., p. 256; Tlin., p. 315; Ponca, p. 34; Dogrib p. 319.

186) Attempt to shoot a glowing-red bird. It is finally shot by a despised participant. Kootenay; Ponca, p. 604. Transformer; see Wanderer legend.

187) Transformation of a man whose body is covered with mouths. Com., p. 63; New., p. 202.

188) Transformation of a man into an animal which is given its name and destiny. Chinook, *passim*; Ponca, p. 20.

189) Transformation of a shaman into a fish. Com., p. 63; New.

190) Many shoes and garments made for a journey to the sun or to the spirits. Cathl.; Shus., p. 15; Fra., p. 41; Alaskan Eskimo, *Journal of American Folklore* 1894, p. 205; Central Eskimo, *op. cit.*, p. 624.

191) Bird used as arrow. Tsim.; Tlin. p. 318.

192) Bird caught by a boy who lies down and induces the bird to swoop down on him. Fra., p. 38; C.Sel., p. 61; Tsim., p. 275.

193) Birds have their necks wrung when they are all invited to a dance. They are made to dance with their eyes closed. Nut.; Micmac, p. 264; Ponca, p. 66.

194) Curtain drawn over the world during creation. Bil., p. 241; Hare, p. 108.

195) Whale employed by the animals to kill Thunderbird who attempts to lift it in vain and is drowned instead. Com., p. 83; Nut., p. 104; New., pp. 179, 207; He., pp. 211, 214; Loucheux, p. 66 (Drowning of Thunderbird).

196) Wanderer legend. Transformers as twins. Chinook, p. 20; Nut., p. 98; New., p. 194.

197) Wanderer legend. Four brothers as transformers. Shus., pp. 1, 16; Fra., p. 19; Bil., p. 241.

198) Mouse warns someone in danger. Chinook, p. 35; Com., pp. 85, 90; He., pp. 228, 230, 239; Tsim., pp. 289, 294.

199) Water of Life. Kwa., p. 161; New., pp. 192, 196, 206; He., p. 236; Bil., p. 255.

200) Water refused a woman who consequently is changed into a bird. Cathl.; Nut., p. 109.

201) People getting water are devoured by a monster which is later killed. Com., p. 64; New., p. 196; Bil., p. 259.

202) Spirits dread water. Chinook, p. 214; Bil., p. 251.

203) Eating contest. One of the contestants is able to eat unlimited amounts of poison or red-hot stones since he has put a tube through himself or made similar preparations. Chinook, p. 56; Com., p. 66; New., p. 182.

204) Spear-throwing contest during which a flat fish turns his thin profile towards the opponents when it is the latter's turn to throw. Cathl.; Nut., p. 107.

205) Climbing contest. Chinook, p. 57; Shus., p. 2; Ponca, p. 172.

206) Diving contest. One of the contestants hides on the beach until the other one surfaces. Chinook, p. 57; Com., p. 79; Micmac, p. 324.

207) Resuscitated twin girl is married and thereby the salmon created. New., p. 174; He., p. 209.

208) War made on the Winds in their own house. Nut., p. 100; New., p. 186.

209) Toothed vagina. Fra., pp. 24, 30; Com., p. 66; Kwa.

210) Tongue of a companion ripped out so that he is unable to report events he witnessed. New., p. 176; Bil., p. 244; Tsim.; Tlin., p. 317.

211) Returning traveller heals his relatives, who had stayed behind, and gives them presents. Fra., pp. 33, 38, 42; C.Sel. p. 63; New., p. 193; He., pp. 222, 238.

212) Returning traveller met by a child, who announces him, but is not believed. Fra., p. 37; C.Sel., p. 63; Nut., p. 122; Kwa., p. 153; Bil., p. 250.

213) Observation makes conjuration or other events impossible. Tillamook; Cathl.; Chippewayan, p. 401.

214) Dwarf catches halibut which are stolen from him. Com., p. 88; New., p. 192.

APPENDIX

LISTING OF STORIES

REFERENCES CITED

Akrigg, G.P.V., and Helen B. Akrigg
  1997   *British Columbia Place Names*, 3rd edition. Vancouver: University of British Columbia Press.

Amoss, Pamela
  1978   *Coast Salish Spirit Dancing: the survival of an ancestral religion*. Seattle: University of Washington Press.

Anderson, Alexander, Archibald McKinlay, and Gilbert M. Sproat
  1878   Report of proceedings to the Minister of the Interior, 21st March 1877. Special Appendix D, pp. 1i–1xiii, *Canada Sessional Papers Volume 8, Fifth Session of the Third Parliament of the Dominion of Canada*. Ottawa.

Andrews H.A. *et al.*
  1943   Bibliography of Franz Boas. *American Anthropologist* 45(3):67–119.

Arima, Eugene, and John Dewhirst
  1990   Nootkans of Vancouver Island. Pp. 391–411, *Handbook of North American Indians, Vol. 7: Northwest Coast*. Edited by Wayne Suttles. Washington, DC: Smithsonian Institution.

Arima, Eugene, Louis Clamhouse, Joshua Edgar, Charles Jones, and John Thomas
  1991   From Barkley Sound Southeast. Pp. 205–315, Between Ports Alberni and Renfrew: Notes on West Coast Peoples, by Eugene Arima and Denis St. Claire *et al. Canadian Museum of Civilization, Canadian Ethnology Service, Mercury Series Papers* 121. Hull, Quebec.

Assu, Harry, with Joy Inglis
  1989   *Assu of Cape Mudge: recollections of a coastal chief*. Vancouver: University of British Columbia Press.

Averkieva, Julia, and Mark A. Sherman
  1992   *Kwakiutl String Figures*. Vancouver: University of British Columbia Press.

Banfield, A.W.F.
  1974   *The Mammals of Canada*. National Museum of Natural Sciences, National Museums of Canada. Toronto: University of Toronto Press.

Barbeau, Marius
  1928   *The Downfall of Temlaham*. Toronto: MacMillan Company of Canada.

Barnett, Homer G.
  1935–1936
          Coast Salish Field Notebooks 1–8. Originals held by the Special Collections Division, University of British Columbia Library, Vancouver, BC.
  1940   Tsimpshian Field Notebooks 1–3, Port Simpson. Originals held by the Special Collections Division, University of British Columbia Library, Vancouver, BC.
  1955   The Coast Salish of British Columbia. *University of Oregon Monographs, Studies in Anthropology* 4. Eugene. (Reprinted: Greenwood Press, Westport, Conn., 1975.)
Blackman, Margaret B.
  1979   Northern Haida land and resource utilization. Pp. 43–55, *Tales from the Queen Charlotte Islands*. Edited by Senior Citizens of the Queen Charlotte Islands. Cloverdale, BC: D.W. Friesen and Sons.
  1990   Haida: traditional culture. Pp. 240–260, *Handbook of North American Indians, Vol. 7: Northwest Coast*. Edited by Wayne Suttles. Washington, DC: Smithsonian Institution.
Boas, Franz
  n.d.1   [Cat'oltq-English vocabulary.] National Anthropological Archives, Smithsonian Institution, Washington, DC. Ms.#711-b.
  n.d.2   Çalō'ltq texts. National Anthropological Archives, Smithsonian Institution, Washington, DC. Ms. #719.
  n.d.3   Comox vocabulary. National Anthropological Archives, Smithsonian Institution, Washington, DC. Ms. #350-c.
  n.d.4   [Nanaimo Grammatical Notes and Texts.] National Anthropological Archives, Smithsonian Institution, Washington, DC. Ms. #738.
  n.d.5   [Pentlatch materials.] American Philosophical Society Library, Philadelphia. Boas Collection, Ms. #497.3, B63c, S 2j.3.
  n.d.6   [Pentlatch texts.] National Anthropological Archives, Smithsonian Institution, Washington, DC. Ms. #740.
  n.d.7   [Snanaimuq vocabulary.] National Anthropological Archives, Smithsonian Institution, Washington, DC. Ms. #712-a.
  n.d.8   [Tsimshian texts, with interlinear translation, and word list.] American Philosophical Society Library, Philadelphia. Boas Collection, Ms. #Pn 5a.6.
  1886a   The language of the Bilhoola in British Columbia. *Science* 7:218.
  1886b   Sprache der Bella-Coola-Indianer. *Verhandlungen der Berliner Gesellschaft für Anthropologie, Ethnologie und Urgeschichte* 18:202–206.
  [1886–1887]
          English-Pĕnl'atc vocabulary. National Anthropological Archives, Smithsonian Institution, Washington, DC. Ms. #711-a.

Boas, Franz

[1886–1888]   [Tlingit notes with Mrs. Vine.] National Anthropological Archives, Smithsonian Institution, Washington, DC. Ms. #4118-b.

1887a   Census and reservations of the Kwakiutl nation. *Bulletin of the American Geographical Society* Vol. 19(3):225–232.

1887b   Die Vancouver-Stämme. *Verhandlungen der Berliner Gesellschaft für Anthropologie, Ethnologie und Urgeschichte* 17:64–66. Berlin.

1887c   Letter to Major F.W. Powell, Director, Bureau of Ethnology, 12 June 1887. BAE Letters received 1887. National Anthropological Archives, Smithsonian Institution, Washington,DC.

1887d   Notes on the ethnology of British Columbia. Pp. 422–428, *Proceedings of the American Philosophical Society*, Vol. XXIV.

1887e   The coast tribes of British Columbia. Science: *Journal of the American Association for the Advancement of Science*, 9(216):288–289.

1887f   Zur Ethnologie Britisch-Kolumbiens. *Petermanns Geographische Mitteilungen* Vol. 33 (5): 129–133.

1888a   The Central Eskimo. *Sixth Annual Report of the Bureau of American Ethnology for the Years 1884–1885*. Pp. 399–669. Washington, DC.

1888b   The Development of the Culture of Northwest America. *Science: Journal of the American Association for the Advancement of Science* 12(299):194–196.

1888c   Die Mythologie der Nordwest-amerikanischen Küstenvölker. *Globus* 53(8):121–127, (10):153–157, (19):299–302, (20):315–319; 54(1):10–14, (6):88–92, (9):141–144, (14):216–221.

1888d   Die Tsimschian. *Zeitschrift für Ethnologie: organ der Berliner Gessellschaft für Anthropologie, Ethnologie und Urgeschichte* 20(9):231–247.

1888e   Einige Mythen der Tlingit. *Zeitschrift der Gesellschaft für Erdkunde zu Berlin* 23:159–172.

1888f   [Haida materials.] National Anthropological Archives, Smithsonian Institution, Washington, DC. Ms. #4117-b.

1888g   The Indians of British Columbia. *Transactions of the Royal Society of Canada for the Year 1888* 6(2):47–57.

1888h   Myths and legends of the Çatloltq of Vancouver Island. *American Antiquarian and Oriental Journal* 10(4):201–211, (6):366–373.

1888i   Omeatl und Hălāqa. *Verhandlungen der Berliner Gesellschaft für Anthropologie, Ethnologie und Urgeschichte* 20:18–20.

1888j   On certain songs and dances of the Kwakiutl of British Columbia. *Journal of American Folk-lore* 1:49–64.

1889a   Introductory letter and preliminary notes on the Indians of British Columbia. Pp. 233–255, 58th *Report of the British Association for the Advancement of Science for 1888*. London.

Boas, Franz

1889b Notes on the Snanaimuq. *American Anthropologist* 2(4):321–328.

1890a First General Report on the Indians of British Columbia. Pp. 801–893, 59th *Report of the British Association for the Advancement of Science for 1889*. London.

1890b [Notebooks, including Lower Fraser River and Bella Coola shorthand notes, and Massett Haida-German vocabulary.] American Philosophical Society Library, Philadelphia. Boas Collection, Ms. #Pn 4b.5.

1891a Dissemination of tales among the Natives of North America. *Journal of American Folk-Lore* 4:13–20.

1891b Ein Besuch in Victoria auf Vancouver. *Globus* 59 (5):75–77.

1891c Sagen aus Britisch Columbien. *Verhandlungen der Berliner Gesellschaft für Anthropologie, Ethnologie und Urgeschichte* 23:532, 628–636. Berlin: Verlag von Asher & Co.

1891d Second General Report on the Indians of British Columbia. Pp. 562–715, 60th *Report of the British Association for the Advancement of Science for 1890*. London.

1891e Vocabularies of the Tlingit, Haida and Tsimshian Languages. *Proceedings of the American Philosophical Society* 29:173–208.

1892a The Bilqula. Pp. 408–424, *61st Report of the British Association for the Advancement of Science for 1891*. London.

1892b Sagen aus Britisch Columbien. *Verhandlungen der Berliner Gesellschaft für Anthropologie, Ethnologie und Urgeschichte* 24:32–66. Berlin: Verlag von Asher & Co.

1892c Sagen der Indianer in Nordwest-America. *Verhandlungen der Berliner Gesellschaft für Anthropologie, Ethnologie und Urgeschichte* 24:314–344, 383–410.

1893 Sagen der Indianer an der Nordwest-America. *Verhandlungen der Berliner Gesellschaft für Anthropologie, Ethnologie und Urgeschichte* 25:228–265, 430–477. Berlin: Verlag von Asher & Co.

1894a Chinook texts. *Bureau of American Ethnology, Bulletin 20.* Smithsonian Institution. Washington, DC: Government Printing Office.

1894b The Indian tribes of the Lower Fraser River. Pp. 454–463, *64th Report of the British Association for the Advancement of Science*. London.

1894c Sagen der Indianer an der Nordwest-America. *Verhandlungen der Berliner Gesellschaft für Anthropologie, Ethnologie und Urgeschichte* 26:281–306. Berlin: Verlag von Asher & Co.

1895a Die Entwicklung der Mythologien der Indianer der Nordpacifischen Küste Amerikas. *Verhandlungen der Berliner Gesellschaft für Anthropologie, Ethnologie und Urgeschichte* 27:487–523.

1895b *Indianische Sagen von der Nord-Pacifischen Küste Amerikas.* Berlin: Verlag von A. Asher & Co.

Boas, Franz

1895c   Sagen der Indianer an der Nordwest-America. *Verhandlungen der Berliner Gesellschaft für Anthropologie, Ethnologie und Urgeschichte* 27:189–234. Berlin: Verlag von Asher & Co.

1895d   Salishan texts. Pp. 31–48, *Proceedings of the American Philosophical Society* 34 (147). Philadelphia.

1896   The growth of Indian mythologies. *Journal of American Folk-Lore* 9:1–11.

1897   The social organization and the secret societies of the Kwakiutl Indians. Pp. 311–738, *Report of the U.S. National Museum for 1895*. Washington, DC: Government Printing Office. (Reprinted in 1970 by Johnson Reprint, New York.)

1898   The mythology of the Bella Coola Indians. *Memoirs of the American Museum of Natural History* 2(1):25–127. New York.

1902   Tsimshian texts, Nass River dialect. *Bureau of American Ethnology Bulletin 27*, Smithsonian Institution. Washington, DC: Government Printing Office.

1905   The mythologies of the Indians. *International Quarterly* Vol. 11:327–342; Vol. 12:157–173.

1910   Kwakiutl tales. *Columbia University Contributions to Anthropology (new series)* Vol. 2. New York. (Reprinted by AMS Press, New York, 1969.)

1912   Tsimshian texts (New Series). *Publications of the American Ethnological Society* 3:65–285. Leyden, the Netherlands: E.J. Brill.

1914   Mythology and folk-tales of the North American Indians. Pp. 374–410, *The Journal of American Folk-Lore*, Vol. XXVII. (Reprinted in 1963 by Kraus Reprint Corporation, New York.)

1916   Tsimshian mythology. *Thirty-First Annual Report of the Bureau of American Ethnology to the Secretary of the Smithsonian Institution, 1909–1910*. Washington, DC: Government Printing Office.

1917   Introduction, International Journal of American Linguistics. Pp. 199–210, *Race, Language and Culture*. Franz Boas. New York: The Free Press; London: Collier-MacMillan.

1921   Ethnology of the Kwakiutl, based on data collected by George Hunt. 2 parts, pp. 43–1481. *Thirty-Fifth Annual Report of the Bureau of American Ethnology to the Secretary of the Smithsonian Institution, 1913–1914*. Washington, DC: Government Printing Office.

[1925]   [Alphabetical listing of Kwakiutl names of persons, tribes, and places.] American Philosophical Society Library, Philadelphia. Boas Collection, Ms. #W.1a.12.

1928   Bella Bella texts. *Columbia University Contributions to Anthropology 5*. New York.

1932   Bella Bella tales. *Memoirs of the American Folk-Lore Society* 25:1–178.

Boas, Franz
1934 Geographical names of the Kwakiutl Indians. *Columbia University Contributions to Anthropology* Vol. 20. New York: Columbia University Press. (Reprinted in 1969 by AMS Press, New York.)
1935 Kwakiutl culture as reflected in mythology. *Memoirs of the American Folk-Lore Society* Vol. 28. New York. (Reprinted in 1969 by Kraus Reprint, New York.)
1940 *Race, Language and Culture*. New York: The Free Press; London: Collier-MacMillan.
1948 Kwakiutl dictionary. Edited by Helene Boas Yampolsky. American Philosophical Society Library, Philadelphia. Boas Collection, Ms. #30 W1a.21.
1966 *Kwakiutl Ethnography*. Edited by Helen Codere. Chicago: The University of Chicago Press.
1981 Indian folktales from British Columbia. Translated for the BC Indian Language Project by Dietrich Bertz from *Indianische Sagen von der Nord-Pacifischen Küste Amerikas*. Pp. 45–77, *The Malahat Review* No. 60. Victoria, BC: University of Victoria.
1999 Native legends of Oregon and Washington Collected by Franz Boas. Translated by Richard Bland, and edited and annotated by Ann Simonds. *Northwest Anthropological Research Notes* 33(1):85–104.
Boas, Franz, and George Hunt
1902–1905
Kwakiutl texts. *Publications of the Jesup North Pacific Expedition* 3(1–3); *Memoirs of the American Museum of Natural History* 5(1–3). New York: G.E. Stechert (Reprinted in 1975 by AMS Press: New York.)
1906 Kwakiutl texts (Second Series). *Memoirs of the American Museum of Natural History* Vol. 14 (1):1–269. (Reprinted in 1975 by AMS Press: New York.)
Boas, Franz and Herman Haeberlin
1927 Sound shifts in Salishan dialects. *International Journal of American Linguistics* 4:117–136.
Boelscher Ignace, Marianne
1998 Shuswap. Pp. 203–219, *Handbook of North American Indians, Vol. 12: Plateau*. Edited by Deward E. Walker Jr. Washington, DC: Smithsonian Institution.
Bouchard, Randy
1992 Notes on Nanaimo Ethnography and Ethnohistory (revised in 1993). Report prepared for I.R. Wilson Consultants Ltd., Victoria, British Columbia, in conjunction with the Departure Bay Indian Village Archaeological Project. (Copy on file with the Heritage Resource Centre, BC Ministry of Communities, Aboriginal and Women's Services, Victoria.)

Bouchard, Randy, and Dorothy I. Kennedy

1977   Lillooet Stories. Edited by Randy Bouchard and Dorothy I. Kennedy. *Provincial Archives of British Columbia, Sound Heritage Series* 6(1). Victoria, BC: Queen's Printer.

1979   *Shuswap Stories*. Edited by Randy Bouchard and Dorothy I. Kennedy. Vancouver, BC: CommCept Publishing.

1988a   Indian land use and Indian history of the Stein River Valley, British Columbia. Appendix I, pp. 79–167, Stein River Haulroad: Heritage Resources Inventory and Impact Assessment. Report prepared for I.R. Wilson Consultants Ltd. and BC Forest Products Ltd., Boston Bar Division (revised in February 1988 from the October 1985 draft). (Copy on file with the Heritage Resource Centre, BC Ministry of Communities, Aboriginal and Women's Services, Victoria.)

1988b   The Indian history of the Robson Bight area. Appendix 3, Robson Bight Archaeological Resource Inventory. Prepared for Millennia Research, Sidney, BC and the Archaeology and Outdoor Recreation Branch of the BC Ministry of Municipal Affairs, Recreation and Culture, Victoria. (Copy on file with the Heritage Resource Centre, BC Ministry of Communities, Aboriginal and Women's Services, Victoria.)

1989   Indian knowledge and use of the Khutzeymateen area. Report prepared for Millennia Research, Sidney, BC, and the Archaeology and Outdoor Recreation Branch, BC Ministry of Municipal Affairs, Recreation and Culture, Victoria, BC (Copy on file with the Heritage Resource Centre, BC Ministry of Communities, Aboriginal and Women's Services, Victoria.)

1990   Clayoquot Sound Indian land use. Report prepared for MacMillan Bloedel Limited, Fletcher Challenge Canada, and the BC Ministry of Forests. (Copy on file with the Heritage Resource Centre, BC Ministry of Communities, Aboriginal and Women's Services, Victoria.)

1991a   Preliminary notes on Ditidaht land use. Report prepared for Millennia Research, the Ditidaht Indian Band, and the BC Heritage Trust. (Copy on file with the Heritage Resource Centre, BC Ministry of Communities, Aboriginal and Women's Services, Victoria.)

1991b   Tsawwassen ethnography and ethnohistory. Section 6, pp. 97–170, Archaeological Investigations at Tsawwassen, BC, Volume 1: Introduction. Report prepared for the BC Ministry of Transportation and Highways by Arcas Consulting Archaeologists, Coquitlam, BC (Copy on file with the Heritage Resource Centre, BC Ministry of Communities, Aboriginal and Women's Services, Victoria.)

1995   A review of the Native Indian history of the Craig Bay area, Parksville, BC Report prepared for the Archaeology Branch, British Columbia Ministry of Small Business, Tourism and Culture, Victoria, BC (Copy on file with the Heritage Resource Centre, BC Ministry of Communities, Aboriginal and Women's Services, Victoria.)

Bringhurst, Robert
  1999   *A Story as Sharp as a Knife: the classical Haida mythtellers and their world*. Vancouver and Toronto: Douglas & McIntyre.
  2001   Personal communication from Robert Bringhurst, Vancouver, BC to Randy Bouchard, July–August 2001.

Brown, Robert
  1873   *The Races of Mankind: being a popular description of the characteristics, manners and customs of the principal varieties of the human family*. Vol. 1. London: Cassell, Petter, & Galpin.

Codere, Helen
  1990   Kwakiutl: traditional culture. Pp. 359–377, *Handbook of North American Indians, Vol. 7: Northwest Coast*. Edited by Wayne Suttles. Washington, DC: Smithsonian Institution.

Cole, Douglas
  1982   Franz Boas and the Bella Coola in Berlin. *Northwest Anthropological Research Notes* 16(2):115–124. (Originally published as Kapitän Jacobsen's Bella-Coola Indianer. *Berliner Tageblatt*, 25 January 1886.)
  1999   *Franz Boas: the early years, 1858–1906*. Vancouver and Toronto: Douglas & McIntyre; Seattle and London: University of Washington Press.

Compton, Brian
  1993   Upper North Wakashan and Southern Tsimshian Ethnobotany: the knowledge and usage of plants and fungi among the Oweekeno, Hanaksiala (Kitlope and Kemano), Haisla (Kitamaat) and Kitasoo peoples of the central and north coasts of British Columbia. Unpublished Ph.D. dissertation in Botany, University of British Columbia, Vancouver.

Comox Argus
  1940   Before the White Man came. *Comox Argus*, April 11, 1940. Comox.

Costenoble, Hermann
  1887   Letter to Franz Boas, 21 November 1887. Professional correspondence of Franz Boas. Microfilm. Wilmington, Delaware: Scholarly Resources Inc. (1972).

Cowan, Ian McTaggart, and Charles J. Guiguet
  1973   The Mammals of British Columbia. 5th edition. *British Columbia Provincial Museum. Handbook* 11. Victoria.

Crosby, Thomas
  1914   *Up and Down the North Pacific Coast by Canoe and Mission Ship*. Toronto: The Missionary Society of the Methodist Church, the Young People's Forward Movement Department.

Curtis, Edward
  1915   The Kwakiutl. *The North American Indian: being a series of volumes picturing and describing the Indians of the United States, the Dominion of Canada, and Alaska.* Vol. 10. Editor, Frederick W. Hodge. Norwood, Massachusetts: Plimpton Press. (Reprinted in 1970 by Johnson Reprint Corporation, New York.)
Dalzell, Kathleen
  1973   *The Queen Charlotte Islands, Book 2: of places and names.* Prince Rupert, BC: Cove Press.
Dauenhauer, Nora Marks, and Richard Dauenhauer
  1990   *Haa Tuwunáagu Yís, for Healing Our Spirit: Tlingit oratory.* Seattle and London: University of Washington Press; Juneau: Sealaska Heritage Foundation.
Dauenhauer, Richard, and Nora Marks Dauenhauer
  2002   Personal communication from Dick and Nora Dauenhauer, Juneau, Alaska, to Randy Bouchard, February, 2002.
Dawson, George
  1885   Diary, 1885. George Dawson Papers. Originals held by McGill University Archives and McGill University Special Collections, Montreal.
  1887a   *Kwakiool Indian Names of Places [indicated on] Geological Map of the Northern Part of Vancouver Island and Adjacent Coasts.* Geological and Natural History Survey of Canada. Montreal: Dawson Brothers. (Published with the maps accompanying the *Annual Report for 1886*, Vol. II.)
  1887b   Letter to Franz Boas, 30 March 1887. Professional correspondence of Franz Boas. Microfilm. Wilmington, Delaware: Scholarly Resources Inc. (1972).
  1888   Notes and observations on the Kwakiool people of the northern part of Vancouver Island and adjacent coasts, made during the summer of 1885. Pp. 63–98, *Proceedings and Transactions of the Royal Society of Canada for the Year 1887.* Montreal: Dawson Brothers.
  1889   Letter to Franz Boas, 10 January 1889. Professional correspondence of Franz Boas. Microfilm. Wilmington, Delaware: Scholarly Resources Inc. (1972).
  1892   Notes on the Shuswap people of British Columbia. *Proceedings and Transactions of the Royal Society of Canada for the Year 1891.* Vol. 9, Section 2:3–44. Montreal: Dawson Brothers Publishers.
De Laguna, Frederica
  1972   Under Mount Saint Elias: the history and culture of the Yakutat Tlingit. 3 Pts. *Smithsonian Contributions to Anthropology* 7. Washington, DC.
  1990   Tlingit. Pp. 203–228, *Handbook of North American Indians: Vol. 7: Northwest Coast.* Edited by Wayne Suttles. Washington, DC: Smithsonian Institution.

Drucker, Philip
  1951   The Northern and Central Nootkan tribes. *Bureau of American Ethnology Bulletin* 144. Washington, DC.
Duff, Wilson
  1952   The Upper Stalo Indians of the Fraser Valley, British Columbia. Anthropology in British Columbia. *Memoirs* 1. Victoria.
  1953–1954
          Kwakiutl tribes and villages: notes from MM [Mungo Martin], maps, etc. Wilson Duff Collection. Anthropological Collections, Royal British Columbia Museum, Victoria.
  1953–1956
          Miscellaneous notes on local Salish. Wilson Duff Collection. Anthropological Collections, Royal British Columbia Museum, Victoria.
  1965   The Southern Kwakiutl. Unpublished manuscript, Wilson Duff Collection. Anthropological Collections, Royal British Columbia Museum, Victoria.
  1969   The Fort Victoria treaties. Pp. 3–57, BC Studies 3 (Fall 1969). Vancouver.
Dunn, John A.
  1995   *Sm'algyax: a reference dictionary and grammar for the Coast Tsimshian language.* University of Washington Press and Sealaska Heritage Foundation.
Ellis, David W.
  1991   The Living Resources of the Haida: birds. Report prepared for Historical Services Division, Parks Canada, Western Region, Calgary, Alberta.
Ellis, David W. and Luke Swan
  1981   *Teachings of the Tides: use of marine invertebrates by the Manhousat people.* Nanaimo: Theytus Books.
Ellis, David, and Solomon Wilson
  1981   The Knowledge and Usage of Marine Invertebrates by the Skidegate Haida People of the Queen Charlotte Islands. Monograph Series 1. Queen Charlotte City: Queen Charlotte Islands Museum Society.
Emmons, George
  1991   *The Tlingit Indians.* Edited by Frederica De Laguna. Seattle and London: University of Washington Press; New York: American Museum of Natural History.
Enrico, John J.
  1989   The Haida language. Pp. 223–247, *The Outer Shores.* Edited by Geoffrey G.E. Scudder and Nicholas Gessler. Queen Charlotte Islands: Museum Press.
  1995   *Skidegate Haida Myths and Histories.* Edited and translated by John J. Enrico. Skidegate, BC: Queen Charlotte Islands Museum Press.

Foster, Michael K.
1996   Language and the culture history of North America. Pp. 64–110, *Handbook of North American Indians: Vol. 17: Languages*. Edited by Ives Goddard. Washington, DC: Smithsonian Institution.

Freeman, John F.
1966   A guide to the manuscripts relating to the American Indians in the library of the American Philosophical Society. *Memoirs of the American Philosophical Society* 65. Philadelphia.

Galois, Robert
1994   *Kwakwaka'wakw Settlements, 1775–1920: a geographical analysis and gazetteer*. Vancouver, BC: University of British Columbia Press.

Galloway, Brent G.
1993   *A Grammar of Upriver Halkomelem*. Berkeley, Los Angeles and London: University of California Press.
2001   Personal communication from Brent Galloway (Department of Indian Languages, Literatures, and Linguistics, Saskatchewan Indian Federated College, University of Regina, Regina) to Randy Bouchard, July 2001.

Galloway, Brent G., and Coqualeetza Elders
1980   *The Structure of Upriver Halq'eméylem*, and, *A Classified Word List for Upriver Halq'eméylem*. Sardis, BC: Coqualeetza Education Training Centre for the Stó:lō Nation.
1982   *Upper Stó:lō Ethnobotany*. Sardis, BC: Coqualeetza Education Training Centre for the Stó:lō Nation.

Gerland, G.
1887   Letter to Franz Boas, 19 May 1887. Professional correspondence of Franz Boas. Microfilm. Wilmington, Delaware: Scholarly Resources Inc. (1972).

Goddard, Ives
1996   The classification of the native languages of North America. Pp. 290–323, *Handbook of North American Indians: Vol. 17: Languages*. Edited by Ives Goddard. Washington, DC: Smithsonian Institution.

Golla, Susan
2000   Legendary history of the Tsisha?ath: a working translation. Pp. 133–171, *Nuu-chah-nulth Voices, Histories, Objects & Journeys*. Edited by Alan L. Hoover. Victoria: Royal British Columbia Museum.

Goldschmidt, Walter R., and Theodore H. Haas
1998   *Haa Aaní, Our Land: Tlingit and Haida land rights and use*. Edited by Thomas F. Thornton. Seattle and London: University of Washington Press; Juneau: Sealaska Heritage Foundation. (First issued in 1946 as a mimeographed report to the U.S. Commissioner of Indian Affairs, entitled "Possessory Rights of the Natives of Southeastern Alaska.")

Grubb, David
    1977   A practical writing system and short dictionary of Kwakw'ala (Kwakiutl). *National Museum of Man, Mercury Series, Canadian Ethnology Service Papers* 34. Ottawa.

Gruber, Jacob
    1967   Horatio Hale and the development of American anthropology. *Proceedings of the American Philosophical Society* 111(5):5–37. Philadelphia.

Guédon, Marie-Françoise
    1984   An introduction to Tsimshian worldview and its practitioners. Pp. 137–159, *The Tsimshian: images of the past, views for the present.* Edited by Margaret Seguin. Vancouver: University of British Columbia Press.

Gunther, Erna
    1977   Personal communication from Erna Gunther, Bainbridge Island, Washington, to Randy Bouchard and Dorothy Kennedy, March 1977.

Halpin, Marjorie M. and Margaret Seguin
    1990   Tsimshian Peoples: Southern Tsimshian, Coast Tsimshian, Nishga, and Gitksan. Pp. 267–284, *Handbook of North American Indians, Vol. 7: Northwest Coast.* Edited by Wayne Suttles. Washington, DC: Smithsonian Institution.

Hill-Tout, Charles
    1899   "Sqaktktquaclt," or the benign-faced, the Oannes of the Ntlakapamuq, British Columbia. *Folk-Lore* 10 (June 1899) pp.195–216.
    1900   Notes on the Sk·qṓ´mic of British Columbia, a Branch of the Great Salish Stock of North America. Pp. 472–549 (Appendix II), *70th Report of the British Association for the Advancement of Science for 1900.* London.
    1903   Ethnological studies of the Mainland Halkōmē´lem, a division of the Salish of British Columbia. Pp. 335–449, *72nd Report of the British Association for the Advancement of Science for 1902.* London.
    1905   Some features of the language and culture of the Salish. *American Anthropologist* 7(4):674–687.
    1907   Report on the Ethnology of the South-eastern Tribes of Vancouver Island, British Columbia. Pp. 306–374, *Journal of the Royal Anthropological Institute of Great Britain and Ireland* 37. London.

Hilton, Susanne
    1990   Haihais, Bella Bella and Oowekeeno. Pp. 312–322, *Handbook of North American Indians, Vol. 7: Northwest Coast.* Edited by Wayne Suttles. Washington, DC: Smithsonian Institution.

Hilton, Susanne, and John C. Rath

1982   Objections to Franz Boas' referring to eating people in the translation of the Kwakwala terms bax̣ⁿbakʷālanux̣ⁿsĩ wē˜ and hamats!a. Pp. 98–106, *Working Papers for the 17th International Conference on Salish and Neighboring Languages*, 9–11 August 1982. Portland: Portland State University.

Hilton, Susanne, John C. Rath and Evelyn W. Windsor

1982   Oowekeeno oral traditions as told by the late Chief Simon Walkus, Sr. Transcribed and Translated by Evelyn W. Windsor. *National Museum of Man, Mercury Series. Canadian Ethnology Service Papers* 84. Ottawa.

Hunt, George and Franz Boas

1916   Myths of the Nootka (collected by George Hunt and edited by Franz Boas). Appendix I, pp. 888–935. Tsimshian Mythology. *Thirty-First Annual Report of the Bureau of American Ethnology to the Secretary of the Smithsonian Institution, 1909–1910*. Washington, DC: Government Printing Office.

Jilek, Wolfgang G.

1974   *Salish Indian Mental Health and Cultural Change: psychohygienic and therapeutic aspects of the guardian spirit ceremonial*. Toronto: Holt, Rinehart and Winston.

1982   *Indian Healing: shamanic ceremonialism in the Pacific Northwest today*. Surrey, BC: Hancock House.

Johnson, Samuel V.

1978   Chinook Jargon: a computer assisted analysis of variation in an American Indian pidgin. Unpublished Ph.D. thesis in Anthropology, University of Kansas.

Jonaitis, Aldona

1988   *From the Land of the Totem Poles: the Northwest Coast Indian art collection at the American Museum of Natural History*. New York: The American Museum of Natural History.

1991   *Chiefly Feasts: the enduring Kwakiutl potlatch*. Edited by Aldona Jonaitis. New York: American Museum of Natural History; Vancouver and Toronto: Douglas & McIntyre.

Kennedy, Dorothy I., and Randy Bouchard

1983   *Sliammon Life, Sliammon Lands*. Vancouver: Talonbooks.

1990a   Bella Coola. Pp. 323–339, *Handbook of North American Indians, Vol. 7: Northwest Coast*. Edited by Wayne Suttles. Washington, DC: Smithsonian Institution.

1990b   Northern Coast Salish. Pp. 441–452, *Handbook of North American Indians, Vol. 7: Northwest Coast*. Edited by Wayne Suttles. Washington, DC: Smithsonian Institution.

Kennedy, Dorothy I., and Randy Bouchard
   1998   Lillooet. Pp. 174–190, *Handbook of North American Indians, Vol. 12: Plateau*. Edited by Deward E. Walker Jr. Washington, DC: Smithsonian Institution.

Kew, J.E. Michael
   1970   Coast Salish ceremonial life: status and identity in a modern village. Unpublished Ph.D. thesis in Anthropology, University of Washington, Seattle.

Kinkade, M. Dale
   1986   Blackcaps and Musqueam. Pp. 60–62, *Working Papers for the 21st International Conference on Salish and Neighbouring Languages*. Seattle: University of Washington.
   1992   Translating Pentlatch. Pp. 163–175, *On the Translation of Native American Literatures*. Edited by Brian Swann. Washington, DC: Smithsonian Institution Press.

Kinkade, M. Dale *et al.*
   1998   Languages. Pp. 49–72, *Handbook of North American Indians: Northwest Coast, Vol. 12: Plateau*. Edited by Deward E. Walker, Jr. Washington, DC: Smithsonian Institution.

Kortlandt, Frederik
   1973   Word list of the Heiltsuk language. Unpublished draft manuscript prepared by F. Kortlandt, with William Freeman. Leiden, Holland.

Krause, Aurel
   1885   Die Tlingit-Indianer: Ergebnisse einer Reise nach der Nordwestküste von Amerika … ,in den Jahren 1880–1881. Jena, Germany: Hermann Costenoble.

Kuipers, Aert
   1967   *The Squamish Language: grammar, texts and dictionary*. The Hague: Mouton.
   1974   *The Shuswap Language: grammar, texts, dictionary*. The Hague: Mouton.
   1982   Shuswap-English dictionary. Unpublished manuscript. Leiden, Holland.
   1989   A Report on Shuswap, with a Squamish lexical appendix. *Langues et Sociétés D'Amérique Traditionnelle* 2. SELAF 310, Centre National de al Recherche Scientifique. Paris: Peeters/SELAF.

Lawrence, Erma, Jeff Leer, *et al.*
   1977   *Haida Dictionary*. The Society for the Preservation of Haida Language and Literature and The Alaska Native Language Center. Fairbanks: University of Alaska.

Levine, Robert Daigon.
   1977   The Skidegate Dialect of Haida. Unpublished Ph.D. thesis in Linguistics, Columbia University, New York.
   1979   Haida and Na-Dene: a new look at the evidence. *International Journal of American Linguistics* 45(2):157–170.

Lévi-Strauss, Claude
  1973   *Anthropologie structural deux.* Paris: Plon.
  1976   Structuralisme et empirisme. *L'Homme, revue française d'anthropologie*
         XVI (2–3). Paris.
  1984   Un témoignage de C. Lévi-Strauss sur Franz Boas (Claude Lévi-Strauss'
         testimony on Franz Boas). *Inuit Studies* 8(1):3–10.
Lincoln, Neville J., and John C. Rath
  1980   North Wakashan Comparative Root List. *National Museum of Man,*
         Mercury Series, Canadian Ethnology Service Papers 68. Ottawa.
Lowie, Robert E.
  1908   The test-theme in North-American mythology. *Journal of American*
         Folklore 21(1908):97–148.
MacDonald, George F.
  1983   *Haida Monumental Art: villages of the Queen Charlotte Islands.*
         Vancouver: University of British Columbia Press; Seattle: University of
         Washington Press.
McClellan, Catharine
  1981   Inland Tlingit. Pp. 469–480, *Handbook of North American Indians, Vol.*
         6: Subarctic. Edited by June Helm. Washington, DC: Smithsonian
         Institution.
McIlwraith, Thomas
  1948. *The Bella Coola Indians.* 2 vols. Toronto: University of Toronto Press.
McNeary, Stephen
  1976   Where Fire Came Down: Social and Economic Life of the Niska.
         Unpublished Ph.D. dissertation in Anthropology. Bryn Mawr College,
         Bryn Mawr, Pennsylvania.
Malin, Edward
  1961   The Social Organization of the Koskimo Kwakiutl. Unpublished M.A.
         thesis in Anthropology, University of Colorado.
Matthews, J.S.
  1955   *Conversations with Khahtsahlano: 1932–1954.* Compiled by Major J.S.
         Matthews, City Archivist. Vancouver: Published by the City of Vancouver.
Maud, Ralph
  1982   *A Guide to B.C. Indian Myth and Legend: a short history of myth-collect-*
         ing and a survey of published texts. Vancouver: Talonbooks.
Mauzé, Marie
  1984   Enjeux et jeux du prestige des Kwagul méridionaux aux Lekwiltok (côte
         nord-ouest du Pacifique). 2 vols. (Thèse pour le doctorat de troisième
         cycle, Ecole des Hautes Etudes en Sciences Sociales, Paris.)
  1992   *Les fils de Wakai: une histoire des Indiens Lekwiltoq.* Paris: Editions
         Recherche sur les Civilisations.

Mayne, R.C.
1859   Sketch of Part of British Columbia By Lieutnt R.C. Mayne, R.N. of H.M.S. Plumper, 1859. Maps and Plans Vault, Surveyor General's Branch, Ministry of Sustainable Resource Management. Miscellaneous 14T2.

Naish, Constance M., and Gillian L. Story
1963   *English Tlingit Dictionary: nouns.* Compiled by Constance Naish and Gillian Story. Fairbanks, Alaska: Summer Institute of Linguistics.

Olson, Ronald L.
1940   The social organization of the Haisla of British Columbia. *University of California Anthropological Records* 2(5):169–200. Berkeley.
1954   Social life of the Owikeno Kwakiutl. *University of California Anthropological Records* 14(3):213–259. Berkeley.
1955   Notes on the Bella Bella Kwakiutl. *University of California Anthropological Records* 14(5):319–348. Berkeley.

Palmer, Garry
1975   Shuswap Indian ethnobotany. *Syesis* 8:29–81. British Columbia Provincial Museum, Victoria, BC

Powell, Jay V.
1991   Our World, Our Ways: T'aat'aaqsapa cultural dictionary. Compiled and edited by Jay Powell. Port Alberni, BC: Nuuchahnulth Tribal Council.

Rath, John
1981   A practical Heiltsuk-English dictionary. Two Volumes. *National Museum of Man, Mercury Series, Canadian Ethnology Service Paper* 75. Ottawa.

Recalma-Clutesi, Kim
1992   The Qualicums. Pp. 20–24, *Qualicum Beach: a history of Vancouver Island's best kept secrets.* Edited by Brad Wylie. Qualicum Beach, BC: Brad Wylie and the Qualicum Beach Historical and Museum Society.
2001   Personal communication from Kim Recalma-Clutesi (Qualicum Indian Reserve, Qualicum Beach, BC) to Randy Bouchard, May 2001.

Rigsby, Bruce J.
1989   A later view of Gitksan syntax. Pp. 245–260, *General and Amerindian ethnolinguistics: in remembrance of Stanley Newman.* Edited by Mary Ritchie Key and Henry M. Hoenigswald. Berlin and New York: Mouton de Gruyter.

Rohner, Ronald P.
1966   Franz Boas: ethnographer on the Northwest Coast. Pp. 149–212, *Pioneers of American Anthropology.* Edited by June Helm. Seattle and London: University of Washington Press.
1967   The People of Gilford: a contemporary Kwakiutl village. *National Museum of Canada, Bulletin No. 225, Anthropological Series No. 83.* Ottawa: National Museums of Canada.

Rohner, Ronald P.
   1969   *The Ethnography of Franz Boas: letters and diaries of Franz Boas written on the Northwest Coast from 1886 to 1931.* Compiled and edited by Ronald P. Rohner. Chicago, Ill.: The University of Chicago Press.

Rozen, David L.
   1978   The ethnozoology of the Cowichan Indian people of British Columbia: Vol.1: Fish, Beach Foods and Marine Mammals. Unpublished report in author's possession, Vancouver, BC. (Copy on file with the BC Indian Language Project, Victoria, BC).
   1985   Place-names of the Island Halkomelem Indian People. Unpublished M.A. thesis in Anthropology, University of British Columbia, Vancouver.

St. Claire, Denis E.
   1991   Barkley Sound tribal territories. Pp. 14–202, Between Ports Alberni and Renfrew: Notes on West Coast Peoples, by Eugene Arima and Denis St. Claire *et al. Canadian Museum of Civilization, Mercury Series, Canadian Ethnology Service Papers* 121. Hull, Quebec.

Sapir, Edward
   1910–1914
            [Nootka Notes.] American Philosophical Society Library, Philadelphia. Boas Collection (Edward Sapir Papers), Ms. #372.7, W2a.18, Microfilm No. 26.

Sapir, Edward, and Morris Swadesh
   1939   *Nootka Texts: tales and ethnological narratives, with grammatical notes and lexical material.* Philadelphia: University of Pennsylvania, Linguistic Society of America. (Reprinted: AMS Press, New York, 1978.)

Schulenburg, A.C. Graf von der
   1894   *Die Sprache der Zimshīan-Indianer in Nordwest-America.* Braunschweig: Verlag von Richard Sattler.

Shotridge, Louis and Florence Shotridge
   1913   Indians of the Northwest [including information on the Koskimo and Quatsino gathered by B.W. Leeson.] *University of Pennsylvania Museum Journal* 4(3):71–100, September 1913. Philadelphia.

Silverstein, Michael
   1996   Note on Chinook Jargon, In, Dynamics of Linguistic Contact. Pp.117–136, *Handbook of North American Indians, Vol. 17: Languages.* Edited by Ives Goddard. Washington, DC: Smithsonian Institution.

Smith, Marian
   1950   The Nooksack, the Chilliwack, and the Middle Fraser. *Pacific Northwest Quarterly* 41(4):330–341.

Spalding, David
  1990   The early history of moose (Alces alces): distribution and relative abundance in British Columbia. *Contributions to Natural Science* 11 (March 1990):1–12. Royal British Columbia Museum, Victoria, BC.
  1992   The history of elk (Cervus elaphus) in British Columbia. *Contributions to Natural Science* 18 (October 1992):1–24. Royal British Columbia Museum, Victoria, BC.

Spradley, James P.
  1969   *Guests Never Leave Hungry: the autobiography of James Sewid, a Kwakiutl Indian.* Edited by James P. Spradley. Yale University Press. (Reprinted by McGill-Queen's University Press, Montreal, 1978.)

Stevenson, David
  1980   A History of the Oowekeeno People of Rivers Inlet. Unpublished report prepared for the National Museum of Man, Ottawa.
  1981   One Large Family: the ceremonial names of the Oowekeeno people of Rivers Inlet. Unpublished report prepared for the National Museum of Man, Ottawa.

Stumpf, Carl
  1886   Lieder der Bellakula-Indianer. *Vierteljahres-schrift für Musikwissenschaft* 2:405–426. Leipzig, Germany.

Suttles, Wayne P.
  1951   Economic Life of the Coast Salish of Haro and Rosario Straits. Ph.D. dissertation in Anthropology, University of Washington, Seattle.
  1955   *Katzie Ethnographic Notes.* Victoria: Royal British Columbia Museum.
  1987   On the Cultural Track of the Sasquatch. Pp. 73–99, *Coast Salish Essays.* Vancouver: Talonbooks; Seattle: University of Washington Press.
  1990   Central Coast Salish. Pp. 453–475, *Handbook of North American Indians: Vol. 7: Northwest Coast.* Edited by Wayne Suttles. Washington, DC: Smithsonian Institution.
  2001   Some Questions About Northern Straits. Pp. 291–310, Papers of the 36th International Conference on Salish and Neighbouring Languages. Edited by Leora Bar-el, Linda Tamburri Watt, and Ian Wilson. *University of British Columbia Working Papers in Linguistics*, Vol. 6.
  2002   Personal communication from Wayne Suttles, Friday Harbour, Washington, to Randy Bouchard, February 2002.

Swanton, John R.
  n.d.   [Check List of British Columbia Birds, annotated with equivalent Haida bird names.] National Anthropological Archives, Smithsonian Institution, Washington, DC. Ms. #4117-a(3).
  1905a   Contributions to the ethnology of the Haida. *Publications of the Jesup North Pacific Expedition* 5; *Memoirs of the American Museum of Natural History* 8(1):1–300. New York.

Swanton, John R.

1905b   Haida texts and myths, Skidegate dialect. *Bureau of American Ethnology Bulletin* 29. Washington, DC (Reprinted: Scholarly Press, St. Clair Shores, Mich., 1976.)

1908a   Haida texts, Masset dialect. *Publications of the Jesup North pacific Expedition* 10(2); *Memoirs of the American Museum of Natural History* 14(2). New York. (Reprinted: AMS Press, New York, 1975.)

1908b   Social conditions, beliefs, and linguistic relationships of the Tlingit Indians. Pp. 391–485, *26th Annual Report of the Bureau of American Ethnology for the Years 1904–1905*. Washington, DC.

1909   Tlingit myths and texts. *Bureau of American Ethnology, Bulletin* 39. Washington, DC (Reprinted: Scholarly Press, St. Clair Shores, Mich., 1976.) [Copy of this 1909 publication annotated by Tlingit Indian William L. Paul held by the National Anthropological Archives, Smithsonian Institution, Washington, DC, Ms. #4823.]

Taylor, Herbert C. and Wilson Duff

1956   A post-contact southward movement of the Kwakiutl. Pp. 56–66, *Research Studies, State College of Washington*, Vol. XXIV.

Teit, James A.

1898   Traditions of the Thompson River Indians of British Columbia. *Memoirs of the American Folk-Lore Society* 6:1–137. Boston and New York. (Reprinted by Kraus Reprint, New York, 1969.)

1898–1910
        [Salish ethnographic notes.] American Philosophical Society Library, Philadelphia. Boas Collection 372, Roll 4, No. 1, Item 61.

1900   The Thompson Indians of British Columbia. Edited by Franz Boas. *Memoirs of the American Museum of Natural History* 2, *Anthropology* 1(4); *Publications of the Jesup North Pacific Expedition* 1(4). New York. (Reprinted by AMS Press, New York, 1975).

1906   The Lillooet Indians. *Memoir of the American Museum of Natural History*. Volume II(5):193–300.

1909   The Shuswap. Edited by Franz Boas. *Memoirs of the American Museum of Natural History* 4(7); *Publication of the Jesup North Pacific Expedition* 2(7). New York. (Reprinted: AMS Press, New York, 1975.)

1912   Mythology of the Thompson Indians. Edited by Franz Boas. Pp. 199–416, *Memoirs of the American Museum of Natural History*, Vol. XII, Part II (reprinted from Vol. VIII, Part II, *Publication of the Jesup North Pacific Expedition*). Leiden: Brill.

1914   Indian tribes of the Interior. Pp. 283–312, *Canada and its Provinces*. Edited by Adam Shortt and Arthur G. Doughty. Toronto: T. & A. Constable.

Thompson, Laurence C., and Dale Kinkade
  1990   Languages. Pp. 30–51, *Handbook of North American Indians, Vol. 7: Northwest Coast.* Edited by Wayne Suttles. Washington, DC: Smithsonian Institution.

Thompson, Laurence C., and M. Terry Thompson (compilers)
  1996   Thompson River Salish dictionary: Nłeʔkepmxcín. *University of Montana Occasional Papers in Linguistics, No. 12.* Missoula, Montana: University of Montana.

Thornton, Thomas F.
  1995   Place and Being Among the Tlingit. Unpublished Ph.D. thesis in Anthropology, University of Washington.

Turner, Nancy J.
  1995   *Food Plants of Coastal First Peoples.* Vancouver: University of British Columbia Press; Victoria: Royal British Columbia Museum.
  1997   *Food Plants of Interior First Peoples.* Vancouver: University of British Columbia Press; Victoria: Royal British Columbia Museum.

Turner, Nancy J., and Marcus A. M. Bell
  1973   The ethnobotany of the Southern Kwakiutl Indians of British Columbia. *Economic Botany* Vol. 27(3):257–310.

Turner, Nancy J., John Thomas, Barry Carlson, and Robert Ogilvie
  1983   Ethnobotany of the Nitinaht Indians of Vancouver Island. *Occasional Papers of the British Columbia Museum* 24. Victoria: British Columbia Provincial Museum.

Turner, Nancy J., Laurence C. Thompson, M. Terry Thompson, and Annie York
  1990   Thompson ethnobotany: knowledge and usage of plants by the Thompson Indians of British Columbia. *Royal British Columbia Museum Memoir* 3. Victoria: Royal British Columbia Museum.

Wallas, Chief James, and Pamela Whitaker
  1981   *Kwakiutl Legends.* North Vancouver, BC and Blaine, Washington: Hancock House.

Wells, Oliver N.
  1987   *The Chilliwacks and their Neighbors.* Edited by Ralph Maud, Brent Galloway and Marie Weeden. Vancouver, BC: Talonbooks.

Wyatt, David
  1998   Thompson. Pp. 191–202, *Handbook of North American Indians, Vol. 12: Plateau.* Edited by Deward E. Walker Jr. Washington,DC: Smithsonian Institution.